Dictionary of Literary Biography

Documentary Series

Yearbooks

Concise Series

Concise Dictionary of American Literary Biography, 7 volumes (1988-1999): *The New Consciousness, 1941-1968; Colonization to the American Renaissance, 1640-1865; Realism, Naturalism, and Local Color, 1865-1917; The Twenties, 1917-1929; The Age of Maturity, 1929-1941; Broadening Views, 1968-1988; Supplement: Modern Writers, 1900-1998.*

Concise Dictionary of British Literary Biography, 8 volumes (1991-1992): *Writers of the Middle Ages and Renaissance Before 1660; Writers of the Restoration and Eighteenth Century, 1660-1789; Writers of the Romantic Period, 1789-1832; Victorian Writers, 1832-1890; Late-Victorian and Edwardian Writers, 1890-1914; Modern Writers, 1914-1945; Writers After World War II, 1945-1960; Contemporary Writers, 1960 to Present.*

Concise Dictionary of World Literary Biography, 20 volumes projected (1999-   ): *Ancient Greek and Roman Writers; German Writers; African, Carribbean, and Latin-American Writers.*

American Novelists Since World War II
Sixth Series

Dictionary of Literary Biography® • Volume Two Hundred Twenty-Seven

American Novelists Since World War II

Sixth Series

Edited by
James R. Giles
and
Wanda H. Giles
Northern Illinois University

A Bruccoli Clark Layman Book
The Gale Group
Detroit • San Francisco • London • Boston • Woodbridge, Conn.

Printed in the United States of America

The paper used in this publication meets the minimum requirements
of American National Standard for Information Sciences–Permanence
Paper for Printed Library Materials, ANSI Z39.48-1984. ∞™

ISBN 0-7876-3136-1

10 9 8 7 6 5 4 3 2 1

*To the people who taught us to read, the greatest gift we have had, for their grace
and their passion, and in respect*

Matthew J. Bruccoli
Edwin Harrison Cady
Jim Corder
James Melville Cox
Orville Clements
Earley Davis
J. Hubert Dunn
Georges Edelen
Richard Ellmann
Warren G. French
Roger and Eva Walker Giles
Rudolph P. Gottfried
Georgia M. and Knofel P. Hancock
Joseph W. Jones
Lyle Kendall
Gordon Mills
Alene Payton
Wallace Stegner
Clara Stephens
Edna Copeland Teaford
Maxine Turnage
Ruth Farlow Uyesugi
Yvor Winters
Samuel Yellen

And, always in hope, for Morgan

Contents

Plan of the Series

The advisory board, the editors, and the publisher of the *Dictionary of Literary Biography* are joined in endorsing Mark Twain's declaration. The literature of a nation provides an inexhaustible resource of permanent worth. We intend to make literature and its creators better understood and more accessible to students and the reading public, while satisfying the standards of teachers and scholars.

To meet these requirements, *literary biography* has been construed in terms of the author's achievement. The most important thing about a writer is his writing. Accordingly, the entries in *DLB* are career biographies, tracing the development of the author's canon and the evolution of his reputation.

The purpose of *DLB* is not only to provide reliable information in a convenient format but also to place the figures in the larger perspective of literary history and to offer appraisals of their accomplishments by qualified scholars.

The publication plan for *DLB* resulted from two years of preparation. The project was proposed to Bruccoli Clark by Frederick G. Ruffner, president of the Gale Research Company, in November 1975. After specimen entries were prepared and typeset, an advisory board was formed to refine the entry format and develop the series rationale. In meetings held during 1976, the publisher, series editors, and advisory board approved the scheme for a comprehensive biographical dictionary of persons who contributed to North American literature. Editorial work on the first volume began in January 1977, and it was published in 1978. In order to make *DLB* more than a reference tool and to compile volumes that individually have claim to status as literary history, it was decided to organize volumes by

topic, period, or genre. Each of these freestanding volumes provides a biographical-bibliographical guide and overview for a particular area of literature. We are convinced that this organization—as opposed to a single alphabet method—constitutes a valuable innovation in the presentation of reference material. The volume plan necessarily requires many decisions for the placement and treatment of authors who might properly be included in two or three volumes. In some instances a major figure will be included in separate volumes, but with different entries emphasizing the aspect of his career appropriate to each volume. Ernest Hemingway, for example, is represented in *American Writers in Paris, 1920–1939* by an entry focusing on his expatriate apprenticeship; he is also in *American Novelists, 1910–1945* with an entry surveying his entire career, as well as in *American Short-Story Writers, 1910–1945, Second Series* with an entry concentrating on his short stories. Each volume includes a cumulative index of the subject authors and articles. Comprehensive indexes to the entire series are planned.

Since 1981 the series has been further augmented by the *DLB Yearbooks*, which update published entries and add new entries to keep the *DLB* current with contemporary activity. There have also been *DLB Documentary Series* volumes which provide biographical and critical source materials for figures whose work is judged to have particular interest for students. One of these companion volumes is devoted entirely to Tennessee Williams.

We define literature as the *intellectual commerce of a nation:* not merely as belles lettres but as that ample and complex process by which ideas are generated, shaped, and transmitted. *DLB* entries are not limited to "creative writers" but extend to other figures who in their time and in their way influenced the mind of a people. Thus the series encompasses historians, journalists, publishers, book collectors, and screenwriters. By this means readers of *DLB* may be aided to perceive literature not as cult scripture in the keeping of intellectual high priests but firmly positioned at the center of a nation's life.

DLB includes the major writers appropriate to each volume and those standing in the ranks behind them. Scholarly and critical counsel has been sought in deciding which minor figures to include and how full their entries should be. Wherever possible, useful references are made to figures who do not warrant separate entries.

Each *DLB* volume has an expert volume editor responsible for planning the volume, selecting the figures for inclusion, and assigning the entries. Volume editors are also responsible for preparing, where appropriate, appendices surveying the major periodicals and literary and intellectual movements for their volumes, as well as lists of further readings. Work on the series as a whole is coordinated at the Bruccoli Clark Layman editorial center in Columbia, South Carolina, where the editorial staff is responsible for accuracy and utility of the published volumes.

One feature that distinguishes *DLB* is the illustration policy–its concern with the iconography of literature. Just as an author is influenced by his surroundings, so is the reader's understanding of the author enhanced by a knowledge of his environment. Therefore *DLB* volumes include not only drawings, paintings, and photographs of authors, often depicting them at various stages in their careers, but also illustrations of their families and places where they lived. Title pages are regularly reproduced in facsimile along with dust jackets for modern authors. The dust jackets are a special feature of *DLB* because they often document better than anything else the way in which an author's work was perceived in its own time. Specimens of the writers' manuscripts and letters are included when feasible.

Samuel Johnson rightly decreed that "The chief glory of every people arises from its authors." The purpose of the *Dictionary of Literary Biography* is to compile literary history in the surest way available to us–by accurate and comprehensive treatment of the lives and work of those who contributed to it.

The *DLB* Advisory Board

Introduction

The isolationist foreign policy to which the United States had been largely committed since the end of World War I was abruptly shattered on 7 December 1941 by the Japanese attack on Pearl Harbor. By the end of World War II, the nation stood unchallenged as one of two world superpowers; its involvement in international affairs had become a given. Under the leadership of President Harry S Truman, the United States undertook the rebuilding of Europe. But even as the most clearly powerful and intact of countries, the United States could not escape being touched by the profound insecurity and moral uncertainty that were part of the war's legacy. The full disclosure of the horrors of the Holocaust forced the West to question, as never before, the inherent decency of human beings; and Hiroshima forced humanity to confront the real possibility of the extinction of all life. Americans could hardly ignore the fact that this potential for human annihilation was the clear result of technology, in which they had for so long posited an almost religious faith.

Moreover, at the end of World War II, the United States found itself, as the leader of the West, engaged in a new order of international conflict, a "cold war" that continued for more than four decades. The nation assumed the responsibility to stop the spread of communism and so became involved in an undeclared conflict with the Soviet Union. The first crisis of the Cold War was the Soviets' construction of the Berlin Wall, creating an enforced separation of East and West Berlin. International tension escalated even more dramatically in 1950 when Communist North Korea invaded South Korea, and President Truman deployed American troops as part of a United Nations "police action" to drive out the invading North Koreans. The first, but not the last, tragically indecisive post–World War II experience for the United States in Asia, the Korean conflict lasted until 1953, with more than 150,000 Americans killed or wounded.

The Korean War forced Americans to realize that there were real limitations to the power of even the strongest of nations, and this awareness of national mortality contributed significantly to a pervasive sense of instability and uncertainty in the United States. In 1952 Americans elected Dwight D. Eisenhower, the former commander in chief of the Allied forces in Europe, as president. The Eisenhower election represented in part a national need for reassurance and stability. The 1950s, however, were haunted by another kind of nightmare: McCarthyism. Joseph McCarthy, the junior senator from Wisconsin, inspired an obsessive national crusade to expose Communists in places of influence in America. Writers and other creative people soon found themselves the favorite targets of McCarthy's "witch hunt," and "blacklists" were utilized to isolate and destroy the careers of suspected Communists in the motion-picture industry, in radio, and in academia.

The young American writers who began publishing in the late 1940s and early 1950s were inevitably touched by this national mood of insecurity and loss of faith in moral certainty. Not surprisingly, several of them–Norman Mailer, James Jones, and Gore Vidal, for instance–first published war novels; and a recurrent theme in this early World War II fiction is a warning against the imminent danger of an American fascism. Mailer and Jones, in *The Naked and the Dead* (1948), and *From Here to Eternity* (1951), respectively, create American generals who quite openly and unapologetically preach the necessity of strong leaders controlling the weak and directionless masses. Moreover, this thematic concern was hardly limited to the war novelists; writers such as Saul Bellow, William Styron, and Chester Himes also produced fiction that expressed anxiety about the existence of grave internal threats to the preservation of American democracy. In *The Catcher in the Rye* (1951), certainly not a political novel, J. D. Salinger created an emblematic figure for the entire decade of the 1950s in Holden Caulfield, a youth in rebellion against a corrupt society and the "phonies" who personified it. In his short stories and novel *The Troubled Air* (1951), Irwin Shaw specifically protested against McCarthyism.

It is impossible to estimate the cost of self-censorship to American literature during the 1950s. What is clear, however, is that the national mood of the decade inspired a withdrawal by several American writers from any sense of involvement in, or commitment to, the dominant culture of the nation. The clearest example of a literary repudiation of mainstream American society came from the talented group of writers known as "the Beat Generation." Jack Kerouac, William S. Burroughs, Allen Ginsberg, and Lawrence Ferlinghetti were among the best known of "the Beats," writers who sought—in Zen Buddhism, jazz, and drugs—antidotes to what they perceived as the sterile conformity of American life. California, specifically San Francisco and its City Lights bookstore, served as the West Coast center of the Beat movement. Columbia University occupied a similar position on the east coast.

Zen was not the only "foreign" philosophy to significantly influence American literature and American culture in the years after World War II. French existentialism, with its emphasis on the absence of any external ethical system and the resulting need for each individual to discover or create his or her own moral truths, had a strong appeal for postwar writers. Fiction that can somewhat loosely be labeled as existential realism began to appear on the American literary scene during the 1950s. It is not at all difficult to see existential overtones in the work of most of the important writers to emerge in America since 1945. For instance, perhaps the main consistency in the constantly evolving literary career of Norman Mailer has been his self-definition as an American existentialist.

Despite the considerable importance of the 1950s to American literature, it seems possible to argue that 1961 and 1962 more clearly represented the end of one era of the American novel and the beginning of a new one. In these two years—at the beginning of what would prove to be one of the most turbulent decades in American history—Ernest Hemingway committed suicide and William Faulkner died. The work of these men constituted the triumph of modernism in American fiction; they had dominated the national literary scene for more than three decades. Indeed, only the "American Renaissance" group of writers (Nathaniel Hawthorne, Herman Melville, Ralph Waldo Emerson, Walt Whitman, Henry David Thoreau, and Edgar Allan Poe) had been so central and vital to American literature for as long as the brilliant generation of writers that emerged in the 1920s. Hemingway and Faulkner, leading literary figures in their generation, produced a body of writing distinguished by its revolutionary sophistication in narrative technique and approach to characterization. Strongly influenced by the innovations in narration associated with James Joyce, their work pointed the way for American fiction to go beyond William Dean Howells's "reality of the commonplace."

By the 1960s, the dominance of Hemingway and Faulkner had begun to have a somewhat inhibiting effect on the American novel. It seemed increasingly difficult to surpass the innovations in modernist technique

found in such masterpieces as *The Sound and the Fury* (1929), *Absalom, Absalom!* (1936), and *The Sun Also Rises* (1926). Modernism hardly disappeared from American literature after the war. It continued to be practiced, often brilliantly, by many writers, including John Cheever, James Baldwin, Ralph Ellison, and William Styron. Cheever, who had been turning out his remarkable short stories since the 1930s, published his first novel, *The Wapshot Chronicle,* in 1957 and followed it with *The Wapshot Scandal* in 1964 and *Falconer* in 1977. With his rich and inventive masterpiece *Invisible Man* (1952), Ellison redirected the African American novel away from the naturalism of Richard Wright. Ayn Rand explored the traditions of both realism and naturalism in her overtly political novels. Throughout the decade of the 1960s, American novelists searched for innovative structures that liberated them from the dictates of formalism—the conscious narrative control—of modernism.

The social and political turbulence of the 1960s contributed to the intensely felt need of many writers to escape virtually any kind of limitations on their art. Few, if any, decades in American history have begun as hopefully or ended as pessimistically as the 1960s. Shortly after his election to the presidency in 1960, John F. Kennedy was confronted with the Civil Rights movement led by Dr. Martin Luther King Jr. Not wanting to offend the Southern wing of the Democratic Party, President Kennedy was initially reluctant to offer much more than verbal support to the cause of civil rights. Soon, though, graphic pictures of "Freedom Riders" and other civil rights protesters being attacked in the South with water hoses, clubs, and police dogs began to dominate the national news on television screens throughout the nation. The Civil Rights movement quickly became the central beneficiary of the youthful idealism to which Kennedy had appealed since the beginning of his administration. Increasingly, the president and his brother, Attorney General Robert Kennedy, saw the inevitability of their playing a more direct role in the struggle for the civil rights of African Americans. The civil rights issue culminated on 17 June 1963 when King delivered his "I Have A Dream" speech to a crowd of more than two hundred thousand in Washington, D.C. The president and the attorney general recognized the necessity of passing a federal civil rights bill to end the old barriers of racial segregation in America. The civil rights struggle was the inspiration for many American writers, artists, and entertainers, especially those of African American descent, to become political activists.

Domestically then, the nation was already in a state of turmoil when, on 22 November 1963, John F. Kennedy was assassinated in Dallas, Texas. The assassination of the president seemed to threaten the most deeply held certainties of American life; and the new national uncertainty inevitably encompassed aesthetics. The television coverage of the assassination and its aftermath–especially the on-camera shooting of Lee Harvey Oswald by Jack Ruby–caused writers and critics to wonder if such a passive medium as the novel could remain viable to an audience trained to respond in such a shockingly instantaneous manner. The murders of Kennedy and Oswald resulted in an obsession with conspiracy theories that is still central to the American consciousness. In 1988 Don DeLillo, probably the American writer most obsessed with the Kennedy assassination and its aftermath, responded to the paranoia resulting from the tragic events of November 1963 with his powerful tour de force, *Libra,* which fictionalizes the life of Oswald, depicting him as a pathetic agent of a conspiracy organized by disaffected CIA agents and organized crime.

As a result of the accelerating involvement in Vietnam, the national mood was to darken even more. Few Americans had even known that in the 1950s the United States, attempting once again to halt the spread of communism in Asia, had committed itself to defending a corrupt and authoritarian regime in South Vietnam against Communist North Vietnam. The political situation continued to deteriorate, but it was not until after Lyndon Johnson's election in 1964 that the United States became heavily involved in a brutal and confusing war in the Southeast Asian nation that few Americans had previously known anything about. Throughout the Johnson presidency, increasing numbers of American resources and troops were poured into a struggle that was destined from the beginning to fail.

One consequence of the Vietnam legacy was the emergence in the United States of a counterculture. More and more young Americans of draft age refused to accept induction into the armed services, and antiwar demonstrations became almost a ritual of daily life on college campuses across the nation. Almost before anyone had noticed its beginnings, a counterculture of young men and women devoted to opposition to the war, experimentation with sex and drugs, and rebellion against everything associated with the middle-class establishment became highly visible throughout urban America. The residential section of San Francisco bounded by Haight and Ashbury Streets was soon identified as the center of the youth-dominated counterculture. Middle-class and middle-aged Americans had, on the whole, little understanding of, and therefore no sympathy for, the rebellious young; and so the nation was fragmented by a sharp generational division. In addition, a new kind of racial conflict ripped apart the fabric of national unity in the last half of the 1960s. Increasingly, African Americans, especially those in northern urban centers and on the West Coast, were outraged and alienated by the war in Vietnam; they saw a disproportionate number of young black men being drafted to serve in Vietnam and, in addition, came to believe that resources of potential use in America's inner cities were being wasted in Southeast Asia. The Watts section of Los Angeles in 1966 and parts of Detroit in 1967 suffered massive outbreaks of rioting and looting.

It seemed that all the tensions that had been building throughout the 1960s exploded in the years between 1968 and 1970. On 4 April 1968, King was assassinated in Memphis, Tennessee; and on 5 June of that same year, Robert Kennedy, in a campaign for the presidency, was shot and killed in Los Angeles the night he won the California primary. Also in 1968, national television audiences saw antiwar demonstrators being brutally assaulted by police at the Democratic National Convention in Chicago. In 1970 National Guard troops shot and killed student protestors at two universities, Kent State in Ohio and Jackson State in Mississippi. In the midst of such national trauma, it was almost difficult to feel the long-anticipated elation when the United States, in 1969, did indeed land a man on the moon. Neil Armstrong's "moon walk" represented one of the few seemingly unequivocal triumphs for American technology in the decade. Yet, for the novelist, and especially for the writer of science fiction, even this revolutionary scientific breakthrough had ominous overtones. What had recently belonged to the world of imaginative fantasy had become one more aspect of known reality. As with so many other major historical events during the 1960s, Americans witnessed Armstrong's adventure on the moon as it occurred. From then on, *astronaut* became a part of the vocabulary of ordinary Americans rather than a concept reserved for science fiction.

Inevitably, a decade marked by such relentless and unsettling turmoil dramatically affected the American novel. In fact, the traditional mimetic role of the novel was called into serious question. American writers and critics began to wonder whether fiction could hope to capture such an elusive reality. Even at the beginning of the decade, novelist Philip Roth expressed genuine doubt concerning this question, in his essay "Writing American Fiction" (1961):

> The American writer in the middle of the 20th century has his hands full in trying to understand, and then describe, and then make *credible* much of the American reality. It stupefies, it sickens, it infuriates, and finally it is even a kind of embarrassment to one's own meager imagination. The actuality is continually outdoing our talents, and the culture tosses up figures almost daily that are the envy of any novelist.

Throughout the rest of the decade, echoes of Roth's pessimistic analysis, usually with some variations in emphasis, became commonplace in literary magazines.

Norman Mailer wondered if the mass media's daily barrage of "information and news" effectively buried any objective and potentially verifiable reality that might exist. In the 1960s it became fashionable to issue pronouncements of "the death of the novel." But a genre that had been so central to Western culture for so long would not pass so quickly into oblivion. Seeking alternatives to modernism and traditional realism, American novelists began to search for ways to revitalize the novel. The most inventive found ways to use creatively the chaos and contradictions of the time. First in short stories and then in a novel, *Snow White* (1967), Donald Barthelme perfected his technique of narrative "collage," a device that deliberately appeared to echo the fragmentation and randomness of American culture and society. In his first novel, *V.* (1963), Thomas Pynchon transformed the national obsession with plots and conspiracies into an innovative and elaborate narrative; in *Gravity's Rainbow* (1973), Pynchon explored an even darker and more complex landscape.

Two World War II novels, one published at the beginning and the other at the end of the 1960s and based on different modes of narrative experimentation, depicted what almost seemed another war than the one described in the late 1940s and early 1950s by writers such as Mailer and Jones. With his first novel, *Catch-22* (1961), Joseph Heller coined a phrase, which has since become part of the English and American vocabulary, to describe bureaucratic and technological irrationality and insanity. Kurt Vonnegut had been a prisoner of war in Dresden, Germany–a city of irreplaceable cultural importance and absolutely no military significance–when the British and U.S. air forces destroyed it in a technique known as firebombing. In *Slaughterhouse-Five* (1969), Vonnegut combined literary realism with science fiction to capture and convey the technological horror that he had witnessed.

John Barth, in a 1967 essay provocatively called "The Literature of Exhaustion," concisely expressed the rationale for the decade's continuous search for innovation in fictional technique. Careless readers saw the essay as simply another pronouncement of the death of the novel; and Barth, in places, seems to encourage precisely this kind of misinterpretation. At one point, for instance, he says he is "inclined to agree" with those who believe "the novel, if not narrative literature generally, if not the printed word altogether, has by this hour of the world just about shot its bolt. . . ." The essay, in fact, turns out to be a plea for the revitalization of the novel. Barth asserts that contemporary writers of fiction who ignore the work of such literary innovators as the Argentine writer Jorge Luis Borges, the Irish playwright Samuel Beckett, and the Russian-born novelist Vladimir Nabokov are doomed to create outdated and irrelevant fiction. Self-consciousness in narration is the key to creating the kind of art that Barth believed has validity; we need, he says, "novels which imitate the form of the Novel, by an author who imitates the role of Author."

The self-conscious, experimental fiction that Barth advocated and that he and others practiced was given different labels, the most common one probably being "metafiction." Assuredly, their work marked a movement of the American novel away from the controlled formalism of modernism and toward narrative openness and play. Whereas Hemingway and Faulkner had perfected techniques ranging from narrative minimalism to complex variations on stream of consciousness to prevent any overt intrusion of an authorial presence that would destroy the reader's suspension of disbelief, the 1960s practitioners of metafiction devised elaborate methods to expedite precisely such intrusions. In his critical study *City of Words* (1971) Tony Tanner provides an excellent analysis of the fascination that such elaborate and often self-reflective alternative "realities" as labyrinths, mirrors, and libraries held for these writers. In many ways, Barth's novel, *Giles Goat-Boy* (1966), epitomizes 1960s metafiction.

Barth's fellow metafictionists include William H. Gass, John Hawkes, Robert Coover, and Ishmael Reed. Gass published *Omensetter's Luck* in 1966 and debated the morality of metafiction with John Gardner. Hawkes produced a horrifying metafictional allegory of World War II in *The Cannibal* (1949) and followed it with *Second Skin* (1964) and *Blood Oranges* (1971). Reed revolutionized African American fiction even more completely than had Ellison, with his experiments in elaborately constructed and resolutely nonmimetic fables, *Yellow Back Radio Broke Down* (1969) and *Mumbo Jumbo* (1972).

There were other ways to respond to the sense that contemporary reality had become too complex and chaotic to be captured by traditional realistic fiction. For instance, one could attempt to erase the commonly accepted boundaries between fact and fiction. Describing contemporary events, Truman Capote in *In Cold Blood* (1965) and Mailer in *The Armies of the Night* (1968) combined objective reporting with fictional subjectivity to produce a genre variously called "nonfiction fiction," "faction," or "the New Journalism." Other writers, for instance Styron in *The Confessions of Nat Turner* (1967), chose instead to fictionalize the past. Styron's book was not at all the same thing as the standard historical novel; it was instead a meditation on the connections between past and present American racial hatred and guilt. Yet, for all the speculation during the 1960s that traditional literary realism could no longer capture external reality, Hubert Selby's *Last Exit to Brooklyn* (1964) and Joyce Carol Oates's *them* (1969) revitalized the tradition of American literary naturalism. Selby combined narrative experimentation with an uncompromisingly brutal vision of life in a marginal blue-collar neighborhood in Brooklyn, while Oates merged the legacy of western romance with a grim account of life in a Detroit slum. Both writers worked out of the pervasive and dehumanizing determinism that had characterized American literary naturalism since the turn of the century, while still managing to invent fresh modes of narration.

Too many sweeping generalizations about the influence of the 1960s on the American novel may have been made, but it seems safe to say that the decade was a climactic and defining one for the novel and for American literature in general. It at least resulted in the necessity to closely reexamine long-standing assumptions about the viability of literary realism and modernism, even if such examination resulted in the reaffirmation of either or both of these modes of writing.

For the United States, the 1970s, while inevitably a calmer decade than the 1960s, still witnessed its share of trauma. By the time a peace settlement was finally negotiated in 1973, 56,000 American troops had died in the remote Southeast Asian nation, and the war left a legacy of division and recrimination. The men and women who served in the Vietnam conflict did not receive the kind of homecoming that had traditionally been the reward for returning American veterans of overseas combat. Some were openly denounced by antiwar demonstrators, while most were ignored. No clear, easily comprehensible justification of the U.S. involvement in Vietnam was ever articulated, and the nation wanted above all to try to forget the entire experience as quickly as possible.

Only in the late 1970s did the American mass media begin a realistic evaluation of the war and its legacy. Between 1978 and 1990, such award-winning American movies as *The Deer Hunter, Coming Home, Platoon,* and *Born on the Fourth of July* graphically depicted the horrific nature of military combat in Vietnam and the postwar suffering of those who survived it. In addition, a group of young American writers, most of them veterans of the conflict in Southeast Asia, have produced a relatively small but distinguished body of fiction about the war. They have done so through a variety of literary approaches that echo both the early realistic-naturalistic World War II novels of Mailer, Jones, and Shaw, as well as the later postmodernist works of Heller and Vonnegut. For instance, Larry Heinemann's two novels, *Close Quarters* (1977) and *Paco's Story* (1987), are writ-

ten in a predominantly realistic mode, while Tim O'Brien's *Going After Cacciato* (1978) experiments with postmodernist narration. Robert Stone and Robert Olin Butler also have produced probing studies of the homefront legacy of the Vietnam War.

The 1970s also witnessed the Watergate scandal and the forced resignation from office of President Richard M. Nixon, and the resulting sense of national insecurity lingered into the 1980s. The Nixon presidency was followed by the administrations of Gerald Ford and Jimmy Carter, which remained largely scandal free, but were nevertheless perceived as unfocused and ineffectual; Ford and Carter were both defeated in their bids for reelection. But as the 1980s began, a politician adroit in utilizing the potential of television for creating dramatic and instantaneous images assumed the presidency: Ronald Reagan, a former motion-picture actor, dubbed "the Great Communicator" because of his intuitive mastery of the mass media, became the first American president since Eisenhower to complete two terms in office. The Reagan presidency represented a return to political conservatism and a repudiation of much of the liberal Democratic agenda that had dominated national politics since Franklin D. Roosevelt's "New Deal." This conservatism was the direct result of a national movement away from political activism; though it represented something of a new national consensus, it offended much of the old liberal, intellectual establishment.

During the late 1970s and most of the 1980s, the serious American writer became more alienated from the national mainstream than at any time since the 1920s. This alienation was partly but certainly not entirely the result of national politics, and to a significant degree was related to an evolving ideology in academic circles that denied the traditional role of the novel as the literary genre of the middle class. In fact, the influence of the French thinkers Michel Foucault and Jacques Derrida led to new theories–first structuralism and then deconstruction–that questioned traditional assumptions about the nature and purpose of literature and of writing itself. Most structuralists argued that literary "texts" were interrelated and were not primarily the creation of individual writers, but the product of the "structure" of society's dominant ideas and values. Deconstructionists held that because of the uncertainty of language itself, all writing inevitably negates its own apparent "meanings." Since these two theories assert that the traditional belief in an individual "author" of a novel is merely a convention, and that the elusiveness of language constantly negates the possibility of any consistent theme or intent in any piece of writing, they challenged and repudiated the traditional view of the novel as a controlled individual work designed to speak to a mass audience. Following in the tracks of Barth, Gass, Hawkes, and Reed, other exponents of postmodernist experimentation emerged. Walter Abish published two especially radical narrative experiments, *Alphabetical Africa* (1974) and *How German Is It* (1980). Nicholson Baker is known for his extraordinary interpretations of ordinary and even mundane subject matter. In *The Public Burning* (1977), Robert Coover crafted a postmodern absurdist version of the trial and execution, in the early 1950s, of accused atomic spies Julius and Ethel Rosenberg and, in 1982, an elaborate variation on Victorian pornography in *Spanking the Maid*. Paul Auster, an incomparable and powerful urban voice, published three remarkable novellas under the umbrella title *The New York Trilogy* (1987), in which he weds elements of the detective novel, literary history, and metaphysical speculation into a distinctive narrative form.

This new emphasis on the fundamentally arbitrary nature of literature and thus of critical judgments about it led to an extensive reexamination of the accepted canon of American literature. Beginning in the 1970s, feminist critics, merging some aspects of structuralist theory with the ideas of the French psychiatrist Jacques Lacan, argued that the canon had traditionally been established by white males and so reflected an arbitrary and limited approach to American writing. The feminist critical agenda resulted in more than one kind of benefit for American literary studies. This agenda led to the rediscovery of a few previously undervalued American women writers of the past: for instance, feminist writers Kate Chopin, Zora Neale Hurston, and Anzia Yezierska. It also inspired new thinking about the proper subject matter for the novel by asserting that books written by men have tended to minimize, if not completely ignore, the customary roles of women in society. Critical feminism brought as well a new awareness of the stereotypes that male writers have often imposed on their women characters, and a search for contemporary women writers to counter such stereotypes. Finally it paved the way for a brilliant new group of women writers. Marge Piercy published *Gone to Soldiers* (1987), an epic version of World War II as experienced by female protagonists. Jane Smiley viewed midwestern farm life from a Shakespearean perspective in *A Thousand Acres* (1991), and wrote a satire of the midwestern land grant university in *Moo* (1995).

The same impulses that produced feminist literary thinking have inspired, especially in academia, a view of literature and the novel in particular as being most important as a form of cultural study. This approach to literature has resulted in a new interest in writers from traditionally marginalized social groups. Beginning in the 1970s, such richly talented black

women writers as Toni Morrison, Jamaica Kincaid, Alice Walker, Gloria Naylor, Gayl Jones, Toni Cade Bambara, and more recently Bebe Moore Campbell, exercised an influence on the American novel comparable to that already enjoyed by such Jewish American writers as Saul Bellow, Philip Roth, and Bernard Malamud. Bellow and Roth have continued their central and prolific work. Roth, in his Zuckerman trilogy and his other elaborate experiments in merging fact with fiction, has produced an especially rich and complex body of work. Asian American novelists such as Maxine Hong Kingston, Amy Tan, and Gus Lee have appeared since the 1970s, as have Mexican American practitioners of the genre, including Tomás Rivera, Sandra Cisneros, Rolando Hinojosa, Rudolfo Anaya, and Ana Castillo. Finally, the fiction and poetry of N. Scott Momaday, Louise Erdrich, James Welch, Sherman Alexie, Leslie Marmon Silko, and Gerald Vizenor have inspired a Native American literary movement, with Vizenor functioning also as a major scholar of the movement.

It is obvious then that the contemporary American novel reflects a rich cultural diversity. This considerable benefit has inevitably resulted in the questioning of old assumptions about the role of the American novelist as the voice of national consensus. It is difficult to imagine anyone speaking today about the national mission of the American writer with the confident assurance of Ralph Waldo Emerson or William Dean Howells. It is even difficult to imagine anyone successfully playing the part of a national man of letters, as did Edmund Wilson for so long. For different reasons, and in different ways, postmodernist novelists such as Pynchon and even writers speaking for socially marginalized groups must assume that they are addressing much more restricted and limited audiences than the traditional middle-class readership of fiction. There are, in addition, more prosaic reasons for the contemporary alienation of the serious American novelist from the middle class.

Television has been the communications and entertainment medium of choice for middle-class America for four decades; and for almost that long writers and other intellectuals have bemoaned its shallowness and superficiality. Inevitably, the ubiquitous presence of television in America has trained its audience to respond more readily to instantaneous visual images than to the printed page. (Certainly, the American television audience was as intensely involved in learning who shot J. R. on the prime-time soap opera *Dallas* as Victorian English magazine readers were in following new installments of Charles Dickens's novels.) For an ever-increasing number of Americans, serious reading seems to be a lost art requiring too much solitary concentration.

In spite of such barriers, it must be said that a few serious and important postwar novelists continue to speak to, and sometimes on behalf of, middle-class America. John Updike's centrality to the postwar American novel is due in no small part to his evocation in four volumes of the financial and spiritual troubles of his fictional Toyota dealer, Rabbit Angstrom. In *Rabbit, Run* (1960), *Rabbit Redux* (1971), *Rabbit Is Rich* (1980), and *Rabbit at Rest* (1990), Updike depicts the morally ambiguous social rise of an ordinary American and thus echoes the fictional agendas of William Dean Howells and Sinclair Lewis. It is a tribute to the versatile nature of Updike's considerable talent that he can in other works echo, usually for satiric purposes, the methodology of literary deconstruction, as in *Memories of the Ford Administration* (1992).

Other postwar American novelists of impressive talent have revitalized old fictional genres, many traditionally associated with popular culture. For instance, regionalism has reemerged as a dominant force in American writing. Continuing a long and illustrious career, William Maxwell, whose eloquent *They Came Like Swallows* appeared in 1937, published another lyrical re-creation of the small-town Midwest, in *So Long, See You Tomorrow* (1980). Lee Smith, Clyde Edgerton, and Madison Smartt Bell, for example, helped revive Southern regionalism. The prolific and widely read Tom Clancy perfected his own fictional invention, the "techno-thriller," which combined the traditional elements of the suspense novel with detailed accounts of technological innovation.

In fact, it seems safe to say that, all the late 1950s and 1960s pronouncements of the novel's demise to the contrary, American fiction since World War II has been, and continues to be, quite healthy indeed. A 1968 anthology of post-1945 American fiction, *How We Live: Contemporary Life in Contemporary Fiction*, edited by Penny Chapin Hills and L. Rust Hills, illustrates this point by closing with a list of three hundred living American fiction writers of at least some significance. An even longer list might easily be developed today. Even if it is true that no contemporary American writers can be said to hold the kind of Olympian prominence enjoyed by modernist giants Hemingway and Faulkner, post–World War II American fiction is distinguished by a richer diversity of achievement than at any other time in the nation's history.

–James R. Giles and Wanda H. Giles

Acknowledgments

This book was produced by Bruccoli Clark Layman, Inc. Karen L. Rood is senior editor. Carol Fairman was the in-house editor.

Production manager is Philip B. Dematteis.

Administrative support was provided by Ann M. Cheschi, Dawnca T. Williams, and Mary A. Womble.

Accountant is Kathy Weston. Accounting assistant is Amber L. Coker.

Copyediting supervisor is Phyllis A. Avant. Senior copyeditor is Thom Harman. The copyediting staff includes Brenda Carol Blanton, James Denton, Melissa D. Hinton, William Tobias Mathes, Jennifer S. Reid, and Nancy E. Smith. Freelance copyeditor is Rebecca Mayo.

Editorial associates are Margo Dowling, Richard K. Galloway, and Michael Martin.

Layout and graphics supervisor is Janet E. Hill. Graphics staff includes Karla Corley Brown and Zoe R. Cook.

Office manager is Kathy Lawler Merlette.

Photography editors are Charles Mims, Scott Nemzek, and Paul Talbot. Digital photographic copy work was performed by Joseph M. Bruccoli and Zoe R. Cook.

SGML supervisor is Cory McNair. The SGML staff includes Linda Dalton Mullinax, Frank Graham, and Alex Snead.

Systems manager is Marie L. Parker.

Typesetting supervisor is Kathleen M. Flanagan. The typesetting staff includes Kimberly Kelly Brantley, Mark J. McEwan, Patricia Flanagan Salisbury, and Alison Smith. Freelance typesetters are Wanda Adams and Delores Plastow.

Walter W. Ross did library research. He was assisted by Steven Gross and the following librarians at the Thomas Cooper Library of the University of South Carolina: circulation department head Tucker Taylor; reference department head Virginia W. Weathers; Brette Barclay, Marilee Birchfield, Paul Cammarata, Gary Geer, Michael Macan, Tom Marcil, and Sharon Verba, reference librarians; interlibrary loan department head John Brunswick; and Robert Arndt, Jo Cottingham, Hayden Battle, Marna Hostetler, Nelson Rivera, Marieum McClary, and Erika Peake, interlibrary loan staff.

American Novelists Since World War II
Sixth Series

Dictionary of Literary Biography

Walter Abish

(24 December 1931 –   )

Julian Cowley
University of Luton

See also the Abish entry in *DLB 130: American Short-Story Writers Since World War II.*

BOOKS: *Duel Site* (New York: Tibor de Nagy Editions, 1970);
Alphabetical Africa (New York: New Directions, 1974);
Minds Meet (New York: New Directions, 1975);
In the Future Perfect (New York: New Directions, 1977; London: Faber & Faber, 1984);
How German Is It (New York: New Directions, 1980; Manchester, U.K.: Carcanet, 1982);
99: The New Meaning, photographs by Cecile Abish (Providence, R.I.: Burning Deck, 1990);
Eclipse Fever (New York: Knopf, 1993; London: Faber & Faber, 1993).

OTHER: "Self-Portrait," in *Individuals: Post-Movement Art in America,* edited by Alan Sondheim (New York: Dutton, 1977), pp. 1–25;
"The Shape of Absence," in *Firsthand,* introduction by Abish, photographs by Cecile Abish (Dayton, Ohio: Fine Arts Gallery, Wright State University, 1978), n. pag.;
"Auctioning Australia," in *Text–Sound Texts,* edited by Richard Kostelanetz (New York: Morrow, 1980), pp. 27–30;
"The Idea of Switzerland," in *The Best American Short Stories, 1981,* edited by Hortense Calisher and Shannon Ravenel (Boston: Houghton Mifflin, 1981), pp. 1–28;
"Is this really you?" from *As If,* in *Facing Texts: Encounters Between Contemporary Writers and Critics,* edited by Heide Ziegler (Durham, N.C.: Duke University Press, 1988), pp. 153–167;

Walter Abish (photograph by Cecile Abish)

Twenty Stories by Eighteen Authors, edited by Abish (New York: Cooper Union for the Advancement of Science and Art, 1995).

SELECTED PERIODICAL PUBLICATIONS–
UNCOLLECTED: "Happiness," *Parenthèse,* 2 (1979): 107–112; revised in *New Directions,* 50 (Spring 1985): 101–107;

3

"The Writer-To-Be: An Impression of Living," *Sub-Stance*, 27 (1980): 101–114;

"Alphabet of Revelations," *New Directions*, 41 (1980): 66–78;

"Family," *Antaeus*, 52 (Spring 1984): 149–169;

"Just When We Believe That Everything Has Changed," *Conjunctions*, 8 (1985): 25–31;

"The Fall of Summer," *Conjunctions*, 8 (1985): 110–141;

"I Am the Dust Under Your Feet," *Conjunctions*, 10 (1987): 7–33;

"Furniture of Desire," *Granta*, 28 (Autumn 1989): 131–145;

"Reading Kafka in German," *Conjunctions*, 14 (Winter 1989): 21–39;

"The Coming Ice Age," *Salmagundi*, 85–86 (Winter–Spring 1990): 152–171;

"House on Fire," *Antaeus*, 64–65 (Spring–Autumn 1990): 146–160.

Walter Abish is a writer who has managed to resolve successfully some of the prominent contradictions facing authors of contemporary fiction. He is a boldly innovative, critically acclaimed writer committed to ludic compositional procedures; yet, Abish's fiction has been found to yield sharp social criticism.

He has been the recipient of many prestigious awards, some of which are: fellow of National Endowment for the Arts, 1979 and 1985; Guggenheim Fellowship, 1981; PEN/Faulkner Award for Fiction, 1981, for *How German Is It* (1980); John D. MacArthur Foundation Fellowship, 1987–1992; and Award of Merit Medal for the Novel, American Academy and Institute of Arts and Letters, 1991.

A collection of poetry, two experimental texts, two collections of short stories, two novels, and occasional fictions in various magazines constitute Abish's literary output over thirty years. This measured approach to publication has prompted Harold Bloom to call him "a patient, immensely careful craftsman." Paul West, a writer admired by Abish, has designated him "an ostentatious parsimonist of himself," pointing out that Abish "has more prizes to his name than he has books." West describes the Abish style as "a touch mincing, but also sardonic and austerely fastidious," adding that "something sleek and taunting emerges when Abish writes," suggesting perhaps that Abish gives priority to aesthetic concerns. But Diane Johnson has asserted that Abish is "a moralist masquerading as a formalist." Jerry A. Varsava concurs emphatically: Abish's writing "effectively rebuts the argument that contemporary, innovative writers neglect history in their preoccupation with formalistic vanguardism."

Abish has listed some of the contemporary writers he admires: Donald and Frederick Barthelme, Samuel Beckett, Thomas Bernhard, Robert Coover, William Gaddis, William Gass, John Hawkes, Joseph McElroy, Thomas Pynchon, Victor Segalen, and West. His work takes its place in this company, comparable in terms of the quality of writing, and of the challenges and excitements it presents to readers.

Walter Abish was born into a Jewish, middle-class family in Vienna, Austria, on 24 December 1931. Following the annexation of Austria by Nazi Germany in 1938, Adolph and Frieda Rubin Abish fled with their son to Nice, France, where Abish attended school. In 1939 his father, a performer, was interned as an enemy alien in Les Milles until shortly before the German invasion in May 1940, when the Abish family was able to leave on one of the last ships to sail from Marseille to Shanghai. The Abishes remained in China until December 1948, when they departed for Israel before the communist defeat of the Kuomingtang. In conversation with Jerome Klinkowitz, Abish reflected on his childhood experiences in China and suggested that his reluctance to employ "straightforward explanatory action" in his work derives in part from "growing up in a world that was bewildering in its profusion of stylized drama, a drama that remained forever highly elusive." Recognizing this quality in the fiction, West has characterized Abish as a writer "who sedulously attends to the guesswork in life."

Abish was serving in the tank corps of the Israeli army when he began writing poetry at age eighteen. In an autobiographical piece, "The Writer-To-Be: An Impression of Living," published in *Sub-Stance* in 1980, Abish recalls the epiphanic moment from which his career as a writer stems: "I was crossing the parade ground in Ramle during my second year in the Tank Corps when quite suddenly the idea of becoming a writer flashed through my mind. A moment of pure exhiliration." After leaving the military, he undertook formal study to develop his interest in architecture, and subsequently he became involved in the design of small communities. In 1955 he met Cecile Gelb, an American working as a city planner in Israel. She later became a distinguished sculptor and photographer. They married, and while living in London he wrote a play, "He Came to Witness." Abish was heavily influenced by T. S. Eliot, and this play, written in verse despite its communist China setting, was his first completed work. As Abish told Maarten van Delden in a 1993 interview, "He Came to Witness" exemplifies the "preference for the foreign as a means of examining the familiar," which remains a highly significant aspect of his work.

For six months following his arrival in 1957 in New York, Abish was sequestered in a sanatorium at the foot of the Rocky Mountains as a result of a spot detected on his lung in London. There he wrote "The Burning of a Misfit child," a play set in a small midwestern community that feels threatened by anything not conforming to the familiar.

Abish took American citizenship in 1960. He had established a career in urban planning, designing and producing master plans, while continuing to cultivate his skills as a writer. His first published work was a fiction piece called "Frank's Birthday Confrontation," which appeared in a magazine called *Confrontation*, issuing in Spring 1970 from Long Island University in New York. Also in 1970, while living near the site in Weehawken, New Jersey, of the duel between Alexander Hamilton and Aaron Burr in 1804, Abish published his first book, *Duel Site,* a collection of poems. He had written novels before 1970 but could not find a publisher for them.

In 1972 Abish received an award from the New Jersey State Council for the Arts. The experimental text *Alphabetical Africa* was published by New Directions in 1974. In *The Life of Fiction* (1977), Klinkowitz remarked that Abish was, in the early years of his literary career, "preeminently a New Directions writer." Indeed, despite rejecting an early novel, New Directions publisher James Laughlin encouraged Abish's work, and his pieces appeared in fifteen anthologies issued by the publishing house between 1971 and 1986. Abish continued to channel his work through a range of small press publications and adventurous literary magazines based not only in the United States and in England, but also in Austria, France, Germany, Holland, Israel, Italy, Poland, Spain, and Sweden.

Alphabetical Africa resembles the radical work of European writers of the Oulipo group, such as Raymond Queneau and Georges Perec, in that it is written under blatant, and arbitrary, constraint. The initial chapter comprises only words that begin with the letter "a." The second chapter adds words beginning with "b," the third adds "c," and so on until the alphabet is completed. The process then operates in reverse, from the full range of available words, back to those starting with "a." In effect, chapters become longer as the centre of the book is approached, with the briefest at either end. In an interview with Larry McCaffery and Sinda Gregory in 1987, Abish explained that the attraction to him of working within self-imposed constraints is that "from the start they present a journey past and over obstacles."

Abish relished in particular the restriction of being unable to write in the first person until he reached the ninth chapter. This ostensible handicap suited Abish's purpose extremely well. In discussion with Klinkowitz, he noted that in this extraordinary prose work, and in his story titled "This is not a film, this is a precise act of disbelief," he aimed for "a neutral value" in his writing, seeking to avoid "the inten-

Abish with his wife, Cecile, in London, 1957 (courtesy of Walter Abish)

tional and sometimes unintentional hierarchy of values that seem to creep in whenever lifelike incidents are depicted." By containing subjectivity within the artifice of verbal play, Abish clearly was taking a major step toward attainment of his aesthetic goal.

Specifically, *Alphabetical Africa* began with a request from Laughlin for an anthology piece comparable to "Minds Meet," a story that had appeared in *TriQuarterly* (1973) before being collected in the volume that bears its name. In that story, formed from sections of a page or less in length, a keyword in the alphabetically ordered subtitle that headed each section acted as a catalyst for composition. In response to Laughlin's request, Abish set out to produce a story of fifteen or twenty pages, but the work assumed its own momentum. Laughlin embraced the expanded project and agreed to publish it.

In further explanation of the genesis of the novel, Abish told Klinkowitz of an African diary advertised for sale, its price reduced from around $90 to $5. Curious to discover what an African diary might be, Abish sought to buy one. The last copy was sold, wrapped, as he reached the counter to make his purchase. In retrospect, as he remarked to McCaffery and Gregory, "the unseen diary was the precursor for the structured novel that I wrote a year later." Additionally, Abish told them he was drawn to Africa as "a continent of taboos that seem to have little bearing on the taboos we encounter in the West." He is fascinated by the unspoken rules that govern behavior, and by their diversity within differing cultures.

He has suggested that the struggle involved in addressing the compositional constraints he had imposed paralleled the difficulties facing his imagination in confronting Africa. Anthony Schirato, in his 1992 essay "Comic Politics and Politics of the Comic: Walter Abish's *Alphabetical Africa*," has argued for a politically inflected content, on the grounds that "the narrative is produced out of a rigid and limiting system in much the same way that Western colonial discourse determines what we can 'see' of Africa." For Abish, the continent was certainly colored by his reading of Joseph Conrad, André Gide, Ernest Hemingway, Sir Richard Burton, and Andrew Turnbull, by Edgar Rice Burroughs, and by the concoctions of Hollywood. Surprisingly perhaps, he had not read Raymond Roussel's *Impressions of Africa* (1966) before writing his own "African" work. He has encountered Roussel's system-generated fictions subsequently, but finds the legend behind the books more stimulating than the books themselves, which he considers excessively mechanical in conception and execution.

Klinkowitz, in *The Life of Fiction*, quotes Abish saying that he feels "a distrust of the understanding that is intrinsic to any communication," and adding that he decided to write a book in which his distrust "became a determining factor upon which the flow of narrative was largely predicated." Nonetheless, *Alphabetical Africa* does have a discernible storyline, despite the foregrounding of structural constraint. Briefly put, it follows the adventures of two jewel thieves, as they trek across Africa, searching for their nymphomaniac lover, who has been abducted by Bantus. Claire Fox, in her 1990 essay "Writing Africa With Another Alphabet: Conrad and Abish" argues that Abish is parodying formulaic representation of "woman as enigma," while also undermining the familiar characteristics of the detective story. Fantastic elements certainly subvert conventional expectations, as Abish's Africa is attacked by driver ants who have discovered a fourth dimension, while Tanzania has been painted orange by the transvestite Queen Quat to match its appearance on maps. The book's comic exuberance exceeds any attempt to delineate plot or trace parodic intent.

In 1974 Abish received an award from the Rose Isabel Williams Foundation. In 1975 his first collection of short stories, *Minds Meet,* was published. The volume includes significant fictions, such as the title story and "This is not a film, this is a precise act of disbelief," which is of novella length. The latter begins: "This is a familiar world. It is a world crowded with familiar faces and events. Thanks to language the brain can digest, piece by piece, what has occurred and what may yet occur. It is never at a

loss for the word that signifies what is happening this instant." The human capacity to filter experiential data to form coherent and stable patterns has remained a source of fascination to Abish. But he is alert to the stultifying effect of attributing to such a familiar world the status of truth. Beyond conventional ordering structures, extensively reliant upon language, the turbulent energies of living are continually engaged in endlessly creative and destructive processes. To ignore these vital processes is to diminish the life experience and to live within illusions, which Abish recognizes as fundamentally harmful.

The story is in three parts, and in thirty-one sections. Varsava, in his book, *Contingent Meanings: Postmodern Fiction, Mimesis, and the Reader* (1990), has remarked that here, as elsewhere in his writing, "Abish skillfully marries fragmentation and allusivity to such conventions of realism as natural plot chronology, symbolism, and surface description." He adds that this story "defamiliarizes both the reassuring surfaces of conventional realist fiction and the reassuring surfaces of the quotidian." Here, Varsava concurs with Klinkowitz who, in *The Life of Fiction*, noted that "Abish disrupts the smooth system of language, so that superficial conventions are revealed as just that." Both critics recognize the world of Abish's shorter fiction as one of familiar surfaces, lurking needs, and sexual predation.

The story "Non-Sites," also in *Minds Meet,* was inspired by the landworks of Robert Smithson. Abish is acutely sensitive to developments in visual art, being drawn to the work of such artists as Cy Twombley, Agnes Martin, Richard Artschweiger, Bruce Naumann, Neil Jenny, Sol Levitt, and Robert Ryman. With his wife, he has long been based in Manhattan, and the couple have been immersed in the city's fertile art milieu. Interviewed in his East Village loft by Maarten van Delden, Abish restated his admiration for the determined inventiveness and the willingness to take risks he has found among practitioners of visual and plastic arts. In the 1970s, a number of his other stories responded explicitly to the creativity of painters and sculptors. "With Bill in the Desert," for example, was based on a gallery installation by Terry Fox. In 1993 he told van Delden: "I would go so far as to say that I privilege the arts—for their ability to skirt the familiar and thereby elude the easy explanation."

Although Abish works sedulously with a verbal surface, he does not rely on style or vocabulary to fix attention at that level of material. Abish is not a writer who performs pyrotechnics on the page. Richard Martin, in his 1983 essay, cites a review of *Minds Meet* by Daniel Levinson that appeared in *Aspect* in 1976. Levinson observed that "By rendering words as neutral as paint on film, Abish transforms them into whatever emotionally charged surface he chooses. Images, not words or phrases, linger in the mind." Martin properly notes that "The last sentence is peculiarly applicable to Abish's later work."

In the spring of 1977, Abish was a writer in residence at Wheaton College in Norton, Massachusetts. During the fall of that year, he was visiting Butler Professor of English at the State University of New York at Buffalo. Also in 1977, he was recipient of an award from the Ingram Merrill Foundation, and he published his second collection of stories, *In the Future Perfect*. In this book, he instigated a literary investigation of contemporary Germany's relationships with its past, which reached its culmination in the novel *How German Is It,* three years later. The roots of that novel clearly reside in a story whose title, "The English Garden," is derived from John Ashbery's *Three Poems* (1972). In an interview with Sylvère Lotringer (1982), Abish comments: "The story describes an American who has come to Germany to interview a German writer. On his arrival the American buys a coloring book, really a children's coloring book, at the airport. During his brief stay he keeps questioning the signs in the coloring book and comparing them to other signs in Germany. That immediately reduces the landscape, everything I describe, to a set of signs and images and also introduces, not the interpretation itself, but the need for interpretation as well as the level on which the speculation is to be conducted. A level of seriousness is implied and suggested."

The pieces assembled for *In the Future Perfect* are, as in Abish's previous short-story collection, oblique fictions, composed from fragments, resisting facile summary or easy exposition. They are metafictional in the sense that they require readers to recognize the artifice of form, and the contrivance that informs perception of coherence. Many of his characters manifest a concern for preservation of order, or (as in the volume's punning title) for formal perfection, which acts as a kind of anesthetic. The many references in his work to photography reflect an interest he understandably shares with his wife Cecile, but they also function thematically as images of stability, of life artificially frozen and preserved from change. The limits to satisfaction granted by such instances of arrested motion are invoked in both "Parting Shot" and "In So Many Words," where Abish quotes Alfred North Whitehead's dictum: "Even perfection will not bear the tedium of infinite repetition."

Ironically, in "Parting Shot" the quotation is played against a glimpse of the contents of a shop window, and it is followed by the question: "Did Whitehead know that wealth enables people to

Dust jacket for Abish's 1980 novel, about a West German town built on the ruins of a World War II concentration camp

acquire the perfect apartment, the perfect country house, the perfect haircut, the perfect English suits, the perfect leather and chrome armchair, the perfect shower curtain, the perfect tiles for the kitchen floor, and a perfect quiche available only from a small French bakery near Madison Avenue, and the perfect Italian boots that look like English boots but are more elegant, and the perfect mate, and the perfect stereo, and the perfect books that have received or undoubtedly are just about to receive a glowing review in the *Saturday Review*."

Ownership and consumption are presented in Abish's fiction as means to fortify selfhood. Identity is delineated in part by the capacity to possess. In his contribution to the volume *Facing Texts: Encounters Between Contemporary Writers and Critics,* published in 1988, Christopher Butler identifies Abish's perception that the self is "perpetually attempting to make the world familiar, comfortable, and conformable to its organizing desires." He cites a paper titled "On Aspects of the Familiar World as Perceived in Everyday Life and Literature," delivered in 1981 at the Second International Conference on Innovation/Renovation in Contemporary Culture, held at the University of Wisconsin, Milwaukee. Here Abish suggested, "All that is required to depict the 'familiar' is that the possessive pronoun, singular or personal, be introduced in a sentence or attached to a word: Our doorway, our neighborhood, my grandeur, his view." Possession is the constant goal of the self and its vocabulary, and perfection is ownership's utopia.

In 1979 Abish was granted a fellowship by the National Endowment for the Arts. From 1979 until 1988, he lectured on English and Comparative Literature at Columbia University. In 1981, he received a C.A.P.S. Grant, as well as a Guggenheim Fellowship, and *How German Is It* won the PEN/Faulkner Award as the most distinguished work of fiction for that year.

If the Africa of his first novel bears scant resemblance to any geographical reality, the Germany of this more conventionally realistic work seems more closely related to an actual place. Yet, despite the ostensible shift away from the linguistic plane toward narrative realism, Abish is essentially concerned here also with a structure of signs, the structure that constitutes the category "Germany" within contemporary understanding. His focus is on what falls within this category in the aftermath of World War II. In fact, he had no firsthand experience of the country at the time he wrote *How German Is It*. It was a fellowship from a German academic exchange program that enabled him in 1987 to visit and to spend six months in Berlin.

Consciously precluding personal familiarity with the culture and topography of which he writes, Abish finds it easier to engage in the practice that Ihab Hassan, in a review of Abish's *How German Is It,* has called "decreation." This entails "a kind of formal cruelty toward things as they seem." In other words, Abish subjects the terms of our everyday understanding to textual pressures, which fracture comfortable explanation and easy exposition. Abish's fiction discomforts readers. It does so not only by denying a neatly packaged meaning that can be easily abstracted from the verbal surface, but also by making the reader aware of the customary reliance on such abstractable meaning.

How German Is It succeeds to the extent that it draws the reader into a familiarly novelistic world, while simultaneously denying that ready satisfaction of knowing, which is the foundation of literary realism. Hence, the author's pleasure at Sylvère Lotringer's recognition, during their 1982 interview, that *How German Is It,* despite superficial appearances, is a ludic novel. Abish remarks that "so far, the critics who have reviewed the book in Germany have failed to understand it. They cannot see the element of play in the book. The 'history' is too close." Play should not be understood here as aesthetic detachment; rather, it is the key to the novel's moral and political engagement.

Schirato, in his essay on *Alphabetical Africa,* finds in that text "a play between, on the one hand, the notion of textual discourse as nothing more than the product of a system that is only capable of reproducing that system and is, therefore, ontologically empty, and, on the other, a notion of discourse as being full of references to its connections with the world outside language and of its dealings with politics, colonialism, and exploitation." His reading then aspires to show how an oblique political content is "consanguinous with narrative practices."

Arguably, Schirato presses the point a little too far in an effort to contain the ludic aspects of *Alphabetical Africa* within a coherent model of understanding its political content. Readers and critics of Abish's work face the constant risk that they will succumb to the temptation to explain it away.

In his shorter fiction, in particular, Abish foregrounds structural elements in order to make such assimilation difficult. Varsava remarks that "Abish would risk unintended, unfortunate self-parody were he to discuss the 'familiar' in familiar literary-generic terms. The 'familiar' can only be effectively depicted through a representational mode that denudes it of its familiarity, making of it something foreign, something unsettling, something perhaps even hateful to the reader." But this formulation, while appropriate to much of the shorter fiction, misses the teasing element that West and others have recognized in the novels; an element that depends largely on a radically equivocal response to the allure of the familiar. The mode of *How German Is It* is a highly sophisticated and refined form of parody that invites readers to feel at home at the same time that it systematically unsettles and disorients them.

In chapter 14 of the novel, Anna Heller writes the word "familiar" on a blackboard, before inviting her class to enter into discussion of the topic. She says,

> "One might even venture to say that the familiar is reassuring. We more or less know what to expect. What it will be like. It will be familiar. which may be a good reason why we, every once in a while, wish to get away, to escape from the familiar, to visit some far-off place, China or India for instance, because we are willing . . . no . . . because we are eager to stretch our imaginations and see something for the first time, something that is not yet entirely familiar. And so, if we are open-minded, we want to introduce to our existence something that is new, something that is different."

As Richard Walsh has pointed out in his book *Novel Arguments: Reading Innovative American Fiction* (1995), that particular scene is a variant on his paper, "On Aspects of the Familiar World as Perceived in Everyday Life and Literature." Alert to Abish's fascinated engagement with structures of signs, Walsh suggests that his recurrent use of the term, "the familiar," is comparable to "the natural" as it occurs in Roland Barthes's politically committed handbook for semiotic analysis, *Mythologies* (1957).

Butler, in *Facing Texts: Encounters Between Contemporary Writers and Critics,* recognizes that Abish's fictions "do not easily create any consensus as to their interpretative meaning," and he makes a case for their being, in consequence, an index of postmodern relativism. Nonetheless, Butler adopts the view that they "show us how this disruptive relationship of the text to our assumed knowledge of the world can still have a moral effect over which we might be able to agree." He has suggested that the uneasiness of reading Abish involves an element of guilt, proceeding from our sense of complicity in stereotyping. As Butler says, "However much we may like to think we can resist Abish's obliging anatomy of cultural stereotypes, in the very act of recognizing them we are made their accomplices." Indeed, he goes so far as to compare Abish to Jonathan Swift in terms of the way he manages "to convict us of harboring prejudices, which he seems positively to encourage us to hold."

Butler espouses, then, the view that Abish is "an insidiously didactic and even moralizing writer" who, like Swift, is preeminently an ironist and a humorist. Expanding on his opinions, he accurately sums up the writer's three main concerns as "(1) an attack on the notion of the self wishing to order the world in its own interests, (2) the defamiliarization of the world that results once the incorporating self is dethroned, and (3) the uncertainties thus produced, in his characters and in the reader, by the sense of relativism and conflict of cultures that results from this new relation."

Varsava's overview in his article "Walter Abish and the Topographies of Desire" is that "*How German Is It* considers the production, maintenance, and reception of the field of signs in the context of a small West German town in the seventies, paying particular mind to the ideological bias that responses to signs betray." Importantly, the title has no question mark to signal the interrogative mode. In response to a question from Lotringer, Abish stressed that the title "is not primarily a question." He proceeded, in the interview, to denounce "our preoccupation with depth," which he recognizes as further manifestation of "a desire for resolution, for explanation." In defiance of such desire, Abish asserts that "everything is on the surface." The book is an encounter with structures of signification rather than a quest for answers.

Dust jacket for Abish's 1993 novel, which examines cultural contrasts between Mexico and the United States

In practice Abish is committed to the seemingly obsessive registration of small details, rather than the excavation of large meanings. This characteristic is most appropriately and forcefully demonstrated when, in *How German Is It,* a mass grave is uncovered. It is a singularly resonant event; yet, Abish resists the temptation to unpack its significance in the manner of a grand exposition of human behavior. He points out to Lotringer that, "In life we are forever, it seems, confronted by situations that defy explanation. We simply do not have sufficient information about them. Yet we interpret and explain. Anything. Everything." His fictions illuminate the kinds of investment made in this activity, and at the same time, as a corollary of this insight, he is conscious that "Puzzles and mysteries, if used well, energize the text." He reiterated this point in conversation with McCaffery and Gregory, where he spoke of the energizing value of ambiguity as a means to counter the reproduction of "formula truths."

Still, Abish's meticulous concern for the surface of the quotidian results in a potentially disconcerting evenness, or flatness, in the construction of his narratives. As Varsava observes in *Contingent Meanings:* "Not a lot happens in Abish's fiction, typically. He juxtaposes a series of short, narrowly enframed scenes involving, for example, a character considering the contents of a shop window, or a sparse narratorial description of an interior, or a bland conversational exchange." It is perhaps more accurate to say that events do occur, but Abish does not allow them to assume the role of obvious focal points for interpretation. Such conventional attribution of significance has become second nature for most of us, and, as Abish stressed in the interview with McCaffery and Gregory, he aims "to undermine the so-called political stability of everyday life that is, in essence, implied in most fiction." He appreciates that such stability relies upon the channeling of energy into narratives that identify peaks and troughs of experience in fixed patterns that invite our passive acceptance.

The epigraph for *How German Is It* is taken from Jean-Luc Godard: "What is at stake is one's image of oneself." Abish has acknowledged the stimulation to creative work he receives from cinema. Among the directors he favors are Eric Rohmer, Paolo Pasolini, Alain Tanner, Rainer Werner Fassbinder, and Stanley Kubrick, but Godard is who he most readily cites as a conscious influence. He has been intrigued by the manner in which the movie director has struggled to achieve and to maintain an appropriate balance between his political beliefs and his involvement with aesthetic issues. Such a balancing act assumed a different complexion in the case of Martin Heidegger, whose work has also fascinated Abish. Heidegger provides a model for Brumhold, a fictional philosopher from whom Brumholdstein, the city in which the novel is set, takes its name. Through Brumhold, Abish expounds the coexistence, in a typical image of German character, of inveterate dedication to order and of attraction to irrationality and of mystification.

If *How German Is It* can be said to have a protagonist, it is Ulrich Hargenau, a novelist and one of Brumhold's former students, whose father was executed for his active opposition to Hitler. Ulrich's brother, Helmuth, is a successful architect, a leading designer of the new town. Among Helmuth's connections are Anna Heller, the schoolteacher; Egon, a book publisher, and his partner, Gisela; and a photographer named Rita Tropf-Ulmwehrt. In the midst of their relative normality, Abish places Ulrich's former wife, Paula, and other members of a left-wing terrorist group called the Einzieh, whose violent gestures defy easy interpretation. Abish spoke to McCaffery and

Gregory of his admiration for Godard's ability to create in his early movies an "uneasy product, in which the gratuitous act of violence was perfectly framed." As is so often the case in his work, a placid surface is ruptured by intimations or instances of lurking chaos. Near the beginning of Part Two of *How German Is It,* the narrator observes: "One runs little or no danger in speaking of the weather, or in repeating what others may have said on that subject. It is safe to conclude that people discussing the weather may be doing so in order to avoid a more controversial subject, one that might irritate, annoy, or even anger someone, anyone, within earshot."

As noted earlier, the novel dramatically expands an earlier fiction, "The English Garden," the story which opens *In the Future Perfect.* There, an American travels to Brumholdstein to interview the German writer Wilhem Aus. During the visit he becomes involved with Ingeborg Platt, a local librarian whose father had been a Nazi. Shortly before his departure, she disappears. The American and Aus search her apartment for clues to her whereabouts, but find only a photograph of inmates of the former concentration camp on which the new town is built. Though the American feels that he is suspected of causing Platt's disappearance, no one prevents him from leaving.

As in *How German Is It,* Brumholdstein is a new town, constructed to embody coherent design but also to conceal the site of a former concentration camp, Durst. This attempt at suppression of the past through a strategy of concealment is characteristic of life in modern Germany, as portrayed in both fictions. Abish is always alert to the potentially damaging effects of such precarious imposition of consoling rational structures. The cosmetic nature of such concealment is exposed in the novel's concluding sentence: "Is it possible for anyone in Germany, nowadays, to raise his right hand, for whatever reason, and not be flooded by the memory of a dream to end all dreams?"

Abish, concerned as ever to outlaw cliché as a presence with any potency in his work, remarked to McCaffery and Gregory that he considers the raising of the arm to be a gesture that now belongs as much to Hollywood as to German reality, where it is repressed through taboo. That concluding sentence follows the physical raising of an arm by Ulrich, in the office of a hypnotherapist. Abish told his interviewers that the incident was based on his own experience on a visit to a New York hypnotist. But while this anecdote seems to deprive the gesture of its Barthesian mythological power, Abish immediately restores that power with the observation that Ulrich "was thrust back into a period when the outstretched arm signified a unanimity—it was the icon that lay at

19

proof of man's interminable moral striving. No one saw any reason

to take issue with his inference... for that matter, no one see-

med to realize that Alejandro, admittedly in a most circuitous

fashion, was mocking the American author whose novels were peopled

by a once glamorous WASP upper-middle class whose values, much

like their present-day interiors, were decidedly dated and more

than a little frayed. Still, these novels about a class whose

political power and influence was on the wane, still made it to the

best seller list. Was it because Jurud, not a Wasp himself, with

a Proustian delight, depicted their shortcomings, much as Proust

had depicted the shortcomings of the Guermantes, only in order to

elevate them to their proper place in history. Alejandro con-

sidered *Intimacy*, at best a grandiloquent entertainment but not, as

the US publisher claimed, a serious contemplative work of Ameri-

can literature.

The month his article on Jurud appeared, anyone in a position

to observe the critic and his girlfriend, Mercedes ascend the Py-

ramid of the Sun on what proved to be the hottest days that June

could have foretold what Alejandro failed to realize, namely that

their relationship, for lack of a better word, was not a promising

one!

Why had he insisted that they climb the pyramid that particu-

lar day with the temperature hovering at 92 degrees? Half-way up

the steep slope of the *Pyramid of the Sun*, Alejandro had stopped

to allow Mercedes to catch her breath. Dejected, she sat down,

resting her elbows on her knees, hands supporting the weight of

Page from the revised typescript for Eclipse Fever *(Collection of Walter Abish)*

the heart of Nazism. In time, even for believers, the salute must have become a perfunctory greeting; nevertheless, at first, with Hitler in power, if one is to trust photographic evidence, the salute embodied a tremendous ecstatic affirmation, a belief, a sense of unity, a sense of being one with the Volk."

This sentence, with its tellingly placed conditional clause, is indicative of Abish's desire to hold in suspension explanatory procedures that might themselves create a momentum for the establishment of ideological unanimity. Van Delden, in an essay on *How German Is It,* notes how the novel combines "the relentless refusal of all certainties," which he associates with the ludic in postmodernist practice, with "an obsessive evocation of the subterranean presence of the horrors of the Third Reich underneath the surface placidity of the new Germany." He suggests that this literary strategy is "precisely suited to the evocation of a past that is perhaps not so much unknowable as unspeakable, and so is best approached through methods of indirection." It might be added that for Abish such indirection seems always to be salutary.

Van Delden's crucial concern in the essay is with treatment of the past within postmodernism, and he affirms that the period in history addressed in *How German Is It* "clamors for a sense of moral discrimination." He holds it, then, to be particularly significant that this is "a novel of withheld information and intriguing omissions." He elaborates, observing that "The constant generation of new enigmas, most of which are left unresolved, as well as the narrator's habit of posing endless questions, even about the most trivial matters, questions that remain largely without answers, are devices for luring the reader into the text, but they also constitute a method of representation. These techniques deconstruct the familiar world of contemporary Germany in order to depict it as a place of evasion and deception, of discontinuities between past and present, a place haunted by an unresolved history, where the past is continually being evoked and then side-stepped."

Van Delden's analysis is an insightful distillation of Abish's remarkable and virtuosic handling of "formal and semantic instability" in this novel. He points out with equal acuity that the narrative's success owes a great deal to its author's distinctive use of point of view which, "in circulating from character to character in a largely inconclusive motion, impedes the creation of a strong personal and moral center to the novel. The novel's standard method is to introduce new characters, often without a great deal of explanation, and eventually to drop them again, without having established a clear relationship to the overall plot, which, in any case, remains extremely shadowy." In

spite of this tenebrous quality, *How German Is It* has been translated into twelve languages and has received widespread critical acclaim, which installs Abish's novel among the major works of fiction produced in North America during the past half century.

Between 1981 and 1983, Abish acted as a panelist advising on literature for the New York State Council on the Arts. From 1982 until 1988, he was a member of the Executive Board for the PEN American Center. In 1985 he received a second National Endowment for the Arts Fellowship. In the mid 1980s Abish assumed a series of Guest Professorships: Yale in 1985; Brown in 1986; and The Cooper Union in 1987, to which he returned in both 1993 and 1994.

Between 1987 and 1992, Abish held a fellowship from the John D. and Catherine T. MacArthur Foundation; this award enabled him to commit himself to writing full time. A citation from the American Academy and Institute of Arts and Letters, issued in 1991, recognized Abish as at once "a relentless experimenter" and "a permanent figure" in the landscape of American literature. Accompanying the award of a Merit Medal for the Novel, this citation affirmed that the essence of his work has been inventiveness, but also characterized him as "a Swiftian ironist, and an authentic representative of the great tradition of skeptical questioning of national identitites, with their spurious myths of shared values."

Diane Johnson pointed out in her piece "How Mexican Is It?" in *The New York Review of Books* (23 September 1993) that in Abish's work one finds the conjoint perceptions that "History, because it is narrated, is subjective and interpretative like fiction, and fiction cannot escape the didactic implications of history." Within this perspective, Abish may be placed alongside other contemporary writers who practice "historiographic metafiction," to use the term popularized by academic critic Linda Hutcheon in her book *A Poetic of Postmodernism* (1988). But there is in Abish's work a distinctive antiepic orientation that channels his ironies in a concentrated rebuttal to those "spurious myths of shared values." In recognition of this orientation, Christopher Butler observes that "Abish likes societies where things seem to work but which have an underlying unease, and he likes the source of that unease to be a past history, and bygone ideologies that haunt the present."

Butler was thinking of *How German Is It* in particular, but his judgment is equally applicable to Abish's novel, *Eclipse Fever* (1993). *Eclipse Fever* is set in Mexico. Once again, Abish pursues his interest in "the everyday in a foreign setting." The point is made clear, once more, in what Abish expressed to van Delden: "What is instantly understood and explained in our culture reverberates differently in our head when it occurs in an alien context." Once again, the author's choice of location was based on the fact that Mexico was a country he had never visited. It was his conscious aim to avoid and help dispel the mystique surrounding the country, as it is portrayed in works by writers including D. H. Lawrence and Malcolm Lowry. As Abish told van Delden, "The exotic can become an outright entrapment. It promises gratification, but it is difficult to sustain and the allure wears off all too quickly."

In the same interview, he cast light on the title by remarking that "the eclipse was a time of high anxiety for the pre-Columbians who believed that in order to replenish the sun's waning power the gods would descend to earth and devour men. A serious reading of the novel must take into consideration that it is the muse, the source of our inspiration, that is being eclipsed." In that respect it resembles numerous American novels of recent decades, which have assumed an apocalyptic air, and have pursued images of cultural entropy. A more immediate, political interpretation is possible. Johnson suggests that eclipse is "a suitable metaphor for the erosion of the Mexican by the American culture, and the triumph of non-history (America) over history (Mexico)."

In his article "Ecliptic Art" for the *Southern Review* (Summer 1994), Ihab Hassan indicated elegantly its multifarious nature: "The book may be read as an international thriller (two murders), a geo-political fiction (Yanquí economic imperialism), a study of cultural contrasts (Mexico and America), a Proustian interrogation of sex, class, and society (on both sides of the border), a meditation on power, both public and personal (*chingar,* the constant Mexican jostling for superiority), a reflection on human obsessions (with homes, places, memories, iterative patterns), a quest for identity (of Bonny, the runaway American teenager; of Alejandro, the Mexican literary critic; and of the American and Mexican nations), a hidden portrait of the artist as fabulator (Abish himself), and a metaphysical novel about the yawning absence at the heart of reality (the titular eclipse)."

The principal characters are a girl named Bonny; her father, Jurud, who is a North American writer; Alejandro, a Mexican critic; and his wife, Mercedes. The relationship between father and daughter is complex in its mix of dependency and exploitation. Wendy Lesser, writing in *The New Republic* (21 June 1993), suggests that *Eclipse Fever,* like *How German Is It,* had its genesis in a short story; in this case, "Parting Shot," from *In the Future Perfect.* In that story an American writer systematically plunders the personal life of his daughter, Maude, to furnish raw material for his

fiction. In this novel, Bonny is similarly forced into realization that "in one guise or another she appeared in each one of her father's novels." As Abish remarked to van Delden, "To her everything she does, becomes an extension of her father's writing." Yet, as Lesser proceeds to explain, "the repetitions of phrase and image and character, both among and within Abish's works, are not signposts to guide us to his meaning; they are introduced with the intent to complicate." In other words, the reader is proffered a sign to suggest entry into a familiar world, only to have that consoling sense abruptly removed.

Abish acknowledged to van Delden that he regards subversion of character as a way of "demonstrating social instability." Coherence breaks down because of surprising behavior or unpredictable utterance. "Comments are made and then unmade." *Eclipse Fever* is, then, as resistant to satisfactory summary as the earlier fictions. Despite the fact that two murders occur, it is not that action which occupies the reader's attention. Rather, Abish again manages to create evocations of physical turbulence, while keeping his audience preoccupied with the problems of interpretation that arise from the verbal surface. Indeed, the consistent achievement of his fiction has been to confront the reader's habitual modes of mapping the terrain of quotidian experience, while sustaining the constant and radical threat of disruption arising from subterranean sources.

Van Delden suggested to Abish that, when reading *Eclipse Fever,* "one has the sense that in each individual scene there is something going on just outside the frame, whether it be some emotion that a character is unable or unwilling to express directly, or some event taking place at some distance from the main line of action." The novel persistently manages to intimate that more is occurring than is revealed through its evident action and that impression is intensified by Abish's disarmingly chaste prose. An apparent transparency conflicts with an opacity that at a certain point confronts, and ultimately baffles, any efforts to paraphrase or explain.

Abish responded to van Delden by noting how this structural tension is focused in the character of Alejandro, the literary critic, who is "the prime interpreter, the analyzer, the questioner even as he goes out of his way to overlook everything that is injurious to the functioning of the self." He is imbedded within a highly competitive group of "upwardly mobile intellectuals." Yet, the novel has no central character who, as van Delden put it, "anchors the action." He is properly insistent that, despite the presence of Alejandro, the narration "provides information in a way that reveals almost nothing about how the information ought to be evaluated." Hassan shrewdly commented that the novel has "a detachment that is the quality of intelligence itself in the face of existence." This detachment is perhaps what Abish himself had especially in mind when, talking with Klinkowitz, he observed of his approach to characterization: "I am convinced that the characters' actions are open to psychological interpretation, but my writing, and the kind of information that is made available to the reader, does not invite it."

Abish went on to reject humanist aesthetics in terms that seem to echo the fiction and the theoretical pronouncements of Alain Robbe-Grillet and Michel Butor, writers for whom Abish has expressed admiration: "Humanism with its specific values imposes a kind of center from which everything radiates . . . in the novel it affects the most diverse things . . . a scuffed carpet, a crack in the wall becomes intentionally or unintentionally incorporated in that humanistic field, presenting to the reader a kind of pattern he can instantly recognize and evaluate. This in itself is enough to destroy the possibilities I see in the novel." In his 1985 essay titled "Walter Abish's *How German Is It:* Language and the Crisis of Human Behavior," Dieter Saalmann drew attention to qualites shared by Abish's prose and the *nouveau roman:* "Like Alain Robbe-Grillet, Abish sets down physical details with a degree of flat precision, laconic brevity, and matter-of-factness that suggest a menacing emptiness."

Steven G. Kellman's article "Walter Abish's Metaphysical Mexico," in *Forward* (11 June 1993), noted the "anecdotal allure" of *Eclipse Fever* while taking stock of those "many absences, occlusions and displacements," that render the novel "as transparent as a galaxy of black holes." Lesser registered "the deep chasms of obsession that run through this seemingly accessible book." West, writing in *The Boston Phoenix* (June 1993), evoked the contesting qualities of the book in the adjectival melee of his reference to "this miasmal, ratiocinative, silky novel." Johnson sought to provide a more analytical overview, asserting that "this is, in fact, a novel written in the interrogative mood, in both the grammatical and psychological senses." She affirms that this mood communicates the author's view "that to question reality is perhaps a more appropriate mode of relating to it than understanding or judging it." Johnson perceived that Abish had accomplished a feat of textual construction that left readers "positioned deep in the subjective uncertainties of the protagonists' experience. No question is ever answered."

A Mexican ambassador's wife voices criticism of Jurud's work as lacking in life-affirming qualities. Abish is sensitive to comparable criticism directed at his own work, and this scene was consciously con-

trived as a response. As he told van Delden, he "wanted to show that people who themselves have little regard for life-affirming values will make use of the term whenever they find it convenient."

During the 1980s, Abish published regularly in various journals, notably *Conjunctions*. Since 1981 he has been a member of the distinguished panel of contributing editors to that fine showcase for new writing. Some of his pieces, composed from excerpts taken from works by other writers, were collected as *99: The New Meaning* (1990), a collection consisting of five works published by Burning Deck, the adventurous small press in Providence, Rhode Island. The title piece of these five verbal assemblages was to take the ninety-ninth page from ninety-nine texts by ninety-nine authors. As he explained to McCaffery and Gregory, the basis for ninety-nine is that "Literature is used as a vast dictionary from which what is extracted, according to a system, is assembled to create a so-called story." This exercise in applied intertextuality utilizes strategies of displacement and combination found extensively in twentieth-century visual arts. It also demonstrates that Abish's ongoing exploration of compositional possibilities has not been at all diminished by the critical acclaim afforded his ostensibly more conventional work.

Between 1990 and 1993 Abish served on the Board of Governors for the New York Foundation for the Arts. The American Academy and Institute of Arts and Letters presented him with the Award of Merit Medal for the Novel in 1991. He held a Lila Wallace-Reader's Digest Fellowship from 1992 until 1995. In May 1996 he was awarded an honorary Doctor of Letters by the State University of New York College at Onconta, and in 1998 Abish became a fellow of the American Academy of Arts and Sciences.

West proposes Henry James and Marcel Proust as Abish's true lineage. He suggests that "this is the literature of the salon, the fiction of the subtle scrutineer, the voyeur with the monocle." Bloom has remarked that *Eclipse Fever* combines "the very different fictional modes of Proust and of Kafka, the two writers from whom Abish most stems. Abish's sense of social reality is Proustian: The power relations between his characters arise from Proust's transformations of Flaubert's imagination of societal relations." His two full-length novels in particular (*How Germans Is It* and *Eclipse Fever*) have established awareness of Abish as a major contemporary writer. The body of critical work addressing Abish's fiction remains surprisingly limited at present, given the broad consensus with regard to his status evident among academic commentators and intelligent reviewers.

Interviews:

Jerome Klinkowitz, *Fiction International,* 4–5 (1975): 93–100;

Sylvère Lotringer, "'Wie Deutsch ist es'. Interview of Walter Abish," *Semiotext(e): The German Issue,* 4 (Spring 1982): 160–178;

Larry McCaffery and Sinda Gregory, *Alive and Writing: Interviews with American Authors of the 1980s* (Urbana: University of Illinois Press, 1987), pp. 7–25;

Maarten van Delden, "An Interview with Walter Abish on *Eclipse Fever,*" *Annals of Scholarship,* 10 (Fall 1993): 381–391.

References:

Alain Arias-Misson, "The 'New Novel' and TV Culture: Reflections on Walter Abish's *How German Is It,*" *Fiction International,* 17 (Spring 1987): 152–164;

Arias-Misson, "The Puzzle of Walter Abish: In the Future Perfect," *Sub-Stance: Current Trends in American Fiction,* 27 (Fall 1983): 115–124;

Kenneth Baker, "Restricted Fiction: The Writing of Walter Abish," *New Directions,* 35 (1977): 48–56;

Christopher Butler, "Walter Abish and the Questioning of the Reader," in *Facing Texts: Encounters Between Contemporary Writers and Critics,* edited by Heide Ziegler (Durham, N.C.: Duke University Press, 1988), pp. 168–185;

Claire Fox, "Writing Africa with Another Alphabet: Conrad and Abish," *Conradiana,* 22 (1990): 111–125;

Jerome Klinkowitz, "Walter Abish," in his *The Life Of Fiction* (Urbana: University of Illinois Press, 1977), pp. 59–71;

Richard Martin, "Walter Abish's Fictions: Perfect Unfamiliarity, Familiar Imperfection," *Journal of American Studies,* 17 (1983): 229–241;

Thomas Peyser, "How Global Is It: Walter Abish and the Fiction of Globalization," *Contemporary Literature,* 40 (Summer 1999): 240–262;

Dieter Saalmann, "Walter Abish's *How German Is It:* Language and the Crisis of Human Behavior," *Critique,* 26 (Spring 1985): 105–121;

Anthony Schirato, "Comic Politics and Politics of the Comic: Walter Abish's *Alphabetical Africa,*" *Critique,* 33 (Winter 1992): 133–144;

Schirato, "The Politics of Writing and Being Written: A Study of Walter Abish's *How German Is It,*" *Novel,* 24 (Fall 1990): 69–85;

Robert Siegle, "On the Subject of Walter Abish and Kathy Acker," *Literature and Psychology,* 33 (1987): 38–58;

Tony Tanner, "Present Imperfect: A Note on the Work of Walter Abish," *Granta* (Autumn 1979): 65–71;

Maarten van Delden, "Walter Abish's *How German Is It:* Postmodernism and the Past," *Salmagundi,* 85–86 (Winter–Spring 1990): 172–194;

Jerry A. Varsava, "Walter Abish and the Topographies of Desire" in his *Contingent Meanings: Postmodern Fiction, Mimesis, and the Reader* (Tallahassee: University of Florida Press, 1990), pp. 82–108;

Richard Walsh, "'One's Image of Oneself': Structured Identity in Walter Abish's *How German Is It,*" in his *Novel Arguments: Reading Innovative American Fiction* (Cambridge: Cambridge University Press, 1995), pp. 111–134;

Paul Wotipka, "Walter Abish's *How German Is It:* Representing the Postmodern," *Contemporary Literature,* 30 (1989): 503–517.

Paul Auster

(3 February 1947 –   )

Dennis Barone
Saint Joseph College

BOOKS: *Unearth: Poems 1970–72,* series 3 (Weston, Conn.: Living Hand, 1974);

Wall Writing: Poems (Berkeley, Cal.: The Figures, 1976);

Fragments from Cold (Brewster, N.Y.: Parenthèse, 1977);

Facing the Music (Barrytown, N.Y.: Station Hill, 1980);

White Spaces (Barrytown, N.Y.: Station Hill, 1980);

The Art of Hunger and Other Essays (London: Menard, 1982); enlarged as *The Art of Hunger: Essays, Prefaces, Interviews* (Los Angeles: Sun & Moon Press, 1992); enlarged again as *The Art of Hunger: Essays, Prefaces, Interviews & The Red Notebook* (New York: Penguin, 1993; enlarged, 1997);

Squeeze Play, as Paul Benjamin (New York: Alpha-Omega Books, 1982; London: Faber & Faber, 1991);

The Invention of Solitude (New York: Sun Press, 1982; London: Faber & Faber, 1988);

City of Glass (Los Angeles: Sun & Moon Press, 1985);

Ghosts (Los Angeles: Sun & Moon Press, 1986);

The Locked Room (Los Angeles: Sun & Moon Press, 1986);

In the Country of Last Things (New York: Viking, 1987; London: Faber & Faber, 1989);

Moon Palace (New York: Viking, 1989; London: Faber & Faber, 1989);

The Music of Chance (New York: Viking, 1990; London: Faber & Faber, 1991);

Augie Wren's Christmas Story (Birmingham, U.K.: Delos Press, 1992; New York: William Drenttel, 1992);

Leviathan (New York: Viking, 1992; London: Faber & Faber, 1992);

Mr. Vertigo (New York: Viking, 1994; London: Faber & Faber, 1994);

The Red Notebook and Other Writings (London: Faber & Faber, 1995);

Smoke & Blue in the Face: Two Films (New York: Hyperion Press, 1995);

Why Write? (Providence, R.I.: Burning Deck, 1996);

Paul Auster (photograph by Arturo Patten; from the dust jacket for Leviathan, *1992)*

Hand to Mouth: A Chronicle of Early Failure (New York: Holt, 1997);

Lulu on the Bridge: A Film (New York: Holt, 1998);

Timbuktu (New York: Holt, 1999).

Collections: *The New York Trilogy* (London: Faber & Faber, 1987; New York: Penguin, 1990);

Disappearances: Selected Poems (Woodstock, N.Y.: Overlook Press, 1988);

Ground Work: Selected Poems and Essays, 1970–1979 (London: Faber & Faber, 1990); republished as *Selected Poems* (London: Faber & Faber, 1998).

PLAY PRODUCTIONS: *Eclipse: A Play in One Act,* New York, Artists Theater, March, 1977.

PRODUCED SCRIPTS: *Smoke,* motion picture, Miramax, 1995;

Blue in the Face, motion picture, by Auster and Wayne Wang, Miramax, 1995;

Lulu on the Bridge, motion picture, Redeemable Features, 1998.

OTHER: *The Random House Book of Twentieth-Century French Poetry; With Translations by American and British Poets,* edited, with an introduction, by Auster (New York: Random House, 1982);

Selected Poems of Jacques Dupin, edited by Auster (Winston-Salem, N.C.: Wake Forest University Press, 1992).

TRANSLATIONS: *A Little Anthology of Surrealist Poems,* edited and translated by Auster (New York: Siamese Banana Press, 1972);

Jacques Dupin, *Fits and Starts: Selected Poems of Jacques Dupin* (Weston, Conn.: Living Hand, 1974);

André du Bouchet, *The Uninhabited: Selected Poems of André du Bouchet,* series 7 (New York: Living Hand, 1976);

The Notebooks of Joseph Joubert: A Selection, edited and translated by Auster (San Francisco: North Point Press, 1983);

Stéphane Mallarmé, *A Tomb for Anatole* (San Francisco: North Point Press, 1983);

Philippe Petit, *On the High Wire* (New York: Random House, 1985);

Maurice Blanchot, *Vicious Circles* (Barrytown, N.Y.: Station Hill, 1985);

Joan Miró, *Joan Miró: Selected Writings,* edited by Margit Rowell (Boston: G. K. Hall, 1986);

Translations (New York: Marsilio, 1997);

Pierre Clastres, *Chronicles of the Guayaki Indians* (New York: Zone Books, 1998; London: Faber & Faber, 1998).

On the back cover of the December 1995 issue of the Parisian journal *magazine littéraire* there is an impressive full-page, color advertisement for the French editions of Paul Auster's work. The ad features fourteen book covers above which are the words: "Auster Dix Ans (1985–1995) Une Oeuvre." This endorsement illustrates a curious fact about Auster: during the mid 1980s and early 1990s, he became one of America's major new novelists; yet, his reputation in other countries far exceeds that which he has at home. For example, *magazine littéraire* devotes almost sixty pages to Auster in an article titled "Le Monde est Dans Ma Tête, Mon Corps est Dans le Monde" (The World is In My Head, My Body is In the World). In the first sentence of the editor's intro-

duction, the magazine proclaims, "Paul Auster, né en 1947, est l'un des écrivains américains les plus brillants de sa génération" (Auster, born in 1947, is one of the most brilliant American writers of his generation). His works have been translated into twenty languages. In the United States it was perhaps the success of his 1995 film *Smoke* that most encouraged a general audience to read his work. Although his fiction oftentimes shows the stylistic influence of the twentieth-century European avant-garde, his themes are unmistakably American, and his sentences are always clear and artful in their carefully wrought simplicity.

Perhaps there is no theme more central in canonical American literature than success and failure. Auster told Mark Irwin that his work "has come out of a position of intense personal despair, a very deep nihilism and hopelessness about the world, the fact of our own transience and mortality, the inadequacy of language, the isolation of one person from another. And yet, at the same time," he added, "I've wanted to express the beauty and extraordinary happiness of feeling yourself alive, or breathing in the air, the joy of being alive in your own skin."

At the start of his memoir *Hand to Mouth* Auster says that "all along, my only ambition had been to write. I had known that as early as sixteen or seventeen years old, and I had never deluded myself into thinking I could make a living at it." Three events in Auster's life have had great significance for his writing. First was the financial difficulties he and his family endured before he received an inheritance–a period when he was "literally on the brink of catastrophe," as Auster said in a 1992 interview with Larry McCaffery and Linda Gregory. The second was a gradual process of moving from poetry to prose, for although Auster always knew that he wanted to write, he was not always sure what kind of writer he wanted to be or what sort of writing he wanted to do. Auster credits his marriage to Siri Hustvedt as the third event that rescued him from the edge of despair.

Born in Newark, New Jersey, on 3 February 1947 to Sam and Queenie (nèe Bogat) Auster, Paul Auster grew up along with one sister in New Jersey suburbs and attended Columbia University. He traveled to Europe during the summer after his high-school graduation and again while a student at Columbia. After six months as a seaman on a tanker in the Gulf of Mexico, he spent the next four years in France. He married writer Lydia Davis and they had a son, Daniel. Then, as Auster neared the age of thirty-two, he felt the burden of failure. He felt that in the decade since graduating from college he had accomplished little and that although he never

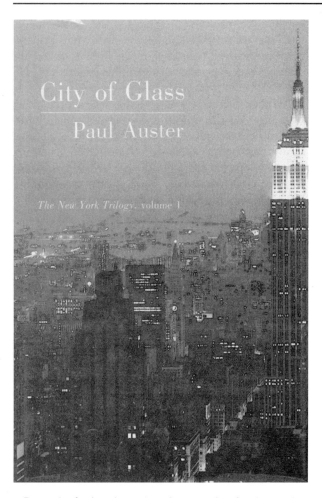

Dust jacket for Auster's 1985 novel, a postmodern detective story in which the author appears as a character

he had translated twentieth-century French prose and poetry into English, written many reviews and literary essays, and published four slim volumes of poetry. In his 1992 interview with Joseph Mallia, Auster said that "having to write prose for publication disciplined me, I think, and convinced me that ultimately I was able to write prose." During this period of "useful apprenticeship," as he called it, his poetry began to "open up" and become "more discursive." He wrote four one-act plays in 1976–1977; three are included as an appendix to *Hand to Mouth,* as is his baseball card game (which is reminiscent of J. Henry Waugh's game in Robert Coover's novel *The Universal Baseball Association, Inc.,* 1968) and his baseball detective novel, *Squeeze Play* (written in the summer of 1978, published 1982). Then in December 1978 he attended the rehearsal of a dance piece that inspired him to write *White Spaces* (1980), "a little work of no identifiable genre," as he described it to McCaffery and Gregory. In a later interview with Marc Chenetier he called it "the breakthrough for me; *that* was the movement into prose. And it was a revelation."

Auster wrote *Squeeze Play* under the pseudonym Paul Benjamin. "The book was an exercise in pure imitation, a conscious attempt to write a book that sounded like other books, but just because I wrote it for money doesn't mean I didn't enjoy myself," he says in *Hand to Mouth.* In 1982 he also edited *The Random House Book of Twentieth-Century French Poetry,* which includes a lengthy introduction by Auster and his translations of forty-two poems by various poets. Most important, however, in that same year, is his publication of *The Invention of Solitude.*

The Invention of Solitude is similarly difficult to pin down. Penguin Books lists it as autobiography. Writer Pascal Bruckner refers to it as a "novel-manifesto." And Auster's primary Japanese translator, Motoyuki Shabata, has said that "most reviewers in Japan identified, I think rightly, *The Invention of Solitude* as a novel; almost no one called it a memoir or an autobiography." Paul Auster himself has said that "I don't feel that I was telling the story of my life so much as using myself to explore certain questions that are common to us all." Many of these questions, often probed by canonical American authors of the nineteenth century such as Nathaniel Hawthorne, Herman Melville, and Henry David Thoreau—the nature of solitude, the improbability of speaking the truth about another, the way the past through memory affects the present, the search by sons for lost fathers, the everyday reality of coincidence and chance—become repeated themes in Auster's subsequent writings. It is because of this, Bruckner says in *Beyond the Red Notebook: Essays on Paul Auster* (1995), that "*The Invention of Solitude* is both the

expected to earn much from his writing, he could not continue to live on the paltry income that translation, literary journalism, and assorted odd jobs provided. As he told McCaffery and Gregory, "I had a small child, a crumbling marriage, and a miniscule income that amounted to no more than a fraction of what we needed." He invented a baseball card game that went unsold, and he wrote a detective novel that took several years to be published. As he recounted in *Hand to Mouth,* Auster was desperate. "Then," as he told McCaffery and Gregory, "out of nowhere, with absolutely no warning at all, my father dropped dead of a heart attack and I inherited some money. That money changed everything for me; it set my life on an entirely different course." If his material needs could now be met, his emotional needs and artistic desires still went unfulfilled. He divorced Lydia Davis and in 1982 married writer Siri Hustvedt, with whom he has a daughter, Sophie.

During the years 1979 through 1982, he made a significant breakthrough in his writing. Up to this time

ars poetica and the seminal work of Paul Auster. To understand him we must start here; all his books lead us back to this one."

In a 1994 interview with Mark Irwin Auster revealed that paradox "gets very much to the heart of what novel writing is for me." He said that "unlike poetry, which for me was always a univocal act. . . . Novel writing is a way of speaking out of both sides of your mouth at once. It's multi-voiced. And I think this suits me better." *The Invention of Solitude* is a multi-voiced work full of paradox. It is composed of two parts: "Portrait of an Invisible Man" and "The Book of Memory." The first section, in first-person narrative, lays out the contradictory facts that Auster knows about his father and the discovery he makes that his grandmother murdered her husband. What he finds tells him much about his father, but not all. He says of the articles he reads about this tragedy: "I do not think they explain everything, but there is no question that they explain a great deal. A boy [his father] cannot live through this kind of thing without being affected by it as a man." Nonetheless, all he knows, all he learns is not sufficient to enable him to enter and understand his late father's solitude: "the essence of this project," he says, "is failure," and later in the section he concludes: "The rampant, totally mystifying force of contradiction. I understand now that each fact is nullified by the next fact, that each thought engenders an equal and opposite thought. Impossible to say anything without reservation. . . ."

In the second section, "The Book of Memory," he turns from the other to the self. If it is not possible to know another, might it be possible to understand oneself? The father of part one differs from his son ("Paul Auster" or "A.," as he is referred to throughout) in part two. In part one the father is invariably apart from others, is invisible. In part two the central figure is ultimately connected to others, and memory is central to this connectedness. Yet, the second part is told in third-person narration. In his 1992 interview with Joseph Mallia, Auster explains why he did this: "I began writing it in the first person, as the first part had been written, but couldn't make any headway with it. . . . In order to write about myself, I had to treat myself as though I were someone else. It was only when I started all over again in the third person that I began to see my way out of the impasse." This is an extraordinarily beautiful but complex prose work that uses a collage method of brief detailed narrative episodes, poetic quotations, repeated motifs, and literary exegesis to explore the relation of the one to the many. A most extraordinary thing about "The Book of Memory" is that everything between the first page and the last page can be read as but a moment of

Dust jacket for Auster's 1992 novel, in which the narrator tries to make sense of how a mild-mannered friend became a terrorist

intense thought and recollection, a life that flashes before the eyes. The first page ends, "Then he writes. It was. It will never be again." And the last page ends, "He finds a fresh sheet of paper. He lays it out on the table before him and writes these words with his pen. It was. It will never be again. Remember."

When it was published, not every reviewer found *The Invention of Solitude* extraordinary. Poet W. S. Merwin, writing in *The New York Times Book Review* (27 February 1983), said that Auster "turns from his subject to an examination of the attempt to write about it, self-consciously tracing a self-consciousness that occasionally affects the style and form of his account without benefiting them" and that the second part is "marred, more than the first part, by recurrent pointless mannerisms apparently suggested by contemporary French 'experimental' writing." Responding directly to Merwin in his review published in *Sulfur,* 3 (1983), Norman Weinstein said that Merwin misread *The Invention of Solitude* and that it "should be read as a philosophical reverie about using writing as a mode to deal with existential anguish." Weinstein also praised

Auster's "exquisitely cadenced" language, an opinion shared by Michael Walters who, in his *Times Literary Supplement (TLS)* review (17 February 1989), called Auster's book an "elaborately crafted memoir." In the Paul Auster half-issue of *The Review of Contemporary Fiction* (Spring 1994), authors such as Robert Creeley, Charles Baxter, and Curtis White praised the book. Derek Rubin, in his essay in the collection *Beyond the Red Notebook,* found that the longing, the yearning, "the hunger at the center of *The Invention of Solitude* links Auster in a fundamental way to his Jewish past and to earlier Jewish American writers. . . ."

Begun immediately after completing *The Invention of Solitude,* Auster's next work, *City of Glass* (1985), is the first volume of *The New York Trilogy* (1987). Auster told McCaffery and Gregory that "in some sense, *City of Glass* was a direct response to *The Invention of Solitude.*" Auster's works are filled with interconnections. In *Hand to Mouth* Auster says that in the late 1970s he "developed an admiration for some of the practitioners" of the detective fiction genre. "One of the conventional plot gimmicks of these stories," he writes, "was the apparent suicide that turns out to have been a murder. . . . I thought: why not reverse the trick and stand it on its head? Why not have a story in which an apparent murder turns out to be a suicide?" *Squeeze Play* makes use of this reversal, and *City of Glass* plays with more conventions of detective fiction. The essential difference between *City of Glass* (and the other novels of *The New York Trilogy*) and *Squeeze Play* is revealed in the comment Auster made in his interview with McCaffery and Gregory: "Mystery novels always give answers; my work is about asking questions." The novels of *The New York Trilogy* ask questions rather than provide answers, and in this sense they are a continuation of the exploratory nature of *The Invention of Solitude.*

City of Glass begins with a chance event. A writer of conventional detective fiction, Daniel Quinn, receives a phone call from a desperate person looking for Paul Auster, not the Auster who is the author but the one "of the Auster Detective Agency." Quinn hangs up, but when the person calls back a few nights later, Quinn assumes the identity of Paul Auster. Peter and Virginia Stillman hire Quinn ("Auster") to protect them from Peter's father, who has just been released from prison. The elder Peter Stillman had locked his son in a room for nine years in an attempt to discover the "original language of innocence." Instead of attempting to harm his son or Virginia, the elder Stillman roams Manhattan collecting broken items such as the handle of an umbrella so that he can create "a language that will at last say what we have to say," a more precise language. Quinn obsessively follows

Stillman on his walks and records all of Stillman's activities in a red notebook. Quinn seeks out the "real" Paul Auster's advice on the case, but when he finds him, he discovers that Auster is a writer and not a detective. Auster invites Quinn to stay for lunch and proceeds to describe his theory regarding the true authorship of *Don Quixote.* At the end of the novel Quinn disappears and the reader discovers that a friend of Auster's, another writer, has used Quinn's red notebook to tell the story that is *City of Glass.*

Perhaps because *City of Glass,* like the entire Auster oeuvre, is about "asking questions" and not about providing easy solutions to simple dilemmas, many publishers rejected this new and unusual work before Douglas Messerli, publisher of Sun & Moon Press (a Los Angeles firm specializing in innovative writing), accepted it. After publication the novel received both acclaim and condemnation. This would be the pattern for the reception of all of Auster's work. Among those who enthusiastically praised *City of Glass,* novelist Toby Olson said in *The New York Times Book Review* (3 November 1985) that Auster's "prose moves with grace and sureness," and Olson called the novel "remarkable." Gary Gach reported in *American Book Review* (September 1986) that as the first volume in a trilogy *City of Glass* is so good "that we may be witnessing something auspicious enough to compare to Samuel Beckett's fictional trilogy. . . ."

Ghosts (1986) also features a man hired to follow another man. Whereas *City of Glass* takes place in contemporary New York, *Ghosts* is set in the same city, but in the year 1947. Although characters have abstract names—Blue, White, Black—there is nothing abstract about this tightly structured, richly detailed story. Indeed, in her review of *Ghosts* for *The New York Times Book Review* (29 June 1986), Rebecca Goldstein called it "nearly perfect."

As Auster writes at the start of the novel, "The case seems simple enough. White wants Blue to follow a man named Black and to keep an eye on him for as long as necessary." But Black is White, and he has hired Blue to watch him. Why this is so the reader never finds out for certain. The novels of *The New York Trilogy* raise questions rather than answer them, and like *The Invention of Solitude* these novels explore the boundary between one person and others. "The only way for Blue to have a sense of what is happening is to be inside Black's mind, to see what he is thinking," Auster writes for example in *Ghosts,* "and that of course is impossible."

The final volume of Auster's trilogy, *The Locked Room* (1986), returns to contemporary New York. As in the two prior volumes, doubling is central to this novel. In this instance Sophie Fanshawe contacts the unnamed first-person narrator of this novel after the mysterious disappearance of her husband, the narrator's childhood best friend. The narrator has not been in touch with his old friend for years, and during this time Fanshawe has become a writer. The narrator agrees to become literary executor when it is assumed that Fanshawe is dead. He gets Fanshawe's works published and establishes his friend's posthumous reputation as a major writer. Then the novel takes a sudden turn when the narrator receives a letter informing him that Fanshawe is alive. He hides this fact from Sophie, with whom he has fallen in love. At the urging of Fanshawe's publisher, the narrator tries to write a biography of his friend. As in the prior two novels of the trilogy, the attempt to look inside the mind of another leads to a loss of one's own good sense. While doing research in France, the narrator has a breakdown during which he feels "as though I was no longer inside myself," as though "I couldn't feel myself anymore." He returns to New York, quits writing the biography, and tries to live in domestic happiness with Sophie, but is haunted once more by Fanshawe. He travels to Boston to meet with Fanshawe, where the latter insists they speak through closed doors and not see one another. Fanshawe reveals that he has taken a fatal dose of poison but has left a notebook for the narrator to read, which, when he reads the notebook, explains nothing.

Near the end of *The Locked Room* there is a direct reference to the other novels of *The New York Trilogy.* The "three stories are finally the same story," Auster's narrator claims, "but each one represents a different stage in my awareness of what it is about. I don't claim to have solved any problems." Whereas detective novels offer solutions, the novels of *The New York Trilogy* do not; and if they do not—if they are not detective fictions of a sort—what are they?

More academic essays have been written about these three books than any other work by Auster. Scholars read them as fictional embodiments of postmodernist or poststructuralist thought. For example, Allison Russell, in "Deconstructing *The New York Trilogy: Paul Auster's Anti-Detective Fiction*" (1990), sees the trilogy as a Derrida-like deconstruction of logocentrism. In a 19 January 1994 letter to Dennis Barone, Auster responded to such interpretations of his work: "Who cares about finding the right label for my books?. . . To read these critics, my novels somehow become aesthetic tracts—when in fact they're *stories* about flesh and blood people. Contradictions abound: there's no one line of thought I'm pushing."

Many reviewers praised *The Locked Room,* though they differed on its overall place in the trilogy. For example, in *The New York Times Book Review* (4 January

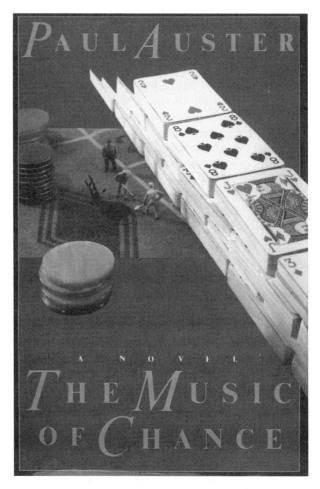

Dust jacket for Auster's 1990 novel, involving a game of chance and its consequences

1987) Stephen Schiff called it "a brilliant leap forward" and the best of the three novels, while in *The Washington Post Book World* (29 March 1987), E. F. Bleiler noted that "*The Locked Room* is well worth reading" but added "it lacks the brilliance and wild imagination of *City of Glass.* . . ." Finally, Colin Greenland in his *TLS* review (11 December 1987) compared Auster favorably to Alain Robbe-Grillet and Beckett; yet, he found *The Locked Room* "the only story [in the trilogy] that is satisfying as a whole, partly because it is the only one that pretends to be a whole."

Although published in 1987—five years after *The Invention of Solitude* and one year after *The Locked Room*—Auster began writing his next novel, *In the Country of Last Things,* in 1970 and completed it in 1985. It is a different book than those in *The New York Trilogy* or *The Invention of Solitude.* Yet, it shares with the latter a deep concern for the importance of memory. Memory is crucial for Auster, and if this age is one prone to a sort of cultural amnesia as some commentators have suggested, then it is more important than ever to recall the past. Why this is so for Auster is perhaps best explained in *In the Country of Last Things.*

The novel tells the story of Anna Blume's search for her missing brother in an unnamed city and her struggle to survive in this postapocalyptic urban environment filled with horror, destruction, and despair. At first it is difficult for Anna to know what to believe in this barren place. "It's not that people make a point of lying to you," she says, "it's just that where the past is concerned, the truth tends to get obscured rather quickly. Legends crop up within a matter of hours, tall tales circulate, and facts are soon buried under a mountain of outlandish theories. In the city the best approach is to believe only what your eyes tell you. But not even that is infallible. For few things are ever what they seem to be, especially here, with so much to absorb at every step, with so many things that defy understanding." Auster directly connects walking with both memory and self-knowledge. As he wrote in *The Invention of Solitude,* "To wander about in the world, then, is also to wander about in ourselves. That is to say, the moment we step into the space of memory, we walk into the world." But to wander is not enough. One must record, must write, as well as wander and remember. (Quinn, Blue, and Fanshawe become still after a certain point.) Anna notes that "unless I write down things as they occur to me, I feel I will lose them for good." These last things that she observes and records do not become lost things. This novel, which may seem to be written in first-person narration, is actually told in a third-person narration. Someone has received Anna's story-as-letter, has read it, and, in turn, is now telling Anna's story. Occasionally, especially near the beginning, there are phrases such as "her letter continued" and "she wrote." Anna worries that her "story starts and stops, goes forward and then loses itself, and between each word, what silences, what words escape and vanish, never to be seen again." The powers that exist here, that manufacture and perhaps control all the chaos, want both things and words to vanish so that people might always feel themselves, like "A." at the start of "The Book of Memory," "sliding through events," estranged.

In this novel memory provides the only subversion of the social engineering and rational planning, and of the social regulation and rational control, that has instituted such final solutions as Transformation Centers, huge crematoria where trucks dump the city's dead each morning. "This is the chief function of the government," the reader is told, "and more money is spent on it than anything else." This is a culture of death, and it is so because it has no memory. The elimination of memory is the triumph of death. The city portrayed in this novel mirrors the world

depicted in the "Enlightenment as Mass Deception" chapter of *Dialectic of Enlightenment* (1972). "The individual who is thoroughly weary," they write, "must use his weariness as energy for his surrender to the collective power which wears him out." That statement well describes life in Auster's unnamed city. In such a world of estrangement, memory enables Anna to bear witness to all those who die invisible deaths. Anna's project and A.'s project in the second part of *The Invention of Solitude* is the same: it is simply to remember. For to forget is to die.

Response to *In the Country of Last Things* was in the main enthusiastic. E. F. Bleiler said in a *Washington Post Book World* review (29 March 1987) that the novel "is powerful, original, imaginative and handled with artistry. It is one of the better modern attempts at describing Hell." Both Katharine Washburn and Sven Birkerts praised this novel in their essays in *The Review of Contemporary Fiction* (Spring 1994). Washburn asserted, "Auster has succeeded with Swiftian guile and ferocity in constructing a world of demolished things which we are forced, immediately and painfully, to recognize as our own." And Birkerts said: "Auster's novel unfolds with menacing simplicity, almost as if the stages of Anna's plight are but a pretext for Auster to vivify the nightmare of social collapse." Anna's story, he added, "holds us through its numb frankness, its determination to bear witness."

In his essay on *In the Country of Last Things,* Birkerts also claims this novel marks an advancement in Auster's overall artistry. He said that the self-reflexive works such as the trilogy, though he enjoyed and admired them, would have led to an artistic dead end if Auster had persisted with that style. Birkerts feels that in Anna Blume's story Auster "reasserts the traditional rights of the genre, exploring the real by way of the invented. This is not to say that Auster has gone back to naturalism . . . but he does allow us to forget that the story is the product of a superintending author."

Similarly Bruce Bawer wrote in his review of Auster's next novel, *Moon Palace* (1989), that "Auster has grown more adept at translating his preoccupations into the language of action and form. . . . It is certainly more realistic than *The New York Trilogy.* . . ." (*The New Criterion,* April 1989). Birkerts commented in his essay on *Moon Palace* (*The New Republic,* 27 March 1989) that "it is almost as if the author needed to put himself through a winnowing process . . . before he could find a way to begin writing." He goes on to say that *Moon Palace* is that beginning for which Auster's earlier work was practice.

There is, however, a problem to such a linear reading of Auster's work–experimentation to mature artistry. As noted above, Auster began *In the Country of Last Things* before he wrote the novels that comprise *The New York Trilogy*, whereas *City of Glass* was begun immediately after completing part two of *The Invention of Solitude*. Furthermore, Auster began *Moon Palace* long before *The New York Trilogy*. Auster told author Marc Chénetier that he "started working on the book as early as around 1968, while I was still a student." In his book *Paul Auster as the Wizard of Odds: Moon Palace* (1996) Chénetier argues that it is the central book in the author's oeuvre, while in his interview with Auster the author grants only that "it's a central book." What this complex chronology means is that Auster's creativity is more prodigious and various than heretofore acknowledged.

Auster's works may be united by the repetition of themes such as the relationship between fathers and sons, the nature of solitude, the meaning of coincidence in everyday life, and disappearance as a result of obsession. His works may be related by a playful intertextuality, too. For example, Daniel Quinn, the writer/detective in *City of Glass,* keeps showing up in other novels. Anna, during one of her walks in *In the Country of Last Things,* finds "the passport of a man named Quinn," and in *Mr. Vertigo* (1994) the main character has a nephew named Daniel Quinn, a nephew who "will know what to do with the book" Walt has written, and that book is *Mr. Vertigo* itself. Although linked by theme and reference, Auster's books differ more than they are alike. A chronological interpretation that traces his development in simple progressive terms will be marred by facts that establish a complex web of thought, and because of this web lacking a center, it may be as unwise to argue for the centrality of any single Auster book as it is to find just the right classification for them. Of most importance is the amount of high-quality, diverse fiction Auster has produced in such a short period of time, all the while continuing his involvement in editing, translating, and moviemaking projects.

Auster's next novel, his longest, *Moon Palace,* is different from all his other prose work. *Moon Palace* is a novel of generations and complex genealogy, a novel about inheritance—needing it, getting it, losing it—and a novel about searching for oneself, but it is also a novel about searching for America. The novel's narrator-protagonist is Marco Stanley Fogg. Even in his name we see the theme of exploration delineated in that it alludes to two historical travelers and one fictional adventurer: Marco Polo, Henry Stanley, and Jules Verne's Phineas Fogg. As the novel begins, Fogg, an orphan, is a student at Columbia University. He has in his possession 1,492 books that his Uncle Victor left with him. At first he uses these boxes of books

Auster in Brooklyn, 1995 (photograph by Ashkan Sahihi)

for furniture; then he reads the books; then he sells a few at a time until his resources dwindle to zero. Distraught because of his uncle's death, he soon becomes a homeless person in Central Park. He is rescued by a young woman named Kitty Wu, also an orphan. Next he takes a job as a companion to Thomas Effing, a sometimes bitter, sometimes comic old man. Effing asks Fogg to help him prepare his obituary, which leads him to tell Fogg the story of his life. This story-within-the-story is an incredible one.

The response to *Moon Palace* was enthusiastic but with some qualification. Bruce Bawer, writing in *The New Criterion* (April 1989), found it "a strange and arresting new novel," but the many references to the moon he thought a "distraction, and even (at times) to the point of ludicrousness." Sven Birkerts, writing in *The New Republic* (27 March 1989), found "the forward motion" of the novel "kinetic; the language," he said, "feels inhabited from within, is self-propelling." Birkerts, however, thought the narrator "steps aside for too long" for Effing's "increasingly improbable tale," an opinion shared by Bawer. Michiko Kakutani, on the other hand, had only praise for the novel: "The book reads like a composite of works by Fielding, Dickens and Twain, with a faint 20th-century gloss of Ionesco and Camus" (*The New York Times,* 7 March 1989).

Auster's next work of fiction, *The Music of Chance* (1990), has its origins in an earlier work. In 1976–1977 Auster wrote a play, "Laurel and Hardy Go to Heaven," in which the two comedians must build a wall. Such is the situation in *The Music of Chance*. Nashe, the straight man, and Pozzi, the jokester, must build a wall, ostensibly to pay off a gambling debt. (Another source for the novel may have been Maurice Blanchot's story "The Idyll," one of the two fictions included in *Vicious Circles* (1985), which Auster translated.) Again, this novel is different from others by Auster. Whereas *Moon Palace* is expansive and episodic, *The Music of Chance* is tightly structured and centers on a single narrative event and setting. Auster told McCaffery and Gregory that fairy tales have been the greatest influence on his work, and he compared these "bare-bones narratives" to *The Music of Chance*: "When I was about two-thirds of the way through the first draft, it occurred to me that the story had the same structure as a fairy tale . . . if you reduce the book to its skeleton, then you wind up with something that resembles a typical story by the Brothers Grimm. . . . A wanderer stumbles onto an opportunity to make his fortune; he travels to the ogre's castle to test his luck, is tricked into staying there, and can win his freedom only by performing a series of absurd tasks that the ogre invents for him."

The Music of Chance is a novel that considers the relationship of money to freedom. A Boston fireman, Jim Nashe, receives an unanticipated inheritance. He quits his job and wanders about America in his new Saab until he picks up a small-time, fast-talking gambler named Pozzi. Pozzi tells Nashe that he has a sure thing; he just needs a backer. Pozzi tells him about two rich fools who want to play a high-stakes poker game. Nashe agrees to stake Pozzi. They go to Flower and Stone's estate in the countryside. These two men, another pair of Laurel and Hardy characters, won the Pennsylvania lottery, and after giving their guests a tour of their unusual house and sharing a bizarre dinner together, they settle down to the game, during which fortune falls on Flower and Stone once more. Pozzi loses, and, unable to pay their debt after one last double-or-nothing cut of the cards, the two guests sign an agreement to build a wall in a field on Flower and Stone's property.

The response to *The Music of Chance* was quite favorable. Bawer said in his *Wall Street Journal* review (21 September 1990) that "the novel is a tour de force about freedom and imprisonment, motion and stasis, order and randomness." He added that it "is no drab, schematic novel of ideas" but "is a rich, dazzling performance. . . ." Paul Bray, writing in *The Review of Contemporary Fiction* (Spring 1994), enthusiastically wrote

that "with *The Music of Chance* Auster, perhaps the most significant author to emerge during the nineteen eighties, has quite simply invented a whole new kind of fiction." Similarly, Jonathan Yardley noted in *The Washington Post* (10 October 1990) that *The Music of Chance* offers "evidence that Auster is one of the few contemporary American novelists whose work is both original and interesting." Auster "can write," Kakutani said in a *New York Times* review of this novel (2 October 1990), "with the speed and skill of a self-assured pool player, sending one bizarre event ricocheting neatly and unexpectedly into the next." Moviemakers Philip and Belinda Hass adapted this novel for the screen in 1992, starring Mandy Patinkin as Jim Nashe and James Spader as Pozzi. Auster makes a brief appearance at the end of the film.

Auster's next two novels, *Leviathan* (1992) and *Mr. Vertigo*, received less praise than his prior one. *Leviathan* is dedicated to novelist Don DeLillo, and in his review in *The New Criterion* (December 1992), Bawer compares these two contemporary American writers. He argues that Auster is the better novelist because he is concerned with the art of fiction, whereas DeLillo is "concerned more with the parochial than with the eternal, more with the making of sociopolitical statements than with the making of art. . . ." Yet, Bawer adds that "alongside *Moon Palace* and *The Music of Chance*, *Leviathan* seems less pure and passionate, more facile and familiar. . . ."

The story of *Leviathan* primarily concerns the lives of two close friends who are both writers. Peter Aaron is the narrator, and he wants to tell—and by telling, to understand—what happened to his friend Benjamin Sachs. The novel begins with Sachs's death, resulting when a "bomb he was building accidentally went off." Sachs, once a promising author, had been traveling the country as the Phantom of Liberty, a sort of mild-mannered terrorist who blew up replicas of the Statue of Liberty located in town squares and parks throughout America. The people and events that touch these two men's lives form the substance of this narrative.

In fact, writing in *The Review of Contemporary Fiction* (Spring 1994), Mark Osteen noted that *Leviathan* suggests "that only through others can one gain access to the locked room of self. If each person remains ultimately unfathomable, nevertheless his or her secrets inevitably chain him or her to the lives of others." Perhaps Auster has populated this novel with too many personalities. Robert M. Adams (*The New York Review of Books*, 3 December 1992) said that it is "a thoroughly confused and confusing story," and Kakutani (*The New York Times*, 8 September 1992) found "a hollowness at the core of this novel." For Bawer, usually

First page of the manuscript for The Locked Room *(Henry W. and Albert A. Berg Collection of English and American Literature, New York Public Library, Astor, Lenox and Tilden Foundations)*

Auster and his wife, writer Siri Hustvedt, circa 1995 (photograph by Arturo Patten)

a supportive advocate for Auster's work, that hollowness is the narrator of *Leviathan*, Peter Aaron: "*Leviathan* is an unengaging experience," according to Bawer, and "part of the problem, undoubtedly, is that instead of hearing about Sachs's life from Sachs himself or from a third-person narrator who is privy to Sachs's thoughts and actions, we hear about it from Aaron, who has in turn heard about it mostly from others. Nothing much happens to *him:* though he's supposedly absorbed in his memories of and concern for Sachs, his own conflicts or torments, whatever they may be, are hardly present in this book." On the other hand, in an article in *The Review of Contemporary Fiction* (Fall 1992) Barone commented that "Aaron is like one of Melville's narrators: the more he writes of the other, the more he reveals of himself." Indeed, there were many reviewers who had positive things to say about *Leviathan*. For example, Richard Locke remarked in *The Wall Street Journal* (15 September 1992) that evident in this "ambitious" novel is Auster's increasing narrative skill.

Mr. Vertigo is the story of a boy who could fly; the inspiration for this novel may have been the French aerialist Philippe Petit, whose book *On the High Wire* Auster translated (Random House, 1985). Like *Moon Palace*, *Mr. Vertigo* uses a retrospective first-person narration. Divided into four sections, the protago-

nist, Walter Claireborne Rawley (Auster has had a lifelong interest in Sir Walter Raleigh) begins writing the story of his life in the final section, a story that traverses the entire twentieth century, a story that describes the implausible with complete seriousness. This tale is an American success story, except that rather than trace a character's rise from rags to riches, *Mr. Vertigo*, like other Auster stories, chronicles an endless cycle of success and failure.

The response to *Mr. Vertigo* was mixed. Some reviewers enjoyed the work overall, but deemed the ending abrupt and dissatisfying. While Jay Cantor (*The New York Times Book Review,* 28 August 1994) found the story "witty, inventive in its language and invitingly playful with its metaphor," Paul Gray (*Time,* 5 September 1994) said that Auster's "clever parable about innocence and its loss comes down to a bumpy landing." It was the ending that critics most often cited as the novel's central weakness. The fourth section, just 16 pages in a 278-page book, is by far the shortest. Peter Blake, for example, noted "the success of this novel" in his *TLS* (8 April 1994) review but also noted that it has a disappointing end. The end may be seen as a coda of sorts, and some reviewers may have missed the various rhythms of this novel. Though the shortest section, Auster elevates his style at the end, a bit like an ancient orator, and this seems appropriate to the fictional voice of the aging Walt, who has completed all his adventures and has almost finished his tale. Walt's peroration is also an invitation: "Deep down, I don't believe it takes any special talent for a person to lift himself off the ground and hover in the air," he says on his final page. "We all have it in us—every man, woman, and child—and with enough hard work and concentration, every human being is capable of duplicating the feats I accomplished as Walt the Wonder Boy."

Whereas *Mr. Vertigo* relates the story of a boy who could fly, *Timbuktu* (1999) describes the adventures of a dog, Mr. Bones, so intelligent it can fully comprehend, though not speak, the English language. Mr. Bones and his master, the loquacious Willy G. Christmas, travel from New York to Baltimore so that Willy can find his former high-school English teacher and leave his legacy to her before he dies: seventy-four notebooks filled with his writings from the past twenty-three years. Willy has warned Mr. Bones that his death is imminent and that he is soon destined to an afterlife in a place called Timbuktu. At the steps of the Edgar Allan Poe house in Baltimore, Willy gives Mr. Bones some final instructions and warnings before departing this life.

In the second half of this short novel, Mr. Bones finds himself two new residences: first with an urban

Chinese American boy, Henry Chow, whose father dislikes dogs, and then with an almost saccharine suburban family named Jones. Mr. Bones's identity changes in each of these situations. Henry calls him Cal, and in the Jones family he is known as Sparky. During his time with Henry, Mr. Bones lives in a box; the Jones family keeps him chained in the yard and not only emasculates his name but neuters him as well. Mr. Bones's circumstances get more and more circumscribed. From the vagabond life he lived with Willy to the kennel where the Jones family take him to board while they go to Disney World, Mr. Bones's world is ever shrinking. But he knows from Willy about the promise of an afterlife in Timbuktu, and so, somewhat like Nashe at the end of *The Music of Chance,* he brings his life to a sudden and abrupt end.

The reviews of *Timbuktu* were quite mixed. The book provoked strong reactions either of praise or disfavor. Christopher Taylor, writing in *TLS* (28 May 1999), found the book to contain many faults, such as "often embarrassing stabs at wordplay," and he concluded that the end is "too slim and whimsical for an adult novel." On the other hand, Paul Kafka, in his *Boston Globe* review (30 May 1999), linked Auster with Robert Coover and Thomas Pynchon and noted that "after reading *Timbuktu,* we ramble through our world with reawakened senses and newly alert minds. This is the Auster magic."

In *The Invention of Solitude* Auster explains that "the superiority of the Collodi original [*Pinocchio*] to the Disney adaptation lies in its reluctance to make the inner motivations of the story explicit. . . . in Disney these things are expressed—which sentimentalizes them, and therefore trivializes them." There is nothing trivial in *Timbuktu;* rather, there is much that haunts the reader. There is a desperation and urgency in this book that is reminiscent of Anna Blume's in *In the Country of Last Things.* There are troubling allusions and references to the Holocaust in *Timbuktu.* For example, when Willy settles down to die on the steps of Poe's house, the reader is reminded that Willy's Jewish parents narrowly escaped a certain death in Poland. Now this front stoop in present-day Baltimore has become Willy's and Mr. Bones's "Poe-land"—a meaningful parallel, perhaps, with Baltimore representing their own nightmare of death.

The fact that Auster wrote *Timbuktu* from a dog's perspective may catch readers off guard at first, but the precision of the meticulous, crystal-clear prose pulls the reader into this intriguing narrative. Auster has perhaps been "reluctant to make the inner motivations of the story explicit," but this is precisely what separates it from a lesser work. In a letter to Barone on 6 June 1999, Auster wrote that *Timbuktu* is "admit-

tedly . . . a little strange–but it insisted on being written." It is a book that only Paul Auster could have written.

According to Marc Chénetier, Auster stated it is the people who hear the rhythm of his books who like them and that, in Auster's words, "people who don't like them at all . . . are not able to hear the language. . . ." In an interview with Michel Contat (1996) he describes the painstakingly slow process he uses to achieve the rhythm of his seamless and distractionless prose. He describes how he concentrates on paragraphs, one paragraph at a time. "I don't go on to the next paragraph until I'm satisfied with the paragraph I'm writing . . . " he says, adding, "I keep writing it over again from the start, from scratch, to make it feel so familiar and so organic that it begins to feel indestructible. . . . I write out the paragraph, and then I look it over and start crossing out words and making changes. Then it becomes hard to read. So I copy it out again, and then I go through the same thing all over again." What results from such intensity of work led Robert Hughes, in his introduction to William Drenttel's *Paul Auster: A Comprehensive Bibliographic Checklist* (1994) to remark, "when you are reading [Auster] you know that he is writing: you are conscious of a refined narrative technique, a tone of voice which is somewhat glassy, hard and transparent, and at the same time supple and colloquial, so that it carries you along. This combination of distance and intimacy is a gift as rare in writers as perfect pitch in musicians or an instinctive grasp of tonal structure in painters."

Interviews:

Joseph Mallia, "Interview," in *The Art of Hunger* (Los Angeles: Sun & Moon Press, 1992), pp. 256–568;

Larry McCaffery and Linda Gregory, "Interview," in *The Art of Hunger,* pp. 269–312;

Mark Irwin, "Memory's Escape: Inventing *The Music of Chance*–A Conversation with Paul Auster," *Denver Quarterly,* 28 (1994): 111–122;

Annette Insdorf, "The Making of *Smoke,*" in *Smoke & Blue in the Face* (New York: Hyperion Press, 1995), pp. 3–11;

Marc Chénetier, "Around *Moon Palace:* A Conversation with Paul Auster," *Sources* (Autumn 1996): 5–35;

Michel Contat, "The Manuscript in the Book: A Conversation," *Yale French Studies,* 89 (1996): 160–187.

Bibliographies:

William Drenttel, *Paul Auster: A Comprehensive Bibliographic Checklist of Published Works, 1968-1994* (New York: William Drenttel, 1994);

Drenttel, "Paul Auster: A Selected Bibliography," in *Beyond the Red Notebook: Essays on Paul Auster,* edited by Dennis Barone (Philadelphia: University of Pennsylvania Press, 1995), pp. 189–198.

References:

Dennis Barone, ed., *Beyond the Red Notebook: Essays on Paul Auster* (Philadelphia: University of Pennsylvania Press, 1995);

Barone, ed., *Review of Contemporary Fiction,* special *Paul Auster–Danilo Kis* issue, 14 (1994): 7–96;

Marc Chénetier, *Paul Auster as the Wizard of Odds: Moon Palace* (Paris: Didier Erudition, 1996);

Gerard De Cortanze, "Le Monde est Dans Ma Tête, Mon Corps est Dans le Monde," *magazine littéraire,* 338 (December 1995): 16–63;

Annick Duperray, ed., *L'Oeuvre de Paul Auster: Approches et lectures plurielles* (Arles: Actes Sud, 1995);

William Lavender, "The Novel of Critical Engagement: Paul Auster's *City of Glass,*" *Contemporary Literature,* 34 (1993): 210–239;

William G. Little, "Nothing to Go On: Paul Auster's *City of Glass,*" *Contemporary Literature,* 38 (1997): 133–163;

Norma Rowen, "The Detective in Search of the Lost Tongue of Adam: Paul Auster's *City of Glass,*" *Critique: Studies in Contemporary Fiction,* 32 (1991): 224–235;

Allison Russell, "Deconstructing *The New York Trilogy:* Paul Auster's Anti-Detective Fiction," *Critique: Studies in Contemporary Fiction,* 31 (1990): 71–84;

Arthur Saltzman, *Designs of Darkness* (Philadelphia: University of Pennsylvania Press, 1990), pp. 56–70;

Saltzman, *The Novel in the Balance* (Columbia: University of South Carolina Press, 1993), pp. 60–82.

Papers:

Paul Auster's papers are housed in The Berg Collection at the New York Public Library and at Columbia University Library in New York.

Nicholson Baker

(7 January 1957 –   )

Arthur Saltzman
Missouri Southern State College

BOOKS: *The Mezzanine* (New York: Weidenfeld & Nicolson, 1988; London: Granta, 1989);

Room Temperature (New York: Grove-Weidenfeld, 1990; London: Granta, 1990);

U and I: A True Story (New York: Random House, 1991; London: Granta, 1991);

Vox (New York: Random House, 1992; London: Granta, 1992);

The Fermata (New York: Random House, 1994; London: Chatto & Windus, 1994);

The Size of Thoughts: Essays and Other Lumber (New York: Random House, 1996; London: Chatto & Windus, 1996);

The Everlasting Story of Nory (New York: Random House, 1998; London: Chatto & Windus, 1998).

OTHER: "K.590," in *The Best American Short Stories 1982,* edited by John Gardner and Shannon Ravenal (Boston: Houghton Mifflin, 1982), pp. 116–123.

SELECTED PERIODICAL PUBLICATIONS–
UNCOLLECTED:

POETRY

"From the Index of First Lines," *New Yorker,* 70 (26 December 1994 – 2 January 1995): 83.

FICTION

"Playing Trombone," *Atlantic Monthly,* 249 (March 1982): 39–58;

"Subsoil," *New Yorker,* 70 (27 June – 4 July 1994): 67–78;

"My Life as Harold," *New Yorker,* 71 (26 June – 3 July 1995): 92–93;

"The Remedy," *New York Times Magazine,* 145 (18 August 1996): 38–39;

"China Pattern," *New Yorker,* 72 (3 February 1997): 68–69.

NONFICTION

"The Author vs. the Library," *New Yorker,* 70 (14 October 1996): 50–53, 56–62.

Nicholson Baker is a novelist and essayist whose reputation rests on two distinct talents. First, he is an

Nicholson Baker (photograph © by Jerry Bauer; from the dust jacket for The Everlasting Story of Nory, *1998)*

exquisite miniaturist, unmatched among his contemporaries in terms of his lavishly detailed attention to the minute particulars of everyday objects and activities. His signature strategy is to slow down and super-magnify. As Thomas Mallon put it in his profile of Baker for *Gentleman's Quarterly* (May 1996), he "doesn't just count the angels on the head of a pin; he does long division with the feathers in their wing tips." From shoelaces to paper towels to the pleasures of writing on a rubber spatula with a ballpoint pen, nothing is too small to escape Baker's scrupulous eye and elegant prose. He coaxes layered etymologies and rich histories out of mundane materials, showing by example the surprising and abundant rewards of refusing to take anything for granted. Relentlessly meditative, an eloquent spokesman on behalf of cultural preservation, Baker cannot bear to dispose of things—neither card catalogues shouldered aside by computer terminals nor small thoughts whose radiance belies their size. Yet, Baker refuses to be restricted by the confines of conventional good taste or traditional definitons of literature. He is also well known as a composer of highbrow erotica, where his penchant for lingering description and secret depths results in explicit examinations of sexual urges, practices, and some of the most outrageous fetishes one may ever encounter. This second reputation derives from the first, the quality of meticulous care and intense imaginative investment that informs all his prose. Baker's deft prose reveals the subtle textures of the world. He makes the ordinary extraordinary and, as a result, all the more precious. Impressed by the "broad, jaw-droppingly knotty matrix of usable reference" at Baker's command, James Kaplan, writing for *Vanity Fair* (January 1992), concludes that among American writers of his generation, "pure octane-wise, not many are in Baker's league."

Nicholson Baker was born in Rochester, New York, on 7 January 1957 to Douglas and Ann Nicholson Baker, who had met as art students at Parsons School of Design and who encouraged Baker's childhood fascination with inventions, mechanisms, and the arts. Music was the first of the arts to captivate Baker, whose proficiency with the bassoon enabled him to attend in 1974–1975 the prestigious Eastman School of Music, where he intended to focus on composition. In the fall of 1975, Baker enrolled at Haverford College, earning a degree in English in 1980. In *U and I: A True Story* (1991), and the essay "Books as Furniture," collected in *The Size of Thoughts: Essays and Other Lumber* (1996), he says his change from music to literature was inspired in part by his perception that writers make more money than musicians and in part by his belief that books represent the highest order of human conservationism—a conviction that fueled his well-publicized campaign to save card catalogues and books themselves from oblivion (a subject discussed in "Discards" in *The Size of Thoughts* and in "The Author vs. the Library"). After short stints as a Wall Street oil analyst and a stockbroker, Baker moved to Berkeley, California, where on 30 November 1985 he married Margaret Brentano. He attended a two-week writing workshop conducted by Donald Barthelme at the University of California, and soon some of his short fiction was published in *The Atlantic* and *The New Yorker*. Baker next traveled to Boston, finding work as a word processor

and technical writer (the job shared by the narrator of *Room Temperature* [1990]). By 1987 he was devoting himself to full-time writing. He lives in Berkeley with his wife and two children, Alice and Elias.

Baker has said that his breakthrough as a writer—the inception of his own style—came from his decision to dispense with the demands of plot in favor of the elaboration of metaphor, excessive rumination, and other forms of self-conscious verbal "loitering." These are the "clogs" he refers to in *U and I,* which in Baker's revised hierarchy are not to be purged so as to facilitate the smooth transmission of the conventional story but rather prized, even aggrandized, for the intrigues they deliver under examination. This quality, along with Baker's droll, ubiquitous wit, clearly unites the author with Barthelme and the lyrical and high-mannered "U" of *U and I,* John Updike. Among other affinities and influences, Baker numbers Flann O'Brien, Ronald Firbank, Samuel Johnson, Howard Moss, Stanley Kunitz, Iris Murdoch, Gerard Manley Hopkins, Henry and William James, and Vladimir Nabokov, as well as several stage and film comedians and Doctor Seuss, Marcel Proust, and Stanley Elkin. The *Encyclopaedia Britannica* could also be reasonably added to this list. Nicholson Baker weds the meganovelist's inclusiveness and appetite for excess to the minimalist's quiet intricacy and belief that art and wonder exist at the molecular level of contemporary society.

The Mezzanine (1988), Baker's first novel, is a masterpiece of smallness whose compression of plot results in some startling densities of descriptive vigor and what might be called archaeological patience and delicacy. The real heroes of the novel are the flotsam and jetsam of the protagonist's lunch hour—the ice-cube trays, the straw, the paper towels, the office supplies, and the other unremarkable items that rise to prominence through the narrator's formidable insight. In *The Mezzanine,* Howie's modest plans to get a bite to eat and to replace his broken shoelace swell to epic dimensions. Everything he sees earns his inventory of its traits, his appreciation of its genesis of manufacture, and its own special dignity. Howie deems himself "the sort of person whose biggest discoveries were likely to be tricks to applying toiletries while fully dressed. I was a man, but I was not nearly the magnitude of man I had hoped to be." Yet, magnitude proves ubiquitous in *The Mezzanine.* The lyricism Howie discovers in the gleam of light off the escalator's rubber rail and the sheer conscientiousness of his homage to otherwise humble products of anonymous technology—to things so regular and reliable as to have grown invisible—have the effect of undermining his remorse. In short, he never allows familiarity to breed neglect. With so devoted an investment in trivia, nothing in *The Mezzanine* can be dismissed as trivial. Howie's asides, his explanatory footnotes, those "finely suckered surfaces that allow tentacular paragraphs to hold fast to the wider reality of the library," often overwhelm the so-called proper text of the novel. The narrative potential of popcorn and the waters coursing down the porcelain wall of a urinal are inexhaustible. Thus when Howie congratulates and aligns himself with "that excellent low-key sort of man who achieves little by external standards but who sustains civilization for us knowing, in a perfectly balanced, accessible, and considered way, all that can be known about several brief periods of Dutch history, or about the flowering of some especially rich tradition of terra-cotta pipes," he raises his status from fetishist to champion of human consciousness.

In his essay "The Size of Thoughts," Baker admits that most thoughts are of limited stature: "about three feet tall," he muses, "with the level of complexity of a lawnmower engine, or a cigarette lighter, or those tubes of toothpaste that, by mingling several hidden pastes and gels, create a pleasantly striped product." But to have such thoughts is no real diminishment, for "major thoughts, like benevolent madonnas, are sustained aloft by dozens of busy, cheerful angels of detail." *The Mezzanine* exemplifies the virtues and the rewards of sustained examination, promoting the idea—in its impact, no small thought, after all—that instead of reserving studious, lingering attention for events and items that merit it, the imagination can extract nutritional content from anything on which it visits that quality of attention. For example, Howie notices a chrome date stamper, which leads to one of perhaps fifty or so digressions on microscopic topics. After pointing out the cunning of its armature and its self-inking mechanism, he lectures on the way "you set the square base of the machine down on the piece of paper you wished to date and pressed on the wooden knob (a true knob!)—then the internal element, guided by S curves cut out of the gantry-like superstructure, began its graceful rotational descent, uprighting itself just in time for landing like the lunar excursion model, touching the paper for an instant, depositing today's date, and then springing back up to its bat-repose." The miraculous resides in Howie's exactitude and steady gaze. When Howie lists his major accomplishments or develops his thought-frequency chart, he provides a true democracy of enthusiasms, in which Pez is as capable of provoking analysis as Plato, and a trip to the corporate bathroom or to the local drugstore becomes a transcendental adventure. When seen through his eyes, nothing is commonplace.

As it transfers the reader from the vocational to the domestic realm, *Room Temperature* serves as a sequel to and reaffirmation of the ingrown interests of *The Mezzanine*. If possible, the intricacies of the second novel

are more tightly ratcheted than those of its predecessor. The narrator, Mike, a Boston-area part-time technical writer and reviewer of television commercials, is not afforded even Howie's modest lunch-hour excursion out of doors (he has the sleeping baby to look after while his wife is at work). Moreover, the time period of *Room Temperature* has been compressed to twenty minutes. Mike does most of his mental delving into "parental sensation" and trains his relentlessness on household objects and homely affairs: the baby's breathing, peanut butter jars, air pumps, Sir Robert Boyle's *General History of the Air* (1692), French horns, flatulence, and the aerodynamics of his pregnant wife's body. These components of a typical associative linkage are proof that this shortening of the radius of awareness of *The Mezzanine* cannot abridge the power of concentrated interest. As Mike puts it, "everything in my life seemed to enjamb splicelessly into everything else." This condition—coupled with the commitment Baker declares in his essay "Changes of Mind" that "I want each sequential change of mind in its true, knotted, clotted, viny multifariousness, with all of the colorful streamers of intelligence still taped on and flapping in the wind"—makes Mike's babysitting a vivid drowse indeed. Like the infant in his arms, who gently flails in search of passing textures of the "various fugal inversions and augmentations" of Mike's sweater, Mike is a texture addict, and almost anything—from classical music to the art of personal hygiene to the "lumpily tangible chiasmus" of the rocking chair—is likely to amplify before him.

There are moments in *Room Temperature* during which Mike gives way to doubt about the legitimacy and healthiness of his dreamy erudition and predilection for freewheeling metaphorical connection. His analyses of frog replication out of single cells taken from other frogs and of the idiosyncratic hybrid model planes he constructed as a child from several kits hint at the dangers of sterility and strain in the relations he imagines throughout the novel. A juxtaposition junkie, Mike momentarily worries about the unruliness of the images he creates. His optimism is soon restored, however, by the ascendancy of yet another image: the mobile, another ephemeral construction, whose loosely harnessed motions make it a fit emblem for Mike's narrative style. Baker calls it a "loopy" plotlessness, which proceeds principally by feel from one "thoughtlet" to the next. He admits that it is the only way he knows how to operate, and he finds its satisfactions undeniable and lasting.

Mike has found validation in his wife's receptivity to his quality of mind. She, too, is keen about subtleties, especially those arising from toys and colors and those coined for bodily functions; not only does she accept

Dust jacket for Baker's first novel (1988), which takes place during the protagonist's lunch hour

her husband's preoccupation with nosepicking and masturbation but she also shares her own secrets on those subjects. A man who savors rubber door stoppers, the baby's nose-aspirator bulb, and varieties of bowel movements could hardly hope for a better mate. The discovery that his six-month-old daughter delights in the overhead ventilation jets on the airplane suggests that she has inherited this gift, having come by it rightly from both sides. Family grounds this narrator and focuses his responsibilities; still, his responsiveness and the pleasures he takes in every "golden, shade-pulled moment of retrospective suspension" are not sacrificed to the trappings of maturity.

U and I: A True Story is an autobiographical account of artistic paternity and smiling parasitism. In this quirky "true story" Baker dispenses with narrative guises to confess and evaluate his ongoing admiration of, corruption by, and competition with John Updike. In this novel the meticulous researcher who created *The Mezzanine* and *Room Temperature* sets himself a surprising constraint: he specifically avoids checking the quota-

tions he remembers from Updike's fiction, because he is more interested in the nature of his absorption and retention of Updike than in their verbatim accuracy. Therefore, Baker's Updike is a strategically qualified figure against whose established stature Baker measures his own legitimacy. The paradox of seeking affinities with a writer he worships and of reaffirming his own originality at the same time makes this manipulation, which he variously refers to as "memory criticism," "phrase filtration," and "closed book examination," especially appealing to Baker, for it keeps the "I" of the title at least as prominent as the muse he hosts. In other words, it is not Updike so much as the author's consciousness of Updike that accompanies Baker throughout the book. As a result, *U and I* not only flouts generic boundaries between fact and fiction, it confesses the opportunism at the root of comparison and the competitive vigor that inspires its praise.

As Baker orbits Updike, he shifts between wishing to be Updike's golfing partner and chiding Updike for his unsavory characterization of his wife in the short story "Wife-Wooing," between disparaging hagiography and his announcing that the Great Writer "exists above the threshold of assent." On the one hand, Baker exhibits something akin to Harold Bloom's "anxiety of influence"; on the other hand, he is simultaneously troubled by the possibility that he cannot endure comparison with Updike without being eclipsed altogether. His neurotic projections aside, Baker meaningfully reveals many of the qualities of Updike's fiction for which both writers are notable (and in which, say some reviewers, both writers occasionally indulge excessively): "flea-grooming acuity" visited on incidentals; "verbal tact," or tactile verbosity, exotic, supercharged imagery; and obsession with the high comedy of human sexual behavior. Both men suffer from psoriasis and insomnia; both suffer an uneasy self-consciousness about public performance (an occasion Baker further develops in his essay "Reading Aloud," in *The Size of Thoughts*); both love to fondle words and details.

In *U and I,* Baker does chronicle two brief meetings with Updike, one at a book signing, another at a party when Updike praises a piece Baker had published in *The New Yorker,* Updike's own long-standing outlet and employer. Because Baker thinks that early work flawed, he ponders whether Updike shares his critical taste. Moreover, Baker lies about being a fellow graduate of Harvard University, so eager is he to impress Updike or rather to press affiliation on him. But neither of these moments ultimately threatens his faith in their "friendship," nor does the fact that Baker's wife, while she tells her husband that he is smarter, deems Updike the better writer. Baker gets a small measure of satisfaction in the end when he thinks he detects evidence of Updike's having incorporated a brief passage of that *New Yorker* story in *The Witches of Eastwick* (1984), thereby gratifying the younger writer with a small claim to having influenced his master. In truth, however, Baker is out for fun; loving generosity, rather than crabbiness, is the ruling mood of *U and I.* The book is ultimately not the account of a rivalry between authors for esteem but proof of their essential aesthetic solidarity.

In his next two novels Baker anatomizes eccentric (many would say perverse) sexual activities with the same patient precision and obvious relish that he accorded environmental specifics in *The Mezzanine* and *Room Temperature.* Whether *Vox* (1992) and *The Fermata* (1994) represent the fatal distortion of Baker's method or epitomize its fertile pleasures has been the principal source of considerable controversy among reviewers. Does microdescription do for secret sexual habits what it does for staplers and doorstoppers? Can the writer's civilizing wit manage masturbation as well as perforated paper and nosepicking? The debate is defined by a

given reader's willingness to perceive the reduction of sexual processes and proclivities to clinical scrutiny as a natural reversal of Baker's eroticization of soda straws and paper towels. Baker's point seems to be that the reader may justifiably and profitably experience anything human. As Jim and Abby, the complete cast of *Vox,* both decide, nothing is strange after all. Creativity can render anything proper–and seductive.

Vox is a book-length telephone conversation between Jim and Abby, who have serendipitously called the same phone sex number at the same time. If the reader appreciates the relationship between husband and wife in *Room Temperature* as a marriage of true minds, the explicit exchanges between strangers in *Vox* are likewise made compelling because of the comparably charged intelligences that inform them. Sexual arousal is a narrative challenge here, for the characters reveal themselves only through language, not action. As their conversation expands beyond typical turn-on ploys to include matters of diction, the visceral impact of noodles, the moment of visual ignition when the television set first comes on, the poetics of streetlights and stereo components, and bookish matters, the constraints of simulated connection on the phone are overshadowed by the erotic privileges afforded by voice alone. How ingeniously one exploits this access determines the level of pleasure. As Jim says, in celebration of their obvious rapport, "An orgasm in a complicated mind is always more interesting than one in a simple mind." Put another way, triggering the orgasm itself is no less satisfying than exploring complexity. Successful intercourse, whether sexual, social, or textual, combines alertness to details, imaginative intrepidity, clever complicity, and enthusiasm.

As consenting adults spared more profound consequences of their fantasies by the physical distance between them, Jim and Abby may escape serious criticism for preferring surrogacy, masturbatory incentives, and conversation to the comprehensive requirements of a full-fledged sexual relationship. Nevertheless, to the extent that their dialogue is understood as artistic collaboration rather than as an attempt to equate their indirect intimacies with mature love, *Vox* logically extends the premises of Baker's earlier books. As Jim adds his euphoric elaborations on certain key images to Abby's stories of sexual intrigue, and as Abby uses Jim's desires as prompts for her verbal delineation of provocative scenes, candor and verbal acuity lead to rapture. Jim's exclamation that he "will feast on that revelation for weeks to come" at once marks the gratitude of a satisfied sexual partner and the acknowledgment of a connoisseur. If the virtues of verbal contact are expressed effectively enough, they may initiate, tutor, and fulfill desires ranging from the cerebral to the coarse.

Vox is maintained by the dialogue it is constrained to, but no such restriction applies to Baker's next novel. *The Fermata* probes the issues of risk, taste, and political correctness even further, for in this novel the narrator, Arno Strine, possesses a supernatural and unprecedented means of sexual transgression. The title, a term for the prolongation of a musical note or rest, refers to Strine's ability to halt time and space around him while he retains the capacity to function as usual. One hesitates to say "function normally," for Strine devotes himself almost exclusively during these "Fold" episodes to licentious invasions and luxurious adventures in self-abuse. After restoring the scene of his sexual manipulations to order (typically a matter of straightening rooms and reclothing his unwitting prey), he usually leaves behind some cryptic bit of evidence of his incursion, some telling alteration. *The Fermata,* then, is Strine's operations manual, confession, and, ultimately, validation.

Partly to accommodate his compulsions, Strine relies exclusively on temp work. Indeed, he occasionally resorts to the Fold to enable him to catch up on work he has let slide during especially protracted sexual encounters, which mandate the same sort of research, plotting, and reconnaissance as the composition of good fiction. Strine's ability is the fulfillment of Jim's dream in *Vox* of being able to watch women invisibly, coupled with his wondering if he could strobe television channels in such a way as to fix images to leer at in a more leisurely fashion. (The comparison to fiction is no less appropriate in this instance, although the implications for the reader are undoubtedly more unsettling.) The Fold is also a more extreme and more outrageous version of Baker's technique of unremitting inspection, as female undergarments replace office equipment and household appliances as targets of microscopic examination. Strine explains that "only an artificially induced pensive force of hundreds of thousands of gravities can spin down some intelligible fraction of one's true past self," whether the suspension be lurid or literary. To readers who would complain that he turns women into objects, Strine counters that he turns objects into women, which is to say that he lavishes passion and exacting prose on them as if they were all equally worthy of being beheld and beloved. Dismantling its gadgets, masturbating before its exposures, or writing about it are similar reasons for wanting to stop the world; they are all means of increasing the "visual happiness" of the learned voyeur. When Strine describes the stealthy insertion of his porn manuscript into the hands of a woman on the beach (through expert manipulation of fermata "holds" and releases reminiscent of an animator's painstaking setting up and shooting of individual frames or of a proficient lover's delaying

technique), he similarly joins sexual and literary successes. When on another occasion he places a taped version of his erotic story into the car cassette player of a strategically "stopped" woman and sees her throw it out the window, both his Fold powers and his confidence as a writer are temporarily diminished.

If violation is half of Strine's delight, vigilance is the other. For all his vulgarity and secret molestation, Strine is as likely to fall in love with the way a woman squeezes the liquid from her teabag by strangling it with its string as he is with her physical allure. Common objects and processes have not lost their enchantment in *The Fermata* as things that give pause (or to which Strine gives pause). Toggle switches, audio cassettes, toad hibernation, tape guns–these merit coverage in the novel just as bodies do; towels spinning in the washing machine can trigger a fermata of their own, not simply because they may once have touched a woman's body but because they likewise turn "time's cattle-drive" into "quality time." Furthermore, Strine's talent passes the test of poetry, as seen, for instance, in the brace of euphemistically inventive synonyms he creates for his special indulgence and which compete with erogenous zones and sexual practices for his attention: "instigating an Estoppel," "hitting the clutch," "dropping in." To be sure, Joyce Collier, Strine's superior at the office and current infatuation, is verbally as well as anatomically stunning. He lathers over her dictation tapes as he transcribes them, gleefully imagining (in keeping with *Vox*) more than one sort of intimacy with her. His first deliberate Drop, which he accomplished in reaction to a provocative grade-school teacher, was a response not only to her flashes of sexual appeal but also to her spelling of *Esquimaux* on the blackboard–two mutually fortifying stimuli. Throughout the novel, then, the predictable thrashing of pornography is upgraded by a hyper-resolved sensual contemplation; conversely, the exaltation of ordinary matters–of ordinary *matter*–makes daily surroundings marvelous, even sexy.

The Fermata alternates between Strine's stories of depravity and a strained defense of his theoretically unsullied moral nature, based in part on the belief that his "curiosity has more love and tolerance in it" than the primitive dreams of other men, in part on the fact that his perpetrations are limited to "momentary pico-states of timeless inconsequence." He is, by his own account, smart, likable, and lyrical (as can be appreciated, for example, in his description of swimming through the gelatinous waves of a Fold-arrested ocean). Yet, for many readers, Strine clumsily finesses issues of power, dignity, and consent. When he talks about "the almost horrified excitement of my wrongdoing," the distance seems to close between his intricately directed plots and rape. If anything stops Strine, it is not regret but carpal-tunnel syndrome from too much self-stimulation.

His reformation, as it were, is highly qualified: he decides to share his secret with Joyce Collier, his evident soul mate, and as a result, his fermata abilities are miraculously transferred to her. Joyce employs them to keep their lovemaking innovative, while Strine contents himself with the alternative pleasures of participating fully in a relationship in which neither partner is dominant nor an automaton.

If the reader deems "childlike" the capacity of Baker's protagonists for finding unself-conscious delight and fascination in the anatomies, relationships, manners, and diction that govern things so small, it should seem natural indeed that the author would select as the heroine of *The Everlasting Story of Nory* (1998) a nine-year-old girl, Eleanor (Nory) Winslow—an actual child, who can practice and enjoy those tendencies without apology. Precocious, contemplative, and endlessly engaged by the world in and around Threll Junior School in England, where she and her younger brother, "Littleguy," have moved with their parents from America, Nory is a prodigy in the crucial matters of proper application of toothpaste, salt, double-jointedness, tailless cats, claymation, erasers, and all sorts of paraphernalia lying close to the nose. She is also an alter ego for Baker in that she has the writer's passion for precise revision of the confusing, the ungainly, and the unjust. (She is seriously considering dentistry as a future career, in part because the terminology it provides is so arresting, in part because it is so obviously dedicated to the work of salvation.) An eager fabulist, she redreams herself through stories that expand the options of family, classroom, and playground. If lunchroom slights and school conformities and rules, rules, rules are the normal ration at Threll, nurture, adventure, and rescue are the order of the day in the stories she creates (complete with a healthy dose of "dear childs" to help shepherd her reader through). A lexical wizard, she invents words that establish coherence and flair: the "pillish" girl at school, the "scrabjibs" of information she dockets, the "eargnashing" noises, the "discombobbledied" moments all attest to the specific wonder of Nory's "angel-may-care" life and keep feelings from brushing by too fast. Oblivion is still the curse to be contended with, even in the delicate, enchanted realm of little girls. Thus for Nory, books, cathedrals, graves, gardens, and letters are all houses of worship, for they are all means of—monuments to—perpetuation: "'Neverending' and 'everlasting' were good words for the job because they last and last when you say them, like 'forevermore.'" Little notes she pens to herself are headed REM, which consolidates references to both the rapid eye movement

Dust jacket for Baker's novel told from the point of view of a nine-year-old girl

of another inveterate collector of minutiae and the sacred, ongoing commitment to remembrance.

The novel's chief appeal is to be found in Baker's talent for channeling Nory's breathless concerns. Her triumphs, insights, perplexities, and crises are lifted into consequence by her sheer irrepressibility: "The two main chitter-chatterers for most of the time were Paul and Ovaltine, who was called Ovaltine, since basically everyone likes Ovaltine and you wouldn't normally make a big thing out of liking it and, for instance, stand up on a chair and say, 'Hi, everybody, I like Ovaltine!' —and his last name was Dean, and his face was oval, and maybe another reason that Nory couldn't remember, but that covered most of it." In describing Littleguy's head as "still basically a construction site," since her brother's avidity is mostly restricted to trucks and heavy machinery, Nory has hit on a compelling metaphor for her own imaginative fevers. Imagination is not just idle fancy but the work of cherishing and recuperation. She is the rightful heir of "that excellent low-key sort of man" championed by Howie in *The Mez-*

zanine (raised to a child's more vivid pitch) and proof that, at least for one more generation, the task of cultural prospecting is in good hands.

In *The Size of Thoughts,* Baker collected the essays that serve as a critical foundation for his fictions. From the etymological odyssey of "Lumber," a 150-page survey of the history and character of a single word, to an evolutionary study of nailclippers, to fastidiously nostalgic commemorations of model airplanes and outmoded movie projector reels, to a plea on behalf of library card catalogues, Baker makes literal Jane Austen's reference, simultaneously modest and satisfied, to "the little bit (two Inches wide) of Ivory on which I work with so fine a Brush, as produces little effect after much labor." In a sense these essays liberate Baker from having to defer to the typical components of fiction, enabling him to concentrate exclusively on the descriptions that have always obsessed him and that best exhibit his talents as a roving consumer reporter. As Thomas Mallon writes, he "has never been a novelist at all. He has been writing essays the whole time, has been, in fact, a small master, the genre's American Faberge."

Baker may poke fun at the size of his own thoughts, but there is no mistaking their density or tenure. Beneath his jeweler's loupe any fixation impressively blossoms. Any "rareme"–a term Baker invents to refer to a rare phenomenon or subtle pleasure, such as the exquisite sensation of writing on a rubber surface with a ballpoint pen or the unpatented poetry of boxes of brass fittings–may prove imperative to a mind poised for the poetry that inheres in the everyday. An ardent observer and sentence-builder, Baker details the "richer under-thrumming" of some of the most surprising fixations to be found in American literature. Nicholson Baker takes the measure of the reader's daily habitats and shows the true depths of their preciousness.

Interviews:

Alexander Laurence and David Strauss, "An Interview with Nicholson Baker," *Alternative-X* (1994), Internet on-line posting: <www.alt-x.com/interviews/nicholson.baker.html>;

Laura Miller, "Lifting Up the Madonna," *Salon,* 10 (23 March – 5 April 1996), Internet on-line posting: <www.salon1999.com/10/bookfront/salon.html>;

David Dodd, "Requiem for the Discarded," *Library Journal,* 121 (15 May 1996): 31–32.

References:

Ross Chambers, "Meditation and the Escalator Principle," *Modern Fiction Studies,* 40 (Winter 1994): 765–806;

Lynn Darling, "The Highbrow Smut of Nicholson Baker," *Esquire,* 121 (February 1994): 76–80;

Peter Evans, "Tiny Curlicues: Nicholson Baker's Room Temperature," *Bulletin of Faculty of Letters,* 37 (Hosei University, 1991);

Dennis Hall, "Nicholson Baker's *Vox:* An Exercise in the Literature of Sensibility," *Connecticut Review,* 17 (Spring 1995): 35–40;

James Kaplan, "Hot *Vox,*" *Vanity Fair,* 55 (January 1992): 118–121, 125–127;

Thomas Mallon, "The Fabulous Baker Boy," *Gentleman's Quarterly,* 66 (May 1996): 82–85;

Arthur Saltzman, "To See a World in a Grain of Sand: Expanding Literary Minimalism," *Contemporary Literature,* 31 (Winter 1990): 423–433;

Saltzman, *Understanding Nicholson Baker* (Columbia: University of South Carolina Press, 1999);

David Shields, "Ludd's Labor's Lost," *Voice Literary Supplement,* 41 (May 1996): 8;

Philip E. Simmons, "Toward the Postmodern Historical Imagination: Mass Culture in Walker Percy's *The Moviegoer* and Nicholson Baker's *The Mezzanine,*" *Contemporary Literature,* 33 (Winter 1992): 601–624;

Bert O. States, "On First Looking into Baker's Index," *Salmagundi,* 109–110 (Winter–Spring 1996): 153–162.

John Barth

(27 May 1930 –   )

William Nelles
University of Massachusetts, Dartmouth

See also the Barth entry in *DLB 2: American Novelists Since World War II.*

BOOKS: *The Floating Opera* (New York: Appleton-Century-Crofts, 1956; revised edition, Garden City, N.Y.: Doubleday, 1967; London: Secker & Warburg, 1968);

The End of the Road (Garden City, N.Y.: Doubleday, 1958; London: Secker & Warburg, 1962; revised edition, Garden City, N.Y.: Doubleday, 1967);

The Sot-Weed Factor (Garden City, N.Y.: Doubleday, 1960; London: Secker & Warburg, 1961; revised edition, Garden City, N.Y.: Doubleday, 1967);

Giles Goat-Boy; or, The Revised New Syllabus (Garden City, N.Y.: Doubleday, 1966; London: Secker & Warburg, 1967);

Lost in the Funhouse: Fiction for Print, Tape, Live Voice (Garden City, N.Y.: Doubleday, 1968; enlarged edition, New York: Bantam, 1969; London: Secker & Warburg, 1969);

Chimera (New York: Random House, 1972; London: Deutsch, 1974);

Todd Andrews to the Author: A Letter from LETTERS (Northridge, Cal.: Lord John Press, 1979);

LETTERS An old time epistolary novel by seven fictitious drolls & dreamers, each of whom imagines himself actual (New York: Putnam, 1979);

The Literature of Exhaustion, and The Literature of Replenishment (Northridge, Cal.: Lord John Press, 1982);

Sabbatical: A Romance (New York: Putnam, 1982);

Don't Count on It: A Note on the Number of the 1001 Nights (Northridge, Cal.: Lord John Press, 1984);

The Friday Book: Essays and Other Nonfiction (New York: Putnam, 1984);

The Tidewater Tales: A Novel (New York: Putnam, 1987; London: Methuen, 1988);

The Last Voyage of Somebody the Sailor (Boston: Little, Brown, 1991; London: Hodder & Stoughton, 1991);

Once Upon a Time: A Floating Opera (Boston: Little, Brown, 1994; London: Sceptre, 1994);

John Barth (photograph by Robert Faber; from the dust jacket for On with the Story, *1996)*

Further Fridays: Essays, Lectures, and Other Nonfiction, 1984–1994 (Boston: Little, Brown, 1995);

On with the Story: Stories (Boston: Little, Brown, 1996).

Editions: *The Sot-Weed Factor* (New York: Grosset & Dunlap, 1964);

The Floating Opera and The End of the Road (New York: Anchor Press, 1988);

Lost in the Funhouse: Fiction for Print, Tape, Live Voice (New York: Anchor Press, 1988);

LETTERS (Normal, Ill.: Dalkey Archive Press, 1994);

Sabbatical: A Romance (Normal, Ill.: Dalkey Archive Press, 1995).

RECORDINGS: *John Barth Reads from Giles Goat-Boy,* N.p., CMS Records 551, 1968;

Two Narratives for Tape and Live Voice, read by Barth, New York, J. Norton 23161, circa 1974.

OTHER: Tobias Smollett, *The Adventures of Roderick Random,* afterword by Barth (New York: Signet, 1964), pp. 469–479;

"A Tribute to Vladimir Nabokov," in *Nabokov: Criticism, Reminiscences, Translations and Tributes,* edited by Alfred Appel Jr. and Charles Newman (Evanston, Ill.: Northwestern University Press, 1970), p. 350;

Rust Hills, ed., *Writer's Choice,* preface by Barth (New York: McKay, 1974).

SELECTED PERIODICAL PUBLICATIONS–UNCOLLECTED: "Lilith and the Lion," *Hopkins Review,* 4 (Fall 1950): 49–53;

"Landscape: The Eastern Shore," *Kenyon Review,* 22 (Winter 1960): 104–110.

In a writing career that spans five decades, John Barth has established himself as the premier writer of the postmodern novel in America. Perhaps more than any other contemporary writer, Barth has managed to combine consistently cutting-edge formal experimentation and theoretical sophistication with a deep commitment to the renewal and replenishment of traditional narrative genres and styles.

John Simmons Barth and his twin sister, Jill, were born on 27 May 1930 in Cambridge, Maryland, to John Jacob Barth and Georgia Simmons Barth; they had an older brother, William. At Cambridge High School he played drums in the band and wrote for the school newspaper. After graduating in 1947 he studied harmony and orchestration in summer school at the Juilliard School of Music in New York City. His interest and training in music are often seen as having influenced his approach to writing fiction, which he frequently discusses in terms of "arrangements" and "orchestrations."

In the fall of 1947, Barth entered Johns Hopkins University in Baltimore on an academic scholarship to study creative writing. He took few literature courses but read voraciously during his leisure time and while working in the university's Classics Library. His job, filing books in the Oriental Seminary collection, exposed him to the vast scale and intricate construction of such frame narratives as *The Ocean of Story, The Panchatantra,* and *The Thousand and One Nights' Entertainments,* stimulating a lifelong critical and artistic interest in the possibilities of narrative framing and embedding.

On 11 January 1950 Barth married Harriette Anne Strickland. That year he published two short stories in the university's student literary magazine and one in *The Hopkins Review.* He received his B.A.

in the spring of 1951. That summer he and his wife had a daughter, Christine Anne. Needing to provide for his family but lacking interest in finding a "real" job, he compromised by taking an assistantship in the graduate writing program at Johns Hopkins in the fall. His 1952 M.A. thesis was "Shirt of Nessus," a realistic novel set in Maryland. His first agent, Lurton Blassingame, was unable to find a publisher for the work, which Barth later characterized as "a neo-primitive miscarriage, justifiably unpublished." In 1952 the Barths had a son, John Strickland.

In 1953, while studying for a doctorate in the aesthetics of literature, Barth took a position as an instructor of freshman English at Pennsylvania State University. Another son, Daniel Stephen, was born in 1954. At Penn State, Barth began work on the "Dorchester Tales" (his hometown is the seat of Dorchester County). This projected series of one hundred stories–echoing Geoffrey Chaucer's *Canterbury Tales* (circa 1387–1400) in its title and Giovanni Boccaccio's *Decameron* (circa 1348–1353) in its scope–combined for the first time what became two of his most durable literary interests: the form of the frame tale and the setting of his native Maryland. He abandoned the scheme after writing fifty of the tales; but in 1960 he published one of them, "The Song of Algol," in *The Kenyon Review* as "Landscape: The Eastern Shore" and incorporated another, "The Invulnerable Castle," into his novel *The Sot-Weed Factor* (1960), which features several characters originally conceived for the "Dorchester Tales."

In 1954 Barth ran across an old photograph of a showboat, *The Floating Theater,* that he had seen as a child. Inspired by the picture, he wrote *The Floating Opera* (1956) between January and March 1955. His planned "nihilist minstrel show" turned into a novel, while retaining both the philosophical seriousness and the vaudeville comedy of his original conception. The narrative takes the form of an autobiographical letter written in 1954 by Todd Andrews that centers on the day in 1937 when he resolved to kill himself. The letter is addressed to Andrews's father, who had hanged himself on Groundhog Day 1930, ostensibly because of his financial ruin in the 1929 stockmarket crash. In the letter Andrews inquires into his father's real motives, as well as into his relationship with his father. The use of a self-conscious and playful narrator was influenced by the Brazilian novelist Joaquim Maria Machado de Assis's *Dom Casmurro* (1899; translated, 1953), which had, in turn, been influenced by Laurence Sterne's *Tristram Shandy* (1759–1767)–a connection with the eighteenth-century novelistic tradition that became central with Barth's third novel. The root cause of Andrews's despair is the diagnosis he received in 1919 that he has a heart condition that might kill him at any moment. He has gone through several phases of denial, becoming successively a rake, a saint, and a cynic, before finally arriving at the nihilistic conclusion that "There's no final reason for living (or for suicide)." His closing meditation—"I considered too whether, in the real absence of absolutes, values less than absolute mightn't be regarded as in no way inferior and even be lived by"—has struck many readers as cautiously affirmative, justifying Barth's labeling the book a "nihilistic comedy." Critics have usually assumed that Andrews's final position represents Barth's own outlook at the time, despite the overt unreliability of the similar narrator in his next book and Stanley Edgar Hyman's warning that "Beneath this cheery narrative surface, Barth offers a very different view of Todd Andrews. He is a victim of his Oedipus complex, a latent homosexual, a cold fish, and a malicious sadist."

Barth's manuscript was rejected by five publishers before Appleton-Century-Crofts accepted it with the stipulation that Barth change the climax, in which Andrews resolves to kill himself and 699 other people, including his former lover, Jane Mack, and her daughter (who may be his own), Jeannine, by blowing up the crowded showboat of the title. In the original ending Andrews is unmoved either by the thought of Jane and her husband, Harrison, "crisped to ash" or by the consideration of Jeannine's "small body, formed perhaps from my own and flawless Jane's, black, cracked, smoking." Barth made the requested changes in the ending, so that, instead of simply feeling "no sense either of relief or disappointment" when the explosion fails to kill everyone on the boat, Andrews finds an acceptable reason to live when gas from the opened jets, meant to cause the explosion, induces a seizure in Jeannine and sparks his sentimental concern for her.

The remarkably well-crafted first novel, published on 24 August 1956, sold only 1,682 copies but earned favorable reviews and was second runner-up for the National Book Award. Several reviewers, however, criticized the new sentimental ending as a weakness, and Barth recognized that in the future he would be better off following his own judgment rather than that of publishers and editors. Given the opportunity in 1967 to revise his early novels for republication by Doubleday, Barth restored the original ending, which is more consistent with his theme and with the characterization of Andrews.

Much of the appeal of the novel for readers and reviewers lay in the intricate structure of the book, with its multiple flashbacks and convoluted—and usually comic—digressions. When Andrews mentions that he is a lawyer, for example, his ensuing explanation of how he came to choose the profession leads into an

Dust jacket for Barth's 1958 novel, about a man who suffers from "psychological paralysis"

extended subplot that includes Harrison Mack's father's seventeen contested wills and the disposition of 129 dill-pickle jars full of human excrement.

Initiating his practice of writing novels in contrastive or complementary pairs—Barth playfully attributes this tendency in part to his having been born an opposite-sex twin—he followed his "nihilist comedy" with a "nihilist tragedy" (or, as he prefers to call it, "nihilist catastrophe"). He had completed *The End of the Road* (1958)—originally titled "What to Do until the Doctor Comes"—by the end of 1955. The narrator is Jacob Horner, who is writing the work in 1955 at the Remobilization Farm, a clinic for the psychologically paralyzed run by the Doctor. Horner seems to be writing the novel as therapy for his paralysis ("Scriptotherapy" is one of the Doctor's standard approaches). In David Morrell's analysis, Todd Andrews's movement from nihilism to relativism is here split between two characters: Horner, a nihilist who considers that the arbitrary nature of values constitutes a rationale for having none, and Joe Morgan, who agrees that values are relative but insists that one must commit to them as though they were absolute. As Barth has explained the connection, "I deliberately had [Andrews] end up with that brave ethical subjectivism in order that Jacob Horner might undo that position in [novel] #2 and carry all non-mystical value-thinking to the end of the road." Their philosophical conflict is acted out physically and emotionally, with Joe's marriage as a test case. His wife, Rennie, commits adultery with Horner, becomes pregnant (though she is not sure by which man), and dies during an illegal abortion arranged by Horner. This shocking demonstration of the extent to which it does matter how he acts leaves Horner psychologically paralyzed, unable to perform any actions whatsoever. Horner explains his condition memorably:

> My eyes, as Winkelmann said inaccurately of the eyes of the Greek statues, were sightless, gazing on eternity, fixed on ultimacy, and when that is the case there is no reason to do anything–even to change the focus of one's eyes. Which is perhaps why the statues stand still. It is the malady *cosmopsis,* the cosmic view, that afflicted me.

Or, in Barth's own deflationary comment, "The hero of *The End of the Road,* Jacob Horner, is supposed to remind you first of all of Little Jack Horner, who also sits in a corner and rationalizes."

Appleton was reluctant to publish the work, partly because of several plot similarities with Barth's first novel–which had sold poorly, despite its generally positive critical reception. As Barth noted, "Their situations have in common that they are narrated by the Other Man in a more or less acknowledged adulterous triangle complicated by an ambiguous pregnancy," and "the narrators share a radical alienation that fascinated me at the time." Rather than meet his publisher's request for a different book, Barth instructed his agent to look for a new publisher. It was eventually placed with Edward Aswell, an editor at Doubleday who had assembled Thomas Wolfe's late novels. Barth acceded to Aswell's request for a title change–the editor feared that the novel would be mistaken for a treatise on first aid–although, perhaps because of his experience with *The Floating Opera,* he did not agree to change the race of the black doctor who performs the fatal abortion.

Doubleday published *The End of the Road* in August 1958. It sold only three thousand copies, but the firm was willing to absorb the financial loss in exchange for the positive publicity generated by the enthusiastic reviews the book earned, and it continued to publish Barth's future works. In 1970 the book was made into a movie directed by Aram Avakian that–despite a strong cast that included Stacy Keach, Harris Yulin, Dorothy Tristan, and James Earl Jones–was a complete failure. According to the critic John Simon, "The principal difference between the novel and the film is that the novel concludes with a harrowing abortion, whereas the film is an abortion from start to finish."

Despite the philosophical concerns and bleak outlook that led many critics to classify Barth's first two novels, and especially *The End of the Road,* as "novels of ideas" and examples of black humor, both are in most ways securely within the then-mainstream of realistic novels with contemporary settings. Barth's next work, *The Sot-Weed Factor,* was a clean break with that tradition and set a new course for his next several books. At the time, however, he saw his third book as the logical sequel to the first two, a "nihilist extravaganza" that would end his trilogy with a narrative explosion. The germ of what turned out to be a much longer book than the first two (Barth claims that he wanted to publish a work so thick that the title would fit horizontally across the spine) was the stories in the "Dorchester Tales" that featured the real-life colonial poet Ebenezer Cooke, best known for his long–and not particularly good–satirical poem *The Sot-Weed Factor* (1708; revised, 1730). Barth conflates Cooke with Cooke's naive fictional narrator, who came from England to America to make his fortune as a "sot-weed factor"–that is, a commercial agent in the lucrative tobacco industry–and narrates the poet's misadventures in an imitation of the exuberant style and archaic English, as well as the generous length, of great eighteenth-century British novelists such as Henry Fielding. Barth also set himself the task of constructing a plot as "insanely complicated" as that of Fielding's *Tom Jones* (1749), while still managing to gather all the loose ends together at the end: "if you're going to do it," Barth remarked in an interview with Cynthia Liebow, "then surely part of the game is to rigorously make sure all the springs are sprung, and that you don't miss any bases. . . . "

To create historical verisimilitude Barth did extensive research in contemporary histories, such as those of William Byrd, and he includes quotations–interspersed with occasional fabrications–of Cooke's poetry. He is, however, willing to make up historical facts, as when he offers a revised version of Captain John Smith's 1624 account of Smith's adventure with Pocahontas in the "Privie Journall" of the fictional Henry Burlingame, whom he has accompany Smith. In the final chapter the narrator, referring to the muse of History, implicitly defends such liberties: "this Clio was already a scarred and crafty trollop when the Author found her." Barth also incorporates motifs from a wide range of authors of other times and places, from Homer to Chaucer to Walt Whitman, thereby adding intertextual to historical depth.

The Sot-Weed Factor continues the series of Barth's novels about protagonists who are themselves writers, but his adoption of third-person narration and an historical setting with a real–however imaginatively and freely re-created–protagonist provides him with opportunities to exploit additional levels of parallelism and contrast: between narrator and historical author, between past and present, and between fiction and reality. As Elaine B. Safer explains in 1987, *The Sot-Weed Factor* "combines an eighteenth-century setting with a twentieth-century sensibility," and Barth has always found this earliest period of the novel more central to his interests than the nineteenth century. He noted in the Liebow interview, "After all, there *are* a lot of affinities between the 18th century and the 20th century–many modernist or post-modernist writers may feel closer to *Tristram Shandy* than they do to, say, Dostoevsky or Tolstoy. . . ."

Cooke's desire, as the poet laureate of Maryland, to write its epic, a *Marylandiad,* parallels Barth's desire to stake his claim as the state's "novelist laureate"; and Barth's books become increasingly likely to be set in the author's home state (Ebenezer Cooke's property, Cooke's Point, lies some fifteen miles from Barth's birthplace). *The Sot-Weed Factor* begins an exploration of the region in historical depth that eventually invited comparison with William Faulkner's creation of the mythical Yoknapatawpha County, Mississippi.

During the four years it took him to write the book, Barth realized that its theme was the potentially tragic relationship of innocence to experience. Rather than the sentimental or nostalgic celebration of innocence so often found in literature, however, the innocence depicted in *The Sot-Weed Factor* is reprehensible. Barth remarks in the foreword to the 1988 paperback edition that innocence "can become dangerous, or even culpable; that where it is prolonged or artificially sustained, it becomes arrested development, potentially disastrous to the innocent himself and to bystanders innocent or otherwise; that what is to be valued, in nations as well as individuals, is not innocence but wise experience." He has Cooke, who has matured considerably by the end of the novel, further characterize it as "the crime of innocence, whereof the Knowledged must bear the burthen. There's the true Original Sin our souls are born in: not that Adam *learned,* but that he *had* to learn–in short, that he was innocent." Cooke's intellectual trajectory from innocence to experience in colonial America is meant to be read at least in part as an allegory of the nation's own history and character, and the manifold connections between art and life broached here came to provide Barth's most durable theme. More importantly, as he told Joe David Bellamy, Barth realized the considerable artistic potential that lay in

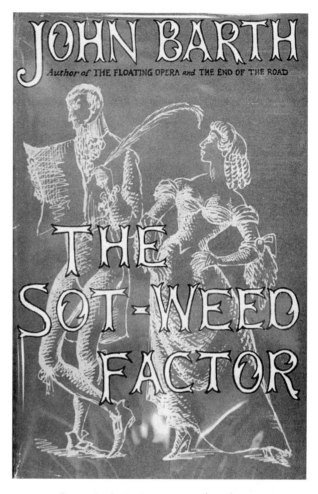

Dust jacket for Barth's third novel (1960), set in eighteenth-century Maryland

"the idea of writing a novel which imitates the form of the Novel," an insight that took him beyond traditional realism for the rest of his career.

The critical response to Barth's third novel was more mixed than it had been to the first two, with some reviewers finding the work prolix and repetitive (Barth reduced the length of the book from 806 to 756 pages when he revised his first three novels for republication in 1967). The eminent critic Leslie Fiedler, on the other hand, conceded that its length was an obstacle but nevertheless found *The Sot-Weed Factor* "something closer to the 'Great American Novel' than any other book of the last decades." Although the initial sale of five thousand copies was not much better than that of the first two novels, *The Sot-Weed Factor* gathered a cult following, and the 1964 Grosset and Dunlap paperback edition quickly sold twenty thousand copies. In 1965 *Book Week* ranked it eighteenth among the twenty best American novels of the previous twenty years.

After completing *The Sot-Weed Factor,* Barth began a novel with the working titles "The Seeker" and "The Amateur," but abandoned it. In 1965 he became professor of English at the State University of New York at Buffalo.

Shortly after *The Sot-Weed Factor* appeared, Philip Young, a colleague at Penn State, had mentioned to Barth that he had noticed parallels between Cooke's adventures and the twenty-two-stage pattern of the myth of the wandering hero described in FitzRoy Richard Somerset, Baron Raglan's *The Hero: A Study in Tradition, Myth, and Drama* (1936). Young assumed that the correspondences were intentional, but Barth had never heard of Raglan's work. After he read it, as well as several other examples of mythic and archetypal criticism, he used the structure of the heroic myth—this time consciously—as the organizational principle for the picaresque comic novel *Giles Goat-Boy; or, The Revised New Syllabus* (1966), producing a book that is about literature and literary analysis rather than about life. The novel warns its readers of the disorientation in store for them with two fictitious prefatory documents in which Barth undermines his own authority: a "Publisher's Disclaimer" by "The Editor-in-Chief" that includes four editors' reports on the novel (two vote against publishing the book, one in favor, and the fourth resigns his position as a result of having read the manuscript) and a "Cover-Letter to the Editors and Publishers," signed "J. B.," in which a struggling academic writer explains how Giles Stoker's book, *The Revised New Syllabus,* was delivered to him by a mysterious young man.

In Barth's own later synopsis in *Further Fridays: Essays, Lectures, and Other Nonfiction, 1984–1994* (1995), the book by Stoker that follows these documents narrates

> the adventures of a young man sired by a giant computer upon a hapless but compliant librarian and raised in the experimental goat-barns of a universal university, divided ideologically into East and West Campuses. Assigned a riddling series of tasks upon his matriculation, he must come to terms with both his goathood and his humanhood (not to mention his machinehood) and, in the very bowels of the University, transcend not only the categories of East and West but all the other categories as well; transcend language itself—and then return to the daylight campus, drive out the false Grand Tutor (whom he understands to be an aspect of himself), and do his best to eff the ineffable.

Giles Goat-Boy sets out to demythologize scriptural writing in much the same way that *The Sot-Weed Factor* dismantled historical writing. The book invites readings, or perhaps decodings, at multiple levels, of a dizzying array of topics: it is a political allegory of the Cold War and a mystical allegory of spiritual enlightenment; it expresses concerns about the role of computers in

society; it is a roman à clef about American popular culture; it includes elaborate and sustained parodies of world myths, especially the Bible and medieval saints' lives; and it is a satire of 1960s academia (though Barth had moved to the State University of New York in 1965, the geography of Universal University is based on Penn State). Safer comments in 1981 on Barth's radical reclamation of the allegorical method: "While traditional writers like Dante develop correspondences between this world and a new Jerusalem on earth, Barth and other black humorists suggest and then collapse allusions in order to disorient the reader who looks for meaningful connections."

Shortly before the publication of *Giles Goat-Boy,* Doubleday persuaded *The New York Times Book Review* to run a retrospective piece on his first three novels; the resulting essay by the respected critic Robert Scholes praised Barth generously and may have contributed to a critical backlash against the new novel, which received several scathing notices characterizing it as tedious and frustrating. In a review of the work in the same periodical (7 August 1966), Scholes defended his evaluation of Barth and extended it to the new novel: "This is not an experiment but a solution—an achievement which . . . stamps Barth as the best writer of fiction we have at present, and one of the best we have ever had." Such important critics as Granville Hicks in the *Saturday Review* (6 August 1966) and Richard Poirier in the *Chicago Sun-Times Book Week* (7 August 1966) also found the book important and rewarding despite its obvious difficulty, and Dabney Stuart in *Shenandoah* (Autumn 1966) went so far as to judge "that *Giles Goat-Boy* ranks with *Moby-Dick* as the best fiction yet written by an American." Despite the mixed reviews—or, perhaps, because of the controversy—the book sold fifty thousand copies, much better than Barth's three previous novels combined; it appeared on best-seller lists, was featured as an alternate selection of the Literary Guild, and resulted in a $2,500 grant to Barth from the National Institute of Arts and Letters. The complex allegorical novel proved to be such hard going for most readers, however, that Barth's commercially most successful novel to that time may actually be one of his least-read books. Nevertheless, the work is important in marking Barth's evolution from realism to the self-conscious foregrounding of literary artifice and form: that is, from modernism to postmodernism.

A third contribution by Scholes to Barth's critical reputation was *The Fabulators* (1967), which identifies Barth with an antirealism Scholes labels "fabulism" or "fabulation." "Fabulators" are characterized by their designing of structures of words and ideas rather than by their expression of themes. This insight fruitfully

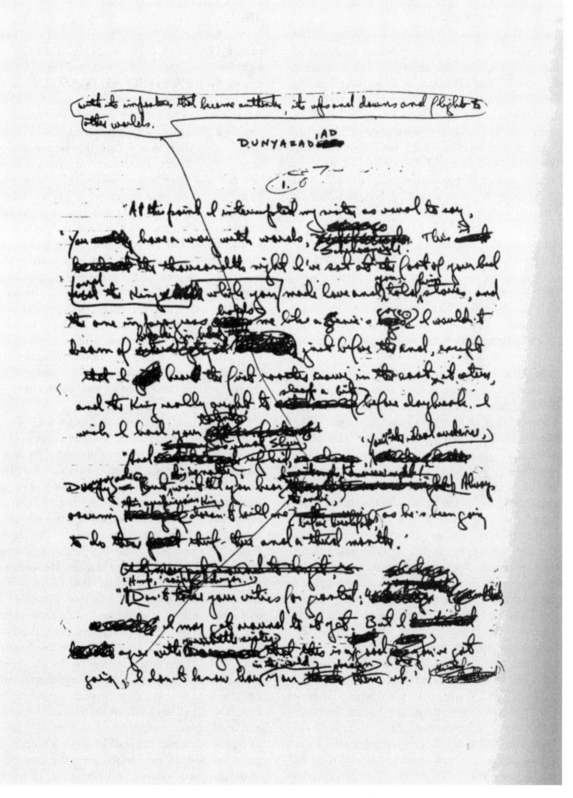

First page of the manuscript for the first novella in Barth's Chimera *(from George Plimpton, ed.,*
Writers at Work, *seventh series, 1986)*

redirected criticism of Barth's novels from thematic explications to formal analyses.

Barth himself entered into the discussions of the state and value of contemporary fiction (specifically including his own) with the influential and frequently reprinted essay "The Literature of Exhaustion" in *The Atlantic Monthly* (August 1967). Although the piece has frequently been cited as a proclamation of the "death of the novel," Barth's intention was to speculate about the future stages of a form to which he was thoroughly committed: "By 'exhaustion' I don't mean anything so tired as the subject of physical, moral, or intellectual decadence, only the used-upness of certain forms or exhaustion of certain possibilities—by no means necessarily a cause for despair." His models of the contemporary author are the Argentine short-story writer Jorge Luis Borges and the Irish playwright Samuel Beckett; he sees them as the successors to great modernist writers such as James Joyce and Franz Kafka, who had seemingly taken fictional forms as far as they could go. Borges's "artistic victory, if you like, is that he confronts an intellectual dead end and employs it against itself to do new human work."

Barth's interest in Borges, combined with his avowed desire to produce some work that could be included in classroom texts—"I wanted to be in those anthologies. Not all of a writer's motives are pure," he writes in *Further Fridays*—led him to publish a book of his short stories, *Lost in the Funhouse: Fiction for Print, Tape, Live Voice* (1968). Although several of the stories had been published separately, Barth insists in his "Author's Note" that the book is "neither a collection nor a selection, but a series . . . meant to be received 'all at once' and as here arranged"—an instance of what has come to be called the "composite novel." The book, his most successful by far, quickly sold twenty thousand copies in hardcover and more than one hundred thousand in a 1969 Bantam paperback edition that included "Seven Additional Author's Notes" in response to the wide range of early critical reaction and was nominated for the 1968 National Book Award. The fourteen stories range in form from traditional to radically unconventional; for many critics they constitute the theoretical centerpiece of Barth's career, the place where he most clearly addresses the "real technical question" he poses in "The Literature of Exhaustion": "how to succeed not even Joyce and Kafka, but those who've *succeeded* Joyce and Kafka." Despite his apparent dismissal of Joyce, the dominant prose writer of modernism, as an "already-succeeded" writer, critics were quick to notice that Joyce is mentioned twice in the collection; and Michael Hinden has argued that "in an attempt to exhaust the possibilities of its own tradition, *Lost in the Funhouse* begins as an elaborate parody, revival and refutation of

Joyce's masterpiece, *A Portrait of the Artist as a Young Man*."

The opening story, "Frame-Tale," consists of the phrase "ONCE UPON A TIME THERE" on the right-hand margin of the recto of one leaf and the phrase "WAS A STORY THAT BEGAN" on the left-hand margin of the verso of the same leaf; the top of the leaf was to be cut out, twisted, and the ends glued together to form a Möbius strip that would read "Once upon a time there was a story that began once upon a time . . ." endlessly. Barth later explained in *Further Fridays* that the story was an adaptation, with—literally—a twist, of the circular structure of Joyce's final novel, *Finnegans Wake* (1939), which begins in the middle of a sentence that is broken off at the same point at the end of the book. Critics have taken this piece—as Barth directs them to do in the common foreword to the 1988 paperback editions of his early works—as a figure for many aspects of the book, including its emphasis on paradox, self-reflexive content, and circular structure. The title story provides another unifying metaphor for the book, that of literature as a maze of distorting mirrors and echo chambers, an alternate reality constructed by writers within which readers can find themselves by temporarily—and productively—disorienting themselves.

In "The Literature of Exhaustion" Barth had made an observation about Borges's concept of the labyrinth that applies to his own notion of the fun house: "A labyrinth, after all, is a place in which, ideally, all the possibilities of choice . . . are embodied and . . . must be exhausted before one reaches the heart." The protagonist of the title story (and of two others in the collection, as well as of the abandoned novel "The Seeker") is Ambrose, a boy who is literally lost in a funhouse but knows that he will become a writer: "He wishes he had never entered the funhouse. But he has. Then he wishes he were dead. But he's not. Therefore he will construct funhouses for others and be their secret operator—though he would rather be among the lovers for whom funhouses are designed." The third-person narrator, who sometimes seems to be Ambrose, the Joycean "artist as a young man" writing as an adult, underscores the parallel between constructing fun houses and fictions by such metafictional (or, in Richard Bradbury's terminology, "autocritical") techniques as reproducing a drawing of Freitag's Triangle (the diagram traditionally used to represent the narrative stages of development, climax, and resolution) as he attempts to figure out how to construct his own narrative. The penultimate story in the collection, "Menelaiad," finds a form to represent both the Möbius strip and the fun house in its intricate embedding of eight narrative levels, each paralleling and intersecting with the others

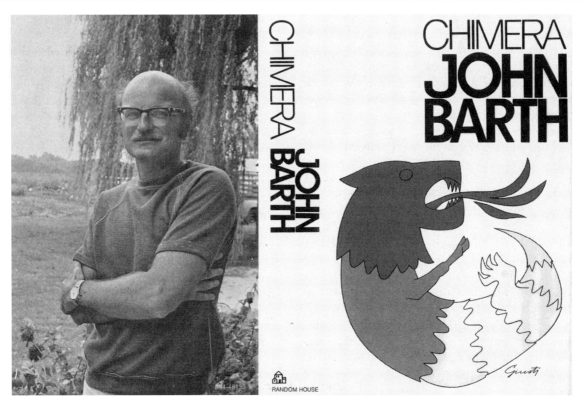

Dust jacket for Barth's 1972 collection of three complexly interrelated novellas

and reaching a formal climax when the word """"""Love!"""""" is spoken simultaneously by all eight narrators (this device also provides a framing connection to the second story, "Night-Sea Journey," which ends with the same word).

Barth followed his first venture outside the form of the novel with its "twin," *Chimera* (1972), a collection of three related novellas (the tripartite mythical beast had the head of a lion, body of a goat, and tail of a serpent) that continues the rewriting of classical stories through postmodernist language and formal devices that Barth began with "Menelaiad" and another story, "Anonymiad," in *Lost in the Funhouse*. The book ignited considerable critical controversy, and a split among the judges for the 1973 National Book Award in fiction led to the unprecedented sharing of the award between Barth's novella suite and John Williams's *Augustus*. *Chimera* sold well, however–seventeen thousand hardcover copies and eighty-five thousand paperbacks in the first year–adding further popular support to increasing respect for Barth among academics that included an honorary doctorate of letters from the University of Maryland in 1969. *Chimera* has come to be widely regarded by critics as one of his finest achievements.

The first novella, "Dunyazadiad," is narrated by Dunyazade, the younger sister of Scheherazade, the narrator of *The Thousand and One Nights' Entertainments*. Here Scheherazade is given the tales with which to occupy the sultan by a genie from the twentieth century, a middle-aged academic writer much like Barth, who has been working on a series of three novellas in which he hopes to find a way to recapture the glories of narratives such as Scheherazade's. Barth's identification with Scheherazade extends into several of his later novels, in which she becomes a mythic representative of all writers.

The novellas "Perseid" and "Bellerophoniad" recount the similar struggles of two middle-aged mythical heroes, Perseus and Bellerophon, to recapture in the second half of their lives the power and purposefulness of the first half. The theme has closer than usual autobiographical relevance: Barth's own middle age had by this time included divorce in 1969, marriage to Shelly I. Rosenberg on 27 December 1970, a period of writer's block, and a self-conscious search for redirection. He continues to explore new options for narrative voice and point of view in the two novellas: Perseus narrates his tale to Medusa after both have been turned into constellations; Bellerophon narrates his story–which is modeled on the "Perseid," which he has read—after having been turned into the bundle of pages on which his story is written, which now float in a Maryland marsh, ready, presumably, for Barth to find them. In Barth's original conception "Dunyazadiad" was the third work in the sequence, but his editor at Doubleday, Anne Freedgood, persuaded him that it was the best and most accessible piece, well suited to lead readers into the book. The rearrangement had its advantages—it resulted in the works growing progressively longer, echoing one of the book's key metaphors, the image of the ever-increasing spiral. But it also had its disadvantages, among them that the book now closed with the pessimism, misogynism, and confusion of Bellerophon's section rather than the optimism, feminism, and clarity of Dunyazade's narrative.

After spending the academic year 1972–1973 at Boston University, Barth returned to his undergraduate institution, Johns Hopkins, to teach in the Writing Seminar in the building that had housed the Oriental Seminary collection where he had begun reading about Scheherazade. He was named to the American Academy of Arts and Sciences in 1977.

Barth returned to his literary origins with *LETTERS* (1979), a tour de force in which he recycles his first six books within the framework of the seventh. He also returns to the origins of the novel, adopting the epistolary form of Samuel Richardson's hugely influential multivolume novels *Pamela* (1740–1741) and *Clarissa* (1747–1749). His seventh novel is made up of letters from seven correspondents writing in seven different styles, six of whom are drawn from his first six books: Todd Andrews, the narrator (and here, the author) of *The Floating Opera;* Jacob Horner, the narrator (and author) of *The End of The Road;* Andrew Burlingame Cook VI, a descendant of Ebenezer Cooke, the protagonist of *The Sot-Weed Factor;* Jerome Bray, a character from *Giles Goat-Boy;* Ambrose Mensch, featured in three of the stories (of which, it turns out, he was really the author) in *Lost in the Funhouse;* and John Barth, who made an appearance (albeit unnamed) in the "Dunyazadiad" section of *Chimera* and who has published under his own name the works that were really written by his "characters." Each writer takes up his original story more or less where it left off and extends it forward and backward into complex interrelationships with the stories of all the other writers (Cook's story even extends back in time to the historical milieu of *The Sot-Weed Factor*). As Max F. Schultz put it in 1990, the writers "acquire antecedent and posterior histories, individual biographies growing into family sagas of generations." The characters are, thus, not merely repeated but brought to fuller development as they are reimagined by their author, much in the manner of Honoré de

Balzac's or Faulkner's characters in those authors' extended novel cycles.

The new correspondent not featured in any of the first six books is Germaine Pitt, Lady Amherst, a middle-aged British academic who represents both the strong modern version of the delicate damsel in distress of the eighteenth-century epistolary novel, as typified by Richardson's Pamela and Clarissa, and also an allegorical figure for the tradition of humanistic letters (another implication of the title), particularly of the novel. In the course of the narrative she becomes pregnant by the experimental writer Ambrose Mensch; at the allegorical level the implication is that the union of the traditional novel and the postmodern novel—of which Barth is presenting *LETTERS* itself as a paradigmatic model—will also be fruitful. Lady Amherst also continues the motif of the union of male and female principles in authorship begun in the "Dunyazadiad" and developed more fully in Barth's next novels. Several of the correspondents are familiar with Barth's writing and their own appearances in it, providing opportunities for Barth to embed interpretive clues and artistic pronouncements about his work within his work. Lady Amherst, for example, provides Barth with a means of setting readers straight on his intent in "The Literature of Exhaustion" when she informs him that Ambrose "assures me that you do not yourself take with much seriousness those Death-of-the-Novel or End-of-Letters chaps, but that you *do* take seriously the climate that takes such questions seriously; you exploit that apocalyptic climate, he maintains, to reinspect the origins of narrative fiction. . . ."

A relatively straightforward example of such reinspection may be seen in Barth's innovative reordering of the traditional epistolary-narrative form. The letters are arranged in seven sections, one for each letter of the title—the book is structured in multiple patterns of sevens—in a complicated sequence that reflects the eighty-eight letters of the "subtitle," *An old time epistolary novel by seven fictitious drolls & dreamers, each of whom imagines himself actual,* in which Barth has their dates of composition spell out the full title of the book on seven pages of a calendar (March through September 1969) after the pages have been turned ninety degrees, which means that the letters are not always presented in the book in the order in which they were written. Some are only a day or so out of sequence; at the other extreme, some of the letters from Cook include letters from his ancestors, which are for the "right" day and month but for the "wrong" year: 1812 instead of 1969. As Barth explained in 1981 to Charlie Reilly,

There are letters responding to other letters that the reader hasn't seen yet, and that occurs because I'm convinced there is a nice dramatic effect achieved by departing from chronological order. . . . If you think about it, you might see that there's a kind of metaphor for the plot—a metaphor of waves crashing ashore on a tidal beach. The plot surges up to a given point, then seems to recede a little, then crashes back on the beach.

This arrangement exemplifies the aesthetic philosophy that Barth had called for in the "The Literature of Exhaustion," in which the postmodern writer reinvents and renews the most traditional literary genres through formal innovation. Barth also rewrites two hundred years of American history, with particular focus on the War of 1812, and offers a detailed satirical representation of American cultural and literary mores at the bicentennial. Furthermore, he accomplishes all of it while limiting himself to writing about his own previous writings, extending the concepts of metafiction and intertextuality toward what may be their limits. The result is an encyclopedic novel that seemed at the time both virtually unreadable and also a monumental (772-page) capstone to Barth's literary achievement, prompting critical comparisons to Joyce's *Finnegans Wake*. A key difference, of course, is that Barth was at a much earlier point in his literary career than Joyce had been.

In keeping with his preoccupation with revisiting earlier works, Barth returned to "The Literature of Exhaustion" in "The Literature of Replenishment: Post-modernist Fiction," published in *The Atlantic Monthly* (January 1980), in which he both defends his earlier piece against widespread misinterpretations and extends it to reaffirm his conviction that literature is far from exhausted. He says that he thought he had made clear from the start that his first essay was about "the effective 'exhaustion' not of language and literature but of the aesthetic of high modernism." He affirms what he had always taken to be the positive message that "artistic conventions are liable to be retired, subverted, transcended, transformed, or even deployed against themselves to generate new and lively work." Barth's own recent synthesis in *LETTERS* of virtually the entire history of the novel, from traditional realism to avant-garde formalism, provides an example of the working out of this theory.

With *Sabbatical: A Romance* (1982) Barth circles back toward the realistic mode (and more modest length, at 366 pages) of his first two novels. Fenwick Scott Key Turner, a former Central Intelligence Agency operative who has written *KUDOVE,* an exposé of the agency, and his wife, Susan Rachel Allan Seckler, a literature professor, are returning in their sailboat to the Chesapeake Bay at the end of her sabbatical leave, during which they have revisited scenes

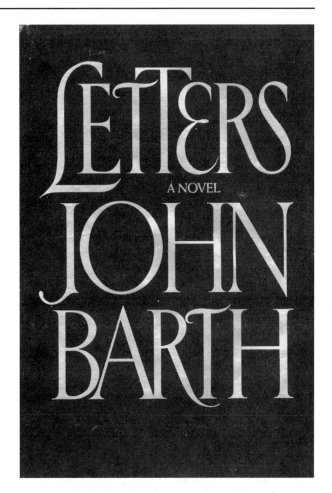

Dust jacket for Barth's 1979 epistolary novel, in which six of the seven correspondents are characters from his previous novels

from the history of their relationship in an attempt to find answers to questions about their future, particularly whether they will have children (in this respect they are like their creator, who said of himself in *Further Fridays* that he decides "where to go by determining where I am by reviewing where I've been"). Both have twin siblings who play important roles in the book, as do Fenwick's former wife and offspring and Susan's mother, providing a depth of realistic context that allows Barth to pay more extensive attention than usual to domestic matters—provoking the critic Zack Bowen to complain about "a celebration of familial ties reminiscent of the Brady Bunch." Even at the level of realistic narrative, however, Barth finds ways to explore his favorite theme of the interpenetration of life and art, incorporating stories from *The Baltimore Sun* about former CIA official John Paisley, whose mysterious death—first mentioned on the final page of *LETTERS* and woven into Barth's next novel, *The Tidewater Tales* (1987)—is worked into one of the complicated spy-novel subplots in the book: Fenwick's brother, Manfred, works for the CIA, and most of the other characters seem to have ties to the agency.

Within this relatively realistic narrative framework, Barth continues his trademark experimentation with point of view and inclusion of metafictional commentary and speculation: the husband-and-wife protagonists are sometimes characters in a third-person narrative and sometimes first-person singular and plural narrators of their own story; and they are writing, and discussing their writing of, a book that may well be *Sabbatical* itself. The merging of two voices into one, a subtype of the theme of convergence explored in several of Barth's works, is emblematized by the form of the letter *Y*, a stylized version of which appears on the title page and cover. The novel explores many related *Y*-shaped analogues from anatomy (fallopian tubes and uterus), the topography of the bay (Wye Island, the confluence of the east and west forks of Langford Creek into Chesapeake Bay), and even astronomy ("from the perspective of Earth—say from Baltimore—our galaxy looks like the capital letter Y"). The *Y* also serves as a symbol both of divergence and of convergence as the characters are forced to make difficult choices between incompatible alternatives. Susan and Fenwick finally decide to stay at the precise point of decision-making, at an island at a point created by three rivers; this decision to make no decision seems comparable to the paralysis of the characters of Barth's early books, especially that of Jacob Horner in *The End of the Road,* but, as Bradbury points out, "The crucial difference between this and his earlier version of the same crisis, presented as cosmopsis in the first three novels, is that here the choice is productive; it leads to fiction and not silence." Another of the central conceits in the book that plays on this fertility/sterility theme is the identification of the Chesapeake Bay as a gigantic womb within which the male and female protagonist, like a sperm and an ovum in their watery environment, are attempting to conceive a novel as well as a child. But as reviewer John Aldridge noted in *Washington Post Book World* (23 May 1982), these elements "are effectively subordinated to the strong realistic thrust of the narrative and so provide the book with an agreeable controlled complexity instead of burying it beneath the old fog-bank of endless equivocation."

Barth has always been a teacher of literature as well as a producer of it; and the highly self-conscious nature of his work makes him even more disposed than most other academic writers to have a strong interest in the theory of his art. In 1984 he collected his miscellaneous writings on the craft of fiction as *The Friday Book: Essays and Other Nonfiction,* so called because of his practice of writing fiction on Monday through Thursday mornings and reserving Friday mornings to "refresh my head with some other sort of sentence-making, preferably nonfiction." In this book and the sequel, *Further Fridays: Essays, Lectures, and Other Nonfiction, 1984–1994,* Barth shows himself to be an acute critic of his own work, as well as one of a handful of creative writers who not only keep abreast of but actively participate in contemporary literary theory. "The Literature of Exhaustion" and "The Literature of Replenishment," both included in *The Friday Book,* have proven seminal documents for the study of postmodern literature.

Barth called his 1987 book *The Tidewater Tales: A Novel* "a sort of opposite-sex twin to *Sabbatical,*" in that it features another married couple but one whose situation is "rather the reverse of Fenwick's and Susan's." Like Fenwick and Susan, Katherine and Peter Sagamore are sailing in the Chesapeake Bay; the storm that ends the earlier novel occurs at the beginning of the later one (the continuity between beginnings and endings, for which Barth used the image of the Möbius strip in *Lost in the Funhouse,* is invoked here by the inclusion of title pages at both the front and back of the book). As in *The Floating Opera* and *The End of the Road,* in which a triangle of somewhat similar characters produces, respectively, a comedy and a tragedy, the two couples in this pair of books take similar situations to different conclusions. Most notably, where Susan aborts the twins she is carrying in *Sabbatical,* Katherine Sherritt Sagamore delivers twins in *The Tidewater Tales* (with the allegorical help of "Jack Bass," another surrogate for Barth). The sequence of Barth's first two books—a "nihilist comedy," in which the narrator apparently fathers a child, is followed by a "nihilist tragedy" that ends with the abortion of a child who may be the narrator's—finds its reversed mirror image in *Sabbatical* and *The Tidewater Tales,* which take the opposite progression: from the abortion of twins to the birth of twins and from tragedy to comedy, in line with what many critics perceive as a growing (though still strongly qualified) optimism in Barth's worldview. For example, Peter is also able to "give birth"—to new literary works; and Bradbury suggests that this "rediscovery of the delights of narrative, as demonstrated both by the stories he tells within the text of *The Tidewater Tales* and by the text itself. . . . is also autobiographical of its author's trajectory over the previous twenty years. . . . It is, in relation to Barth's earlier work, *the* autocritical work."

This optimism is especially evident in Barth's sensitive and increasingly sympathetic depictions of fulfilling marriages (Barth's novels from *Sabbatical* onward are dedicated to his second wife) and of the beauties of nature, particularly the land- and seascapes of the Chesapeake Triangle. The happy marriage is dramatized as Peter, a writer afflicted with writer's block, and his

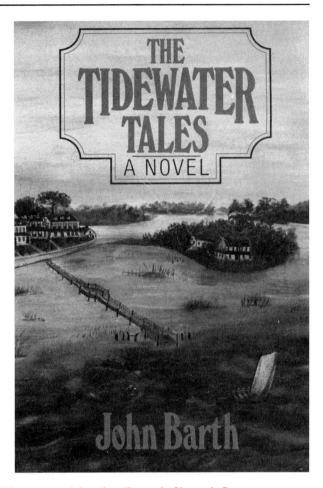

*Dust jackets for Barth's 1982 and 1987 novels, both of which concern married couples sailing on the Chesapeake Bay,
and in both of which the wife is pregnant with twins*

eight-and-a-half-month-pregnant wife help each other with their respective stressful situations through a program of storytelling; and the region is celebrated through their stories, which survey the history of the Chesapeake Bay and mourn a range of contemporary ecological and sociopolitical threats to the bay. Just as Peter has fertilized the biological offspring that his wife will deliver, Katherine, herself a storyteller and founder of the American Society for the Preservation of Storytelling, will fertilize her husband's artistic offspring as he overcomes his writer's block, his literary sterility. As Bowen remarks, in Barth's later novels "the principal dilemma involves how to recount the events successfully rather than how to overcome any obstacle the events themselves impose."

The central metaphor of the bay as a womb persists from *Sabbatical*—the formerly fecund bay itself is threatened with ecological sterility—and the many parallels include not only the gestation of Katherine and Peter's twins and the gestation of their collaborative novel, *The Tidewater Tales*, but the story-within-

the-story *Sex Education*, a manuscript play they find floating on the waters of the bay in two flare canisters. The content of the play, which centers around May and June, two ova from successive ovulations, and their lesbian romance and eventual encounters, both brutal and romantic, with sperm, recapitulates in reverse (and thereby demonstrates the increasingly strong feminist emphasis in Barth's work) the first full story of *Lost in the Funhouse*, "Night-Sea Journey," which tells the story of conception from a sperm's point of view. The method of "publication" of the play similarly recalls the final story from that collection, "Anonymiad," in which a minstrel sends poetry across the water in amphorae. Barth continues his knitting together of his various works by having Katherine and Peter meet the authors of the play, Leah and Franklin Key Talbott, a childless couple who closely resemble Susan and Fenwick of *Sabbatical* (Franklin's book is *KUBARK* instead of *KUDOVE*; Susan's mother, Carmen B. Seckler, is transmuted into Carla B. Silver; and so on).

The Tidewater Tales ranges widely outside its nominal setting as Barth pursues his fascination with incorporating classic literature into his novels. Kept largely in abeyance in *Sabbatical,* this interest returns in its twin as the framing story of Katherine and Peter is woven together with framed stories of Barth's favorite literary characters: Odysseus, Don Quixote, Scheherazade, and Huckleberry Finn. He offers a partial rationale for the frequent recurrence of these figures in his works in "The Limits of Imagination," a 1985 lecture collected in *Further Fridays,* when he identifies those four "cardinal images" as "literary-artistic images . . . of such extraordinary imaginative power—one might say, of such mythic resonance—as to be larger than the works that contain them, or rather fail to contain them" and calls them "the very compass-points of my own narrative imagination."

The Last Voyage of Somebody the Sailor (1991) is the third novel in a row set in the present and, at least in part, aboard a boat; but here Barth periodically shifts the scene from Maryland to the medieval Baghdad of Scheherazade and Sindbad. Extending a progression initiated with the essentially realistic *Sabbatical* and continued with the mixed realism and fabulation of *The Tidewater Tales,* Barth now produces an essentially fantastic novel (albeit one with realistic embedded narratives), a progression that reenacts, though without repeating, the movement from realism to myth of his first six novels. The book opens with Simon William Behler in a hospital room telling a new story about Scheherazade to a young woman who seems to be his doctor and finally seems to be a surrogate for his stillborn twin sister. In the story Scheherazade, now old and sick, will not be allowed the death for which she is ready unless she can tell Death himself, The Destroyer of Delights, a story that he has never heard—an inversion of *The Thousand and One Nights' Entertainments,* in which she had to tell stories to forestall her death. She tells Death about a marathon storytelling contest in which Sindbad the Sailor and Somebody the Sailor tell one story each on consecutive nights. Sindbad retells the tales of his voyages, already familiar to his auditors from frequent repetitions (and to Barth's readership, though they are here somewhat altered, from *The Thousand and One Nights' Entertainments*).

The stories of the mysterious beggar Somebody, however, turn out to be those of Behler himself, who was lost in 1980 off the coast of Sri Lanka attempting to retrace the legendary voyages of Sindbad and eventually found himself a guest in Sindbad's house and the lover of Sindbad's daughter, Yasmin. Somebody/Behler's first four stories take place in Behler's twentieth-century life, describing the "adventures," such as sexual initiation and divorce, that occurred on his sev-enth, fourteenth, forty-second, and fiftieth birthdays. These narratives, which Bowen calls "the most compelling realistic fiction" of Barth's career, are, in an ironic twist, perceived by his Arabian auditors as the most fantastic of fictions, especially with regard to details such as watches and airplanes, which Barth's modern readers take as indices of traditional realism: "Said Sindbad presently, 'Hum: mechanical birds and bracelets that measure time." The medieval audience can nevertheless find compelling the universals of human experience, linking the voyages of Sindbad to Behler's coming-of-age narrative set in East Dorset, Maryland, in 1937 (and metaleptically providing an image to describe Barth's compositional methodology in the novel itself): "that business of your brother's drifting in a leaky vessel that must ceaselessly be bailed: that speaks to my condition! An admirable bit of realism in a sea of fantasy." In the fifth and sixth stories Behler/Somebody fully enters the world of *The Thousand and One Nights' Entertainments,* and it turns out to be Somebody, not Sindbad, who undertakes the famous seventh voyage before returning to the modern world. The treasure he has brought back from his voyages is, of course, the narrative of them. At the end of the novel Behler recognizes the doctor as his twin sister and appears ready to follow her—whether to death or to birth is not clear. The task imposed on and carried out by Behler, Scheherazade, and Somebody of telling a new story after all the stories have been told is the task that Barth believes every writer faces each time he or she writes; and Barth again demonstrates the practicability of his method of replenishing contemporary literature by returning to the only apparently exhausted origins of literature in what is, for Bowen, "perhaps the best one Barth has yet told."

In 1990 Barth took early retirement from Johns Hopkins, where he now holds professor emeritus status in the Writing Seminars. Just as his first series of six progressively more experimental books was capped by the self-reflexive *LETTERS,* which featured Barth himself as a character, the next sequence of three progressively more experimental novels is capped by his eleventh book of fiction, the self-reflexive *Once Upon a Time: A Floating Opera* (1994). In citing his first novel, the title implies that the book also serves as a coda to his previous ten fictions. The "memoir bottled in a novel," as Barth calls it in a prefatory "Program Note," "is not the story of my life, but it is most certainly a story thereof. The better to sing it, I have passed over or scarcely sounded other themes, and have reorchestrated freely to my purpose." The text is presented as the reflections of a fictional character named John Barth, a middle-aged writer who is sailing into the Chesapeake Triangle with his wife. As R. H. W. Dillard remarked in his review (*New York Times Book Review,* 3 July 1994), "True to his life-long fascination with twins and doubles, and his rage for symmetry and fictive order, both Mr. Barth's first and 'last' novels are floating operas, twinned mirror images of each other, reflecting the beginning and end."

Having rounded off his career as a novelist with the elegiac and meditative *Once Upon a Time,* Barth published *Further Fridays: Essays, Lectures, and Other Non-fiction, 1984–1994* in 1995 and *On with the Story,* his third collection of shorter fictions, in 1996. While all twelve stories in the latter had first appeared in periodicals, the collection appeared to many reviewers to have its own integrity and to constitute another example of the composite novel. Ron Loewinsohn (*New York Times Book Review,* 28 July 1996), for example, found a structural principle: "a dozen stories arranged in three groups of four, concerning beginnings, middles, and endings." D. Quentin Miller noted (*Review of Contemporary Fiction,* 1997) the unifying force of Barth's device of "concluding the book with continuations of the eleven stories that precede the conclusion, in reverse order," as well as the coherence provided by "the series of interchapters depicting a vacationing husband and wife who exchange stories in bed," linking the latter to Barth's frequent reliance on the device of the frame tale in his recent novels.

A further principle of coherence is suggested by Barth's two epigraphs, from the physicist Werner Heisenberg and from a standard textbook on narrative (co-authored by Barth's early critical champion Scholes), and by the explicit linking of the laws of physics and of narrative in several of the stories. "Ad Infinitum: A Short Story" and "On with the Story," for example, are adaptations of the pre-Socratic philosopher Zeno's paradoxes of, respectively, Achilles and the tortoise and the arrow that can never hit its target, which pose problems in the physics of relative motion, into stories structured around the literary techniques for the depiction of temporal and spatial relations in narrative. Barth also links *On with the Story* to his first book of short stories, *Lost in the Funhouse.* The narrator of the final story, "Countdown: Once Upon a Time" (the subtitle is a citation of Barth's last novel) was himself "once briefly lost in a funhouse, and a quarter-century later found a story in that loss"; here he finds an additional story in it, rather more than an additional quarter-century later. Even the title of the book connects the two works, as the phrase "On with the story" appeared at the end of the "Author's Note" to *Lost in the Funhouse.* As Loewinsohn stipulated, however, it is the typical Barthian spiral, a repetition with a difference: "There it signified a beginning, meaning 'Let's get the

Barth circa 1987 (photograph by William Denison; from the dust jacket for The Tidewater Tales*)*

story started.' Here it is a plea for continuity: 'Let's not allow the story to end.'"

Hyman wrote of Barth in 1965: "I can hardly conceive a limit to his eventual attainment." Over the next three decades Barth produced a series of increasingly ambitious, innovative, and influential novels that could not have been conceived at the time Hyman wrote. Yet the question of Barth's critical stature remains open, primarily, perhaps, because he has set his sights so high that even his undeniably impressive achievements may seem to fall short of his self-imposed goals. From the beginning the reviews of his books have been surprisingly mixed for a writer of his remarkable craftsmanship. But Barth, much in the manner of such modernist predecessors as Faulkner, Joyce, and Virginia Woolf—all of whom were similarly declared unreadable and perversely experimental by many of their contemporaries—has proven that over the long run he can create and educate his own readership and outlast his detractors. The long and demanding novels that seemed so obscure in the 1960s and 1970s have turned out to be quite lucid now that readers have had time to absorb them (and other writers have had time to imitate them).

The rise of cultural criticism among some academic critics in the 1980s and 1990s has raised the rather different question of the "political correctness" of a writer who has not seemed to share their priorities; as Barth himself admits, "as a white Anglo-Saxon (lapsed) Protestant of just the right age and location to have missed all the wars of our century, I have had the remarkable privilege of being largely left alone by history and politics, and I have largely returned them that courtesy." Barth's typically self-deprecating concession seems to be contradicted, however, by the highly skeptical "deconstructive" view of American historical and political master narratives that he has been developing at least since *The Sot-Weed Factor*–well in advance of the similarly skeptical theories adopted by the academic critics–and, more recently, by the pronounced concern with feminism and, especially, ecology, that has characterized his work at least since *Sabbatical*. Further, much of the work of his more overtly politically engaged contemporaries from each of the five decades of his career has become dated and unreadable, while even Barth's earliest novels continue to appear fresh and bear up under close rereading through new critical tools whose application he always seems to have anticipated.

As Joseph N. Weixlmann observes, "Barth has, on various occasions, indicated that the true measure of his authorial success will not be taken for decades, even centuries; that his attempt, as a writer, is to rival Shakespeare and Cervantes rather than his contemporaries. In this context, Barth scholarship is in its infancy, despite the fact that much serious critical attention has already been focused on his work."

Interviews:

John J. Enck, "John Barth: An Interview," *Wisconsin Studies in Contemporary Literature,* 6 (Winter-Spring 1965): 3–14; republished in *The Contemporary Writer: Interviews with Sixteen Novelists and Poets,* edited by L. S. Dembo and Cyrena M. Podrom (Madison: University of Wisconsin Press, 1972), pp. 18–29;

Alan Prince, "An Interview with John Barth," *Prism* [Sir George Williams University, Montreal] (Spring 1968): 42–62;

Roger Henkle, "Symposium Highlights: Wrestling (American Style) with Proteus," *Novel,* 3 (1970): 197–207;

Joe David Bellamy, "Having It Both Ways: A Conversation Between John Barth and Joe David Bellamy," *New American Review* (April 1972): 134–150; republished as "John Barth," in *The New Fiction: Interviews with Innovative American Writers,* edited by Bellamy (Urbana: University of Illinois Press, 1974), pp. 1–18;

Frank Gado, "A Conversation with John Barth," *Idol* (Union College), 49 (Fall 1972): 1–36; republished in *First Person: Conversations on Writers and Writing,* edited by Gado (Schenectady, N.Y.: Union College Press, 1973), pp. 110–141;

James McKenzie, "Pole-Vaulting in Top Hats: A Public Conversation with John Barth, William Gass, and Ishmael Reed," *Modern Fiction Studies,* 22 (1976): 131–151;

Charlie Reilly, "An Interview with John Barth," *Contemporary Literature,* 22, no. 1 (1981): 1–23;

Heide Ziegler and Christopher Bigsby, "John Barth," in *The Radical Imagination and the Liberal Tradition: Interviews with English and American Novelists,* edited by Ziegler and Bigsby (London: Junction, 1982), pp. 16–38;

"A Dialogue: John Barth and John Hawkes," in *Anything Can Happen: Interviews with Contemporary American Novelists,* edited by Tom LeClair and Larry McCaffery (Urbana: University of Illinois Press, 1983), pp. 9–19;

Cynthia Liebow, "Entretien avec John Barth," *Delta: Revue du Centre d'Etudes et de Recherche sur les Ecrivains du Sud aux Etats-Unis,* 21 (1985): 1–15;

George Plimpton, "John Barth," in *Writers at Work: The Paris Review Interviews, Seventh Series,* edited by Plimpton (New York: Viking, 1986), pp. 225–240;

John Howell, "John Barth," introduction by Sarah Zimmerman, *Papyrus,* 1 (1987): 39–49;

Loretta M. Lampkin, "An Interview with John Barth," *Contemporary Literature,* 29, no. 4 (1988): 485–497;

Bin Ramke and Donald Revell, "Conversation with Prime Maximalist John Barth," *Bloomsbury Review,* 11 (1991): 3, 8.

Bibliographies:

Jackson R. Bryer, "John Barth: A Bibliography," *Critique: Studies in Modern Fiction,* 6, no. 2 (1963): 86–89;

Joseph N. Weixlmann, "John Barth: A Bibliography," *Critique: Studies in Modern Fiction,* 13, no. 3 (1972): 45–55;

Weixlmann, *John Barth: A Descriptive Primary and Annotated Secondary Bibliography, Including a Descriptive Catalogue of Manuscript Holdings in United States Libraries* (New York & London: Garland, 1976);

Richard Allan Vine, *John Barth: An Annotated Bibliography* (Metuchen, N.J.: Scarecrow Press, 1977);

Thomas P. Walsh and Cameron Northouse, *John Barth, Jerzy Kosinski, and Thomas Pynchon: A Reference Guide* (Boston: G. K. Hall, 1977).

References:

Mary Allen, *The Necessary Blankness: Women in Major American Fiction of the Sixties* (Urbana: University of Illinois Press, 1976), pp. 14–37;

Beverly G. Bienstock, "Lingering on the Autognostic Verge: John Barth's *Lost in the Funhouse,*" *Modern Fiction Studies,* 19, no. 1 (1973): 69–78;

Zack Bowen, *A Reader's Guide to John Barth* (Westport, Conn.: Greenwood Press, 1994);

Richard Bradbury, "Postmodernism and Barth and the Present State of Fiction," *Critical Quarterly,* 32 (1990): 60–72;

Jerry H. Bryant, *The Open Decision: The Contemporary American Novel and Its Intellectual Background* (New York: Free Press, 1970), pp. 286–303;

Charles B. Caramello, *Silverless Mirrors: Book, Self, and Postmodern American Fiction* (Tallahassee: University Presses of Florida, 1983), pp. 112–130;

Thomas Carmichael, "A Postmodern Genealogy: John Barth's *Sabbatical* and *The Narrative of Arthur Gordon Pym,*" *University of Toronto Quarterly,* 60 (1991): 389–401;

Jack David, "The Trojan Horse at the End of the Road," *College Literature,* 4 (1977–1978): 159–164;

Robert Con Davis, "The Case for a Post-Structuralist Mimesis: John Barth and Imitation," *American Journal of Semiotics,* 3, no. 3 (1985): 49–72;

Marilyn Edelstein, "The Function of Self-Consciousness in John Barth's *Chimera,*" *Studies in American Fiction,* 12 (1984): 99–108;

Harold Farwell, "John Barth's Tenuous Affirmation: 'The Absurd, Unending Possibility of Love,'" *Georgia Review,* 28 (1974): 290–306;

Leslie Fiedler, "John Barth: An Eccentric Genius," *New Leader,* 44 (1961): 22–24;

Stanley Fogel, "The Ludic Temperament of John Barth," in his *The Postmodern University: Essays on the Deconstruction of the Humanities* (Toronto: ECW Press, 1988), pp. 113–123;

Fogel and Gordon Slethaug, *Understanding John Barth* (Columbia: University of South Carolina Press, 1990);

Jan Gorak, *God the Artist: Novelists in a Post-Realist Age* (Urbana: University of Illinois Press, 1987), pp. 145–191;

Gerald Graff, "Under Our Belt and Off Our Back: Barth's *LETTERS* and Postmodern Fiction," *Tri-Quarterly,* 52 (1981): 150–164;

James T. Gresham, "Giles Goat-Boy: Satyr, Satire, and Tragedy Twined," *Genre,* 7 (1974): 148–163;

John Z. Guzlowski, "No More Sea Changes: Hawkes, Pynchon, Gaddis, Barth," *Critique: Studies in Modern Fiction,* 23 (1981–1982): 48–59;

Charles B. Harris, *Contemporary American Novelists of the Absurd* (New Haven, Conn.: College and University Press, 1971);

Harris, *Passionate Virtuosity: The Fiction of John Barth* (Urbana: University of Illinois Press, 1983);

Richard Boyd Hauch, *A Cheerful Nihilism: Confidence and "The Absurd" in American Humorous Fiction* (Bloomington: Indiana University Press, 1971), pp. 201–236;

John Hawkes, "*The Floating Opera* and *Second Skin,*" *Mosaic,* 8 (1974): 17–28;

Jeffrey Helterman, *John Barth's Giles Goat-Boy: A Critical Commentary* (New York: Monarch, 1973);

Michael Hinden, "Lost in The Funhouse: Barth's Use of the Recent Past," *Twentieth Century Literature,* 19 (1973): 107–118;

Stanley Edgar Hyman, "John Barth's First Novel," *New Leader,* 48 (12 April 1965): 20–21;

Enoch P. Jordan, "'A Quantum Swifter and More Graceful': John Barth's Revisions of The Sot-Weed Factor," *Proof: Yearbook of American Bibliographical and Textual Studies,* 5 (1977): 171–182;

Gerhard Joseph, *John Barth* (Minneapolis: University of Minnesota Press, 1970);

Frederick R. Karl, *American Fictions 1940–1980: A Comprehensive History and Critical Evaluation* (New York: Harper & Row, 1983), pp. 444–487;

Robert F. Kiernan, "John Barth's Artist in the Funhouse," *Studies in Short Fiction,* 10 (1973): 373–380;

Jerome Klinkowitz, *Literary Subversions: New American Fiction and the Practice of Criticism* (Carbondale: Southern Illinois University Press, 1985), pp. 3–17;

Edgar H. Knapp, "Found in the Barthhouse: Novelist as Savior," *Modern Fiction Studies,* 14 (1969): 446–451;

Thomas LeClair, "John Barth's The Floating Opera: Death and the Craft of Fiction," *Texas Studies in Language and Literature,* 14 (1973): 711–730;

Jeanne M. Malloy, "William Byrd's Histories and John Barth's *The Sot-Weed Factor,*" *Mississippi Quarterly,* 42 (1989): 161–172;

Marjorie M. Malvern, "The Parody of Medieval Saints' Lives in John Barth's *Giles Goat-Boy,*" *Studies in Medievalism,* 2 (1982): 59–76;

John T. Matthews, "Intertextual Frameworks: The Ideology of Parody in John Barth," in *Intertextuality and Contemporary American Fiction,* edited by Patrick O'Donnell and Robert Davis (Baltimore: Johns Hopkins University Press, 1989), pp. 35–57;

Frank D. McConnell, *Four Postwar American Novelists: Bellow, Mailer, Barth, and Pynchon* (Chicago: University of Chicago Press, 1977), pp. 108–158;

James L. McDonald, "Barth's Syllabus: The Frame of Giles Goat-Boy," *Critique: Studies in Modern Fiction,* 13 (1972): 5–10;

Peter Mercer, "The Rhetoric of *Giles Goat-Boy,*" *Novel,* 4 (1971): 147–158;

David Morrell, *John Barth: An Introduction* (University Park: Pennsylvania State University Press, 1976);

Douglas Robinson, *John Barth's* Giles Goat-Boy: *A Study* (Jyväskylä, Finland: University of Jyväskylä Press, 1980);

Robinson, "Reader's Power, Writer's Power: Barth, Bergonzi, Iser, and the Post-Modern Period Debate," *Criticism,* 28 (1986): 307–322;

Earl Rovit, "The Novel as Parody: John Barth," *Critique: Studies in Modern Fiction,* 6 (1963): 77–85;

Elaine B. Safer, "The Allusive Mode and Black Humor in Barth's *Sot-Weed Factor,*" *Studies in the Novel,* 13 (1981): 424–438;

Safer, *The Contemporary American Comic Epic: The Novels of Barth, Pynchon, Gaddis, and Kesey* (Detroit: Wayne State University Press, 1988), pp. 50–78;

Safer, "The Essay as Aesthetic Mirror: John Barth's 'Exhaustion' and 'Replenishment,'" *Studies in American Fiction,* 15, no. 1 (1987): 109–117;

Robert Scholes, "Disciple of Scheherazade," *New York Times Book Review,* 8 May 1966, pp. 5, 22;

Scholes, *Fabulation and Metafiction* (Urbana: University of Illinois Press, 1979), pp. 75–102, 118–123;

Scholes, *The Fabulators* (New York: Oxford University Press, 1967), pp. 135–173;

Max F. Schultz, "Barth, *LETTERS,* and the Great Tradition," *Genre,* 14 (1981): 95–115;

Schultz, *Black Humor Fiction of the Sixties: A Pluralistic Definition of Man and His World* (Athens: Ohio University Press, 1973), pp. 17–42;

Schultz, *The Muses of John Barth: Tradition and Metafiction from* Lost in the Funhouse *to* The Tidewater Tales (Baltimore: Johns Hopkins University Press, 1990);

Gordon E. Slethaug, "Barth's Refutation of the Idea of Progress," *Critique: Studies in Modern Fiction,* 13 (1972): 11–29;

Slethaug, "Floating Signifiers in John Barth's *Sabbatical,*" *Modern Fiction Studies,* 33 (1987): 647–655;

John O. Stark, *The Literature of Exhaustion: Borges, Nabokov, Barth* (Durham, N.C.: Duke University Press, 1974), pp. 118–175;

Tony Tanner, *City of Words: American Fiction, 1950–1970* (New York: Harper & Row, 1971), pp. 230–259;

Campbell Tatham, "The Gilesian Monomyth: Some Remarks on the Structure of *Giles Goat-Boy,*" *Genre,* 3 (1970): 364–375;

Tatham, "John Barth and the Aesthetics of Artifice," *Contemporary Literature,* 12 (1971): 60–73;

Jac Tharpe, *John Barth: The Comic Sublimity of Paradox* (Carbondale: Southern Illinois University Press, 1974);

John W. Tilton, *Cosmic Satire in the Contemporary Novel* (Lewisburg, Pa.: Bucknell University Press, 1977), pp. 43–68;

Patricia Tobin, *John Barth and the Anxiety of Continuance* (Philadelphia: University of Pennsylvania Press, 1992);

Joseph J. Waldmier, ed., *Critical Essays on John Barth* (Boston: G. K. Hall, 1980);

Edward P. Walkiewicz, *John Barth* (Boston: Twayne, 1986);

James F. Walter, "A Psychochronology of Lust in the Menippean Tradition: *Giles Goat-Boy,*" *Twentieth Century Literature,* 21 (1975): 394–410;

Deborah A. Woolley, "Empty 'Text,' Fecund Voice: Self-Reflexivity in Barth's *Lost in the Funhouse,*" *Contemporary Literature,* 26 (1985): 460–481;

Heide Ziegler, *John Barth* (London: Methuen, 1987).

Papers:

Manuscript and typescript drafts for John Barth's *The Floating Opera, The End of the Road, The Sot-Weed Factor, Giles Goat-Boy, Lost in the Funhouse,* and a wide range of other Barth materials are in the Library of Congress. Uncorrected galley proofs for *Giles Goat-Boy* and *Lost in the Funhouse* are at Washington University, St. Louis. A handful of miscellaneous items are in the Pennsylvania State University Library.

Bebe Moore Campbell

(18 February 1950 –   )

Jane Campbell
Purdue University, Calumet

BOOKS: *Successful Women, Angry Men: Backlash in the Two-Career Marriage* (New York: Random House, 1986);

Sweet Summer: Growing Up With and Without My Dad (New York: Putnam, 1989; London: Collins, 1990);

Your Blues Ain't Like Mine (New York: Putnam, 1992; London: Mandarin, 1996);

Brothers and Sisters (New York: Putnam, 1994; London: Heinemann, 1995);

Singing in the Comeback Choir (New York: Putnam, 1998; London: Heinemann, 1998).

SELECTED PERIODICAL PUBLICATIONS–
UNCOLLECTED: "Staying in the Community," *Essence,* 20 (December 1989): 96–98;

"Daddy's Girl," *Essence,* 23 (June 1992): 72–74;

"Brothers and Sisters," *New York Times Magazine,* 23 August 1992, pp. 6, 18;

"Remember the 60's? The Protest," *Los Angeles Times,* 13 December 1992, p. 1;

"I Felt Rage–and Then Fear," *Parents,* 68 (February 1993): 94–95;

"Coming Together: Can We See Beyond the Color of Our Skin?" *Essence* (February 1995): 25, 80–82;

"The Boy in the River," *Time,* 153 (8 March 1999): 35.

Bebe Moore Campbell (photograph © 1998 by Barbara DuMetz; from the dust jacket for Singing in the Comeback Choir*)*

Novelist and journalist Bebe Moore Campbell is an African American writer known for her courageous critiques of contemporary society. A contributing editor for *Essence* magazine and a commentator for National Public Radio (NPR), she has published nearly one hundred articles, not only in *Essence* but also in *Black Enterprise, Ms., Seventeen, Parents,* and various newspapers, including *The New York Times,* the *Los Angeles Times,* and the *Detroit Free Press.* The topics addressed in these articles range from feminist advice for black women regarding their business careers or personal lives to commentaries about interracial relationships, electoral and congressional politics, apartheid, the 1992 Los Angeles riots in response to the verdict in the Rodney King case, police brutality,

Medicare, and class prejudice in the African American community. Her major publications include three novels, a memoir, and one volume of social criticism. Her journalism and fiction both demonstrate a commitment to art and social justice.

Campbell has chosen a path long traveled by novelists: creating fast-paced, readable fiction directed to a wide audience. Like Terry McMillan, with whom she is sometimes compared, Campbell explores relationships both between men and women and between women. Her characters are often upwardly mobile professionals. But her fiction has a complexity far beyond its surface appearance and moves in directions that distinguish her from McMillan. An ethnographic journalist, she depicts cultural events in a journalistic style. She is preoccupied with relationships between blacks and whites and often places her fiction within an historical context. Moreover, Campbell's fiction faces problems within the black community, including urban blight, drugs, gangs, single teenage mothers, and absent fathers. She insists that African Americans need to take at least partial responsibility for solving these problems.

Bebe Moore was born to Doris and George Linwood Peter Moore in Philadelphia on 18 February 1950. Her parents separated while she was still an infant, and she and her mother went to live with her maternal grandmother, also of Philadelphia. Her mother's grandparents, who had been sharecroppers in Virginia, migrated north when Bebe's grandmother was a baby, while her father's family remained in the South. As Campbell puts it in her memoir, *Sweet Summer: Growing Up With and Without My Dad* (1989), she was raised in "a household where capable and loving women made sure that I had both culture and Christianity, that I greased my legs and learned the difference between nice children and riffraff, that I was proper." Both her parents were college educated, her father at North Carolina Agriculture and Technical College and her mother at the University of Pennsylvania, where she received a bachelor's degree and two master's degrees. Doris Moore was a social worker, and George Moore was a county farm agent and restaurant owner whose career was interrupted by a car accident that left him a paraplegic when Bebe was ten months old. Despite this tragedy, he remained a spirited, independent man who greatly influenced his daughter. She adored him and, until her late teens, spent every summer with him near Elizabeth City, North Carolina, longing to have him in her life year-round. In *Sweet Summer* she recounts her youthful dissatisfaction that she and her cousin Michael had "only the Bosoms guarding our lives." This belief in the significance of a present father figure emerges again and again in Campbell's novels.

From an early age, Campbell's family expected her to excel in school. Her mother sent her to Logan Elementary rather than the less competitive school in her North Philadelphia neighborhood. Later she attended Wagner Junior High and Girls High School. She graduated summa cum laude in 1971 from the University of Pittsburgh. From 1971 to 1977 she taught public school in Pittsburgh, Atlanta, and Washington, D.C. Her commitment to education has remained an important part of her mission, as she expressed in a 1996 interview with Martha Satz: "I hope I can teach a little bit. . . . [I] have a

forum to preach and I do commentaries for NPR, so I don't use the novel to preach. . . ."

An early marriage to Tiko F. Campbell, about which Campbell has written little, ended in divorce. Even in *Sweet Summer,* in which Campbell describes her wedding, she never mentions her husband's first name. One daughter, Maia Campbell, now an actress, was born during this marriage. Campbell and her second husband, Ellis Gordon Jr., a banker, married in 1984 and live in Los Angeles with their son, Ellis Gordon III.

After writing *Sweet Summer* and another nonfiction book, *Successful Women, Angry Men: Backlash in the Two-Career Marriage* (1986), Campbell turned her talents to fiction. She is best known for her three novels: *Your Blues Ain't Like Mine* (1992), *Brothers and Sisters* (1994), and *Singing in the Comeback Choir* (1998). Commenting on the overriding theme of these works, Campbell notes, "My books are about healing." Admitting to a preoccupation with the impact of history in all three of her novels, she notes that the importance of history is "quieter" in *Singing in the Comeback Choir.* The notion of healing through facing up to one's history is intertwined with an emphasis on the need for personal accountability: Caucasians must continually acknowledge their role in a white supremacist world and their racist actions and thoughts; middle- and upper-class people must acknowledge that they have benefited from class stratification; men must reject chauvinistic values to sustain relationships; and African Americans who have achieved power, status, and wealth must give back to less-privileged black communities. Campbell's novels are grounded in reality, allowing her to explore these issues of personal accountability with unusual courage. Unlike some contemporary African American writers who prefer to explore only the distant past, Campbell asserts the importance of addressing contemporary problems in ways that may arouse discomfort. Her characters are flawed human beings, and although her novels emphasize that the trio of race, gender, and class bias form an oppressive structure, she repeatedly insists that her characters must also look within themselves for solutions to social ills.

Your Blues Ain't Like Mine, winner of the NAACP Image Award for literature, demonstrates clearly that for Campbell, delving into history is an experience both excruciating and freeing. She regards the novel as an effort "to give racism a face." Although the novel fictionalizes the 1955 murder of fifteen-year-old Emmett Till in Mississippi, Campbell views her work as less about history than about the sources of racial hatred: "This is not about color–it's about childhood. We're talking about little boys who grew up not liking themselves. They need a scapegoat." Despite her disclaimer that *Your Blues Ain't Like Mine* is not an historical novel, her perspective that historical tragedies result from the collision of race, class, and gender marks her as a revisionist historian of the first order. The book depicts Till's murder and the subsequent acquittal of his murderer, theorizing about how and why such injustice occurs. *Your Blues Ain't Like Mine* suggests that a history of family dysfunction, combined with underclass status, breeds pathological figures such as the character Floyd Cox, the murderer of Armstrong Todd (the fictional version of Till). Floyd's murder of Armstrong, who innocently speaks French in a pool hall in front of Lily Cox, Floyd's wife, theoretically stems from his desire to protect "white womanhood." The real cause, however, is Floyd's feeling of emasculation, his need to prove himself to his father, who blatantly favors Floyd's brother.

Through a shifting third-person-limited narration, Campbell explores the aftermath of the murder itself, a catalyst for change within each character. The novel moves from the 1950s through the 1980s, from the civil rights movement to affirmative action to the Reagan/Bush era. Though history and politics provide a vital backdrop, the focus, Campbell insists, is on the characters. They must come to terms with the effects of Armstrong's murder, and to move forward they must decide how they fit into the community and face their personal limitations. To the extent that each character does so, he or she heals.

Delotha and Wydell Todd, Armstrong's parents, face the most painful memories and the most difficult healing. They must deal with the horror of their son's victimization, first by racist "crackers," then by the equally racist southern legal system. Furthermore, they must confront their guilt, question their own humanity. Armstrong would not have been living in Hopewell, Mississippi, with his grandmother had not Wydell's alcoholism interfered with his ability to father Armstrong, leading Delotha to separate from Wydell and send Armstrong back home from Chicago until she felt she could care for him on her own.

Wydell clearly bears the blame for his parental irresponsibility, but both parents feel responsible. Eventually, the couple resumes their marriage, determined to begin their lives again. With Delotha's support, Wydell quits drinking and obtains a barber's license. He admits that Delotha has given him his manhood back, and for a time healing appears to be taking place. The couple reconnects with the community, builds a successful business together, and has three more children. Wydell remains sober for twenty years and becomes a model husband and father. But Delotha's effort to heal by raising another son, W. T., thereby resurrecting Armstrong, proves disastrous. Despite Wydell's insistence that she cannot replace one

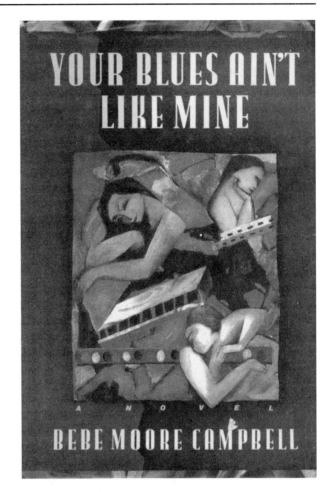

Dust jacket for Campbell's 1992 novel, about racism and murder in the South

son with another, Delotha fails to heed the warning, calling W. T. by his brother's name, overprotecting him, and consequently pushing him and Wydell further away. Wydell sinks back into alcoholism, and the marriage collapses. Stripped of his identity, confused, and resenting both parents, W. T. joins a gang. Delotha realizes: "All her life she'd been defending him against the wrong enemy; she would have to fight the streets to save him, and she didn't have the strength."

Rather than assigning blame, Campbell clearly understands the agony that leads to Delotha's actions, and Wydell, though equally flawed, is as strong and admirable a man as Delotha is a woman. Their marriage works when they support one another and remain sensitive and open to one another's pain; it fails when they refuse to confront their demons and to be accountable for their actions. Wydell, like Floyd Cox, suffers from self-hatred. Eventually Wydell, whose feelings of paternal inadequacy derive from his experiences with his own father, rekindles his relationship with W. T. The novel ends on a healing note, affirming the theme of personal accountability. Wydell reenters W. T.'s life, underscoring Campbell's belief that fathers must remain present and loving if children are to break the cycle of self-hatred.

Armstrong's death galvanizes another character to protect her son. Ida Long is a strong, admirable woman raising her child, Sweetbabe, on her own. Abandoned by Sweetbabe's father, Ida also has never known the identity of her own father, Stonewall Pinochet, perhaps the wealthiest man in Hopewell, who never considered marrying his black mistress. Determined to ensure that Sweetbabe's life is better than hers, Ida uses every available resource. Living with her stepfather, who raised her, Ida seeks a positive male role model for Sweetbabe. When Sweetbabe begins to flounder academically, she persuades Clayton Pinochet, Stonewall's legitimate, white son, to tutor him. In time Sweetbabe realizes Ida's dream of moving to Chicago, where he obtains a college education and then returns to Hopewell to teach. In Mississippi he believes he and his wife can raise their son in a small community to which he can contribute, underscoring Campbell's belief that African Americans need to reconnect with their original communities.

Armstrong's death changes everyone's lives, in the white community as well as the black. In *Your Blues Ain't Like Mine* Campbell portrays white characters, especially Clayton Pinochet and the Coxes, from both ends of the social scale. The Pinochets basically own Hopewell, while the Coxes often starve, especially since Floyd is frequently in jail.

Clayton embodies the weakness and hypocrisy of white liberals who are unable to act ethically despite their empathy for African Americans. Unconsciously following in his father's footsteps, Clayton supports a black mistress, Marguerite, whom he loves but will not marry for fear of losing his inheritance. In fact, Clayton, like Floyd, is completely controlled by his father, whom he does not respect but cannot defy. Clayton's spinelessness epitomizes the paralysis of the old South, until he begins to fight the white supremacist code by tutoring Marguerite, Sweetbabe, and several other black teenagers. Eventually, when Clayton agrees to recognize Ida as his half sister and to share his inheritance with her, he repudiates his father's ugly legacy. Even though Clayton cannot fully change until his father dies, healing comes through a son's refusal to repeat his father's patriarchal, racist values.

Floyd Cox, unlike Clayton, cannot move beyond the limitations of his family. A repellent character, Floyd never accepts responsibility for his actions. He categorically denies to everyone but Lily and his family that he murdered Armstrong. Even in his admission he blames Lily for being in the pool hall and for all their misfortunes and poverty. After Floyd kills Armstrong, the black community refuses to reenter his pool hall, and the business fails. He can neither rent nor sell the pool hall and finally abandons the building. Descending the social scale from small-time businessman to manual laborer, Floyd works alongside black men, a necessity he perceives as humiliating. Because of his frustration, Floyd batters Lily physically and emotionally, continually reminding her of his version of reality:

> He liked her begging him. Why shouldn't she beg him? If it hadn't been for her, he'd still have his business. He wouldn't have to be digging ditches with niggers for two dollars a day. If she'd listened to him and stayed out of the place like he told her to, they wouldn't be eating surplus government food like they was. . . .
> "I ain't trash," he screamed.
> . . . the palms of his hands were lumpy with blisters; he could feel them oozing as he slapped her. He was hurting so bad he almost didn't feel his wife shaking as he punched her. He hit her again to make her stop shaking, and again to shut her up.

Forgetting neither the class struggle that reinforces Floyd's racism and sexism nor the hopelessness and defeat that cripple his spirit, Campbell, however, can never excuse Floyd's inhumanity. His brutality knows no bounds. While his second child is being born, he leaves Lily and their son to starve. When he finally returns, he abuses her for accepting charity and claims that the baby does not look like him. Floyd's repeated incarcerations force Lily to seek public assistance, and when he returns from jail, he punishes her for his inadequacies. Filled with self-loathing brought on by his father's rejection, Floyd is incapable of growth and quickly disintegrates. Unlike Wydell, who, despite inadequate fathering, reinvents himself with Delotha's help, or Clayton, who finally manages to throw off his paternal badge of evil, Floyd has no positive values to pass on to Floydjunior. When Floyd's son becomes selfish, cruel, and hopelessly addicted to crack cocaine—a carbon copy of Floyd's earlier, flawed self—Campbell suggests that negative father figures can be even more destructive than absent ones. Men who cannot accept responsibility for their actions can never heal and will destroy instead. With fathers such as Floyd, poverty, violence, and racism continue indefinitely.

Campbell's creation of Lily is striking. Despite Lily's ignorance, weakness, and racism, she is arguably the most sympathetic and individualized white character in the novel. Speaking of her ability to portray white characters, Campbell notes that readers, both black and white, ask: "How could you get in the white mind, how could you know that? . . . And they kind of look at you and say, 'What kind of black person are you?' Well, I say, I know white people. I go to general parties. I have some white friends. I have some experience. And I get a surprised reaction from black people. And from the white it's the stare. It's the expectation that you'll be hostile and angry. And they are really surprised when you are not."

Lily's vulnerability and oppression as an underclass white woman dominated by a monstrous husband underlie her sympathetic characterization. Surviving repeated beatings, struggling to feed and mother her two children in the face of terrifying poverty, Lily faces life alone most of the time. Her one brief friendship with a woman is with Ida Long. Although Lily tries ineffectually to warn Ida about Floyd and his brothers' plot to "teach Armstrong a lesson," her warning fails to prevent the tragedy, and the murder destroys her friendship with Ida.

Lily's frail self-esteem, further damaged by a childhood of incestuous experiences, causes her to see herself as nothing more than a fading Delta beauty, always a victim. Her fondest memory is being crowned Magnolia Queen of Jefferson Davis High School. Feeling beautiful even though her dress, made out of a secondhand lace tablecloth, had "a faded gravy stain right in the center of the bodice," Lily heeds her mother's advice: "Baby, all a woman has got is her looks, for a thin sliver of time. You squander your beauty, you done lost your life." Hampered by such a fragile worldview, Lily never envisions herself in any situation other than being married to Floyd: "She felt frightened and weak when he was away from her. It was as though she didn't exist when he was absent." Fairly early in their marriage, she realizes that Floyd did not kill Armstrong to protect her, as he originally claimed, but only to win his father's approval. This realization destroys any love she holds for him, and she remains with him only out of dependency. Her life becomes a grinding struggle to keep her family afloat. In a heart-wrenching scene, a welfare caseworker rapes Lily, leading to her mental breakdown and commitment to the state institution. After her release she is further humiliated by having to live with her abusive mother-in-law.

Even if there is no hope for Floydjunior, *Your Blues Ain't Like Mine* suggests that Lily's one accomplishment is her daughter, Doreen, who as an adult joins a union led by Ida and empowers Lily to leave Floyd. Because Lily is also able to nurture Doreen, she raises a daughter who may eventually transcend her family's bankrupt values. Despite Campbell's emphasis on fathers' influences, she clearly recognizes the role of mothers in dismantling patriarchal and racist values through the way they raise their daughters.

Your Blues Ain't Like Mine is a remarkable novel. The title alludes to the narrative voices of the characters, the haunting historical and personal memories embodied in their diverse versions of reality. Although Campbell's black characters would assert that the blues as a musical

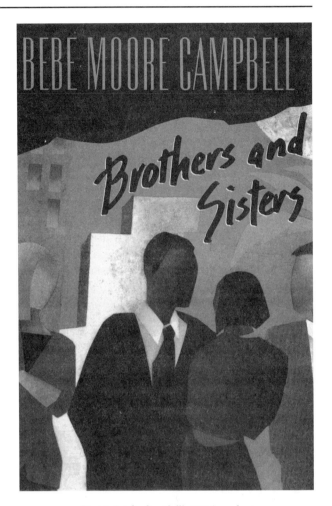

Dust jacket for Campbell's 1994 novel, set during the 1992 Los Angeles riots

form belongs only to African Americans and that their versions of history are far more devastating than those experienced by white characters, Campbell also suggests that pain affects all people, black or white. That sentiment dovetails with the class struggle underscoring *Your Blues Ain't Like Mine*. Except for the Pinochets, most of the characters in the novel are poor, and this poverty leads to self-hatred and, in the case of white characters, scapegoating. "White trash" seek to subjugate people of color in response to their own class subjugation. The only way to break the cycle is for the Pinochets to acknowledge their privilege and change their economic relationship to the working class, which Clayton tries to do.

Brothers and Sisters, like *Your Blues Ain't Like Mine*, was inspired by historical events. The brutal beating of Rodney King in 1991, the subsequent acquittal on 29 April 1992 of the Los Angeles policemen responsible for the beating, and the violent aftermath of the trial, known as the L.A. riots but regarded by many as social protest, represented a crisis in American history. Campbell's goal in *Brothers and Sisters*, published in 1994, is to explore the tensions that led to the racial unrest and to provide a guide for healing those tensions. She asserts, "I hope *Brothers and Sisters* can serve as a kind of blueprint, to help people foster racial understanding. I mean, I'm an integrationist. I am. I'm not a separatist." *Brothers and Sisters* reached *The New York Times* best-seller list just two weeks after publication, but reviewers found Campbell's second novel less carefully crafted than her first. While *Your Blues Ain't Like Mine* is unquestionably a more lyrically written, complex narrative than *Brothers and Sisters,* Campbell's second novel does share many of the same strengths of her first, including its fast-paced, engaging plot and its willingness to tackle serious political and social issues in reference to specific historical events. While predominantly about the attempts of two women, Esther Jackson and Mallory Post, to forge an interracial friendship, *Brothers and Sisters* also explores such issues as the tensions between African Americans and recent immigrants from Asia and Latin America, the plight of single teenage mothers living in the ghetto, the beginnings of the demise of affirmative action in California, the influence of right-wing talk-radio hosts, and the widening gap between rich and poor.

Campbell's decision to focus on Esther and Mallory's relationship within the world of banking, which she no doubt knows well through her husband, Gordon, is an interesting choice. This setting allows her to indict the corporate world, where racism thrives, and to illustrate the difficulties women face in male-dominated professions. In explaining her choice to write about women's friendships, Campbell explains: "I wanted to explore friendship; I wanted to explore the possibilities. Because one of the things that really strikes me about America, and it's kind of the under-reported story, is that in spite of all the racial trauma we go through, there are black and white people who like each other very much, even love each other. And I'm not even talking about romantic love. . . . We don't really talk about those friendships and how to make more of them."

In *Brothers and Sisters* healing derives from Esther and Mallory's learning to understand one another and becoming accountable for their feelings. With Esther's help Mallory begins to unlearn her deeply entrenched racism; Esther, in turn, relinquishes some of the anger she feels toward Mallory's upper-class white privilege. For Campbell *Brothers and Sisters* appears also to represent personal healing, for she invented the relationship between Mallory and Humphrey, an African American banker, partly to work through her own anger at black men in relationships with white women. Esther must acknowledge that Humphrey's pursuit of Mallory, which eventually escalates into sexual harassment, is only partially fueled by Mallory's initial encouragement. In a 1994 conversation with Joyce Carol Oates, Campbell spoke of her desire to let go of her anger: "I did not want to have this anger as a burden any-

more because it was going nowhere. . . ." In a 1996 interview with Martha Satz, she noted, "I think what people who are not black women don't understand is that it feels like the ultimate betrayal and rejection. And what we have to move to is that it's not. It's not our business. It's not personal. It's not a rejection of me. It's this guy's choice—for whatever sick or healthy reasons he makes it."

Campbell admits that black men's attraction to white women grows out of white standards for female beauty, which undermine African American women's self-esteem, but, she insists, "that doesn't make it healthier for me to get enraged every time I see a black man and a white woman. That's very debilitating. . . . I don't think God placed me here to get angry, to be enraged about that. That's not my purpose. So I really want to distance myself." Esther's friend Vanessa Turner, a black woman, insists, "you have to focus on you. Every morning go to the mirror and say, 'My color is my joy and not my burden.'" Although Esther scoffs at Vanessa's advice, Campbell has noted that she intended the advice as a corrective.

Esther represents a different generation from Delotha and Ida's in *Your Blues Ain't Like Mine*. Born in the South Side of Chicago, Esther attends a North Side private school for the same reasons that Campbell's parents enrolled her in an elementary school outside her own neighborhood. After earning an M.B.A. Esther achieves a prestigious position as regional-operations manager at Angel City National Bank in Los Angeles. Living in an upscale neighborhood, driving an expensive car, and sporting designer clothes, Esther adopts the motto "no romance without finance" as a way of ensuring equality in her relationships. She spends a great deal of time educating the sheltered Mallory about unconscious racism.

Mallory, like many white people, has never reflected on why she is always the one to whom white servers speak or give the check to when she and Esther go out to eat. She cannot understand Esther's fury when a white banker addresses Humphrey as "homeboy," and she honestly believes that police never "beat people without provocation." She regards LaKeesha Jones, the young woman from the ghetto whom Esther hires as a teller, as "a little threatening." The character of Mallory embodies white perceptions of African Americans and allows Campbell to explore the reasons racial conflicts reached the boiling point in 1992 in Los Angeles. Even after the Rodney King incident offered a flagrant example of police brutality toward minorities, many whites were unable to fathom African Americans' rage. Mallory's thoughts, triggered by three black youths, exemplify this oblivion; the teenagers, being arrested for merely congregating on a corner,

managed to look menacing even as they stood with their hands locked behind their necks. Good, they caught them, she thought as she sped past. These were

the animals who defiled public property and shot innocent bystanders. They were just like the pigs who beat
Reginald Denny. Just thinking of the helpless white
man being dragged from his truck, for no reason, no
earthly reason, except that he was white, made Mallory
tremble with fear.

Mallory has made little effort to understand life
beyond the narrow confines of her race and class. She represents wealthy whites who are willing to befriend African
Americans who appear to have "made it," such as Esther.
Yet, Mallory and people like her never grasp the reasons
behind social unrest because they cannot empathize with
people whose color and class have deprived them of privilege and hope. Campbell intends *Brothers and Sisters* as a
blueprint for friendship between white and black women,
whereby their friendships can lead to social change.

The two women become friends primarily because
they bond over their previous addictive relationships with
men. With Mallory this addiction stems from an absent,
abusive father, emphasizing Campbell's belief in the damage wreaked by such misguided patriarchy. In Campbell's
work, women must often reject abusive, sexist men in
favor of those men capable of becoming equal life partners. Esther must realize that men such as Humphrey
Boone, despite their education and financial acumen, can
never develop good relationships because they stereotype
and demean women. Instead, she begins to see Tyrone
Carter, a Federal Express deliveryman, as a sensitive,
good-hearted person and a far more suitable partner.

Campbell's awareness of class differences emerges
elsewhere in her novel as well. Demonstrating the importance of successful African Americans giving back to the
working-class black community, Esther not only helps
Tyrone return to school but also serves as a mentor to
LaKeesha. To be sure, LaKeesha has already accepted
accountability for her life and those of her sisters, single
mothers at fifteen and sixteen years old. Also a single
mother, LaKeesha begins using birth control and makes
sure her sisters follow her example because she realizes
that additional babies will hold all of them back. Determined to get herself off welfare, LaKeesha seeks job training, persuades Esther to hire her, and begins saving
money for her own apartment. Although she eventually
betrays LaKeesha, Esther's decision to help the young
woman illustrates Campbell's insistence on the importance
of reconnecting with the black underclass. Even Humphrey decides to become chief executive officer of Solid
Rock, a new black-owned bank in south-central Los Angeles, after he is fired from Angel City.

In *Singing in the Comeback Choir* (1998) Campbell
recapitulates this theme by sending her protagonist,
Maxine McCoy, back to her childhood community.
Whereas *Your Blues Ain't Like Mine* and *Brothers and Sisters*

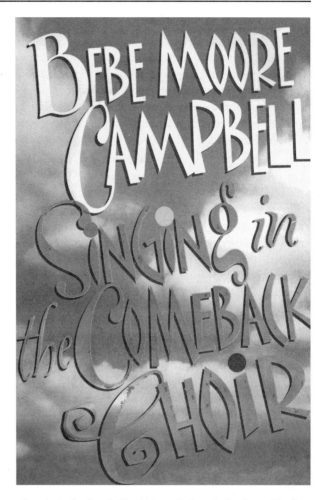

*Dust jacket for Campbell's 1998 novel, about dysfunction and healing
in the African American community of North Philadelphia*

explore the sources of racial hatred, *Singing in the Comeback
Choir* focuses on the despair and dysfunction within certain inner-city African American communities. Relationships with white Americans, preoccupations in
Campbell's first two novels, take a backseat to relationships with other African Americans in her third novel.
Healing must come from within, not only from within
the community but also from within oneself.

For *Singing in the Comeback Choir,* Campbell drew on
elements of her own experience. Maxine, like Campbell,
grew up in North Philadelphia and lived with her maternal grandmother; after teaching public school for a few
years, she has developed a career in broadcasting. As a
talk-show executive producer, Maxine, like Campbell,
tries to eschew fluff for substance in journalism. Pregnant
and married to Satchel, a successful, sensitive man, Maxine lives in a fashionable neighborhood in Los Angeles.

The theme of healing emerges when Maxine
returns to Philadelphia to care for Lindy Walker, her
seventy-six-year-old grandmother, because Lindy's hired
live-in companion has resigned. Recovering from a

stroke, Lindy has disregarded doctor's orders to quit smoking and drinking and, like her neighborhood, seems doomed. Once an acclaimed singer, Lindy suffered exploitation by her agent, and her career toppled in 1971, forcing her to become a nurse to support the motherless Maxine. In the twenty or more years since, Lindy has gradually become more dispirited, and the stroke appears to have defeated her.

Although Lindy insists she can live successfully on her own, Maxine decides to take charge of Lindy's life. Unable to find another caretaker, Maxine intends to move Lindy out of her house and into a senior care facility. She is distraught to see that the respectable working-class neighborhood she grew up in has begun to exhibit "urban blight": trash abounds; houses need painting; and the home across the street, once a child's haven, has become a crack house. Even more alarming to Maxine, teenage neighbor boys behave with open hostility or drugged confusion, while one young unmarried girl has had multiple pregnancies. Gang violence holds everyone hostage, and hope has fled.

As usual, Campbell handles these issues with sensitivity. Maxine's heavy-handed efforts to reform the indomitable Lindy fail miserably at first. Not until Lindy nearly sets the house on fire does she begin to realize that she must take control of her life; but, as always in Campbell's fiction, the changes come with agonizing slowness. When Maxine finds Lindy a singing coach to help her regain confidence to participate in a music festival, Lindy's first attempt fails. Maxine persuades Lindy to begin getting dressed every day and exercising; her drinking and smoking lessen but do not cease. When Maxine returns for a visit a few months later, Lindy has resumed her singing in preparation for the festival, but she has not regained the voice of her youth. Still, Maxine has reawakened Lindy's passion for singing, the cure for her depression and lack of self-esteem.

Maxine's own healing takes place in part because of Lindy's wise mentoring. Her trust in Satchel shattered by an affair he had a year earlier, Maxine has pushed him away. Portrayed, however, as a truly remorseful, exceptional man, Satchel has always supported his mother and sisters financially and continually proves himself a worthy mate. With Lindy's help, Maxine begins to forgive him and allows intimacy to rebuild. Like Lindy, who to resume singing must forget her anger toward the manager who robbed her, Maxine must relinquish her anger toward Satchel before it destroys her. *Singing in the Comeback Choir* reiterates Campbell's belief that women should build partnerships with men who truly strive toward equal and fair relationships.

Singing in the Comeback Choir also reiterates the notion of accountability to the African American community. Maxine gradually realizes that she has sometimes sacrificed ethics and authenticity for ratings, and by the time the network cancels her talk show, she has already considered returning to teaching. Meeting "Motorcycle," a former student whose life she had turned around completely, makes her see how much she loved her earlier career. Lindy also rejoins her community and agrees to let an aspiring rap singer from the neighborhood back her up at the festival. In both instances Campbell suggests that some troubled teenagers simply lack the kind of guidance or attention that will build self-esteem. *Singing in the Comeback Choir* reflects Campbell's belief that one must come to terms with the past by returning home, either literally or figuratively, and giving of oneself to the community.

The sense that healing comes from facing one's limitations and choices resonates through all three of Campbell's novels. Her gift as a writer is her ability to enunciate these themes through a compelling intersection of issues, measuring history and social problems against personal accountability. Her characters' flaws are played out within the context of a distinctly flawed society. Events and human beings cannot be divorced from their political and historical context. A thoughtful writer who interweaves social commentary with entertainment, Campbell writes in the vein of the earlier African American novelist Pauline Hopkins; both merged journalism with fiction to create a public voice, capturing a large audience and provoking their readers to confront personal, social, and political issues.

Interviews:

Joyce Carol Oates, "Which Counts More, Gender or Race?" *New York Times Magazine,* 25 December 1994, pp. 6, 16–22;

Martha Satz, "I Hope I Can Teach a Little Bit: An Interview with Bebe Moore Campbell," *Southwest Review,* 81 (April 1996): 2, 195–213;

Alice Walker, "Heal the Ancestors, Recover the Earth," *Black Issues Book Review,* 1 (March–April 1999): 32–34;

Jane Campbell, "An Interview with Bebe Moore Campbell," *Callaloo: A Journal of African and African American Arts and Letters,* 22 (Fall 1999): 954–972.

Reference:

Kari J. Winter, "Gita Brown's *Be I Whole* and Bebe Moore Campbell's *Brothers and Sisters,*" *African American Review,* 31 (1997): 369–372.

Truman Capote

(30 September 1924 – 25 August 1984)

Helen S. Garson
George Mason University

See also the Capote entries in *DLB 2: American Novelists Since World War II; DLB 185: American Literary Journalists, 1945–1995; DLB Yearbook 1980;* and *DLB Yearbook 1984.*

BOOKS: *Other Voices, Other Rooms* (New York: Random House, 1948; London: Heinemann, 1948);

A Tree of Night and Other Stories (New York: Random House, 1949; London: Heinemann, 1950);

Local Color (New York: Random House, 1950; London: Heinemann, 1950);

The Grass Harp (New York: Random House, 1951; London: Heinemann, 1952);

The Grass Harp: A Play (New York: Random House, 1952; London: Heinemann, 1952);

The Muses Are Heard (New York: Random House, 1956; London: Heinemann, 1957);

Breakfast at Tiffany's: A Short Novel and Three Stories (New York: Random House, 1958); republished as *Breakfast at Tiffany's* (London: Hamilton, 1958);

Observations, photographs by Richard Avedon, commentary by Capote (New York: Simon & Schuster, 1959; London: Weidenfeld & Nicolson, 1959);

Selected Writings (New York: Random House, 1963; London: Hamilton, 1963);

In Cold Blood: A True Account of a Multiple Murder and Its Consequences (New York: Random House, 1965; London: Hamilton, 1966);

A Christmas Memory (New York: Random House, 1966);

House of Flowers, by Capote and Harold Arlen (New York: Random House, 1968);

The Thanksgiving Visitor (New York: Random House, 1967; London: Hamilton, 1969);

Trilogy: An Experiment in Multimedia, by Capote, Eleanor Perry, and Frank Perry (New York: Macmillan, 1969);

The Dogs Bark: Public People and Private Places (New York: Random House, 1973; London: Weidenfeld & Nicolson, 1974);

Truman Capote

Music for Chameleons (New York: Random House, 1980; London: Hamilton, 1981);

One Christmas (New York: Random House, 1983; London: Hamilton, 1983);

Answered Prayers: The Unfinished Novel (London: Hamilton, 1986; New York: Random House, 1987).

Editions and Collections: *The Grass Harp and A Tree of Night and Other Stories* (New York: New American Library, 1956);

Other Voices, Other Rooms, twentieth-anniversary edition, with an introduction by the author (New York: Random House, 1968; London: Heinemann, 1968).

Three by Truman Capote (New York: Random House, 1985);

A Capote Reader (New York: Random House, 1987; London: Hamilton, 1987).

PLAY PRODUCTIONS: *The Grass Harp: A Play,* New York, Martin Beck Theater, 27 March 1952; produced as a musical, New York, Martin Beck Theater, November, 1971;

The House of Flowers, musical based on a short story of the same name, in *Breakfast at Tiffany's: A Short Novel and Three Stories* (1958), libretto by Capote and Harold Arlen, New York, Alvin Theater, 30 December 1954; revised, New York, Theater de Lys, 24 January 1968.

PRODUCED SCRIPTS: *Beat the Devil,* motion picture, script by Capote and John Huston, Santana Pictures/Romulus Films, 1954;

The Innocents, motion picture, script by Capote, William Archibald, and John Mortimer, 20th Century–Fox, 1961;

Trilogy, motion picture, script by Capote and Eleanor Perry, Allied Artists, 1969;

A Christmas Memory, television, ABC, 21 December 1966;

The Thanksgiving Visitor, television, ABC, November, 1968;

The Glass House, television, script by Capote, Tracy Keenan Wynn, and Wyatt Cooper, CBS, 4 February 1972.

RECORDINGS: *Children on Their Birthdays,* read by Capote, Columbia Literary Series, ML 4761, 195;

A Christmas Memory, read by Capote, United Artists Records, UAI 9001, [1959];

In Cold Blood, read by Capote, RCA Victor, VDM 110, 1966;

The Thanksgiving Visitor, read by Capote, New York, United Artists Records, UAS 6682, [1968].

OTHER: Jane Auer Bowles, *The Collected Works of Jane Bowles,* introduction by Capote (New York: Farrar, Straus & Giroux, 1966; London: Owen, 1984).

SELECTED PERIODICAL PUBLICATIONS–
UNCOLLECTED:
FICTION
"The Walls Are Cold," *Decade of Short Stories,* 4 (October–December 1943): 27–30;

"A Mink of One's Own," *Decade of Short Stories,* 6 (July–September 1944): 1–4;

"The Shape of Things," *Decade of Short Stories,* 6 (October–December 1944): 21–23;

"Preacher's Legend," *Prairie Schooner,* 19 (Winter 1945): 265–274;

"Blind Items," *Ladies Home Journal,* 91 (January 1974): 81, 122, 124.

NONFICTION
"This Winter's Mask," *Harper's Bazaar* (December 1947): 100–105, 195–196;

"A House in Sicily," *Harper's Bazaar* (January 1951): 153–155;

"La Divine," *Harper's Bazaar* (April 1952): 148–149;

"Plisetskaya: 'A Two-Headed Calf,'" *Vogue,* 143 (April 1964): 169;

"A Curious Gift," *Redbook,* 125 (June 1965): 52–53, 92–94;

"The 'Sylvia' Odyssey," *Vogue,* 147 (January 1966): 68–75;

"Two Faces and . . . a Landscape . . . ," *Vogue,* 147 (February 1966): 144–149;

"Oliver Smith," in *Double Exposure,* by Roddy McDowell, (New York: Delacorte, 1966), pp. 152–153;

"Extreme Magic: An Awake Dream, Cruising up the Yugoslavian Coast," *Vogue,* 149 (15 April 1967): 84–89, 146–147;

"Death Row, U.S.A.," *Esquire,* 70 (October 1968): 194–196;

"Time, the Timeless and Beaton's Time Sequence," *Vogue,* 152 (1 November 1968): 172–173;

"At the Sea and in the City," *House Beautiful,* 111 (April 1969): 93–98;

"Donna Marella and the Avvocato," *Vogue,* 153 (1 April 1969): 206–209;

"Guests," *McCall's,* 104 (February 1977): 132–137;

"Truman Capote," *Vogue,* 169 (December 1979): 260–262, 312.

When Truman Capote died on 25 August 1984, a month short of his sixtieth birthday, he had few mourners. In a letter to Helen S. Garson after the 1986 publication of *Answered Prayers,* Capote's longtime editor, Joe Fox, stated he was happy not to have to work with Capote anymore. Various reviewers, critics, enemies, and former friends were happy to flay the dead writer in print and on television. Obituaries described bizarre and unattractive aspects of Capote's personality, and pundits predicted that the public had not only seen but also had heard the last of him. Time has proved them wrong. The writer–described mockingly by life-time enemy Gore Vidal in his 1996 memoir *Palimpsest* as someone for whom "an interview is his principal art form"–is gone but not forgotten.

Capote's literary reputation and influence have expanded over the years, with more and more literary figures tipping their hats to him. A few biographers or memoirists have treated him well. Both John Malcolm Brinnin in *Sextet: T. S. Eliot and Truman Capote and Others* (1981) and *Dear Heart, Old Buddy* (1986) and Gerald

Clarke in *Truman Capote* (1988) present a balanced view of the writer (although Vidal gratuitously attacks Clarke's truthfulness in research). Brinnin and Clarke characterize Capote as a complex, charming, volatile, and emotional man who evoked strong feelings in those who knew him. On the other hand, writer Donald Windham and artist Andy Warhol–friends at first and later enemies of Capote–like Vidal, maliciously attack Capote for everything from his appearance to his writing. Warhol even asserts that Jack Dunphy, Capote's longtime lover, probably wrote some of his material. (A quick scan of Dunphy's writings should be enough to convince any reader of the ludicrousness of the charge.) Two relatives of Capote's produced a type of "as told to" reminiscences of the writer's childhood. The earlier book, Marie Rudisill's (with James C. Simmons) *Truman Capote: The Story of His Bizarre and Exotic Boyhood by an Aunt Who Helped Raise Him,* published in 1983, horrified and dismayed him. Not only did he reject it as untruthful, but so did his aunt Mary Ida Carter and his childhood friend Harper Lee, author of *To Kill A Mockingbird* (1965). In 1996 a cousin of Capote's, Jennings Faulk Carter, provided a series of remembrances as the foundation for Marianne M. Moates's book, *Truman Capote's Southern Years: Stories from a Monroeville Cousin.* As with all books of this type, it is impossible to separate the "as I remember" material from the evolved view of Moates. Almost nothing in either of these books prepares the reader for the talented young writer who burst on to the literary scene at an early age.

Truman Capote, whose name and face through the medium of television were even better known than his work during his lifetime, was born 30 September 1924 in New Orleans, the son of Lillie Mae (later known as Nina) Faulk and Archulus (Arch) Persons. His father called him Truman Streckfus Persons, the first name after a friend from military school, the unusual middle name from the New Orleans family for whom Arch Persons worked. Nina Persons married Arch in 1923 and divorced him in 1931. For the first four years of Truman's life he lived in Louisiana. As his parents' relationship foundered, he was taken back and forth between Alabama and Louisiana. Shortly before his sixth birthday his mother left him to be cared for by her family in Monroeville, a rural Alabama town. (Capote called it abandonment.) The marriage of his parents had been fraught with problems from the beginning: Arch was an undependable, untrustworthy liar, and Nina, a former Miss Alabama, was a self-centered, promiscuous social climber who later committed suicide. When the final break came with Arch (there had been several), she moved to New York, where she met and married Joseph Garcia Capote, a well-to-do Cuban-born businessman, who left his wife for her. After several years of having her Faulk relatives look after her son, Nina brought him

Capote at about the age of six in Monroeville, Alabama, where his mother left him in the care of her relatives (Collection of Karen Lerner)

to live with her and Capote in New York. The boy's name was changed when Joseph Capote adopted him in 1935. Truman, whose entire life and work were influenced by the bitterness he felt toward both parents, but particularly his mother, told interviewers the only reason he went to New York when he was about ten was that his mother could not have any more children. An inventive statement of Capote's or not, the reality is that he remained an only child, one shaped forever by his belief that neither parent wanted him.

Capote, a self-proclaimed genius, who also states in his story "Nocturnal Turnings" in *Music for Chameleons* (1980), that he is "an alcoholic . . . a drug addict . . . and a homosexual," had an erratic education. Although teachers recognized his cleverness, he disliked school. In New York he first attended private schools–Trinity, and then for a time St. John's, a military academy to which the Capotes sent him hoping that the discipline would force him to take schooling more seriously. When they moved to Connecticut, he attended a public high school where he was befriended by a teacher, Catherine Wood, whose influence was strong enough for him to dedicate to her his story "A Christmas Memory," first published in *Mademoiselle* in December 1956. (The story was published as a separate book a decade later by Random House.) In spite of his indifference to school, Capote was quite well read, and many of the significant books of the nineteenth and twentieth centuries influenced his writing. Capote also had a spongelike mind, absorbing as his own the information he learned from others and using it in his work. Undoubtedly he was thinking of his erratic education when he describes the P. B. Jones character in his final work, the stories that comprise *Answered Prayers.* Jones, one of many doubles created by Capote throughout his career, is dubbed an "intellectual hitchhiker," a term that describes Capote perfectly. For a period of time in his youth, his lovers, some of whom he had met through the writers' havens Bread Loaf and Yaddo, were scholars whose backgrounds were different from anything the young Capote had ever known. Once his work was published, his circle widened, along with the experiences and knowledge that came with it.

Although Capote had dropped out of high school at seventeen, he returned as a senior in 1942–1943 to the last of his private schools, Franklin, where the Capotes sent him so that he would at least have a diploma. At the same time Capote found a part-time job as a copy boy with *The New Yorker.* Given the job only because World War II had depleted the magazine of employees, Capote was not a typical hiree: a small, blue-eyed, effeminate, pretty boy with blonde bangs and a high-pitched voice (which he was never to lose and which he cultivated for effect in his later years). At eighteen he looked like a twelve-year-old, but he was as worldly wise as any young man in his day. He knew how to seek the society of those who could help him get ahead, a faculty that served him well for much of his life. Capote served in various clerical jobs at *The New Yorker,* always hoping that one of his stories would be published in the magazine. Nobody there was interested in his writing, nor did anyone imagine that he would become one of the magazine's star contributors little more than a decade later.

Primarily a novelist, Capote was also a playwright, essayist, and short-story and screenplay writer. The general public remembers Capote mostly for his 1966 book *In Cold Blood.* Labeled a "nonfiction novel" by the writer, it remains the work linked to his greatest fame and fortune. Although Capote claimed to be the originator of a new genre with *In Cold Blood,* his assertion has been disputed by various other writers and reviewers. Over time, however, the debate has become inconsequential, for it is Capote's book that critics point to as the major example of the "nonfiction novel." Its influence is immeasurable, while the myths surrounding its inception and reception continue to grow.

Some of Capote's writing has been accorded the impressive, though perhaps now outmoded, term "classic." *Breakfast at Tiffany's* (1958), a novella, remains a perennial favorite, and not only because the protagonist, Holly Golightly, has become synonymous with the luminous movie star Audrey Hepburn. Another successful novella, though failed play, *The Grass Harp* (1951), was made into a movie in 1996. At least one story, "A Christmas Memory," usually has an annual seasonal showing on television, and other Capote short stories are heard by the radio audience or seen on television. *In Cold Blood* has become a movie classic and also has been produced as a television movie. Further, in the April 1996 issue of *Washingtonian,* writer Dick Victory places *In Cold Blood* on his list of books so memorable "that one feels moved, by some moral obligation to press them on friends and promising strangers."

Not hampered by a sense of modesty, Capote's own pre-obituary summary of the importance of his work is on target. In televised appearances, shown in flashbacks in a 1987 documentary three years after his death, Capote seems certain of his influence on fiction. Part of his legacy to literature, he says, would be short stories "as good as any in the English language." Various contemporary critics and scholars reevaluating the work today would agree.

Because Capote had both a nonchalant and artistic view of "facts," it is a challenge for critics to sort out truth from fiction. In speaking of the artistic process, Capote noted many times that truth becomes lies and vice versa in the hands of a writer. The artist, he insists, must be free from the restraints of reality. Capote was as casual about the use of biographical information as he was about fiction, and readers should be wary of the contradictory statements that he made for effect, attention, and humor. He felt no compulsion to be truthful. Vidal, though excessively harsh and biased against Capote, is close to the mark in describing Capote in *Palimpsest* as one of those who "keep on inventing themselves before our eyes." When it suited Capote, he justified his choreographing of "facts" to fit the situation. In the introduction to *Truman Capote: Conversations* (1987), a collection of interviews that reporters and reviewers had with Capote over the course of his life, editor M. Thomas Inge warns of Capote's manipulativeness. Capote often made outrageous statements for fun; yet, gullible listeners accepted those as truth. He is, however, one of the most autobiographical of writers, and somewhere in most of his work fragments of reality lurk.

Capote began to write stories—part truth, part fiction—when he was still a youngster. Some relatives have claimed that he got into trouble for his childish, gossipy tales about local townspeople while he was a child living in Monroeville. Whether or not that is true, his penchant for gossip was part of his personality from boyhood on. In adulthood he was the star at many a

Capote (right) with his lover, Jack Dunphy, in Tangier, Morocco, in 1949 (photograph by Paul Bowles)

dinner table, not only because he was a gossip and raconteur but also because he was a man with a biting wit. Katherine Graham describes him as "a magic conversationalist whose sentences were like stories." People enjoyed hearing him talk, just as he took pleasure in exchanging gossip with them. Toward the end of his life he proclaimed, probably truthfully, that he enjoyed gossip more than writing. He even declared, in that sad period of decline when he was being castigated for the type of fiction he was producing, that literature is gossip. The failure to discern the difference played a major role in his literary downfall in his last years and the destruction of his personal life. Apparently he never learned, or he forgot, the lessons of childhood tale-telling, and in the end the price he paid was unendurable.

Encouraged and praised by teachers for his writing, while still in his teens Capote produced several short stories; the first, "The Walls Are Cold" (1943), was published when he was nineteen. Three more stories (uncollected and now forgotten) were printed in

1944 and 1945, before the June 1945 issue of *Mademoiselle* started his meteoric rise to fame. The story "Miriam" brought him his first O. Henry Award in 1946. That year became a highly productive and important one for Capote when two diametrically opposed, yet later equally famed, stories of his were printed: "A Tree of Night," in the October 1946 issue of *Harper's Bazaar,* and "Jug of Silver," in the December 1946 issue of *Mademoiselle.* Reading the three early stories—"Miriam," "A Tree of Night," and "Jug of Silver"—gives some insight into the polarities in Capote's work. The first two stories abound with symbols of despair and disintegration, of loneliness and fear, whereas the third story is about magic, hope, and childhood dreams.

These opposing qualities in his fiction are also revelatory of the writer's dual personality. One side is the droll and humorous Capote whose happier work sometimes expands into the tall-tale exaggeration found in Southern and Western stories. Often these pieces tell of children's illusions that they will be taken out of their humdrum and sometimes unhappy world into one where time stands still, where children are always loved, and where it is possible to live apart from demanding, punitive, harsh adults. The sparkling and witty characteristics of such stories help account for their continuing popularity. On the opposite side, however, is a body of grim and darkly complex stories, which take on a new form of gothicism. These differences in the work led to the recognition that Capote's fiction follows two distinct patterns: one is the light and sunny style; the second is its antithesis, consisting of brooding, psychological explorations into the hidden and secret psyche of its characters. Not only are these stories disturbing, but they are also more difficult to comprehend inasmuch as they function on several levels of meaning.

Because of the techniques and subject matter of his dark stories, Capote has been labeled either a gothicist, a Southern gothicist, or a new gothicist. (At times he angrily rejected all these labels because, inaccurately, he thought them limiting.) Although to some early scholars the use of the term "gothic" was pejorative, in recent years it has been understood as important to the understanding of psychological aberrations. The modern gothic mode, or as critic Irving Malin calls it in his 1962 book of the same name, "New American Gothic," is a prevalent form in Southern literature of the 1940s and 1950s. It exists as well in some Southern fiction of the 1930s—in William Faulkner's work, for example. Also, though gothicism changed and is less popular today, its influence did not disappear by the end of the 1950s in the South or elsewhere.

Capote, also to his annoyance, has been categorized as a Southern writer, although he spoke of himself as a southerner only when it suited him. At other times he pointed out that most of his life had been spent away from the South, and thus his work could not be designated as Southern. Like many of his views, this one, too, is contradictory. Many of his best stories are set in the South or have Southern characters. Although not all of his dark stories take place in the South, they are alike in the neo-gothic techniques associated with Southern writers.

New American Gothic characteristically utilizes dreams, nightmares, fantasies, and distortions as representative of disturbed psychological states. To understand the meanings of new gothic fiction, the reader must unravel repetitive patterns of unusual images and symbols: confused chronology, blurring of the real and imaginary, journeys and rooms that symbolize the longing of the character to escape from the locked room that is the secret self. Like traditional early gothic tales of the eighteenth and nineteenth centuries, terror is part of the new gothic pattern; but in the later gothicism the terror is interior, the disturbances brought on by something happening within rather than by external forces. The characters are narcissistic and obsessive, anxiety-ridden people facing the abyss of disintegration and/or madness. Some precipitating force destroys the self-protective barriers that have allowed them to function; although throughout their lives they have had to cope with the damage inflicted by judgmental, pitilessly cruel, or callously indifferent families, their defenses fail them at a critical juncture, allowing or forcing the hidden self to overcome the protection of the flimsily constructed ego.

Capote's early prize-winning stories became part of a published collection, along with several newer pieces, in 1949. A year before that, his first novel appeared, *Other Voices, Other Rooms,* a work with strong similarities to his dark short stories. Although the novel was an immediate popular success, most literary critics disliked it. It bore no relationship to anything regarded as meaningful. Before World War I Southern literature had been romantic, flowery, and often imitative of chivalric and heroic English poetry and historic romances in the manner of Sir Walter Scott. Only after that war did the literature of the South begin to develop a significant mode of its own, first with poetry and literary criticism in the 1920s and 1930s, then with plays and fiction. Because other regions of the country were producing strongly sociological and often polemical fiction, Southern literature was often misunderstood and suspect. Critical support was almost nonexistent. For example, *The Fathers* (1938), the superb novel by poet and critic Alan Tate, failed to arouse any interest outside of the South. It took the help of the much-respected Malcolm Cowley to establish Faulkner's reputation. Cowley also became one of Capote's early literary supporters.

But Capote's novel is nothing like the fiction of writers such as Faulkner, Tate, or Robert Penn Warren, whose work tracks the decay of the old South, the corruption and destruction of families, and the disappearance of the familiar natural world. *Other Voices, Other Rooms* is narrower in scope than most Southern novels, with their themes of a dying civilization and the causes of its death. Confessional, even intimate, in its narcissism, *Other Voices, Other Rooms* harks back to this earlier mode in one way only—its focus on a taboo subject, forbidden topics introduced by American (Stephen Crane, Frank Norris, Jack London) and French naturalists (Emile Zola and Edmond and Jules Concourt) in the late nineteenth century. Where these naturalists often called attention to the plight of women, particularly those who turned to prostitution, the taboo subject of *Other Voices, Other Rooms* is homosexuality.

In spite of the antagonism of important critics, the book immediately became a best-seller, perhaps in part, as some reviewers claimed, the result of an unusual and memorable photo of a twenty-three-year-old Capote on

TRUMAN CAPOTE was born in New Orleans twenty-six years ago. A first novel, OTHER VOICES, OTHER ROOMS, established him in the front rank of younger American writers. His stories, eight of which are collected in A TREE OF NIGHT, have appeared in the better periodicals here and abroad, and are frequently anthologized. Last year Random House published LOCAL COLOR, a book of Mr. Capote's travel pieces. His work is widely known in Europe, where he has lived the last several years.

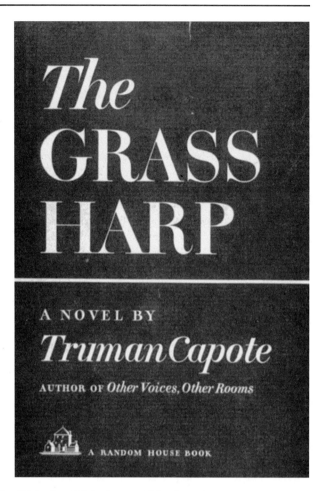

Dust jacket for Capote's 1951 book, one of several works of fiction for which he drew on childhood experiences

the jacket. The provocative portrait of the author, then a beautiful young man, caused a sensation with its suggestiveness and was talked about as much as the novel itself. It remains titillating, as *Vogue* magazine reminded readers many years later with a photograph of a fifty-five-year-old, jaded-looking Capote assuming the same pose. Throughout his life the author knew just how to capture the attention of the public. He and his sometimes outrageous publicity-seeking activities never lacked an audience. But *Other Voices, Other Rooms* is significant in its relationship to the writer's entire body of work. The themes that form the framework of the novel appear again and again in successive writings: the search for love, the devastation that follows betrayal, and the loss of innocence. The poignant young protagonist of the novel, the lonely lost child, resembles many characters not only in Capote's early work but also in his late work—both fiction and nonfiction—through his final autobiographical short story, *One Christmas,* published in 1983. Even as he advanced toward his sixtieth year, Capote was unable to over-

come the despair of the unloved and unwanted child he had been.

Other Voices, Other Rooms is a highly poetic novel filled with often opposing symbols and images—frigidity and overwhelming heat, sunrise and sunset—as well as those of sexuality, death, and dying. Everything reveals the fears of a boy just on the verge of maturity and uncertain of his masculinity. His mother dead, his aunt unable to care for him, his father little more than a vegetable, Joel Knox has to find a way to survive in a terrifying and uncaring world. Each person who rejects him and each episode that frightens him pushes him further into unbearable isolation. Ultimately, he has no choice but to enter the "other room," the world of homosexuality offered to him by Randolph, the man in whose home he lives.

Capote, who liked to think of his work as cyclical, stated that *Other Voices, Other Rooms* came at the end of his first writing cycle. Although he believed that his first published collection of short stories, *A Tree of Night and Other Stories* (1949), was the beginning of a second cycle, there are many similarities between the novel and several of the stories. Of the five dark, neo-gothic stories in *A Tree of Night and Other Stories,* two have male protagonists, and three have female protagonists. "Shut a Final Door" and "The Headless Hawk" are about young men, "Miriam," "Master Misery," and "A Tree of Night" about women.

"Shut a Final Door," one of the most disturbing pieces in Capote's oeuvre, took first prize in the O. Henry Memorial Awards in 1947. At the time of its publication it seemed an unusual and clever work by a young, still unknown author. But today the piece needs to be recognized as an important autobiographical, albeit fictionalized, part of the puzzle of Capote's personality. In this story, as elsewhere in his fiction, Capote gives the reader clues to his identification with the protagonist. Not only is there doubling within the story but also redoubling. The protagonist, Walter Ranney, is a double for Truman Capote, whereas a young man named Irving is a double for Walter. In this and other pieces, one hint of the writer's connection to the characters comes through the names, in which the number of letters may provide an opening suggestion of the author's intention of doubling.

It is not necessary, however, to recognize such pointers to recall that descriptions of places and characters in "Shut a Final Door" fit the author himself. Familiar settings—New York City, Saratoga, New Orleans, as well as references to Connecticut—are autobiographical links. Similar to the author's life, a feared father and a hated mother have a role. Details of appearance—sweet, little, pink-cheeked, and baby-faced—are exact replicas of the youthful Capote. (In *Other Voices, Other Rooms* the boy Joel also resembles the author when young.) Although caution is necessary in interpretation, the more readers have learned about Capote over the course of his lifetime the more they have been able to connect him to the protagonists of several of the stories. In "Shut a Final Door" the confused, disoriented personality that splits from the outwardly confident and popular Walter is the "poor little boy," who is also Walter, the other self. This is the rejected, inadmissable self, terrified of confronting his hidden and denied homosexuality. Dreams of being betrayed and betraying friends, a vicious parent, an employer/lover who has discarded him for another, and a teacher who failed him reveal a tormented, shattered fictional character whose history is close to that of the writers. In the most significant of his many dreams, the protagonist stands naked on an empty street as his betrayers drive past in black cars. When he goes to one car crying "Daddy," his father slams the door on his hand, severing his fingers, a symbolic act of castration.

Capote apparently was aware of the psychoanalytic literature of Sigmund Freud. In discussing father-son relationships, Freud speaks of fears of nakedness and wounding and issues of competition and masculinity. Capote either read or heard about or intuited those Freudian meanings that informed his own use of symbols. (At various times personally and privately he castigated analysts; some of his work openly or symbolically does just that; yet, the author was in therapy on and off throughout his life.)

The actual hotel-room door of the title "Shut a Final Door" symbolizes the protagonist's inability to return to the socially accepted life of heterosexuality. Because of his terror of a disembodied voice that suggests intolerable truths and the contempt of the world outside the room (the room itself allows various symbolic interpretations), he cannot open the door. Thus the protagonist's only way out is through the nonbeing of madness, something the writer explores in other stories as well.

Among Capote's many writings that touch on the matter of homosexuality, the most obvious and also the weakest of these is his story "My Side of the Matter," in *A Tree of Night and Other Stories.* The story is an early attempt at comedy in which the flimsy plot serves as a vehicle for different types of humor: exaggeration, understatement, drollness, vaudevillian slapstick actions, and ridiculous characters. Later, as his artistic control improved, Capote was able to utilize these same elements as delightfully funny parts of novellas. In "My Side of the Matter," however, an unappealing protagonist wants to present a case to the reader about his mistreatment by his wife's family. So certain is he that the listener will take his part, he makes no attempt to disguise the family's belief that he is a misfit, whose major flaw is his lack of "manliness." Whether the young Capote intended it or not, and in spite of all the broad slapstick, homosexuality is a major issue. The fact that the whining, unappealing character has impregnated his teenage wife is beside the point, just as Walter's heterosexual affair in "Shut a Final Door" masks his true nature.

"The Headless Hawk," considered one of Capote's finest stories, is also one of his most complex and somber. It too explores the idea of hidden homosexuality, but it is more than that. The protagonist, Vincent, corresponds to those Capote characters whose narcissism, like that of all people who suffer from the same psychological disorder, is combined with an inner sense of emptiness. And, similar to other Capote protagonists terrified of self-knowledge, he tries to run from it. But there can be no flight from self-revelation, unless it is into madness, the path followed by Walter in "Shut a Final Door," into the nothingness that is the sound of wind. Although Vincent needs love, he lacks the ability to love anyone. He betrays and destroys all who love him. Images and symbols of despair and inertia fill the pages: blindness, drowning in green seas,

She spent entire days slopping about in her tiny, sweatbox kitchen (José says I'm a fabulous cook. Better than the Colony. Who would have thought I had such a great natural talent. A month ago I couldn't scramble eggs.) And she still couldn't, for that matter. The simpler dishes, steak, a proper salad, were beyond her; instead, she fed José outré soups (brandied black Terrapin poured into avocado shells), dubious innovations (chicken and rice served with a chocolate sauce: An East Indian ~~specialty~~ specialty, darling."), Nero-ish novelties

Page from the manuscript for Breakfast at Tiffany's, *published in 1958 (Library of Congress)*

wavering reflections that lack clarity, devastating dreams, rain that does not heal but brings uncrossable barriers. Vincent's soul has a sickness unto death, an incurable illness connoted by the title. "The Headless Hawk" is both image and symbol; its cruel pictorial image dominates a painting and also becomes the symbol of Vincent's lifetime of perfidy and failure.

One of the complexities in "The Headless Hawk" and some of Capote's other work is his use of circularity, a favorite technique in both his light and his dark pieces. With the circular mode the writer begins with the ending that is the result of the actions, though usually the reasons are unknown at that point. Then the time shifts to the beginning of the actions and advances chronologically through the series of events leading to the conclusion. The effect of circularity in the dark and the light stories is totally different. In the dark works the form intensifies the sense of hopelessness often found in absurdist literature. With such patterns one thinks of plays such as Samuel Beckett's *Waiting for Godot* (1956). In Capote's dark pieces, similar to absurdist plays, nothing can or will change because the protagonist suffers from the malaise and paralysis of despair. Contrarily, in the light stories in which the circular technique is effected, enclosure is created, which serves to heighten the sweet/sad sense of nostalgia that goes with remembrance of things past.

Although "Miriam," a story of schizophrenia, was Capote's first prize-winning work (and was also published in *A Tree of Night and Other Stories*), years after its publication Capote dismissively labeled it a "stunt," proclaiming it the piece he liked least. Yet, "Miriam" and the other two dark stories about women in his initial collection have much in common. In fact, they bear many resemblances to the works in which the protagonists are male. The women, like the men, are solitary, isolated figures, uncertain of their own identities, unhappy with their lives. However, major differences also exist between the males and females of the stories. Where the males are cruel and vindictive, the women are not. Rather, the women are weaker, more dependent on others to provide meaning in their lives. The males are uncertain of their inner selves and sexual orientation, but the women are uncertain and fearful about everything, not only who they are but also of the world outside themselves.

The old woman of "Miriam" is only a shell, hollow inside; thus her descent into madness is not as terrible as the fate that befalls the young women in "Master Misery" and "A Tree of Night." All three women are repressed in various ways. The two young ones, uncertain, sexually inhibited, unable to protect themselves, become victims of others, whereas the protagonist in "Miriam" is destroyed by her hidden self. Old Mrs. Miller, who fantasizes a double named Miriam but is also "Miriam," cannot bear the reality of her insular life. A radio, a bird, a trip to the movies provide her only connections with other voices. Married for many years but now widowed, she is nothing without her husband; the clue is her identification as her husband's wife, Mrs. H. T. Miller. When the tenuous links to the external world are snapped, she becomes the victim of her own inner being, the desired, bold, free, and hallucinatory self.

Winter weather requires Mrs. Miller to stay in her own apartment; however, it does more: solitude locks her inside herself. When the emptiness inside the familiar frame becomes unbearable, the secret self emerges. Although intense heat, one type of hell, serves as background and symbol for the dark stories about men in this collection, cold and ice are central symbols in the three dark stories about women. One may only speculate about the author's reasons for envisioning different types of living hell for men and women, but the frigid atmosphere of the stories of the women seems linked to their intense reclusiveness and sexual fears.

Sylvia, in "Master Misery," is a young woman who has left home to seek a more exciting life in New York. But she finds New York actually and psychologically a cold city, where she feels completely cut off from relationships. Although at first she lives with a couple she knows from home, their marital intimacy shuts her out from any real contact, thus adding to her isolation. Sexual dreams and longings frighten her, as does an encounter at dusk in a lonely park. Sylvia's disintegration begins when she seeks out someone known only as "Master Misery," who purchases dreams of clients. Although she is warned about the dangers of selling her dreams by a man who briefly becomes her friend and lover, she cannot help herself. Master Misery takes her dreams and "uses them up," leaving her with nothing. A young woman without a job, money, friends, hope, or love, ultimately she does not even fear the possibility of rape as she wanders aimlessly in the bitter cold of winter.

The reader is left to speculate about the identity of "Master Misery," who takes the dreams of weak, unhappy, lonely clients. Is he representative of the psychiatrist who tears away the protective facades people construct to be able to function in what is portrayed as an icy and indifferent existence? What then is left for someone like Sylvia, who is split between her fears and longings for adulthood and her desire to return to the safe world of the womb? The reader may find in the subtext the author's suggestion that personalities should not be tampered with; for the weak and uncertain human, recognition of the true self is unbearable.

Because of the title of the collection, it is possible that Capote considered "A Tree of Night" the most

important of the eight stories. The last in the book, it is what the reader most remembers at the conclusion. The atmosphere and suggestions behind the images and symbols are those that frightened Capote most when he was a child—fears of the dark, fears of death, the nighttime dangers outside the window. A memory that troubled him throughout his life was of being left alone at night in a locked room when his mother wanted to go out. "A Tree of Night" suggests such fears. Kay, the protagonist, is another of Capote's young characters with a somewhat unformed personality, suggestible and imaginative. On her way south by train after attending a funeral, Kay has a disastrous encounter with a frightening and hostile man and woman. Even though the train has many passengers, Kay feels completely separated and defenseless as she is preyed on by the couple. The strange journey suggests a voyage into the world of death as Capote mixes myth, biblical allegory, and the terrifying memory of a burial act his father had once managed. Known as "The Great Pasha," an actor would take a drug to slow his heartbeat, allowing him to remain in an airtight coffin for several hours. A paying audience that sought the thrill of seeing someone buried alive was ultimately disappointed when the drug failed and "the Great Pasha" died.

Although Kay attempts to escape the couple's psychological and then physical hold on her, she finally succumbs to them. Images and symbols disclose not only the hidden fears people have but also the particular terror women have of physical violation.

Set in the South, "Children on Their Birthdays" and "Jug of Silver," two of the best known of Capote's sunnier short stories, also appear in this first collection. Each evokes the other in its combination of joy and melancholy, but "Jug of Silver" is less complex. Like the later, also Southern "Christmas Memory" (1966), "Thanksgiving Visitor" (1967), and *One Christmas,* "Jug of Silver" is a type of holiday story. Both stories tell of childhood dreams that cannot be fulfilled. In "Jug of Silver" the dream has two parts: a young boy longs to help his sister follow her dream, which is to achieve Hollywood stardom. For this she must get a new set of teeth; however, the family has no money. The boy attains his dream somehow through magical insight when he wins a pot of silver in a contest. But, though the silver pays for his sister's false teeth, her dream of stardom in the never-never land of Hollywood cannot be realized.

In "Children on Their Birthdays" another young girl longs to become a Hollywood star. This story has no supernatural or extrasensory qualities; yet, there are several elements of fantasy present. Holding less vague longings than those of the sister and brother in "Jug of Silver," Miss Lily Jane Bobbit reflects the hopes of glory of all youngsters. Because of the narrator, "Mr. C." (an

unmistakable reference to Capote himself), the interest created by the circular structure, and the specificity of details, the reader becomes more involved with the major character. With all the polish and style of a writer who has found his voice, Mr. C. tells of the little girl who captivates and involves an entire town in her dreams and ambitions for a year. Although Lily Jane is only a child, she is determined, single-minded, and wise beyond her years. If the opening sentence in this circular story had not prepared readers for the melancholy conclusion, we would expect Miss Bobbit to become the star she wants to be. She controls her mother and devoted friends, collects swains, breaks all the rules, and defies those who believe in church and schooling. She is, in fact, the embodiment of the secret longings of children.

Two motifs run parallel courses in this story, as they do in "Jug of Silver" and many of Capote's stories: the fantasies and desires of children and the impossibility of achieving them. With his brilliant use of symbol and imagery to create mood, and in the combination of humor and melancholy, Capote takes a giant step forward in his mastery of style.

Memory and nostalgia, the sweet but sad mix in "Children on Their Birthdays," becomes a central mode in many of the writer's stories of childhood. Capote never limited himself to one genre, and in the year following the publication of the short stories a collection of essays appeared. *Local Color* (1950) is a series of unrelated pieces about places where the author had lived or visited in the United States and Europe. Throughout his life Capote spent long periods abroad. (Generally he traveled with his lifelong companion Jack Dunphy, a dancer who was married when they met in their youth. Dunphy gave up dancing and marriage and turned to writing when he and Capote became lovers.) The prose in *Local Color* is accompanied by brilliant black-and-white photographs taken by noted photographers of the day. In what became typical of his nonfiction, the often lyrical writing includes stories about people, some renowned, some unknown. Different as each place is—Brooklyn and New Orleans, for example—the writer frequently elicits a feeling of loneliness, decay, emptiness, or sterility. He is harshest in his descriptions of Hollywood, shown as a city of total aridity and artificiality. That was the world to which the author was drawn at the end of his life; the area that in youth he saw as a land of death was where, exhausted and depressed, he died.

Capote's first novella, *The Grass Harp,* published in 1951, followed his collection of travel essays. A delicate and warm, yet occasionally didactic story with spelled-out messages about the importance of love, its preachy quality is mitigated by several elements: outstanding humor, both the understated and exaggerated verbal variety and the vaudevillian physical; memorable characters, notably cousin Dolly, modeled after the author's cousin Sook; and, what by then was becoming a hallmark of many Capote stories, a moving, all-encompassing gentle melancholic reminder of time's swift passage. The writer's circular technique encloses the memories of boyhood inviolably as the narrator, like the grass harp, soughs stories of those who are dead.

Capote's initial venture into the theatrical world came when he turned *The Grass Harp* into a play in 1952. Although one of the most famous theater critics of the day, Brooks Atkinson, praised the play, almost everyone else reviled it—and with good reason. The writer had destroyed the very fabric and meaning of the novella by altering the characters and muddying the themes. Where symbols and images form a sweet yet solemn pattern in the novella, built around memories of things past—the lovely years that cannot be restored—they are all pointless and senseless in the adaptation. The play lasted for thirty-six performances.

Capote was somewhat more successful as a playwright two years later with his romantic musical play, *The House of Flowers*. Although the reviews favored Harold Arlen's music, Capote's script was panned. Still, the show ran on Broadway for almost five months. Periodically there is a revival, the most recent one in 1991, receiving mixed reviews. The simple, slight, and humorous tale of love, set on the island of Haiti, where superstition and voodooism are an integral part of life, was published as a short story in 1958 in *Breakfast at Tiffany's: A Short Novel and Three Stories*.

Clearly, playwriting was not Capote's métier even though the opportunities for money, fame, and a more exciting social life had tempted him away from the spartan regime of the novelist. Knowing that solitude is a requirement for a dedicated novelist, he was torn between opposing needs of his personality. Hollywood movie scripts, a television play, and a documentary, as well as several crime shows, provided pleasurable and lucrative work, but those were not at the core of his writing life. Developing movie scripts, though, proved to be closer to Capote's talents than creating plays for the legitimate stage. Over a period of years, he turned out a variety of scripts, of which *Beat the Devil* (1954) and *The Innocents* (1961) brought accolades and continue to interest scholars and movie buffs.

After the initial publication of *The Grass Harp*, Capote and his publisher, Random House, began a practice that would suggest he had written a larger body of work than actually existed. *The Grass Harp* was republished along with the writer's earliest collection of stories. The pattern was followed throughout Capote's life and even after his death, although occasionally one or two new stories or essays were added to a collection.

Readers who subscribed to *The New Yorker* in the 1950s discovered the pleasure of the humorous Capote. As one of three "journalists" accompanying a touring American theater company to the USSR, he wrote a sparkling, extremely funny series of articles for the magazine. Later published as *The Muses Are Heard* (1956), the book tells about the beginning of cultural exchange between the U.S. and the Soviets with a theatrical production of *Porgy and Bess*. Traveling aboard a train and then staying in Russian hotels with the large number of people involved with the show—some only peripherally—Capote was an eyewitness to an historic, yet, ephemeral event that would now be forgotten but for his book. Although serious at times, as in descriptions of the brutality of the Soviet system and his sense of the desperation that exists among its people, he is at his satiric best portraying both Americans and Russians in their arrogance, vanity, and foolishness. Never intrusive, the writer uses quotations, dialogue, and episodes to achieve the humor and flavor of the trip. With his highly sensitive ear for the nuances of speech, Capote captures individual idiosyncrasies through language.

A large collection of some of the writer's best-known nonfiction pieces from the 1950s and 1960s, with one or two from the early 1970s, was published in 1973 as *The Dogs Bark: Public People and Private Places*. Included in the book are prose descriptions by Capote of eight celebrities that appeared in Richard Avedon's *Observations* (1959), *The Muses Are Heard,* and *Local Color;* also appearing in *The Dogs Bark* is "The Duke in His Domain," which *The New Yorker* editor William Shawn calls a "masterpiece" and biographer Clarke labels "a remarkable work of journalism." The work is part narrative, part interview with actor Marlon Brando. Published during the filming of the movie *Sayonara,* the written piece will undoubtedly be remembered much longer than the motion picture.

In his extremely productive period of the 1950s, when Capote was achieving success in almost every genre, he wrote two of his most popular and memorable works, *Breakfast at Tiffany's* and "A Christmas Memory." The stories have different settings, different time frames, and different characters, although given Capote's penchant for autobiographical touches, the young writer in *Breakfast at Tiffany's* is probably the boy of "A Christmas Memory." Still, for all the dissimilarities, both works contain humor, tenderness, love, and an underlying sense of sorrow that is connected to irredeemable loss. The poetic prose is stronger and more joyful in "A Christmas Memory," as the writer describes the child's shared country existence and the delights of the seasons with an elderly "friend," his gentle, simple cousin with whom he lives. Yet, the language of bereavement in both the novella and the short story is comparable in its images and symbols. Both are told within a frame of memory that encloses and separates the story from all that goes before and after.

"A Christmas Memory" also resembles the earlier *The Grass Harp* in its use of a young male narrator who is another fictionalized version of the author as a boy; in the moving and memorable figure of the childlike, warmhearted spinster cousin who protects him against harsher relatives; and in its mood of nostalgia for the lost world of childhood, whose enchantment can only be recovered through memory. Using his familiar circular technique to tell of the brief but deliriously happy memories, the adult teller of the tale looks back over the years to a time when he was a small boy in Alabama, when nature was all to him and his cousin. Abruptly the child's life is altered, as was Capote's, when he is taken away from the only life he knows and plunged into a city world of harshness, concrete, and misery.

Because of its popularity and perhaps to take advantage of Capote's developing reputation, in 1966, years after its inclusion with *Breakfast at Tiffany's,* "A Christmas Memory" was republished as a separate work. It was soon followed by "The Thanksgiving Visitor," a lesser story that seems to piggyback on the success of "A Christmas Memory." As another holiday story with many of the same people as those in "A Christmas Memory," it lacks much of the poetic, symbolic, and mythical qualities of the earlier work and also takes on some of the didacticism of *The Grass Harp.* However, the appeal of the story comes through the picture Capote draws of the rural South in the 1930s, of a slow-paced world now forgotten. Further, at the conclusion there is a brief reminder of the use the writer makes of the seasons to reveal the swift passage of time, similar to what he does in "Children on Their Birthdays," *The Grass Harp,* "A Christmas Memory," *Breakfast at Tiffany's,* and *In Cold Blood.*

Some of the same metaphors of change are used in *Breakfast at Tiffany's* as in "A Christmas Memory." Here again the circular style reveals remembrance of things past. Once upon a time, during World War II, when the narrator (again meant to be Capote) is only hopeful of becoming a writer, he meets and falls in love with a beautiful, fun-loving, elusive girl-about-town. She calls herself Holly Golightly, and her card reads "traveling." Holly fled from her adolescent life of poverty and deprivation, leaving behind her real name, Lulamae Barnes, as well as her elderly husband and his brood of children, to fulfill her dreams of fame and fortune first in Hollywood and then New York. But as with other Capote dreamers, the dream eludes her. When she does become famous for a brief time, it is disastrous. Because she is daring, enthusiastic, and entrancing, she has been able to stay afloat through romantic liaisons and some mob affiliations.

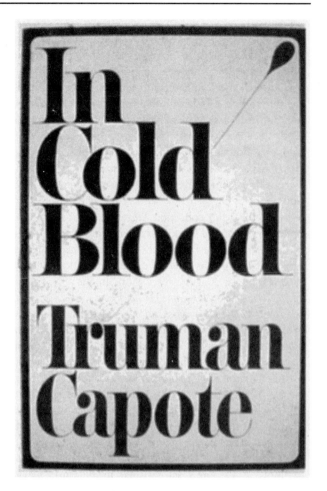

Dust jacket for Capote's 1965 "nonfiction novel" about the murders of four members of a Kansas farm family

However, Holly is surprisingly naive about the penalties for such things. Believing in the possibility of an old-fashioned kind of love, she is devastated when her Latin fiancé abandons her in the aftermath of a mob scandal. Fleeing from the U.S., after warning the narrator and her other brokenhearted admirer that it is a mistake to love her, she disappears from their lives. She has warned her friends never to love a wild thing who lives in the sky because such love brings suffering. Wild things soar higher and higher until at last they disappear. Yet Holly, the uncaged bird and freedom seeker, also seeks the polar opposite, the safety and security represented by Tiffany's. The narrator, who ultimately becomes a successful writer, suggests that Holly never finds her Tiffany's; and that, plus the piling up of images and symbols of the waning day and the waning season, adds to the effect of loss and nostalgia for a past beyond remedy.

Capote's symbolic use of the loner who lives in the sky appears early in his work, with "Master Misery," and in his final story, *One Christmas.* Even though they might wish otherwise, those who live in the sky can never relate for long to people who lead ordinary lives. Holly is kin to all those dreamers in Capote's stories, all whose fantasies and hopes fail. Some, though, are more tragic than others, and the author uses images to reveal the differences. Lily Jane Bobbit dies as she runs toward her future in a shower of yellow roses and a rainbow. Holly escapes from her past in an autumnal shower of rain, abandoning everything she has loved. The memories of Miss Bobbit are wrapped in roses and fireflies and sweet shrub, but those of Holly are caught up in "a downpour of October rain" and yellow leaves.

In the 1963 collection *Selected Writings* a different and unprecedented Capote story appears. Although the piece, "Among the Paths to Eden," has not captured as large an audience as it deserves, several critics have singled it out for lengthy discussion. In his *The Limping Hero: Grotesques in Literature* (1971) Peter Hays, speaks of maiming in the story as symbolic of death and spiritual rebirth, the opposite of maiming in *Other Voices, Other Rooms*. In the novel, says Hays, maiming represents paralysis, whereas in the short story it suggests renewal. Critic William Nance, in his book *The Worlds of Truman Capote* (1970), compares this with earlier stories, claiming that Capote was both enlarging his fictional cast of characters and finally distancing himself from them. In *Truman Capote: A Study of the Short Fiction* (1992) Helen S. Garson focuses on the irony behind the language and symbols as Capote's self-satisfied protagonist, a widower, is able, in the cemetery in which his wife is buried, to avoid confronting his own mortality.

Nance attributes Capote's movement away from his earlier style to the type of research involved in preparation for the nonfiction novel *In Cold Blood*. The story of Capote's desire to try a new form of journalism and his search for an exciting subject has been told frequently, appearing in many of the interviews given after publication of his book. (Most interviews may be found in Inge's compilation of interviews with Capote.) Capote claimed that his interest in writing the book was sparked by a news report of the murder of a wealthy Kansas farmer, his wife, and two of his four children. It was what Capote had been looking for, a dissimilar world from the one he knew, with different kinds of people, as well as an opportunity to hone his journalistic skills and combine them with the writing techniques he had developed for two decades. In an essay, "Dreaming the News," in *Time* (14 April 1997), Roger Rosenblatt notes that writers read the news as "the first draft of a work of art," and he points to Truman Capote and Norman Mailer's discovery of "this opportunity a long time ago."

Linking his enthusiasm to Capote's plans for the project that would become *In Cold Blood*, the editor of *The New Yorker* signed him in 1959 to do a series about the murders of the Clutter family. His Random House publisher, Bennett Cerf, who would later publish the reports as a book, helped get him introductions to people in Kansas. Capote invited his friend Harper Lee to assist him in some of the work, and they were off to Holcomb, Kansas.

At first Capote's reception in Kansas was cold. Few inhabitants of Holcomb knew his books or his name, and fewer had heard of the magazine he was representing. His voice, his appearance, and his mannerisms made him seem "like someone coming off the moon," according to Lee. Because of the initially unfriendly response of townspeople and his own sense of alienation in an unfamiliar milieu (his New York socialite friend Babe Paley sent him caviar to cheer him up), Capote wondered if he would be able to follow through on the story; however, as the community got to know him, he gained their respect and even admiration for his penetrating intelligence and friendliness. A *Hutchinson News* editorial describes him as "a man of grace and intellect." Once he began to make a number of friends in the area, he grew more comfortable and his perspective changed.

Originally, Capote intended to have the series focus on the lives and deaths of the Clutter family and the reactions and changes the murders brought to the people in the small midwestern community. He did not envision anything beyond that goal. Among the people who affected his change of scope was the detective in charge of the case, Alvin Dewey, and his wife. Capote and Lee were at the Dewey home the night the Clutter murderers, Perry Smith and Richard Hickock, were arrested, and with their capture a different shape began to emerge for the planned series. Suddenly it seemed to the writer that there were more persons than the victims to write about in covering the tragedy. Determined to understand the murderers and the forces that brought them to the grisly homicides, he pursued that tack. The decision had far-reaching effects on Capote's life: with the publication of the articles and book, he became richer and more renowned than he had ever imagined, and he gained an enormous audience, which propelled him into the limelight as never before, taking him to heights in his career that he was never again able to reach. Negatively, the aftermath of the experiences, which proved to be traumatic for him, increased his growing dependence on alcohol and drugs.

Capote spent much time on research about crime, meeting not only with Hickock and Smith but also with other criminals as he came to believe there was a particular type of mentality that leads to criminality. He studied the background of everyone involved in the Kansas murder and accumulated thousands of pages of notes for use in the book. Capote and Lee used no tapes nor took notes during the many interviews with the players in the tragedy as well as the Clutter, Smith, and Hickock families, and the Clutters' friends and neighbors in the community. They depended on memory until they were alone and could write down what they had learned, a technique faulted by a number of critics after the publication of *In Cold Blood*. Capote explored everything he could find about the murdered members of the Clutter family–the parents, Herbert and Bonnie Clutter, and two of their four children, Nancy and Kenyon–and the killers, Hickock and Smith, and their families.

The Clutters were a religious, wealthy but unpretentious, closely knit farming family who apparently had no known enemies. Herbert Clutter had served on the Farm Federal Administration Board during the Eisenhower administration. He and his children were active participants in the community, though Bonnie Clutter suffered from psychiatric disorders and spent most of her time in bed. Nancy, the sixteen-year-old daughter, was admired for her kindness and cleverness by everyone who knew her. Kenyon, the Clutter's only son, was fifteen, the youngest child in the family. At first the great puzzle behind the particularly brutal killing of an upstanding family was motivation, for little was taken from the home of the Clutters. When further events unfolded, discovering the names, tracking the murderers, and investigating their lives, the pieces fell into place.

Hickock and Smith met in prison, where a cellmate had told Hickock exaggerated tales about the Clutters and their wealth. Hickock decided that a robbery of the Clutters would be an easy job, but he was wrong. Undoubtedly, Herbert Clutter was well off, but what Hickock did not know was that no money was kept at home. Because he needed an assistant for a robbery, he lied, pretended, and cajoled Smith into joining him. Although he was more disturbed and violent than Hickock, it was Smith who captured the major share of Capote's interest. The writer saw in Smith the results of a terrible and loveless childhood, and he identified closely–too closely–with him. He became emotionally involved in the fate of the two murderers. During the five years the men were in prison, he wrote to each one twice a week, as they did to him, and he supplied them with reading material until their deaths. At the request of Smith and Hickock he attended the executions, even though he claimed that others tried to prevent his being there. Hickock was hanged first, and when Smith's time came he turned to Capote, kissed him, and said goodbye in Spanish. Capote paid for the headstones on the graves. It was over, but Capote took it hard; he wept for days and mourned what he saw as injustice to Smith. Although Hickock had deep character flaws, the writer believed that Smith was mentally ill and should not have been executed. Capote agreed with a doctor's labeling of

Capote about four years before his death
(photograph © by Harvey Wang)

Smith as a "paranoid schizophrenic." Readers might wonder why Capote felt more emotionally attached to Smith than to Hickock and why more pages are devoted to Perry than to any other person in the book. Many explanations have been given: Smith's appearance, small and childlike, reminding the writer of himself; his artistic nature; his similarities to the lost dreamers of Capote's fiction; his loneliness even in groups; his homosexuality; and probably most important of all, his sad, deprived, and harsh boyhood. Neither the writer nor the murderer was able to overcome feelings of abandonment and betrayal. And, in fact, in one of Capote's last essays, "Nocturnal Turnings," he confides to the reader what he most fears: "Betrayal. Abandonment."

In spite of the classification of *In Cold Blood* as a nonfiction novel, stylistically it has many of the markings of other Capote stories: darkness and light, poetry and prose, symbols and images, foreboding atmosphere, and psychological aberrations. However, the writer also makes use of techniques found in some of his nonfiction work, the essays, travel pieces, and interviews. His experiences writing motion picture and play scripts buttress the book; the influence of motion picture technology is seen in flashbacks and close-ups, in crowd scenes, in portraiture, in detailed settings. As if he is writing a mystery novel, he provides information, yet withholds some facts for a time, building tension and suspense that engages the reader. Like many mystery novelists, he goes back and forth revealing bits and pieces about characters and events. Crisp reporting of episodes is interspersed with creative and selective use of details, so that the written page resembles a painter's use of brush and color.

In the telling of the tragic events, Capote makes a change from his earlier work by standing back from involvement; no names or initials link him to the tale, only the impersonal term "reporter." Each of the four divisions of the book has a title that provides a clue to what will follow: part 1, "The Last to See Them Alive"; part 2, "Persons Unknown"; part 3, "Answer"; and part 4, "The Corner," the least effective section in the work. Part 4 lacks the suspense of the other chapters because it is weighted down with too much about the justice system and extraneous stories of other prisoners and their crimes.

The concluding pages, like an old-fashioned novel, provide closure with information about various marriages, births, deaths, and other changes in the lives of all who were a part of the story. However, it is the prose of the last few lines, with its quiet sadness and peerless poetic language, that provides stylistic connection to other endings in some of Capote's finest work. Images of weather, landscape, and season are brought together to mirror and reflect the viewer's sense of loss. *In Cold Blood* concludes in a cemetery, the Clutter graves next to a wheat field, and, as agent Dewey walks away, left behind is "the big sky, and the whisper of wind voices in the wind-bent wheat." Though fearing rightly he would never repeat the success of *In Cold Blood,* typically Capote boasted that he was working on something that would surpass it. A novel he had been planning since 1958, he claimed, would be a masterpiece in the manner of Marcel Proust, unlike anything Capote had written before. He had even selected a title, *Answered Prayers.* As it turns out, that novel, promised for a long time, in fact was never finished. Meanwhile, however, between bouts of depression and bursts of energy he managed to produce other work. In 1973 he put together *The Dogs Bark,* which was not new material but a collection of earlier pieces. During his last decade he continued to write travel and personal confessional essays that were prominently advertised by the magazines that published them. In 1980 *Music for Chameleons* was published, a mixed collection of essays, stories, and further personal reflections. In 1983, a year before his death, a slim, separate volume of forty-one triple-spaced pages appeared, titled *One Christmas,* his most

bitter little story. (The book had a limited printing, with a pathetic misspelling in its dedication—whether it was Capote's error or his editor's or the printer's is unclear—and there were few buyers, perhaps because of its excessive cost.) Then, in 1987, three years after the writer's death, Random House brought out in book form *Answered Prayers: The Unfinished Novel,* which was composed of three of four Capote stories published by *Esquire* in 1975 and 1976. Capote had deceived everyone about the amount of work he was doing on that last novel: no other chapters could be found in spite of the thorough search undertaken by interested parties.

Although he tried to hide it from friends, publishers, and readers, by the 1970s Capote was having great difficulty writing. He was drinking constantly, taking drugs, going from one failed love affair to another, and suffering from a variety of illnesses. In spite of his bravado declarations, he was terrified about his slippage in productivity. Nevertheless, in 1975 he produced for *Esquire* his first piece of fiction in eight years, a short story titled "Mojave," originally intended to be the second chapter in *Answered Prayers.* At some point, though, he decided instead to use "Mojave" to flesh out another collection, *Music for Chameleons* (1980), and when the posthumously published but unfinished *Answered Prayers* appeared, "Mojave" was not included.

Of Capote's four stories that appeared in *Esquire* in the seventies, "Mojave" is the strongest, once again showing touches, as Gerald Clarke puts it, of the writer's "magician's power over words." The effectual and smooth techniques are those of the frame, of doubling and redoubling, and the incorporation of tonal qualities and contrasting images—sand and snow, sunlight and darkness—that remain with the reader after the narrative is forgotten. Proving himself still the stylist, Capote employed methods that had been successful before, but they outperform the story itself. One senses fatigue in the writing and superficiality in the narrative as the writer reaches ineffectively to make connections between one group of characters and another; through the experiences of two disparate sets of people he issues a warning that no matter what wealth, or beauty, or social status exists, everyone at some time is "left out there under the sky," disillusioned and alone. (It is revealing that Capote's old symbol of the sky has mutated in this late story; here the characters—older and without hope or semblance of innocence—lack any resemblance to wild things in flight; and now they are earthbound beneath the vast and pitiless expanse of sky, an unconscious touch perhaps of the influence of writer Paul Bowles.) The last lines of "Mojave" contain flashes of the melancholy, though without the gentle sadness found in Capote's earlier stories, as they close with reminders of the swiftness of time and the symbolic coming on of night. The poet/painter still could create beauty with his pen in a scene here and there and almost invariably with his haunting endings, but the stories themselves do not measure up.

Editors at *Esquire* were so pleased with "Mojave" they placed the first page on the cover of the June 1975 issue. Although a number of reviewers praised the work, there were also detractors, and afterward it became clear with the publication of the next three stories that a shared theme had been sounded in "Mojave." All four stories are about betrayal. And all four reveal strong antipathy toward women through the inclusion of hostile, distasteful sexual jokes, which, combined with the quality of the three stories in *Answered Prayers,* are a clue to the disintegration of Capote himself. Throughout the writer's life he had several close women friends whom he loved and admired, but when the stories in *Esquire* divulged his friends' confidences, injuring them and other people, he also destroyed his own reputation. Furthermore, he lost what by then mattered perhaps as much or more than his role as writer—his place in the jet set, society world. Capote, who was not a naive man, nevertheless was unprepared for the reactions to the *Esquire* stories. Traumatized by hostile reviews and the contempt and rejection by old friends, he drew around himself the mantle of "writer," one who is always free of the constraints imposed on others. Nevertheless, he recovered from his self-inflicted wounds.

The three other 1975–1976 stories, "Unspoiled Monsters," "La Cote Basque," and "Kate McCloud," which later became the unfinished novel and had caused a scandal when they were first published in *Esquire,* are distasteful and disorganized, vulgar, pornographic, and often pointless. Only the power of Capote's name and literary reputation could have led to publication. Still, the stories attracted magazine buyers who were as fascinated as Capote himself had been by the glittering world of the rich and famous.

"La Cote Basque," the second Capote story to be published in *Esquire* in 1975, was placed last in *Answered Prayers.* Placement, however, makes little difference because there is only one element that connects it to the other two stories, a narrator named P. B. Jones. Jones's role in "Unspoiled Monsters" and "Kate McCloud" is larger and more important than in "La Cote Basque," for it is through Jones that the author talks, disjointedly, of many things that have concerned, interested, or angered him over the years. Among them is his vision of himself as artist. As he jabs and sneers at real and perceived enemies, he also works in his views about art: art must be chosen over the artist's life. Is he being defensive about it? At that point, yes. Does he believe it? Perhaps, at times.

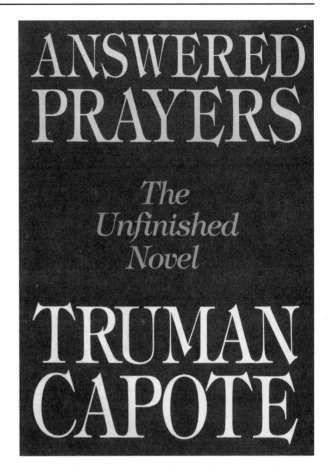

Dust jacket for Capote's "unfinished last novel"—actually a collection of three stories—published posthumously in 1986

Various people, including Capote's editor, have labeled Jones a "dark Doppelgänger" of the writer, and certainly Capote goes to great lengths to draw clear links between himself and his creation. He slips in and out of Jones's skin; sometimes he is Jones, sometimes Capote, sometimes both. Using incidents and experiences from his own life, he turns them into Jones's autobiography. One can only speculate about the reasons behind his doubling with so base a character as Jones, a masseur, prostitute, and failed writer, none of which applies to Capote. The clever, funny, charming writer has disappeared, and in his place stands an unsavory figure resembling the painting of Dorian Gray. The Jones/Capote portrait shows intense self-hatred and rage at the world in which the writer lived, the world he had sought so eagerly and from which he now had been expelled.

Both "Unspoiled Monsters" and "Kate McCloud" have plots of sorts, which read like a combination of true romance and pornography, whereas the plotless "La Cote Basque," though skillfully written, exists as little more than a vehicle for gossip. Yet, even in the two plotted stories, the narrative lines are indecipherable and disconnected and often ridiculous. Many of the names in the stories are familiar, for they belong to actual people, and even when the names are disguised, they are often recognizable to those who follow the lives of the rich and famous.

Although Capote employs his familiar and formerly successful techniques of circularity, time shifts, memory and nostalgia, and cinematic devices and humor, rarely does anything rescue the work. Like the final paragraph of "La Cote Basque," with its language of exhaustion–the rose shedding its petals, and nothing beyond "the failing New York afternoon"–the words mirror the last bleak stage of Capote's life and work.

Still, he struggled on, and in 1980, attempting to regain his reputation, he put together the material for *Music for Chameleons*. The book, surprisingly, is dedicated to Tennessee Williams, with whom Capote was not always on good terms. Williams had praised "Mojave," and it may be that Capote was identifying himself with other creative people. Charles Ruas, in *Conversations with American Writers* (1985), talks of Capote's bitter feeling that writers and painters and composers in the U.S. all suffer the same fate, led to the heights by a public that later destroys them. And Donald Windham writes in his book *Lost Friendships: A Memoir of Truman Capote, Tennessee Williams and Others* (1987) that both Capote and Williams regarded themselves as victims of critics and a fickle public. Yet, in spite of identifying with him, the capricious Capote draws an obscene portrait of Williams in *Answered Prayers*. Since when Capote actually wrote the stories that became *Answered Prayers* is uncertain (he had been assembling parts of the book for years), it may be that he changed his mind about Williams by 1980 when he put together *Music for Chameleons*.

Music for Chameleons is composed largely of pieces Capote had written for various magazines. While not a major work, the collection was favorably reviewed because it shows some of the author's old flair. Once again the reader becomes aware of Capote's fascination with people from opposite ends of the social ladder, the movie stars and the cleaning women. He was always attracted to "the beautiful people" and in writing about them could extract the essences that made them beguiling to the public. One person who intrigued him was Marilyn Monroe. Capote had hoped Monroe would be given the role of Holly Golightly in the motion picture *Breakfast at Tiffany's,* but he had no control over casting. In his prose segments accompanying Avedon's 1959 collection of photographs, *Observtions,* Capote wrote a profile of Monroe. He reprinted it in *The Dogs Bark* in 1973. "A Beautiful Child," another Monroe portrait, which biographer Clarke considers one of Capote's best sketches, appears in *Music for Chameleons.* "Handcarved Coffins," a novella published previously in 1979 as part of a series called "Conversations" in Warhol's magazine *Interviews,* is also reprinted in *Music for Chameleons.* Although the author suggested that it, like *In Cold Blood,* was another fictionalized nonfiction, he was toying, not uncharacteristically, with critics and reviewers who took him seriously. Needing and wanting their approbation after his fall from grace with friends and the reading public, he thought he could intrigue them once again with what he claimed was a true-crime story.

Capote's subtitle for "Handcarved Coffins" is "A Nonfiction Account of an American Crime." So seriously was his categorization taken that his Random House publishers list the novella as "Reportage" in the posthumous *A Capote Reader* (1987). At no time was it ever suggested that the story is a hoax, that Capote is taking vengeance on those critics who had questioned the truths of parts of *In Cold Blood.* However, unlike *In Cold Blood,* the work is pure invention even though the writer labels it reality. At first he claimed the novella was nonfiction, then that it was "mostly fictional." In spite of the outlandish episodes of the novella, it is not difficult to understand why readers and critics alike were deceived: the narrator, Capote himself, is the voice of authority reporting "facts." We believe him, no matter how bizarre the events he relates. Yet, close reading reminds us of other Capote stories, the grotesque and the gothic characteristics of his 1940s fiction published in *A Tree of Night and Other Stories.* In this novella there are many familiar symbols, images, and ideas, but the gothicism is less impressive than in the initial stories. In those dark pieces the gothicism is modern, part of the psychological disintegration of the characters. In "Handcarved Coffins" the author employs an older and less believable type of gothicism, including a mysterious atmosphere complete with an old house, a monstrous villain, romance, adultery, illegitimacy, and five horrifying murders in which the victims are forewarned of their deaths by the receipt of a handcarved coffin. In addition to the literary resemblances to some of his early stories, the gothic and religious scenes and characters seem to be indebted to the fiction of other Southern writers, to Flannery O'Connor and William Styron. Robert Siegle's study of "Handcarved Coffins" finds other fictional influences, those of Charles Dickens, Anthony Trollope, Herman Melville, Mark Twain, Edith Wharton, Jane Austen, and Eric Ambler.

In his preface to *Music for Chameleons,* Capote returns to an idea that he has attempted to define throughout his life, the need to make distinctions between what is true and what is "really" true. For the reader of "Handcarved Coffins," what is apparent or really true is the author's desire to understand the nature of evil, but the story itself is another sleight of hand by Capote.

One Christmas is both Capote's last holiday story and his last work. The other holiday stories are set in Monroeville, but here the city is New Orleans, site of the dark stories Capote wrote as a young author and also the background of another late autobiographical story, "Dazzle." Surprisingly, *A Capote Reader* categorizes "Dazzle" as an essay, probably because the writer makes little attempt at disguising or distancing himself from the unhappy memories he recalls, his boyhood desire and efforts to become a girl. (*One Christmas* is not in *A Capote Reader*.) The confessional "Dazzle" and *One Christmas* are autobiography shaped into the structure of a story, with beginning, middle, ending characters, and plots. In both, the narrator, Capote, is telling a story, albeit about himself.

Because Capote selected New Orleans as the setting for his first dark, unhappy fiction, it becomes clear that the city was not chosen at random but that it is the locus of suffering, fear, and betrayal for the writer. Reading "Dazzle" and *One Christmas* augments a reader's understanding of that which lies beneath the surface in "The Headless Hawk" and "Shut a Final Door"–the ambivalent sexuality in both and the cruelty and betrayal by the father figure in "Shut a Final Door."

In *One Christmas* the author tells of a childhood visit to New Orleans to see his father. Although the boy, Buddy, has no desire to visit him, his cousin Sook persuades the child to go, for there is the possibility he might see something he has only heard about–snow. The promised snow, which fails to materialize, becomes the symbolic link to the unattainable dreams of children in Capote's short stories and the traumatized maid Zoo in *Other Voices, Other Rooms*.

Arch Persons wants his son's love and tries to buy it with presents, but the child fears and mistrusts him in spite of the gift of an expensive toy airplane. Still, back home in Alabama, Buddy sends an affectionate note to "Pop," one that Arch kept until his death. Capote's paradoxical portrait of his father reveals the two opposing sides that made up his character, the likable, proud father and the unreliable, cruel liar. The son draws the figure of a charming, weak, fickle man whom he could never forgive. However, it is toward the mother, Lillie Mae (Nina) Faulk Persons Capote, that the child-adult directs most of his acrimony. Recalling his early longings and need for his mother, he describes her as beautiful, avaricious, and pitiless, a self-centered woman whose behavior to him he never forgave. Writing this story thirty years after his mother's suicide on the "Seconal road," when he is almost sixty and close to death, he remains a conflicted, anguished,

and abandoned boy. No matter how far he has come, no matter the fame, the fortune, and the accolades, he cannot shut the door to the childhood world he left behind.

Alcohol and drugs brought on the illnesses that led to Capote's death, which might have been prevented if he had wanted to be saved. Preventing his friend, Joanne Carson, from calling for medical assistance when he was critically ill from accidentally or deliberately taking an overdose of drugs, Truman Capote died at her California home on 25 August 1984. No longer able to write, yet keeping up a brave pretense, rejected by people he loved and the glittering crowd he had ardently pursued, he sought oblivion. He had, as he told many people, "used up the world."

Interviews:

Pati Hill, "Truman Capote," in *Writers at Work: The Paris Review Interviews,* edited by Malcolm Cowley (New York: Viking, 1958), pp. 283–299;

Lawrence Grobel, *Conversations with Capote* (New York: New American Library, 1985);

Charles Ruas, "Truman Capote," in his *Conversations with American Writers* (New York: Knopf, 1985), pp. 37–56;

M. Thomas Inge, ed., *Truman Capote: Conversations* (Jackson: University Press of Mississippi, 1987).

Bibliographies:

Richard Wall and Carl Craycraft, "A Checklist of Works about Truman Capote," *Bulletin of the New York Public Library,* 71 (March 1967): 165–172;

Jackson R. Bryer, "Truman Capote: A Bibliography," in *In Cold Blood: A Critical Handbook,* edited by Irving Malin (Belmont, Cal.: Wadsworth, 1968), pp. 239–269;

David Vanderwerken, "Truman Capote: 1943–1968–A Critical Bibliography," *Bulletin of Bibliography,* 27 (1970): 57–60, 71;

Robert J. Stanton, *Truman Capote: A Primary and Secondary Bibliography* (Boston: G. K. Hall, 1980).

Biographies:

Ann Taylor Fleming, "The Private World of Truman Capote," *New York Times Magazine,* 9 July 1978, pp. 22–25; 16 July 1978, pp. 12–15;

John Malcolm Brinnin, *Sextet: T. S. Eliot and Truman Capote and Others* (New York: Delacorte Press/Seymour Lawrence, 1981), pp. 3–96;

Marie Rudisill and James C. Simmons, *Truman Capote: The Story of His Bizarre and Exotic Boyhood by an Aunt Who Helped Raise Him* (New York: Morrow, 1983);

Brinnin, *Dear Heart, Old Buddy* (New York: Delacorte Press/Seymour Lawrence, 1986);

Jack Dunphy, *Dear Genius . . . A Memoir of My Life with Truman Capote* (New York: McGraw-Hill, 1987);

Donald Windham, *Lost Friendships: A Memoir of Truman Capote, Tennessee Williams, and Others* (New York: Morrow, 1987);

Gerald Clarke, *Truman Capote: A Biography* (New York: Simon & Schuster, 1988);

Marianne M. Moates, *Truman Capote's Southern Years: Stories from a Monroeville Cousin* (Tuscaloosa: University of Alabama Press, 1996).

References:

John Aldridge, "Capote and Buechner: The Escape into Otherness," in *After the Lost Generation: A Critical Study of the Writers of Two Wars* (New York: Noonday Press, 1951), pp. 194–230;

Aldridge, "The Metaphorical World of Truman Capote," *Western Review,* 15 (Summer 1951): 247–260;

Blake Allmendinger, "The Room Was Locked, with the Key on the Inside: Female Influence in Truman Capote's 'My Side of the Matter,'" *Studies in Short Fiction,* 24 (Summer 1987): 279–288;

Nona Balakian, "The Prophetic Vogue of the Anti-Heroine," *Southwest Review,* 47 (Spring 1962): 134–141;

Nancy Blake, "*Other Voices, Other Rooms:* Southern Gothic or Medieval Quest?" *Delta,* 11 (November 1980): 31–47;

Robert Davis, "*Other Voices, Other Rooms* and the Ocularity of American Fiction," *Delta,* 11 (November 1980): 1–14;

Chester Eisinger, *Fiction of the Forties* (Chicago: University of Chicago Press, 1963), pp. 237–243;

Helen S. Garson, "From Success to Failure: Capote's *The Grass Harp,*" *Southern Quarterly,* 33 (Winter–Spring 1995): 35–43;

Garson, *Truman Capote* (New York: Ungar, 1980);

Garson, "Truman Capote," in *Fifty Southern Writers after 1900,* edited by Joseph M. Flora and Robert Bain (New York: Greenwood Press, 1987), pp. 99–110;

Garson, *Truman Capote: A Study of the Short Fiction* (New York: Twayne, 1992);

Craig M. Goad, *Daylight and Darkness, Dream and Delusion: The Works of Truman Capote* (Emporia, Kan.: Emporia State Research Studies, 1967);

Louise Gossett, *Violence in Recent Southern Fiction* (Durham, N.C.: Duke University Press, 1965), pp. 145–158;

Richard Gray, *The Literature of Memory: Modern Writers of the American South* (Baltimore: Johns Hopkins University Press, 1977), pp. 257–265;

Ihab Hassan, "Truman Capote: The Vanishing Image of Narcissus," in *Radical Innocence: Studies in the Contemporary American Novel* (Princeton: Princeton University Press, 1961), pp. 230–258;

Alfred Kazin, *Bright Book of Life: American Novelists and Story-Tellers from Hemingway to Mailer* (Boston: Little, Brown, 1973), pp. 209–219;

Paul Levine, "Truman Capote: The Revelation of the Broken Image," *Virginia Quarterly Review,* 34 (Autumn 1958): 600–617;

Irving Malin, *New American Gothic* (Carbondale: Southern Illinois University Press, 1962);

Malin, ed., *Truman Capote's "In Cold Blood": A Critical Handbook* (Belmont, Cal.: Wadsworth, 1968);

Albert Moravia, "Truman Capote and the New Baroque," from "Two American Writers," *Sewanee Review,* 68 (Summer 1960): 473–481;

William Nance, *The Worlds of Truman Capote* (New York: Stein & Day, 1970);

Kenneth T. Reed, *Truman Capote* (Boston: Twayne, 1981);

Robert Siegle, "Capote's *Handcarved Coffins* and the Nonfictional Novel," *Contemporary Literature,* 25 (1984): 437–451;

Lee Zacharias, "Living the American Dream: 'Children on Their Birthdays,'" *Studies in Short Fiction,* 12 (Fall 1975): 343–350.

Papers:

Truman Capote's papers are at the Library of Congress and at the New York Public Library.

Ana Castillo

(15 June 1953 –)

Ibis Gómez-Vega
Northern Illinois University

See also the Castillo entry in *DLB 122: Chicano Writers, Second Series.*

BOOKS: *Otro Canto* (Chicago: Alternativa Publications, 1977);

The Invitation (Chicago: Ana Castillo, 1979);

Women Are Not Roses (Houston, Tex.: Arte Público Press, 1984);

The Mixquiahuala Letters (Binghamton, N.Y.: Bilingual Press/Editorial Bilingüe, 1986);

Sapogonia: An Anti-Romance in 3/8 Meter (Tempe, Ariz.: Bilingual Press/Editorial Bilingüe, 1990; revised edition, New York: Anchor Books, 1994);

My Father Was a Toltec (Albuquerque, N.Mex.: West End Press, 1988);

So Far from God (New York: Norton, 1993; London: Women's Press, 1994);

My Father Was a Toltec and Selected Poems, 1973–1988 (New York: Norton, 1995);

Massacre of the Dreamers: Essays on Xicanisma (Albuquerque, N.Mex.: University of New Mexico Press, 1994);

Lover Boys (New York: Norton, 1996);

Peel My Love Like an Onion (New York: Doubleday, 1999).

OTHER: "Mi Maestro," in *Zero Makes Me Hungry,* edited by Edward Sueders and Primus St. John (Glenview, Ill.: Scott-Foresman, 1975), p. 122;

"El ser mujer" and "Euthanasia," in *Second Chicano Literary Prize* (Irvine: University of California Press, 1976), pp. 147–154;

"Napa, California," "1975," "A Christmas Carol: c. 1976," and "Our Tongue Was Nahuatl," in *The Third Woman: Minority Women Writers of the United States,* edited by Dexter Fisher (Boston: Houghton Mifflin, 1979), pp. 386–392;

"Carta," "Seduction of the Poetess," "El sueño," "Thoughts on a Late August Night," "Poem 13," and "Invierno salvaje," in *Canto al Pueblo: Antología* (Mesa, Ariz.: Arizona Canto al Pueblo, 1980), pp. 34–43;

Ana Castillo (photograph by Barbara Seyda; from the dust jacket for Peel My Love Like an Onion, *1999)*

"Napa, California," in *Women Poets of the World,* edited by Joanna Bankier and Deirdre Lashgari (New York: Macmillan, 1983), pp. 395–396;

"Entre primavera y otoño" and "Martes en Toledo," in *Esta puente, mi espalda,* edited by Castillo and Cheríe Moraga (San Francisco: Ism Press, 1988), pp. 94–97;

Esta Puente, Mi Espalda: Voces de mujeres tercermundistas en los Estados Unidos, edited and translated by Castillo with Moraga and Norma Alarcón (San Francisco: Ism Press, 1988);

Third Woman: The Sexuality of Latinas, edited by Castillo with Moraga and Alarcón (Berkeley, Cal.: Third Woman Press, 1989);

"La Macha: Toward a Beautiful Whole Self" and "What Only Lovers," in *Chicana Lesbians,* edited by Carla

Trujillo (Berkeley, Cal.: Third Woman Press, 1991), pp. 24–48, 60–61;

"Massacre of the Dreamers: Reflections on Mexican Indian Women in the U.S.: 500 Years after the Conquest," in *Critical Fictions,* edited by Philomela Mariani (Seattle: Bay Press, 1991), pp. 161–176;

"Nani Worries about Her Father's Happiness in the Afterlife," "Seduced by Natassja Kinski," "An Ugly Dog Named Goya," and "Zoila López," in *After Aztlán,* edited by Ray Gonzalez (Boston: Godine, 1992), pp. 18–22;

"Women Are Not Roses," "From 'A Letter to Alicia,'" "Whole," "The Toltec," and "Paradox," in *Infinite Divisions: An Anthology of Chicana Literature,* edited by Tey Diana Rebolledo and Eliana S. Rivero (Tucson: University of Arizona Press, 1993), pp. 94–95, 105–107, 145, 303–304;

Recent Chicano Poetry/Neueste Chicano-Lyrik, edited by Castillo and Heiner Bus, introduction by Castillo (Bamberg: Bamberger Editionen, 1994);

Mariano Azuela, *The Underdogs,* introduction by Castillo (New York: Signet, 1996);

"Extraordinarily Woman," in *Goddess of the Americas,* edited, with an introduction, by Castillo (New York: Riverhead Books, 1996), pp. 72–78;

"El Chicle," in *El Coro: A Chorus of Latino and Latina Poetry,* edited by Martín Espada (Amherst: University of Massachusetts Press, 1997), p. 37;

"Yes, dear critic, there really is an Alicia," in *Máscaras,* edited by Lucha Corpi (Berkeley, Cal.: Third Woman Press, 1997), pp. 152–160;

"Anaïs Nin, All the Rest Is Origami," in *Conjunctions,* edited by Martine Bellen and others (Annandale-on-Hudson, N.Y.: Bard College, 1997), pp. 260–264.

SELECTED PERIODICAL PUBLICATIONS– UNCOLLECTED:

POETRY

"The Vigil (and the Vow)" and "Untitled," as Castillo Rivera, *Revista Chicano-Riqueña,* 3 (Spring 1975): 11–12.

FICTION

"Antihero," in *Nosotras: Latina Literature Today,* edited by María del Carmen Boza and others (Binghamton, N.Y.: Bilingual Review/Press, 1986), pp. 71–72.

NONFICTION

"Watsonville: A Case of Chicana Activism," *Gulliver,* 26, no. 2 (1989): 25–38;

"A Chicana from Chicago," *Essence* (June 1993): 42, 130;

"Selena Aside," *Nation,* 260 (29 May 1995): 764–766;

"Chicago con Salsa," *New York Times Magazine: Sophisticated Traveler,* 12 November 1995, pp. 22–23, 56–60;

"The Real Frida Kahlo: Flamboyant, Yet Private; The Writings of a Tormented Artist Who Loved Life," *Washington Post,* 11 December 1995, D11;

"A Healing Legacy," *Ms.,* 7 (September–October 1996): 92–95;

"The Overlooked Half of the Farm Workers' Triumph," *Los Angeles Times,* 20 April 1997, M2;

"Bowing Out," *Salon Magazine* [online], 12 April 1999.

Ana Castillo is one of a few Mexican American writers who have attracted the attention of the mainstream reading public. From her earliest writing she has tried to unite those segments of the American population often separated by class, economics, gender, and sexual orientation. Her success is a tribute to her self-discipline, her courage, and her considerable literary ability.

Castillo was born in Chicago on 15 June 1953 to Raymond Castillo and Raquel Rocha Castillo, struggling working-class people. In a 1997 interview Castillo told Elsa Saeta that she attended a "secretarial high school," studying to become a file clerk, which her parents considered a good job. Castillo, however, had other ideas. She said that she was "a lousy typist" and had an "aversion to authority," so she abandoned secretarial training. After attending Chicago City College for two years, she transferred to Northeastern Illinois University, where she majored in secondary education, planning to teach art. She received her B.A. in 1975.

Castillo's experience as a student at Northeastern Illinois was largely negative, she explained in the interview, because "the extent of the racism and the sexism of the university in a city like Chicago discouraged" her from becoming an art teacher. She went on: "by the time I was finishing my B.A.–and it took a lot of work to get scholarships and grants to get through the university system–I was really convinced that I had no talent. I couldn't draw and I had no right to be painting." As a result of these experiences, Castillo stopped painting. During her third year of college, however, she resumed writing poetry.

These first poems were a response to her grandmother's death. In the introduction to *My Father Was a Toltec* (1988) she claims to have been "possessed suddenly to compose from a place so deep within it felt like the voice of an ancestor embedded in a recessive gene." Appropriately written on the "ugly" yellow pages of a utilitarian notepad picked up at the factory where her mother worked, the poems, she says, "were short, roughly whittled saetas [couplets from a poem or song] of sorrow spun out of the biting late winter of Chicago" that allowed the child poet to work through her pain. "If it hadn't been that my mother got it for me, and at no cost, at the factory," she says, "I wouldn't have had a pad on which to give birth to my first poems." Her family's working-class status set the stage for a developing writer who throughout her literary career has examined pervasive social and economic inequities that affect women and Latinos in the United States.

Castillo's literary career began before she finished college. At twenty she gave her first poetry reading at Northeastern Illinois University, and in 1975 *Revista Chicano-Riqueña* published two of her poems, "The Vigil (and the Vow)" and "Untitled." That same year another poem, "Mi Maestro," was included in the anthology *Zero Makes Me Hungry*. The following year the *Revista Chicano-Riqueña* published a second group of her poems about racial injustice, particularly the fate of indigenous peoples in America. Mindful of her previous experience as a painter, Castillo told Saeta, she promised herself never to take writing courses "with anybody or any university . . . because I was so afraid that I would be discouraged and told that I had no right to be writing poetry, that I didn't write English well enough, that I didn't write Spanish well enough." Like many other Latino poets of her generation, Castillo felt that she had "no models that spoke to my experience and in my languages," and she admits in the introduction to *My Father Was a Toltec* that she felt compelled to "carve out for myself the definition of 'good.'" She wanted to be a good poet, but a poet on her own terms, with a political conscience and fluency in the two languages that she used to navigate through a predominantly Anglo world.

Despite her uncertainty about the value of her poems, Castillo continued to write and develop her poetic voice. Caught up in the political fervor of the 1970s and concerned by the plight of Latinos in the United States, she told Saeta in 1997 that she thought of herself as "a political poet, or what is sometimes called a protest poet talking about the economic inequality of Latino people in this country." One of her early poems, "Invierno salvaje" (Savage Winter), written in 1975 and published in the anthology *Canto al Pueblo* (1980), addresses the difficult lives of Latinos during a hard winter. When the worker-poet asks the harsh winter, "¿Intentas matarnos?" (Do you intend to kill us?), the answer is that winter, harsh as it may be, "No tendrás / el honor" (will not have the honor) because "Las fábricas / nos esperan / y la voz / del mayordomo / es aún más fuerte / que la tuya" (The factories / await us / and the voice / of the foreman / is more powerful / than yours). "The New Declaration of Independence," published in *Revista Chicano-Riqueña* in 1976, celebrates the political awareness of "an entire people / who are coming together as ONE! / At last . . . At last!" Castillo's work should be read with an awareness of what Yvonne Yarbro-Bejarano describes in "Chicana Literature from a Chicana Feminist Perspective" (1988) as "the most important principle of Chicana feminist criticism . . . the realization that the Chicana's experience as a woman

Dust jacket for Castillo's 1993 novel, which incorporates elements of magic realism

is inextricable from her experience as a member of an oppressed working-class racial minority and a culture which is not the dominant culture."

In 1975 Castillo moved to Sonoma County, California, where she taught ethnic studies for a year at Santa Rosa Junior College. Returning to Chicago in 1976, she pursued a master's degree in Latin American and Caribbean studies in 1978 and 1979. In 1977 she published a chapbook, *Otro Canto* (Other Song), in which she collected her earlier political poems, including "Napa, California," dedicated to migrant-labor activist César Chávez, and "1975," a poem about "talking proletariat talks." From 1977 to 1979 she was writer in residence for the Illinois Arts Council. In 1979 she published her second chapbook, *The Invitation,* a collection that exhibits for the first time Castillo's interest in sexuality and the oppression of women, especially Latinas. She also received her M.A. degree in 1979 from the University of Chicago and between 1980 and 1981 was poet in residence of the Urban Gateways of Chicago. A son, Marcel Ramón Herrera, was born on 21 September 1983.

In 1984 Arte Público Press published *Women Are Not Roses,* a collection of poems that includes some poems from her chapbooks. In 1986 her first novel, *The Mixquiahuala Letters,* which she had begun writing in 1979, was published by the Bilingual Press; it received the Before Columbus Foundation's American Book Award in 1987. Written as a series of letters from Teresa, a Latina, to her Anglo-Spanish friend Alicia, the novel reveals Teresa's complicated feelings for Alicia during their ten-year friendship. Castillo provides three tables of contents or reading strategies, labeled "For the Conformist," "For the Cynic," and "For the Quixotic."

Regardless of which reading strategy the reader chooses, *The Mixquiahuala Letters* begins with Teresa's description of three trips to Mexico taken by Teresa and Alicia, together or separately, and follows a narrative through which Teresa not only reminds her friend what happened during their time together but also admits her own feelings of love and hate. Anne Bower claims that *The Mixquiahuala Letters* "is very much a quest novel . . . with form and explanation taking us into the women's emotional and artistic searches," while Erlinda Gonzales-Berry argues that in Castillo's "letter writing project, the letter simultaneously functions as a bridge and as a boundary between subject and object." Gonzales-Berry believes that the letter "verbally links the receiver, (Other), to the sender, (Self), but it also posits the other as the impenetrable mirror that reflects the specular image of the speaking-writing subject." She argues that this binary opposition is necessary so that Teresa can exorcise "her rage . . . through the act of writing" because "in the act of sharing [her letters with Alicia], Teresa discovers her love for Alicia."

Castillo pointed out in a 1991 interview with Marta A. Navarro that Teresa compares and contrasts herself with Alicia throughout the novel because she is dealing with "a very real, painful reality for Mexicanas, brown women who don't fit into the aesthetic" of what is considered beautiful in North America. According to Castillo, Teresa's letters address "the fact that in patriarchy, all women are possessions, but the highest possession, . . . is the white woman." Thus, although in one letter Teresa admits to driving "sixteen and a half hours just to ask you to *dance* with me," in another she tries to explain "why I hated white women and sometimes didn't like you." Teresa's ambivalent feelings for Alicia gradually evolve into a homoerotic subtext that recurs throughout Castillo's work, although Castillo told Navarro that her female characters cannot identify themselves as lesbians because they are not "willing to give up that hope for identity through the male" that is so important to them.

By 1985 Castillo was once again in California teaching at San Francisco State University, becoming more and more involved as an editor for Third Woman Press and receiving early praise for *The Mixquiahuala Let-*

ters. After the novel received the Before Columbus Foundation's American Book Award in 1987, Castillo was further honored by the Women's Foundation of San Francisco in 1988 with the Women of Words Award for "pioneering excellence in literature." Still needing money and finding it difficult to raise her son alone, she taught Chicano humanities and literature at Sonoma State University in 1988, creative writing and fiction writing at California State University at Chico as a visiting professor in 1988–1989, and Chicana feminist literature at the University of California at Santa Barbara as a dissertation fellow/lecturer for the Chicano Studies Department during the same school year. In 1989 she received a California Arts Council Fellowship for Fiction and in 1990 a National Endowment for the Arts Fellowship.

Castillo's second novel, *Sapogonia: An Anti-Romance in 3/8 Meter* (1990), was written in Chicago in 1984 and 1985 while she was teaching English as a second language and taking care of her new baby. The novel springs from her passion for flamenco music, which had earlier led her to the Al-Andalus flamenco performance group, with which she performed in 1981 and 1982; Máximo Madrigal is the main male character in the novel and a second-generation flamenco artist. Although Castillo denies that the novel is autobiographical, several aspects of the female protagonist, Pastora Velásquez Aké, are reminiscent of the author's life. Pastora sings her own poems, becomes involved in liberation politics, and questions her Catholic faith. Toward the end of *Sapogonia,* she "rejoices over the child that was sprouting from her very soul," happy even though she has neither married Eduardo, the child's probable father, nor told him that she is with child. She plans to give birth to the child and "teach it to fly," expecting to rear him or her alone, an act of defiance even for a lapsed Catholic.

On the back page of the original Bilingual Press edition of 1990, Rudolfo A. Anaya called *Sapogonia* "a literary triumph." The novel is a complicated narrative about the love/hate relationship between Pastora and Máximo. Yarbro-Bejarano argues in "The Multiple Subject in the Writing of Ana Castillo" (1992) that *Sapogonia* "explores male fantasy, its potential for violence against women and the female subject's struggle to interpret herself both within and outside of this discourse on femininity," a discourse that, in *Sapogonia,* evolves through Pastora's web of connections with both men and women as well as through her commitment to Latino politics.

By the early 1990s Castillo was a fellow at the University of California at Santa Barbara, where she gave a seminar and researched her dissertation. She received her Ph.D. in American studies from the University of Bremen in 1991 with a dissertation on Xicanisma, or Chicana feminism, subsequently published as *Massacre of the Dreamers: Essays on Xicanisma* (1994). Patricia Dubrava describes the book as "a collection of essays on the experience of the 'Mexic Amerindian' (Castillo's term) women living in the United States and a meditation on the recent history of Mexic activism." In this book Castillo advocates "our own mythmaking from which to establish role models to guide us out of historical convolution and de-evolution," and she believes these myths should address "our spiritual, political, and erotic needs as a people." According to Rosaura Sánchez, Castillo is a "cultural feminist" whose book "for the most part focuses on cultural differences," but Sánchez sees "a running thread of biologism in the text that would be difficult to construe as other than deterministic and essentialist."

In August 1990, before completing her Ph.D., Castillo moved to New Mexico, where she began to write her third novel. According to Bill Varble, she "had been mourning the death of her father, and recently read a book on saints to research another novel" when she sat down to write "the first chapter of *So Far from God* one afternoon in September of 1990."

By far her best novel, *So Far from God* (1993) distinguishes itself through Castillo's use of the New Mexicans' English sprinkled with Spanish, a language whose rhythm often makes the characters' English sound like Spanish. In a 1993 interview with Robert Birnbaum, Castillo describes "listening very carefully [to the New Mexicans' speech patterns] because the way you use language is the way you're experiencing life." The characters in this novel use double negatives and "code switch" (alternate) between Spanish and English as they communicate. Reading *So Far from God* prompted Sandra Cisneros to exult on the jacket of Castillo's book,

> This Ana Castillo has gone and done what I always wanted to do—written a Chicana *telenovela*—a novel roaring down Interstate 25 at one hundred and fifteen miles an hour with an almanac of Chicanismo—saints, martyrs, t.v. mystics, home remedies, little miracles, *dichos,* myths, gossip, recipes—fluttering from the fender like a flag. Wacky, wild, y bien funny. ¡Dale gas, girl!

Other Latino critics also praised the Spanish feeling of the novel, and Jaime Armín Mejía called the novel a "contagiously fast-moving, silly, irreverent, yet wise series of tales from Nuevo Méjico." Mejía also praised the voice of the female narrator, who calls herself a "*metiche mitotera,*" the equivalent of a busybody, who "is privy to all that transpires to everyone and everything . . . [and] intrudes into the *novela*'s postmodern narrative to fill it with *chisme* (gossip), *remedios* (remedies), and *recetas* (recipes)." This narrator's Latin voice provides "readers a not always reliable but certainly a culturally rich understanding of the *nueva mexicana* community" where the novel is set.

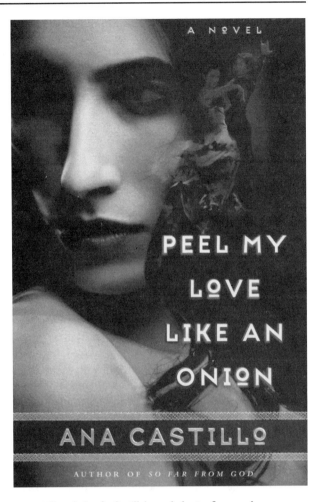

Dust jacket for Castillo's novel about a flamenco dancer with a leg weakened by polio

So Far from God, Castillo's best-known novel, focuses on the lives of a New Mexican mother, Sofia, and her four daughters, who seem doomed to live chaotic lives from page one when la Loca levitates during her own funeral and ascends to the roof of the church. What follows is an intricately developed story through which the four daughters—Fé (Faith), Esperanza (Hope), Caridad (Charity), and la Loca—live their lives and die young. Fé dies from exposure to chemicals at a job that promised to help her achieve the "American Dream" to which she aspired. Esperanza, the only one of the four sisters who leaves her hometown in Tome and, thereby, the safety offered by the family, disappears during Desert Storm as she covers the war for a news station. Caridad is first attacked and left disfigured by "la malogra," the evil that lurks out in the night, and then is miraculously healed during one of la Loca's seizures. Caridad not only becomes herself again but also becomes a healer; shortly after falling in love with a woman, she takes the woman's hand and plunges off a mountain to become, perhaps, a mythological character. La Loca, a character who never leaves home, contracts AIDS from no apparent source and dies, leaving Sofia, alone and angry, to become a radical political organizer.

So Far from God is simultaneously funny and sad, as Castillo examines several different issues at once. Fé's story illustrates what can happen to Latinas who turn their backs on their culture to pursue material possessions. Sofia's story is probably the most poignant; even before she loses all four daughters, she becomes a community activist, hoping to improve the lives of the people of Tome. Because spirituality also plays a significant role in this novel, many critics consider it Castillo's homegrown version of Mexican American magic realism, but So Far from God is actually a work in which the lives of five women are realistically defined not by their imaginations but by their connections to each other and the world around them. In 1993 the novel won the Carl Sandburg Literary Award in Fiction and the National Association of Chicano Studies Certificate of Distinguished Recognition for "Outstanding Contributions to the Arts, Academia, and to Our Community." The following year, So Far From God won the Mountains and Plains Bookseller Award, and Castillo also received a second National Endowment for the Arts Fellowship in fiction.

In 1996 Castillo published Lover Boys, an uneven but interesting collection of short stories. Brian Evenson, writing for the Review of Contemporary Fiction (Spring 1997), claims that "as intriguing as the book's cultural depictions is the complex way in which gender and desire are figured and refigured from story to story." Evenson recognizes in the stories a theme that runs through much of Castillo's work, "desire of all types, heterosexual and homosexual, from women who flirt with other women despite feeling themselves largely heterosexual, to the lesbian in the title story who finds herself drawn irresistibly to a young man." Reviewing the book in Library Journal (July 1996), Barbara Hoffert called the stories "terse, fragmentary pieces" but added that Castillo's "strength would seem to be in capturing character through a well-sketched situation." Likewise, Catherine Bush in The New York Times Book Review (8 September 1996) complained that Castillo has "grown a little too enamored of the sound of her own voice," which Bush described as a "discursive, conversational style," but she added that "this voice has a vibrancy that compels attention, jamming ribald humor up against pathos and melancholy desire." Donna Seaman in Booklist (August 1996) found Castillo's work "defiant, satirically hilarious, sexy, and wise," as well as "tirelessly inventive." Seaman also noted that "Castillo's strong women tend to be creative . . . , well traveled, independent, resourceful, sensual, given to drink and laughter and solitude, and wildly skeptical about the possibilities of finding happiness anywhere other than deep within their own vibrant souls."

In Peel My Love Like an Onion (1999), Castillo returns to one of her favorite themes: flamenco dancing and music. Castillo creates Carmen, "La Coja" ("the cripple"), whom she invests with an obsession to become a flamenco dancer although she is not a gypsy and one of her legs is afflicted by polio. As she laments at the beginning of the novel,

> Nothing sadder than a washed-up dancer. I was beyond sad. One day you turn thirty-six years old. The sum of your education is a high school diploma. No other skills but to dance as a gimp flamenco dancer, and your polio-inflicted condition is suddenly worsening. Nowhere to go but down.

The trip down, however, is filled with convoluted love stories about Carmen and Manolo and Carmen and Agustín, both dancers and gypsies as well. These two men dance in and out of Carmen's life without ever committing to much more than a good time. Máximo Madrigal, the main character from Sapogonia, makes an appearance as a flamenco musician who becomes Carmen La Coja's gallant, but temporary, lover. Peel My Love Like an Onion is the first of Castillo's novels to be deeply concerned with the erotic lives of its main characters.

Carmen is in many ways defined by her nonsupportive, selfish family. They recognize her passion for dancing only when she becomes a singer earning good money. That she could become a flamenco dancer in spite of her "condition" escapes them, and they are not capable of giving her more than occasional reassurance, a lack of support that might explain why Carmen expects nothing of the men in her life. Her one purpose and joy in life is to be onstage dancing to flamenco music.

Castillo's novels, short stories, and poetry all emerge from a working-class, Latina sensibility; yet, her work has crossed social and ethnic lines to examine issues common to all people regardless of their cultural backgrounds or ethnicity. Her detailed descriptions of a specifically Latino culture are the backdrop for a body of literature that speaks to people of all cultures.

Interviews:

Wolfgang Binder, "Ana Castillo," in Partial Autobiographies, edited by Binder (Erlanger: Verlag Palm & Enke Erlangen, 1985), pp. 28–38;

Marta A. Navarro, "Interview with Ana Castillo," in Chicana Lesbians, edited by Carla Trujillo (Berkeley, Cal.: Third Woman Press, 1991), pp. 113–132;

Jacqueline Mitchell and others, "Entrevista a Ana Castillo," MESTER, 20, no. 2 (1991): 145–156;

Robert Birnbaum, "Ana Castillo," *Stuff* (June 1993): 53–56;

Simón Romero, "Interview," *Nu-City,* 18 June – 1 July 1993, pp. 1, 8;

Elsa Saeta, "Interview with Ana Castillo," *Texas College English,* 26 (Fall 1993): 1–7;

Bill Verble, "¡Xicanisma!" *Mail Tribune,* 27 February 1994, pp. 1C, 7C;

Patricia Dubrava, "Ana Castillo: Impressions of a Xicana Dreamer," *Bloomsbury Review,* 15 (November–December 1995): 5, 13;

Saeta, "A *MELUS* Interview: Ana Castillo," *MELUS,* 22, no. 3 (1997): 133–149.

References:

Norma Alarcón, "The Sardonic Powers of the Erotic in the Work of Ana Castillo," in *Breaking Boundaries,* edited by Asunción Horno-Delgado and others (Amherst: University of Massachusetts Press, 1989), pp. 94–107;

Elyette Benjamin-Labarthe, "L'Amour et la haine dans un roman chicano contemporaine: *Sapogonia* d'Ana Castillo," in *Etats-Unis/Mexique: Fascinations et repulsions reciproques,* edited by Serge Ricard (Paris: L'Hamarttan, 1996), pp. 193–208;

Benjamin-Labarthe, "*Sapogonia* d'Ana Castillo, ou le feuillete des identifications," *Annales du Centre de Recherches sur l'Amerique Anglophone,* 20 (1995): 157–170, 237–238;

Tanya Long Bennet, "No Country to Call Home: A Study of Castillo's *Mixquiahuala Letters,*" *Style,* 30 (Fall 1996): 462–478;

Anne L. Bower, "Remapping the Territory: Ana Castillo's *The Mixquiahuala Letters,*" in her *Epistolary Responses* (Bloomington: Indiana University Press, 1996), pp. 132–150;

Debra A. Castillo, "Borderliners: Federico Campbell and Ana Castillo," in *Reconfigured Spheres,* edited by Margaret R. Higonnet and Joan Templeton (Amherst: University of Massachusetts Press, 1994), pp. 147–170;

Barbara Brinson Curiel, "Heteroglossia in Ana Castillo's *The Mixquiahuala Letters,*" *Discurso: Revista de Estudios Iberoamericanos,* 7, no. 1 (1990): 11–23;

Theresa Delgadillo, "Forms of Chicana Feminist Resistance: Hybrid Spirituality in Ana Castillo's *So Far from God,*" *MFS: Modern Fiction Studies,* 44 (Winter 1998): 888–916;

Ibis Gómez-Vega, "Debunking Myths: The Hero's Role in Ana Castillo's *Sapogonia,*" *Americas Review,* 22 (Spring–Summer 1994): 244–258;

Erlinda Gonzales-Berry, "*The* (Subversive) *Mixquiahuala Letters:* An Antidote for Self-Hate," *L'Ici et ailleurs,* 16 (1987): 227–240;

Carmela Delia Lanza, "Hearing Voices: Women and Home in Ana Castillo's *So Far from God,*" *MELUS,* 23 (Spring 1998): 65–79;

Jaime Armin Mejía, "*So Far from God* by Ana Castillo," *Southwestern American Literature,* 19 (Fall 1993): 94–95;

Colette Morrow, "Queering Chicano/a Narratives: Lesbian as Healer, Saint, and Warrior in Ana Castillo's *So Far from God,*" *MMLA,* 30 (Spring 1997): 63–80;

Silvia Novo Peña, "Ana Castillo," in *¡LATINAS! Women of Achievement,* edited by Diane Telgen and Jim Kamp (Detroit: Visible Ink, 1996), pp. 63–66;

Rafael Pérez-Torres, *Movements in Chicano Poetry* (Cambridge: Cambridge University Press, 1995);

Kamala Platt, "Ecocritical Chicana Literature: Ana Castillo's 'Virtual Realism,'" *Isle: Interdisciplinary Studies in Literature and Environment,* 3 (Summer 1996): 67–96;

Alvina E. Quintana, "Ana Castillo's *The Mixquiahuala Letters:* The Novelist as Ethnographer," in *Criticism in the Borderlands,* edited by Héctor Calderón and José David Saldívar (Durham, N.C.: Duke University Press, 1991), pp. 72–83; republished as "Shades of the Indigenous Ethnographer: Ana Castillo's *Mixquiahuala Letters,*" in Quintana's *Home Girls: Chicana Literary Voices* (Philadelphia: Temple University Press, 1996), pp. 75–92;

Elsa Saeta, "Ana Castillo's *Sapogonia:* Narrative Point of View as a Study in Perception," *Confluencia,* 10 (Fall 1994): 67–72;

Alberto Sandoval Sánchez, "Breaking the Silence, Dismantling Taboos: Latino Novels on AIDS," *Journal of Homosexuality,* 34 (March 1998): 155–175;

Rosaura Sánchez, "Reconstructing Chicana Gender Identity," *American Literary History,* 9, no. 2 (1997): 350–363;

Roland Walter, "The Cultural Politics of Dislocation and Relocation in the Novels of Ana Castillo," *MELUS,* 23 (Spring 1998): 81–97;

Yvonne Yarbro-Bejarano, "Chicana Literature from a Chicana Feminist Perspective," in *Chicana Creativity and Criticism: Charting New Frontiers in American Literature,* edited by Maria Hererra-Sobek and Helena Maria Viramontes (Houston, Tex.: Arte Público Press, 1988), pp. 139–145;

Yarbro-Bejarano, "The Multiple Subject in the Writing of Ana Castillo," *Americas Review,* 20 (Spring 1992): 65–72.

Papers:

Ana Castillo's papers for 1973–1990 are housed at the University of California, Santa Barbara.

John Cheever

(27 May 1912 – 18 June 1982)

Patrick Meanor
State University of New York College at Oneonta

See also the Cheever entries in *DLB 2: American Novelists Since World War II; DLB 102: American Short-Story Writers, 1910–1945, Second Series; DLB Yearbook 1980;* and *DLB Yearbook 1982.*

BOOKS: *The Way Some People Live* (New York: Random House, 1943);

The Enormous Radio and Other Stories (New York: Funk & Wagnalls, 1953; London: Gollancz, 1953);

The Wapshot Chronicle (New York: Harper, 1957; London: Gollancz, 1957);

The Housebreaker of Shady Hill and Other Stories (New York: Harper, 1958; London: Gollancz, 1959);

Some People, Places, and Things That Will Not Appear in My Next Novel (New York: Harper & Row, 1961; London: Gollancz, 1961);

The Brigadier and the Golf Widow (New York: Harper & Row, 1964; London: Gollancz, 1965);

The Wapshot Scandal (New York: Harper & Row, 1964; London: Gollancz, 1964);

Homage to Shakespeare (Stevenson, Conn.: Country Squire, 1968);

Bullet Park (New York: Knopf, 1969; London: Cape, 1969);

The World of Apples (New York: Knopf, 1973; London: Cape, 1974);

Falconer (New York: Knopf, 1977; London: Cape, 1977);

The Day the Pig Fell into the Well (Northridge, Cal.: Lord John, 1978);

The Stories of John Cheever (New York: Knopf, 1978; London: Cape, 1979);

The Leaves, the Lion-Fish and the Bear (Los Angeles: Sylvester & Orphanos, 1980);

Oh What a Paradise It Seems (New York: Knopf, 1982; London: Cape, 1982);

The National Pastime (Los Angeles: Sylvester & Orphanos, 1982);

Atlantic Crossing: Excerpts from the Journals of John Cheever (Cottondale, Ala.: Ex Ophidia, 1986);

John Cheever

The Journals of John Cheever, edited by Robert Gottlieb (New York: Knopf, 1991);

Thirteen Uncollected Stories of John Cheever, edited by Franklin H. Dennis (Chicago: Academy Chicago Publishers, 1994).

Edition: *The Wapshot Chronicle,* with a new introduction by Cheever (New York: Time, 1965).

Few American writers have been so clear in mapping their recurrent subject matter and themes as John Cheever. From his first published story, "Expelled," he has been concerned with the Fall from a condition of Edenic childlike innocence into the painful chaos of adult knowledge. Most of his novels and stories share the theme of the Fall or are variations on the same theme. This recurring concern is so ingrained in Cheever's work that he can be considered a mythopoeic writer, as was William Faulkner, that is, a writer who managed to create a mythic world of his own. Faulkner's Yoknapatawpha County is instantaneously recognizable, and so, too, is Cheever's early mythopoeic world of St. Botolphs and its later Westchester equivalents of Shady Hill, Proxmire Manor, and Bullet Park. Though Cheever told Scott Donaldson in a 1987 interview that fiction was "never crypto-autobiography," a reader even slightly familiar with his work notices clear correspondences that form themselves into unmistakable patterns. And once a reader examines the letters, the journals, the interviews, and Donaldson's 1988 biography, Cheever seems to contradict himself. Certainly much of Cheever's fiction comes directly out of his own life experience and is autobiographical, but autobiographical in the patterns of those experiences rather than echoes of actual events. Most importantly, Cheever's fictive treatments of these events create rather than record what those experiences meant to him. What strikes the reader of Cheever most is the incomparable way in which he transforms the commonplace events of daily life into some of the wittiest and most profoundly moving stories in modern American literature.

John Cheever was born into a middle-class New England family on 27 May 1912 in the seaside community of Quincy, Massachusetts, a few miles south of Boston. His mother, an English-born woman named Mary Devereaux Liley, was ten years younger than John's father, Frederick Lincoln Cheever. Both of his parents figure throughout his fiction but are never so identified. Rather, they appear as types—the hard-drinking, charming, storytelling, father figure in conflict with the emotionally reserved, class-conscious workaholic mother or grandmother. They are frequently involved in the fall of a respected family from a socially prominent position because of the father's irresponsible behavior in financial or sexual matters. The mother is never the cause of the family's disintegration and is usually the agent of recovery—much resembling Mary Cheever's role in sustaining the family by creating her own businesses after her husband lost both his job and then his home during the Depression.

John Cheever's talent for mythologizing his family's background became an integral part of his storytelling reputation throughout his life. He told friends and interviewers that his father had owned a shoe factory in Lynn, Massachusetts, but scholars have never been able to find any record of such a company. His father had been, though, a successful traveling shoe salesman throughout New England and was so listed in the Quincy city directory for many years; after 1922 he was listed as a shoe manufacturer. Cheever was not content to romanticize his immediate family background, however. He accepted the family legend handed down to him by his father and embellished it with his best storyteller's voice. Though he rarely altered the facts of his family background, he did choose a remote branch of the Cheever genealogy and made himself its direct heir. He claimed that he was descended from a famous Cheever named Ezekiel, a schoolmaster at the Boston Latin School. Cotton Mather, a former student of Ezekiel Cheever, preached the latter's funeral sermon and alluded to him as Master Socrates. The actual ancestor of John Cheever was instead Daniel Cheever, the real founder of the American branch of the family. He was not a schoolmaster at Boston Latin but was, rather, a prison warden in Cambridge, Massachusetts, as was his son, Israel. Daniel was a cousin of the legendary Ezekiel, which made Ezekiel a cousin of John Cheever's great-great-great-great-great-great grandfather. John Cheever claimed to have seen his father's genealogical papers but said that they had later been accidently thrown away. One of the consistent patterns throughout John Cheever's life was his increasing inability to adhere to historical facts if alluring fictive embellishments contributed to a more compelling version of the story. And, in fact, Cheever used Ezekiel Cheever as a prototype of Ezekiel Wapshot, the founder of the Wapshot dynasty in *The Wapshot Chronicle* (1957). Indeed, the opening chapter of the novel uses the genealogical information as it appears in the Cheever family history. The main character of Cheever's final novel, *Falconer* (1977), is also named Ezekiel Farragut and echoes some characteristics of his ancestor. Both John Cheever's father and grandfather had reputations as alcoholics, which both Cheever and his brother, Fred, shared.

Cheever's mother had emigrated from England with her parents when she was six. Though Cheever resented his strong-willed mother, there is little doubt that her family, especially her mother, Sarah Liley, was responsible for fostering John's artistic gifts. One of his fondest memories is that of his maternal grandmother reading Robert Louis Stevenson, Jack London, and Charles Dickens to him before he attended Wollaston Grammar School. And it is difficult to overlook the obvious Dickensian wit in much of Cheever's work.

Indeed, the young Cheever was one of the best story-tellers at his grammar school. His teachers used his storytelling gift as a reward for their students' good behavior. Many of the stories became serials because, as Cheever later admitted, he had no clear idea of where they were heading and followed his innate feel for how effectively the story held the attention of his classmates. Cheever's daughter, Susan, in her 1984 biography of her father, *Home Before Dark,* remembers her father telling her about those early storytelling adventures: "With luck, and increasing skill, he could spin the story out over two or three periods so that the teacher and his classmates forgot all about arithmetic and geography and social studies. He told them stories about ship captains and eccentric old ladies and orphan boys, gallant men and dazzling women in a world where the potent forces of evil and darkness were confounded and good triumphed in the end. He peopled his tales with his own family and friends and neighbors." The subject matter and themes of his first novel, *The Wapshot Chronicle,* and some of his early short stories were clearly foreshadowed in those grammar school narratives. Captain Leander Wapshot and Honora Wapshot were later embodiments of Cheever's grammar school fictions.

Though there are few orphans as such in Cheever's fiction, many young boys and men feel orphaned by their loveless childhoods and are unable to express their feelings because of a New England Puritanism built into their characters. These characters surface in what Donaldson calls in his biography the "unwanted-child motif" that can be found in many typical Cheever stories and that originated in information from Cheever's own father, after several strong drinks, concerning the circumstances under which John was conceived. Frederick Lincoln Cheever told him the story repeatedly, to remind John that the only child his mother and father truly wanted was his older brother, Fred. Had his father not had two manhattans one afternoon, John would not have been conceived. His parents had wanted only one child and even invited an abortionist to dinner one evening. So wounded was John Cheever by that story that he transcribed the imagined scene of the abortionist's dinner visit into both *The Wapshot Chronicle* and *Falconer.* As Donalson's biography quotes Cheever as saying, "The greatest and most bitter mystery of my life was my father."

Tied to the recurring unwanted-child motif was Cheever's relationship with his brother, Fred. As Cheever admitted to his daughter, Susan, according to her 1984 biography: "It was the strongest love in my life." His brother and he were inseparable during their childhood and remained so well into their twenties. After a while, the brotherly relationship between John and Fred simply became too close. They had shared an apartment in Boston for two years and had planned to buy a house together in Boxford, Massachusetts, in the mid 1930s, but John later claimed that their relationship had become "morbidly close," suggesting that it was incestuous. Their love-hate impulses combined with their heavy drinking created many family crises, and the brother theme is the most important theme in all of Cheever's fiction. Though Hammer and Nailles, the two major characters in *Bullet Park* (1969), are not related by blood, their relationship is grounded in mutual destruction. Cheever himself insisted that "Goodbye, My Brother" appear first in the strict chronological arrangement of *The Stories of John Cheever* (1978), even though it postdated many stories in that collection. The brothers Moses and Coverly Wapshot are principal characters in both *The Wapshot Chronicle* and *The Wapshot Scandal* (1964). And the murder of his brother Eben by Ezekiel Farragut becomes the cause of Ezekiel's imprisonment in *Falconer.* Family relationships became the major content for most of Cheever's fiction: his mother, father, and brother became prototypes for most of the mothers, fathers, and brothers in his short stories and novels.

Though the young Cheever was a grammar school storytelling celebrity, he was never an outstanding student; he failed algebra and French in his middle-school and high-school years at the prestigious Thayer Academy in South Braintree, Massachusetts. In fact, his grades were so poor at Thayer that he dropped out and attended Quincy High School during 1928–1929, returning to Thayer in 1929 as a probationary student. His grades did not improve, and he was expelled in 1929. There were other explanations, however, as to why Cheever left Thayer Academy. Cheever later admitted that he was really thrown out of school because he was caught smoking. Then his story changed, and he said he was actually expelled for seducing the son of one of the faculty members. But, as Donaldson cautions in his biography, "it was not unusual for him to supply alternative accounts of events in his own life." The sooner students of Cheever's work begin to understand that so-called facts are not important in Cheever's world, the better will they begin to appreciate his creativity. Cheever's ability to entertain the fictive possibilities of any situation or to reveal the truth of a character's personality are much more important than facts in understanding his genius as a writer.

Undoubtedly, the most important failure of young Cheever's life—his expulsion from Thayer Academy—became the genesis of his first published short story, appropriately titled "Expelled." Cheever's ability to transform failure into success established a pattern that he repeated throughout his life. He could transform failure into success by writing honestly and openly about his own academic failure. He wrote a story about an actual event, changing some details here and there, and sent it to the literary editor of the *New Republic,* Malcolm Cowley, who accepted it for publication. Cheever's story appeared in the 1 October 1929 issue, and Cheever and Cowley remained close personal friends and professional colleagues for the rest of their lives. Indeed, Cheever often went to Cowley for advice, particularly when he was having trouble getting published. Cowley's advice, if Cheever followed it, was inevitably correct.

The publication of "Expelled" and the continuing fall of Cheever's family into financial ruin–the family lost their home when the bank foreclosed in 1932–were landmark experiences for young Cheever. Cheever's mother and father did not discuss the family's obvious financial difficulty, and John's alcoholic father retreated into his own fantasy world. His mother's solution was to start a business career by opening a gift shop in Quincy, starting a rewarding business career. Frederick resented her success and saw it as a form of humiliation. And in later years, John Cheever himself regarded his mother's "unfeminine" behavior as an embarrassment that rekindled feelings of hostility when he remembered himself as a neglected child who had to cook for himself and take care of household chores. His father drank more heavily as his mother's business success made her a proudly independent woman. Mary, who had previously been a successful head nurse at Massachusetts General Hospital, also involved herself in many charitable and civic organizations. Young John vividly recalls the lack of affection between his parents and later in life complained of his mother's icy indifference toward her husband and children. With the fall of the family into both financial and emotional chaos, Cheever decided to move to Boston with Fred.

After leaving his boyhood home, Cheever ceased any formal education but continued to read voraciously on his own, recalling years later the influences of writers who shaped his youthful imagination. He cites Gustave Flaubert's *Madame Bovary* (1856) as the book that most influenced him and claimed to have read it more than twenty-five times, calling it his "Yale College and his Harvard." He read Fyodor Dostoyevsky; Leo Tolstoy; Marcel Proust; John Donne; T. S. Eliot; W. B. Yeats; John Keats; George Gordon, Lord Byron; and Percy Bysshe Shelley. Of these, his favorite was Keats, and he had Coverly Wapshot, in *The Wapshot Scandal,* feed all of Keats's poetry into a computer to discover significant linguistic patterns. During the four years that John lived with his brother, he met important members of the literary set in Cam-

Cheever with his older brother, Fred (Cheever family collection)

bridge and Cape Cod; his most important introduction was to E. E. Cummings, with whom he struck up a warm friendship. Two older scholars helped support him for a short time. The first was Harry Dana, a Harvard professor and son of novelist Richard Henry Dana, and Hazel Hawthorne Werner, a fiction writer. Through these influential figures, he met the editors of the Boston avant-garde literary journals *Pagany* and *Hound & Horn,* where he published two early stories based on family conflicts resembling his own.

Also during these years in Boston he began to keep a journal, which eventually reached more than four million words. The appearance of his story "Bock Beer and Bermuda Onions" in the April–June 1932 issue of *Hound & Horn,* edited by Lincoln Kirstein, further promoted his burgeoning career since authors such as Eliot, Marianne Moore, Wallace Stevens, and Cummings frequently appeared in its pages. Cummings, however, warned Cheever that Boston was not the place to establish a serious literary career. According to Donaldson, Cummings told Cheever quite bluntly: "Get out of Boston. It's a city without springboards for people who can't dive." Though it took him four years to take Cummings's advice seriously, he spent those years trying to get his stories published. He also worked in department stores and as a reporter on a Quincy newspaper, but he continued to live off his brother and several charitable patrons.

Cowley suggested that Cheever apply to Yaddo, the artists' colony in Saratoga Springs, New York, so that he would have the time to write, meet other writers, artists, and musicians, and be able to pay his bills. His first application to Elizabeth Ames, Yaddo's manager, was turned down in 1933, but his next, in 1934, was approved, and he began a relationship with Ames that would last for nearly fifty years. He also established some enduring contacts there with writers such as James T. Farrell, Josephine Herbst, and Muriel Rukeyser and composer Ned Rorem. After a successful summer at Yaddo, Cheever moved to Greenwich Village in New York City, where, though desperately poor, he managed to continue writing stories. Previewing books for the *New Republic* and writing synopses of novels for M-G-M helped pay his bills. Werner, a former patron, offered him a sofa in her Waverly Place flat. Through her and Cowley, Cheever also came into contact with important writers in the city. He renewed his acquaintance with Cummings and became friendly with John Dos Passos. He also met Sherwood Anderson, James Agee, critic Edmund Wilson, the painter Milton Avery, sculptor Gaston Lachaise, and photographer Walker Evans. When not writing synopses for M-G-M, Cheever worked on his short stories and a novel he called "Empty Bed Blues." Most of his short stories were rejected, and he sought once again the counsel of Cowley. The advice Cowley offered him changed the direction of his career when he told Cheever that his stories were too long—six to seven thousand words—and that the market demanded shorter stories. He suggested writing a story a day for four days, each no longer than a thousand words. Cheever took his advice and a week later gave Cowley four stories. Cowley took one for publication in the *New Republic,* and sent two to *The New Yorker* (which accepted them), and the fourth was published in a little magazine the next year. "Brooklyn Rooming House" became the first of the 121 stories that *The New Yorker* published of Cheever's work over a forty-year period. From 1935 on, *The New Yorker* and Cheever's literary career were inextricably connected. With the exception of John O'Hara, Cheever published more stories in that magazine than any other writer in its history.

By 1937 Cheever's literary career was quickly rising; he was publishing stories in *The New Yorker, Collier's, New Republic, Yale Review,* and *Story.* In 1938 he also landed a writing job with the Federal Writers' Project at $50 a week and moved to Washington, D.C., for half a year. He worked as a junior editor on one of President Franklin Roosevelt's Works Projects Administration (WPA) projects, which employed thousands of unemployed teachers and writers to write guides for all forty-eight states.

By 1939 Cheever, at age twenty-seven, felt the need for a permanent relationship, and as he put it, "didn't want to sleep alone anymore." He was emotionally ready to settle down and raise a family. By chance, he met Mary Winternitz, who happened to work for Cheever's agent, Maxim Lieber. He was struck by her beauty and grace and asked Lieber to introduce them. They immediately began dating. Both of Mary's parents were well-known physicians. Her mother, Helen Watson, had been one of the first women in America to earn a medical degree, and her father, Milton Winternitz, a respected pathologist, eventually became dean of the Yale University Medical School. Mary, educated at Sarah Lawrence College, was intensely interested in literature and was herself an excellent poet. After living together for two years, John and Mary were married on 22 March 1941. Living with his beloved energized Cheever's creativity, because he published, in 1940 alone, fifteen stories—eleven in *The New Yorker,* two in *Harper's Bazaar,* one in *Mademoiselle,* and one in *Collier's.* All of those magazines paid well, and *The New Yorker,* in particular, paid within a week of a story's publication.

Cheever's literary reputation was quickly growing, but just as his writer's hopes were becoming a reality, World War II broke out, and Cheever immediately enlisted in the army. His letters to his wife from military training camps in South Carolina and Georgia indicate that Cheever was quite naive when it came to seeing how working-class and poor people managed to live their lives. And although he kept up with the rugged physical training, he was not an athletic person. His letters to friends and Mary demonstrated Cheever's talent, which lasted throughout his writing career, for employing everyday characters and occurrences around him for literary purposes. A dozen of his stronger early stories came out of his military training, the most notable a piercing psychological study of a sadistic basic-training sergeant titled "Sergeant Limeburner."

As Cheever's unit was preparing to confront the Germans in the North African desert, he got word that Random House was publishing a collection of his stories. He confessed years later that his lunch with Random House publisher Bennett Cerf celebrating the signing of a contract for his first book of stories in September 1942 was the happiest day of his life. He called the collection *The Way Some People Live* (1943), a title that suggests Cheever's continual amazement at what ordinary people can endure. Many of the stories address the change in the lives of middle-class people brought on by World War II, though none of them involve actual combat. Rather they tell of the homesickness of young men away from their families for the first time, the emotional and financial hardships of young wives, and the starkness of barracks life. The other stories deal with victims of the Depression, particularly those who had lost jobs and homes because of that disaster. The collection received both enthusiastic and cautious reviews. Struthers Burt predicted in the 19 April 1943 issue of the *New Republic* that Cheever, if he avoided certain stylistic affectations, would undoubtedly become "one of the most distinguished writers." Weldon Kees, of the *New Republic,* warned that the sameness in the stories' tone and situation made them almost generic *New Yorker* stories and that Cheever ran the risk of formulaic writing.

More importantly, however, were first appearances of autobiographical patterns that ran through Cheever's fictions throughout his writing career. Character types such as the wanderer, the exile, and the alienated lover and the themes of loneliness and isolation are evident throughout *The Way Some People Live,* as is the mythic pattern of the attempt to regenerate an Edenic happiness that many of these victims had lost in their fall from ignorance to knowledge.

Not only did Cheever's literary reputation begin to thrive, but it immediately created advantages for him even as a private first class. Because several of his superior officers saw copies of his book in local book-stores, they decided to reassign him to Astoria, Queens, to work with other writers in the Signal Corps Photographic Center. Cheever had spent four years at a number of dull jobs during his military career and hoped to become an officer, but his weak mathematical skills precluded that possibility. As events worked out, that failure probably saved his life. Had Cheever remained with his original infantry unit, he might well have become one of its many casualties. Four out of five enlisted men were wounded and half were killed in combat by the end of the war.

As a result of his first published book, Cheever, now a Random House author, was able to work with other literary celebrities in a relaxed atmosphere. Hollywood director Stanley Kramer was the administrative head of the unit that boasted such writers as William Saroyan and Irwin Shaw, who, with Cheever, worked on scripts for antifascist propaganda films. Because of the contacts he made through his fellow writers, he attended parties with celebrities Frederic

Dust jacket for Cheever's first novel, an autobiographical family saga published in 1957

March, Abe Burrows, and Moss Hart. Cheever also became famous for his obsessive devotion to his writing projects. Leonard Spigelgass, the head writer for the project, claimed that Cheever always finished his tasks before anyone else and became easily bored. He called Cheever "a writing machine." But Cheever's discipline enabled him to produce a huge body of work over many years in spite of his heavy drinking and extramarital affairs.

Because of the general informality of his work with the Signal Corps, he was able to live off-base in a townhouse on East Ninety-second Street. Since it was too expensive for one family, the Cheevers shared the five floors with two other couples and their babies. Mary Cheever had given birth to their first child, Susan, in May 1943, just before their move to East Ninety-second Street. Their life in their new home became humorously complicated, and Cheever was able to use some of the incidents in six stories that he published in *The New Yorker* in 1945 and 1946. They came to be known as the "Town House" stories and attest to Cheever's ability to transform insignificant domestic problems into memorable art. So popular were these stories that one of Broadway's most influential directors and producers, George S. Kaufman, produced a play out of them called *Town House* on Broadway in the fall of 1948; it lasted only twelve performances. Cheever made only a little more than $50 on the play, but his name became well known not only in the relatively small world of the short story but also in the larger and more rewarding spotlight of Broadway.

After a military writing assignment sent Cheever to Guam and the Philippines, he returned to New York just in time to be honorably discharged from the army shortly after the atomic bombs were dropped on Hiroshima and Nagasaki. The family moved to a smaller apartment on the Upper East Side, where Cheever immediately began a work routine that he would repeat throughout his life. He would rise early in the morning, dress in a business suit and hat, and ride the elevator with the other businessmen. They would get off on the first floor, and Cheever would take the elevator to the basement, where he would enter a storage room, remove his clothes down to his shorts, and work all day, taking only a short break for lunch. He felt that writing was as responsible and demanding a profession as any other and treated it with complete respect. By keeping his writing separate from his domestic life, he could define his goals clearly and devote the proper amount of time and effort to accomplish them. While he was always a consistently disciplined writer, his vocation as a family man and the energies he devoted to those responsibilities were vitally important in keeping him emotionally centered in a daily routine. And in this devotion to the quotidian, he resembles Wallace Stevens and William Carlos Williams, whose professional duties as a lawyer and doctor, respectively, kept both of them from being overwhelmed by the chaos of the world.

Cheever began working on a novel with a hefty advance from Random House. The outline of the novel chronicled the disintegration of a respected New England family named Field, of which the mother, father, and two sons bore striking resemblances to the Cheever family and its problems during the Depression. This narrative became, eventually, the principal plot of his first novel, *The Wapshot Chronicle*. More importantly, however, were several stories that signaled a major change in Cheever's style, fictive voice, and tone. He had moved away from the short short stories that Cowley had urged him to write in the mid 1930s and began writing much longer and psychologically more sophisticated stories such as "The Enormous Radio" and "Torch Song." These two stories, published in 1947, came in time to be considered two

of his greatest and most popular works not only for his new highly developed lyrical style and brilliant character portraiture but also for his ability to evoke deep mythic resonance within the most mundane circumstances. Few of Cheever's female characters are as outwardly normal as Joan Harris of "Torch Song," but no other Cheever figure takes on so ominously—or subtly—the obvious vampiric characteristics of the fatal woman as she. From 1947 on, deeper and richer textures emerge in his stories principally because he was permitting prototypical figures to enter his fiction—like Joan Harris—who gave common, everyday occurrences a deeper significance; his best stories from these years frequently operate on two levels simultaneously: the mythic and the everyday. At age thirty-five, Cheever's stories began to operate not only as probing psychological studies but also as archetypal revelations, revealing Joan Harris as a modern-day Hecate.

Eventually the Cheevers found a comfortable apartment at 400 East Fifty-ninth Street, where they lived until 1951. Though Cheever himself had lived in Manhattan for seventeen years, once he married and the children arrived, it became too expensive and distracting for him to continue living in Manhattan any longer. Another child, Benjamin, had been born in May of 1948, and the family decided that they needed more room and less chaos and moved to Scarborough, a Westchester suburb some thirty miles outside New York City. The house they moved into was actually a large garage that had been converted into servants' quarters on the vast estate of National City Bank founder Frank A. Vanderlip. The surrounding estate was pastoral, with sheep grazing in a pasture with brooks, fields, and wooded areas. Adjoining the Cheever house there was a large Italian garden, a rose arbor, and a swimming pool that Cheever used frequently. True to Cheever's habit for using his immediate surrounding as settings for his stories, he began a series of narratives about the joys and sorrows of suburban life, which were published seven years later under the title *The Housebreaker of Shady Hill and Other Stories* (1958). In keeping his professional life separate from his home life, he did some of his writing in a rented room at the train station in Scarborough. Cheever never needed the rarefied library atmosphere that many authors insist on. Rather, he moved his portable typewriter to any quiet place; the closer he was to the actual pulse of everyday life—but not so close as to be distracted—the more productive he remained. The financial troubles that had plagued the family in Manhattan were relieved both by their move to Scarborough and also by a generous Guggenheim Fellowship in 1951.

Cheever himself enthusiastically entered into the mores of upper-middle-class suburban males, which included heavy drinking–especially of gin. Exhausted husbands emerged from their commuter trains after six and tranquilized themselves with martinis, a favorite of Cheever and many of his protagonists. He joined the local volunteer fire department, where heavy drinking sometimes accompanied drills, became a member of the local school board, and attended dances at the country club. In short, he performed all the social rituals that young, ambitious, successful businessmen pursued in the 1950s and 1960s.

In 1953 his next collection of short stories was published under the title *The Enormous Radio and Other Stories,* a collection that contained some of his finest stories, comprising the title story, "Goodbye, My Brother," "The Pot of Gold," "O City of Broken Dreams," "Torch Song," and nine others. Amazingly enough, Cheever had great difficulty finding a publisher for these stories, which many critics would later call his greatest single collection. These are the stories that made Cheever famous and defined his singular style and tone for the rest of his writing career. Random House rejected them even though he had received an O. Henry Award in 1951 for "The Pot of Gold." Eventually Funk & Wagnalls published the collection to mostly negative reviews. Because much of Cheever's work was published in *The New Yorker*, his name had become identified with the magazine. And as a result of that identification, his work was tarred with the same brush as that of many other *New Yorker* writers.

Many book reviewers belonged to the New York intellectual elite, university professors in Eastern schools whose attitudes were unapologetically socialist or leftist. These brilliant first-generation college-educated scholars, who had escaped the ghettos of the Lower East Side of Manhattan, the Bronx, Brooklyn, or Chicago, favored fiction with a proletarian edge that was closer to their childhood and adolescent experiences. They looked on Cheever's *New Yorker* stories as elitist indulgence that unemotionally chronicled the shallow manners and morals of the upper middle class. Other critics considered his work depressing because some of the stories dealt with shabby lives mired in urban hopelessness. In short, Cheever's second collection of short fiction, containing stories that virtually defined what eventually became known as "Cheeveresque" (five of which would become known as his best work), met with mixed reviews.

At this point in Cheever's career, he decided to pursue his novel-in-progress to earn some much needed money for his expanding family responsibilities. He accepted a position at Barnard College to teach creative writing in the fall of 1954. He was, by most accounts, a superb and encouraging teacher. One of his former students reported that he was most concerned

with transforming dull and lifeless sentences into highly effective rhetorical structures whose balance would impress and move readers. He also insisted that they write about their own lives–much as he himself did–and that they should "mythologize the commonplace"–again, a consistent and major part of his own writing patterns. It was also about this time that he began to feel the painful effects of his heavy drinking. He consulted a psychiatrist about both his drinking and his homosexual tendencies, which, as *The Journals of John Cheever* (1991) reveal, became more troubling to him as he got older. Fortunately, Harper and Brothers offered to buy out Cheever's contract with Random House and gave him a substantial advance on his novel-in-progress and five years in which to finish it. He had decided to call it *The Wapshot Chronicle*.

In spite of the hostility of the academic critics, Cheever started winning literary prizes for his outstanding work in the short-story form. In 1955 he won the Benjamin Franklin Magazine Award for his brilliant portrait of suburban living in "The Five-Forty-Eight," and in January 1956 he won the even more prestigious O. Henry Award for what many critics consider his best story, "The Country Husband." However, two distressing events took place within the same week in February of 1956. The first was the death of his mother at the age of eighty-two (the same age at which his father died), and the second was the death of his editor at *The New Yorker,* Gus Lobrano, who, having edited Cheever's early stories, became a close friend by teaching Cheever how to fish. After these emotional blows, Cheever returned to Yaddo and worked nonstop on *The Wapshot Chronicle*. Still under some financial pressure, he sold off four major portions to *The New Yorker* and sent off the entire manuscript to Harper in June 1956.

Other financial rewards began arriving, the first of which was $40,000 from the head of M-G-M, Dore Schary, for the film rights to his recently published *New Yorker* story called "The Housebreaker of Shady Hill," a title that also became the name of his next short-story collection. He had been elected to the board of directors at Yaddo, where he had intermittently spent twenty years under the care of Elizabeth Ames and where he wrote some of his best work. With the money from the film rights, the Cheevers decided to spend a year in Italy, a vacation they had been planning for many years. They had also been encouraged by fellow writers Robert Penn Warren and his wife, Eleanor Clark, who had had a second home in Rome for many years.

After an uneventful trip on the ocean liner *Conte Biancamano* (though Cheever was gathering details for several stories involving adulterous affairs on ocean liners), the family arrived in Rome in November of 1956. It happens that Cheever's story "The Country Hus-

Cheever with his wife, Mary Winternitz Cheever, and their daughter, Susan (photograph © by Nancy Crampton)

band" was aired on the television drama series *Playhouse 90* the day the family arrived in Rome, an event that showed his work had become commercially as well as literarily successful. They settled into a huge apartment in the Palazzo Doria, where they spent the year. With occasional trips to Roman ruins outside the city walls and to seaside resorts such as Port'Ercole, a place that Cheever called the single most beautiful place he had ever visited, the family decided to rent a ruined castle there called "La Rocca" during the summer of 1957.

An even more important event, though, was the birth of another son, Federico, on 9 March 1957. They also hired a maid, Iole Felici, who not only cleaned, cooked, and cared for the family but also took over the management of the entire Cheever household. So successful were her management skills that the family brought her back to the United States, where she remained with them for the next twenty-five years. Though Cheever wrote little during his year in Rome, he enjoyed Italian culture immensely and studied Italian with several teachers. He absorbed all the important cultural details and wrote, over the next several years, a

series of stories that showed Americans confronting the Italian way of life. Though most critics would not include them in his best work, stories such as "The Bella Lingua," "The Duchess," "The Golden Age," and "Boy in Rome" would certainly rank as some of his most entertaining and witty, particularly in the way he uses Graeco-Roman myths to build several later stories on and creates satiric Italian names for many of his Italian characters. Evidently the Italian language greatly appealed to Cheever's musical sensibilities.

Cheever's first novel, *The Wapshot Chronicle,* a work he had spent twenty years writing, was published by Harper. The critics were divided over its merits. Some found fault with its episodic structure; it appeared not to follow a neat, orderly Aristotelian plot. Still others were put off by its dark vision. Joan Didion praised it highly and in a 1961 article in *The National Review* intelligently placed it within a novelistic tradition: "*The Wapshot Chronicle* surprised some, troubled others, seemed not even a novel to those brought up on twentieth century fiction. What it was not was a sentimental novel; what it was not was a novel of manners. It was a novel more like *Tom*

Jones than *Madame Bovary,* more like *Tristram Shandy* than *Pride and Prejudice* (And more like any one of them than the novels commonly written by *New Yorker* writers)." Most earlier critics felt as Didion later would, and awarded it the National Book Award in 1958 (Cheever had already been elected to the National Institute of Arts and Letters in 1957). The novel's principal themes were the same as many of his earlier stories: love in various guises, specifically between brothers, among families, and between men and women. The Wapshot family saga bears uncanny resemblances to the history of the Cheever family, with appearances of fairly obvious Cheever family ancestors such as Ezekiel Cheever as Leander Wapshot and his two sons, Moses and Coverly, who resemble John and his brother, Fred. Sarah Wapshot, Leander's wife, also possesses many of the same character traits that John Cheever's mother exhibited, so much so that Cheever would permit publication only after her death. Most importantly, however, is that the fall of the Wapshot family–like the fall of the Cheever family–from a prominent position in the community structures the novel. The novel is not built on the kind of linear framework that conservative critics prefer. It is obviously cyclic–certainly a more appropriate form to chronicle the rise and fall of a distinguished New England family. The novel concludes where it began, and family history repeats itself seven years later in his next novel, *The Wapshot Scandal.* Happily for Cheever's financial condition, the Book-of-the-Month Club chose it as a selection, thus insuring Cheever substantial royalties.

With the publication of his first novel in 1957, John Cheever's career began a steady ascent. The financial success, the honors he was garnering, and the high critical praise made him more productive. Between 1957 and the mid 1960s he published five new books: three short-story collections and two novels. His financial situation improved to such an extent that he was able to buy a large, old house in one of the more affluent neighborhoods of Ossining, New York. He also was awarded a second Guggenheim Fellowship in 1960 to write another novel. In the meantime, he published *The Housebreaker of Shady Hill and Other Stories* (1958), a short-story collection that was one of his most highly praised collections, containing such masterpieces as "The Sorrows of Gin," "The Country Husband," and "The Five-Forty-Eight." That collection established him, once and for all, as the bard of suburban angst. Though much of his earlier work detailed middle-class lives in the Upper East Side of Manhattan, *Housebreaker* became what readers to this day consider archetypal Cheever stories, earning him the label as "Ovid in Ossining" in *Time* magazine.

Again, some critics found Westchester cocktail parties shallow and decadent and suggested that Cheever lacked the moral courage to criticize these lifestyles of the rich and bored. Cheever merely presented such lives and left ethical judgments to the readers themselves, an objectivity that later readers and critics admired him for. Part of Cheever's reputation for being nonjudgmental was his consistently objective attitude toward his characters. What many critics failed to detect was the obvious mythical subtexts that Cheever subtly delineated and explored in suburbia. Shady Hill is both Eden and Hades, paradoxes Cheever's characters are perpetually torn between. Using what Eliot called "the mythical method"–that is, a continual par-lelling of the present with the past–Cheever insists that his readers make their own moral judgments; he seemed uncomfortable upholding one philosophical belief and condemning another. He trusted his readers, with the aid of mythic allusions, to share the spiritual dilemmas that his characters often underwent. Indeed, he came to mythologize important parts of his own life, especially his growing hostility toward his wife's father, Milton Winternitz. Mary spent a large part of her time with her family even after their marriage, and Cheever viewed her absence in unmistakably mythic terms: "I have come to think of Winter as the king of a Hades where M [Mary] must spend perhaps half her time," alluding to his father-in-law as one who became "a source of darkness" in their life.

There is also no doubt that buying a large house in Ossining gave Cheever what he needed most to become more productive; he established a solid familial base located in the middle of a forest-like area. He loved dogs and enjoyed taking them on long daily hikes through the woods. Though he no longer had a swimming pool, he used his next-door neighbor's. His obsession with nature often serves as a backdrop for the stories and the novels in which nature's perfection becomes the pristine Edenic condition by which his characters measure their lives. Indeed, all of his recurrent themes of brotherly love and conflict, family strife, sexual celebration and failure, and existential musings are grounded in a natural context that becomes a consistent metaphor for paradise. Often his characters experience a sense of oneness with this natural paradise if they make themselves available to its restorative powers.

In 1961 Cheever published his fourth collection of short stories, titled *Some People, Places and Things That Will Not Appear in My Next Novel.* Most critics were not pleased with the quality of the stories in this collection, and only "The Death of Justina" and "Boy in Rome" were favorably compared to earlier masterpieces such as "The Country Husband" or "The Sorrows of Gin."

The tone of most of these stories is acidic, and a disturbing apocalyptic air pervades the collection. David Boroff in *The New York Times Book Review* (16 April 1961) called Cheever "a Gothic writer whose mind is poised at the edge of terror." It became clear that Cheever's heavy drinking was beginning to show its deleterious effects by the dramatic change of tone and attitude in a bitter reassessment of standard themes and character types, which he catalogued in the book's final story, "A Miscellany of Characters That Will Not Appear." In this uncharacteristically postmodern story, Cheever promises to omit from any future stories such topics as "The pretty girl at the Princeton-Dartmouth game . . . All parts for Marlon Brando . . . All scornful descriptions of American landscapes [i.e., Wasteland details such as ruined tenements, polluted rivers, etc.] . . . All lushes . . . all those homosexuals who have taken such a dominating position in recent fiction. . . . " Ironically, several stories contain the very topics he had promised to exclude from his work. His troubling response to homosexual fiction and his abhorrence of homosexuals in general found a different attitude in his frank homosexual confessions throughout *The Journals* of John Cheever. He was finally able to accept his own homosexuality during his later years of sobriety.

From 1959 until 1964 Cheever worked on his second novel, *The Wapshot Scandal,* but his journals show that his excessive drinking created severe family and writing problems. Cheever had always prided himself on his capacity to drink vast amounts of hard liquor and not let it interfere with his writing. He usually rose early even after a heavy night of drinking and put in five or six hours of writing, stopping for lunch at noon. But it was becoming increasingly difficult for him to delay his first drink of the day until noon, often moving it back to eleven o'clock so that he would be able to stop shaking. His drinking began to concern his friends, who noticed that Cheever, until then a cheerful and celebratory drinker, had become hostile after a few drinks. He was known to ruin dinner parties with embarrassing drunken scenes.

Mary Cheever became exhausted nursing her husband through his hangovers; she took a job teaching English at nearby Briarcliffe College, a move that saved her sanity. John was adamantly against the idea of his wife working. Also about this time, Fred had to be hospitalized for excessive drinking. In spite of his own troubles with alcohol and his wife's independence, John continued to work on *The Wapshot Scandal,* a dark book that chronicles the complete collapse of the family. He also continued to publish short stories in *The New Yorker,* managing to produce some of his greatest works, such as "The Swimmer," "The Music Teacher," and "The Angel of the Bridge."

Cheever also published six sections of *The Wapshot Scandal,* from 1959 to 1964 in *The New Yorker,* so close observers of Cheever's work should not have been overly disturbed at the darkening vision of the bleakest book he ever wrote when Harper and Row published it in January of 1964. He confessed during the writing of this novel that he had seriously contemplated suicide, so deep was his depression. His drinking was out of control and his phobias were debilitating him.

The critical response to *The Wapshot Scandal* was generally positive even though the tone of the novel differed greatly from *The Wapshot Chronicle.* In *Critical Essays on John Cheever* (1982) George Garrett best describes the major differences between the two novels: "The sins of *Chronicle* are original sin. *Scandal* moves inexorably toward the end of the world." Garrett detects a notable lack of sensuousness, particularly of smells; Cheever's prose was famous for its sensuous celebration. He also points out that love had given way to lust, and the sensuous had become the sensual. Cowley was alarmed at Cheever's anger, calling his world in an October 1963 letter one of "emotional squalor and incongruity." Though *The Wapshot Chronicle* detailed the decline of an old, respected New England family in the mythical St. Botolphs, *The Wapshot Scandal* shows the remainder of the family, especially the brothers Moses and Coverly, attempting to find new suburban Edenic structures to replace the sacred center of St. Botolphs. Conflicts with editors at *The New Yorker* increased to such an extent that Cheever engaged, almost on a whim, a new agent who immediately acquired a lucrative promise from *The Saturday Evening Post* of $24,000 for four stories a year from Cheever, which he delivered regularly from 1963 until he died in 1982. Cheever published only six more stories with the *The New Yorker.*

Though his family life was on the verge of collapse and his drinking out of control, *Time* magazine chose him for a March 1964 cover story after the great success of *The Wapshot Scandal.* His reputation enabled him to sell his stories to the highest-paying magazines such as *Esquire, Playboy,* and *The Saturday Evening Post.* Cheever also published one of his finest short-story collections in 1964, *The Brigadier and the Golf Widow,* which contained some of his most compelling stories. The title story, "The Swimmer," "The Music Teacher," and "The Seaside Houses" certainly qualify as some of Cheever's best work. And "The Swimmer" catapulted him into the world of Hollywood and high living that he enjoyed immensely. As soon as "The Swimmer" appeared in *The New Yorker,* he was contacted by film director Frank Perry, who proposed a film version. Eventually Burt Lancaster starred in the moderately successful film, which earned Cheever a small fortune. It was also during his Hollywood stay

sovereign

Government   *the steps of the courts*   *something*   *cooler text*   *Byzantine*

The main entrance to Falconer--the only entrance for
convicts, their visitors and the staff--was crowned by an
esuctheon representing Liberty,Justice and,between the two,
the power of legislation. Liberty wore a mob-cap and carried a
pike. Legislation was the federal eagle,armed with hunting arrows.
Justice was conventional;blinded,vaguely erotic in her clinging
robes and armed with a headsman's sword. The bas-relief was
bronze but black these days--as black as unpolished anthracite or
onyex. How many hundreds had passed under this--this last
souvenir they would see of man's struggle for cohreence. Hundreds,
one guessed,thousands,millions was close. Above the escutchen was
a declension of the place-names:Falconer Jail 1871,Falconer
Reformatory,Falconer Federal Penitionary,Falconer State Prison,
Falconer Correctional Facility and the last,which had never
caught on:Daybreak House. Now cons were inmates,the assholes
were officers and the warden was a superindendent. Fame is
chancey,God knows but Falconer--with it's limited accomodations
for two thousand miscreants was as famous as Old Bailey. Gone
was the water-torture,the striped suits,the lock-stepkthe balls
and chains and there was a soft-ball field where the gallows had
stood but at the time of which I'm writing leg-irons were still
used in Auburn. You could tell the men from Auburn by the noise
they made.

        Farragut (fratracide,zip to ten #734-508-32)was brought

Page from the manuscript for Falconer, *published in 1977 (from* Paris Review, *Fall 1976)* that he met and fell in love with film actress Hope Lange, a liaison that continued over many years. The affair with Lange was but one of many he conducted throughout his lifetime; he also became less guarded about affairs he was having with several young men.

In 1964 Cheever traveled to Russia to participate in a cultural exchange program and met Tanya Litvinov, who became the translator of his short fiction. He also became friends with John Updike during that trip. Though Updike was nearly twenty years younger than Cheever, the older author recommended Updike for membership in the National Institute of Arts and Letters and also helped him win the National Book Award for *The Centaur* (1963), a novel whose mythic structures appealed to Cheever's archetypal sensibilities. In 1965 the American Academy of Arts and Letters awarded Cheever its William Dean Howells Medal for *The Wapshot Scandal,* an award that was given for the best piece of fiction during a five-year period. Cheever was honored to be in the company of such distinguished earlier recipients as Willa Cather, Faulkner, and Eudora Welty.

Though he appeared to be operating at the top of his creative powers, recognized and honored with major literary prizes and awards, his drinking was destroying his family and his sanity. Having admitted to friends that his obsession for alcohol was growing stronger, he sought help in the summer of 1965 by consulting a psychiatrist and undergoing some psychotherapy. The therapy gave him an opportunity to examine some of his early childhood traumas and their possible connections to his suicidal drinking habits.

His life had moved into a typical alcoholic paradox: he could tolerate neither isolation nor company for any prolonged period of time. Yet, much of the despair and the deadly mixture of self-pity and self-loathing would not come out until the publication of segments of his journals in *The New Yorker* in the early 1990s. Many admirers of his work were astonished at the interminable rationalizations and the shameless way he manipulated both family and friends.

Wracked by guilt, he somehow made progress on his new novel, *Bullet Park*. He also had a serious falling-out with his longtime *New Yorker* editor, William Maxwell, over the effect his drinking was having on the quality of his stories. After acquiring one of the New York literary world's most powerful agents, Candida Donadio, who arranged a highly lucrative contract for *Bullet Park* with Alfred A. Knopf, he severed his long affiliation with Harper and Row, a company with which he had published three of his story collections and two of his novels over an eleven-year period.

True to a consistent pattern in Cheever's work in which his own spiritual conflicts are mirrored in his latest fiction, *Bullet Park* is his most sharply divided novel.

Critic Samuel Coale, in his 1977 book on Cheever, characterizes the conflicts throughout the novel as "distinctly Manichean." Nowhere in his earlier work is there such a clear division between such warring opposites as body and spirit, the light and the dark, good and evil. In mythic terms Cheever's conflicts can be best understood as the Dionysian at war with the Apollonian impulses, but the Dionysian in its most dangerously self-consuming manifestations. Suicidal thoughts run throughout his journals during these years. The mythic *Bullet Park* is a minefield of families and characters in conflict. Updike, an admirer of Cheever's work, but also a writer who explores the negative effects of the Puritan ethic, found the deepest level of Protestant male melancholy celebrating the Emersonian pleasures of life in the midst of the crucifying agonies of a meaningless world. Cheever most assuredly wants the reader to detect the Christian cross as the backdrop on which the story is played out by "comically" giving the two principal families the names Hammer and Nailles. The reviews were mixed, and some critics simply confessed that they were confused over the theme of the novel. Though John Leonard gave it a highly favorable review in *The New York Times* (29 April 1969), Benjamin DeMott suggested (*The New York Times Book Review,* 27 April 1969) that Cheever's irksome habit of unnecessarily inflating a short story into a novel weakened the work's structure.

Because of the novel's mixed critical reception, Cheever's drinking increased, as did the problems that it spawned. Though he consulted a psychiatrist throughout 1969 and openly admitted his alcoholic dependency, he did little to modify his destructive behavior and continued to suffer deep guilt over his drinking. His confusion over his bisexual impulses continued. His public drunkenness and insensitive behavior alarmed his friends, and he was also arrested for driving while intoxicated in 1969. His drinking dramatically affected his literary output. During his best years he published five short stories a year; he published only one in 1970, none in 1971, two in 1972, and one in 1973—a drastic reduction for a writer known for the volume of his literary production. It was clear to most of his friends that he was on the verge of losing everything: his family, his reputation, his capacity for work, and possibly his life.

Since Cheever had no idea of future novelistic projects, he decided to teach a creative-writing class at Sing Sing Prison or what was officially called the Ossining Correctional Facility. At a Westchester cocktail party he heard that the two thousand prisoners there had only six teachers. According to Donald Lang, a prisoner who became a close friend of Cheever's, Cheever gained the prisoners' respect when he courageously showed up to teach his class immediately following the devastating 1971 riots at Attica Prison. Consciously or unconsciously, however, Cheever recorded with great accuracy many details of prison life that would eventually surface in what many critics would call his greatest novel, *Falconer*. Cheever taught at Sing Sing until the spring of 1973, but his drinking continued unabated and did not allow him to produce any significant material for publication.

He had enjoyed his teaching experience at Sing Sing and, after a successful reading at the University of Iowa, was invited by Jack Leggett, the director of the Iowa Writing Program, to teach there during the fall semester of 1973. He was pleased by both the positive critical reception given his latest collection of short stories, *The World of Apples* (1973), and his nomination for membership to the prestigious American Academy of Arts and Letters. Cheever had hoped for what some alcoholics call a geographical cure of some kind since his marriage was collapsing and his drinking had thwarted any serious literary output; he casually discussed suicide. His physical health had deteriorated to such an extent that he thought he had a heart attack in May of 1973 and ended up in Phelps Memorial Hospital in Tarrytown, New York. In reality it was a condition common to alcoholics called cardiomyopathy, with symptoms of shortness of breath and erratic heartbeat. His doctor had made the mistake of prescribing Seconal, a strong sleeping medication, which Cheever mixed with alcohol, causing pulmonary edema. Because he could not drink in the hospital, he began to hallucinate and was put in a straitjacket. Both his family and his doctor suggested Alcoholics Anonymous (AA), which he flatly rejected.

In spite of his precarious physical condition and his denial of his "drinking problems," Cheever traveled to the University of Iowa, where he immediately became close friends with fellow instructors John Irving and Raymond Carver, with whom he spent much time drinking and mixing with the student population. He also met some other students who later became prominent writers, Allan Gurganus and T. Coraghessan Boyle, both of whom acknowledge a great debt to Cheever for helping them publish their early work and for giving them practical suggestions to improve their writing. Though he did collapse once during his stay at Iowa, he was able to finish the semester and return to Ossining, where his wife announced that she could no longer live with his drunken behavior; he was drinking in the morning, and nothing she could do would stop him.

He accepted a teaching position at Boston University for the fall of 1974 even though his drinking had rendered him emotionally and spiritually impotent. Financially, he was bringing in only half of what was needed to operate his household. He frequently could not meet his students at Boston University and was barely able to finish his teaching duties before Fred, whom John had once helped sober up, took him for detoxification at Phelps Hospital in Tarrytown. Cheever again suffered through delirium tremens and, with the strong insistence of his doctor, his wife, and his children, admitted himself into one of New York City's most famous drying-out facilities, the Smithers Alcohol Rehabilitation Center on the Upper East Side of Manhattan. After initial negative feelings about having to be in close contact with "common folks" of all kinds, an uncharacteristic response from Cheever, who loved to mix with all levels of society—and a measure of how radically his alcoholism had transformed him—he settled into the routine of the institute and emerged from the program a sober and hopeful person.

Though initially hostile to the idea of attending AA meetings, he relented and went three times a week. He became there an eloquent participant in discussions and a popular speaker. His wife noted that he acted as if he were a prisoner who had been released from bondage, an observation that explains why Cheever may have been attracted to teaching at Sing Sing. He realized that his alcoholic addiction was as enslaving as being in prison. His renewed emotional and physical response to life quickly resulted in major transformations in his daily routine. He threw out the medication that his doctors had prescribed: He stopped taking Seconal to sleep and Valium to "relieve stress" and never touched a drop of alcohol again. Instead, he drank huge quantities of iced tea, and though he continued to smoke heavily, he was able to break that addiction five years later.

Once Cheever stopped his suicidal drinking, he resumed work, and in May 1975, just a month after his release from Smithers, he began writing *Falconer*. Donaldson states that he was able to complete about seven pages a day in that many hours, a production rate he had been able to reach only in his earliest work. Cheever's attitude changed completely as he resumed many of the recreational activities he loved, especially hiking, skating, and swimming (in three different neighborhood pools). He took up healthy new hobbies such as cross-country skiing and bicycling. He was also able to become more open about his homosexual feelings and affairs and had learned through regular attendance at AA meetings that honesty about every aspect of his life was necessary for him to maintain his serenity and sobriety.

Cheever finished *Falconer* in less than a year, and it was published in 1977 to mostly favorable reviews. The novel serves as an allegory of the writer's life with particular resonance to forms of enslavement Cheever himself suffered throughout his life: his self-entombing alcohol-

Dust jacket for Cheever's final novel

ism, his agonizing bisexuality, his divided feelings about his parents, and, most dramatically, his pathological love-hate relationship with his older brother, Fred. *Falconer* addressed what Donaldson called Cheever's bifurcated life and the painful issues caused by those struggles within himself.

From 1977 until his death in June 1982, Cheever's reputation grew enormously as he garnered many awards and prizes for his superb writing. The success of *Falconer* brought him renewed fame when he appeared on the cover of *Newsweek* in March 1977 and on the *Dick Cavett Show,* where he spoke with great candor about his self-destructive drinking, his troubled marriage, and other problems. All of these public appearances contributed to hefty sales of not only *Falconer* but also his earlier work; he found himself a wealthy man in his mid sixties. Paramount Pictures bought the movie rights for *Falconer* for $40,000 but decided not to make the picture; Cheever was delighted.

In 1978 he was awarded an honorary doctorate from Harvard University, and in 1979 he received the Pulitzer Prize and the National Book Critics Circle Award for *The Stories of John Cheever,* which Alfred A. Knopf had published the year before. *The Stories of John Cheever* renewed interest in Cheever's writings on a huge scale primarily because both readers and critics had never seen so many of his stories—sixty-one of them—together in one volume. The reviews were excellent; John Leonard called the book "not merely the publishing event of the 'season' but a grand occasion in English literature" (*The New York Times,* 7 November 1978). As a result of the generally ecstatic critical reception, his agent was able to negotiate a $500,000-advance from Knopf for Cheever's next two books.

Unfortunately, Cheever would write only one more novel, *Oh What a Paradise It Seems* (1982), a work closer to a novella, though he had intended it to be much longer. While on a visit to Yaddo, he suffered a grand mal seizure in the fall of 1980. During urological surgery for a cancerous kidney his doctors discovered that it had spread to the bone. He had further surgery for tumors on his bladder, but by early December of 1981 his doctor advised his family that he had six months to live. Though weak and quite ill, he attended a Carnegie Hall ceremony at which he was given the National Medal for Literature (and $15,000) in late April 1982.

His last days were serene, and surrounded by family and friends, he died quietly on 18 June 1982 at

his home in Ossining. His funeral was held in Norwell, Massachusetts, where he was buried in the Cheever family plot. Though Cheever struggled with alcohol, a loveless childhood, and his homosexual feelings, he considered himself a lucky man. He faced his self-destructive impulses directly when he quit drinking and joined Alcoholics Anonymous. Cheever also faced his feelings for men; until his death, he unashamedly maintained a long-term relationship with a younger man. He never lost the ability to change literary direction and moved away from the content of his earliest work—the fall of New England families into the shabbiness of the modern world—to the alienation, despair, and redemption of his last great novel, *Falconer*.

Letters:

The Letters of John Cheever, edited by Benjamin Cheever (New York: Simon & Schuster, 1988);

Glad Tidings: A Friendship in Letters: The Correspondence of John Cheever and John D. Weaver, 1945–1982, edited by John D. Weaver (New York: Harper-Collins, 1993).

Interview:

Scott Donaldson, ed., *Conversations with John Cheever* (Jackson: University Press of Mississippi, 1987).

Bibliographies:

Dennis Coates, "John Cheever: A Checklist, 1930–1978," *Bulletin of Bibliography,* 36 (January–March 1979): 1–13, 49;

Deno Trakas, "John Cheever: An Annotated Secondary Bibliography (1943–1978)," *Resources for American Literary Study,* 9 (1979): 181–199;

Francis Bosha, *John Cheever: A Reference Guide* (Boston: G. K. Hall, 1981);

Coates, "Cheever Bibliographical Supplement, 1978–1981," in *Critical Essays on John Cheever,* edited by R. G. Collins (Boston: G. K. Hall, 1982), pp. 279–285;

Bosha, ed., *The Critical Response to John Cheever* (Westport, Conn.: Greenwood Press, 1994).

Biographies:

Susan Cheever, *Home Before Dark* (Boston: Houghton Mifflin, 1984);

Scott Donaldson, *John Cheever* (New York: Random House, 1988).

References:

Samuel Coale, *John Cheever* (New York: Ungar, 1977);

R. G. Collins, ed., *Critical Essays on John Cheever* (Boston: G. K. Hall, 1982);

George Hunt, *John Cheever: The Hobgoblin Company of Love* (Grand Rapids, Mich.: Eerdmans, 1983);

Patrick Meanor, *John Cheever Revisited* (New York: Twayne-Macmillan, 1995);

James O'Hara, *John Cheever: A Study of the Short Fiction* (Boston: Twayne, 1989).

Papers:

Many of the typescripts of John Cheever's short stories and books are at Brandeis University, Waltham, Massachusetts, and a substantial collection of Cheever's manuscripts and letters is at Harvard University.

Tom Clancy
(12 April 1947 –   )

Helen S. Garson
George Mason University

BOOKS: *The Hunt for Red October* (Annapolis, Md.: Naval Institute Press, 1984; London: Collins, 1985);

Red Storm Rising (New York: Putnam, 1986; London: Collins, 1987);

Patriot Games (New York: Putnam, 1987; London: Collins, 1987);

The Cardinal of the Kremlin (New York: Putnam, 1988; London: Collins, 1988);

Clear and Present Danger (New York: Putnam, 1989; London: Collins, 1989);

The Sum of All Fears (New York: Putnam, 1991; London: HarperCollins, 1991);

Without Remorse (New York: Putnam, 1993; London: HarperCollins, 1993);

Submarine (New York: Putnam, 1993; London: HarperCollins, 1993);

Armored Cav: A Guided Tour of an Armored Cavalry Regiment (New York: Putnam, 1994); republished as *Armoured Warfare: A Guided Tour of an Armoured Cavalry Regiment* (London: HarperCollins, 1996);

Debt of Honor (New York: Putnam, 1994; London: HarperCollins, 1994);

Fighter Wing: A Guided Tour of an Air Force Combat Wing (New York: Berkley, 1995; London: HarperCollins, 1996);

Executive Orders (New York: Putnam, 1996; London: HarperCollins, 1996);

Marine: A Guided Tour of a Marine Expeditionary Unit (New York: Berkley, 1996; London: HarperCollins, 1997);

SSN: Strategies of Submarine Warfare (New York: Berkley, 1996; London: HarperCollins, 1997);

Into the Storm: A Study in Command, by Clancy and General Fred Franks Jr. (New York: Putnam, 1997);

Airborne: A Guided Tour of an Airborne Task Force (New York: Berkley, 1997);

Rainbow Six (New York: Putnam, 1998; London: Joseph, 1998);

Carrier: A Guided Tour of an Aircraft Carrier (New York: Berkley, 1999);

Every Man a Tiger, by Clancy and Chuck Horner (New York: Putnam, 1999);

Tom Clancy (photograph by John Earle; from the dust jacket for Debt of Honor, *1994)*

The Bear and the Dragon (New York: Putnam, 2000).

Collections: *Two Complete Novels: Red Storm Rising; The Cardinal of the Kremlin* (New York: Putnam, 1993);

Three Complete Novels: Patriot Games, Clear and Present Danger, The Sum of All Fears (New York: Putnam, 1994).

OTHER: "Before Anyone Gets Carried Away"; "Five Minutes Past Midnight–and Welcome to the Age

106

of Proliferation," by Clancy and Russell Seitz; "Getting Our Money's Worth"; "Back to the Frontier"; "But I Like to Shoot"; "The Federal News Service"; "Isvestia–1"; "Isvestia–2. Capitalism"; "Isvestia–3. Principles"; "Funeral"; "Dinosaurs"; and "Turn Back," in *The Tom Clancy Companion,* edited by Martin H. Greenberg (New York: Berkley, 1992, pp. 87–155; London: Fontana, 1992), pp. 87–155.

Tom Clancy's books have been given various labels—thrillers, suspense novels, science fiction—but the most accurate and frequently used designation is techno-thrillers. Even though Clancy insists he is not the creator of the genre, he is the writer most closely identified with it. Taking elements from both suspense novels and science fiction, he combines them with technological information to create a new type of thriller. Hallmarks of Clancy's fiction are the use of current and futuristic scientific developments, lengthy discussions and explanations of computer abilities and possibilities, and modern weapons systems. His characters are drawn from the upper echelon of government as well as branches of the U.S. military, intelligence, and industrial complex. His intense patriotism and conservative political ideas permeate all his writing.

Clancy's impact on popular literature has become so strong that he has achieved instant name recognition and has followings throughout much of the world. As a best-selling author of techno-thrillers he has impressive numbers of loyal, devoted fans, including presidents, vice presidents, and members of Congress. With his books assigned as texts in some college courses and his frequent appearances as guest lecturer before military and intelligence groups, Clancy has at times played a role in establishment politics and influenced many readers. Not only do military people generally say that Clancy gets the military world right in his novels, but many nonmilitary readers accept his views about terrorism, the Cold War, the Vietnam War, trade wars, and the drug culture.

An American of Irish descent, Thomas L. Clancy Jr. was born into a working-class family in Baltimore, Maryland, on 12 April 1947, the second of three children. The son of Thomas Clancy, a mail carrier and credit clerk in a department store, Clancy has always taken pride in his Irish heritage, his Catholic religion, and his hardworking and self-sacrificing parents. His father served in the navy during World War II, and Tom Jr. longed for the chance to become a navy man himself. The closest brush he had with military service, however, was a brief stint in ROTC at Loyola College in Baltimore. The poor eyesight that prevented his joining any branch of the military also cut short his partici-

pation in ROTC. His interest in warfare–land, sea, and air–later came to full fruition in his fiction and nonfiction, and in his friendships. Even his choice of military-style clothing reflects the attraction for him of all martial objects. And on the lawn beside the sweeping driveway leading to his home sits an army tank, a gift from his former wife.

Despite Clancy's reputation for brilliance, particularly in technological matters, he has admitted that he was not much of a student. Prepared for no particular career he became an insurance broker after graduating from college in 1969. In the same year he married Wanda Thomas, manager of her family's insurance business. Both Tom and Wanda worked in insurance, and she continued for a time after he turned to writing as a career. They are the parents of four children: Michelle, Christine, Tommy, and Katie. (Clancy's fictional stand-in, Jack Ryan, who has something of a parallel life to Clancy's, also has a young daughter named Katie.)

Clancy's work in insurance provided a living but failed to satisfy him, for he harbored a dream of becoming a writer. Always fascinated by ships, science fiction, and works of technology, Clancy developed a compelling interest in computers and computer war games. He became friendly with Larry Bond, an expert on war games, who later advised Clancy on his first book and collaborated on the second. As he searched for a plot in which he could use his technological knowledge, Clancy became fascinated by an actual event—the attempted defection of a Soviet frigate, the *Storojeroï,* in 1975. The parts came together for him as he realized there was a story to be told, one that could encompass excitement, suspense, technology, and politics. Using an old typewriter he carried home nightly from his insurance office, he worked at the dining-room table on the manuscript that became the remarkably successful *The Hunt for Red October* (1984). Nothing in his past or his daily routine suggested what was to happen with the publication of this first novel. President Ronald Reagan read the book, and his enthusiastic recommendation of *The Hunt for Red October* launched the novel and changed Clancy's life from that of middle-class insurance broker to multimillionaire novelist.

The Hunt for Red October takes place during the Cold War. The commander of the Soviet submarine *Red October,* Captain First Rank Marko Ramius, filled with bitterness over the brutality, corruption, and inefficiency of his government, decides to defect to the West and makes a thrilling and ultimately successful run for Norfolk, Virginia, where the vessel is taken over by American naval experts. The nuclear submarine furnishes much information about advances in

Dust jacket for Clancy's first novel, about a Soviet naval officer who defects to the West with his nuclear submarine

ladder, change jobs, marry, have children, lose spouses. Some retire. Mentors age, get sick, and die, and then they are replaced by those who worked for them or sometimes by less worthy political appointees. Clancy's first published novel introduces his favorite character, Jack Ryan, former marine, who at this juncture is a professor at the Naval Academy in Annapolis, Maryland, and a civilian employee of the CIA. In later novels he becomes indispensable to the American government, serving in different capacities.

Clancy often refers to Ryan as his alter ego. As a result the reader inevitably sees a conflation of opinions of the fictional character and his creator. Ryan's personality, as it develops with each novel, seems to mirror Clancy's as he has prospered over the years. Clancy seems to use Ryan as his model and yardstick of achievement. A former businessman and shrewd investor, Ryan is a millionaire, something Clancy only dreamed of when he began his writing career. He soon, however, caught up with and even surpassed his protagonist financially.

At times Clancy seems to be in competition with his hero. Both men own similar estates named Peregrine Cliff on Chesapeake Bay in Maryland. Ryan's house was "built" first, but Clancy has pointed out that his is larger. After the success of *The Hunt for Red October,* Clancy remained in the insurance business for a few more years until he was certain he could make a living as a writer. By 1986 he had moved from his modest home to a larger one, had given up his typewriter for a computer, and had purchased a Rolex watch and a Mercedes. Within a few years Clancy could afford to build his Peregrine Cliff dream house. A fifteen-thousand-square-foot stone mansion, it includes an underground pistol range because shooting is one of Clancy's interests.

The Hunt for Red October remains the favorite of many readers and reviewers. Clancy thinks less of his first novel than more-recent ones, believing he has become a better novelist over the years. Adverse criticism of Clancy's later work has grown as the novels have become longer; the number of plots, characters, and pronouncements has increased; and the main plot has become more and more complex.

Clancy's second novel, *Red Storm Rising* (1986), was a collaboration with Larry Bond, and its publication was greeted with enthusiasm by critics and the public. Although Clancy gives Bond credit in the introduction, his name does not appear as co-author. Clearly, by his second book, Clancy's name had become the selling point, an attribute not missed years later with the launching of three paperback series: *Tom Clancy's Op Center* (1995), *Tom Clancy's Power Plays* (1997), and *Tom Clancy's Net Force* (1998). Several books in each

Soviet naval technology. Of special interest is a new and exceptionally quiet drive system, "the caterpillar," whose major function is to elude enemy ships undetected. So ingeniously does Clancy describe his imaginary system that a large number of readers, including members of the U.S. Congress, believed it to be an actual component of new Soviet submarines. This kind of convincing technical description occurs throughout Clancy's work. Other than the invented drive system in *Red October,* Clancy asserts that almost all the technology in his novels is fact based. Few readers challenge his understanding of technology. Nevertheless, some critics find his descriptions and claims of military efficacy misleading.

The Hunt for Red October introduces several characters who appear in later Clancy novels: people in the U.S. Navy, the CIA, and other government agencies, as well as their various Russian counterparts. Clancy treats his players as if they actually exist, aging and advancing them in their professions over a period of years from novel to novel. They move up the career

series have since been published. The title pages state that the novels were "Created by Tom Clancy and Steve Pieczenik," but a third person is also credited with preparation of the manuscript. Thus, the extent of Clancy's contribution is not clear.

While *Red Storm Rising* owes some small debt to Clancy's interest in science fiction, he and most critics agree that he is not a science-fiction writer. The novel is futuristic, envisioning a third world war started by the Soviet Union. At the time the book was written, neither Clancy nor U.S. intelligence groups predicted the breakup of the Soviet Union. The Soviets were viewed as an implacable and dangerous enemy, the most dangerous threat to world peace and stability. This novel, like Clancy's first, echoes the views of many in the U.S. government during the 1980s before the collapse of the Soviet superstructure. Again, Clancy describes a harsh, amoral country willing to sacrifice anyone, its own citizens as well as foreigners, and even Soviet children. The government, manipulated by the KGB, will do anything to maintain power, even if it means destruction of large areas of the world.

With a structure modeled after the war games that Clancy enjoys, the novel begins when Muslim terrorists destroy a major Soviet oil refinery. The Politburo of the Soviet Union, fearful of the effect of insufficient oil supplies on the economy of its various republics, but particularly Russia, decides to attack several European countries to gain control of the oil fields of the Persian Gulf. The Allied countries, including the United States, are caught by surprise, and for a time it appears the Soviets will achieve their goals. Ultimately, however, the Russian forces' need for oil to operate their military equipment brings the war to an end.

The war machinery deployed in the novel includes submarines and other vessels, tanks and the paraphernalia of large invading armies, as well as various types of missiles. So large an operation in fiction or reality requires an enormous cast of characters, which Clancy provides, with the risk of overwhelming the reader. Reviewers voiced complaints that became more frequent with later Clancy novels. Although the work is exciting, it has too much of everything—too many subplots and too many people engaging in too many activities. Criticism of Clancy's characterizations also began with this work, and faultfinding has increased with each novel. Clancy seems most irritated by complaints about characters. He considers them true representations of military and government figures. Nevertheless, reviewers have repeatedly said his depictions of technology are better than his portrayals of humans. One critic has gone further, stating that Clancy's descriptions of machinery have more sexual suggestion than his love scenes. Clancy has

given credence to this assertion in interviews. Carried away by his enthusiasm when he has tried out new types of military equipment, he has called the experiences better than sex.

Heroes exist on both sides in *Red Storm Rising,* but, as in his first book, there are more American "good guys" (a Clancy term) than Russians. Apart from a few decent men, Clancy's Soviet Union is the "evil empire"–as defined by Reagan in the 1980s. A major difference between this novel and his first is the lack of a central unifying character. When Clancy was writing *The Hunt for Red October,* he used Jack Ryan, whom he had begun to develop earlier in his then unpublished manuscript *Patriot Games,* as the focal point. *Red Storm Rising,* however, lacks a hero to pull the multiple plots together. One man is the hero of one of the longer, more-cohesive plots, but it has only a limited connection to other parts of the work. Air Force first lieutenant Mike Edwards is the designated stouthearted man in this plotline. A meteorologist stationed in Keflavik, Iceland, Edwards leads the few American survivors to safety after a Russian surprise attack demolishes the base. He also rescues a young Icelandic woman who has been raped by Russians, and he provides intelligence information that ultimately leads to the recovery of Iceland by Allied forces.

Eventually, the multiple plots are brought to a satisfactory solution with Allied victories, as well as a successful coup in the Soviet Union. All ends with restoration of peace in the world, the promise of a wedding, and the expectation of a child.

Although the world of which Clancy writes is masculine, he is fond of concluding his novels with an actual or soon-to-occur birth. In *Red Storm Rising* the baby is not yet born, but in the closing segment of the next novel, *Patriot Games,* a son is born to the Ryans while Jack is on assignment, chasing and capturing Irish terrorists. An anticipated birth also ends his fourth novel, *The Cardinal of the Kremlin* (1988). In Clancy's sixth novel, *The Sum of All Fears* (1991), Cathy Ryan spends much of her time trying to get her tired and temporarily impotent husband to impregnate her during her carefully charted fertile days. A baby is anticipated in the seventh novel, *Without Remorse* (1993), and in *Executive Orders* (1996). Women have no other visible role in Clancy's first novel and little more in the second. He is notably weak in creating male-female relationships.

Clancy's third novel, *Patriot Games,* has a larger number of women in the major plot. Cathy Ryan now serves as more than an appendage to Jack. As a physician, wife, and mother, she participates in several actions in the two segments of the story that take place in London and Maryland. Although male characters in

Clancy at the time of The Hunt for Red October

Clancy's works appear either as loners or as part of a masculine world, the women are generally shown as parts of couples.

Clancy has called *Patriot Games* a love story, a view probably based on his intention of showing the close relationship of Cathy and Jack Ryan. Not only does the book include more romance than is usual in Clancy's work, it is also less a techno-thriller than an espionage novel. This characteristic points to its being an earlier piece of work, for at the time of the writing the author had not yet made technology the focus of his tales. The hero of *Patriot Games* is younger than the Ryan of *The Hunt for Red October*. Providing much of the Ryan background taken for granted in *The Hunt for Red October*, *Patriot Games* reveals more about him personally, including the reasons behind the queen's bestowal of a knighthood on Ryan.

The major plot concerns terrorism in Great Britain and the United States. The action begins when a fictional Irish Maoist group, the Ulster Liberation Army (ULA), attempts to capture the Prince and Princess of Wales and their infant son. In London with his family, Jack Ryan successfully foils the ULA and is seriously wounded. After his recovery, he and his family return home unaware that the terrorists now consider them targets. The ULA plan is expanded to include assassination of the Ryans and the Waleses while the prince and princess are visiting the Ryans in America. (The prince and Ryan have become steadfast friends, a friendship that continues through subsequent novels.)

In an action-packed conclusion, typical of the Clancy style, Ryan outthinks and outmaneuvers the ULA, killing some and capturing others, who are tried and found guilty in Clancy's next book. This thread linking one work to another and providing some sense of continuity from novel to novel is typical of Clancy's work, as history, politics, and current world events shape and alter identities.

At this beginning stage of his government career, Jack Ryan is not the figure the reader sees in later novels. He seems to evolve over time into a quick-tempered and arrogant hero. As the years pass, Ryan is certain he has a better understanding of national and international events than the officials elected or appointed to administer them. In *Patriot Games* Ryan appears naive, much in awe of pomp and circumstance. By the sixth, eighth, and ninth novels, written in the 1990s, nothing fazes Ryan as he brashly gives orders to clerks and presidents alike. (Clancy's seventh novel, *Without Remorse*, has a different hero.) After publication of his first books, Clancy developed friendships at home with presidents and vice presidents, as well as members of the U.S. Congress, the military, and various intelligence agencies, and he also formed attachments with people from other countries, including Great Britain. In spite of his Irish heritage, Clancy's novels reveal him, like Ryan, to be an Anglophile. Nevertheless, some of his most interesting villains are the Irish terrorists in *Patriot Games*. They are less stereotypical than most of his Russian malefactors. Sean Miller, the cold, vengeful ULA assassin, and one of the Clancy's most memorable characters, has been described by some critics as a Clancy double, the dark and dangerous opposite of the open, often humorous Ryan, who is not yet the all-knowing, didactic, and often imperious character he becomes in the later novels.

In *The Cardinal of the Kremlin,* Ryan is special assistant to the deputy director of the CIA, whose job Ryan will be given in the next book when the director dies. Ryan represents the CIA in arms-control negotiations between the United States and Russia. Extremely skeptical, he does not believe the Russians' proclaimed interest in peace. Neither does he want to bargain with the Russians over the Strategic Defense Initiative (SDI, also known as Star Wars). As might be expected in a Clancy plot, Ryan's distrust proves to be correct; for even as the Russians negotiate, they are secretly building an antiballistic-missile-defense system in Dushanbe, near the Afghan border.

The main plot of *The Cardinal of the Kremlin* hinges on the hush-hush race between the Americans and the Russians to develop antiballistic-missile systems. Current information suggests the Russians never had such a system. While the Americans were moving in that direction, work on the project was suspended on SDI, though some members of the military and the government have continued to press for the funds for the development of such a system. Clancy has shown great confidence in the possibilities of SDI–a not-unexpected belief for someone focused on the power of technology–and continues to urge the funding of various other costly technological projects. In "Back to the Frontier," a 1989 essay collected in *The Tom Clancy Companion* (1992), he excoriates "social reformers" who would give priority to poverty programs (which he considers failures) over scientific experimentation.

The Cardinal of the Kremlin is set during the Afghan-Russian War (1978–1992). The story moves back and forth from Afghanistan to Russia to the United States, from conference tables to laboratories, from cities to deserts to mountains, from diplomats to scientists to secret agents on both sides. Among the many spies in the novel, the most important is the "Cardinal" of the title, a Russian general named Filitov. Of all the Russian characters Clancy has created, Filitov is one of the most appealing. A highly respected war hero, Filitov remains in a position of power that enables him to provide intelligence to the United States, particularly information about the developing Russian antiballistic-missile facility. His reasons for betraying his country to the United States are similar to those of Ramius in *The Hunt for Red October.* When at last his secret actions are revealed at home, the Americans rescue him and bring him to the United States. The Archer, another important figure, is an Afghan guerrilla fighter supported covertly by the U.S. government. He loses his life during his attack on Dushanbe, which cripples the Russian missile facility, bringing to an end the threat of another military crisis between East and West.

John Clark, who makes a first brief but impressive appearance in *The Cardinal of the Kremlin,* is a major player in *Clear and Present Danger.* Though a dangerous and ruthless man in action, Clark is intensely honorable and loyal to friends. Because of the dark, violent side of his nature, critics see him in contrast to Ryan. In *Clear and Present Danger,* though not in other novels, Clark's unflinching and forceful personality and clarity of purpose are more impressive than Ryan's. Still, Ryan always comes through eventually. Whereas Ryan has a Ph.D., Clark has not gone to college. Ryan is rich; Clark is not. Clark saw action in Vietnam, but Ryan had only a brief stint in the marines and no combat experience.

Much of *Clear and Present Danger* is set in Colombia, South America, in the area controlled by the Medellín drug cartels. Alarmed by the large quantities of drugs and drug money coming into the country, the U.S. president, running for reelection and eager to improve his chances, decides to enlarge the area of action against drug dealers further than his legal mandate from Congress permits by launching a covert, unauthorized military operation to destroy cartel operations. After the operation fails and the men are stranded in enemy territory, the weak president and his amoral advisers, fearing a damaging leak about their activities, decide to scrap the plan, leaving the men to their fate. Clark, Ryan, and others save what is left of the troops, among them a young soldier named Domingo "Ding" Chavez, another hero whom Clancy uses in later novels.

Clancy's irritation with Congress—declared frequently and openly in interviews, essays, and his fiction—grows stronger with each successive novel. He expresses the view that individuals may have to take matters into their own hands if the law is "wrong." In addition to his contentious remarks about Congress, Clancy indicts gays as undependable and welfare recipients as taking unscrupulous advantage of the system. He also expresses contempt for certain sorts of government employees. In many of his novels he scorns people who come from wealthy Yankee backgrounds, have gone to Ivy League schools, and have used connections to get good jobs. He usually rates secular education as inferior to Jesuit institutions. The products of Jesuit schools, Ryan and Clark are always more logical and better trained than other men.

Education is important, writes Clancy, but so too is military service, as is demonstrated by the rise of

Ding Chavez. Born into poverty, Chavez becomes a leader of military men and in successive books joins the CIA, gets a good education, and eventually becomes engaged to one of Clark's daughters. Nevertheless, a fine education does not always turn out an admirable person, as Clancy reveals through a favorite scapegoat, Elizabeth Elliot, who becomes national security adviser to the president.

In the *The Sum of All Fears* Ryan considers Elliot his greatest adversary. As President Fowler's close adviser and mistress, she wields a lot of power. Ryan feels that she opposes, obstructs, or ignores his proposals and input. His hostility toward her, shared by almost everyone Elliot deals with–deceptive and unscrupulous as she may be–is out of proportion to her significance in the novel and calls attention to Clancy's contradictory attitudes toward women.

The many subplots in *The Sum of All Fears* have led to adverse comments from critics. Yet, at the end he brings together all the pieces. The major plot of this novel involves a group of Arab terrorists who want to start a war between the United States and Russia, hoping to distract the United States from its support of Israel and thus make Israel vulnerable to attacks from its enemies. Planning to create suspicion of Russia, the terrorists explode a bomb at a Super Bowl game in Denver. They kill large numbers of people but do not succeed in bringing about another war.

One of the two Clancy novels in which Ryan does not appear, *Without Remorse,* like some of the earlier novels, has been faulted for its style, length, and melodrama. The most significant criticism is of its moral code. John Kelly (known previously to readers as Clark) espouses a credo similar to what Jack Ryan only hints at, and in some limited way acts on, in *The Sum of All Fears.* Both men believe that people must take a stand against evil even if it means breaking the law. Each person may decide on an individual code of justice. Although logic makes plain that the ultimate end of such a stance is anarchy, neither Clancy nor any of his characters seems to consider that possibility.

Without Remorse has two plots and fewer subplots than most Clancy novels. Equal in importance, the two major plots at first seem to have no relationship, but soon it becomes apparent that the important connection is war, foreign and domestic. The country of Vietnam and American prisoners of war–missing or declared dead–are the focus of one plot. *Without Remorse* could be labeled Clancy's Vietnam novel; it reveals in dramatic fashion Clancy's views about that war and the people on both sides who fought it. The second plot, equally forceful, tells of domestic war brought on by the drug culture in the United States.

Kelly, as the only character who acts in both parts of the story, provides the direct link between them, but there are also more subtle connections. Clancy shows that a shooting war and a drug war involve many of the same kinds of people, the victims and persecutors, the heroes and villains, the loyal and the traitorous. Cruelty and greed destroy large numbers of lives, whether on city streets or in foreign jungles. Violence is pervasive and gratuitous in the amoral worlds of both wars. No one person can save the world (even in a thriller novel), but good and great men must try.

John Kelly/John Clark is such a man. In the 1970s John Kelly, a young man just out of the navy, not long married but soon widowed, has his life transformed by harsh events. He falls in love with a young prostitute who is murdered by the drug dealers she tries to escape. Kelly avenges her death by destroying the drug ring, but his illegal actions require that his name disappear from all records. Thus he assumes the name John Clark. His true name is *almost* restored twice in later novels. Clark's other heroic efforts in *Without Remorse* center on the rescue of American military prisoners from Vietnam. At the end of the book, in typical Clancy style, a newly married Clark is about to become a father.

Without Remorse employs devices and strategies reminiscent of James Bond movies. One reviewer of the novel commented, "Inside every Tom Clancy novel is a thin Ian Fleming waiting to get out." Clark, like Bond and other fantasy heroes, is a one-man army. Constantly tested, he always comes through and wins out against evil. The dark and handsome daredevil and avenger is a superhero. More a man of action than Ryan, he moves behind the scenes, undercover and chameleon-like when necessary. In Clancy's next novel, Clark manages to fit quietly into a Japanese environment without arousing suspicion.

Debt of Honor (1994) has several plots, characters, and settings. A long book, it is made longer by Clancy's expository remarks throughout. The main theme is economic competition between the United States and Japan. Clancy depicts an aggressive, hostile Japan led by secretive, vengeful men who desire greater economic power and military control over territory outside Japan. In many ways these archvillains seem much like the Russians of Clancy's earlier books but further repugnant qualities are assigned to the Japanese–including a proclivity for pornography, a desire for Western women, and breast fetishism. A minor subplot exposes some U.S. senators as sexually decadent but not as depraved as the Japanese.

Trade relationships create problems between the two countries, both competing for world markets. After

Dust jacket for Clancy's 1998 novel, about an elite international group of antiterrorist commandos

several Americans die in accidents in Japanese cars, the United States passes punitive trade restrictions that threaten the Japanese financial situation. In response, imperialistic groups that have taken control in Japan launch economic and military attacks on the United States, drawing the surprised and unprepared Americans into an undeclared war. Victory comes to the "good guys" thanks to the wisdom and dedication of people such as Jack Ryan. Yet, in one last Japanese action, an attack on the U.S. Capitol, the president and many members of Congress are killed. Ryan becomes the new president only hours after being sworn in as vice president. In Clancy's next novel the narrative picks up with Ryan serving as president.

Ryan's standing is greater than ever in *Debt of Honor.* Essential to the government, more brilliant than anyone else, he no longer hesitates to take action in any situation. Among the larger-than-life American heroes– and a few admirable Japanese–in this novel, Ryan looms largest, though Clark is an impressive player.

Clancy has generally followed the pattern of publishing a novel each year, usually in August, but after *Debt of Honor* he chose to write one of his several nonfiction technological instructional guides. He then turned to the creation of his paperback fiction series and television movies based on his books. In 1995 he told several talk-show hosts that Jack Ryan would be back, but first

he would produce a collection of nonfiction essays titled *Reality Check: What's Going On Out There?* In August 1995, Clancy's publishers listed the book as available, but it was never released. The only explanation given to prospective buyers was that Putnam recalled the book.

In Clancy's ninth novel, *Executive Orders,* a massive 874 pages, Ryan is established in the White House. One reviewer notes with tongue in cheek that the presidency is the only job left for him. Clark also has a role, along with Chavez–the George Mason University graduate and soon-to-be son-in-law of Clark. (Clancy often plugs his favorite schools in his writings while also expressing his intense dislike of Ivy League institutions.)

With Russia no longer the chief adversary of the United States, Clancy has turned to other areas of trouble, inflating actual hostilities into major or minor wars. In *Executive Orders* the chief enemy is an imaginary, newly united Iran and Iraq, whose leader, the Ayatollah, and his followers use every method from weaponry to biological warfare in their attempts to destroy enemies. The Ayatollah is responsible for terrorists' attempt to kidnap the Ryan's youngest child, for a bodyguard's efforts to kill Ryan, and for the planting of the Ebola virus in several areas of the United States, resulting in widespread infection and death. As China and Taiwan move close to combat and India expresses hostility toward the United States, Iran-Iraq goes to war against its neighbors and the United States. Other subplots cover events in Sudan, Uganda, Khartoum, Israel, Turkmenistan, Russia, Saudi Arabia, and France–while various domestic problems seem insurmountable, but predictably Ryan overcomes them all–while, true to form, a multitude of characters heap praise on him. As Clancy's persona, Ryan has an agenda for change. Clancy frequently sacrifices suspense to lecture the reader in unremitting detail about the need for tax reform, the inefficiency of the Congress, the amorality of the mass media, or whatever other political issue occupies his thoughts at the moment.

In Clancy's 1998 novel *Rainbow Six,* Ryan is still president and presumably has not yet stood for election. Another John Clark novel, *Rainbow Six* is set mainly in England. Clark and a group of specially trained men from many nations have been brought together to fight worldwide terrorism. Eventually, they go to North and South America to defeat the source of world terror–a group of American scientists who have the knowledge, money, power, and connections with which they attempt to control the planet.

In the course of his victories Clark becomes more aware of his younger self in son-in-law Ding Chavez. With so much emphasis placed on Clark's aging and the prowess of Chavez in the novel, the reader cannot help but speculate that Clancy may be grooming the younger man to be his next superhero.

Interviews:

Tom Mutter, "PW Interviews Tom Clancy," *Publishers Weekly,* 230 (8 August 1986): 53–54;

Cynthia Ward, "Author Tom Clancy and His Novels in Defense of America," *Conservative Digest,* 14 (April 1988): 5–12;

Marc Cooper, "Interview: Tom Clancy," *Playboy* (April 1988): 55–57, 60–63, 160–163;

"The Write Stuff," *American Legion,* 131 (December 1991): 16–17, 49–51;

Martin H. Greenberg, "An Interview with Tom Clancy," in *The Tom Clancy Companion,* edited by Greenberg (New York: Berkley, 1992), pp. 57–86;

Peter Carlson, "What Ticks Tom Clancy Off?" *Washington Post Magazine,* 7 June 1993, pp. 12–15, 26–32.

Bibliography:

Helen S. Garson, *Tom Clancy: A Critical Companion* (Westport, Conn.: Greenwood Press, 1996).

References:

Patrick Anderson, "King of the Techno-Thriller," *New York Times Magazine,* 1 May 1988, pp. 54–55, 83–85;

Larry Bond, Introduction to *The Tom Clancy Companion,* edited by Martin H. Greenberg (New York: Berkley, 1992), pp. 1–4;

Marc Cerasini, "Tom Clancy's Fiction," in *The Tom Clancy Companion,* pp. 5–55;

Tad Friend, "The Pentagon's Favorite Novelist," *Gentlemen's Quarterly,* 58 (June 1988): 220–223;

Helen S. Garson, *Tom Clancy: A Critical Companion* (Westport, Conn.: Greenwood Press, 1996);

Walter Hixson, "*Red Storm Rising:* Tom Clancy's Novels and the Cult of National Security," *Diplomatic History,* 17 (Fall 1993): 599–613;

Michael Knight, *Tom Clancy's Rainbow Six: Prima's Official Strategy Guide* (Rocklin, Cal.: Prima, 1998);

Art Levine, "The Pentagon's Unlikely Hero," *U.S. News and World Report,* 101 (15 September 1986): 66;

William Ryan, "The Genesis of the Techno-Thriller," *Virginia Quarterly Review,* 69 (Winter 1993): 24–40;

Richard Sandza, "Does the Word Warrior Get His Facts Right?" *Newsweek,* 112 (8 August 1988): 62–63;

Scott Shuger, "Paperback Fighter," *Washington Monthly,* 21 (November 1989): 10–18;

Evan Thomas, "The Art of the Techno-Thriller," *Newsweek,* 112 (8 August 1988): 60–65.

Robert Coover

(4 February 1932 –   )

Julian Cowley
University of Luton

See also the Coover entries in *DLB 2: American Novelists Since World War II* and *DLB Yearbook 1981.*

BOOKS: *The Origin of the Brunists* (New York: Putnam, 1966; London: Barker, 1967);

The Universal Baseball Association, Inc., J. Henry Waugh, Prop. (New York: Random House, 1968; London: Hart-Davis, 1970);

Pricksongs & Descants (New York: Dutton, 1969; London: Cape, 1971);

A Theological Position: Plays (New York: Dutton, 1972);

The Water Pourer (Bloomfield Hills, Mich.: Bruccoli Clark, 1972);

The Public Burning (New York: Viking, 1977; London: Allen Lane, 1978);

Hair O' the Chine (Columbia, S.C.: Bruccoli Clark, 1979);

After Lazarus: A Filmscript (Bloomfield Hills, Mich.: Bruccoli Clark, 1980);

A Political Fable (New York: Viking, 1980);

Charlie in the House of Rue (Lincoln, Mass.: Penmaen Press, 1980);

Spanking the Maid: A Novel (Bloomfield Hills, Mich.: Bruccoli Clark, 1981; London: Heinemann, 1987);

The Convention (Northridge, Cal.: Lord John Press, 1982);

In Bed One Night & Other Brief Encounters (Providence, R.I.: Burning Deck, 1983);

Gerald's Party: A Novel (New York: New American Library, 1985; London: Heinemann, 1986);

Aesop's Forest, with *The Plot of the Mice and Other Stories,* by Brian Swann, Capra back-to-back series, volume 8 (Santa Barbara, Cal.: Capra Press, 1986);

A Night at the Movies: Or, You Must Remember This (New York: Linden/Simon & Schuster, 1987; London: Heinemann, 1987);

Whatever Happened to Gloomy Gus of the Chicago Bears? (New York: Linden/Simon & Schuster, 1987; London: Heinemann, 1988);

Pinocchio in Venice (New York: Linden/Simon & Schuster, 1991; London: Heinemann, 1991);

Robert Coover (photograph © by Stathis Orphanos; from the dust jacket for Ghost Town, *1998)*

Briar Rose (New York: Grove, 1996);

John's Wife: A Novel (New York: Simon & Schuster, 1996);

Ghost Town: A Novel (New York: Holt, 1998).

PLAY PRODUCTIONS: *The Kid,* New York, American Place Theater, 17 November 1972; London, 1974;

Love Scene, produced as *Scène d'amour,* Paris, Troglodyte Theater, 1973; produced again as *Love Scene,* New York, 20 March 1974;

Rip Awake, Los Angeles, 1975;

A Theological Position, Los Angeles, 1977; New York, 1979;

Bridge Hand, Providence, R.I., 1981.

PRODUCED SCRIPT: *On a Confrontation in Iowa City,* motion picture, University of Iowa, 1969.

OTHER: Ricardo Estrada, "The Osprey and the Sparrowhawk," translated by Coover, *Quarterly Review of Literature,* 15 (1968): 259–262;

"The Last Quixote: marginal notes on the Gospel according to Samuel Beckett," in *New American Review,* 11 (New York: Simon & Schuster, 1971), pp. 132–143;

The Stone Wall Book of Short Fiction, edited by Coover and Kent Dixon (Iowa City: Stone Wall Press, 1973);

Minute Stories, edited by Coover and Elliott Anderson (New York: Braziller, 1976);

"The Clemency Appeal," in *Statements 2: New Fiction* edited by Jonathan Baumbach and Peter Spielberg (New York: Fiction Collective, 1977), pp. 87–94;

"Statement," in *Statements 2: New Fiction,* edited by Jonathan Baumbach and Peter Spielberg (New York: Fiction Collective, 1977), pp. 7–9.

SELECTED PERIODICAL PUBLICATIONS–UNCOLLECTED: "One Summer in Spain: Five Poems," *Fiddlehead* (Autumn 1960): 13–14;

"Blackdamp," *Noble Savage,* 4 (October 1961): 218–229;

"The Square Shooter and the Saint," *Evergreen Review,* 25 (July–August 1962): 92–101;

"Dinner with the King of England," *Evergreen Review,* 27 (November–December 1962): 110–118;

"The Second Son," *Evergreen Review,* 31 (October–November 1963): 72–88;

"The Neighbors," *Argosy* (January 1965);

"The First Annual Congress of the High Church of Hard Core (Notes from the Underground)," *Evergreen Review,* 89 (May 1971): 16, 74;

"McDuff on the Mound," *Iowa Review,* 2 (Fall 1971): 111–120;

"Lucky Pierre and the Music Lesson," in *New American Review,* 14 (New York: Simon & Schuster, 1972), pp. 202–212;

"The Dead Queen," *Quarterly Review of Literature,* 18 (1973): 304–313;

"Lucky Pierre and the Cunt Auction," *Antaeus* (Spring–Summer 1974): 13–14;

"The Master's Voice," *American Review,* 26 (November 1977): 361–388;

"Hyperfiction: Novels for the Computer," *New York Times Book Review* (29 August 1993): 1, 8–12.

Robert Coover is one of America's most distinguished writers. His eminence is to be measured not by the size of his current readership, which remains select, but in terms of the technical resourcefulness that has enabled him to produce a series of virtuosic works in a dazzling array of styles and forms. Coover is a consummate artist who has invested immense literary labor in the production of work of enduring quality.

His creative energy is assiduously directed. Most of his writing has been done away from the United States, and his custom has been to work mainly in the early hours of the morning. Writing in *New Times* in 1977, Geoffrey Woolf remarked: "More than any writer, more than any man I have met, he is invincibly self-assured and secure in his professional self-esteem. This he expresses not through stridency or arrogance but through a relentlessness of purpose; he knows what he means to do, and does neither less nor more. He has outlined sufficient work to occupy himself for the next 200 years." It should be added that Coover is able to do things in fiction that few of his contemporaries, indeed few writers at any time, have had the capacity to accomplish.

Lois Gordon, in her 1983 study, *Robert Coover: The Universal Fictionmaking Process,* cites a discussion she had in 1981 with Fred Jordan, a senior editor at Grove Press, who remarked: "Most writers are torn between the marketplace and their vision. I've never encountered that in him. The marketplace is immaterial to him." Although the artistic integrity this comment discloses is undoubtedly a factor contributing to the relatively limited sphere of his current readership, his editor at Viking for *The Public Burning* (1977), Richard Seaver, has affirmed to Gordon, "In the long haul, when we look back over the end of the century, he will have sold more books than his contemporaries. Like any good writer, he's not necessarily in tune with his time or catering to his time."

Profoundly engaged with fictional structures, Coover is nonetheless alert to the physical realities of the world in which the reader lives, and in crucial ways he is emphatically responsive to his time. In a 1973 interview with Frank Gado, published in *First Person,* Coover asserted: "I've always been contentious with my writing; I've never turned away from unpleasantness in order to provide escapism. The world itself being a construct of fictions, I believe the fiction maker's function is to furnish better fictions with which we can re-form our notions of things."

This understanding has remained essential to his work. In an interview with Larry McCaffery in 1979, he returned to the point, arguing that "Men live by fictions. They have to. Life's too complicated, we just can't handle all the input, we have to isolate little bits and make reasonable stories out of them." An engagement with this "human need for pattern" underlies all his writing, but his function as an author is not merely reflective; rather, he assumes a pungently critical position. Coover continued, "If some stories start throwing their weight around, I like to undermine their authority a bit, work variations, call attention to their fictional natures." His persistent concern has been to counter empty ritualistic forms which, if accepted without question, diminish or distort human energies.

Robert Lowell Coover was born in Charles City, Iowa, on 4 February 1932, the son of Grant Marion and Maxine (Sweet) Coover. His family moved to Bedford, Indiana, when he was nine, then later to Herrin, Illinois, where he graduated from high school. At school Coover manifested an early interest in writing and in drama. He was a member of Quill and Scroll, as well as the National Honor Society, and he became high-school class president. His father was managing editor of the *Herrin Daily Journal;* following this paternal lead he edited various school papers as "Scoop" Coover and contributed a column titled "Koover's Korner." He was a member of the school band and enthusiastically followed sports, supporting the local basketball team and the Cincinatti Reds. He also played tabletop baseball games, and these imaginative examples of emulatory ritual fed into his second novel, *The Universal Baseball Association, Inc., J. Henry Waugh, Prop.* (1968).

Coover entered Southern Illinois University in 1949. While there he wrote for the campus newspaper, *The Egyptian,* and continued to work for the *Herrin Daily Journal* until he graduated. Herrin was the scene of a mining disaster in 1951, and Coover helped cover the story. Recollection of this incident furnished raw material for the story "Blackdamp," which appeared in the magazine *Noble Savage* ten years later, and then for his first novel, *The Origin of the Brunists* (1966). Also in 1951 he transferred to Indiana University, graduating with a Bachelor of Arts degree in 1953. He majored in Slavic studies. On the day of his graduation he was drafted into the armed forces and chose to join the navy. He attended Officer Candidate School, then spent three years in Europe at the rank of lieutenant. During a one-year tour of the Mediterranean, he met Maria del Pilar Sans Mallafré, a student at the University of Barcelona, who later became his wife.

After leaving the navy, and prior to attending graduate school at the University of Chicago, Coover began writing with a new seriousness. In the summer of 1957 he spent a month in a cabin beside Rainy Lake on the Canadian border. He refers to the experience in

Coover at the time of The Origin of the Brunists *(1966)*

"The Magic Poker," a story that appeared in the collection *Pricksongs & Descants* (1969). That summer was a significant period for Coover in terms of formative reading, the discovery of Samuel Beckett's work being of particular importance. Coover recorded the impact of Beckett's example in an essay, "The Last Quixote," published in *New American Review* in 1971. Beckett, he says, "offered me, in those days, a way of going on, of making art, without affirmation." More specifically, "He was wonderful at odd abrupt transitions between different functional levels, at ironic echoes and parallels, funny games with numbers, names, and logogriphs." All these characteristics are plentiful in Coover's subsequent work. Coover studied at the University of Chicago from 1958 until 1961, eventually receiving his master's degree in 1965.

In "The Last Quixote," Coover alludes to his mentor at the University of Chicago, Richard McKeon, professor of classics and philosophy. McKeon's courses on the history of discourse in physical science, social science, and humanities persuaded Coover that "the fashion of the world was indeed changing." McKeon highlighted a widespread sense among contemporary intellectuals of a cosmos in transition. This understanding has subsequently informed all of Coover's fictional investigations of the fiction-making nature of human understanding. His first book, *The Origin of the Brunists,* is dedicated to McKeon.

Between 1958 and 1959, Coover traveled in Spain. In the summer of 1959 he married Maria del Pilar Sans Mallafré, and the couple journeyed through southern Europe on a motorbike. In remarks to Julian Cowley in 1998, Coover referred to that time as " . . . our wedding summer." This experience furnished material for "One Summer in Spain: Five Poems," his first published work—"little love poems of a sort," he told Cowley. The Coovers have three children: Diana Nin, Sara Chapin, and Roderick Luis. Coover is fluent in Spanish. Knowing the language has undoubtedly enhanced his enthusiasm for Miguel de Cervantes Saavedra. Coover has published translations of his own work into Spanish and the literature of others from Spanish into English. Coover has expressed admiration for Latin American authors such as Jorge Luis Borges, Miguel Angel Asturias, Julio Cortázar, and Gabriel García Márquez.

In the early 1960s, publication of Coover's short stories began to appear regularly in magazines, including *Evergreen Review.* From 1962 until 1965 he lived in his wife's hometown of Tarragona, working on *The Origin of the Brunists, The Universal Baseball Association,* and some short stories. At this time Coover developed an interest in older modes of storytelling, such as those found in Ovid's *Metamorphoses* and in *The Arabian Nights.* He has valued this immersion in ancient literatures as vital engagement with remarkable imaginative responses to problems arising in the composition of fiction. He recognizes the enduring power of myth and suggested in his 1973 interview with Frank Gado that "the crucial beliefs of people are mythic in nature; whether at the level of the Cinderella story or of the Resurrection, the language is mythopoeic rather than rational." Far from viewing his investigation of mythic structures as some form of pure research, Coover argues that this "means of navigating through life" informs one's reception of information in daily life through contemporary media such as newspapers, film, and television.

In 1965, "The Neighbors" was published in *Argosy* in London. The next year Coover began a teaching career at Bard College, New York, that provided some financial security, enabling him to write without compromise; that same year Coover's first novel, *The Origin of the Brunists,* was published.

Coover told Gado that during the reworking of his first novel, he read *Moby-Dick* (1851) for the first time. From Melville he took "a lesson in perserverance: I thought that if a writer could go that far in exploring an idea, then I could go the distance with my book." Coover admires such unswerving dedication to the craft of writing; he reads as a writer, not as a professional critic or an academic, and is acutely conscious of the struggles and triumphs of literary labor involved in the work of other writers. Among his North American contemporaries Coover has stated his interest in the novels of such writers as Stanley Elkin, William Gass, John Barth, Thomas Pynchon, John Hawkes, and Sol Yurick.

The Origin of the Brunists is a novel that conforms, more than any of his later fictions, to recognizable conventions of realism. Coover told Gado: "I thought of it, a bit, as paying dues. I didn't feel I had the right to move into more presumptuous fictions until I could prove I could handle the form as it now was in the world." Nonetheless, there are significant technical departures, and this novel already marks Coover as a metafictionist in that it is a study of how a system of beliefs, analogous to a fictional construct, is generated and developed, shaping social behavior in the process.

The action centers on a mining disaster in which ninety-seven members of a small, closely knit midwestern community die. Giovanni Bruno, one of the survivors, is an enigmatic figure, who soon finds himself at the heart of a religious cult, "The Brunists," delineated in terms that inevitably recall Christianity. The cult's subsequent history is traced as it prepares for imminent apocalypse. These preparations reach, in the novel's penultimate chapter, a frenzied climax at the Mount of Redemption. The apocalyptic moment fails to materialize, and Bruno has been consigned to an asylum. Nonetheless, the influence of the new religion continues to spread.

In his characterization of the main character, Justin "Tiger" Miller, Coover introduces a thematic concern that has persisted through later work: "Games were what kept Miller going. Games, and the pacifying of mind and organs." Games constitute an appropriate metaphor because they require their own sets of rules, which are arbitrary and have no reference to any reality beyond the games, yet constrain the participants. Coover finds the game a cogent metaphor for the ways in which most social forms and institutions operate.

The characterization continues: "Miller perceived existence as a loose concatenation of separate and ultimately inconsequential instants, each colored by the actions that preceded it, but each possessed of a small wanton freedom of its own. Life, then was a series of adjustments to these actions and, if one kept his sense of humor and produced as many of these actions himself as possible, adjustment was easier." Within a fiction, Coover asserts the need for fiction-making to be sufficiently flexible to accommodate indeterminate aspects of the living process. *The Origin of the Brunists* traces the genesis and development of a ritualistic structure as a community gives birth to a religion.

Coover has a long-standing interest in the work of Emile Durkheim, particularly in the sociologist's explanation of the manner in which mediation occurs between an isolated individual existence and the sense of belonging to a group. This novel is a compelling work of fiction, not merely an exercise in fleshing out ideas, and that achievement was recognized when *The Origin of the Brunists* received the William Faulkner Award for the best first novel of 1966.

In 1967 Coover taught at the University of Iowa while continuing to publish stories. Since the mid 1960s he has managed to divide his time effectively between teaching in America and residing in Europe (predominantly Spain and England). Talking with Gado he observed: "I realized long ago that the process of asserting and creating your life is made much more difficult where the familiar vibrations are strong."

Coover returned to the University of Iowa as writer in residence for a month in the summer of 1968. That same summer his second novel, *The Universal Baseball Association, Inc., J. Henry Waugh, Prop.*, was published. Like its predecessor the novel evolved from a short story, "The Second Son," published in *Evergreen Review* in 1963. Coover's career has been marked by occasions of such transformation of his own work into another form, or an alternative realization. In "The Second Son," which closely corresponds to the important second chapter of the novel, Coover relates the story of a middle-aged accountant, J. Henry Waugh, who becomes obsessed with his invention of a tabletop baseball game. Waugh becomes so involved with the people and events of his game that he begins to believe in their literal existence. Specifically he grows attached to one of the imaginary players, Damon Rutherford, who assumes the importance of a "second son" for Waugh. A throw of the dice necessitates Damon's death. He is struck by a ball on the field of play, and Waugh is driven to despair by the loss.

As in the novel, the accountant in the short story is a man who takes comfort from numbers; he is bored by actual baseball games, but finds compelling the statistics generated from his own concocted league. The game metaphor in the novel takes the foreground, while Christian parallels of sacrifice and salvation resonate strongly around it. Waugh, whose name puns on Jehovah, is a god who does play dice with his tabletop universe, and when the result is the sacrifice of a favored son, he is traumatized.

In the expanded version of the short story that forms the novel, much space is devoted to meditations on death, the void that is masked by ritual and metaphor, the formless abyss that lies beyond pattern. Waugh takes revenge by killing Jock Casey, the player whose pitch felled Rutherford, and he experi-

Dust cover for the first edition of Coover's first novel (1967), about the founding of a religious cult (Bruccoli Collection, University of South Carolian)

ences catharsis. He has broken the rules, which have supported him for so long, but Coover's point is that they have proven inadequately responsive to changing needs. The novel articulates a paradoxical lesson, "that perfection wasn't a thing, a closed moment, a static fact, but process, yes, and the process was transformation." It is a lesson that Coover has found forcefully made in Ovid.

The year 1969 was an important one for Coover. He wrote, directed, and produced a motion picture, *On a Confrontation in Iowa City;* for a brief time was writer in residence at Washington University in St. Louis; was recipient of a Brandeis Creative Arts Award and of a grant from the Rockefeller Foundation; and his book of fictions titled *Pricksongs & Descants* was published. Most of the pieces collected were written prior to the composition of his first novel. In response to Gado's question concerning the meaning of the title, Coover has explained that it alludes to musical terms: "'Pricksong' derives from the physical manner in which the song was printed—the notes were literally pricked out; 'descant' refers to the form of music in which there is a *cantus firmus,* a basic line, and variations that the other voices play against it. The early descants, being improvisations, were unwritten; when they began writing them, the idea of counterpoint, of a full, beautiful harmony emerged." In addition to their obvious availability for sexual punning, the terms attracted him because they refer back to "art forms that have been shunted aside by the developments of the last three hundred years. The choice of title had to do with my decision to focus on Cervantes as a turning point." The spirit of the author of *Don Quixote* presides over this volume of bold innovation.

Coover had hoped to publish a collection of stories some years previously but had been dissuaded on the grounds that novels would more firmly establish his career. By the time publication of such a book seemed appropriate, he had pared down the number of fictions he considered suitable. A section headed "Seven Exemplary Fictions" is prefaced by an address to Cervantes. It confides that just as his novellas "were 'exemplary,' in the simplest sense, because they represented the different writing ideas you were working with from the 1580s to 1612, so do these seven stories—along with the three 'Sentient Lens' fictions also included in this volume—represent about everything I invented up to the commencement of my first novel in 1962 able to bear this later exposure." In *Pricksongs & Descants,* Coover aspired to emulate Cervantes, whose stories "exemplified the dual nature of all good narrative art: they struggled against the unconscious mythic residue in human life and sought to synthesize the unsynthesizable, sallied forth against adolescent thought-modes and exhausted art-forms, and returned home with new complexities." In retrospect it appears that this program has fueled Coover's own adventures in fiction for more than thirty years.

This dedicatory preface also registers Coover's commitment to design as a principle of composition. In 1973 he explained to Gado that from the start of his writing career he had made "an arbitrary commitment to design." The commitment is arbitrary because it does not spring from "some notion of an underlying ideal order which fiction imitates"; rather it testifies to his "delight with the rich ironic possibilities that the use of structure affords. Any idea, even one that on the surface doesn't seem very interesting, fitted with a perfect structure, can blossom into something that even I did not suspect was there originally. Engaging in that process of discovery is the excitement of making fiction." Self-conscious design displaces the given, and once that displacement is underway all kinds of exciting possibilities are activated.

Pricksongs & Descants is a celebration of those possibilites in a richly varied collection of twenty-one virtuosic fictions. A striking aspect of many of these fictions is their initial reliance on materials drawn from folklore, fairy tales, and Bible stories as well as from popular culture. At the same time that he deploys recognizable, even familiar, figures from such sources, Coover draws attention to the act of writing through linguistic play or through disruption of conventional narrative forms. The lens of language through which the borrowed figures are seen grows opaque, and it is evident that they are in fact constituted through language. Wielding the power that this recognition confers on him, Coover then works spinning variations on the well-known stories.

"The Brother" is a retelling of the story of Noah from the point of view of his unnamed brother who helped build the ark but was denied the salvation it offered. "J's Marriage" presents Joseph's view of the birth of Christ, which combines confusion and anger at the unexpected impregnation of his young wife. In such cases Coover is challenging the authority of unitary narratives by indicating limits to the received versions. The truth offered by the familiar stories becomes precariously provisional and so more truly human. The fact that Noah's brother addresses the audience in an unpunctuated monologue, employing a working-class idiom, and that Joseph has been reduced to an initial, a victim within a Kafkaesque world of suspected persecution by unseen forces, heightens the effect of salutary defamiliarization by unsettling "unconscious mythic residue." These pieces involve the working of a literary counterpoint against well-known narratives.

Another set of fictions found here are regularly cited as exemplary of postmodern compositional practice. In *The Metafictional Muse,* Larry McCaffery refers to them as "cubist stories," built around "a deliberate ambiguity of event." Fictions such as "The Elevator" and "The Babysitter" offer multiple realizations of a given situation. The available realizations contradict or even negate one another. But this is not just a case of presenting contesting perspectives on an empirically verifiable reality. Rather, Coover's acts of invention demand recognition that no version can justifiably claim priority; none holds a reassuringly privileged position to help coordinate an authoritative reading. Coover writes in a world where, as McCaffery puts it, "the assurance of the existence of the objective nature of reality has faded."

In "Ideas of Order at Delphi," his contribution to the 1988 volume *Facing Texts,* Marc Chénetier also notes Coover's persistent resistance to naive faith in objective description: "Perhaps because one of our dominant fictions has forever consisted in naturalizing the objectivity of our perceptions and measuring all other registering devices in terms of their closeness to or distortion of 'natural' perception, Coover's strategy at all times, although in an admirable variety of manners, consists in demonstrating the illusory stability, the essential inadequacy and incompleteness of our fictional optics, its founding plasticity and lack of resilience under the creative assaults of imagination and desire."

Perhaps the most explicit treatment in *Pricksongs & Descants* of this concern to counter the tendency to naturalize perceptions is to be found in three stories collectively titled "The Sentient Lens." These fictions are composed as if filtered through a camera lens, but as the title indicates that is not regarded as a neutral medium but as inescapably caught up in a process of translation. Ostensibly less involved with "fictional optics," a story such as "The Babysitter" is in fact a more radical departure from the conventions that anchor any commitment to objective realism.

Given that Coover's perception is that the world is unstable, in constant flux, and subject to "the creative assaults of imagination and desire," his next major fictional work appears all the more extraordinary. *The Public Burning* did not appear until 1977, and when published, it generated furious controversy of a kind that only incisive engagement with historical and political reality can produce. But that reality is in fact entirely consistent with the world of *Pricksongs & Descants,* and that volume of fictions may tellingly elucidate some of the less obvious sources for the hostility and anxiety with which, in certain quarters, the novel was received.

The 1970s started well for Coover but ultimately was not an easy decade. In 1971 Coover received a Guggenheim Fellowship and a citation in fiction from Brandeis University. In 1972 he taught at Princeton University, and Dutton published *A Theological Position,* a collection of four one-act plays, all of which have been produced. Coover assisted in the staging of *The Kid* at New York's American Place Theater. It was directed by Jack Gelber, who received an Obie award for his work. *Love Scene* premiered in Paris at the Troglodyte theater and was performed in French as *Scene d'amour,* directed by Henri Gilabert. When *Rip Awake* premiered in Los Angeles, Rip was played by Ron Sossi, whose Odyssey group also premiered *A Theological Position.* Also in 1972 Coover published a small book, *The Water-Pourer,* originally written as a chapter for *The Origin of the Brunists* but omitted from the finished novel.

In 1974 Coover again received a Guggenheim Fellowship, and published in *TriQuarterly,* "The Public Burning of Ethel and Julius Rosenberg: An Historical Romance," which provided a glimpse of his major work in progress. Further indication of the shape *The Public Burning* was taking was given in the story "Whatever Happened to Gloomy Gus of the Chicago Bears?" that appeared in *New American Review,* in 1975. It registered the increasingly central position the figure of Richard Nixon had come to occupy in the composition of Coover's American epic. In 1976 Coover received an American Academy of Arts and Letters Award in literature.

The Public Burning was begun as a play in 1966. Coover found that the form did not suit the materials, so he reconceived it as a fiction. He returned to his plan for a fiction handling the Rosenberg case but found he could not contain the project within the limits he had initially conceived. It became a novel of more than five-hundred pages. The manuscript circulated among New York publishers for several years before its eventual acceptance by Richard Seaver for Viking Press. The publishing houses were unsettled by the book's provocative treatment of sensitive political materials. The book was actually finished in 1975, and Coover intended that it should be published to coincide with America's Bicentennial and the 1976 presidential election. But Knopf, who had energetically negotiated the manuscript away from Dutton, jettisoned the book fearing possible libel actions.

In 1977 Coover published "Statement" as a prefatory piece to the anthology *Statements 2.* This meditation on the status of literary art in contemporary America is manifestly colored by the anguish and frustration he experienced while attempting to bring *The Public Burning* into print under the aegis of a major publishing house. Coover has always insisted on the priority of preserving the integrity of his work. In *Statements 2* he writes that "America is, at best, a strange place for an artist to work in. On the one hand there is the illusion of artistic freedom, constitutionally protected; on the other, there's the operative dogma of the marketplace: will it sell? In America, art—like everything else (knowledge, condoms, religion, etc.)—is a product. The discovery of this is the capstone to the artist's alienation process in America. He knows there is no relation between what is good and what sells, nor between what he's made and how it's used by the market managers." The bitterness he felt during these years is channeled into the caustic declaration: "No need for censorship: trust the general banality of the marketplace."

The Public Burning was published two and a half turbulent years after its completion. Seaver was tenacious in persuading Viking of the book's outstanding literary quality, despite its potentially inflammatory handling of the Rosenberg case and still more provocatively its irreverent use of Richard Nixon as a narrator and principal character. Coover has disclosed that Viking nonetheless withheld money for several years to cover possible legal battles and ensured that in such an

Cover for Coover's 1985 novel, a murder-mystery parody

event the author would be held entirely responsible. Still, the novel established Coover unequivocally as a major force in contemporary fiction.

The book has twenty-eight sections, with Nixon narrating alternating sections. Critics have noted how the publicly discredited politician becomes, in significant ways, a sympathetic figure within Coover's text. His narration is surprisingly introspective, disclosing a sensitivity that assumes a certain poignancy amidst the novel's insistent physicality. The Rosenbergs, on the other hand, are presented less sympathetically than one might expect, largely because as they act out the roles the situation assigns to them, the suspicion is raised that they were to some extent complicit in their own persecution. Coover is not interested in the corroboration of received wisdom, whether it originates from liberal or from reactionary sources. He is not making a banal political point. Rather, he is involved in the more fundamentally political and ethical procedure of investigating how human beings are shaped by the roles available

to them, how actions are constrained and determined by patterns and rituals, and how a sense of history is conditioned by narrative forms and media channels.

The Universal Baseball Association includes a scene in which Coover's view of the constructed nature of historical understanding is expounded: "The paper spoke blackly of bombs, births, wars, weddings, infiltrations, and social events. 'You know, Lou,' Henry said, 'you can take history or leave it, but if you take it you have to accept certain assumptions or ground rules about what's left in and what's left out.'" In *The Public Burning,* a comparable observation is made by Nixon: "What was fact, what intent, what was framework, what was essence? Strange, the impact of History, the grip it had on us, yet it was nothing but words. Accidental accretions for the most part, leaving most of the story out. We have not yet begun to explore the true power of the Word, I thought. What if we broke all the rules, played games with the evidence, manipulated language itself, made History a partisan ally?"

Coover's fiction displays a connoisseur's attention to language, played against evocations of physical activity that is often gross, inclines to perversity, and continually hints at latent violence that occasionally erupts into view. Most of the action in *The Public Burning* occurs during the two days and nights preceding the execution. Coover shifts its location from Sing Sing to Times Square, rendering it a spectacle; that is, at once circus and ritual sacrifice to Uncle Sam. Talking with McCaffery in 1983, Coover spoke of his interest in the phenomenon of "a ritual return to the mythic roots of a group of people." He went on to explain that "This idea of a ritual bath of prehistoric or preconscious experience was very attractive to me as I began developing the Rosenberg book." He views this as a procedure for radical defamiliarization, as "one of the great disruptive functions of art: to take the tribe back into dream time, pulling them in, letting them relive the preconscious life as formed for them by their tribe." *The Public Burning* aspires, then, to precipitate a collective investigation of "the formative elements" of selfhood, as it is recognized in contemporary America.

The Public Burning ends with a riot of orgiastic excess and sexual extravagance. Coover is attracted to social situations that are structured in such a way that they preclude representation according to the principles of Aristotelian linearity or goal-oriented narrative: the orgy and the carnival, but also the party, a night at the movies, or a circus. Coover told Gado that it was the "circus aspect" of the Rosenberg trial that initially interested him most. Nixon was initially introduced as the clown.

Uncle Sam is personified as the incarnation of American folk consciousness. Discussing the composition of *The Public Burning,* Coover indicated the epic scope of his ambition: "One of the peculiarities of *The Public Burning* was that it was made up of thousands and thousands of tiny fragments that had to be painstakingly stitched together, and it was not hard to lose patience with it. It was like a gigantic impossible puzzle. I was striving for a text that would seem to have been written by the whole nation through all its history, as though the sentences had been forming themselves all this time, accumulating toward this experience. I wanted thousands of echoes, all the sounds of the nation." The result is a powerful, stunningingly accomplished fiction that transcends the occasion of its composition and amply repays the concerted literary labor of its composition.

"Whatever Happened to Gloomy Gus of the Chicago Bears?" evolved as a project separate from *The Public Burning,* but Coover has indicated that he used it to work off some of the frustrations he experienced in composing the more demanding and considerably more substantial work of *The Public Burning.* The initial stimulus to write the novella was a request from a popular magazine for a sports story. Coover saw the perversity of this particular response to his "baseball" novel and declined the invitation, but it generated the idea of a fiction in which Nixon follows an alternative career as a professional football player. Coover has said that, "As this would had to have taken place in the 1930s, it suddenly opened up for me the possibility of writing a good old-fashioned 1930s-style novella, full of personal material, thoughtful asides, and so on." It provided a productive form of respite from his more arduous task: "Everything fell into place like magic, and I sat down at the machine and for the first time in years just banged away happily. It was the most joyful writing experience I ever had." An expanded version, the book *Whatever Happened to Gloomy Gus of the Chicago Bears?* was published in 1987.

In 1976 Coover taught a semester at Virginia Military Institute. Then, after a visit to Barcelona, Coover lived in London and Kent during 1978 and 1979. Later in 1979 the family settled in Providence, Rhode Island, where Coover was offered a professorship at Brown University. Pieces written earlier in his career were published at this time. *Hair O' the Chine* (1979) and *After Lazarus* (1980) were both written in the late 1960s, in the form of film scripts. The former performed variations on the tale of the "Three Little Pigs." *After Lazarus* is a reworking of the biblical story. *Charlie in the House of Rue* (1980) improvises on Chaplin's gestures, choreography, acrobatics, and story lines. Meanwhile, Viking published *A Political Fable* (1980), Coover's slightly revised version of *The Cat in the Hat for President,* a short story that appeared in *New American Review* (1968) to coincide with the 1980 election.

The most significant of this cluster of fictions was *Spanking the Maid,* published in a limited edition by Bruccoli Clark in 1981 and by Grove Press the following year. Coover has identified Victorian "Guides for Domestics," setting out the rules governing conduct for servants, as a model for the novella. They share its repetitiousness and its eroticism, albeit in suppressed form. Repetition is of course a crucial element in pornography, and critic Jackson I. Cope has identified the book as a "pastiche of nineteenth-century styles from the literature of pornography." Jerry Varsava's 1990 essay on *Spanking the Maid* gives some sense of its sophistication and conceptual complexity when he remarks that the novella addresses "the significance of empirical evidence, the capacity of language to be 'truthful,' the efficacy of reason, the limits of traditional theories of knowledge, and the definability of space-time."

The novella is formed by thirty-nine sections. It has two characters. Repeatedly, a maid enters her master's bedroom at the start of the day and discovers him in a variety of postures or engaged in a range of activities. Sometimes they talk. She wears a uniform and carries equipment for cleaning, but her intention to establish order is invariably frustrated. She finds strange, menacing objects in the master's bed. The master, who has awakened from troubled dreams, administers chastisement and formulates suitable admonitions.

In a 1986 interview in *Publishers Weekly,* Coover spoke about the literary usefulness of eroticism: "We are never more susceptible to our own doubts and fears and anxieties than when we are approaching the erotic, and so are most apt—and part of art is process—to discover something going that route and not being too programmatic and self-censoring. Understanding the self, approaching 'the other' by way of its erotic impulses is a way of understanding everything—philosophy, religion, history. But this is what has led me over and over to the use of it. And I think it's led *all* artists to it in a way that is ultimately not prurient but revelatory." The scenario here is of course adjacent to that "ritual bath of prehistoric or preconscious experience" he spoke of in relation to *The Public Burning,* a point to which his fictions repeatedly return.

Between 1981 and 1982 Coover taught one semester at Brandeis. In 1983 the small Providence press, Burning Deck, published *In Bed One Night & Other Brief Encounters,* drawing together nine varied pieces that had previously appeared through such magazines as *Antaeus, Harper's, The Little Review,* and *Playboy.* The pieces range from lyrical Beckettian fragments, such as "Debris" and "The Old Man," to the colloquial comedy of "The Convention" and the self-reflective musings of the longest composition, "Beginnings." This latter fiction also echoes of Beckett, while its island landscape resembles that of "The Magic Poker" in *Pricksongs & Descants*.

Gerald's Party, a novel of more than three hundred pages, was published in 1985 to critical acclaim. The book is dedicated to fellow novelist John Hawkes. It is a remarkable parody of the murder mystery although Christopher Ames has argued that the novel's success actually derives from a "collision of different narrative codes." He suggests, "The narrative structure of *Gerald's Party* is composed from the patterns associated with the detective story, slapstick comedy, carnivalistic celebration of the body, masquerade, dream tale, and ritual sacrifice," and he adds, "None of these codes is allowed to dominate." The initial focus for the action is the discovery of a body, but the narrative does not develop toward the familiar resolution promised by the novel of detection. The expectations readers hold are consequently frustrated or transformed through surprising variations.

Coover combines realistic elements with palpable absurdities, usually entailing the eruption of violence or sexual energy as social forms disintegrate. The police, who are called to the scene of the crime, beat the newly widowed husband to death with croquet mallets and torture other guests. The party continues unabashed, with Gerald acting the role of urbane middle-class host, despite further deaths. If the novel evokes the classic tale of detection, it is equally redolent of the absurd world of Eugene Ionesco's plays. The arrival of a theatrical troupe adds an additional challenge to efforts to unravel what is real.

Coover seizes on the party as a social situation in which discourses inevitably overlap or interrupt one another. Readers are placed as eavesdroppers within an environment where voices contest for attention and are subjected to noise. This sophisticated and consciously ironic marriage of form and thematic concerns is characteristic of Coover's fiction. The party's resistance to linear representation, its dissonance and intractable simultaneity, are held in an uneasy tension with the customarily unidirectional narrative dynamic of the investigative process, even though that process is in this case evidently a sham.

Gerald's Party is a parodic investigation of how facts are habitually formed through abstraction from life's processes, and it continues Coover's interest in the artifice through which one arrives at a sense of the past. The metaphysical point underlying the novel is encapsulated by Inspector Pardew: "Well, I've been in homicide a very long time now, and I can tell you, the more I run into all the surface codes and structures–as we say in the business–that people invent for themselves, the more it seems to me that the one common invariant behind them all is, quite frankly, *murder itself!*" Death is conceived metaphorically, here, as the stasis caused by imposition of inadequate or outmoded forms on the dynamic processes of living.

A Night at the Movies: Or, You Must Remember This was published in 1987, bringing together "After Lazarus" and "Charlie in the House of Rue" with shorter pieces that had earlier appeared in *Evergreen Review, TriQuarterly, Frank, Paris Exiles,* and *Playboy*. The volume attains coherence through its reflection of Coover's enduring interest in cinema and cinematic forms. In an interview in 1979 he remarked: "I work with language because paper is cheaper than film stock. And because it's easier to work with a committee of one." Still, his attraction to film is undiminished, a legacy of the recollected "Saturday morning religious experience in the local ten-cent cinemas."

The French poet and critic Pierre Joris, in an essay published in 1993, points out that "although the formal reference of the writing is to the medium of film, and although each one of the individual fictions that make up the book is directly related to film, the book as a whole tries to suggest the complex social occasion of 'going to the movies,' of spending 'a night at the movies.'" Coover's evocation of cinema-going in the 1940s and 1950s allows him to make strategic use of nostalgia, while presenting a full and varied program in the manner of the social practice of that time. As with *Gerald's Party,* the structure of the represented setting offers a ready-made form, characterized by diversity and discontinuity, around which Coover can work his virtuosic variations.

Diversity and discontinuity make summary difficult, but Joris suggests that the opening fiction, "The Phantom of the Movie Palace," can serve as a paradigm for the entire book: "It is, simultaneously, a comic parody of just about every imaginable movie genre, a stern fable on the porous boundaries between 'fiction' and 'reality,' an astute analysis and critique of the author's role, a philosophical meditation on the illusory nature of time and the effectuation of the apocalypse announced in the text's first sentence." This multifarious fiction is held together by the presence of an old projectionist, who is alone in an otherwise deserted movie palace.

In *Gerald's Party,* Coover seems to intimate that the host may be construed as a metaphor for the author. In *A Night at the Movies,* the projectionist can also be seen to assume metaphoric status, but there is a twist in the tale, for the projectionist goes mad and finally believes himself to be a character in an old historical movie, facing execution. At the end of "The Phantom of the Movie Palace," the projectionist is escorted to the guillotine in the midst of a crowd that screams, "The public is never wrong!" Over the public address system a disembodied voice recounts the crimes of the condemned: "hauteur is mentioned, glamour, dash and daring." There is irony in Coover's depiction of the marginalization of the artist within the context of a night at the movies, at a palace of popular entertainment. The irony extends further into recognition of lessons derived from the popular medium and recycled into the revitalizing procedures of self-conscious and self-reflexive art.

Pinocchio in Venice, published in 1991, is a fantasia of transformation. An aging, increasingly decrepit academic has left America to revisit in mid winter his native Italy. In Venice it soon becomes apparent that the old professor is in fact Pinocchio, and the perception of the character by the reader modulates between the venerable human being and Collodi's puppet, as remembered from childhood reading or from Walt Disney's movie version. The old man's quest for a culminating image to finish *Mamma,* his literary tribute to the Blue-Haired Fairy, is accompanied by physical metamorphosis, as he turns back into his wooden former self.

Pinocchio in Venice plunges into the world of carnival. That world finds its verbal equivalent in Coover's virtuosic wordplay. Commitment to verbal adventure adds an important dimension to this novel, in which Coover challenges not only the forms of familiar fictions but also the deadening linguistic formulas of cliché. The lesson of *Pinocchio in Venice* is perhaps encapsulated in the old man's musings on the work of the Venetian masters: "The illusory, that is to say, *was,* for the great Venetian painters, *what was real. Change* was *changeless.* Becoming *was* Being. For them, 'persistence' of vision was active, not passive: they *saw through.* Theirs was the art of intense but reposeful acceptance of the turbulent wonderful." Such, it should be said, is also the art of Robert Coover. Failure to accept the processual nature of life is surely to court the fate suggested in the title's echo of Thomas Mann's 1912 novella *Death in Venice.* Coover pauses to admire the old masters; yet, he remains attentive to the changes history brings.

A 1992 issue of *The New York Times Book Review* carried a piece by Coover, in which he addressed "The End of Books and Hypertext." The following year the *Review* published a second set of observations, "Hyperfiction: Novels for the Computer." It is not surprising that Coover is drawn to this creative extension of electronic writing, as some of his best-known fictions ("The Babysitter," "The Elevator") embrace the nonlinearity and potential narrative multiplicity on which hypertext thrives. By the time the piece appeared, he had been conducting experimental hyperfiction workshops for three years, at Brown Uni-

JOHN'S WIFE

Once, there was a man named John. John had money, family, power, good health, high regard, many friends. Though he worked hard for these things, he actually found it difficult not to succeed; though not easily satisfied, he was often satisfied, a man whose considerable resources matched his considerable desires. A fortunate man, John. He was a builder by trade: where he walked, the earth changed, because he wished it so, and, like as not, his wishes all came true. Closed doors opened to him and obstacles fell. His enthusiasms were legendary. He ate and drank heartily but not to excess, played a tough but jocular game of golf, roamed the world on extended business trips, collected guns and cars and exotic fishing tackle, had the pleasure of many women, flew airplanes, contemplated running for Congress just for the sport of it. In spite of all that happened to his wife and friends, John lived happily ever after, as though this were somehow his destiny and his due.

[A NOVEL]

ROBERT COOVER

Dust jacket for Coover's 1996 novel, which the Publishers Weekly *reviewer called "a spicy blend of erudition and scatology, epic and farce"*

versity, as well as organizing conferences to debate issues arising from the new medium.

The essay introduces a wider readership to works composed using hypertext. It also includes general observations on the creative possibilities opened up by the technology; Coover's remarks are characterized by guarded enthusiasm. He affirms that "Hyperfiction is a new narrative art form," noting that the "unidirectional" dynamic espoused by "book culture" is here replaced by "a network of alternate paths through a set of text spaces by way of designated links." He writes with the authority of a practitioner who has at times pushed the printed medium to its limits: "The conventional nature of most of the fictions so far written in it probably reflects the apprehension felt in adjusting to a new medium (it took a century and a half after the Gutenberg revolution before Don Quixote first sallied forth, did it not?) but this transitional phase will soon pass. Hyperfictions of the future will not necessarily have printbound analogue. With each foray into hyperspace something new is added to the craft, the orbits widen, the technical manuals expand."

Dedicated readers of Coover will also find a resonance in his assertion that "As one moves through a hypertext, making one's choices, one has the sensation that just below the surface of the text there is an almost inexhaustible reservoir of half-hidden story material waiting to be explored. That is not unlike the feeling one has in dreams that there are vast peripheral seas of imagery into which dream sometimes slips, sometimes returning to the center, sometimes moving through parallel stories at the same time."

Coover published two books in 1996. *Briar Rose* is a text that appeared in a different version in *Conjunctions.* Coover works inventive variations on the basic materials of the "Sleeping Beauty" story. The third-person narration alternates between the points of view of the male and female protagonists, as the tale unfolds with a characteristic mix of verbal richness, eroticism, humor, and self-conscious storytelling.

John's Wife is dedicated to the late English novelist Angela Carter, "whose infamous illusionist Doctor Hoffman believed, like Ovid, that 'the world only exists as a medium for our desires,' and that 'Nothing . . . is ever completed; it only changes'" (*The Infernal Desire Machines of Dr. Hoffman,* 1972). Coover then extends the dedication to Ovid, also. The message may be familiar, but the book is yet another daring stylistic and formal departure.

Reviewers of *The Origins of the Brunists* noted that Coover presented many characters in considerable detail. In *John's Wife,* also more than four hundred pages long, Coover is again concerned to portray an entire social group. In this novel it is a well-to-do, middle-class community, and the approach to character is much more fragmentary. *John's Wife* is a novel of multiple perspectives, and in place of more conventional characterization Coover presents brief notations of point of view, involving, it seems, the entire population of a small town. As patterns form through the repetitions, a narrative emerges and the unconscious dynamics that drive the community come to light.

The agitated shifting viewpoint of the novel runs the risk of narrative disintegration, but Coover gives his novel a center of gravity in the eponymous John's wife. Like Virginia Woolf's Mrs. Dalloway, she exemplifies the multiform nature of social existence, at the point where varying perspectives converge into some kind of coherence. This parallel may be conscious: John and his wife have a daughter who shares Mrs. Dalloway's name, Clarissa. But as in his earlier work, Coover deviates from the modernist position by refusing to allow the convergence of points of view to isolate

an essential being beyond the play of the text. John's wife remains elusive, and that is necessary if life is to be other than "a dream dreamt by the dead in which the living were condemned to mythic servitude."

Coover is again addressing the human need for stability. The character Kate observes that "it's scary for everybody to imagine getting turned into something entirely different from what we think we are, even if we don't much like what we are, just as it would frighten us to have the world we live in change its basic rules in incomprehensible ways all of a sudden." Her own route to security is through the movie theater; she likes to go to "the commercial genre movies, the westerns and romances, the gangster movies, thrillers, screwball comedies, because she said it was like going in for a tune-up: they reset the basic patterns."

The interrogation of those patterns is mainly channeled through two citizens with aspirations to artistry. Gordon is a photographer, whose commitment to registration, through his medium, of the life of the community, taps into transgressive subterranean desires in ways that put him in constant jeopardy. His photographs freeze time, capturing the moment by appearing to elude process. Contrary to Coover's own creed, Gordon lays claim to "objective artistic principles."

The photographer's principles are challenged within the novel through the criticism made by his friend, Ellsworth, a novelist. Ellsworth's evaluation of the photographer is that he is a man who "loved less flesh than form, more pattern of light than what tales or implied excitements those patterns might bespeak, one who sought to penetrate the visible contours of the restless world, ceaselessly dissolved by time, to capture the hidden image beyond, the elusive mystery masked by surface flux, and the name he gave that which he pursued was Beauty." Gordon shares Kate's view that art's function is "to shield us from the dusky terrors of the flux." Coover concedes that art may accomplish this goal, but his work has always sought to resist the stultification that follows such insulation from reality.

In 1998 Coover published *Ghost Town,* a parodic Western in which a nameless lone rider enters a continually shape-shifting frontier town. A predictable round of violent action ensues, but the extent of that violence is exaggerated beyond all expectations. This excess is matched verbally by Coover's indulgence in relentlessly stereotyped cowboy dialogue. The novel complicates the Western genre's characteristic reliance on instantly recognizable binary oppositions incarnated in the hero and the villain, the law-enforcer and the outlaw, the virgin and the whore, and in abstract qualities such as innocence and experience. Most tellingly, the opposition between life and death is collapsed as characters are killed and then resurrected. Coover draws on familiar props and stock events but deploys them in unexpected ways in order to unsettle the coherence of conventional Western fiction, and to interrogate the values that such fiction may endorse. In a 1979 interview with Christopher Bigsby, Coover said: "I see self-conscious fiction as a willed passage beyond the functional definitions of the world, out where it can wrestle with the shapeshifting universe. That, for me, is a moral act."

Coover is a morally responsive writer but not merely a novelist of ideas. Chénetier observes that Coover "always gathers enough narrative momentum, always makes us wallow enough in opulent textures to make us take his allegorical theoretical asides in stride." It is that blend of critical acuity and writerly skill that has made Robert Coover a significant figure in contemporary literature.

Interviews:

Leo J. Hertzel, "An Interview with Robert Coover," *Critique,* 11 (1969): 25–29;

Alma Kadragic, "An Interview with Robert Coover," *Shantih,* 2 (Summer 1972): 57–60;

Frank Gado, "Robert Coover," in *First Person: Conversations on Writers and Writing* (Schenectady, N.Y: Union College Press, 1973), pp. 142–159;

Geoffrey Woolf, "An American Epic," *New Times* (19 August 1977): 48–57;

Christopher Bigsby, "Robert Coover," in *The Radical Imagination and the Liberal Tradition: Interviews with English and American Novelists,* edited by Christopher Bigsby and Heide Ziegler (London: Junction, 1982), pp. 79–92;

Larry McCaffery, "An Interview with Robert Coover," in *Anything Can Happen: Interviews with Contemporary American Novelists,* conducted and edited by McCaffery and Tom LeClair (Urbana: University of Illinois Press, 1983), pp. 63–78;

Peter Nelson, "An Interview with Robert Coover," *Telescope,* 4 (Winter 1985): 23–28;

Amanda Smith, "Robert Coover," *Publishers Weekly* (26 December 1986): 44–45;

Farhat Iftekharuddin, "Interview with Robert Coover," *Short Story* (Fall 1993): 89–94.

References:

Christopher Ames, "Coover's Comedy of Conflicting Fictional Codes," *Critique,* 31 (Winter 1990): 85–99;

Richard Andersen, *Robert Coover* (Boston: Twayne, 1981);

Marc Chénetier, "Ideas of Order at Delphi," in *Facing Texts: Encounters Between Contemporary Writers and Critics,* edited by Heide Ziegler (Durham, N.C. & London: Duke University Press, 1988), pp. 84–108;

Jackson I. Cope, *Robert Coover's Fictions* (Baltimore & London: Johns Hopkins University Press, 1986);

Lois Gordon, *Robert Coover: The Universal Fictionmaking Process* (Carbondale: Southern Illinois University Press, 1983);

Phillip Brian Harper, "Robert Coover and Metafictional Baseball," in *Framing the Margins: The Social Logic of Postmodern Culture* (New York & Oxford: Oxford University Press, 1994), pp. 156–164;

Pierre Joris, "Coover's Apoplectic Apocalypse or 'Purviews of Cunning Abstractions,'" *Critique,* 34 (Summer 1993): 220–231;

Thomas E. Kennedy, *Robert Coover: A Study of the Short Fiction, Twayne's Studies in Short Fictio*n (New York: Twayne, 1992);

Thomas LeClair, "Robert Coover, *The Public Burning,* and the Art of Excess," *Critique,* 23 (Spring 1982): 5–28;

Paul Maltby, "Robert Coover," in *Dissident Postmodernists: Barthelme, Coover, Pynchon,* Penn Studies in Contemporary American Fiction (Philadelphia: University of Pennsylvania Press, 1992), pp. 82–130;

Jerry Varsava, "Gender Relations and the Ways of Paradox in Coover's *Spanking the Maid,*" in *Contingent Meanings: Postmodern Fiction, Mimesis, and the Reader* (Tallahassee: Florida State University Press, 1990), pp. 109–141.

Papers:

A collection of Robert Coover's manuscripts is located at Houghton Library, Harvard University. The Department of Rare Books and Special Collections, Thomas Cooper Library, the University of South Carolina, Columbia, also holds Coover manuscripts.

Ralph Ellison

(1 March 1914 – 16 April 1994)

Mark Busby
Southwest Texas State University

See also the Ellison entries in *DLB 2: American Novelists Since World War II; DLB 76: Afro-American Writers, 1940– 1955;* and *DLB Yearbook 1994.*

BOOKS: *Invisible Man* (New York: Random House, 1952; London: Gollancz, 1953);

Shadow and Act: Essays (New York: Random House, 1964; London: Secker & Warburg, 1967);

Going to the Territory: Essays (New York: Random House, 1986);

Flying Home and Other Stories, edited by John F. Callahan, preface by Saul Bellow (New York: Random House, 1996; London: Penguin, 1998);

Juneteenth: A Novel, edited by Callahan (New York: Random House, 1999; London: Hamilton, 1999).

Edition and Collection: *Invisible Man,* Thirtieth Anniversary Edition, with a new introduction by Ellison (New York: Random House, 1982);

The Collected Essays of Ralph Ellison, edited, with an introduction, by Callahan, preface by Saul Bellow (New York: Modern Library, 1995).

OTHER: Stephen Crane, *The Red Badge of Courage and Four Great Stories,* introduction by Ellison (New York: Dell, 1960);

"Out of the Hospital and Under the Bar," in *Soon, One Morning: New Writing by American Negroes 1940– 1960,* edited by Herbert Hill (New York: Knopf, 1963), pp. 242–290;

"The Music of Invisibility," in *City of Words: American Fiction 1950–1970,* edited by Tony Tanner (New York: Harper & Row, 1971), pp. 50–63;

"And Hickman Arrives," in *Black Writers of America: A Comprehensive Anthology,* edited by Richard Barksdale and Kenneth Kinnamon (New York: Macmillan, 1972), pp. 693–712;

Leon Forrest, *There Is a Tree More Ancient Than Eden,* foreword by Ellison (New York: Random House, 1973);

"Backwacking: A Plea to the Senator," in *Chant of Saints: A Gathering of Afro-American Literature, Art, and*

Ralph Ellison (UPI/Bettman Newsphotos)

Scholarship, edited by Michael S. Harper and Robert B. Stepto (Urbana: University of Illinois Press, 1979), pp. 445–446.

SELECTED PERIODICAL PUBLICATIONS– UNCOLLECTED: "Slick Gonna Learn," *Direction* (September 1939): 10–11, 14, 16;

"The Birthmark," *New Masses,* 37 (2 July 1940): 16–17;

"Did You Ever Dream Lucky?" *New World Writing,* 5 (April 1954): 134–145;

"The Roof, the Steeple and the People," *Quarterly Review of Literature,* 10 (1960): 115–128;

"It Always Breaks Out," *Partisan Review,* 30 (Spring 1963): 113–128;

"Night-Talk," *Quarterly Review of Literature,* 16 (1969): 317–329;

"A Song of Innocence," *Iowa Review,* 1 (1970): 30–40;

"Cadillac Flambe," *American Review,* 16 (1973): 249–269.

At his death on 16 April 1994, Ralph Ellison had come to be recognized as one of the world's most distinguished men of letters, primarily on the strength of the only novel published during his lifetime, *Invisible Man* (1952). For this powerful first novel Ellison received the Russwurm Award, the Certificate of Award from the *Chicago Defender,* and the National Book Award, whose citation from the jury of Martha Foley, Irving Howe, Howard Mumford Jones, and Alfred Kazin read: "With positive exuberance of narrative gifts, he has broken away from the conventions and patterns of the tight 'well-made' novel. Mr. Ellison has the courage to take many literary risks, and he has succeeded with them." In 1954 he won a Rockefeller Foundation Award and was selected to tour and lecture in Germany and at the Salzburg Seminar in Austria. He received Prix de Rome Fellowships from the American Academy of Arts and Letters and lectured and toured Italy with the U.S. Information Agency in 1955 and 1956.

From 1958 to 1961 Ellison taught Russian and American literature at Bard College. He served as Alexander White Visiting Professor at the University of Chicago in 1961, then as visiting professor of writing at Rutgers and fellow in American Studies at Yale from 1962 to 1964. He was selected as Gertrude Whittall Lecturer at the Library of Congress and delivered Ewing Lectures at University of California at Los Angeles in January and April 1964. He also taught African American folklore, creative writing, and literature at various colleges and universities. From 1970 to 1980 Ellison was the Albert Schweitzer Professor of Humanities at New York University, and his hometown of Oklahoma City erected a public library in his name in 1975.

Ralph Waldo Ellison was born in Oklahoma City, Oklahoma, on 1 March 1914, the son of Lewis Alfred and Ida Millsap Ellison. His mother grew up on a plantation in White Oak, Georgia, and his father was from Abbeville, South Carolina. Ellison's maternal and paternal grandparents had been slaves. Lewis Ellison became a soldier and served in Cuba, the Philippines, and China, fighting in the 1900 Boxer Rebellion there. After operating a candy kitchen, and later a restaurant, in Chattanooga, Tennessee, Ellison's father became a construction foreman, the job that brought his family to Oklahoma. They settled in a rooming house on First Street on Oklahoma's east side, and Ellison's father later went into business selling ice and coal. He died in an accident when Ellison was three years old.

The Ellisons left the South to raise their family on the Oklahoma frontier because they wanted better conditions for their children. After settling in Oklahoma Territory, his parents fought hard to keep segregationist laws, like those in neighboring Texas, out of the Oklahoma constitution. Unlike Texas and Arkansas, Oklahoma had no tradition of slavery. Additionally, there was a sense of connection between Native Americans, who constituted a significant proportion of Oklahoma's population, and African Americans. Ellison's geographical fate was to be born in Oklahoma, where the experience of "Southwestern blacks differs from that of *Southeastern* blacks. . . ." In the South, Ellison noted in an interview with Hollie West, the slave past was embodied in "buildings, patterns of movement about the cities, in manners, in signs, in monuments," but the traditions of the Oklahoma frontier were in the "attitudes and memories of individuals." In Oklahoma, Ellison continued, "the atmosphere of the place there was a sense that you had to determine your own fate, and that you had a chance to do it"–that the world was possibility.

In fact, Ellison and his boyhood friends achieved positive aspects of the American frontier belief in a free and open territory. This experience of the world as possibility that was later contradicted by his experience of oppression has been central to Ellison's imaginative attempts to confront the reality of a seemingly free world that actually provides restraints, as he wrote in *Shadow and Act* (1964). "One thing is certain, ours was a chaotic community, still characterized by frontier attitudes . . . which [encouraged] the individual's imagination–up to the moment 'reality' closes in upon him–to range widely and, sometimes, even to soar."

Another significant part of Ellison's past is his name. Being named for Ralph Waldo Emerson led to complex and confusing questions of identity. He recalled the humor revolving around "a small brown nubbin of a boy carrying around such a heavy moniker. . . ." After he wrote *Invisible Man,* he learned that his father had named him for Emerson and hoped for his son to become a poet.

To support Ralph and his younger brother, Herbert, Ellison's mother, known as Brownie by her friends, worked at various jobs as a domestic and as stewardess of the Avery Chapel Afro-Methodist Episcopal Church. Because the minister had his own home, Ellison's family moved into the parsonage, which housed more books than Ellison had seen before in one

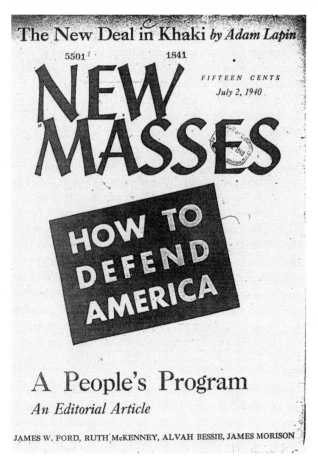

Cover for the issue of the magazine in which Ellison's second published story, "The Birthmark," appeared

place. In addition, his mother often brought home magazines such as *Vanity Fair* and *Literary Digest* from the houses she cleaned. Ellison read voraciously and eclectically, beginning with fairy tales, then junior fiction, Westerns, detective stories, the Haldeman Julius Blue books, the Harvard Classics, G. B. Shaw, Guy de Maupassant, Thomas Hardy's *Jude the Obscure* (1895), and Emily Brontë's *Wuthering Heights* (1847). His interest in the frontier continued; for example, he read James Fenimore Cooper's *The Last of the Mohicans* (1826) ten times. His grade-school teacher, Mrs. L. C. McFarland, taught him of the New Negro Movement of the 1920s, and he read those authors who excited his interest about "the glamour of Harlem," such as Langston Hughes, Countee Cullen, Claude McKay, and James Weldon Johnson.

Initially, Ellison was drawn to music as a career primarily because of the diverse and extensive music program at the Frederick Douglass School in Oklahoma City, where Ellison attended for the first twelve years of his schooling. He began playing the trumpet at the age of eight. One teacher at Douglass, Mrs. Breaux, influenced Ellison's musical interests, and her

father, Dr. Inman Page, the principal, oversaw his academic pursuits. A former slave, Page was an 1877 graduate and class orator at Brown University. In an address at Brown in 1979, Ellison recalled Page's reading of St. Paul's Epistles during daily chapel exercises, and he also remembered receiving a stern remonstrance from Page after he caught Ellison in horseplay during chapel. Like Page, other teachers at Douglass brought extensive academic training to Oklahoma. For example, Ellison studied Latin for four years with a teacher educated in Latin, Greek, and Hebrew. Although music was Ellison's primary interest in school, he played both tackle and running back on the football team—an example of the importance he placed on becoming a Renaissance man.

When the state of Oklahoma awarded Ellison a scholarship (actually a device for keeping minority students out of state colleges), he decided to study music at Tuskegee Institute in Tuskegee, Alabama, after discovering that the school's choir, directed by William L. Dawson, had opened Radio City Music Hall. Booker T. Washington, who founded Tuskegee in 1881, set forth the early principles of vocational education central to Tuskegee's mission. Washington later became an important figure in Ellison's writing. For example, the narrator in *Invisible Man* quotes from Washington's speech during his address after the battle royal, and the narrator's college as well as Dr. Bledsoe, Homer Barbee, and other characters and events are obviously drawn from Ellison's experience at Tuskegee.

By the time Ellison arrived in 1933, Tuskegee was a school with an unusual duality. Although the atmosphere that Washington created continued at the school, the institute had moved far from its founder's original conception of a trade school and had developed a strong liberal arts component and an especially impressive music department headed by composer and choir director Dawson. Ellison's literary training at Tuskegee was more informal than formal. Still, Morteza Drexel Sprague, the head of the English department, earned the dedication in *Shadow and Act,* where Ellison calls Sprague a "dedicated dreamer in a land most strange." On his own, Ellison read T. S. Eliot's *The Waste Land* (1922) and, he noted in *Going to the Territory* (1986), was "caught up in a piece of poetry which moved me but which I couldn't reduce to a logical system." The poem, he decided, was similar to jazz because the jazz musician, like Eliot, had to know the tradition out of which he worked, but he also had to improvise on that tradition. Ellison also concluded that Eliot's "range of allusion was as mixed and as varied as that of Louis Armstrong." When he asked Sprague about the poem, she explained to him how he could find Eliot's sources and the criticism he needed to understand the poem, and he was profoundly affected by reading Eliot's appended notes and studying Eliot's sources: "That really was a beginning of my literary education and, actually, it was the beginning of my transformation (or shall we say, metamorphosis) from a would-be composer into some sort of novelist."

Working part-time in the college library, he first read modernists such as Ezra Pound, Gertrude Stein, Sherwood Anderson, Ford Madox Ford, James Joyce, F. Scott Fitzgerald, and Ernest Hemingway and then turned to nineteenth-century writers Herman Melville and Mark Twain, as well as to influential works by Karl Marx and Sigmund Freud. "Books which seldom, if ever, mentioned Negroes," he noted, "were to release me from whatever 'segregated' idea I might have had of human possibilities." He found studying writing familiar after the time he had spent learning music. "Besides," he commented, "it was absolutely painless because it involved no deadlines or credits."

Ellison left the South by chance and was not expelled like the narrator in *Invisible Man*. When confusion about his scholarship at the end of his junior year left him without money for school, he decided to go to New York City to seek funds to complete his senior year and to study sculpture. After his arrival in New York on 5 July 1936, he took a room at the Harlem Annex of the Young Men's Christian Association (YMCA). When he went across the street for breakfast the next morning, he recognized Alain Locke, whom he had met just a few weeks earlier in Tuskegee. Through Locke, Ellison met Langston Hughes and then Richard Wright. Ellison's relationship with Wright was one of the most important and complex relationships of his life.

Wright's friendship eventually led Ellison to the craft to which he devoted the rest of his life. Ellison and Wright talked about literature and writing, and Ellison read the manuscripts of *Uncle Tom's Children* (1938). Ellison was in awe of the accomplished writer, for Ellison at the time had only written classroom assignments and a few poems. Still, Wright seemed interested in discussing his ideas with someone of a similar background. Recognizing Ellison's keen interest in literature, Wright asked him to write a book review for *New Challenge,* and Ellison reviewed Waters Edward Turpin's novel *These Low Grounds* for the Fall 1937 issue.

Wright soon challenged him further. Needing a story for the next issue of *New Challenge,* Wright asked Ellison to write one, and Ellison's fiction-writing career was under way. He continued writing book reviews for several journals such as *New Masses, Direction, Negro Quarterly,* and *New Challenge,* publishing more than twenty signed reviews and literary essays between 1937 and 1944, as well as many political and social essays. In 1939 Ellison began a novel titled "Slick Gonna Learn," a section of which became his first published story in 1939. His second story, "The Birthmark," appeared in *New Masses* on 2 July 1940. These two early stories concerned with police brutality reflect the leftist ideological influence toward which Ellison leaned at the time. From 1940 to 1944 Ellison published six more stories, three set in Oklahoma, about the adventures of two young black characters, Buster and Riley, and three stories that show Ellison's maturation, "In a Strange Country," "Flying Home," and "King of the Bingo Game."

Ellison worked on the Federal Writer's Project in New York City from 1938 to 1942 and had a number of experiences that affected his writing and his outlook on life. Working there gave him time to concentrate on writing as a craft and to work on his own as well. His major assignment was a book to be titled *Negroes in New York*. Another project, headed by B. A. Botkin, was to collect folklore such as children's rhymes, games, and songs.

Ellison resigned from the Federal Writer's Project in 1942 to become managing editor of *Negro Quarterly*. He worked there for almost a year, but the money was irregular, and the journal ceased publication. Ellison also did freelance writing and covered one of the significant events of the early 1940s, a riot in Harlem in 1943, which he reported for the *New York Post*. The riot serves as the partial basis for the apocalyptic climax in *Invisible Man*.

The United States was then deeply involved in World War II. After unsuccessfully trying to enlist in the U.S. Navy band and then deciding that he did not want to be in a "Jim Crow army," Ellison joined the Merchant Marine in 1943 and served as a cook until 1945. As a merchant seaman, Ellison would go to sea, where he could concentrate on his writing, and then return home for significant amounts of time before going out again. On one layover in 1944 Ellison met Fanny McConnell through a mutual friend who knew that both of them were interested in books, and they were married in 1946.

While in the Merchant Marine, Ellison worked on a novel set in a German prisoner-of-war camp about a black American pilot appointed camp leader who, because of his rank, achieves enormous power over other American prisoners, many of whom are white Southerners. Ellison tried to work on the prison-camp novel on his next voyage in the winter of 1944 during the Battle of the Bulge as he served on a ship taking war supplies across the North Atlantic. The ship's water supply had become contaminated with rust, and when he reached Le Havre, Ellison had a kidney infection. Because his condition worsened on the return trip, he took sick leave as the war wound down in the summer of 1945 and went with Fanny to a friend's farm in Vermont to write and recuperate.

Setting up his typewriter in the open doorway of a large old barn there, he struggled with his prison-camp novel. He found that "creatures from Afro-American fables–Jack-the-Rabbit and Jack-the-Bear–blended in my mind with figures of myth and history" about whom he had been reading in Lord Raglan's *The Hero* (1936) and distracted him from his novel. "Images of incest and murder, dissolution and rebirth whirled in my head," he recalled in the introduction to the thirtieth anniversary edition of *Invisible Man*. In such a state, he sat at the typewriter and suddenly typed what were to become the first words of his novel: "I am an invisible man." Starting to destroy the page, he then reread it and began to wonder what kind of voice would speak such words.

When Ellison returned to his one-room ground-floor apartment on St. Nicholas Avenue in New York City, he found himself preoccupied with the voice. By that time, Fanny had become executive director of the American Medical Center for Burma. Ellison supplemented her regular salary by building high-fidelity audio systems and by selling book reviews, articles, short stories, and photographs. Additionally, he received monthly support from an art patron, Mrs. J. Caesar Guggenheimer. Ellison worked on *Invisible Man* for seven years, and the novel finally appeared in April 1952.

During the 1960s and 1970s, however, Ellison was criticized on several fronts. A decade had passed since the publication of *Invisible Man,* and Ellison's publisher was suggesting that the next novel, sections of which began appearing in 1960, would soon be ready. The literary world speculated about why the author of a promising first novel had not yet finished a second one. But the most sustained and significant attacks accused Ellison of not calling loudly enough for social change. Because Ellison remained staunchly integrationist, militants during the growth of the "black is beautiful" and Black Aesthetic movements denigrated Ellison and labeled him an Uncle Tom. A *Negro Digest* survey of important black writers in 1968 ranked Ellison fourth, with Richard Wright designated as the "most important black American writer of all time." At Oberlin College in 1969, Ellison was jeered by black students.

Ellison also found himself isolated from the majority of black intellectuals' ideas about Vietnam. While black leaders such as Martin Luther King Jr. opposed the war, Ellison supported it and President Lyndon Johnson. As was usual with Ellison, his reasons for supporting the war were complex. Ellison's South-

western past contributed to his support for Johnson. Ellison's Oklahoma background led him to "listen to the individual intonation, to *what* was said as well as to *how* it was said." Johnson valued Ellison's support and awarded him the Medal of Freedom in 1969. Despite the attacks, Ellison maintained a high profile and accepted several public appointments. He served as vice president of the American PEN Club and the National Institute of Arts and Letters, trustee of the Citizens' Committee for Public Television and the John F. Kennedy Center in Cambridge, and member of the National Council on the Arts and the Carnegie Commission on Educational Television. Other awards continued as well. In 1964 Tuskegee awarded Ellison an honorary doctorate in humane letters, and he received honorary degrees from no less than fourteen colleges and universities, including Rutgers, Michigan, Williams, Harvard, and Wesleyan. In 1970 André Malraux, who greatly influenced Ellison's work, serving as the Minister of Cultural Affairs in France, awarded Ellison the Chevalier de l'Ordre des Artes et Lettres.

From 1960 to 1980 he published eight excerpts of the work-in-progress in such varied publications as *Noble Savage, Quarterly Review of Literature,* and *Massachusetts Review.* These eight stories total almost 150 pages of the second novel in print during his lifetime.

Despite verbal assaults on his work and personal beliefs during the 1960s and 1970s, Ellison was moved to the forefront of American literature in the 1980s. Whenever arguments about expanding the American canon dominated discussion, Ellison was often mentioned as a black writer who must be included. He was elected to the American Academy of Arts and Letters in 1975, awarded the Langston Hughes medallion for contribution in arts and letters by City College in New York in 1984, and presented the National Medal of Arts in 1985. A second essay collection, *Going to the Territory,* was published in 1986 and includes Ellison's essays written from 1964 to 1985, as well as some essays left out of *Shadow and Act.* In *The Collected Essays of Ralph Ellison,* edited by John F. Callahan in 1995, selections from both published books of essays are included, as well as previously uncollected nonfiction works.

Behind Ellison's nonfiction, throughout his career, is a voice of reason, concern, optimism, and intelligence. From his earliest to his last essays Ellison returned repeatedly to those issues that compelled him as an artist, most of which resulted from his acute awareness of the unity and diversity of American life: the one and the many, order and chaos, ideal and reality, masks and identity. Among the other themes that appear often in his nonfiction are Ellison's regard for history and the past, antipathy toward racial stereotyping, consequence of identity, emphasis on the power of

.1

INVISIBLE MAN

BY RALPH ELLISON

I am an invisible man. No, I am not a spook such as those
who haunted Edgar Allan Poe; nor one of your Hollywood movie ecto-
plasms. I am a man of substance, of flesh and bone, fiber and
liquids--I might even be said to possess a mind. I am invisible, you
see, simply because people refuse to recognize me. I am not complaining, nor am I protesting either. It is sometimes advantageous
to be unseen, although it is most often rather wearing on the
nerves. Then too, you're constantly being bumped by those of
poor vision. Or again, you ~~sometimes~~ *often* doubt if you really exist.
You wonder whether you aren't simply a phantom in other people's
minds. Say a figure in a nightmare which the sleeper tries with
all his strength to destroy. It's when you feel this ~~way~~ *like* that, out
of resentment, you begin to bump people back. And, let me confess,
you feel that way most of the time. You ~~feel~~ *ache with the* need to convince
that you're a part of all the
yourself that you <u>do</u> exist in the real world, and you strike out
with your fists, you curse and swear to make them recognize you.
And it *alas, seldom* ~~isn't always~~ successful.

Once I accidently bumped into a man in the dark, and perhaps
because of the darkness he saw me and called me an insulting name.
I sprang at him, seizing his coat lapels and demanded that he apolo-
gize. He was a tall blond man and as my face came close to his he
looked insolently out of his blue eyes and cursed me, his breath hot
in my face as he struggled and I pulled his chin down sharp upon
the crown of my head, butting him as I had seen the West Indians
do, and I felt

First page of the setting copy, with Ellison's revisions in pencil, for the only novel he published during his lifetime (Ralph Ellison Papers, Manuscript Division, Library of Congress)

art to transform, awareness of the richness of African American culture, and belief in amalgamation. In most essays he summoned his own experience, or at least the created persona, "Ralph Ellison," to support his points.

Ellison's nonfiction falls into four general groups: uncollected political and literary essays written in the late 1930s and 1940s, primarily for Marxist publications such as *New Masses;* essays, speeches, and interviews from 1942 to 1964 collected in *Shadow and Act;* essays, speeches, and interviews collected in *Going to the Territory,* most written from 1964 to 1985; and a few final pieces written between the publication of *Going to the Territory* and Ellison's death in 1994. Within these four groups, Ellison's nonfiction focuses on three general concerns: literature, music, and African American social and political life.

As a writer Ellison often examined the purpose of the novel, and he stated that American fiction must regain the moral resolve that America's best nineteenth-century writers—Herman Melville, Mark Twain, and Henry James—demonstrated in their best work as they attempted to use the novel to promote democratic principles. These writers understood the significance of slavery in the American experience and portrayed African Americans as representing the most meaningful aspects of democracy. As a former musician and aspiring composer, Ellison returned to his musical background for comparisons of artistic purpose and discipline. Southwestern jazz and blues musicians provided the basis for his understanding of the complex intertwining of tradition and individual talent, the given and the improvised, from which American art, as Ellison perceived it, springs. As an African American, Ellison was acutely aware of the disparity between American ideals and opportunity and the restrictions forced on black people, first through slavery, then through Jim Crow laws, and always through racism. Ellison refused to accept sociologists' conclusions that black life is stilted and reduced because of the burdens placed on African American culture. Ellison agreed with his friend and Tuskegee classmate Albert Murray, who called these views "social science fiction." There is, Ellison insisted, a flourishing black culture, despite the reality of racism in America, and it is through African American culture—folklore, art, music, dance—that young black men and women discover what is intrinsically valuable about being African American, American, and human.

Much of Ellison's work in short fiction is aesthetically significant. He published eight short stories during his fiction writing apprenticeship from 1939 to 1944. The first two political protest stories, "Slick Gonna Learn" and "The Birthmark," grew out of his relationship with Richard Wright and such journals as *New Masses.* Although he stated that his early work had a

persuasive purpose, he never acknowledged he was writing "the official type of fiction" and refused to accept that he wrote from a narrowly leftist viewpoint: "I wrote what might be called propaganda—having to do with the Negro struggle—but my fiction was always trying to be something else; something different even from Wright's fiction. I never accepted the ideology which the *New Masses* attempted to impose on writers." Although Ellison tried to move these stories beyond limited naturalism, they provide only glimpses of the concerns of the mature writer. Set in the South where Ellison had experienced limitation, they concentrate on human constraints and racial tension.

However, Ellison abandoned the narrowly political in his next three stories—"Afternoon" (1940), "Mister Toussan" (1941), and "That I Had the Wings" (1943). In these stories he returned to his Southwestern past and created two young boys, Buster and Riley, whose adventures in Oklahoma draw heavily from black Southwestern folklore. Although their lives reveal racial injustice and bigotry in the background, foremost is the two boys' sense of hope and possibility, particularly as they build on the Southwestern and African American folklore available to them. They are a black Huck Finn and Tom Sawyer, ready to shape their experiences into adventure and excitement. Restrictions are apparent, but they originate primarily through the adults who supervise them.

By returning imaginatively to the Southwest, Ellison created stories about the power of the human imagination to reach beyond limits, an important theme in his longer work as well. In the Southwest the frontier myth of freedom and possibility inspires the boys, but they often find themselves confronted by older blacks conditioned by a slave past. Through humor, wit, and verbal games, Buster and Riley assert their own identities and resist being confined by others' definitions of reality. These are initiation stories in which the boys learn to test the boundaries of their limitations—sometimes to soar and sometimes to fall and fail.

In his three stories published in 1944 ("In a Strange Country," "Flying Home," and "King of the Bingo Game") Ellison concentrates on the themes of racial identity and alienation and uses African American folk materials in a stylistic combination of irony and symbolism. Together, these eight pre-*Invisible Man* stories demonstrate how Ellison shaped his experiences in the Southwest, the South, and the North and began to achieve his mature artistic vision.

"Flying Home," perhaps Ellison's most successful short story, consolidates several Ellison themes, images, and techniques: isolation, estrangement, racial strife, initiation, and search for identity themes; bird, wing, and flying imagery; laughing, judgmental men; fram-

ing, myth, folklore, and distorted, surreal–or magic
realism–passages. The story draws from a specific historical event that concerned Ellison during World War
II, the establishment of a Negro air school at Tuskegee
whose pilots never got out of training. In this story a
black pilot trainee, Todd, while attempting to correct a
dangerous maneuver, hits a buzzard, crash-lands in a
field, and breaks his ankle. An old black "peasant"
sharecropper, Jefferson, sends his son for help and then
tells the pilot two folktales. The first is a story about
seeing two buzzards arising from a horse's carcass, and
the second, catalogued by folklorists as early as 1919 as
the "Colored Man in Heaven" tale, is about a black
angel who, because of his pride, was expelled from
heaven. The second story offends Todd, who thinks
Jefferson is mocking him. During this time Todd recalls
his childhood fascination with flying. Jefferson's stories
indicate he is one of Ellison's wise fools, like Jim Trueblood, Peter Wheatstraw, and the narrator's grandfather in *Invisible Man.*

In his story "King of the Bingo Game," Ellison
looks both backward and forward. Like the early stories,
this one ends pessimistically. It is the first Ellison story
concerning a young black man from the South who discovers a lack of community support after the great
migration north. In this story a nameless young man desperately needs money for his critically ill wife, Laura.
Unable to get a job with no birth certificate, he hopes to
win money offered as a sales promotion at a local movie
theater. To win the prize of $36.90, he must first win a
bingo game and then cause an electrically controlled
wheel to land on the appropriate (ironic) number–double zero. By playing five cards he gets his chance at the
wheel, but feeling such exhilaration at being in control of
something, he cannot let loose of the power line. The
button that controls the wheel is connected by a wire,
and as the main character holds it, he feels immense
power and identity, yelling "This is God!" and decides
that he has been "reborn" as "The-man-who-pressed-the-
button-who-held-the-prize-who-was-the-King-of-Bingo."
Finally, as he is dragged off the stage to the hoots of the
audience, the wheel lands on the winning number.

Themes of control and freedom are central to the
story and to *Invisible Man,* as are images of light and
electricity. Also central to the story is the search for
identity as the unnamed narrator lacks a birth certificate to validate his being. While the pessimistic conclusion looks back to earlier stories, "King of the Bingo
Game" foreshadows the universal applications of these
Ellison concerns as they reappear in the novel. On one
level the story is about the absence of black identity
caused by white racism. But it is also about the universal existential position of twentieth-century men and

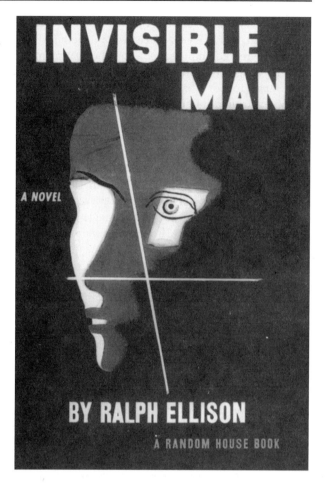

*Dust jacket for Ellison's first novel, which established
his reputation as an important American writer*

women who feel themselves alone in a world controlled
by large mechanical forces and by mere chance.

"Out of the Hospital and Under the Bar" was
originally chapter 11 of *Invisible Man,* but because of
space limitations the original 17,500-word chapter was
replaced by the 5,600-word hospital machine chapter.
In the story the narrator awakens from the explosion in
the machine and sees Mary Rambo, wearing a uniform
of a cleaning lady, looking in at him and trying to open
the machine and release him. Mary eventually helps
him escape, and he falls into and hides in a coal bin,
climbs out, helps an old blind man who reminds him of
his grandfather, and finally returns to Mary's house.
The story contains many of the themes and images
from the novel, such as invisibility, rebirth, restriction,
blindness, running, the underground, and folklore references such as Jack-the-Bear and John Henry.

The second Mary Rambo story, "Did You Ever
Dream Lucky?," is concerned with storytelling, the
human response to dashed expectations, initiation, the
value of humor, and unrealistic dreams. As the story

begins, Mary Rambo and her boarders finish a Thanksgiving meal, and Mary tells them a story about the time two cars wrecked on the street below the apartment she and her daughter Lucy shared. Mary and Lucy rushed below and found a bag that "clinked" loudly with a "sweet metal-like sound," which they hid in the toilet flush box. Frightened they would be discovered, they waited to open it, spending their money in their dreams. Finally, Mary opened the bag and discovered that it contained two sets of auto chains.

In polls conducted in *Book Week* in 1965 and the *Wilson Quarterly* in 1978, *Invisible Man* was selected by critics as "the most distinguished single work" published since World War II, returning the novel to the forefront of American critical thought. As the twentieth century drew to a close, critical discussions of the making and unmaking of the American canon reemphasized the novel's importance. African American literary theorists who apply varieties of European literary theories to African American literature also underscore Ellison's stature. The strength of *Invisible Man* derives from Ellison's integrative and wide-ranging imagination. He drew from classical works in the European tradition, major works in the American canon, African American literature and folklore, native American mythology, children's games and rhymes, and his own experience—in short, from wherever his imagination led him.

Although most of *Invisible Man* is set in Harlem, the narrative relies on frontier imagery associated with the duality between freedom and restriction often presented in American literature through the opposition between east and west. Ellison, who was raised in Oklahoma when it was still a territory, sensed the power of a frontier world of possibility. When he moved to the South, he encountered a world where the frontier ethos did not prevail, at least for an African American adult. *Invisible Man* dramatizes this revelation: it is an American bildungsroman in which the narrator moves from a frontier belief in freedom, simplicity, possibility, and harmony to a confrontation with the reality of restriction. The awareness that results emphasizes the "personal moral responsibility for democracy," which Ellison states is the significance of the fiction.

The Prologue, set at the end of the action, introduces most of the major themes and images. There the nameless writer-narrator—called variously by critics Invisible Man, Invisible, IM, Jack-the-Bear, Jack, "P," and "N"—explains the title as a reference to poor sight, a recurring metaphor in contemporary American fiction for innocence and ignorance: "That invisibility to which I refer occurs because of a peculiar disposition of the eyes of those with whom I come in contact. A matter of the construction of their *inner* eyes, those eyes with which they look through their physical eyes upon

reality." Living in an underground basement "in the great American tradition of tinkers," the narrator has rigged it so that he has 1,369 lights powered by electricity drained illegally from "Monopolated Light & Power," thus introducing the light/darkness duality as well as the image of electricity that recurs throughout the novel. But he is also a "thinker-tinker" who writes and shapes the story of his experience. It is a narrative answering Louis Armstrong's question, "What Did I Do to Be So Black and Blue?" As he listens to Armstrong and prepares to tell his tale, the narrator eats vanilla ice cream with sloe gin poured over it, adding black to the traditional American colors of red, white, and blue. Both the story and Armstrong's pun are concerned with innocent suffering to which both respond in the tragicomic language of the blues.

Ellison emphasizes the narrator's innocent belief in the outer world of appearance. His first hint that something exists beneath the surface comes when he overhears his dying grandfather, "a quiet old man who never made any trouble," tell his father: "Live with your head in the lion's mouth. I want you to overcome 'em with yeses, undermine 'em with grins, agree 'em to death and destruction, let 'em swoller you till they vomit or bust wide open." His grandfather's words confront him with the enigma of contradiction between appearance and reality, between mask and identity. Although he is puzzled by his grandfather's statement (there will be a long gap between hearing and understanding), he ultimately achieves the complex sense of identity that mediates between appearance and reality.

Ellison associates the narrator with the American Adam by having him recall his college. The narrator's memories flow with a flood of nostalgia for what he later refers to as "this Eden" with its harmonious garden imagery. Overwhelmed by his own sense of purpose as a student, he fails to see that this garden contains mockingbirds and a rumbling black powerhouse, an image that suggests the black college president, Dr. Bledsoe, for whom power is the goal. In his innocence the narrator bungles the responsibility of keeping the white school trustee Mr. Norton from seeing the squalid nearby environment: the incestuous sharecropper Jim Trueblood and the apocalyptic, Blakean world of chaos, the Golden Day, a whorehouse tavern visited by black inmates of an insane asylum for veterans. Trueblood, a character who combines the abilities of blues singers from African American culture with humor and tale-telling from Southwestern culture, offers the narrator a model for overcoming his own invisibility.

The narrator's dilemma is the familiar American crux that posits the open frontier against the restricted civilized world, the isolated Adam versus the communal

Ellison with his wife, Fanny McConnell Ellison, in the mid 1950s (Ralph Ellison Papers, Manuscript Division, Library of Congress)

Christ: "Our fate is to become one, and yet many. . . ." How does the one realize self without jeopardizing the allegiance to the many? How does one find freedom without falling into shapeless anarchy? How does one become committed to brotherhood without denying individuality? Ellison's oxymoronic answer is that these goals are achieved through organized chaos, through unified diversity, through restricted freedom.

By recognizing another's reality, the narrator is ready to discover freedom in artistic creation, a restricted freedom combining tradition and the individual talent. However, before rebirth comes a symbolic death through a second descent into the underworld. The descent and rebirth take place in various stages. First, by understanding, the narrator realizes he has been accepting as true subjective versions of reality articulated and imposed on him by others, "each attempting to force his picture of reality upon me and neither giving a hoot in hell for how things looked to me." He now recognizes that models of reality that deny the past are not acceptable: "I began to accept my past and, as I accepted it, I felt memories welling up within me."

Ellison began working on his second novel in 1958. With Saul Bellow's urging, Ellison planned to teach at Bard College, and since Bellow was spending the year in Minnesota, he offered the Ellisons his house. There Ellison began seriously writing the novel originally conceived in 1955. Additionally, Bellow asked Ellison for a contribution to the *Noble Savage,* and Ellison sent the first excerpt, "And Hickman Arrives" (1960), also his working title for the book. Between 1960 and 1977 Ellison published seven more stories, usually with a line stating "Excerpt from a novel in progress": "The Roof, the Steeple and the People" (1960), "It Always Breaks Out" (1963), "Juneteenth"

(1965), "Night-Talk" (1969), "A Song of Innocence" (1970), "Cadillac Flambe" (1973), and "Backwacking: A Plea to the Senator" (1977).

The author states that the novel takes place "roughly from 1954 to 1956 or 1957" and is set primarily in Washington, D.C., but it goes back "to some of the childhood experiences of Hickman, who is an elderly man in time present." The setting for the time past is various southern states, as the traveling evangelist Hickman moves throughout the South–from Georgia to Alabama to Oklahoma–as he takes his show on the road. In readings around the country Ellison identified Oklahoma as the setting for several of the stories set in the past. The main characters are the Reverend Alonzo Zuber Hickman and the orphan Bliss, a light-skinned boy of indeterminate race raised by Hickman to be a traveling evangelist. During sermons the boy hides in a white coffin until Hickman begins preaching of Christ's agony on the cross, and Bliss rises up from the coffin. Bliss eventually disappears into the white community and later reappears as the racist Senator Sunraider from an unidentified New England state (probably Massachusetts) who is later shot by another character, a young man from Oklahoma named Severen. In an interview Ellison said of the characters: "One man learns how to operate in society to the extent that he loses a great part of his capacity for, shall we say, poetry or for really dealing with life. And another man who seems caught at a very humble stage of society seems to have achieved quite a high level of humanity."

A second story line concerns the senator's activities. He makes a blatantly offensive speech in which he suggests that so many blacks are driving Cadillacs that the cars have lost their appeal to whites. In protest a black jazz musician burns his Cadillac on the senator's lawn. The speech inspires a racist southerner to write the senator a letter about some obscure sexual practice among blacks. The lawn burning also leads a group of journalists to discuss political acts of black people.

The published excerpts indicate that Ellison's second novel was to be a complex, carefully crafted work concerned with themes of interest to Ellison throughout his career: the spiral of history as the past boomerangs into the present, identity, resurrection, showmanship, amalgamation, and the positive and negative power of language and narrative to transform. Like *Invisible Man*, Ellison's second novel would examine the dialectic of freedom and restriction, dramatizing the restricted freedom that language and democracy provide for achieving wholeness and the chaos resulting from forgetting history.

In the mid 1980s Ellison began transcribing the novel on a word processor, and by the time of his death the manuscript was almost two thousand pages. Ellison had not selected a literary executor before he died; Ellison's wife, Fanny, asked John F. Callahan, Morgan S. Odell Professor of Humanities at Lewis and Clark College in Portland, Oregon, a friend of Ellison and author of a well-respected book on African American literature, *In the African-American Grain: Call and Response in 20th Century Black Fiction,* to edit the second novel. Callahan pared down the kaleidoscopic novel to a single story line for a modest novel rather than the massive one Ellison planned, and in 1999 *Juneteenth* was published.

Callahan had no special connection to Ellison's past nor to the African American experience that is central to Ellison's work. African American author Stanley Crouch, often called the clear heir to Ellison's intellectual legacy, labeled the book "John Callahan's *Juneteenth*," not Ellison's. Callahan was sensitive to these concerns and in the foreword and afterword to *Juneteenth* tries to anticipate the issues. He explains that he took Ellison's massive, two-thousand-word manuscript written over forty years and pared the "multifarious, multifaceted, multifocused, multivoiced, multitoned" work into a single, coherent, chronological story. He claims that every word is Ellison's and that he merely arranged sections, cut off extraneous parts, and selected what might have been a title Ellison would use. Callahan's editorial decisions about what to include in the story Ellison had worked on for years particularly limit the Southwestern focus that Ellison had in mind during the years he worked on the novel. When asked about his second novel, Ellison often said he was working on a Southwestern or Oklahoma novel, and in 1975, when asked about the importance of the Southwest to his work, he said, "Every night I dream of Oklahoma City."

Callahan selected *Juneteenth* for a title with a Southwestern emphasis but left out most of the particularly Southwestern sections of the story. Callahan's title for the novel refers to 19 June, the day in 1865 when slaves in Texas received word of their emancipation. Most of the rest of the edited novel explores Hickman's and Bliss's backgrounds, tracing Bliss's life from young evangelist to moviemaker to senator and Hickman's change from jazzman to minister, all told with language influenced by Ellison's reading of James Joyce and William Faulkner. One of the most effective parts details Hickman's visit to the Lincoln memorial with Hickman "mounting the steps and feeling a sudden release from the frame of time, feeling the old familiar restricting part of himself falling away as when, long ago, he'd found himself improvising upon some old traditional riffs of the blues, or when, as in more recent times, he'd felt the Sacred Word surging rapturously within him, taking possession of his voice and tongue."

Bliss/Senator Sunraider is like the shady character Rinehart in *Invisible Man,* a shape-changer, a trickster who is the master of chaos because he lacks a moral center to sustain him. Disconnected from a meaningful past, "passing for white," Bliss loses his identity and his soul and achieves a kind of death. His death requires a rebirth, an ascension, and certainly there are many images of death and rebirth with the central visual image of Bliss rising out of the coffin. The ironic Christ imagery, indeterminate race, and identity crisis suggest Ellison's debt to Faulkner's Joe Christmas in *Light in August* (1932). The various literary and biblical allusions demonstrate that in the second novel Ellison continues the theme of amalgamation and eclecticism from *Invisible Man* with the same cautions as before made more emphatic now. Just as Rinehart's eclecticism crossed over the border into chaos, so Bliss's protean shape-changing yields disorder. The Oklahoma frontier where Ellison grew up allowed and required possibility, but as Ellison made clear in *Invisible Man,* the American frontier's emphasis on ignoring the past was one of the negative aspects of the frontier myth. Perhaps the predominant theme of the second novel is the necessity of applying to the present the moral judgments validated by history. Ultimately, *Juneteenth* demonstrates how former jazzman Ellison spent the last forty years of his life riffing on race, identity, and freedom as he struggled to finish a second novel that would be large enough to surpass the first and would both resonate with and unite America's voices.

Going through Ellison's papers as he edited the second novel, Callahan discovered two previously unpublished stories that were then published in the 29 April – 6 May 1996 special issue of *The New Yorker* on "Black in America." These two early stories, "Boy on a Train" and "I Did Not Learn Their Names," provide new insight into the early Ellison. Most of Ellison's published early stories were harshly didactic, attacking American classism and racism, many published in left-leaning publications. Callahan edited *Flying Home and Other Stories,* which included these two stories, four other previously unpublished stories, and seven of Ellison's best short fiction; the collection was published posthumously in 1996.

Although it became fashionable in post-1960s America to dismiss the melting pot motif, Ellison, throughout his life, believed that America is a mixture. Just as the American language is not English but a transformation of English, American life reveals the diversity of various cultures, all drawing from one another to alter and color the whole. Believing this truth, Ellison resisted black nationalist and back-to-Africa movements and extolled the strength of the

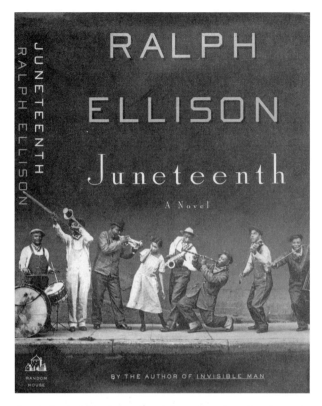

Dust jacket for Ellison's second novel, begun in 1958 and posthumously published in 1999 as edited by John F. Callahan

American amalgamation, a powerful force he originally discovered on the Southwestern frontier. Coming from the region where his fate was to develop frontier attitudes about freedom and possibility, Ralph Ellison charted new frontiers in American literature in language that forces chaos to reveal its truth.

Interviews:

Allen Geller, "An Interview with Ralph Ellison," in *The Black American Writer: Volume I, Fiction,* edited by C. W. E. Bigsby (Baltimore: Penguin, 1969), pp. 153–168;

Michael S. Harper and Robert B. Stepto, "Study and Experience: An Interview with Ralph Ellison," in *Chant of Saints,* edited by Harper and Stepto (Urbana: University of Illinois Press, 1979), pp. 451–469;

John Hersey, "'A Completion of Personality': A Talk with Ralph Ellison," in *Speaking for You,* edited by Kimberly W. Benston (Washington, D.C.: Howard University Press, 1987), pp. 285–307;

Hollie West, "Growing Up Black in Frontier Oklahoma . . . From an Ellison Perspective," in *Speaking for You,* edited by Benston (Washington, D.C.: Howard University Press, 1987), p. 12.

Maryemma Graham and Amritjit Singh, eds., *Conversations with Ralph Ellison* (Jackson: University Press of Mississippi, 1996).

References:

Jervis Anderson, "Going to the Territory," *New Yorker,* 52 (22 November 1976): 55–108;

Kimberly W. Benston, ed., *Speaking For You: The Vision of Ralph Ellison* (Washington, D.C.: Howard University Press, 1987);

Mark Busby, *Ralph Ellison* (Boston: Twayne, 1991);

Busby, "The Significance of the Frontier in Contemporary American Fiction," in *The Frontier Experience and the American Dream,* edited by Busby, David Mogen, and Paul Bryant (College Station: Texas A & M University Press, 1989), pp. 95–103;

Robert J. Butler, *The Critical Response to Ralph Ellison* (New York: Greenwood Press, 2000);

David L. Carson, "Ralph Ellison: Twenty Years After," *Studies in American Fiction,* 1 (Spring 1973): 17;

George Garrett, ed., *The Writer's Voice: Conversations with Contemporary Writers* (New York: Morrow, 1973), pp. 221–227;

Trudier Harris, "Ellison's 'Peter Wheatstraw': His Basis in Black Folk Tradition," *Mississippi Folklore Register,* 6 (1975): 117–126;

Harris, *Exorcising Blackness: Historical and Literary Lynching and Burning Rituals* (Bloomington: Indiana University Press, 1984), pp. 17, 31, 35, 40–49, 53, 76–77, 119, 184;

Richard Kostelanetz, "The Politics of Ellison's Booker," *Chicago Review,* 19 (1967): 5–26;

Kostelanetz, "Ralph Ellison: Novelist as Brown-Skinned Aristocrat," in his *Master Minds* (New York: Macmillan, 1969), pp. 36–59;

Zbigniew Lewicki, *The Bang and the Whimper: Apocalypse and Entropy in American Literature* (Westport, Conn.: Greenwood Press, 1984), pp. 47–58;

Robert G. O'Meally, *Ralph Ellison: The Craft of Fiction* (Cambridge, Mass.: Harvard University Press, 1980);

O'Meally, ed., *New Essays on Invisible Man* (New York: Cambridge University Press, 1988);

Susan Resneck Parr and Pancho Savery, eds., *Approaches to Teaching Ellison's Invisible Man* (New York: MLA, 1989);

Edith Schor, *Visible Ellison* (New York: Greenwood Press, 1993);

Joseph Trimmer, ed., *A Casebook on Ralph Ellison's Invisible Man* (New York: Crowell, 1972);

Jerry Gafio Watts, *Heroism and the Black Intellectual: Ralph Ellison, Politics, and Afro-American Intellectual Life* (Chapel Hill: University of North Carolina Press, 1994).

Richard Ford

(16 February 1944 –   )

Tamas Dobozy
University of British Columbia

BOOKS: *A Piece of My Heart* (New York: Harper &
Row, 1976; London: Collins Harvill, 1987);

The Ultimate Good Luck (Boston: Houghton Mifflin,
1981; London: Collins, 1989);

The Sportswriter (New York: Vintage, 1986; London:
Collins Harvill, 1986);

Rock Springs: Stories (New York: Atlantic Monthly
Press, 1987; London: Collins Harvill, 1988);

My Mother, in Memory (Elmwood, Conn.: Raven Editions, 1988);

Wildlife (New York: Atlantic Monthly Press, 1990;
London: Collins Harvill, 1990);

Independence Day (New York: Knopf, 1995; London:
Harvill, 1995);

Women With Men: Three Stories (New York: Knopf,
1997; London: Harvill, 1997);

Good Raymond (London: Harvill, 1998).

PLAY PRODUCTION: *American Tropical,* Louisville,
Actors Theater, 1983.

PRODUCED SCRIPT: *Bright Angel,* motion picture,
Hemdale Film Corporation, 1991.

OTHER: *The Best American Short Stories 1990,* edited
by Ford and Shannon Ravenel, with an introduction by Ford (Boston: Houghton Mifflin,
1990);

Juke Joint: Photographs by Birney Imes, introduction by
Ford (Jackson: University Press of Mississippi,
1990);

The Granta Book of the American Short Story, edited by
Ford (London: Granta/Viking, 1992; New York:
Penguin USA, 1992);

The Granta Book of the American Long Story, edited by
Ford (London: Granta, 1998);

The Essential Tales of Chekhov, translated by Constance
Garnett, edited, with an introduction, by Ford
(Hopewell, N.J.: Ecco Press, 1998);

Richard Ford (photograph © by Miriam Berkley)

Eudora Welty, *Complete Novels,* edited by Ford and
Michael Kreyling (New York: Library of America, 1998);

Welty, *Stories, Essays & Memoir,* edited by Ford and
Kreyling (New York: Library of America,
1998);

The Best American Sports Writing 1999, edited by Ford
(Boston: Houghton Mifflin, 1999).

SELECTED PERIODICAL PUBLICATIONS–
UNCOLLECTED: "Walker Percy: Not Just Whistling Dixie," *National Review,* 29 (13 May 1977): 558–564;

"Country Matters," *Harper's,* 263 (July 1981): 81–84;

"The Three Kings: Hemingway, Faulkner, and Fitzgerald," *Esquire,* 100 (December 1983): 577–584;

"The Boss Observed," *Esquire,* 104 (December 1985): 326–329;

"My Mother, in Memory," *Harper's,* 275 (August 1987): 44–57;

"Accommodations," *Harper's,* 276 (June 1988): 38, 42–43;

"First Things First: One More Writer's Beginnings," *Harper's,* 277 (August 1988): 72–76;

"Heartbreak Motels," *Harper's,* 279 (August 1989): 12–15;

"American Tropical," *Antaeus,* 66 (Spring 1991): 75–80;

"An Urge for Going: Why I Don't Live Where I Used to Live," *Harper's,* 284 (February 1992): 60–68;

"What We Write, Why We Write It, and Who Cares," *Michigan Quarterly Review,* 31 (Summer 1992): 373–389;

"A Minor's Affair," *Harper's,* 285 (September 1992): 32–34;

"What Happened Next," *New Yorker,* 71 (26 June 1995): 121–122;

"Sanctuary for Ideas We Love–And Hate," *Library Journal,* 20 (1 July 1995): 40–41;

"Privacy," *New Yorker,* 72 (22 July 1996): 58–59;

"In the Face," *New Yorker,* 72 (16 September 1996): 52–53;

"The Master of Ambiguity," *New York Times,* 17 October 1996, p. A27;

"Where Does Writing Come From?," *Granta,* 62 (Summer 1998): 249–255;

"Good Raymond," *New Yorker,* 74 (28 December 1998): 70–79;

"Our Moments Have Been Seized," *New York Times,* 27 December 1998, p. 4;

"Crèche," *New Yorker,* 74 (28 December 1998): 72–85.

Richard Ford's place in American letters has been established by his five novels, and many critics consider him one of the finest contemporary short-story writers as well. While he is often discussed as a "regionalist" author, Ford rejects that designation. His fiction examines America as a whole through its constituent parts, employing a wide-ranging perspective that accords with his ambition–echoing William Dean Howells–"to create a literature worthy of America."

A self-described "Aristotelian" and realist, Ford nevertheless delves into abstract philosophical concerns, such as transcendentalism, solipsism, and the ways in which people employ language to create their own versions of reality. His major theme may be contradiction, as it manifests itself between doing and saying, prescription and symptom, event and its subsequent reporting. His writings, fiction and nonfiction, address the limits and efficacy of individualism. Examining the conflicting forces acting on individuals, Ford's writing underscores the inconsistency of American life at the close of the twentieth century, celebrating the Whitmanesque "multitudes" and their inevitable contradictions.

Rather than lamenting what has been lost in the technocratic, postwar world, Ford values what remains, refusing to accept the disappearance of human will and agency. As he told Gregory L. Morris in 1994: "Not that you can always be responsible for what happens to you. But you can try to be. I've always disliked the sense of disempowerment." Ford presents an optimistic picture of human endeavor. His characters, especially in his later works, do their best with the options available in a world of strip malls, small towns, and interstate highways. Ford's fiction chronicles the human imagination striving to conceive a better life with the often scanty resources provided by society. In a 1998 interview with Huey Guagliardo, Ford connects this striving with the phrase "secular redemption," explaining that "what we are charged to do as human beings is to make our lives and the lives of others as livable, as important, as charged as we possibly can." Ford's fiction records the success or failure of various characters to live up to this humanist imperative.

Ford rejects categorization of his work, and the many critical pigeonholes in which it has been placed indicate that his writing covers a wide band of the realist spectrum. Bill Buford and Frank W. Shelton consider Ford a writer of "dirty realism," which Buford characterizes as a writing of "low-rent tragedies" depicting lower-class "drifters in a world cluttered with junk food and the oppressive details of modern consumerism." Vivian Gornick and Michael Trussler associate Ford with Raymond Carver and other writers of the so-called minimalist school of fiction, which is given to stylistic terseness and plain narrative surfaces. Bruce Weber, Ted Solotaroff, and Fred Hobson, however, place Ford in opposition to the "minimalist" set. As Hobson says, "No one could call *The Sportswriter* minimalist fiction. It is extravagant fiction." In fact, Ford's themes–such as language, epistemology, and mutability of identity–suggest a postmodern realism. Hobson and Jeffrey J. Folks, as well as Ford, have applied the designation "postmodern" to his writing.

Richard Ford was born in Jackson, Mississippi, on 16 February 1944, in a house located across the street from the home of Eudora Welty, a major literary influence. His father, Parker Carrol Ford, worked as a traveling starch salesman, and Ford and his mother, Edna Akin Ford, often joined Parker Ford on the road. At other times Edna Ford traveled with her husband, and her son stayed with his maternal grandparents at the Marion Hotel in Little Rock, Arkansas, which was run by his grandfather. As Ford wrote in "Accommodations" (*Harper's,* June 1988), at the Marion, watching guests come and go, he realized, "Home is finally a variable concept." This itinerant lifestyle informs the rootlessness of many of Ford's fictional characters, people dislocated not only geographically or domestically, but epistemologically as well, picking through the conceptual bric-a-brac of society and not permanently adopting one cognitive framework.

Much of Ford's fiction deals with the extent to which people's conceptions of home exert power—physical or philosophical—over them. The constant change associated with travel—which Ford, in "An Urge for Going: Why I Don't Live Where I Used to Live" (*Harper's,* February 1992), defines as "painstakingly subtle internal accommodations to contingency"—is internalized within Ford's fiction, as characters such as Frank Bascombe in *Independence Day* (1995), try to "accommodate" themselves to their various dependencies, to variations in luck, and to events set in motion with or without their consent. Travel serves as a panacea for the accumulation of facts that build up around the sedentary dweller, offering a constant shedding of the facts of the known location for the mystery of unlived-in locales.

Parker Ford died of a heart attack in 1960, when his son was sixteen years old. Having always been dependent on her husband's income, Ford's mother had to find employment, leaving her son to, in his words, "grow up in a hurry." As described in "My Mother, in Memory" (*Harper's,* August 1987), Parker Ford's death precipitated his son's awakening to responsibility. Ford reevaluated his circle of friends and, in the process, his character, making necessary social adjustments. With this shift came the notion of character as a conscious decision—as not fixed but mutable—a notion prominently featured in *Independence Day,* where Frank contemplates his son, Paul:

> I just think he's got some problems figuring out a good conception of himself . . . and I want to offer a better one so he doesn't get too attached to the one he's hanging onto now, which doesn't seem too suc-

cessful. . . . He has to risk trying to improve by giving up what's maybe comfortable but not working.

Character is not solely the product of the unconscious. It is also the creation of an individual's will to trade "comfort" for change, to break off unproductive "attachments" in an attempt at "figuring out" a "better" conception of oneself. Ford's fiction continually addresses accountability, the extent to which individuals must accept responsibility for their actions.

In 1962 Ford enrolled at Michigan State University, where he majored in literature and graduated with a B.A. in 1966. Following a brief, unrewarding stint in law school at Washington University, he decided to study writing at the University of California at Irvine, earning an M.F.A. in 1970. In 1968 he married Kristina Hensley, a research professor in the field of urban and regional planning, whom he had met while at Michigan State. After earning his M.F.A., Ford taught at the University of Michigan (1974–1976), Williams College (1978–1979), and Princeton University (1979–1980).

As Ford told Bruce Weber in 1988, "I couldn't be a writer if it weren't for Kristina." All Ford's books are dedicated to her, and Ford often refers to his marriage as a primary influence on the development of his writing. He decided to become a writer in January 1968. As he told Weber, "Being a writer just seemed like a good idea. It was just casting off into the dark. But I think that's the way people make themselves into whatever they finally make themselves, good or otherwise." Ford told Bonnie Lyons in a *Paris Review* interview (Fall 1996), that his early models were "Donald Barthelme, Robert Coover, William Gass." As Ford explains in "First Things First: One More Writer's Beginnings" (*Harper's,* August 1988), after most of his early stories were rejected outright by publishers of literary magazines, he began work on a novel in the realistic tradition, a direction suggested by his teachers at Irvine. In this undertaking he drew on models such as William Faulkner, Eudora Welty, and Walker Percy, as well as "Cheever and Richard Yates and Bellow and Roth. Plus Babel. Plus Chekhov"— and his contemporaries: "Ray Carver, Joy Williams, Mary Robison, Ann Beattie and others." After six years of arduous work, this shift in aesthetic resulted in Ford's first novel, *A Piece of My Heart* (1976).

Apart from a few flashbacks, *A Piece of My Heart* takes place during one week of the annual turkey-hunt season on an uncharted island in the Mississippi River, between the states of Arkansas and Mississippi. The novel chronicles the meeting of two men—Sam Newel, a Chicago law student, and Robard Hewes, a sometime construction worker—and their interaction

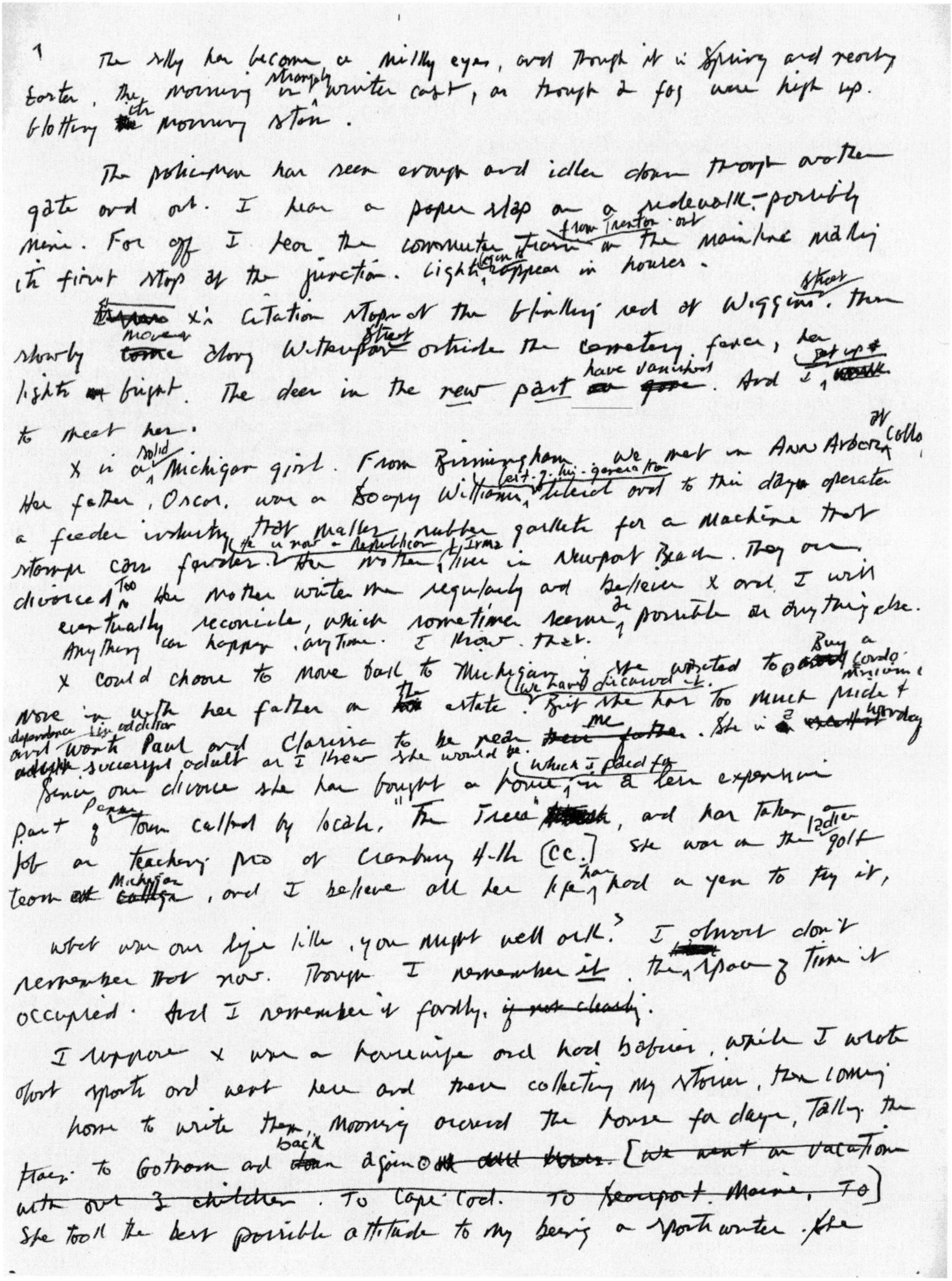

[Handwritten manuscript draft page — partially legible]

The sky has become a milky cyan, and though it is Spring and nearly Easter, the morning is through in winter cast, as though a fog were high up, blotting the morning stars.

The policeman has seen enough and idles down through another gate and out. I hear a paper slap on a sidewalk—possibly mine. Far off I hear the commuter train from Trenton on the main line making its first stop at the junction. Lights begin to appear in houses.

X's Citation stops at the blinking red of Wiggins. then slowly moves along Witherspoon outside the cemetery fence, her lights bright. The deer in the new part have vanished. And I get up to meet her.

X is a solid Michigan girl. From Birmingham. We met in Ann Arbor. Her father, Oscar, was a ... Williams ... to this day operates a feeder industry ... rubber gaskets for a machine that stamps car fenders ... the mother lives in Newport Beach. They are divorced too ... the mother writes her regularly and believes X and I will eventually reconcile, which sometimes seems as possible as anything else. Anything can happen, anytime. I know that.

X could choose to move back to Michigan ... wanted to buy a condo ... move in with her father on the estate ... But she has too much pride and ... to be near me. She is ...

Since our divorce she has bought a house, which I paid for, in a less expensive part of town called by locals "The Trees" ... and has taken a job as teaching pro of Cranbury 4th [CC.] She was on the golf team at Michigan, and I believe all her life has had a yen to try it.

What was our life like, you might well ask? I almost don't remember that now. Though I remember it. The space of time it occupied. And I remember it fondly.

I suppose X was a housewife and had babies, while I wrote about sports and went here and there collecting my stories, then coming home to write them, mooning around the house for days, taking the train to Gotham and back again ... [we went on vacation with our 3 children. To Cape Cod. To Seacoast Maine, To]
She took the best possible attitude to my being a sportswriter. She

Manuscript page and corrected typescript page for Ford's 1986 novel, The Sportswriter
(Special Collections, Michigan State University Libraries)

144

"It was Mr. Balch."

"I shoulda guessed that. What's he?"

Bump hits the window beside us with a crackly stream of

hose water. He is visible blurrily behind the pane, his face

stern, his K. of C. cap low over his villain's eyes. Bump is a

Catholic. Pauline is A.M.E. I am a Presbyterian, though not

a usable Christian, any longer. We ignore him as usual.

"He couldn't say. But I have to go to Brielle to help

him do something."

"Brielle?" I might as well have said Normandy.

"It is mysterious. He called from New York."

"New York! He's also full of mysteries, Mr. Balch is.

He ain't acted right now a year. I didn't say it. through.

You did." Bump has left us for other windows now, and the

breakfast nook pane begins to dry up in little islands left

by the bright spring sunlight. The nook grows silent.

"O.K. What do you mean?"

"Somethin strange about that man." Mrs. Bump stares

at a biscuit she holds in her fingers as if an ant is on it.

"Somethin bout a tall man, you know when he ain't right."

Street Balch is six-seven, a bean pole, but in excellent

shape. He played basketball for the Rebels. "Somethin bout

how see him standin out."

"I think maybe he has a girlfriend. It's going around

now, I hear."

"Sho am." Mrs. Bump gives me her old white-eyed look.

I know its meaning well enough. She is no friend to Rosy

Rizzuto whose company I have kept for better than a year now.

with the grizzled, ornery Mark Lamb, the owner of the island.

Constructed in sections alternately titled "Robard Hewes" and "Sam Newel" and told from the third-person-limited points of view of the two men, the narrative presents Hewes and Newel as mirror images, or Doppelgängers: Hewes, the sensual, physical man driven by sexual appetites, versus the cerebral, spiritually paralyzed Newel, trying to weather an existential crisis.

Flashbacks throughout the Sam Newel sections illustrate his failure to reconcile past and present, and he ultimately fails to grasp that freedom comes not through dwelling on the past but through accepting a place in the present. At one point Newel incredulously asks Hewes, "You don't really think the best way to solve a problem is just forget about it, do you?" Hewes's reply expresses the problems inherent in his visceral way of living and also offers a remedy for Newel's obsessiveness: "If you're to where there ain't nothing else, it is." If a particular problem or line of thought leads to a spiritual vacuum, it must be abandoned. But Ford's narrative does not dismiss rational thinking, nor does it endorse an easy acceptance of uncertainty; rather it critiques a reliance on given linguistic formulations: "Just cause you think up some question don't mean there's an answer," says Hewes.

Conversely, Hewes makes no attempt to order experience into narrative, and the randomness of his death underlines the dangers of a visceral existence. Newel warns Hewes against believing that "the whole world just boils down to a piece of mysterious nooky." But his wholesale rejection of history—especially his history with his married lover, Beuna—deprives him of the necessary tools for coping with present contingency: "If I was to try to pin together my past and make something intelligent out of it I'd damn sure be in one then. I'd either get bored to tears or scared to death. . . . Except as far as I'm concerned, things just happen. One minute don't learn the next one nothin." In Hewes's ethos, action precedes reason. While Newel fixates on trying to determine the exact coordinates of his being in history, Hewes rejects any sense of being at all.

The third major character in the novel, Mr. Lamb—a grotesque, comic sage and a vital personality—synthesizes the two protagonists' characteristics in his ability to hold contrary elements in equipoise. As Frank Shelton notes, Mr. Lamb serves as a model of stability in contrast to the disorderly conduct of Newel and Hewes. He offers Hewes the responsibility he cannot survive for long without and Newel the critique of epistemological structures necessary for retaining a vital interest in life. A repository of "Southern tradi-

tion," Mr. Lamb functions, paradoxically, as a source of possible renewal rather than as an allegorical figure of a defeated South. As his glass eye suggests, he manufactures "seeing," constantly questioning perception.

Having caught two military surveyors poaching on his island, Mr. Lamb has bribed the men—against pain of arrest—to remove the island from their official charts. This action offers a potent metaphor for the ways in which individuals carve out niches for themselves in an overwhelmingly regulated culture. Lamb's accidental death by electrocution awakens the reader, if not Newel, to the unpredictability of occurrence and the failure of history to prepare for happenstance. At the same time it offers a lesson on consequence to Hewes, whose death appears equally random. He is killed, not by Beuna's husband, but by a boy who shoots him for trespassing.

A Piece of My Heart reevaluates the stereotypical view of the South. In Ford's view, which he expressed in "Walker Percy: Not Just Whistling Dixie" (*National Review,* 13 May 1977): "The south is not a place any more: it's a Belt, a business proposition, which is the nearest thing to anonymity the economy recognizes." *A Piece of My Heart,* then, tells of a South unattached from its past and deluded in presenting itself as a place permeated by history and portentous significance. Near the end of the novel Hewes tells Newel: "Down in Jackson there ain't nothing but a bunch of empty lots and people flying around in Piper Comanches looking for some way to make theirselves rich. It wouldn't feel like nothing at all anymore, to *you.*" *A Piece of My Heart* depicts the South as a place of transaction rather than event, where Newel—despite his protestations to the contrary—does not find history incarnate in daily living, only a dailiness no different from the Chicago of his present circumstance.

A Piece of My Heart was a modest critical success. Nolan Miller, in *The Antioch Review* (Winter 1977), and Susan Wood, in *The Washington Post* (20 February 1977), both criticized the indebtedness of the work to Faulkner, but they went on to recognize Ford's considerable potential. Victor Gold, writing in the *National Review* (12 November 1976), offered generally favorable observations on the novel, but along with Miller and Wood, he faulted the overuse of symbolism. The sternest criticism appeared in Larry McMurtry's review for *The New York Times* (24 October 1976). While recognizing the latent "promise" of the novel, McMurtry felt that its strengths lay buried under "the characteristic vices of southern fiction."

Writing in *Newsweek* (11 May 1981), Walter Clemons categorized Ford's second novel, *The Ultimate Good Luck* (1981), as an "existential thriller." The book follows Harry Quinn, a veteran of the Vietnam War, on a quest to free Sonny—the brother of Quinn's lover, Rae—from prison in Oaxaca, Mexico. Accused by Deats, a Los Angeles drug dealer, of stealing the drugs he was meant to deliver, Sonny is a target of inmates employed by local drug contacts. Finally, a rendezvous with an underworld contact whom Quinn considers his last hope for freeing Sonny, results in a bloodbath. Quinn has to shoot his way to freedom, killing two people. The novel ends with Quinn and Rae abandoning Sonny's cause.

At one point in *The Ultimate Good Luck* Quinn wonders "if it still ran in his character to get lucky." In these words Ford is simultaneously evoking and binding contrary ideas: on one side, the deterministic notion of "character"—that the conditions of one's life generate one's opportunities—and, on the other, a metaphysical notion of "luck" as a power to which individuals can appeal but which they cannot control. Standing contradictions exist throughout the novel.

The Ultimate Good Luck also examines the concept of "faith," particularly the belief in realities outside sensual perception. Quinn, for instance, puts his faith in luck as the necessary precondition for survival. As Ford told Guagliardo in 1998, survival in his fiction relies on belief "in the efficacy of things you can't predict or see the evidence of, in the faith that if you invent them they will cause you to survive, literally survive. And maybe more: survive with dignity, survive with pleasure, survive with a sense of life's being worthwhile." Such survival depends on imaginative invention—crafting a conceptual or narrative vision adequate to describe and overcome the contingencies of life. Quinn's faith in luck relates directly to his experiences during the Vietnam War: "It was always a war, . . . and when it was over you felt lucky, even left by yourself."

The war is responsible for Quinn's damaged, "lonely" psyche and for the concept of "luck" to which he clings. At the same time Ford portrays Quinn as sorting through the experiences that impinge on, and determine, his character, suggesting that character is both determined and self-determining.

Through the metaphor of expatriation, *The Ultimate Good Luck* examines the effect of the Vietnam War on a generation of American men. Quinn says: "Mexico was like Vietnam or L.A., only more disappointing—a great trivial abundance of crap the chief effect of which wasn't variety but sameness." He encounters the fragmentation of Vietnam everywhere, not just in the foreign locale of Mexico but in American cities such as Los Angeles. Vietnam has become a way of thinking for him and an entire segment of the population. In a maze of "trivial abundance"—a consumer culture cluttered with identical options—dis-

tance, impersonality, and isolation become the norm. In writing of Quinn's experience in Vietnam, Ford captures the disorientation of ordinary Americans: "But that patterned feel [of American life] had gotten disrupted somehow, as though everything whole had separated a little inch, and he [Quinn] had dropped back in between things, to being on the periphery without a peripheral perspective." Quinn knows that he stands outside, on the "periphery" and lacks "perspective" necessary to see inside the culture that excludes him. He cannot even tell the difference between Los Angeles and Oaxaca, or Vietnam and Mexico. Borders have disintegrated, and he is lost in a fragmented world. Even the physical immediacy of violence makes "everything the same." Isolation remains the only possible means of sustaining self in an undifferentiated milieu.

Yet, other forms of faith are open to Quinn. A tourist woman at the beginning of the novel tells him: "You know trust is at the heart of love and art and all kinds of shit." Through the course of the novel he comes to reject his imaginary concept of luck for a belief in the consolations offered by Rae. This different sort of faith—one that leads away from the bloodbath at the end of the novel—provides a richer sort of "survival" than the bare bones of Quinn's isolationism. As the tourist points out, without trust Quinn's existence "excludes" the "love and art and all kinds of shit" necessary to dignify life.

At the same time as *The Ultimate Good Luck* depicts the dislocation of Quinn's generation, it also argues that the impulse to fix one's coordinates in the culture may, in fact, be a misguided desire: "You can always think everything's on a grid and somebody's responsible for everything. But it isn't true." The nostalgia for a firm grasp on one's "place"—for a reliable explanation—can anaesthetize the individual to what is available in present circumstances. Quinn's long-range, "distanced" vision occludes and desensitizes him to the comforts of friends and lovers. With Rae, Quinn establishes "an intimacy that doesn't need an outside frame." Rae and Quinn lose their peripheral status by forming their own nucleus, and Quinn escapes from the "grids" and "systems" he wishes to impose on experience. As Rae tells him, such cognitive frameworks only further subordinate an everyday reality that constantly overflows patterns: "Those self-contained systems just get smaller . . . they don't tolerate enough."

Rae prefers narrative to theory, openness to control, and love to luck. Under her influence, Quinn trades his prophetic, utopian vision of control for an active engagement with occurrence. Ford clearly believes in the importance of individual experience

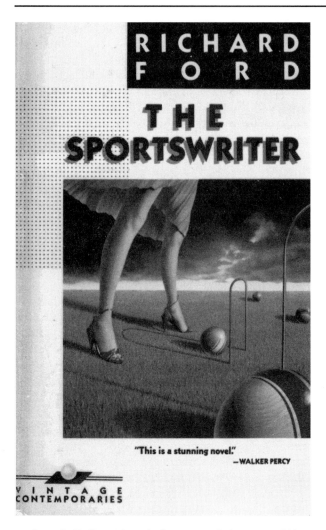

Cover for Ford's 1986 novel, about a man who is content to drift through life

and that a focus on particulars is a remedy for, rather than a symptom of, the atomization evident in post-1960s America.

The Ultimate Good Luck was not well received. While C. D. B. Bryan, in *The New York Times Book Review* (31 May 1981), praised Ford's characterization of Quinn as "exactly right," most reviewers focused on Ford's inadequacy in handling the thriller genre. Gilberto Perez, in *The Hudson Review* (Winter 1981–1982), faulted the novel for indulging in "gratuitous violence" and the "tough-guy mystique." Writing for *Newsweek* (11 May 1981), Walter Clemons recognized Ford's weakness in portraying "a macho hero less intelligent than he is," while offering constructive criticism by highlighting Ford's "sacrifice of his robust gift for comedy"—a comment that Ford admitted to Lyons, "was one of the most significant things I'd ever read about something I'd written."

Ford's comedic sensibility returned full force with *The Sportswriter* (1986). Regarded as a breakthrough work, the novel followed a brief hiatus from writing. Dissatisfied with his life in New Jersey, disappointed with the reception of *The Ultimate Good Luck,* and, most important, grappling with his mother's terminal illness, Ford gave up writing novels in 1981 and instead wrote articles for the magazine *Inside Sports.* Speaking to Weber in 1988, Ford credited his resumption of literary writing to *Inside Sports* going out of business and his wife's challenge "to write a book about a happy man." Thinking over her challenge, Ford decided that the perfect occupation for a man living a happy life would be sportswriting. He views the novel as a career benchmark: "My writing life changed after I began *The Sportswriter,*" he told Weber, "I felt much more encouraged." Encouragement characterizes the novel.

The Sportswriter takes place over an Easter weekend. It opens on Good Friday, with the protagonist, Frank Bascombe, and his former wife, called only "X," visiting the grave of their son Ralph, who died of Reye's syndrome just over two years before the beginning of the narration. A week short of his thirty-ninth birthday, Frank—who published one collection of short stories before quitting literary authorship—now writes for a "glossy New York sports magazine" and continues to live in the house he once inhabited with his wife and three children. The novel examines Frank's past as well as his immediate future. Though he attempts to make the best of things, events often test the limits of his optimism. Yet, despite the many trying circumstances he experiences in the course of the novel—many of them attributable to mistakes on his part—he remains characteristically confident at the close of *The Sportswriter,* filled with the "modest hopes" that allow him to continue seeking solace in a world not always fair or kind to him.

The Sportswriter represents a massive departure for Ford. Unlike Robard Hewes, Sam Newel, or Harry Quinn, Frank Bascombe undergoes harrowing experiences not in the exotic locales of Mr. Lamb's island or Oaxaca, but in the everyday world of the malls, highways, and restaurants of Haddam, New Jersey. Also, Ford abandoned the heavy symbolism of his first two novels for a more literal, philosophical rendering of the world. To facilitate this rendering, he created a lyrical voice whose long, decorative sentences mirror Frank's more-generous worldview. For the first time, as well, Ford employed a first-person narrator, giving his protagonist's consciousness an immediacy lacking in the first two novels.

The Sportswriter stood out amid other novels of its time for what Weber calls "its overarching lack of irony." Like Weber, Fred Hobson has highlighted Ford's sincerity in dealing with the redemptive aspects of an America glutted with consumer culture. He praises Ford's refusal to take an elitist, condescending view of popular culture, adding: "It is precisely this resistance to easy irony, a resisting the temptation to be ironic in dealing with popular culture, that distinguishes Ford from numerous other contemporary writers; for if an ironic vision is generally assumed to be a literary virtue, such a transcendence of accessible irony—or, perhaps, a deeper irony that turns on itself, ironizing the ironists—may be even more desirable." Hobson praises Ford's discovery of transcendent values in religious bric-a-brac and mail-order catalogues, a rejection of the clichéd view that consumer culture is the repository of all that is meaningless and illusory in American life.

In mail-order catalogues Frank finds not the adman's continually withheld promise of enrichment through material possessions but rather a mystery that leads to "solace," an "odd assurance that some things outside my life were okay still. . . . Things were knowable, safe-and-sound. Everybody with exactly what they need or could get. A perfect illustration of how the literal can become the mildly mysterious." Frank finds an "assurance," not that his life will somehow become more interesting, exciting, or glamorous through acquisition, but that the straightforwardness of consumer advertising—not purchase itself—can temporarily overturn the terrible factuality of his life with the mystery of possibility, appealing to a belief in an "outside" world where things are "safe-and-sound." Catalogues show Frank that the world is not entirely defined by his experience. They make him realize the limits of his perspective, dissolving the boundaries within which he views his existence.

Throughout the novel Frank continually sorts various strategies for apprehending experience in the best possible way, and more often than not he finds it in ordinary living. Ford offers a further nonironic approach in his 1987 article "My Mother, in Memory." In this memoir Ford praises his parents for encouraging him to "seek the normal in life" as a response to adversity, for portraying "a world, a private existence, that *could be* that way." Rather than inciting a need for material acquisition, advertising reconciles Frank to existing material conditions.

Despite Frank's rejection of literary endeavor, he remains a writer. As Raymond A. Schroth has said, Frank "is the individualist as writer, who must learn to turn his loneliness into creative energy rather than self-pity." Having stopped crafting narratives on the page, he applies a writerly attitude to life itself. The lyricism of the novel exemplifies Frank's willful transformation of pain into an affirming aesthetic display. Yet, this transformation is also a means by which Frank avoids commitment to anything but the free play of rendering.

By continually sorting through the means of representing experience, Frank remains essentially passive, an observer rather than an agent. His admiration for athletes is based entirely on their apparent possession of a decisiveness he lacks. They are "happy to let their actions speak for them" and "never likely to feel the least bit divided, or alienated, or one ounce of existential dread." However, his interview with Herb Wallagher, a wheelchair-bound former football player, calls into question Frank's initial view of athletes. Deprived of an existence in action, Wallagher finds himself without the tools necessary to accept the world.

Literature allows Frank an escape from the permanence of fact. Speaking of the brief time in which he taught at Berkshire College, he sharply criticizes the misuse of writing to promote permanence rather than mystery: "Real mystery—the very reason to read (and certainly write) any book—was to them [the faculty at the college] a thing to dismantle, distill and mine out into rubble they could tyrannize into sorry but more permanent explanations. . . ." In contrast, Frank believes that literature prepares a person for what "can't be foreseen," the accidents that the athletic life fails to consider. Ford's unwillingness "to say . . . that anything is ever the sole cause of anything else," his reluctance to adopt a clear-cut deterministic view of occurrence, permeates *The Sportswriter*. As long as there is another way of saying, another way of representing experience, Frank will never have to struggle with accountability. He can offer a wide variety of explanations for his actions, picking from among them the one that suits him best at any given time. He is unwilling to choose between often mutually exclusive options because choosing would confine him to a fixed set of responsibilities. He moves from one idea to the next, adopting various strategies for remaining unencumbered by any specific set of demands. As Alice Hoffman noted, in *The New York Times Book Review* (23 March 1986), Frank never "trades theorizing for action."

Ford's portrayal of Frank as a man who prefers the delayed "promise" of mystery and accident to the specificity of history, allows readers, as Michiko Kakutani noted in *The New York Times* (26 February 1986), to view Frank as he "sees himself" and also "as he must appear to others"—at once flexible and open to contingency and also unwilling to face, or even admit, the facts. While Frank's open-ended strategy permits him the freedom of contradiction and a conceptual

Ford with his wife, Kristina Hensley Ford (photograph by Bob Adelman)

mobility that evades fixity and accountability, it leaves him unable to adhere to the standards necessary for the maintenance of community. His happiness comes at the cost of reliability, without which he is unable to sustain relationships.

The Sportswriter is an instructive novel insofar as it shows how narrative indeterminacy can facilitate optimism and revitalize a life dispirited by historical fact. The novel also celebrates how the human imagination enables survival and the derivation of happiness from the most banal of sources. Yet, Ford also offers a case study of the problems facing the ordinary citizen. Frank's response to bewildering events suggests not so much a way by which one may know or guide life, but means through which one may accept its conditions without succumbing to despair. The meandering lyricism and abstract speculation are simultaneously symptomatic of Frank's situation and a strategy against it. As Edward Dupuy commented in 1990, "Frank's act of telling becomes a confession. It

not only discloses and acknowledges the events of his life but also reconciles him to those events." Dupuy also points out that Frank's relenting to "life's inherent sadness," his acceptance of occurrence, ultimately allows him a "woundedness" that "does not preclude happiness." Frank knows that only acceptance of loss eases its pain.

The Sportswriter was well received. *Time* magazine named the novel one of the five best books of 1986. It won a PEN/Faulkner citation for fiction in 1987, the same year in which Ford received a literature award from the Mississippi Academy of Arts and Letters. Writing for *Newsweek* (7 April 1986), Walter Clemons called Frank's narrative voice "a superlative achievement," and other critics agreed. Robert Towers, in *The New York Review of Books* (24 April 1986), praised Ford's "vision" and "embrace," calling *The Sportswriter* "a reflective work that invites reflection, a novel that . . . touches us with the perplexities of a . . . hopeful man adrift in his own humanity."

The Sportswriter did encounter some criticism, particularly from female reviewers. Alice Hoffman was an exception to the many reviewers who found Frank an essentially happy man. For Hoffman the novel was full of an "unsettling irony." Her contention that "Bascombe's attempt at arranging an unexamined life for himself is thwarted" opposed the praise lavished on the novel by Kakutani, Towers, and Weber, who viewed Frank's self-examination as its chief contribution to American literature. She saw him as a man lost in "sorrow." Jonathan Yardley, in *The Washington Post* (30 March 1986), criticized the novel, saying it "drones on" without ever "getting fully engaged." Vivian Gornick, in *The New York Times Book Review* (16 September 1990), took the most notable exception to *The Sportswriter,* however, accusing Ford of being "in love with" "Bascombe's depression." She found the book meandering and directionless, referred to Frank as unconscious of his dilemma ("Frank's not knowing what is happening to him is the story"), and strongly criticized Ford's presentation of women.

Published only a year after *The Sportswriter, Rock Springs* (1987), a collection of ten short stories, includes some of Ford's most critically acclaimed fiction to date. Set mainly in the small towns of Montana, these stories are again a departure for Ford, taking the reader from the civic-minded, suburban milieu of New Jersey to the windswept, bleak, semirural, and often extremely limited economic horizons of the American West.

Ford's next novel, *Wildlife* (1990), begins as Joe Brinson, the sixteen-year-old narrator, recounts the temporary dissolution of his family during the fall of 1960. His father, Jerry, goes to fight the forest fires raging in the mountains outside the town of Great Falls, Montana. Left behind, Joe and his mother, Jeanette, must come to grips with the possibility that Jerry may not return, and Jeanette eventually begins seeing a married man. Throughout the narrative, Joe copes with his sudden and unwanted independence and with the realization that he can no longer rely on his parents for steadfast counsel. As Shelton suggests, the novel focuses on "the moments when characters seem to lose control of their lives—when connections fall apart and chaos threatens."

The fire burning in the hills around the town, threatening its populace, impinges on and destabilizes established patterns of existence, while at the same time it serves a hidden, though inaccessible, order. From the devastation of fire springs the possibility of renewal, as well as the preconditions for disastrous recurrence. Joe associates the fire with the vastness of life outside the limited familial framework. Jeanette tells him "that the whole fire was just a lot of little sep-

arate fires? . . . Well, I guess I think nothing's that important by itself." This statement suggests the impossibility of recovering original causes, of obtaining definitive empirical evidence to explain occurrence, echoing a belief Ford expressed to Morris: "Fate and family and affection . . . all kinds of things are not final causes; they are contributive causes to all kinds of human actions, and finally all that we have left are ourselves and our responsibility for our own actions." Thus, the fire refers primarily to itself. Its root causes cannot be replicated, nor can one account for its existence. Absolute order, the sequential chain of events, cannot be ascertained. The totality always remains fragmentary, as does Joe's conception of the fire as "just a lot of little fires." Joe can no more locate a trigger for the events in the novel than he can find anyone outside himself to rely on in his moment of crisis. *Wildlife* does not deny that forces act on a situation, but that the specific forces cannot be discovered in their totality.

The many symbolic permutations for the fire in the novel—including chaos, sexual passion, masculine endeavor, and recurrence—show how the human mind fastens onto actuality and imposes on it the meanings and identifications it presently requires. Yet, over the long term these meanings may not cohere into a unified symbolic pattern. The fire ultimately calls attention not to what it stands for but rather to the many things for which it is made to stand. The fire becomes a metaphor for metaphor itself. By calling attention to the process of creating metaphors, the fire emphasizes the characters' need for them. Ford peels back the symbolic layer or "meaning" that people cast over things. He aims at the erasure of symbols, dissolving them back into the immediate and specific moments of his characters' histories.

The young narrator must rise from a safe familial structure and hazard his own view on the world, one governed not by preset rituals and metaphors, but according to his own historical specifics:

> I wondered if there was some pattern or an order to things in your life—not one you knew but that worked on you and made events when they happened seem correct, or made you confident about them or willing to accept them even if they seemed like wrong things. Or was everything just happening all the time, in a whirl without anything to stop it or cause it—the way we think of ants, or molecules under the microscope, or the way others would think of us.

Ford indefinitely suspends contrary interpretations. Joe does one over the other. Just articulating the conflict seems to console Joe, at least allowing him to view two possibilities. Ford does not deny that a pattern or

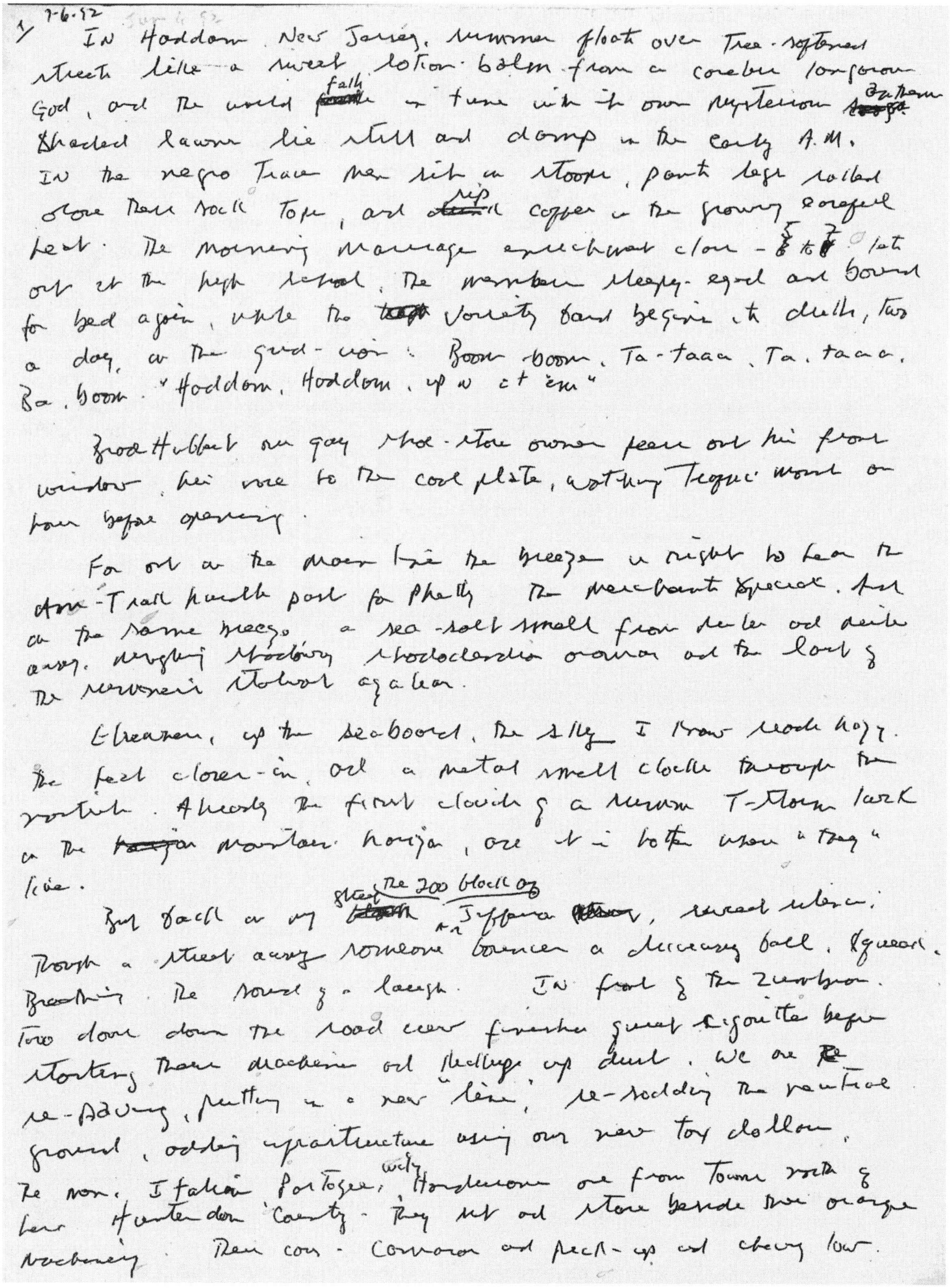

In Haddam, New Jersey, summer floats over tree-softened streets like a sweet lotion balm from a careless, languorous God, and the world falls into tune with its own mysterious anthems. Shaded lawns lie still and damp in the early A.M. In the negro trace men sit on stoops, pants legs rolled above their sock tops, and sip coffee in the growing, sorrowful heat...

(remainder of handwritten manuscript largely illegible)

Manuscript page and corrected typescript page for Ford's 1995 novel, Independence Day
(Special Collections, Michigan State University Libraries)

granted, given them a bad name, ~~never really getting past the~~
~~surface.~~ ~~And~~ in point of fact, the ~~scared-shitless~~ anxiety they
feel is ~~really a~~ pioneer worry that there are reasons not to
venture too far for fear of the unknown: ~~too much excitement, too~~
~~many cinema and yogurt venues,~~ a faster paced existence, ~~the ante~~
~~raised to dizzier and dizzier~~ heights.

My job -- and I only rarely succeed -- is to draw them back
closer to a chummier feeling that we're really doing pretty much
exactly the same things twenty-four hours a day, thinking the same
things, dreaming the same dopey dreams, longing the same longings;
make them less anxious about how they're like their neighbors and
the few insignificant ways they're not. When I fail -- and I ~~of~~
~~course~~ usually sell a house ~~anyway~~ -- I leave the buyer with an
intact pioneer ~~spirit~~ which means that he'll ~~probably~~ be ~~up~~ and on
the road again in 3.86 years, instead of settling in and letting
time slip past him -- the way people do who have something really
important on their mind. [~~reduce 3 prev paras~~]

Does ~~this~~ mean I'm cynical? A cultural ~~anesthetist~~? ~~Is~~
realty itself basically as cynical and leering as an oriental
massage, ~~only less pleasant?~~

No. ~~I'm~~ simply ~~in~~ a phase of life, in which a sense of
anticipation, of something being out there promised-but-you-don't-
know-what-it-is seems harder to rely on; ~~the phase when it's seems~~
~~smart to make a project out of worrying less,~~ the phase ~~in your~~
life which when you think back on it, at the end of life's journey,
you'll have a hard time remebering much ~~distinctly~~; the time you'll

order might exist, only that if it does, it must reside somewhere beyond what "one . . . knew." The reconciliation of these two opposing ideas comes not as a newfound scientific or epistemological awareness but rather in the ability of words to sustain opposing ideas in a single paragraph.

Set in 1961, the last chapter, in which Joe recounts the reconciliation of his parents, does not clarify whether the events of the fall of 1960 represent a break in the Brinson family's life pattern or merely a fluctuation implicit to the pattern itself. Joe comes to understand that he cannot count on life to supply ready-made answers to the dilemmas it raises. The last sentence of the novel describes Joe's narrative as a personal, rather than omniscient, transcription of events: "They lived together—that was their life—and alone. Though God knows there is still much to it that I myself, their only son, cannot fully claim to understand." In this way Joe takes responsibility for the narrative, stepping forward as the author of the tale, albeit an author with limitations of perspective.

Wildlife did not receive as enthusiastic or widespread a response as *Rock Springs* or *The Sportswriter;* neither has the novel received much critical or scholarly consideration. Paul Gray in *Time* (4 June 1990), however, found the novel faithful "to the texture of experience," eschewing programmatic morality or explicit abstractions for "how it feels to be enlightened." Similarly, Peter S. Prescott, in *Newsweek* (11 June 1990), praised the "elegance" of Ford's prose, comparing him favorably to "early Hemingway." However, Jonathan Yardley, in the *Washington Post* (20 June 1990), criticized the book for its "pop psychology," and Victoria Glendinning in *The Times* (London) on 9 August 1990 found the writing "obsessional" and "over-tidy." Trevor Ferguson, in *The Globe and Mail* (7 July 1990), addressed the central paradox of *Wildlife,* calling it "strangely contradictory—at once affirmative and self-limiting."

For most of the next five years Ford was immersed in the gestation and writing of his most-successful novel to date, *Independence Day.* Published in 1995—the same year Ford won the Rea Short Story Award—the novel picks up the story of Frank Bascombe five years after *The Sportswriter.* Still as preoccupied and erratic as ever, Frank has changed professions from sportswriting to real estate. The novel charts Frank's activities during the Fourth of July weekend in 1988, the year of the Bush-Dukakis presidential elections.

While *The Sportswriter* recalls the personal advantages of an unrestricted individualism, *Independence Day* critiques the indeterminacy that enabled Frank's earlier individualism. *Independence Day* expands Ford's

frame of reference to include a more comprehensive vision of contemporary America than in the earlier novel. Ford explained this shift of scope to a reporter for the *New Orleans Times-Picayune* (2 July 1995): "I was trying to address the country in as large a way as I can imagine—intellectually as well as spiritually." Unlike *The Sportswriter, Independence Day* begins with a description not of Frank but of Haddam, a town suffering the loss of communal values and the recent economic downturn and its fallout: joblessness, destabilization of accepted values, and heightened criminal activity. The opening of the novel recounts Frank's recent mugging one street over from where he lives. His coworker Clair Devane, who was his love interest in *The Sportswriter,* was raped and murdered while showing real estate to a client.

The first half of the novel deals primarily with Frank's realty business and his other entrepreneurial interests. While following Frank around as he tries to find a suitable dwelling for his clients Phyllis and Joe Markham, Ford introduces Frank's vision of real estate as a pragmatic rather than idealist solution to the disparity between desire and reality: "The premise [of real estate] is that you're presented with what you might've thought you didn't want, but what's available, whereupon you give in and start finding ways to feel good about it and yourself." Real estate offers a metaphor for acclimatizing to a world that does not coincide with one's dreams. The novel, then, is concerned not so much with Frank as an individual but with the societal context in which he attempts to navigate.

The reader learns that Frank's former wife, now called Ann rather than "X," has remarried and relocated to Deep River, Connecticut, with her and Frank's children, Paul and Clarissa. Paul has recently been arrested for shoplifting condoms and assaulting a security guard. The second half of the novel focuses on the relationship between father and son. Intending to teach Paul a few valuable lessons about selfhood, Frank devises a trip for the two of them, a visit to the Basketball Hall of Fame in Springfield, Massachusetts, and the Baseball Hall of Fame in Cooperstown, New York, over the long Fourth of July weekend. The trip is as much of a learning experience for Frank as for Paul and almost ends disastrously in Cooperstown, when Paul purposely steps in front of a batting machine and nearly loses an eye. Through his relationship with his son, Frank comes to realize the weakness of adopting a position that straddles the "fissures between the literal and the imagined." Because Paul so equally matches his father at wordplay, free association, and the strategically deployed evasions and ambiguities of narrative, Frank's educational attempt fails. He discovers the isolationism and ineffectuality of his admitted strategy, which he had described earlier by stating, "I rely on how I make things seem." In Cooperstown reality in the form of a baseball ultimately rebounds on Frank until "there is no *seeming* now. All is *is*." The accident deprives Frank of his ability to overwrite reality; too many people are directly involved in the event, and it is too manifest for him to superimpose his own "take" on it. Ultimately, Frank accedes to Ann's wishes for Paul's treatment and, by doing so, regains a place in the family. *Independence Day* critiques what Jeffrey J. Folks, in *World Literature Today* (Winter 1998), called "The illusory myths of individualist society." In the end Frank trades personal license for mutual agreement. The family, like society, is predicated on a shared language.

Frank's division of life into distinct "periods" supports the view that he undergoes a transformation. As the novel opens, he defines his current condition as the "Existence Period," a time of inertia, when "you tell yourself you'll have to change your way of doing things. Only you don't. You can't. Somehow it's already too late." His solution to the "things" to which he cannot "adapt," the "unfixable crises" of life, is to let them go. This passivity, this willful lack of agency, is exactly the message he wishes to impart to Paul, when his son clearly needs a proactive and concrete means of grappling with problems. Frank is aware of the contradictions in his lassitude: "interest can mingle successfully with uninterest . . . , intimacy with transience, caring with obdurate uncaring." He keeps all his options open, while at the same time expecting others, such as Paul, to play along. By the end of the novel the drawbacks inherent to this position have become clear. Frank calls the next stage in life the "Permanent Period," which is antithetical to the rampant individuality characteristic of the "Existence Period": "The Permanent Period . . . that long stretching-out time when my dreams would have mystery like an ordinary person's; when whatever I do or say, who I marry, how my kids turn out, becomes what the world—if it makes note at all—knows of me." Paul's accident forces Frank to readjust to the status quo. Abandoning his carefully engineered outsider status, he engages with the society around him. The novel ends on Frank's submersion in the sea of ordinary life: "I feel the push, pull, the weave and sway of others."

Frank's acceptance of the status quo comes at the cost of his narrative primacy. As D. G. Myers pointed out in *Commentary* (November 1995), Frank "talks about writing itself just as much as he ever did, and still regards himself as the author." He masters events through narrative. In Barbara Ehrenreich's words, Frank is a man intent on "writing his life

Dust jacket for Ford's sequel to The Sportswriter

instead of living it" (*The New Republic,* 13 September 1995). By overwriting reality to accord with his contradictory impulses and actions, Frank becomes the sole arbiter of "story," demanding of others that they fall in with the twists and turns of his contrived plot. Frank "simulates" reality rather than experiencing it. Frank depends on words being "close" to reality, on their inexactness in rendering, giving him room to maneuver between what actually happened and its verbal representation. Ambiguity permits him to ascribe different meanings to what he has said, as required by the moment. Frank's evasiveness explains his preference for history over psychiatry: "History's lessons are subtle lessons, inviting us to remember and forget selectively, and therefore are much better than psychiatry's, where you're forced to remember everything." Frank always prefers "selectivity," provided he is the one selecting. By casting himself in an authorial role, he continually selects and reselects his meanings to elude verbal capture and fixity of position. It takes Paul nearly losing an eye to remind him that some things cannot be forgotten. There are events history will not allow him to bury.

Independence Day debunks what Schroth, in *Commonweal* (6 October 1995), denigrated as "the American virus of excessive individuality." Through Frank's individual story, Ford expresses the "universal" condition of "contingency," which, in its accidents and specific dependencies, constitutes, at the same time, a reality in which general rules do not apply. By the end of the novel Frank arrives at some understanding of a contingent, mutually evoked reality, in which events instigated by himself and others have repercussions far beyond his predictions. Try as he might, he cannot contain the effects of his actions, nor can he establish and maintain a clear demarcation between himself and those around him: "We want to feel our community as a fixed, continuous entity . . . as being anchored to the rock of permanence; but we know it's not. . . . We and it are anchored only to contingency like a bottle on a wave, seeking a quiet eddy. The very effort of maintenance can pull you under."

The only "universal" rule is that there is no universal rule, only the particulars of time and place, the intricate machinery of interpersonal connections in a particular historical moment. Ford's "anchor," contingency, is no "anchor" at all, and his universalism, paradoxically, is anti-universal. In "contingency" Ford expresses a view of America as a process rather than as a fixed idea.

Frank's political affiliation reflects Ford's presentation of America. Throughout the novel Frank cites his preference for the Democrats, describing them as "the party of no tradition, no influence, no nothing." Conversely, he sees the Republican Party as standing for "money, tradition and influence." Frank finds "tradition"—in the form of a false "continuity"—inappropriate to present-day America, "a society in need of new ideas." He is equally critical of the ideals of the 1960s, which he views as partially responsible for the dissolution of the American social fabric. He blames the drop-out ethic of the so-called counterculture movement for promoting a complacency and isolationism inadequate to the task of living in late-twentieth-century America. Frank recognizes the combination of liberal and reactionary attitudes in his viewpoint, calling himself a "liberal in a conservative's zoot suit." Ultimately his attitude calls for engagement, rejecting the antiestablishment hippie ethic and at the same time the lofty and equally unrealistic disengagement from the vicissitudes of everyday life evident in the Republican devotion to tradition and continuity. In this context freedom does not mean "license" or "isolationism" or "preservation" of order, a definition Ford ridicules in his essay "Sanctuary for Ideas We Love—And Hate" (*Library Journal,* 1 July 1995): "Freedom often means 'my' right to do anything 'I' want—no matter what 'you' want. Freedom is for 'me'; whereas the restraints of law, the rule of the reasonable 'man,' the pressing need for moderation in order that calm heads might prevail—that part's for you." Initially, Frank clings to his own freedom while demanding participation of everyone else, but finally *Independence Day* offers an entirely different definition of freedom—one not based on the politics of rights, procedures, and individualism, but rather on a willingness to take responsibility for one's decisions.

In 1996 *Independence Day* became the first novel ever to win both the Pulitzer Prize and the PEN/Faulkner award. The novel received glowing reviews. Elizabeth Hardwick, in *The New York Review of Books* (10 August 1995), called it "the confirmation of a talent as strong and varied as American fiction has to offer." Jeff Giles, in *Newsweek* (12 June 1995), viewed Frank as "a great mythic American character" and called the novel "exhilarating." Douglas Kennedy, in *The New Statesman & Society* (14 July 1995), called *Independence Day* "a great American novel." The reviewer for *The Economist* (12 August 1995) saw the book as "full of hope and the prospect of redemption."

Unlike some critics who perceived *Independence Day* as continuing to portray an essentially "happy" man seeking hope and redemption, Paul Gray, in *Time* (19 June 1995), called Frank a man who "does not devote much thought or comment to his potential role in causing [events]." John Shelton Reed, in the *National Review* (25 September 1995), referred to Frank as "a caricature," and the novel as "a book in which nothing much does happen."

With his most ambitious and successful novel completed, Ford turned to the novella. *Women With Men* (1997) comprises three narratives—"The Womanizer," "Jealous," and "Occidentals." While the first two revisit themes of infidelity, maturation, and the conflict between personal and communal narrative, the third portrays Ford's first truly nonsolipsistic protagonist. A writer still at mid career, Ford seems likely to explore such uncharted regions in the future.

Interviews:

Kay Bonetti, ed., "An Interview with Richard Ford," *Missouri Review,* 10 (1987): 71–96;

Gregory L. Morris, "Richard Ford," in his *Talking Up a Storm: Voices of the New West* (Lincoln: University of Nebraska Press, 1994), pp. 102–119;

Bonnie Lyons, "Richard Ford: The Art of Fiction CXLVII," *Paris Review,* 140 (Fall 1996): 42–77;

Matthew Gilbert, "Interview with Richard Ford," *Writer,* 109 (1 December 1996): 9–12;

Huey Guagliardo, "A Conversation with Richard Ford," *Southern Review,* 34 (Summer 1998): 609–620.

Bibliography:

Frank W. Shelton, "Richard Ford," in *Contemporary Fiction Writers of the South: A Bio-Bibliographical Sourcebook,* edited by Joseph M. Flora and Robert Bain (Westport, Conn.: Greenwood Press, 1993), pp. 147–155.

References:

Bill Buford, "Editorial," *Granta,* 8 (1983): 4–5;

David Crouse, "Resisting Reduction: Closure in Richard Ford's *Rock Springs* and Alice Munro's *Friend of My Youth,*" *Canadian Literature,* 146 (Autumn 1995): 51–64;

Edward Dupuy, "The Confessions of an Ex-Suicide: Relenting and Recovery in Richard Ford's *The Sportswriter,*" *Southern Literary Journal,* 23 (Fall 1990): 93–103;

Jeffrey J. Folks, "Richard Ford: Postmodern Cowboys," in *Southern Writers At Century's End,* edited by Folks and James A. Perkins (Lexington: University of Kentucky Press, 1997), pp. 212–225;

Folks, "The Risks of Membership: Richard Ford's *The Sportswriter,*" *Mississippi Quarterly,* 52 (Winter 1998–1999): 73–88;

Nick Gillespie, "Bye-Bye American Pie," *Reason,* 28 (December 1996): 53–58;

Fred Hobson, "Richard Ford and Josephine Humphreys: Walker Percy in New Jersey and Charleston," in his *The Southern Writer in the Postmodern World* (Athens: University of Georgia Press, 1991), pp. 41–58;

Raymond A. Schroth, "America's Moral Landscape in the Fiction of Richard Ford," *Christian Century,* 106 (1 March 1989): 227–230;

Michael Trussler, "'Famous Times': Historicity in the Short Fiction of Richard Ford and Raymond Carver," *Wascana Review,* 28 (Fall 1994): 35–53;

Bruce Weber, "Richard Ford's Uncommon Characters," *New York Times Magazine,* 10 April 1988, pp. 50, 59, 63–65.

Papers:

The Michigan State University Library has a collection of Richard Ford's papers.

William H. Gass

(30 July 1924 –   )

Arthur Saltzman
Missouri Southern State College

See also the Gass entry in *DLB 2: American Novelists Since World War II.*

BOOKS: *Omensetter's Luck* (New York: New American Library, 1966; London: Collins, 1967);

In the Heart of the Heart of the Country, and Other Stories (New York: Harper & Row, 1968; London: Cape, 1969);

Willie Masters' Lonesome Wife, TriQuarterly Supplements, no. 2 (Evanston, Ill.: Northwestern University Press, 1968);

Fiction and the Figures of Life (New York: Knopf, 1971);

On Being Blue: A Philosophical Inquiry (Boston: Godine, 1976; Manchester, U.K.: Carcanet New Press, 1979);

The World Within the Word: Essays (New York: Knopf, 1978);

The First Winter of My Married Life (Northridge, Cal.: Lord John Press, 1979);

Culp (New York: Grenfell Press, 1985);

Habitations of the Word: Essays (New York: Simon & Schuster, 1985);

The Tunnel (New York: Knopf, 1995);

Finding a Form: Essays (New York: Knopf, 1996);

The Dual Muse: The Writer as Artist, the Artist as Writer, by Gass and Johanna Drucker (St. Louis, Mo.: Washington University Gallery of Art/International Writers Center, Washington University / Philadelphia: John Benjamins, 1997);

Cartesian Sonata and Other Novellas (New York: Knopf, 1998);

Reading Rilke: Reflections on the Problems of Translation (New York: Knopf, 1999).

Edition: *Willie Masters' Lonesome Wife* (New York: Knopf, 1971).

RECORDING: *William Gass Reads "The Old Folks" and "The Tunnel,"* read by Gass, American Audio Prose Library, GA I 1381-R, 1981.

OTHER: "A Letter to the Editor," in *Afterwords: Novelists on Their Novels,* edited by Thomas McCormack (New York: Harper & Row, 1969), pp. 88–105;

William H. Gass (photograph © by Joyce Ravid)

Gertrude Stein, *The Geographical History of America; Or, The Relation of Human Nature to the Human Mind,* introduction by Gass (New York: Vintage, 1973);

"The Old Folks," in *The Best American Short Stories, 1980,* edited by Stanley Elkin and Shannon Ravenel (Boston: Houghton Mifflin, 1980), pp. 159–175;

"Uncle Balt and the Nature of Being," in *The Pushcart Prize 7,* edited by Bill Henderson (Yonkers, N.Y.: Pushcart Press, 1982), pp. 384–387;

John Hawkes, *Humors of Blood & Skin: A John Hawkes Reader,* introduction by Gass (New York: New Directions, 1984);

The Best of Intro, edited by Gass and Charles Simic (Norfolk, Va.: Associated Writing Programs, 1985);

"The Sunday Drive," in *Facing Texts: Encounters Between Contemporary Writers and Critics,* edited by Heidi Ziegler (Durham, N.C.: Duke University Press, 1988), pp. 186–204;

Robert Walser, *"Masquerade" and Other Stories,* translated by Susan Bernofsky, foreword by Gass (Baltimore: Johns Hopkins University Press, 1990);

A Temple of Texts: Fifty Literary Pillars: An Exhibit to Inaugurate the International Writers Center, selected by Gass (St. Louis, Mo.: Special Collections, Olin Library, Washington University, 1991);

The Writer in Politics, edited by Gass and Lorin Cuoco (Carbondale: Southern Illinois University Press, 1996);

The Writer and Religion, edited by Gass and Cuoco (Carbondale: Southern Illinois University Press, 2000).

SELECTED PERIODICAL PUBLICATIONS–
UNCOLLECTED:

FICTION

"Mad Meg," *Iowa Review,* 7 (Winter 1976): 77–95;

"Koh Whistles Up a Wind," *TriQuarterly,* 38 (Fall 1977): 191–209;

"Susu, I Approach You in My Dreams," *TriQuarterly,* 42 (Spring 1978): 122–142;

"Summer Bees," *Paris Review,* 79 (1981): 231–236;

"Life in a Chair," *Salmagundi,* 55 (Winter 1982): 3–60;

"The Barricade," *Conjunctions,* 8 (Fall–Winter 1985): 122–124;

"Family Album," *River Styx,* 21 (1986): 5–47;

"Sweets," *Review of Contemporary Fiction,* 11 (Fall 1991): 46–64;

"Quotations from Chairman Flaubert," *Paris Review,* 36 (Fall 1994): 270–315;

"Foreskinned," *Esquire,* 123 (March 1995): 130–132.

NONFICTION

"The Snares of Meaning," *New Republic,* 158 (11 May 1968): 34–35;

"Written with a Hose," *New York Times Book Review,* 22 September 1968, pp. 4–5, 40;

"The Anatomy of Mind," *New York Review of Books,* 22 (17 April 1975): 3–5;

"The Scientific Psychology of Sigmund Freud," *New York Review of Books,* 22 (1 May 1975): 24–29;

"The Battered, Triumphant Sage," *New York Review of Books,* 22 (15 May 1975): 9–12;

"Monumentality / Mentality," *Oppositions,* 25 (Fall 1982): 126–144;

"A Portrait of Elias Canetti: The Road to the True Book," *New Republic,* 187 (8 November 1982): 27–33;

"China Through a Writer's Eye," *Washington University Magazine,* 55 (Spring 1985): 10–17;

"Seine and Sensibility: Portrait of Rilke as a Young Man," *New Republic,* 192 (4 March 1985): 27–32;

"East vs. West in Lithuania: Rising Tempers at a Writers' Meeting," *New York Times Book Review,* 2 February 1986, pp. 3, 29, 31;

"The Face of the City: Reading Consciousness in Its Tics and Wrinkles," *Harper's,* 272 (March 1986): 37–44;

"Some Snapshots from the Soviet Zone," *Kenyon Review,* 8 (Fall 1986): 1–43;

"A Visit with Yevtushenko," *Harper's,* 274 (January 1987): 36–37;

"The First Seven Pages of the Boom," *Latin American Literary Review,* 15 (January–June 1987): 33–56;

"On Thinking Through a Little Problem," *Harper's,* 276 (February 1988): 18–22;

"The Polemical Philosopher," *New York Review of Books,* 35 (4 February 1988): 35–41;

"A Life at Death's Door: Review of *Wittgenstein: A Life; Young Ludwig, 1889–1921,* by Brian McGuinness," *New Republic,* 200 (1 May 1989): 35–40;

"Where East Meets West–to Boogie!" *New York Times Magazine,* 4 March 1990, II: 63, 66–67;

"Tribalism, Identity, and Ideology," *Profession* (1994): 54–56;

"On Experimental Writing: Some Clues for the Clueless," *New York Times Book Review,* 21 August 1994, pp. 3, 27;

"Mississippi," *Yale Review,* 83 (January 1995): 1–18;

"Stanley Elkin: An Anecdote," *Review of Contemporary Fiction,* 15 (Summer 1995): 38–41;

"The Hovering Life," *New York Review of Books,* 43 (11 January 1996): 56–62;

"I've Got a Little List," *Salmagundi,* 109–110 (Winter-Spring 1996): 20–38;

Review of *Uncollected Poems: Rainer Maria Rilke, Nation,* 262 (1 April 1996): 27–31;

"The Trapezoidal Mind," *New Letters,* no. 62 (Fall 1996): 9–19;

"Shears of the Censor: Notes on Excision, Imprisonment, and Silence," *Harper's,* 294 (April 1997): 59–65;

"The Test of Time," *Alaska Quarterly Review,* 15 (Spring-Summer 1997): 69–87.

William Gass is one of the foremost theoreticians, champions, and practitioners of postmodern literature, and has also earned considerable eminence as an essayist and as a writer of fiction. Often grouped with such contemporary American authors as John Barth, Donald Barthelme, Robert Coover, Stanley Elkin, William Gaddis, John Hawkes, Thomas Pynchon, and Paul West, Gass shares with them a fundamental concern with the self-evident, self-sufficient status of language itself–in short, with

Dust jacket for Gass's first novel, published in 1966, about a mysterious stranger who disrupts a small Ohio River town in the 1890s

the metafictional imperative. His fiction and his nonfiction conspire in an obsession with the primacy of words, glamorized by Gass's inimitable stylistic flourishes. According to Gass, words do not principally serve as vehicles conveying the reader to some external reality they imitate; they also constitute a reality–a "world within the word"–and, hence, are foregrounded as a destination unto themselves. In this sense, language is viewed as being more opaque, more centripetal, than naive notions of literary realism would allow. Accordingly, fiction is not merely to be understood as a depiction of experience but as a competitive addition to experience, another new thing that the writer's craft allocates to the world. What Gass advocates is the reader's "kindly imprisonment" within texts whose formal gymnastics and startling metaphors few save William Faulkner can rival. A so-called writer's writer of strenuous beauty and probing intellect, Gass has earned greater critical esteem than popular success. It is an uncompromising love Gass lavishes on language, and the lavish language that results from this enterprise has done as much as the work of any contemporary author to reveal "the soul inside the sentence."

William Howard Gass was born in Fargo, North Dakota, on 30 July 1924 to William Bernard and Claire (Sorensen) Gass. His family soon afterward moved to Warren, Ohio, where he grew up in the company of an alcoholic mother and a severely arthritic father. Gass's rejection of that environment led him to become emotionally detached, which eventually became reflected in his formalist aesthetic principles, as well as in the often suffocative, if word-drunk, introversion of his most notorious fictional narrators. He began college at Ohio Wesleyan, then served as an ensign in the navy during World War II before resuming his college career at Kenyon, the home of New Critic John Crowe Ransom. Gass earned a degree in philosophy in 1947 and took his graduate studies in philosophy at Cornell University. While at Cornell, Gass was influenced by Ludwig Wittgenstein, whom he heard lecture on several occasions, and by Max Black, who directed Gass's graduate work. Gass's dissertation, *A Philosophical Investigation of Metaphor,* evidences these influences and served as prelude to the author's career-long preoccupation with the nature of language and aesthetic models. He completed the dissertation in 1954 while teaching at the College of Wooster (Ohio). From there Gass went on to Purdue University, where he taught philosophy for fifteen years. By the end of the decade, some of the stories that were included in *In the Heart of the Heart of the Country* (1968) or became incorporated into *Omensetter's Luck* (1966) were appearing in *Accent* magazine. In 1969 Gass moved to Washington University in St. Louis, where he still teaches as the David May Distinguished University Professor in the Humanities and where, since 1990, Gass has also served as director of the International Writers Center.

Many of the writers who recur as touchstones in Gass's essays, such as Faulkner, James Joyce, Marcel Proust, Rainer Maria Rilke, Samuel Beckett, Colette, Gertrude Stein, and Paul Valéry, share Gass's passion for the rhythms, intricacies, and ordeals presented by the medium in which they operate. Writing about Ralph Waldo Emerson, Gass championed the essay for its conduciveness to "the act of thinking things out" and for its availability to "the mind in the marvels and the miseries of its makings." These are qualities consistently on view in Gass's nonfiction; indeed, many readers know William Gass not as a novelist but as a reviewer and essayist for many of the tonier periodicals, including *Harper's* and *The New York Review of Books.* His essay collections—*Fiction and the Figures of Life* (1971), *The World Within the Word* (1978), *Habitations of the Word* (1985), and *Finding a Form* (1996), the last two of which earned the National Book Critics Circle Award—represent an ongoing critical project to evaluate language as "a container of consciousness" and to treat the page as a laboratory in which to conduct experiments on the English language: its etymologies, its sonic textures, its transports of fluency. This concentration is perhaps nowhere more apparent than in *On Being Blue: A Philosophical Inquiry* (1976), Gass's book-length rumination on the historical, poetic, and philosophical implications of that single word, color, and concept, which expands into a consideration of the erotics of language, of the flesh made visceral word:

> The word itself has another color. It's not a word with any resonance, although the *e* was once pronounced. There is only the bump now between *b* and *l*, the relief at the end, the whew. It hasn't the sly turn which crimson takes halfway through, yellow's deceptive jelly, or the rolled-down sound in brown. It hasn't violet's rapid sexual shudder, or like a rough road the irregularity of ultramarine, the low puddle in mauve like a pancake covered with cream, the disapproving purse to pink, the assertive brevity of red, the whine of green. What did Rimbaud know about the vowels we cannot also find outside the lines in which the poet takes an angry piss at heaven? The blue perhaps of the aster or the iris or the air a fist has bruised.

While the typical use of language is casual and unreflective, Gass encourages the reader by argument and example to live up to the rigorous elegance of the best sentences and not be willing to subsist "on broken phrases and syllable gristle." Indeed, what unites Gass's fictions and essays is the belief that the page is first and foremost "a field for the voice," so that presence is determined by the efficacy of verbal expression. Moreover, Gass's metafictional insistence keeps the reader consistently apprised of the fact that, as he explains in "The Medium

of Fiction," "literature is language, that stories and the places and people in them are merely made of words as chairs are made of smoothed sticks and sometimes of cloth or metal tubes," a realization as remarkable to some readers, Gass continues, as would be the discovery "that your wife were made of rubber: the bliss of all those years, the fears . . . from sponge." Thus, not only are most of Gass's best-known protagonists linguistic artists, they are also overtly linguistic artifacts.

Gass's first novel, *Omensetter's Luck,* finally appeared after the legendary setback of the robbery of the sole typescript and the rejections that followed. It immediately introduces readers to Gass's formal experimentalism and rhetorical lushness, developed here within the context of long-standing American literary themes of pastoral idealism, guilt and innocence, and spiritual redemption. The novel traces the disruptions occasioned by the arrival of Brackett Omensetter and his family in Gilean, a small Ohio River town in the 1890s. Omensetter's "luck" is really his unnatural naturalness: he has a seemingly prelapsarian self-possession and unself-conscious ease so extraordinary as to earn the worshipful envy of some of the citizenry and the suspicion and denunciation of others. Prominent among the first camp is Henry Pimber, Omensetter's landlord, who sees in this mysterious stranger the embodiment of all he is not and cannot have— serenity, fecundity, grace, and guiltless, unmediated experience. When Omensetter "magically" cures Pimber of lockjaw, Pimber follows him as if he were "a dream he might enter"; however, Omensetter is either indifferent to or blissfully unaware of Pimber's urgent attentions, and in despair, the "rejected" suitor commits suicide. This catastrophe gives the local preacher, Jethro Furber, a means whereby to turn his animosity toward Omensetter into a town conspiracy against him. A haunted, repressed, perverse man—the prototype for Gass's isolated, word-girdled consciousnesses living behind "beautiful barriers" of rhetorical abstraction—the preacher takes Omensetter's natural intimacy as a threat to his own founding principles: arid intellectuality and strident Christian doctrine. In a sense, Furber also loves his enemy, for Omensetter suffers none of that fatal separation from God and his Creation that so obsesses Furber; yet the preacher must destroy Omensetter, he reasons, in order to authenticate himself, his practices, and more broadly, human life after the Fall. Implicating Omensetter in Pimber's death, Furber also embroils him in awareness, perpetrating a Fall that scuttles his "luck" by making him aware of it. Omensetter and his family are expelled from Gilean, leaving Furber to decline into recrimination and madness.

It is the linguistic achievement of *Omensetter's Luck* that impressed the critics, led by Richard Gilman, who pronounced the novel "the most important work of fiction by an American in this literary generation." Gass was

Gass, circa 1976

favorably compared to Herman Melville, Joyce, and Faulkner for his lyrical intrepidness. Not surprisingly, given the density of the prose, popular success did not measure up to such acclaim, a fact that Gass regularly dismisses by arguing that he is less interested in catering to an audience than in furthering an art. As he once noted in one of his several debates with John Gardner on morality and fiction, he does not want everyone to love his books, just as he does not want everyone to love his daughter.

His second book, the collection *In the Heart of the Heart of the Country,* shows Gass continuing to wrestle with the possibilities of technique and the concept of character; it is chiefly populated by alienated personalities who, like Reverend Furber, justify and compensate themselves with elaborate rhetoric. The best known of these fictions, "The Pedersen Kid" and "In the Heart of the Heart of the Country," are at once psychological and linguistic investigations. These stories also serve as arenas for the ongoing contest in Gass's writings between antimimetic principles and mimetic compromises. "The Pedersen Kid" features an adolescent narrator, Jorge Seagren, and his harrowing initiation into moral and aesthetic independence. He and his family's hired man, Big Hans, discover a neighbor's child nearly frozen to death in the Dakota winter; reviving him, they are told of the murder of the Pedersen Kid's

family by a yellow-gloved stranger. This precipitates a reluctant journey through a winter wasteland by Jorge, his drunken lout of a father, and Big Hans to verify the tale, a journey made all the more difficult by the open animosities among the three of them. On their arrival at the Pedersen farmhouse, Mr. Seagren is shot, Hans deserts, and Jorge takes up refuge in the Pedersen's basement. Apart from the symbolic exchange of the Pedersen kid for the Seagren kid, the plot of the narrative is left unresolved; more accurately, perhaps, it is abandoned to the psychological focus on Jorge's redemptive arrival in a "new, blank land" that he finds hospitable despite the cold and danger.

The title story of the volume concerns another sort of strategic recoil, but its rewards are even sparser than those Jorge nurses in his burrow. If the heart of the country is the anonymous, remorselessly uninspiring Midwestern town to which the unnamed narrator has retired from love, the "heart of the heart" may be the spiritual reflection of environmental circumstances. "So I have sailed the seas and come . . . to B . . . a small town fastened to a field in Indiana," he begins, punning on the opening to Yeats's "Sailing to Byzantium" by equating himself with the town whose bitter genius and voice he has "come to be." But this Byzantium provides no saving artifice for old men. "In the Heart of the Heart of the Country" is set out in thirty-six separately titled mini-sections, ranging from Weather to Politics to other (dubiously dubbed) Vital Data, and all attesting to stifled prospects. The imagination festers in retreat. Transcendence is more stylistic than spiritual, as evidenced by the vindictiveness of the narrator's descriptions of the surrounding population and his announced desire (in the Education section) "to rise so high . . . that when I shit I won't miss anybody." So in spite of some wonderfully evocative set pieces, which are largely responsible for Gass's having received so many letters over the years from small-town inhabitants claiming their own community to be Gass's model, the story exclusively reserves its pleasure for its own ingenuity–its richly imaged, precisely rendered sense of rural malaise and personal defeat:

> For we're always out of luck here. That's just how it is–for instance in the winter. The sides of the buildings, the roofs, the limbs of the trees are gray. Streets, sidewalks, faces, feelings–they are gray. Speech is gray, and the grass where it shows. Every flank and front, each top is gray. Everything is gray: hair, eyes, window glass, the hawkers' bills and touters' posters, lips, teeth, poles and metal signs–they're gray, quite gray. Horses, sheep, and cows, cats killed in the road, squirrels in the same way, sparrows, doves, and pigeons, all are gray, everything is gray, and everyone is out of luck who lives here.

To be sure, with its striking assaults upon conventions of plot, character, and action, "In the Heart of the Heart of the Country" remains the most renowned of Gass's fictions.

The remaining three stories in the collection likewise present characters in various predicaments of recoil: the unemployed, voyeuristically inclined narrator of "Mrs. Mean," whose revulsion at the nature and habits of his neighbor intensify his passion to enter her premises; Fender, the feckless real estate salesman of "Icicles," who becomes figuratively and literally "iced in" as the story progresses; and the frustrated housewife of "The Order of Insects," who discovers in an infestation of dead insects a surprising beauty and preemptive fascination that disqualifies her domestic role and leaves her with "a pair of dreadful eyes." In each of these impersonations, Gass delivers conditions of psychic isolation in terms of often stunning metaphors; all are committed to versions of the provisionality of interaction defined in "In the Heart of the Heart of the Country": "We meet on this window, the world and I, inelegantly, swimmers of the glass; and swung wrong way round to one another, the world seems in." But who suffers a lonesomeness more remarkable than the protagonist in *Willie Masters' Lonesome Wife* (1968)? One of the truly essential metafictions in contemporary literature, this essay/novella is at once a tale of the promiscuous Babs Masters, who pines for a worthy partner, and a meditation on and enactment of art's seduction of the reader. Undeniably, good books are starved for practiced, patient, imaginative attention in much the same way as good lovers are. Appropriately enough, central among Babs's many aliases in the book is that of Language Herself, a sinuous, sensuous mistress (one who demands more responsiveness than Phil Gelvin, her woeful partner, can provide). *Willie Masters' Lonesome Wife* is an extravaganza of unabashed wordplay and acrobatic allusion, an orgy of fonts and (rather explicit) graphics, and basically, experimental showmanship. Gass demolishes the willing suspension of disbelief in favor of anti-illusionism par excellence, with fanciful shapes, textures, and colors adorning a dizzying fall into art.

If *Willie Masters' Lonesome Wife* serves as the foundational text for contemporary American metafiction, Gass's novel *The Tunnel* (1995), portions of which appeared in literary journals over the course of some thirty years, may well be its culminating achievement. Certainly the book provides another set of formal eccentricities and subversions to contend with, and Gass's signature stylistic effusiveness is regularly on display. But what has made *The Tunnel* so immediately controversial a work is Gass's exercising of his rhythmic brilliance in the context, or at the expense, of the greatest trauma of modern history. William Frederick Kohler, the dominant consciousness of the novel, is an historian teaching at a midwestern university during the 1960s. He is nearly finished with his academic masterpiece, *Guilt and Innocence in Hitler's Germany,* and is in the process of devising the introduction. However, he keeps getting derailed into relating all manner of incendiary personal confession about his colleagues, his unavailing family relationships, his starved childhood, his squalid affairs, and his aesthetic and philosophical reflections, until the added pages, which he keeps secreting within the pages of the project proper, overwhelm his original intention. This postponement grows into an epidemic of subjectivity and studied reproachfulness, as the historian displaces his purported historical subject. (Call him a swimmer of the *broken* glass, whose participation in *Kristallnacht* reverberates through the years and pages of the book as his defining instance of guilt.) If Kohler is erudite and full of figurative wizardry–he states that he gave up poetry for history, but the two pursuits continuously interpenetrate here–he is also vicious, bigoted, and, by his own account, morally bankrupt. His interest in "the fascism of the heart" not only fuels his theory that sociopolitical atrocities are rooted in the ordinary brutalities of private life, it also derives from the litany of abuses large and small constituting his autobiography–the ever-interfering concern of his "tunnel vision." The title also refers to an actual tunnel Kohler is evidently digging in his basement as well as through heaps of horrifying data, an effort bereft of the purpose or dignity of those desperate survival tactics of the World War II prisoners it imitates. In a sense, then, Kohler stands out as the most outrageous in Gass's line of solitary, driven, misanthropic word-churners, whose tunnel is the most elaborately conceived withdrawal of all.

In the roiling, scandalous confines of *The Tunnel,* sublime rhetoric mingles with corpses, unwholesome limericks and puns, and bodily functions; Kohler's consciousness mixes disastrous memory with corrupted desire. Despite Gass's claims that Kohler must be regarded as a literary construction and challenge–the author has termed his mission in the novel "to bring grandeur to a shit"–several reviewers have derogated Gass for what they see as his exploitation of the Holocaust, calling it unconscionable to make rhetorical capital out of the death camps or to trivialize the Holocaust by reducing it through postmodern antics and equations with the narrator's sour home and professional life. Are Gass's luxuriant catalogues proper memorials to the terror of their occasion, or are they examples of fetishistic excess? In an exemplary passage, "dry spiteful speech, jailed conjunctions, metaphors machine-gunned where they stood" inspire "tides of verse and floods of piss," as well as waves of alliterative rage and remorse; this leads into a field of rotting corpses and exposed bones, followed by "copulation with cliches, with the elderly and infants," that further triggers references to violence, disease, and "symbolic rapes by the same vague smegma's shape"–coherence and convention having become casualties of "total word war." The critical reception of *The Tunnel* has been polarized by the question of whether this sort of production demonstrates opportu-

are a blaze of brandy

in the clear only in

at least the

call the cows, for god's sake

ugh you ordered chocolate, a childhood sweet, but didn't put a spoon in, perhaps +4
fearing you might spill that conflagration from the spoon and burn down the place; ok
I suppose it's because I'm a little older, a bit fat (I didn't say that aloud); and it's −1
certainly not because I cuff you around, or because I won't leave my wife, because −1
you want less of me, not more; you want to rezip our relationship, close up every +4
opening, put a cork on it, call the cows in: goodby. [Culp: be a good guy and do ok
a zipper closing.] You did say something finally about why: you had found a rea- +1
son - rather, you had found a reason for a feeling, a feeling you had recently found, −14
well, something which had been bothering you for... um... a while - anyway, you +2
now knew why: it was because I had a loathsome mind. Loathsome, was it? a word +1
from an English movie, a word popular with girls age 14. I said I love you, though −3
rather wearily, and you said no - quite firmly - however, I've never been sure if +7
you were refusing my avowal or denying its truth. Then your spoon went swiftly +5
and silently into your cup (not a tick); I felt fat thickening me, moment by moment, −6
like some god damn gravy; and I became the man I now am.

ugh you ordered chocolate, a childhood sweet, but didn't put a spoon in, perhaps +4
fearing you might spill that conflagration in the spoon like a blaze of brandy, and +5
burn down the place; I suppose it's because I'm a little older, a bit fat (I didn't say −6
that in the clear, only in code); and it's certainly not because I cuff you around, or xx+6
or because I won't leave my wife, because you want less of me, not more; you want −1
to rezip our relationship, close up every opening, put a cork on it, call the cows in: −9
goodby. [Culp: be a good guy and do a zipper closing; at least call the cows, for +2
god's sake.] You did say something finally about why: you had found a reason - +7
rather, you had found a feeling which became a reason, something which had been +2
bothering you for... well... a while - anyway, you now knew why: it was because +2
I had a loathsome mind. Loathsome, was it? a word from an English movie, a word +3
popular with girls age 14. I said I love you, though somewhat wearily, and you said −9
no - quite firmly - still, I've never been sure if you were refusing my avowal or de- −7
neying its truth. Then your spoon went swiftly and silently into your cup; I felt +6
fat thickening me, moment by moment, like some god damn gravy; and I became the −2
man I now am.

ugh you ordered chocolate, a childhood sweet, but didn't put a spoon in, perhaps +4
fearing you might spill that conflagration from the spoon like a blaze of brandy, and −7
burn down the place; I suppose it's because I'm a little older, a bit fat (I didn't say −6
that in the clear, only in code); and it's certainly not because I cuff you around, +6
gone limp, lost my job, fancy another, or because I won't leave my wife, because +9
you really want less of me, not more; you want to rezip out relationship, close up +6
every opening, put a cork on it, call the cows in: goodby. [Culp: be a good guy +5
and do a zipper closing (sad sound); at least call the cows, for god's sake.] You +5
did say something finally about why: you had found a reason; rather, you had found −11
a feeling which became a reason, something which had been bothering you for... +10
well... a while; anyway, you now knew why: why? it was because I had a loathsome −5
mind. Loathsome, was it? a word from an English movie, a word popular with girls ok
age 14. I said I love you, though somewhat wearily, and you said no - quite firm- ok
ly - still, I've never been sure whether you were refusing my avowal or denying its −5
truth. Then your spoon went swiftly and silently into your cup; I felt fat thicken- −3
ing me, moment by moment, like some god damn gravy; and I became the man I now −2
am.

Page from the revised typescript for Gass's 1995 novel, The Tunnel *(Collection of William H. Gass)*

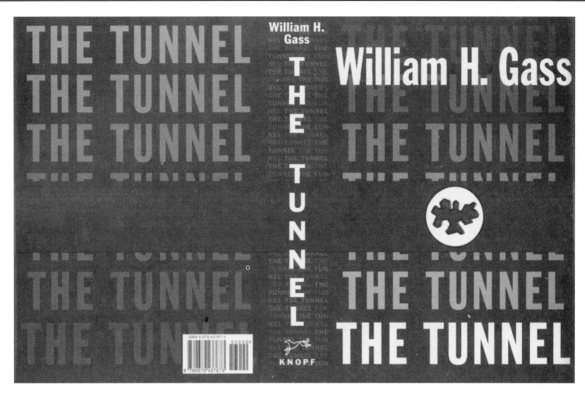

Dust jacket for Gass's controversial novel about the Holocaust

nistic violation of the dead or art's dauntless initiative and appetite. On the one hand, there are those who echo Robert Alter's complaint in *The New Republic* (27 March 1995) that there emerges from *The Tunnel* "an inadvertent complicity between author and protagonist" and, worse, a reduction of "the enormity of genocide . . . into the nickel-and-dime nastiness that people perpetrate in everyday life." In other words, as Robert Kelly concluded in *The New York Times Book Review* (26 February 1995), to say that one has known "bedrooms bad as Belsen," shows alliteration running away with proportion. On the other hand, many reviewers side with Steven Moore's assessment in *The Review of Contemporary Fiction* (Spring 1995) that Gass has produced "truly one of the great books of our time," in which "rhetorical energy and excess redeem personal failure and emptiness. The sheer beauty and bravura sentences are overwhelming, breathtaking; the novel is a pharaoh's tomb of linguistic treasures." From this perspective, Gass is to be congratulated for sustaining meticulously conceived rapture under such grisly conditions. What no one seems to doubt, regardless of other convictions about the book, is that *The Tunnel* immediately joins other encyclopedic postmodern novels such as Thomas Pynchon's *Gravity's Rainbow* (1973), William Gaddis's *The Recognitions* (1955), and John Barth's *Giles Goat-Boy* (1966) as one inevitably to be reckoned with by students of the contemporary epic.

Whether or not *The Tunnel* sins against the gravity of its concerns is largely a matter of whether or not the reader grants Gass his enduring prioritization of language composed for its own sake. In his essays, Gass has earned consistent praise for the subtlety and rigor of his interpretations of other writers; in his own fictions, he has been recognized for his venturesome topics and techniques. In the final analysis, however, Gass's reputation begins at the level of the sentence–the suppleness and physicality of the prose itself. For Gass, love scrupulously made to and through language is the writer's foremost ethical contribution. Countering the demands of "lead eared moralists," Gass supports what he calls "The Music of Prose," collected in his 1996 essays, *Finding a Form,* whereby resonance and cunning relation are the most reliable criteria of virtue. In Gass's estimation, language "is not the lowborn, gawky servant of thought and feeling; it is need, thought, feeling, and perception itself. The shape of sentences, the song in its syllables, the rhythm of its movement, is the movement of the imagination too. . . ." Meanwhile, his characters, inwardly driven and self-confessed wordsmiths all, are sentenced to some of the most nuanced, rhapsodic sentences on display in today's fiction, notwithstanding the dire particulars they typically endure. As Gass routinely reminds his audience, form is philosophy, the method is the message and the muse, and figural endowments are their own best argument: "Without impudent comparisons, without freewheeling fancy, without dreams, without invention, without the transformations of metaphor, the burglaries of meaning that symbols commit: without such aeration, prose deflates, our tires turn on air," he contends in the essay titled "Finding a Form." "Flat" sentences "will only leave their rubber on the highway; but, in addition, the other elements of the good sentence–desire, feeling, sensation, thought–require the imagination for their construction." It is no coincidence that these elements of the good sentence are components of compelling character, not to mention standards of extratextual fulfillment. It is hard to match Gass for the enchantments of excess. Even in the dankest consciousness he creates, the delights of the confinements he effects–of the reader's kindly imprisonment, of habitation in the word–are difficult to resist.

Interviews:

Gary Mullinax, "An Interview with William Gass," *Delaware Literary Review*, 1 (1972): 81–87;

Ned French and David Keyser, "Against the Grain: A Conversation with William H. Gass," *Harvard Advocate*, 106 (Winter 1973): 8–16;

Carol Spearin McCauley, "Fiction Needn't Say Things–It Should Make Them Out of Words," in *The New Fiction: Interviews with Innovative American Writers*, edited by Joe David Bellamy (Urbana: University of Illinois Press, 1975), pp. 32–44;

James McKenzie, "Pole-Vaulting in Top Hats: A Public Conversation with John Barth, William Gass, and Ishmael Reed," *Modern Fiction Studies*, 22 (Summer 1976): 131–151;

Jeffrey L. Duncan, "A Conversation with Stanley Elkin and William H. Gass," *Iowa Review*, 7 (Winter 1976): 48–77;

"A Symposium on Fiction: Donald Barthelme, William Gass, Grace Paley, Walker Percy," *Shenandoah*, 27 (Winter 1976): 3–31;

Thomas LeClair, "A Conversation with William Gass," *Chicago Review*, 30 (Spring 1978): 97–106;

Regis Durand, "An Interview with William Gass," *Delta*, 8 (May 1979): 7–19;

G. A. M. Janssens, "An Interview with William Gass," *Dutch Quarterly Review of Anglo-American Literature*, 9 (1979): 242–259;

Jan Garden Castro, "An Interview with William Gass," *ADE Bulletin*, 70 (Winter 1981): 30–34;

Heide Ziegler, "Interview with William H. Gass," in *The Radical Imagination and the Liberal Tradition: Interviews with English and American Novelists*, edited by Heide Ziegler and Christopher Bigsby (London: Junction, 1982), pp. 151–168;

Brooke K. Horvath and others, "A Colloquy with William Gass," *Modern Fiction Studies*, 29 (Winter 1983): 587–608;

Bradford Morrow, "An Interview with William Gass," *Conjunctions*, 4 (Spring–Summer 1983): 14–29;

Tom LeClair and Larry McCaffery, "A Debate: William Gass and John Gardner," in *Anything Can Happen: Interviews with Contemporary American Novelists*, edited by LeClair and McCaffery (Urbana: University of Illinois Press, 1983), pp. 20–31;

LeClair, "An Interview with William Gass," in *Anything Can Happen: Interviews with Contemporary American Novelists*, pp. 152–175;

Arthur M. Saltzman, "An Interview with William Gass," *Contemporary Literature*, 25 (Summer 1984): 121–135;

Lorna H. Domke, "An Interview with William Gass," *Missouri Review*, 10 (Fall 1987): 53–67;

Jo Brans, "Games of the Extremes," in her *Listen to the Voices: Conversations with Contemporary Writers* (Dallas: Southern Methodist University Press, 1988), pp. 193–214;

"'Nothing but Darkness and Talk?': Writers' Symposium on Traditional Values and Iconoclastic Fiction," *Critique*, 31 (Summer 1990): 233–255;

Saltzman, "Language and Conscience: An Interview with William Gass," *Review of Contemporary Fiction*, 11 (Fall 1991): 15–28;

Ramona Koval, "A Conversation with William Gass on *The Tunnel*," *Quadrant*, 40 (July–August 1996): 26–32.

Bibliographies:

Larry McCaffery, "A William H. Gass Bibliography," *Critique*, 18 (Summer 1976): 59–66;

Ned French, "William Gass Bibliography," *Iowa Review*, 7 (Winter 1976): 106–107;

Arthur M. Saltzman, "A William H. Gass Checklist," *Review of Contemporary Fiction*, 11 (Fall 1991): 150–158.

References:

Bruce Bassoff, "The Sacrificial World of William Gass: *In the Heart of the Heart of the Country*," *Critique*, 18 (Summer 1976): 36–58;

Robert Boyers, "Real Readers and Theoretical Critics," in his *After the Avant-Garde: Essays in Art and Culture* (University Park: Pennsylvania State University Press, 1988), pp. 81–90;

Elizabeth Bruss, "The Creative Impasse," in her *Beautiful Theories: The Spectacle of Discourse in Contemporary Criticism* (Baltimore: Johns Hopkins University Press, 1982), pp. 135–202;

Frederick Busch, "But This Is What It Is to Live in Hell: William Gass's *In the Heart of the Heart of the Country*," *Modern Fiction Studies*, 19 (1973): 97–108;

Charles Caramello, "Fleshing Out *Willie Masters' Lonesome Wife*," *Sub-Stance*, 27 (1980): 56–69;

Kevin J. H. Dettmar, "'yung and easily freudened': William Gass's 'The Pedersen Kid,'" *Review of Contemporary Fiction,* 11 (Fall 1991): 88–101;

Reginald Dyck, "William Gass: A Purified Modernist in a Postmodern World," *Review of Contemporary Fiction,* 11 (Fall 1991): 124–130;

Melanie Eckford-Prossor, "Layered Apparitions: Philosophy and 'The Pedersen Kid,'" *Review of Contemporary Fiction,* 11 (Fall 1991): 102–114;

Eckford-Prossor, "Shattering Genre / Creating Self: William Gass's *On Being Blue,*" *Style,* 23 (Summer 1989): 280–299;

Ned French, "Against the Grain: Theory and Practice in the Work of William H. Gass," *Iowa Review,* 7 (Winter 1976): 96–106;

Richard Gilman, "William H. Gass," in his *The Confusion of Realms* (New York: Random House, 1969), pp. 69–81;

Donald Guttenplan, "The Wor(l)ds of William Gass," *Granta,* 1 (1979): 147–160;

Charlotte Byrd Hadella, "The Winter Wasteland of William Gass's 'In the Heart of the Heart of the Country,'" *Critique,* 30 (Fall 1988): 49–58;

Ihab Hassan, "Wars of Desire, Politics of the Word," *Salmagundi,* 55 (Winter 1982): 110–118;

David Hayman, "Surface Disorders / Grave Disturbances," *TriQuarterly,* 52 (Fall 1981): 182–196;

Paul Hedeen, "A Symbolic Center in a Conception Country: A Gassian Rubric for *The Sound and the Fury,*" *Modern Fiction Studies,* 31 (Winter 1985): 623–643;

Watson L. Holloway, *William Gass* (Boston: Twayne, 1990);

Patricia Kane, "The Sun Burned on the Snow: Gass's 'The Pedersen Kid,'" *Critique,* 14 (Fall 1972): 89–96;

Michael Kaufmann, "The Textual Body: William Gass's *Willie Masters' Lonesome Wife,*" *Critique,* 35 (Fall 1993): 27–42;

Larry McCaffery, *The Metafictional Muse: The Works of Robert Coover, Donald Barthelme, and William H. Gass* (Pittsburgh, Pa.: University of Pittsburgh Press, 1982);

James Phelan, "Design and Value in a World of Words: Umberto Eco and the Language of *Willie Masters' Lonesome Wife,*" in his *Worlds from Words: A Theory of Language in Fiction* (Chicago: University of Chicago Press, 1981), pp. 184–220;

Alvin H. Rosenfeld, "The Virtuoso and the Gravity of History," *Salmagundi,* 55 (Winter 1982): 103–109;

Arthur M. Saltzman, *The Fiction of William Gass: The Consolation of Language* (Carbondale: Southern Illinois University Press, 1986);

Saltzman, "Where Words Dwell Adored: An Introduction to William Gass," *Review of Contemporary Fiction,* 11 (Fall 1991): 7–14;

Richard J. Schneider, "The Fortunate Fall in William Gass's *Omensetter's Luck,*" *Critique,* 18 (Summer 1976): 5–20;

Schneider, "Rejecting the Stone: William Gass and Emersonian Transcendence," *Review of Contemporary Fiction,* 11 (Fall 1991): 115–123;

Ilan Stavans, "Kafka, Cortazar, Gass," *Review of Contemporary Fiction,* 11 (Fall 1991): 131–136;

Philip Stevick, "William Gass and the Real World," *Review of Contemporary Fiction,* 11 (Fall 1991): 71–77;

Susan Stewart, "An American Faust," *American Literature,* 69 (June 1997): 399–416;

Tony Tanner, "William Gass's Barns and Bees," in his *Scenes of Nature, Signs of Man* (New York & Cambridge: Cambridge University Press, 1987), pp. 248–273;

John M. Unsworth, "William Gass's *The Tunnel:* The Work-in-Progress as Post-Modern Genre," *Arizona Quarterly,* 48 (Spring 1992): 63–85;

Robert F. Waxman, "Things in the Saddle: William Gass's 'Icicles' and 'Order of Insects,'" *Research Studies,* 46 (December 1978): 214–222;

Ray Levis White, "The Early Fiction of William H. Gass: A Critical Documentary," *Midamerica,* 7 (1979): 164–177;

Lucy Wilson, "Alternatives to Transcendence in William Gass's Short Fiction," *Review of Contemporary Fiction,* 11 (Fall 1991): 78–87;

Heide Ziegler, "On Translating 'The Sunday Drive,'" *Review of Contemporary Fiction,* 11 (Fall 1991): 137–149.

Papers:

The major collection of William H. Gass correspondence and manuscripts is in the Modern Literary Manuscripts Collection, the Special Collections of the Washington University Libraries, St. Louis, Missouri.

John Hawkes

(17 August 1925 – 15 May 1998)

Carol MacCurdy
California Polytechnic State University

See also the Hawkes entries in *DLB 2: American Novelists Since World War II; DLB 7: Twentieth-Century American Dramatists; DLB Yearbook: 1980;* and *DLB Yearbook: 1998.*

BOOKS: *Fiasco Hall* (Cambridge, Mass.: Harvard University Printing Office, 1943);

The Cannibal (Norfolk, Conn.: New Directions, 1949; London: Spearman, 1962);

The Beetle Leg (New York: New Directions, 1951; London: Chatto & Windus, 1967);

The Goose on the Grave, and The Owl (New York: New Directions, 1954);

The Lime Twig (New York: New Directions, 1961; London: Spearman, 1962);

Second Skin (Norfolk, Conn.: New Directions, 1964; London: Chatto & Windus, 1966);

The Innocent Party (New York: New Directions, 1967; London: Chatto & Windus, 1967);

Lunar Landscapes: Stories & Short Novels, 1949–1963 (New York: New Directions, 1969; London: Chatto & Windus, 1970);

The Blood Oranges (New York: New Directions, 1971; London: Chatto & Windus, 1971);

Death, Sleep & the Traveler (New York: New Directions, 1974; London: Chatto & Windus, 1975);

Travesty (New York: New Directions, 1976; London: Chatto & Windus, 1976);

The Universal Fears (Northridge, Cal.: Lord Jim Press, 1978);

The Passion Artist (New York: Harper & Row, 1979);

Virginie: Her Two Lives (New York: Harper & Row, 1981; London: Chatto & Windus, 1983);

The Bestowal (West Lafayette, Ind.: Sparrow, 1983);

Adventures in the Alaskan Skin Trade (New York: Simon & Schuster, 1985; London: Chatto & Windus, 1986);

Innocence in Extremis (Providence: Burning Deck, 1985);

Island Fire (Providence: Burning Deck, 1988);

Whistlejacket (New York: Weidenfeld & Nicolson, 1988; London: Secker & Warburg, 1989);

Sweet William: A Memoir of Old Horse (New York: Simon & Schuster, 1993; London: Penguin, 1994);

John Hawkes

The Frog (New York: Viking, 1996);

An Irish Eye (New York: Viking, 1997).

Collections: *Humors of Blood & Skin: A John Hawkes Reader,* with autobiographical notes by Hawkes (New York: New Directions, 1984);

Hawkes Scrapbook: A New Taste in Literature, edited by Hawkes, A. J. Guerard, and others (Virginia Beach: Dawson, 1990);

The Lime Twig, Second Skin, Travesty (New York: Penguin, 1996).

OTHER: "Charivari," in *New Directions in Prose and Poetry,* 11 (1949): 365–436.

SELECTED PERIODICAL PUBLICATIONS–
UNCOLLECTED: "Notes on Violence," *Audience,* 7 (Spring 1960): 60;

"The Voice of Edwin Honig," *Voices: A Journal of Poetry,* no. 174 (January–April 1961): 39–47;

"Flannery O'Connor's Devil," *Sewanee Review,* 70 (Summer 1962): 395–407;

"Notes on the Wild Goose Chase," *Massachusetts Review,* 3 (Summer 1962): 784–788;

"Notes on Writing a Novel," *Tri-Quarterly,* 30 (Spring 1974): 109–126;

"The Floating Opera and *Second Skin,*" *Mosaic,* 8 (Fall 1974): 17–28;

"A Stationary Traveler," *Delta: Revue de Contre D'Etudes et de Recherche,* 22 (February 1986): 1–11.

A writer of highly experimental, nightmarish fiction, John Hawkes was one of the most original and uncompromising artists to come out of the post–World War II generation of writers. Challenging established American fiction with its limitations of realism (verifiable settings, logical plots, and recognizable themes), Hawkes aggressively pursued the irrational, the erotic, the disruptive, and the comic. In a 1965 interview with John Enck, Hawkes talked about his artistic vision: "I take literally rather than figuratively the cliché about breaking new ground. . . . the idea that the imagination should always uncover new worlds for us. I want to try to create a world, not represent it." For this reason his fiction is "nearly pure vision," relying more on dreams and the unconscious than on strictly historical or autobiographical material. The result is highly poetic prose that asserts the primacy of art and the imagination.

Born to John Clendennin Burne Hawkes and Helen Ziefle Hawkes in Stamford, Connecticut, on 17 August 1925, John Clendennin Burne Hawkes Jr., an only, asthmatic child, spent the first eight years of his life in New England. In 1935, after living briefly in New York City, Hawkes and his mother joined his father, an adventurer and businessman, in Juneau, Alaska, where they spent five years. They moved back to New York in 1940. In 1943, when Hawkes entered Harvard University, he began writing poetry, producing the privately printed *Fiasco Hall* (1943). After a disappointing semester he left Harvard to serve as an American Field Service ambulance driver in Italy and Germany in 1944–1945 (toward the end of World War II), an experience that often shaped the war-torn European settings of his fiction. Following his return to Harvard in 1945, he began writing fiction, met Sophie Goode Tazewell, and followed her to Fort Peck, Montana, where they

married on 5 September 1947. During this time he began his first work of short fiction, "Charivari," which gained him admission to Albert J. Guerard's creative writing class at Harvard. Under Guerard's mentorship and with his wife's support, Hawkes began his formal writing career.

Guerard introduced Hawkes to James Laughlin, the publisher of New Directions, who developed a long-standing relationship with the writer and published his first ten books. In 1949 Hawkes graduated from Harvard. He worked at the university press (1949–1955) and taught briefly at Harvard (1955–1958). In 1958 he began teaching creative writing at Brown University, retiring in 1988. Throughout this time he and Sophie Hawkes lived in Providence, Rhode Island, and raised four children: John, Sophie, Calvert, and Richard. Often during his career Hawkes traveled abroad with his family to write. He published sixteen novels, a volume of plays (written primarily during the 1960s), and two collections of fiction. Over the years he received many fellowships and honors, including being elected to the American Academy of Arts and Letters. In 1973 he received Le Prix du Meilleur Livre Etranger, one of the most distinguished French literary prizes, for *The Blood Oranges* (1971), and in 1986 he was awarded the Prix Medicis Etranger for the best foreign novel translated into French for *Adventures in the Alaskan Skin Trade* (1985). He was writer in residence or visiting professor at the Massachusetts Institute of Technology (1959), the University of Virginia (1965), Stanford University (1966–1967), and the City College of the City University of New York (1971–1972). He was supported by a Guggenheim Fellowship (1962–1963), a National Institute of Arts and Letters Grant (1962), a Ford Foundation Fellowship (1964–1965), a Rockefeller Foundation Fellowship (1966), and the Lannon Foundation Grant.

Nothing in Hawkes's biography prepares one for the radical nature of his fiction. His best-known statement on the art of the novel, made to Enck in 1965, continues to raise eyebrows: "I began to write fiction on the assumption that the true enemies of the novel were plot, character, setting, and theme, and having once abandoned these familiar ways of thinking about fiction, totality of vision or structure was really all that remained. And structure–verbal and psychological coherence–is still my largest concern as a writer." Although Hawkes's fiction does not completely abolish traditional elements of the novel, these conventions are certainly subjugated to his visionary prose. This definitive characteristic indicates a desire to liberate fiction from the constraints of realistic representation.

Discussing his experimental goals with Enck, Hawkes explained his wish to give fiction new life: "Every fiction of any value has about it something new.

*Dust jacket for Hawkes's first novel, which established his
reputation as an experimental writer*

At any rate, the function of the true innovator or specifically experimental writer is to keep prose alive and constantly to test in the sharpest way possible the range of our human sympathies and constantly to destroy mere surface morality." Challenging not only the conventions of the novel but of society as well, he wanted to mine the nightmare, to confront humankind's potential for violence, believing that there is a "terrifying similarity between the unconscious desires of the solitary man and the disruptive needs of the visible world." This pursuit of individual and collective nightmares led to horrifying descriptions—such as a man cutting up a child or a gangster truncheoning a woman to death. Never apologizing for the "disturbing nature" of his work, Hawkes aimed "never to let the reader (or myself) off the hook, so to speak, never to let him think that the picture is any less bleak than it is or that there is any easy way out of the nightmare of existence." For Hawkes the psychic journeys into "all the fluid, germinal, pestilential 'stuff' of life itself" are moral because they lead to sympathy. In an interview with John Kuehl he explained, "If the point is to discover true compassion, true sympathy, then clearly the task is to sympa-

thize with what we ordinarily take to be truly repulsive in life." He identified American authors such as Nathanael West, Djuna Barnes, and Flannery O'Connor as other writers who, like him, tried to maintain a detachment from violence while simultaneously generating sympathy.

By situating his fiction in what Hawkes described as "the psychic and literal spot where life is most difficult, most dangerous, most beautiful," he brought to this opening, no matter how uncomfortable or disorienting, a "saving comic spirit and the saving beauties of language." The comic elements of Hawkes's fiction have often been overlooked as early reviewers focused on the shocking. For Hawkes the comic response and use of poetic language were affirmations. Both bring to "the fractured picture" an energy that may seem inappropriate but in effect releases the vitality and futurity of life. Thus, the imagination is expanded, compassion is encouraged, and life becomes possible. He told Enck, "Comic vision always suggests futurity, I think, always suggests a certain hope in the limitless energies of life itself." Not identifying himself with black humorists, Hawkes explained his use of comedy to Kuehl: "it's clear that we need to experience drastic shifts in what we perceive—hence, the comedy. Comedy violates normal expectations, and it also ameliorates pain through language. No doubt laughter is sometimes sadistic and victimizing. . . . But at least through laughter there is release, vilification, possible purification, and, finally, identification with the victim." One trademark of Hawkes's fiction throughout his career was this paradoxical mixture of comedy and terror.

When Hawkes began writing his first fiction, he was anticipating marriage, living in a Montana wasteland, and suffering from a bad case of athlete's foot from his new cowboy boots. In "Charivari" (1949) he employed parody to capture his feelings of dislocation, sexual desire, and fear. By writing about Henry and Emily, a naive, childless, middle-aged couple who fearfully attempt to adjust to an unexpected pregnancy, he satirizes the institutions of marriage and parenthood. The joke is that after considerable anxiety and horror, the pregnancy is discovered to be hysterical, or false, and the couple resume acting like children themselves. According to Hawkes, "the butt of [the story's] satire is innocence." Innocence is a major theme in all Hawkes's works, but in his early novels in particular he satirizes the innocence of characters who, because they will not acknowledge their fears and desires, are victimized by them. Often the innocence is sexual and becomes for Hawkes a sick innocence indicative of sexual apathy and death externalized in his fictional world.

At this early stage in Hawkes's fiction sterility dominates the landscape. All of his fiction from "Charivari" to *The Lime Twig* (1961) presents apocalyptic worlds bereft of life-sustaining energies. Tony Tanner suggests that Hawkes's "landscapes of desolation and decline . . . point to the progress of entropy quite as graphically as the landscapes of [William S.] Burroughs and [Thomas] Pynchon." Indeed, between 1949 and 1964, war dominated Hawkes's novels. Set in post–World War II England, Germany, and Italy, *The Cannibal* (1949), *The Goose on the Grave, and The Owl* (1954), and *The Lime Twig* may seem like standard World War II fare, yet the reader experiences the locales of these novels more as hallucinated visions than as places. In *The Cannibal* the fictional German town of Spitzen-on-the-Dein epitomizes Hawkes's warscapes: "The town, roosting on charred earth, no longer ancient, . . . gorged itself on straggling beggars and remained gaunt beneath an evil cloaked moon." In Hawkes's metaphor this deterministic environment becomes a slumbering vulture that eats its inhabitants. The landscape of the novel is modern consciousness disintegrating.

The Cannibal consists of three parts. Parts one and three take place in post–World War II Germany, framing part two, which depicts a decadent wartime Germany before and during World War I and portrays the marriage of Stella Snow, daughter of a Franco-Prussian war hero, and her husband, Ernst. The first and third sections focus on the omniscient first-person narrator, Zizendorf, a neo-Nazi who calls himself "the leader" and who is also a newspaper editor. He wants to lead Germany from its ashes into another Teutonic uprising by killing Leevey, the American overseer of one-third of Germany. By placing a log across the path of Leevey's motorcycle, Zizendorf restores order to Spitzen-on-the-Dein, symbolically to all of Germany, and brags of his own rise to power in the preface. Moving back and forth from the Germany of World War II to that of 1914 telescopes the two eras and emphasizes the never-ending horror of war. Significantly, Zizendorf's success anticipates a repetition of Nazi domination and a third eruption of worldwide terror. As Hawkes observed in an interview with John Graham, "This juxtaposition at the outset is intended to try to suggest that perhaps we don't move so much in cycles as repetitions or that we have always had these particular problems of violence, destruction, sadism and so on."

As the title suggests, cannibalism becomes the metaphor for a nation that devours itself. However, in the novel Germany is only a microcosm of the modern world; history is really the main character. Its repetitive, irrational nature is so insistent that it crushes any human effort to resist. People trapped in this recurring historical force become depraved and imprisoned conspirators in their own corruption and in the decline of society at large. Thus, Hawkes makes the metaphorical literal. In one of the most memorable episodes in all his fiction he stuns the reader with the description of a starving duke pursuing, dismembering, and eating a young boy. Such an extreme image horrifies and tests Hawkes's call for "extreme fictive sympathy." Yet, clearly the reader is to acknowledge a common humanity in the madness, for the pervasive madness of Duke Zizendorf and war destroys the future. In short, history cannibalizes all who ignore, run from, or vainly attempt to control it.

Convinced that a traditionally structured and written novel might suggest a conventional response to war, Hawkes began his career with a boldness of vision that immediately separated his writing from that of contemporaries such as Saul Bellow, Norman Mailer, William Styron, and J. D. Salinger. Hawkes's obsessive images and radical experimentation are so insistent that reviewers expressed admiration for his cold brilliance as a writer and alarm at the claustrophobic intensity of his writing. From the beginning Hawkes's technique generated critical interest but distanced him from the general reading public.

Hawkes's second full-length novel, *The Beetle Leg* (1951), proved even more challenging than his first. Leaving the war-torn landscape of Europe, Hawkes set the novel in the American West to parody the frontier myth. The far-reaching desert wilderness renders minuscule the small town of Gov City and its inhabitants. Ten years before the novel opens, Mulge Lampson is buried alive while building a dam. This central incident comes from a similar accident that occurred to a laborer when Hawkes worked on the Fort Peck irrigation dam in Montana in 1947. The idea of a man "swimming around in the mud" captured his imagination. This figure of living death epitomizes all characters who are metaphorically buried alive by the landscape. The dam should be a promise of the American Edenic myth but becomes instead the burial ground of Adamic aspirations. This sense of cultural erosion is underscored by the image of a moving, decaying, and devouring dam that creeps toward an apocalyptic end as it inches forward "a beetle's leg each several anniversaries."

While overturning the American dream, Hawkes simultaneously parodies the American Western. He takes the conventions of the classic Western—the sheriff, frontier wife, tight-lipped cowboy, Indian squaw, good "old" doc, the classic poker game, and the inevitable climactic shootout—and comically reverses them until the reader is left with what Patrick O'Donnell calls "the entropic embodiment of the pioneer spirit." For example, in the climactic gunfight the moral distinction between the good guys and bad guys no longer matters,

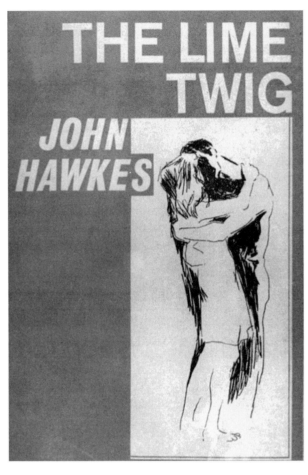

Dust jacket for Hawkes's 1961 book, a nightmarish parody of the detective novel

and the "hero" either shoots himself or his gun backfires. Parodying the myth of the American frontier, *The Beetle Leg* powerfully communicates the betrayal of a national dream, a desperate waste of human spirit, and the need to look more deeply into the myth of the New World.

One of the most memorable examples in Hawkes's canon of his commitment to exposing the extremities present in humankind's shared psychic life is the image of the drowned fetus in *The Beetle Leg*. In a 1977 interview with Anthony C. Santore and Michael Pocalyko, Hawkes explained, "The moment in *The Beetle Leg* when Luke fishes the fetal baby out of the flood and tenderly holds it, then puts it back into the flood, is an analogue for what I think the artist ought to be able to do. We should feel a strong attachment to human life even in its most frightening form." Fishing in what should be life-sustaining waters and retrieving instead a nightmare of lost innocence should horrify and, according to Hawkes, elicit sympathy.

More militantly experimental than *The Cannibal* and more difficult to follow, the still largely overlooked

The Beetle Leg received conflicting reviews, some rejecting individual scenes as incomprehensible while others considered them "extraordinary." In a 1952 study of Hawkes, Kuehl compared Hawkes's pre-1960 novels, written soon after he abandoned poetry writing, to long modern poems such as T. S. Eliot's *The Waste Land* (1922) because, like that poem, the novels rely on images and synecdoche rather than on sequentially arranged incidents that offer motive or even cause-and-effect relationships.

Hawkes's novellas *The Goose on the Grave* and *The Owl,* published together in 1954, were later collected along with "Charivari" in *Lunar Landscapes* (1969). This title describes the barren worlds created in the two novellas, with *The Goose on the Grave* set in war-ravaged Italy and *The Owl* in the medieval Italian town of Sasso Fetore, meaning "Tomb Stench." The terrain of both worlds is in shambles, with such breaches of nature and violations of humanity that Hawkes seems to be still trying to write his way out of the terrors of World War II. In *The Goose on the Grave* a grim, war-scarred Italy leaves an orphan exposed to the degeneracies of a failing Western culture. In *The Owl* the townspeople of Sasso Fetore, after enduring an unnamed war, allow themselves to be intimidated by a ruthless executioner named Il Gufo and his towering medieval fortress. Largely deterministic, these dark hallucinatory landscapes embody Hawkes's early worldview in a tensionless, inert universe.

The Owl was republished separately in 1977 with an introduction by Robert Scholes, who called the novella "one of the very best of Hawkes's fictions, and probably the best introduction to his work." In a 1983 interview with O'Donnell, Hawkes said *The Owl* was "a deliberate effort to rewrite *The Cannibal*." Like Zizendorf, Il Gufo is a fascist ruler and a first-person narrator with a destructive, yet artistic, impulse. The desire of these characters to order chaos is artistic, but their fanaticism (ironically) promotes barrenness. Because no marriageable men survived the war in the wasteland of *The Owl,* the women pin all their hopes for marriage on Il Gufo or, more especially, his new male prisoner scheduled for hanging. Il Gufo, the hangman, is a comic choice for matrimony because he is married to his gallows (referred to as "she") and represents an entire legalistic, death-ridden culture based on an abhorrence of sexuality and life. The prisoner, however, offers untamed creative energy as suggested through his escape by flying Icarus-like from the hangman's citadel. As in the story of Icarus, however, the prisoner fails and is captured, horrifyingly punished, and hanged, thus preventing him from redeeming the town and restoring life. Although obviously a dark novel, *The Owl* has comic elements. Also apparent are Hawkes's emerging

concerns with the paradoxical nature of the artist and the conflict between Eros and Thanatos, between sex and death.

All the promise of Hawkes's initial work culminated in *The Lime Twig,* the best example of his early style. During the seven-year interval between novels, the longest in Hawkes's career, he and his family moved from Harvard to Brown, in Providence, Rhode Island. Although this work depicts yet another spiritually and sexually depleted world (post–World War II England), it offers a more coherent plot with more consistent characters. As he told Enck, Hawkes was continuing in this novel with his desire "to parody the novel form." Specifically, *The Lime Twig* parodies "the soporific plot of the thriller" or detective novel. It has all the trappings–thugs, prostitutes, policemen, an innocent couple, gambling, beatings, and killings–as well as the murky atmosphere of the underworld and "Dreary Station," a shabby postwar environs where the spiritless lower class lodges. Flannery O'Connor effectively described the experience of reading this novel: "You suffer *The Lime Twig* like a dream. It seems to be something that is happening to you, that you want to escape from but can't. This . . . I might have been dreaming myself."

The experience of reading *The Lime Twig* is not only dreamlike, but the novel is actually about dreaming. It considers what might happen if a person's most intimate repressed desires came true, if the boundary between fantasy and reality collapsed. The dreamers in this novel are William Hencher, the first-person narrator who is soon killed, and a married couple, Michael and Margaret Banks. Hencher becomes "the seedbed," according to Hawkes, of the pathetic dreams and lives of the Bankses. Through his contacts with a local gang, Hencher helps Michael achieve his dream of attaining a racehorse. By being the front for the stolen racehorse, Michael unwittingly becomes involved with the ruthless gang that is responsible not only for Hencher's death but also for the kidnapping and fatal beating of Michael's wife. For Michael the horse is the embodiment of power, sexual potency, beauty, and danger–"knowing that his own worst dream, and best, was of a horse which was itself the flesh of all violent dreams." Knowing and yet innocent, Michael pursues his dream, realizes the fulfillment of its sexual pleasures, and is literally destroyed when he plunges in front of the galloping horse to end the race and dash the gang's chance of wealth. Dream and dreamer here merge. As Donald J. Greiner wrote in 1985, "the pursuit of dreams inevitably degenerates to confrontation with nightmare because fantasy cannot be controlled." The unwary dreamer realizes that he cannot restrain what he will not acknowledge, for just beneath the surface of our dreams lie brutality and sexual thrill. As O'Donnell explains, "*The Lime Twig* articulates one of Hawkes's strongest themes: how we are 'limed' by our own desires. Lime twigs snare birds and the innocents in the novel are limed by their own fantasies."

Representing law, order, and rational society, the police cannot possibly comprehend the real mystery–the irrational undersurface of the dream nor Michael's deliberate act of self-sacrifice to prove that he is no longer at the mercy of the dream. The detectives who sift through empirical evidence and Sidney Slyter, the newspaper commentator whose sports column confidently but unreliably recounts the events, are parodies of authorities who believe they deal with the real world.

With *The Lime Twig* Hawkes entered what Greiner calls his "major phase." For the first time Hawkes began to receive notable critical attention. Reflecting on how the appearance of *The Lime Twig* in 1961 challenged established American fiction, Robert Coover described his discovery of the young Hawkes as "like finding, in a stifling lockup, a secret message of imminent liberation." Along with *The Cannibal* and *Second Skin* (1964), *The Lime Twig* was republished in the Penguin Twentieth-Century Classics Series in 1996. In the preface to this edition Coover calls *The Lime Twig* a "startlingly original masterpiece." Along with Thomas Pynchon's *V* (1963), Vladimir Nabokov's *Pale Fire* (1962), and John Barth's *The Sot-Weed Factor* (1960), *The Lime Twig* expands the potentialities of the novel form, a concern of the "metafiction" of the 1960s. It undermines expectations that the novel would present interpretable morals, while calling attention to the nature of fiction, offering imaginative prose, and helping to usher in the postmodern tradition.

Beginning with the publication of *Second Skin* in 1964, Hawkes not only increased his reputation as one of the premier American experimental novelists but also began to shift his emphasis. Rather than concentrating on the depiction of a dark, deterministic, hallucinatory world, he began to stress the modern individual's reaction to the chaos he encounters. The sense of stasis and impersonality of the earlier works gives way to subjective fictions with dramatic form. Skipper becomes Hawkes's first sustained first-person voice, actively shaping his world and commenting directly on the novel he is writing. A memoir, or "naked history," that he finished the previous night, the novel is Skipper's imaginative reconstruction of his past, using lyrical language and humor to triumph over death and sadism. In his interview with Graham, Hawkes comments on his change of emphasis and tone: "In *Second Skin* I wanted to be sure, first, that the comedy would be unmistakable. . . .This is the first time, I think, in my fiction that

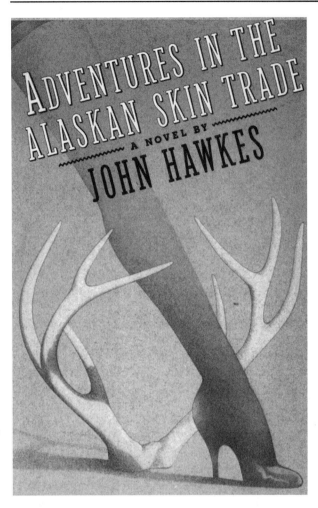

Dust jacket for Hawkes's 1985 novel, which draws on his experiences during the five years of his childhood that he spent in Alaska

there is something affirmative. In other words, even I got very much involved in the life-force versus death."

Hawkes wrote *Second Skin* in 1962 while he and his family lived for ten months on the Caribbean island of Grenada under the auspices of a Guggenheim Fellowship. In "Notes on Writing a Novel" (1962) he explains that his inspirations for *Second Skin* were the suicide of a close friend and time spent on an island off the coast of Maine. A lush tropical island and a cold New England island are the fictional landscapes of *Second Skin,* dramatizing Skipper's struggle with life and death. Writing his memoir from the timeless, "sun-dipped wandering island" of his imagination, Skipper recalls the cold "black island in the Atlantic" where his daughter Cassandra committed suicide. Skipper's past is filled with tragic stories of death and pain: his early childhood living at his father's mortuary, his father's and his mother's suicides, his assault by Tremlow, and other wartime experiences, all of which he has sur-

vived. Blind to his own ineffectuality, passivity, and especially his own culpability in the suicide of his daughter, the fat, middle-aged Skipper becomes an artist figure who imagines his life as a triumph. In telling the tale with the perspective of hindsight he reinterprets his dreadful past. The experimental structure and use of time meet his needs as a storyteller as he journeys from a deadly past to a paradisiacal life to find "love at last." On this self-created island of the imagination he is no longer a guilt-ridden failure but an artificial inseminator of cows, perhaps the father of Catalina Kate's son, and a lover of life.

Although the reader questions Skipper's reliability and sees his failures, the narrator experiences both psychic extremes—of Eros and Thanatos, as illustrated by the two alternating islands—yet manages to choose life over death. In doing so, Skipper assumes a kind of mythic stature. The affirmation of the novel comes from Skipper's act of creative will, a triumph of the redemptive imagination. As Hawkes said to Kuehl, "what we all want to do . . . is to create our own worlds in our own voice." Skipper does so through language, his "second skin" that covers and protects him from the past's brutal scars. Since it serves as a salvatory act, his language heightens, transforms, and redeems experience. Skipper's lyrical language calls attention to itself and continually reminds the reader that this "naked history" is self-consciously fictive and illustrates Hawkes's insistence on the primacy of the imagination.

Second Skin marked the first time in Hawkes's fiction, as he told Enck, that he successfully accomplished his goal of bringing a "saving comic spirit and the saving beauties of language" together and making them the subject of a novel. For this accomplishment *Second Skin* became Hawkes's most celebrated novel and was the runner-up to Saul Bellow's *Herzog* for the National Book Award.

According to Hawkes's 1982 interview with Heide Ziegler, the subject of his work from *Second Skin* on is "the imagination itself." The three novels that follow *Second Skin—The Blood Oranges, Death, Sleep & the Traveler* (1974), and *Travesty* (1976), often referred to as the triad—deal explicitly with "the relationship between sex and the imagination." While Hawkes's early fiction shows how the repression of sexuality contributes to the pain and deathly impulses of the modern world, he examines this subject directly in the triad. The first-person narrators of these novels share an open obsession with sexuality, and each male narrator conflates sexuality and aesthetics. Cyril, Allert, and Papa want to create and control their fictional worlds, as well as the women they desire. By developing each narrator's psychology Hawkes explores perhaps his central concern: the paradoxical nature of the artist. Discussing his treatment of the first-person narrators in the triad, Hawkes told Ziegler: "In each case these figures embody both the victim and, more important, the victimizer; each narrator is both creator and destroyer. . . . For me the poles of the authorial self, or of that self that creates something out of nothing, are precisely these: cruelty, or ultimate power, and innocence." Each novel in the triad intensifies Hawkes's exploration of the narrator's imaginative access to innocence and power.

Just as Hawkes desired to explode the conventions of the novel, Cyril, the narrator of *The Blood Oranges,* desires to destroy sexual conventions. Because Cyril and his wife, Fiona, believe "the only enemy of the mature marriage is monogamy," they have a sexually open marriage and try to initiate another couple, Hugh and Catherine, into the "multiplicity of love" and their vision of love's aesthetic possibilities. This humorous yet tragic picture of a complex relationship between two married couples echoes Ford Madox Ford's *The Good Soldier* (1915). The epigraph from Ford's novel suggests Cyril's desire to construct a "terrestrial paradise . . . where people can be with whom they like and have what they like and take their ease in shadows and in coolness." To underscore the pastoral nature of Cyril's longings, Hawkes sets the story in Illyria, the mythical retreat of William Shakespeare's *Twelfth Night* (1602). In addition, Hawkes layers Cyril's narration with complexities suggesting his unreliability. Cyril's account of what happens reveals the simultaneous loss of his pastoral ideal, his self-defense concerning the validity of his vision, and his belief that he has successfully regained it.

A self-appointed "sex-singer," Cyril blames Hugh for thwarting their erotic harmony and for the onanistic and perverse eroticism that leads to his accidental hanging. With his tapestry in shreds Cyril attempts to re-create his love song with Catherine and thus imagine his "terrestrial paradise" into being. His success depends on the seductive power of his language. In a 1972 interview with Scholes, Hawkes affirms Cyril's vision: Cyril "is simply trying to designate the power, the beauty, fulfillment, the possibility that is evident in any actual scene we exist in. . . . Illyria doesn't exist unless you bring it into being." Although Hawkes defended Cyril, the destructive underpinnings of the narrator's authoritarian imagination emerge. A complex and comic portrait of an artist as a "sex aesthetician," *The Blood Oranges* remains Cyril's version of failed pastoral. Nevertheless, as Lesley Marx points out, "The complexity of the critique of this desire for fictions of concord lies in the passion and beauty with which Hawkes is able to invest that desire, to see it as desirable, even as it is destructive."

From Cyril's questionable rhapsodic vision, *Death, Sleep & the Traveler* moves to a realm of nightmare and stasis. Hawkes commented to Ziegler that he thought this novel to be "the poet's descent into the underworld or into the unconscious in search of the self." Emanating from an unidentified location, the narrator's detached voice suggests isolation and possible madness. More a collection of dreams, memories, and astonishingly imagined sexual tableaux than a traditional narrative, the novel remains exiled in the narrator's suspended dream state. The story Allert tells alternates between two settings, two time sequences, and two sets of menage à trois—one the frigid northern world, where Allert, his wife, Ursula, and a friend Peter form one menage à trois, and the other a southern world of sun and sea, where Allert takes an uncharted ocean cruise with Ariane and Olaf. Rather than opposing landscapes suggesting Eros and Thanatos, each setting ultimately makes sex and death synonymous. All Allert's sexual encounters and erotic landscapes include deathly images; for example, in the explicitly sexual sauna scene the lovers almost die. In fact, both triangles end in a death. Peter dies, and Allert is accused of dropping Ariane overboard. Refusing to admit his culpability, Allert ends with "I am not guilty." So far removed from life, this artist is indeed innocent of life itself and doomed to aestheticize the emerging terrors of his nightmares and his own autoeroticism. Thus, Allert's artistic power is undermined by his own urgent unconscious needs and fears.

Whereas Allert refuses to admit that his pursuit of artistic illusion has evoked devastation, Papa, the voice of *Travesty,* consciously chooses death over life by making death his chosen art form. Delivering an uninterrupted monologue on the aesthetics of death, Papa careens through the night, hell-bent on suicide and murder. Hawkes reduces the landscape of the novel to the confines of a car, making it synonymous with the narrator's mind; the ride suggests an interior journey into the imagination, like Allert's ocean voyage. In another triangle of human relationships, Papa encloses himself in the speeding car with his daughter Chantal and Henri, who is lover to Chantal and to Papa's wife, Honorine. The final novel of the triad is a tour de force, a 125-page monologue in which the narrator explains his plan to crash the car into a brick wall and kill all three of them.

Inspired by Albert Camus's *The Fall* (1956), Hawkes explained to Ziegler that he "subverted Camus's question so that it became, not 'Why not suicide?', but *how* suicide, *when,* and *where*. I was interested in not how to live but in what could be most taxing to the imagination. It came to me that cessation was the only thing unimaginable. Cessation and 'the existence of that which exists no longer' are the only concerns of my narrator. . . ." Papa's pursuit of death is, therefore, not only an imposition of form on chaos but also a creation of something outside of life: "that nothing is more important than the existence of what does not exist; that I would rather see two shadows flickering inside the head than all your flaming sunrises set end to end. There you have it." Although a comic exaggeration of artistic pursuit, Papa's statement nevertheless espouses Hawkes's belief in the artist's need to defy the world around him—echoed in Papa's italicized words: "*Imagined life is more exhilarating than remembered life.*" Papa's car ride, in fact, becomes a metaphor for the absolute artistic experience, and Hawkes suggests that such a romantic endeavor is fatal. As Papa says in his closing words, "there shall be no survivors. None." O'Donnell concludes: "Of the narrators in the triad, Papa goes the farthest in consciously rendering a coherent vision that replaces the disparities of life; ironically, he is not trading one world for another, as is Skipper in *Second Skin*, nor falteringly reconciling two worlds, as does Cyril, but choosing a form of nonbeing and annihilation that, indeed, makes his vision a travesty."

With *Travesty* he took the act of making the world fictive to such extremes that "without a new start, Hawkes may next offer a blank page," according to Graham. Hawkes's experimentation with the nature of fiction and language was so bold that the publication of the triad during the 1970s firmly established him in the avant-garde tradition and garnered some of his best reviews. For example, Thomas McGuane called Hawkes "feasibly our best writer" (*The New York Times Book Review*, 19 September 1971), and Tony Tanner called him "one of the very best living American writers" (*The New York Times Book Review*, 28 March 1976). To Ziegler, Hawkes claimed that *Travesty* was "as close as I've come to perfection"; however, his expectations about the success of that novel were dashed. His critical reputation did not carry over to the general reading public. Sensitive to the charge that his books were "inaccessible," Hawkes frankly admitted, "I am tired of being called America's best unknown writer."

The Passion Artist (1979) signals Hawkes's effort to reach a wider audience. Published by Harper and Row instead of New Directions and written for a larger audience, this novel became his most accessible to date. Hawkes had already begun to ease some of the demands that his early, surreal fiction placed on the reader by offering recognizable characters, settings, and plot. With *The Passion Artist* he also wrote more overtly about his preoccupations with sexuality, the imagination, and psychic journeys. Hawkes returned to the distancing of a third-person narrator, rather than the unreliable first-person narrator he used in his triad.

Like many of Hawkes's other middle-aged protagonists, Konrad Vost is enslaved by unconscious repressions and childhood fears. Throughout his life he has been victimized by women, and he is presently obsessed with his mother, his dead wife, and his daughter. Excessively rigid and seeking control, this timid man lives in an anonymous European city whose bleakness reflects the protagonist's listless existence.

The Passion Artist focuses on sexual repression as the principal source of a man's enslavement to a life without imagination. La Violaine, the local women's prison where Vost's mother resides, suggests the sexual deprivation of a modern authoritarian society in which eroticism, particularly feminine eroticism, is the enemy of order. Hawkes externalizes imprisonment as a symbol not only of the repressive forces in modern civilization but also of the individual's enslavement to his submerged unconscious. The incarceration of women characterizes this society, explicitly reflecting its institutionalized misogyny, and Vost parallels his deficient surroundings as the "man who does not know the woman." When a prison riot breaks out, Vost and other male volunteers enter the prison to quell the riot, but participate in it instead. Hawkes suggests through this eruption the dangers of confining not only unruly sexuality but all disruptive needs lodged in the unconscious.

At first the title of the novel, *The Passion Artist,* seems ironic, for Vost is crippled by his lack of passion and is one of Hawkes's least sympathetic protagonists. However, during the course of the novel one sees Vost's courage as he goes further than any of Hawkes's other protagonists in his willingness to undergo the terrors of the imagination. The novel is structured around Vost's interior journeys that unearth his buried memories and reveal his psychic scars. He clearly illustrates the paradoxical nature of many of Hawkes's previous artist figures; he is characterized by both his innocence (because of his willingness to explore his subconscious) and his brutality (because of his imagination's violent proclivities).

At the end Vost ironically finds himself imprisoned by women. Enclosed in his private cell, Vost exchanges his nightmare for erotic liberation. In the presence of women he has spent his life avoiding, this man of rigid self-control realizes at last how to meet a woman without guilt or fear or repression: "Vost knew at last the transports of that singular experience, which makes every man an artist: the experience, that is, of the willed erotic union." For Vost, passion releases his imaginative vitality and allows him to achieve the ultimate artistic experience—the union of the self and the other. Recognizing the unity of masculinity and femininity that "willed eroticism" offers, Vost reconciles the

Dust jacket for Hawkes's 1988 novel, which juxtaposes a twentieth-century photographer and the eighteenth-century
painter George Stubbs, best-known for his portraits of horses

ambivalences in his unconscious–the terror and the freedom, "the pit of putrescence" and "the bed of stars." Freed from the imprisonment of self, he achieves the ultimate artistic experience through sex (not death). Nevertheless, the cost of such freedom is great, and Vost is shot accidentally by a friend as he emerges from the prison gates. On the other side of completely integrated psychic experience may be annihilation.

Vost's transformation into a "passion artist" occurs through his ability to cross over into the world of women. According to Marx, in *The Passion Artist* Hawkes moved away from depicting the "totalizing" imagination of a first-person male artist toward the incorporation of a feminine voice. This introduction of a female perspective points the way to female narration first in *Virginie: Her Two Lives* (1981) and later in *Adventures in the Alaskan Skin Trade*. The female narrators of these novels each view and re-envision the activity of male author figures.

A novel in the form of a journal, *Virginie* returns to first-person narration and explicitly asserts its form as writing. Virginie, Hawkes's first female narrator, is an eleven-year-old girl who lives and writes her journal in 1740 and 1945 France: the first date being significant as the year of the Marquis de Sade's birth, the second for marking the end of World War II. In 1740 Virginie is the companion of Seigneur, an exquisitely decadent French nobleman who runs a school to prepare lowly women to be mistresses to aristocratic men; in 1945 Virginie is the companion of her brother, Bocage, an earthy Parisian taxi driver who gathers a circle of street-walkers and their companions for the purpose of engaging in "charades of love." Although the two stories differ in time and tone, they are joined by the sensibility of Virginie herself, who remains radically innocent, no matter what she sees or is subjected to.

Intended as a parody of a pornographic novel, *Virginie* plays on the paradox of male vision rendered in female voice. Hawkes pokes fun at various erotic fantasies that men have created through the centuries to portray women as objects of their desire. Although Seigneur and Bocage represent artists of two different times—one, the omniscient author of the eighteenth century who harnesses Eros with the reins of symmetry and order, and the other, the twentieth-century author left operating in a random, disintegrating world—they both function as authors who desire mastery. Virginie's prepubescent eyes seem merely to observe and record the events in her journal, but she does more. She destabilizes Seigneur and Bocage's male authorial power by her writing. Her own desire is the motivation for the journal. She writes: "Marvels come to me and crowd me round, . . . and heat my face and make me clasp my quill in ecstasy! . . . I am thankful I have the power of solacing myself with dreams of creations which neither I nor anyone shall ever see. May I never lose that power." Her pleasure is the erotic engagement with the dreams of her creation and her language. Although the novel appears to end on a destructive note with Virginie in flames in both 1740 and 1945, her essence survives in the beauty of her language because, as Hawkes implies, it does not partake of experience. Virginie, "the insubstantial voice of the page that burns," is both the innocent imagination and the innocent text.

Many critics found that the two novels with which Hawkes attempted to reach a larger audience lacked the power of his earlier work. In the *Washington Post Book World* (29 September 1985) Bob Halliday referred to *The Passion Artist* "as curiously obsessive and shrill" and to *Virginie: Her Two Lives* as "an elegantly written but thin erotic caricature."

Adventures in the Alaskan Skin Trade is a major work that yields surprises for the reader. Two radical changes are immediately evident: a dramatic stylistic break and the inclusion of highly autobiographical elements. Although this novel deals with some familiar Hawkesian concerns (such as innocence and power, storytelling and fictional representation, and the imagination and eroticism), it does so in a different way. Using an expansive canvas filled with lively anecdotes rather than a tight focus on dense imagery, Hawkes invokes the tradition of male adventure stories and the tall tale. Prompting autobiographical comparisons, the novelist John Burne Hawkes names his female narrator Jacqueline Burne Deauville—nicknamed "Sunny" by her father—and gives her his birthday and a similar childhood. Dragged to Alaska at a young age by an ill-equipped mother and a larger-than-life father in search of adventure, Sunny attempts to come to terms with her family history, especially her father's. Told never to call him "father" or "dad," Sunny refers to him as Uncle Jake. An irresistibly magnetic figure, Uncle Jake pur-

sues his Buffalo Bill fantasies, remains oblivious to his family, and disappears mysteriously without a trace in 1940.

The novel opens in 1965 with Sunny reviewing her father's life and contemplating a new life for herself in France. She is trapped in the past as she dreams obsessively about Uncle Jake, whom she describes as "an artist in the life of adventure." A large portion of the novel is Sunny's retelling of her father's Wild West adventures: killing giant bears, pulling teeth for suffering Indian chiefs, and rescuing prospectors driven mad by mosquitoes. Nevertheless, she has been wounded by his abandonment and disappearance, his innocent, yet cruel pursuit of masculine adventure, and his puritanical blindness to sexuality. Not only does her narration reveal her critique of his paternal authority, but so does her lifestyle. All grown up, Sunny has become the proprietress of the Alaska-Yukon Gamelands, a frontier bordello and the state's largest trailer park for prostitutes. While her father's last frontier was Alaska, Sunny tells us, "At an early age I knew that woman, not Alaska, is the last frontier." She therefore counters her father's masculine confrontation with the wilderness with her own exploration into the challenging wilderness within.

Sunny's narrative is composed of her memories, her dreams, her father's tall tales, and pieces of her mother's journal; it is a form of self-therapy. Tortured by seven months of recurring dreams about her absent father, she wishes to come to terms with him. This feat is accomplished by two means: Sutka Charley's climactic revelation of her father's suicide and the process of her own storytelling. While she re-creates Uncle Jake and his stories, she also creates her own narrative. As Sunny says, "no matter that his entire life was my seduction and betrayal—all this aside, Uncle Jake was a storyteller." Rather than being left bereft by her father's death, Sunny decides that she is also important and becomes her own storyteller. Incorporating the two frontiers of woman and Alaska, she realizes the final frontier is storytelling. Deciding against going to France, Sunny says at the end, "So here I am, an Alaskan woman feeling good in her skin in Alaska."

The same year *Adventures in the Alaskan Skin Trade* was published, a small press released *Innocence in Extremis* (1985). Less than a hundred pages and originally part of the previous novel, it makes both an interesting companion to the longer work and at the same time an independent work. The story of twelve-year-old Uncle Jake and his family's visit to the Deauville estate in France provides insight into the character's subsequent failure as a husband and father. The novella differs in style from *Adventures in the Alaskan Skin Trade* by offering

"John Hawkes . . . must be ranked as America's greatest living visionary." —Edmund White

Praise for John Hawkes

Adventures in the Alaskan Skin Trade
"A great bear of a novel."
—San Francisco Chronicle

The Blood Oranges
"Rich, evocative, highly original."
—Anthony Burgess

The Frog
"Challenging, thought provoking, often hilarious."
—Ravina Gelfand, Minneapolis Star Tribune

Sweet William
"A tremendous, truly extraordinary novel."
—The Boston Globe

The Lime Twig
"From the first, John Hawkes's prose has sounded what Henry James would have said was, 'the right note.' . . . His lines are alive as few in our literature are."
—William Gass

John Hawkes

John Hawkes

AN IRISH EYE

a novel

AN IRISH EYE

VIKING

Dust jacket for Hawkes's last novel, a parody of the Cinderella story

finely crafted enclosure. It ends by anticipating Hawkes's next novel.

While Hawkes's female narrators Virginie and Sunny critique the activity of male author figures, *Whistlejacket* (1988) returns to a male narrator, Michael. Michael's role as narrator and fashion photographer allowed Hawkes to focus even more deeply on issues related to aesthetics as well as sexual control because Michael photographs models. Michael's narration is juxtaposed with a middle section third-person narration about artist George Stubbs (1724–1806). By juxtaposing eighteenth- and twentieth-century artists Michael and Stubbs, Hawkes sets up a comparison reminiscent of the one between Seigneur and Bocage in *Virginie*. In *Whistlejacket* both artists appear to be exemplars of representational art, one through realistic painting and the other through photography (a medium supposed to epitomize objectivity), but differences become apparent.

Michael's tenuous position as the unofficially adopted son of the wealthy Van Fleet family corre-

sponds to the decentered status of the postmodern author. Displaced from the true lineage of the patriarch Harold Van Fleet, Michael as his protégé also loves horses, women, and art. However, unlike Harold (Hal) and his father before him, both of whom pride themselves on conquests, Michael has voyeuristic tendencies. He likes to look at women–as well as life–through the lens of his camera. Like previous Hawkes novels, *Whistlejacket* critiques both forms of mastery–sexual and aesthetic–as it investigates issues that Marx refers to as "objectification, appropriation, and violation of the world."

The plot of the novel revolves around the mysterious circumstances of Hal's death at age sixty-two. Asked by his widow "to re-create his life in photographs," Michael constructs a "pictorial biography" of the dead Harold Van Fleet, and as he does so, the novel becomes a photograph album. No continuous narrative develops; Michael describes only the photos, insisting "Story is the anathema of the true photographer." Echoing

Hawkes's early claim that "true enemies of the novel were plot, character, setting, and theme," Michael also wishes to defy conventional art and create his own. Michael's narration reveals the artificiality of visual or fictional representation and the paradoxical nature of artistic vision that is simultaneously innocent and suspect.

Another of Hawkes's profoundly ambivalent narrator-artists, Michael presents himself as "an innocent though not entirely pure photographer." As the camera eye that records surfaces, he is aware that signs refer only to signs and claims the objectivity of his art while simultaneously privileging his vision. Michael's conflict points to the larger tension in the novel between the relationships of the seer, the sign, and meaning. The reader immediately questions the camera's being an innocent eye that translates the real into authentic images.

Through such uses of structure and character, Hawkes explores a key postmodern element: indeterminacy, or the difficulty (some would say the impossibility) of reading "signs" in this world. As both photographer and unwitting detective interested in reconstructing a crime, Michael uses his pictures to capture a surface. However, his naive belief in the purity and autonomy of his art and in his own innocence as an artist and biographer allows him to be seduced (by the camera's image) and ultimately implicated in Hal's death.

The title of the novel, as well as its dominant image, is George Stubbs's well-known painting of a rearing stallion called Whistlejacket. The eighteenth-century British artist becomes a character in the second section of *Whistlejacket*. Renowned for his amazing accuracy of representation, Stubbs becomes an artistic and psychological foil to Michael and his twentieth-century postmodernism. In part two of the novel Hawkes turns from Michael's stagnant photo album to Stubbs's disciplined, yet chilling life as a realistic painter, allowing Hawkes to compare eighteenth- and twentieth-century ideas of artistic and erotic mastery.

Historically Stubbs's body of work was largely devoted to horse portraiture; his many anatomical drawings came from the painstakingly dissected corpses of horses. Like the real George Stubbs, the artist in the novel becomes intimate with the interior of what he paints. Stubbs is committed to portraying a reality that goes beyond complacent acceptance of the exterior sign first seen when viewing an object. His paintings are more than photographic reporting; his aesthetic inspiration and even pleasure come from immersion in the grisly dissection of blood and guts; thus, they contrast with Michael's photographic distance, his voyeurism, and his seeming lack of authority. The ways in which Stubbs and Michael depict their subjects disturbingly connect to erotic desire and mastery.

Whistlejacket remains one of Hawkes's most fascinating treatments of postmodern art from an author considered one of the masters of postmodernism. One of the most cerebral and abstract of Hawkes's novels, *Whistlejacket* was criticized for its lack of tension and self-enclosure. In *The New York Times Book Review* (7 August 1988) Patrick McGrath acknowledged that "design overwhelms debris rather too thoroughly to arouse the terrible tensions of earlier works"; nevertheless, he found it "quite strong enough to maintain John Hawkes's position as the most consistently interesting writer, in terms of formal inventiveness, intelligence, and the sheer grace of the prose, at work in the United States today."

After the unsettling exploration of artistry in *Whistlejacket*, Hawkes's next novel is surprisingly gentle. *Sweet William: A Memoir of Old Horse* (1993) is comic, truly accessible, often touching, yet still experimental. The narrator of this fictional autobiography is a thoroughbred racehorse. The problem, not to mention impossibility, of a horse serving as narrator raises the postmodern controversy of the self or the issue of authorship—issues Hawkes raised previously with other impossible narratives such as *Virginie* and *Travesty*. This comic choice of first-person narrator is the perfect culmination of Hawkes's innovative narrative methods as well as his obsession with horses, which has appeared in varying degrees in nearly all his work.

Not interested in honoring the "great tradition" of beloved horse fables that offer "convention and reassurance," Hawkes has Old Horse admit to "misanthropy" on the first page. Hawkes's equine narrator echoes the author's own (as well as former problematic narrators') opposition to conventional morality, and his behavior demonstrates it. Old Horse's biting, stomping, kicking, mounting, and even killing serves as comical commentary on the necessary defiance of the artistic imagination that exerts its disruptive power, erotic vitality, and cruelty. In addition to this comic defiance, Hawkes also incorporates in Old Horse's narration the feminine voice of Virginie and Sunny or, as Marx contends, the voice of those "whom his totalitarian dreamers have oppressed and tormented." Ridden, mounted, broken, raced, beaten, sold, castrated, resold, named, and renamed, Old Horse tells his story from the perspective of age and a lifelong experience of enforced submission to external authority. However, unlike previous Hawkes artist figures who angrily confront external deterministic forces, Old Horse by the end learns to use his imagination to surrender with dignity. Through these changes Hawkes's readers may also hear the musings of an aging writer and author.

The catalyst for Old Horse's mellowing is his last owner, an elderly eccentric who has never ridden a horse. Ironically referring to him as Master, Old Horse says, "For our few months of life together we shared the silent music of arthritis, his and mine, the ignominy of gaunt frames and aching bones, the brief marriage of his innocence with my misanthropy, the unlikely collaboration of discarded man and discarded horse mutually revived at death's door." Not only does Old Horse offer his decrepit owner a new identity, but Master does the same for Old Horse by renaming him Petrarch, after the fourteenth-century Italian cleric and poet who invented the sonnet sequence. An analogy is immediately established between the horse and the "versifier Petrarch," so it follows that riding a horse is "nothing more or less than writing poetry."

Like Virginie, Old Horse tells his story when facing imminent death. At the conclusion of the novel he finally acquiesces with dignity and enters the vet's death van. Old Master eulogizes him, and Old Horse extorts, "Ride on! Ride through it!" These dynamic final words suggest that if one rides on or writes on, one will perhaps encounter Skipper's "time of no time." In other words, one enters the paradoxical realm of art where life is in death—as suggested by a grotesquely beautiful image evoked near the close of the novel, an image of a horse's corpse covered with a glorious wave of golden maggots.

The Frog (1996) and *An Irish Eye* (1997), Hawkes's fifteenth and sixteenth novels, evoke classic fairy tales such as "The Frog and the Prince" and "Cinderella"; yet, they read like modern fables. Of the two *The Frog* is more somber. Playing with the ageless fairy tales of ugly frogs, Hawkes weaves a tale Franz Kafka might have imagined.

As Hawkes told Greiner, the first-person narrator Pascal is the cherubic baby boy in *Travesty* grown to adulthood, an allusion pointing to the increasing tendency of Hawkes's novels to relate in character, theme, or technique to previous novels. Growing up on a pre–World War I French country estate where his parents work, the two-year-old child becomes secretly inhabited by Armand the frog for the rest of his life. Residing in his stomach, the frog gives the boy intense pain and amazing powers. Pascal confesses, "Exceptional is he who hosts the frog." During the course of Pascal's life, the frog's presence insures his mother's devotion, causes him to be sent to an asylum, prompts his father's death, pleasures many of Pascal's lovers, inspires horror and awe, and finally chokes him, causing an early death. In Pascal's words Armand is the "source of my worst pain and a power that exceeded manhood."

Hawkes seems to be writing indirectly of the pleasure and pain of being an artist. Much like the gift or curse of being an artist, the frog possesses the boy against his wishes, often alienating him from the world,

Hawkes at the time of An Irish Eye

as well as endowing him with psychosexual powers. For Pascal this exacerbates the classic Oedipal conflict by demanding his mother's attention and estranging his father, who later dies from seeing the frog. Near the end Pascal resolves the conflict when he discovers a dozen or so other inmates who possess and follow their frogs. Realizing he is not alone and that he can live without his mother, Pascal writes his tale from the asylum. In addition, he renounces traditional male sexuality as embodied by both his father and a German soldier he knows and lives voluptuously through his senses. As Hawkes told Greiner, "The point of the novel for me is that everybody has his own frog, his own demon within, his own strangeness, which can be a form of beauty itself."

Pascal's acceptance of his difference from others is similar to the accommodation that Old Horse makes at the end of *Sweet William.* At the latter part of his career Hawkes seems to be moving toward a gentler treatment of the artist and away from harsh criticism of ambitious authors. The choice of a prepubescent orphan girl as narrator of *An Irish Eye* (reminiscent of Virginie) also suggests this movement. However, Hawkes's work has always been protean and has never followed a convenient linear progression. His novels may have become more accessible, but they have never been conventional. As a writer, he has always defied traditional novelistic methods and simple morality. He told Greiner: "To me no one is exempt from anything we can imagine or anything we suffer, imagined or otherwise. We are all the same. What I write is fiction that simply tries more specifically, more evocatively, to draw us into consciousness of that fact."

Since 1949 John Hawkes's writing has been variously characterized as avant-garde, postmodern, antirealistic, and new gothic. Always innovative, his fiction explored the nature of fictionality, aesthetic power, paradox, the imagination, the power of language, the role of the artist, eroticism, and the envisioning of psychic processes. His writing also had unmistakable stylistic qualities. From the innovation of his early writing to the elegance of his later prose, his narratives have evoked the sensations and rhythms of dreams. Like most dreams they draw the reader in with unimaginable pictures that dissolve the rational unity of perception, and they allure with their illumination of what lies within. Hawkes made no promises about what will be retrieved from these depths, but the resulting novels testify to his creative vision and his position as one of the leading voices of post–World War II fiction.

Interviews:

John Enck, "John Hawkes: An Interview," *Wisconsin Studies in Contemporary Literature,* 6 (Summer 1965): 141–155;

John Graham, "John Hawkes on His Novels," *Massachusetts Review,* 7 (Summer 1966): 449–461;

David Keyser and Ned French, "Talks with John Hawkes," *Harvard Advocate,* 104 (1970): 6, 34–35;

Robert Scholes, "A Conversation on *The Blood Oranges* between John Hawkes and Robert Scholes," *Novel,* 5 (Spring 1972): 197–207;

Douglas Dunn, "Profile 11: John Hawkes," *New Review,* 12 (1975): 23–28;

John Kuehl, "Interview," in his *John Hawkes and the Craft of Conflict* (New Brunswick, N.J.: Rutgers University Press, 1975), pp. 155–183;

Andrew Fielding, "John Hawkes Is a Very Nice Guy, and a Novelist of Sex and Death," *Village Voice,* 24 May 1976, pp. 45–47;

Paul Emmett and Richard Vine, "A Conversation with John Hawkes," *Chicago Review,* 28 (Fall 1976): 163–171;

Nancy Levine, "An Interview with John Hawkes," in *A John Hawkes Symposium: Design and Debris,* edited

by Anthony C. Santore and Michael Pocalyko (New York: New Directions, 1977), pp. 91–108;

Santore and Pocalyko, "'A Trap to Catch Little Birds With': An Interview with John Hawkes," *A John Hawkes Symposium: Design and Debris,* pp. 165–184;

Roger Sauls, "John Hawkes: I Am Pleased to Talk about Fiction," *New Lazarus Review,* 1 (1978): 5–10;

Thomas LeClair, ed., "Hawkes and Barth Talk about Fiction," *New York Times Book Review,* 1 April 1979, pp. 7, 31–33;

LeClair, "The Novelists: John Hawkes," *New Republic,* 181 (10 November 1979): 26–29;

Heide Ziegler, "John Hawkes," in *The Radical Imagination and the Liberal Tradition: Interviews with English and American Novelists,* edited by Ziegler and Christopher Bigsby (London: Junction Books, 1982), pp. 169–187;

Patrick O'Donnell, "Life and Art: An Interview with John Hawkes," *Review of Contemporary Fiction,* 3 (Fall 1983): 107–126;

Donald Greiner, "Elegant Barbarity: An Interview with John Hawkes about *The Frog,*" *Critique,* 38 (Fall 1996): 3–11.

Bibliography:

Carol A. Hryciw-Wing, *John Hawkes: A Research Guide* (New York: Garland, 1986).

References:

C. J. Allen, "Desire, Design, and Debris: The Submerged Narrative of John Hawkes's Recent Trilogy," *Modern Fiction Studies,* 25 (Winter 1979–1980): 579–592;

Charles Baxter, "In the Suicide Seat: Reading John Hawkes's *Travesty,*" *Georgia Review,* 34 (Winter 1980): 871–885;

Frederick Busch, *John Hawkes: A Guide to His Fictions* (Syracuse, N.Y.: Syracuse University Press, 1973);

Joseph M. Conte, "Design and Debris: John Hawkes's *Travesty,* Chaos Theory, and the Swerve," *Critique,* 37 (Winter 1996): 120–138;

Lois A. Cuddy, "Functional Pastoralism in *The Blood Oranges,*" *Studies in American Fiction,* 3 (Spring 1975): 15–25;

Paul Emmett, "The Reader's Voyage through *Travesty,*" *Chicago Review,* 28 (1976): 172–187;

Rita Ferrari, *Innocence, Power, and the Novels of John Hawkes* (Philadelphia: University of Pennsylvania Press, 1996);

Lucy Frost, "The Drowning of American Adam: Hawkes's *The Beetle Leg,*" *Critique,* 14 (Summer 1973): 63–74;

John Graham, ed., *Studies in Second Skin* (Columbus, Ohio: Merrill, 1971);

Donald J. Greiner, *Comic Terror: The Novels of John Hawkes* (Memphis: Memphis State University Press, 1978);

Greiner, *Understanding John Hawkes* (Columbia: University of South Carolina Press, 1985);

Albert J. Guerard, "The Prose Style of John Hawkes," *Critique*, 6 (Fall 1963): 19–29;

Elisabeth Kraus, "Psychic Sores in Search of Compassion: Hawkes's *Death, Sleep & the Traveler*," *Critique*, 17 (1976): 39–52;

John Kuehl, *John Hawkes and the Craft of Conflict* (New Brunswick, N.J.: Rutgers University Press, 1975);

Christine Laniel, "John Hawkes's Return to the Origin" in *Facing Texts: Encounters Between Contemporary Writers and Critics*, edited by Heide Ziegler (Durham, N.C.: Duke University Press, 1988), pp. 221–246;

Thomas LeClair, "A Pair of Jacks: John Barth and John Hawkes Gamble with New Fiction," *Horizon*, 22 (1979): 64–71;

Carol MacCurdy, "A Newly Envisioned World: Fictional Landscapes of John Hawkes," *Contemporary Literature*, 27 (Fall 1986): 318–335;

Leslie Marx, *Crystals Out of Chaos: John Hawkes and the Shapes of Apocalypse* (Madison, N.J.: Fairleigh Dickinson University Press, 1997);

Harry T. Moore, ed., *Contemporary American Novelists* (Carbondale: Southern Illinois University, 1964);

Patrick O'Donnell, *John Hawkes* (Boston: Twayne, 1982);

O'Donnell, "Self-Alignment: John Hawkes's *Travesty*," in his *Passionate Doubts: Designs of Interpretation in Contemporary American Fiction* (Iowa City: University of Iowa Press, 1986), pp. 23–40;

Earl Rovit, "The Fiction of John Hawkes: An Introductory View," *Modern Fiction Studies*, 10 (Summer 1964): 150–162;

Anthony C. Santore and Michael Pocalyko, eds., *A John Hawkes Symposium: Design and Debris* (New York: New Directions, 1977);

Robert Scholes, *Fabulation and Metafiction* (Urbana & Chicago: University of Illinois Press, 1979);

Scholes, *The Fabulators* (Oxford: Oxford University, 1967);

Tony Tanner, *City of Words: American Fiction, 1950–1970* (New York: Harper & Row, 1971), pp. 202–229;

Stanley Trachtenberg, ed., *Critical Essays on John Hawkes* (Boston: G. K. Hall, 1991);

Arnold Weinstein, *Nobody's Home: Speech, Self, and Place in American Fiction from Hawthorne to DeLillo* (New York: Oxford University Press, 1993), pp. 213–234;

Michaele Whelan, *Navigating the Minefield: Hawke's Narratives of Perversion* (New York: Peter Lang, 1998);

Heide Ziegler, "Postmodernism as Autobiographical Commentary: *The Blood Oranges* and *Virginie*," *Review of Contemporary Fiction*, 3 (Fall 1983): 207–213.

Joseph Heller

(1 May 1923 – 12 December 1999)

David Seed
Liverpool University

See also the Heller entries in *DLB 2: American Novelists Since World War II; DLB 28: Twentieth-Century American-Jewish Writers; DLB Yearbook: 1980;* and *DLB Yearbook: 1999.*

BOOKS: *Catch-22: A Novel* (New York: Simon & Schuster, 1961; London: Cape, 1962);

We Bombed in New Haven: A Play (New York: Knopf, 1968; London: Cape, 1969);

Catch-22: A Dramatization Based on the Novel Catch-22 (New York: S. French, 1971);

Clevinger's Trial (from Catch-22): A Play in One Act (New York: S. French, 1973);

Something Happened (New York: Knopf, 1974; London: Cape, 1974);

Good as Gold (New York: Simon & Schuster, 1979; London: Cape, 1979);

God Knows (New York: Knopf, 1984; London: Cape, 1984);

No Laughing Matter, by Heller and Speed Vogel (New York: Putnam, 1986; London: Cape, 1986);

Picture This (New York: Putnam, 1988; London: Macmillan, 1988);

Closing Time: A Novel (New York & London: Simon & Schuster, 1994);

Now and Then: From Coney Island to Here (New York & London: Simon & Schuster, 1998).

Editions: *Catch-22: A Critical Edition,* edited by Robert M. Scotto (New York: Dell, 1973);

Catch-22: A Dramatization (New York: Delacorte, 1973);

Catch-22, introduction by Malcolm Bradbury, Everyman's Library, no. 220 (London: David Campbell, 1995; New York: Knopf, 1995).

PLAY PRODUCTIONS: *We Bombed in New Haven,* New Haven, Yale School of Drama, 4 December 1967; New York, Ambassador Theater, 16 October 1968;

Catch-22, East Hampton, N.Y., John Drew Theater, 13 July 1971;

Clevinger's Trial, London, Soho Poly Theatre, 2 March 1974.

Joseph Heller (photograph by Joyce Ravid; from the dust jacket for Closing Time, *1994)*

PRODUCED SCRIPTS: *Sex and the Single Girl,* motion picture, screenplay by Heller and David R. Schwartz, Warner Bros., 1964;

Casino Royale, motion picture, screenplay by Heller and others, Columbia, 1967.

RECORDING: *Catch-22,* read by Heller, Caedmon, TC 1418, 1974.

OTHER: "World Full of Great Cities," in *Nelson Algren's Own Book of Lonesome Monsters,* edited by Nelson Algren (New York: Lancer, 1962), pp. 7–19.

SELECTED PERIODICAL PUBLICATIONS–
UNCOLLECTED:

FICTION

"I Don't Love You Any More," *Story,* 27 (September–
October 1945): 40–44;

"Castle of Snow," *Atlantic Monthly,* 181 (March 1948):
52–55;

"Girl from Greenwich," *Esquire,* 29 (June 1948): 40–41,
142–143;

"A Man Named Flute," *Atlantic Monthly,* 182 (August
1948): 66–70;

"Nothing to be Done," *Esquire,* 30 (August 1948): 73,
129–130;

"Catch-18," *New World Writing,* 7 (April 1955): 204–
214;

"MacAdam's Log," *Gentleman's Quarterly,* 29 (December
1959): 112, 166–176, 178.

NONFICTION

"Coney Island: The Fun Is Over," *Show,* 2 (July 1962):
50–54, 102–103;

"Irving Is Everywhere," *Show,* 3 (April 1963): 104–105,
126–127;

"*Catch-22* Revisited," *Holiday,* 41 (April 1967): 44–61,
120, 141–142, 145;

"How I Found James Bond, Lost My Self-Respect, and
Almost Made $150,000 in My Spare Time," *Holi-
day,* 41 (June 1967): 123–125, 128, 130;

"Love, Dad," *Playboy,* 16 (December 1969): 181–182,
348;

"Moths at a Dark Bulb," *New York Times,* 24 May 1976,
p. 29;

"Something Happened," *People Weekly,* 18 (23 August
1982): 24–29;

"Joseph Heller: The Way Back," *New York Times Magazine,* 12 January 1986, pp. 30, 34, 36–37, 50, 52;

"Yossarian Lives," *Smart* (May 1990): 81–96;

"The Day Bush Left," *Nation,* 250 (4 June 1990): 779–
785;

"What Did You Eat in the War, Daddy?" *Forbes FYI*
(11 March 1996): 98–100, 103–104, 106.

Joseph Heller has established himself as a major
satirist in the field of contemporary American fiction. A
new phrase was added to the American lexicon from
the title of his first novel *Catch-22* (1961). The term
"catch-22" has become accepted in *Webster's New World
Dictionary* and the *Oxford English Dictionary* and denotes a
bureaucratic paradox, having the effect of entrapping
the subject. Heller's fiction continues to be examined
for its use of absurdist techniques and more recently for
its critique of Cold War America. Heller was elected to
the American Academy of Letters in 1977; in 1985 he
was awarded two French prizes: the Prix Médicis
Etranger and the Prix Interallie.

Joseph Heller was born in Brooklyn, New York,
to Russian Jewish immigrants, Isaac Heller, a truck
driver, and Lena Heller, on 1 May 1923. He had a basically secular upbringing, his mother being more concerned with social forms than religious observance. His
father died as a result of a bungled operation when
Heller was five, and his friend and journalist Barbara
Gelb feels that this event caused a psychic wound,
revealing itself in the recurrence of death as a central
focus in Heller's writing. Looking back on the Coney
Island neighborhood where his family lived, Heller has
always recalled those years with nostalgia, and indeed
the Coney Island Luna Park must have had a formative
influence on Heller's perception of comic spectacle and
the streetwise banter of the showmen. In his 1962 article "Coney Island: The Fun Is Over" Heller recorded
his memories of the barkers who created a "setup
where the customer could never win." The confidence
tricks recur on a small scale within different contexts in
Heller's novels.

In his youth Heller was an avid reader of Jerome
Weidman's fiction of New York's Lower East Side. At
the age of thirteen, he briefly held a job as a Western
Union messenger boy, an experience he drew on for his
1962 story "World Full of Great Cities." In his teens he
tried his hand at writing short stories while holding
brief jobs as a file clerk in a casualty insurance company, a blacksmith's helper in a naval yard, and a shipping file clerk. In 1942 Heller joined the U.S. Army Air
Corps and from May 1944 to mid 1945 was stationed
on Corsica with the 488th squadron of the 340th Bom-
bardment Group. He flew about sixty combat missions
as a bombardier, earning the Air Medal and rising to
the rank of lieutenant. The 37th mission over Avignon
proved to be one of the most dangerous and was later
written into *Catch-22* in the descriptions of Snowden's
death.

On his discharge from the air corps Heller married Shirley Held and enrolled at the University of
Southern California under the G.I. Bill, but with the
help of Whit Burnett, the editor of *Story* magazine, he
transferred to New York University. New York has
remained Heller's preferred location partly because of
the tempo of life and partly because–as he wisecracked
in a press conference–the people are so unfriendly.
Heller's first published work, "I Don't Love You Any
More," was an account of a returned soldier, which
came out in the servicemen's issue of *Story* in 1945.
Heller's letters from this period suggest that Burnett
played an important part in encouraging his writing, as
did Maurice Baudin, whose course on short story composition Heller took at New York University. "Baudin
pointed out my faults to me," Heller has recalled. "He'd
say throw away the first three or four pages, and he

Heller during his service in the U.S. Army Air Corps during World War II

was right." Although it is generally thought that *Catch-22* was written entirely in the 1950s, as early as 1945 Heller was considering a novel about a "flier facing the end of his missions and thinking over the meaning of the war." Heller's earliest short stories are characterized by the pattern of satiric realism encouraged by periodicals such as *Esquire*. He graduated Phi Beta Kappa in 1948 and during the following year took an M.A. at Columbia University where his professors included Lionel Trilling. In 1949 he received a Fulbright scholarship to St. Catherine's College, Oxford, where, according to his fellow student Edward J. Bloustein, he spent much of his time working on short stories. In 1991 Heller returned to Oxford as a Christensen Visiting Fellow and that same year was elected to an Honorary Fellowship of St. Catherine's.

On his return to the United States he accepted a post as an English instructor at what was then Pennsylvania State College. Finding the place and the teaching uncongenial, Heller left Penn State in 1952 to join *Time* magazine as an advertising copywriter until 1956, when he moved on to *Look,* and then served as promotion manager at *McCall's* from 1958 to 1961. All of this commercial experience fed directly into his second novel *Something Happened* (1974). Two stories that stand out from Heller's pre–*Catch-22* years as showing signs of future promise are "World Full of Great Cities" (written 1947, published 1962) and "MacAdam's Log" (written 1950, published 1959). The first story, somewhat influenced by William Saroyan, describes the chance intersections between characters' destinies as narrated from the perspective of a messenger boy. The second story deals more substantially with the fantasy life of a retired hardware dealer who finds relief from monotony in imaginary voyages.

The opening chapter of *Catch-18,* as Heller's classic was originally called, was published in *New World Writing* in 1955. The chapter was then extensively revised and shortened. Over the years sections from the original version have found their way into print, and Heller's complex schematic outline for the novel has been published in David M. Craig's book *Tilting At Mortality: Narrative Strategies in Joseph Heller's Fiction* (1997). When the novel itself was on the verge of publication in 1961, Heller's editor decided the title would have to be changed because Leon Uris's novel *Mila 18* was scheduled for the same year. Heller came up with the number 22, which actually captures more effectively the motif of duplication. Despite an elaborate promotional campaign, *Catch-22* was slow to sell at first, faring better in Britain. Some reviewers were openly hostile, such as Whitney Balliett in *The New Yorker* complaining that the book gives the impression of having been "shouted onto paper." One of the problems faced by Heller was the lack of preparedness in the reviewers for the unorthodox experimentalism of the work. Heller attacks not only the institutionalized authority of the military but also the conventional decorum of novelistic realism. Accordingly, his novel could be usefully compared with the works of other dark humorists of the 1960s, writers such as Philip Roth and Bruce Jay Friedman, who outraged their readers by bawdily ridiculing Jewish stereotypes, or with Terry Southern, who deployed an anarchic humor against such targets as evangelism and the pornographic movie business. These works characteristically used urban locations, fast-moving and increasingly ludicrous plots, and a humor that respected no sacred cows. The hostility of some reviewers, therefore, represented their anger at seeing their preconceptions challenged. In interviews Heller has explained how he was drawn to novelists such as Evelyn Waugh and Vladimir Nabokov, who apparently invert the relation between triviality and importance found in other works.

At every point *Catch-22* questions the conventions of the American war novel. It includes a farcical reprise of the lake journey to freedom in Ernest Hemingway's *A Farewell To Arms* (1929) when Orr rows to Sweden. While James Jones used the army to represent the stratifications of American society, Heller uses it to demonstrate the paranoia of the McCarthy era. However, Norman Mailer's *The Naked and the Dead* (1948) daunted Heller by being the "masterwork." By his own account Mailer's novel delayed Heller in the composition of his own work, which an early manuscript draft makes quite explicit: "Now they had just about everything to make a perfect plot for the best-selling war novel. They had a fairy, they had a Slav named Florik from the slums, an Irishman, a thinker with a PhD. . ." Here Heller satirizes the formulaic ethnic mix that went into *The Naked and the Dead* and revises many of the elements in the earlier novel for his own purposes. Mailer's Minetta, for instance, is a chronic malingerer whose fake illnesses are related to the existential issue of courage, whereas Yossarian's feigned illnesses exploit and thereby ridicule the processes of military bureaucracy. Indeed, Yossarian himself embodies one important divergence from the pattern of earlier war fiction. Heller drew on James Joyce's *Ulysses* (1922) in using a nonlinear narrative pattern (his outline is reproduced in Frederick Kiley and Walter McDonald's 1973 *A Catch-22 Casebook*) and in creating an outsider hero. Originally Yossarian was planned to be Jewish until Saroyan's story "Twenty Thousand Assyrians" (*The Assyrians and Other Stories,* 1950) alerted Heller to the ultimate ethnic minority. Yossarian was designed therefore as an "open hero" who maneuvers his way through an extended existential present by drawing on roles from popular fiction, seeking to stay alive by remaining disengaged. Yossarian's role in *Catch-22* is both central and ironic. Most of the characters accept bizarre procedures as the norm, but Yossarian's exclamations articulate a minority voice of sanity amid the prevailing absurdity. The games or routines he plays are the very opposite of playful. His masquerade as a hospital case enacts his own likely future; his dialogues with others repeatedly foreground the one thing they are all trying to suppress—death; and his refusal to wear a uniform represents a final symbolic act of noncompliance with officialdom. Yossarian is the supreme individualist; he refuses collectivism, whether of the army or his country; and the unavoidable physicality of Snowden's death leads him to appear at the funeral naked. It would be tempting to read Yossarian as a rebel hero, but the novel gains much of its claustrophobic power by denying its characters any substantial outside where they can find refuge. Yossarian thus dreams of going home, but in the meantime devotes all his energies to staying alive, and in the process mimics a crazy officialism through circular logic games—inventing a character

to sign servicemen's letters (Washington Irving and then Irving Washington)—and in his perception of conspiracy.

Yossarian's distrust of any official statements figures as the culmination of a learning sequence experienced by Chaplain Tappman, the other main outsider of the novel. By the nature of his post, marginalized from the military hierarchy, the chaplain experiences the epistemological doubts of other figures and paradoxically only experiences liberation by lying, separating language from reality. In *Catch-22* the two main defining roles of characters are either exploiters or victims, and the chaplain clearly falls into the latter category as seen when he is interrogated over a stolen tomato. Heller operates on a premise that the war produces caricatures that necessarily demand different expectations of character. Figures might be defined by their prevailing obsessions (Orr with fixing a valve, Aarfy with his pipe, and so on) or take on a comic identity through their designations. Major Major Major represents one instance as a reduplicated title of rank, and the typographical blank in Major____ de Coverley signifies his status as an enigma to the Germans. "Characters" therefore in many cases turn out to be nothing more substantial than titles, indications of roles, as names that, as the novel progresses, display an alarming tendency to slip adrift from any referents. This process is imitated in the novel's use of names as chapter titles, which gives a deliberately misleading impression of a sequence of portraits.

Virtually the only linear process in the novel is the remorseless raising of the number of flights the men have to go on before their tour of duty is over. This sequence gives the reader one helpful marker in an apparently jumbled chronology, but discontinuity is one of Heller's main strategies to force the readers to revise their sense of causality. Heller's refusal to give any preamble embeds the reader, like his characters, within a sequence of events whose logical connections remain just out of reach. Recurrence becomes only one of the devices that simultaneously suggests familiarity and strangeness. For example, the soldier in white disappears from the hospital in the opening chapter and then reappears later in the novel—or does he? Surely the second bandaged figure is a different size from the first. Ultimately the soldier in white remains an enigma, possessing only the outline of a human figure without identifying features.

Repetition in *Catch-22* is never straightforward. Taking Snowden's death as the prime example, Heller scholar Robert Merrill has argued that repetition tends to be incremental. Each time Snowden's death is referred to, more details are added until its full gory horror emerges. Snowden has been eating tomatoes,

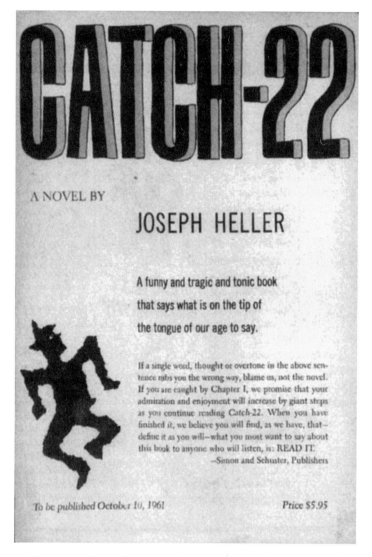

Front wrapper for an advance copy of Heller's first novel (Bruccoli Collection)

which carry the same color code in this novel as blood, so when his wound opens, the contents of his stomach pour out. By a black pun on a quotation from *King Lear* —"ripeness was all"—Heller links this episode with Milo Minderbinder's tomato deals. Milo compulsively commodifies everything, even the humans he has to deal with, so Snowden's death reminds the reader of the human lives Milo's deals erase.

Of course the main sequence designated by the novel's title is a circular one. Catch-22 consists of a juncture between two propositions where the conditions of one contradict or disable the other. Insanity would be one basis for obtaining relief from bombing missions, but the official entailment that this be requested in writing is prima facie proof of the applicant's sanity. The result of this double bind is to entrap

the officers and to preserve intact the obligation to go on the missions. In that sense Catch-22 becomes symptomatic of officialdom's independence of rational scrutiny. As more and more instances occur in the novel, the title phrase comes to represent a sinister principle at work behind the scenes rather than an individual clause. One condition of Catch-22 is that its existence does not have to be demonstrated, with the result that it comes to signal the operation of an authoritarian, if lunatic, administration. Heller's word games and his use of self-canceling propositions ("Yossarian had stopped playing chess with him because the games were so interesting they were foolish") are only two of the many ways in which language is thrown into prominence in this novel. Words determine reality, instead of vice versa. Thus, despite his protests, Doc Daneeka is pronounced "dead" because his name was on the crew list of a crashed plane and a letter of condolence is sent to his "widow."

This self-perpetuating bureaucratic logic is one of the key imperatives in *Catch-22,* others being the profit motive (embodied in Milo) and the need for an enemy. The latter suggests yet another reason why some reviewers were so disconcerted when the novel first appeared. For *Catch-22* presents a hybrid fiction where World War II is merged into the McCarthy era. Heller has stated in interviews, how distressed he has been to witness that the military "retains its enormous influence on affairs in a peacetime situation" and accordingly has deployed anachronisms that make it impossible to limit the events of the book to 1944–1945. The repetition of cue-words like "subversive" by the leading paranoids in the novel, the loyalty oath campaign, and above all the extended interrogation of the chaplain all evoke the political atmosphere of the early 1950s, which was when Heller began work in earnest on *Catch-22.* Drawing partly on Franz Kafka's novel *The Trial* (1937), Heller has stated that in the interrogation he was trying to capture the atmosphere of the congressional hearings; he also found a suggestive similarity between his own novel and Richard Condon's account of conspiracy in *The Manchurian Candidate* (1959). Both novels, he told *The Realist* (November 1962), "are at once serious and at the same time it's almost like watching a kind of burlesque."

This burlesque features prominently in the outrageous activities of Milo Minderbinder. He transforms himself into a grotesquely inflated system ("I'm the people I buy . . . from," he tells Yossarian) designated "M & M Enterprises." This combine represents an expansive capitalism that knows no national boundaries so, despite the war, Milo is constantly flying to other countries to clinch commercial deals, which defy understanding. Milo embodies the boom enjoyed by American commerce in the 1950s, and his "deals" even include the Germans, implying that the new enemy is communism. Milo's activities also anticipate the treatment of World War II in later novels like Thomas Pynchon's *Gravity's Rainbow* (1973), where warfare is presented as a screen erected to conceal the real commercial processes taking place. When the Germans attack the Americans' base, Milo reassures the panicking Americans that it's all part of the "plan." What exactly the "plan" involves only Milo knows, but the military cooperates in its implementation.

For years Heller had been interested in the theater. In his teens he considered writing farces modeled on the collaborations between Moss Hart and George S. Kaufman; when he returned from the war, his interest shifted to the works of playwright Clifford Odets.

He pursued this interest intermittently, devoting his master's thesis at Columbia University to "The Pulitzer Prize Plays from 1918 to 1935." As soon as *Catch-22* was published, Paul Newman invited Heller to consider working with the members of the Actors Studio on adaptations from the novel; Heller declined. During a visit to Yale University in December 1966, Heller mentioned the idea of a dramatic adaptation to Robert Brustein, dean of the Yale Drama School. Brustein was enthusiastic and helped secure Heller a temporary appointment at Yale; Brustein had transformed the drama school into an important location for the theater of protest against the Vietnam War. By this time the commercial success of *Catch-22* had enabled Heller to leave his job at *McCall's.*

Heller's play *We Bombed in New Haven* was first produced at Yale in 1967 and is a work that constantly disrupts the theatrical illusion, the curtain half-rising as if in error to reveal the actors still getting ready for the production. Virtually all the action takes place in an air force briefing room where the Major carries papers doubling as military orders and as the script of the play itself. Heller's plan was to use this device to raise questions about the actors' free will: "Can they break away from the script?" Gaps were left in the script that the actors could fill with improvisations depending on the audience's responses. The play's title links theatrical failure with military combat, and the dialogue moves in and out of different levels of reality (war-as-theater, war-as-game) to prevent the audience ever losing their awareness of watching a stage production. The play draws on *King Lear* to develop a relatively minor motif in *Catch-22:* the relation of parents to children. Major Starkey in effect plays the role of a deity in deciding which figures (always *young* ones) are expendable. The disconcerting formality of the dialogue between Starkey and his son reflects their total estrangement from each other, and in his 1995 study Stephen W. Potts was correctly suggested that the Vietnam War was widely perceived to be a collective betrayal of sons by fathers.

We Bombed in New Haven includes many allusions to other wars, but the common consciousness of the Vietnam War must have been paramount in 1967. By the end of that decade *Catch-22* had established itself as the novel with the most pointed and parodistic relevance to that war. In the play Heller achieves the dislocation of language from reality by having a character declare: "There is no war taking place," only to have his words interrupted by an explosion. At another point a plastic time bomb is thrown into the audience, simultaneously drawing them into the situation of warfare and warning that for America time is running out. As in *Catch-22,* the concept of "enemy" is revised and relocated so that Americans are shown to be killing fellow

Americans. This tragedy is starkly enacted in a scene where a youth named Henderson is shot, partly echoing Snowden's death, and also inverting the traditional analogy between war and sport. Henderson represents the innocents sent to their deaths in Vietnam by the U.S. government. By the end of the play the notion of the script as destiny has emerged as a convenient fiction used to support the continuing operations of the military.

When Heller wrote an introduction for the 1973 Delacorte edition of his dramatization of *Catch-22* in 1971, he carefully stressed the importance of "due process gone awry" in his works, relating this issue to contemporary cases such as that of the Catonsville Nine, who poured animal blood over their draft papers. He saw such prosecutions as being designed to "inflict severe, disabling punishments upon these individuals more for their irreverent opposition to official policy than for actions severely criminal." "Irreverent opposition" sums up Heller's own satirical stance in *Catch-22, We Bombed in New Haven,* and much of his subsequent fiction. In the interviews he gave in the late 1960s Heller repeatedly expressed his conviction that the Cold War had induced the beliefs that communism must be stopped and that American youth would have to die in a war long after any rationale for such beliefs had disappeared. In 1965 he wrote a pointedly sarcastic essay on the Federal Bureau of Investigation's (FBI) bugging of telephones ("This is called National Defence," published 1975). When he contributed to a 1967 collection of statements, *Authors Take Sides on Vietnam,* he was absolutely forthright in his condemnation: "I *am* against the military intervention of the US in Vietnam. It was a ghastly choice, and thousands die each month because of it."

During this same period Heller was working on a dramatization of *Catch-22,* which was first produced in his hometown of East Hampton, New York, in 1971. For this adaptation Heller used cameo scenes with the chaplain and Yossarian playing expository figures and Captain Black a sinister choric role, rubbing his hands with glee as the number of bombing missions is raised. The other adaptation Heller made from the novel was *Clevinger's Trial,* a one-act piece based on chapter 8, produced in 1974. Heller had been invited by the movie industry to write screenplays even as early as his teaching appointment at Penn State. He began a collaboration with his colleague Bernard Oldsey on a screenplay called "The Trieste Manuscripts" about espionage at the end of the war, but the project was abandoned. In the early 1960s he helped launch the television series *McHale's Navy* and briefly went to Hollywood to work with David R. Schwartz on writing the screenplay for the movie comedy *Sex and the Single Girl* (1964). That

experience reportedly left Heller unimpressed with Hollywood, but not as much as his participation in writing for Charles K. Feldman's James Bond spoof, *Casino Royale* (1967). To his astonishment he found that Woody Allen had been working on exactly the same scenes; Heller described these experiences in a comic sketch called "How I Found James Bond, Lost My Self-Respect and Almost Made $150,000 in My Spare Time." Heller wrote two other pieces for the cinema in the 1960s: working on a screen adaptation of his friend George Mandel's novel, *The Breakwater,* and collaborating with Tom and Frank Waldman on the script for *Dirty Dingus Magee* (1970), a Western spoof starring Frank Sinatra.

After its publication, the movie rights to *Catch-22* were bought by Columbia Pictures, who then hired Heller to write the screenplay, but Heller had so little interest in this undertaking that he waived his contractual rights. Buck Henry was next asked to write the screen adaptation, which Henry showed to Heller before filming started. Heller expressed mixed feelings about the script and the finished movie, noting with regret the disappearance of the crucial interrogation scenes, changes to characters, and the use of gratuitous comic effects. On the other hand, he did praise the depiction of Snowden's slow death and what he called the "philosophical weariness" of the old woman in the brothel. Whatever his feelings about the 1970 movie, its release marked a peak in the decade leading up to 1973 when Heller was essentially consolidating the status of his first novel.

Heller's second novel, *Something Happened,* was originally planned to have a much stronger continuity with *Catch-22* than the finished novel displayed. A preliminary sketch published in 1966 under the same title identifies its narrator/protagonist as a former bombardier who has flown missions over Italy and France. These details were removed from the novel, which plays down the importance of wartime memories. *Something Happened* consists of an extended monologue by business executive Bob Slocum, who is going through extended midlife doldrums. One reason for Heller to make these revisions may have been that the subject of the businessman back from the war had already been treated in Sloan Wilson's *The Man in the Grey Flannel Suit* (1955), whose title had become a catchphrase for uniformity in that decade.

The overwhelming emphasis in Slocum's narrative falls on business procedures rather than finished products. When he is asked about his job, Slocum simply replies that he "sells selling." The company where he works is described as a miniature society with its own rules of decorum, hierarchy, and even dress code. Slocum's immediate superior, Jack Green, expresses the

Poster, signed by Heller, for the 1970 movie version of his novel (Bruccoli Collection)

principle of subordination crudely but directly: "I don't trust deference, respect, and cooperation. I trust fear." Slocum's life in the company affects his language, which keeps sliding into the jargon of business reports, and structures his year so that even flirtations are related to fiscal periods. His company is neither blatantly exploitative nor presented through parody. Heller himself explained to *The Houston Chronicle* (2 March 1975) that he "did not want to write a book about economic exploitation," but wanted instead a "neutral corpora-

tion." Heller's novel draws on his experiences at Time, Inc. and other companies in its account of promotional techniques and in its writing of advertising material. Because the company where he works is relatively benign, Slocum is not defined in opposition to it like Yossarian in *Catch-22*, but rather looks to the company for a reassuring repertoire of roles to play. Much of this company's activity seems to be devoted to internal reviews and the respective impacts that different sections make on each other. The novel constantly stresses the company's capacity to manipulate perceptions: "what mattered was what people *thought* was true." Hence Slocum's self-consciousness about his own behavior grows directly out of company practices. His typical narrative tactic is to reverse perspective so that the reader often receives the hypothetical views of the character under discussion. The issue of free will that Heller raised in *We Bombed in New Haven* now figures as a choreographed orchestration of the lives of the staff: "we goose-step in and goose-step out, change our partners and wander all about, sashay around for a pat on the head, and promenade home till we all drop dead."

Slocum would be about the same age as the author, though he comes from a different background. Growing up in white Anglo-Saxon Protestantism in America in the 1930s and 1940s, Slocum bemoans the disappearance of role models like Joe DiMaggio and Babe Ruth, because he has conformed to the paradigm of material success without the satisfaction he expected. It is impossible in practice to divorce Slocum's personal feelings from his perceptions of contemporary America. In a section Heller published separately under the title "From Sea to Shining Sea, Junk" he evokes through Slocum's eyes the spectacle of a nation in entropic decline, a landscape filling with garbage, where spiritual values are displaced by commerce. But then none of these statements can be divorced from Slocum himself, becoming symptoms of his own malaise. One of Slocum's main problems is boredom; in other words, the loss of any purposeful structure to his day. He describes himself as "free-floating," although the term sounds misleadingly positive. The prize of hard work—leisure—has turned into a liability. When the book was published, Heller gave an interview to the *Paris Review* where he explained that Slocum was "utterly unset, undefined, ambivalent." Here again, one of the main differences between him and Yossarian emerges. The latter manifests a comic energy in avoiding the definition of prescribed roles, whereas Slocum yearns for the structure that such roles would give. *Catch-22* parodies the security state; *Something Happened* describes a state of insecurity.

The first section of this novel carries an epigraph from Fyodor Dostoyevsky, and several critics have noted similarities to *Notes from Underground* (1864). Slocum too is caught in a state of "half belief" and, like Dostoyevsky's narrator, constantly leaves his statements unresolved. Contradiction in *Catch-22* was constantly used to block rational explanation, whereas oxymoron becomes the stylistic hallmark of Slocum's ambivalence. He wants to succeed yet ridicules the features of success. Slocum's narration often reads like a sequence of self-canceling propositions. When he is considering the pride and general role of parents, he reflects on his son: "We think so too (we are somewhat vain and braggart about those precious intuitions and idiosyncrasies of his in which we can take proprietary delight) and (like rigid, high-powered machines not really in charge of ourselves) operate automatically to change him." The image of the automaton reflects Slocum's perception of behavior being prescribed by others, a commercial variation on the regimentation characters such as Yossarian try to avoid in *Catch-22*.

Time is one of Slocum's key obsessions. "Everything passes" is one of his catchphrases. Thinking back to one of his first loves, he pictures her sitting under a clock. For each of their abortive encounters, she rationed the young Slocum a few moments at a time; when he remembers her, however, the passage of time accelerates dramatically: "she withers in my mind into what she would be today." Slocum's memories emerge in blocks between which there are long gaps that he considers with ambiguous fascination. Memory is often spatialized in his narrative as primal scenes hidden behind closed doors that open on a series of sexual revelations: his parents making love, and his brother having sex. Slocum has a wife and a mistress and flirts regularly with one of the girls in the art department, but in none of these cases does sex bring satisfaction. It turns out to be an analogue of his job in the company because, as Potts points out, Slocum's "sexual activity is rooted not in passion or pleasure, but in his need to exercise power over others." These others are constantly eluding his attempts to stabilize them through recall or sexual contact.

Something Happened mounts an enquiry into the origins of the narrator's dissatisfactions. The book's apparently rambling digressions make more and more sense as Slocum's main preoccupations reveal themselves. Not surprisingly, his account of things is peppered with references to Freudian analysis, usually with the comically dismissive effect often associated with Roth and Nabokov. In *Something Happened* no effect can be quite straightforward, however. Slocum's double consciousness (self as sufferer, self as observer of that suffering) and general ambivalence make it quite possible for him to ridicule psychoanalysis and at the same time attempt self-diagnosis. One development in his narrative, for instance, lies in his gradual acknowledgment of sadomasochistic impulses in himself; another centers on his representation of his suffering, which reaches its climax when he evokes a private hell: "Vile these evil, sordid, miniature human beings who populate my brain, like living fingers with faces and souls."

For Slocum, both recall and communication in the present become exercises in appropriation. To a large extent, then, the novel can be read as a monodrama where characters represent contrasting or alternative versions of himself. The only member of Slocum's family to be named is his brain-damaged son Derek, who nevertheless is drawn into the role of embodying Slocum's self-image of victim. His daughter, on the other hand, represents the caustic, self-questioning side of Slocum, hence their inevitable arguments every time they are together. Slocum's second son personifies the bonding impulse that draws one side of Slocum to structures like the family or his company. Finally, his colleagues could be taken as more or less successful versions of himself, a view institutionalized by the company's competitive, hierarchical structure.

The literary allusions in *Catch-22* tend to reveal its divergence from the war novel genre or highlight its absurdism. While he was writing *Something Happened,* Heller read Dostoyevsky's works and Beckett's trilogy (*Molloy,* 1951; *Malone Dies,* 1951; and *The Unnamable,* 1953), and the work of both authors had crucial influences on the novel's contradictory narrative progression. Heller also drew on Henry James (particularly *The Ambassadors,* 1903) to shape Slocum's free-flowing style. A specific imagistic echo, this time from *The Turn of the Screw* (1898), occurs in the ambiguous conclusion to Heller's novel. Something happens—probably a traffic accident—and he finds his son lying bleeding by the side of the road. Clutching him in his arms, Slocum unconsciously imitates the embrace of the governess at the end of James's novella when little Miles dies. A protective embrace seems to squeeze the life out of the child and a similar ambiguity informs Slocum's action since he has articulated his "love" for his son at one point as a desire to kill him. At the end of the novel the event occurs so quickly that it gives an additional meaning to its title. *Something* happened, but the reader can never know for sure, especially as Slocum quickly retires back behind the smoke screen of his style.

Good as Gold (1979) partly returns to the parodic methods of *Catch-22* in describing how its protagonist Bruce Gold fluctuates between two worlds: the Jewish context of his family and the political world of Washington, D.C. Heller set out to produce a tongue-in-cheek account of the "Jewish Experience in America" and paints an unflattering but hilarious portrait of the antagonisms running through Gold's family. One member, Joannie, has escaped to Hollywood in pursuit of a movie career and tells Gold that though she belongs to a California temple, they "make it a point never to pray." Each member of the family represents a stereotype, and Gold feels himself infantilized at every gathering. The family is presided over by a Dickensian despot of a father who dresses like a business magnate despite his failure as a tailor. At every meeting Gold seeks approval from his father only to find humiliation. For

instance, when he suggests going to eat at a local fish restaurant, his father immediately queries the idea:

> "What's so good about it?" said his father.
> "So"–Gold declined to argue–"it won't be so good."
> "Why you getting me fish that's no good?"
> "Black," said Gold.
> "White," said his father.
> "White," said Gold.
> "Black," said his father.
> "Cold."
> "Warm."
> "Tall."
> "Short."
> "Short."
> "Tall."
> "I'm glad," said Gold, "you remember your game."
> "Who says it's a game?"

His father refuses everything, even common rules to a verbal game. Contradiction is his typical mode. When he claims to be religious, Gold objects that he is an atheist; but a "Jewish atheist," his father retorts. There is in fact a caustic realism in his posturing. He cuts through Gold's academic ideals, insisting that money is the source of power, thereby reversing one Jewish paradigm of the hard-working father enabling his children to pursue a good education.

Gold's sparring with his father represents the most extreme form of a competitive edge, which comes into his dealings with other members of his family; his brother Sid, for instance. Similarly, Gold keeps in touch with two old friends from his college days—Lieberman, the gluttonous editor of a little magazine, and Pomoroy, a publisher. This trio shares a dream of establishing themselves as intellectuals, but all feel they have missed out on life's opportunities. Gold then is presented as a kind of seeker without the single-minded ambition of the figure who looms large in this novel—Henry Kissinger. Gold plans to write a book on the latter's career but abandons the project. A second, even more symptomatic project he plans is to write a book about the Jewish experience, and here lies one of Heller's main ironies. The seeking, the arguing, the different attempts to merge into perceived mainstream currents of American life may all in themselves constitute the Jewish experience.

Bruce Gold is a study in self-deception. He is constantly encountering figures who try to puncture his social, sexual, or intellectual postures, the strangest of which is an FBI agent named Greenspan who doggedly tracks his steps throughout the novel. In 1995, Potts described his role as that of the "orthodox Jewish conscience," and certainly his main function is a disembod-

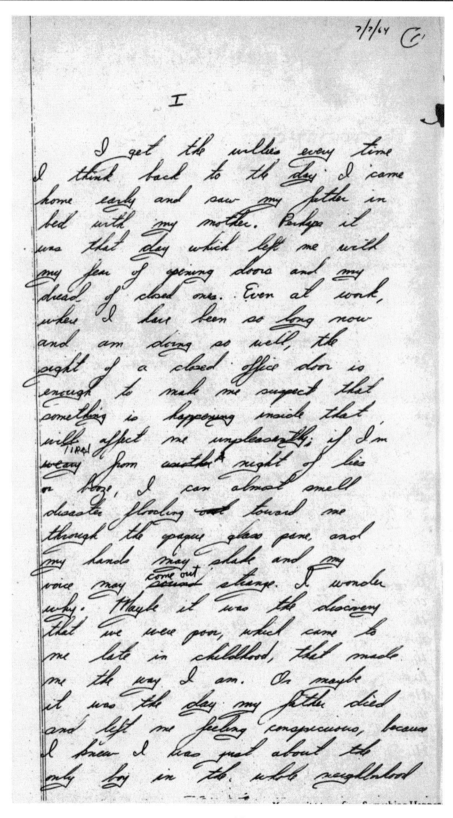

First page of the manuscript for Something Happened *(Thomas Cooper Library, University of South Carolina)*

ied voice urging Gold to remember the moral issues he has tried to rationalize away.

Heller employs comparatively short narrative units to stress the discontinuity between the three worlds Gold inhabits: the university, the family, and Washington, D.C. His verbal register shifts to conform to each new context. Gold's style of speech marks one source of difference. Heller sets up a further contrast of location between the Coney Island of Gold's youth and the Virginia estate of his lover, Andrea Conover, in Washington. Her estate is described as a latter-day plantation ruled by a feudal lord who lays on banquets that include a pig's head on a platter. This is no isolated instance since Heller exploits the cultural symbolism throughout this novel. For instance, despite their antagonisms, the gatherings between Gold's family and friends are communal occasions of noisy shared preparation and consumption. In the Conover mansion, meals are of course prepared by the servants and consumed in silence. Second, food carries the dimension of ethnic diet, usually by default with the Golds, who have no hesitation in eating pork in a Chinese restaurant. Third, food is linked with a way of life that has disappeared. When Gold and his friends squeeze into a small Italian bar, its size reflects the displacement of the old Jewish neighborhoods from Gold's youth. He and those around him are haunted by changes in the ethnic composition of New York, the decay of some areas and the construction of higher and higher office blocks in others.

These blocks tantalize Gold by dominating the city skyline and also raising his expectations of personal success. In the same year that the novel was published Heller wrote an article on American "Inhuman Callousness," making explicit an unpalatable truth that Gold tries to avoid. In the United States, he wrote, "those qualities which are important in achieving public power have little to do with creative intelligence or integrity of purpose." Gold suppresses all the signs of this being the case, clinging to the delusion that his progress is due to personal talent or ability. In order to deny such causality Heller uses three main devices in the novel: running as a metaphor of striving for social advancement, confusions between direction and size, and a play on the rhetorical dimension of names. Gold (like Heller himself in the late 1970s) goes jogging at his local YMCA and implicitly relates running to the achievement of social goals. Such an identification had already been made in Budd Schulberg's 1941 novel, *What Makes Sammy Run?*, the title referring to the tempo of the protagonist's hustling. When Gold collapses on the running track, the event clearly symbolizes the collapse of his hopes.

Heller's second comic device centers on vertical metaphors where rising connotes an increase in hopes, and falling the opposite. The use of elevators is crucial as an extension of the many discussions about social quality that take place in the novel. Gold becomes all too aware of the confusion of values he experiences; after a visit to Andrea Conover's father he wonders: "how much lower would he crawl to rise to the top?" Heller weaves a surreal variation on this motif by literalizing a connection between physical size and status. When Gold meets a Jewish college friend he is astonished to see that his friend has transformed himself into a White Anglo-Saxon Protestant (WASP) "grown lean with rectitude and tall and ramrod-straight with probity." These instances all bear on the social location of the self, and Heller strengthens this issue by playing on names. Bruce Gold, as his two names suggest, stands between two cultural identifications, but when he meets Andrea Conover's father—the very personification of the WASP establishment—he is addressed by a medley of names forcibly reminding him of his ethnic origins (Goldberg, Goldfarb), culminating in the open abuse of "Ikey-kikey." This name-calling occurs at the center of a place of material and sexual plenty and raises the question of how far Gold will compromise his self-respect in the pursuit of status.

The world of Washington where Gold will supposedly achieve this status is one defined partly by the rhetoric of his friend Ralph Newsome, the Milo Minderbinder of this novel. (Newsome promises to "promote" Gold, although the latter does not have any identifiable post; or he will contradict himself, making grandiose offers to Gold that can never be realized. The fact that Heller published a preliminary section of the novel as a news briefing ("Moths at a Dark Bulb") suggests that Newsome is based on Nixon's press secretary Ron Ziegler, who achieved a reputation as a manipulator of Madison Avenue jargon. Within the novel Newsome, like Ziegler, uses verbal tactics to avoid giving out any information whatsoever.

Gold's liaison with Andrea Conover makes explicit the novel's linkage of sexuality with power where neither figure is responding to an individual. To Andrea, Gold appears to be an up-and-coming member of the Washington establishment, while to him she represents the realization of a dream: the blond WASP ministering to his needs. In this and other respects Gold tries to act out a role for himself as a second Kissinger. Heller originally planned to include Kissinger as a minor character, but then he grew in importance. For instance, he is discussed at length by different characters, and news items are quoted referring to him. Parallels are established also between Kissinger's wife and Andrea, all details that suggest Kissinger embodies an

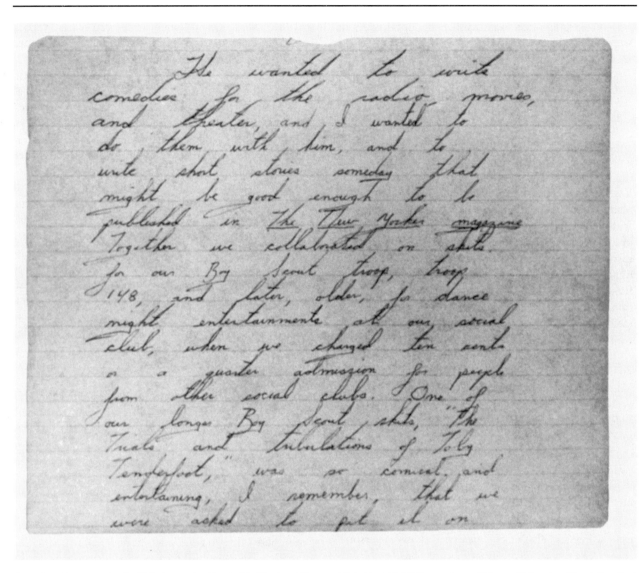

Page from the manuscript for Heller's sequel to Catch-22, Closing Time, *published in 1994 (Thomas Cooper Library, University of South Carolina)*

example to Gold of stature and wealth. At this period in his career Heller, in an interview with the British Broad-casting Corporation (BBC) radio program *Midweek* (14 May 1980), criticized the replacement of an ethic of public service in America with the "apotheosis of money," and the title of his novel suggests exactly this perceived identification of quality with money. In fact, *Good as Gold* implies a substitution supported by the many indications in the novel that America has become a society run on credit. Gold is therefore an absent quality replaced not only by credit, but ultimately by words, which have become the new currency in Washington. Bruce Gold's cynical observations on politicians' use of language unconsciously demonstrates his inability to join this establishment. *Good as Gold* is full of instances where meaningless slogans take on a

spurious significance within the Washington context. Throughout the novel there is an extended play on terms relating to wealth and precious metals, and at one point Gold even dreams while sleeping of transforming himself into a jewelry store. While he was working on *Good as Gold,* Heller read English writers Charles Dickens and Evelyn Waugh in order to apply their methods of caricature, and the allusions to Laurence Sterne's nine-volume work *The Life and Opinions of Tristram Shandy, Gentleman* (1759–1767), help to explain the self-referential dimension to Heller's novel. A phrase that occurs within the text will then reappear as the title of a section, and Heller uses the unifying principle of focusing each section on Gold's own writing. The few pieces he does produce (rather than plan) are either plagiarized or derivative. The novel opens with Gold's decision to write a book about the Jewish experience, but writing for him remains a potential activity. Gold's ambitions shape themselves through the books he will never write.

Heller based his next novel, *God Knows* (1984), on the biblical story of David. Although the book immediately became a best-seller, many of the reviews were hostile, drawing comparisons with the comic monologue, "The Two Thousand-Year-Old Man," by Heller's longtime friend, Mel Brooks. Despite its superficial divergence from Heller's usual preference for contemporary subjects, this novel bears a close thematic relevance to his other works through the related issues of authority and justice. One of the central problems in *God Knows* lies in David's relation to his two symbolic fathers, Saul and God. In *Catch-22* Heller had engaged with this relationship, presenting Major Major Major as the victim of a black joke played on him by his father. The protagonist of *Good as Gold* suffers endless torments at the hands of his sadistic father, and when the death of his elder brother leaves Gold notionally as the head of his family, he is saddled with two parents who reject their relation to him. The position of fathers in the Jewish tradition is absolutely central and bound up with questions of religion and assimilation.

David was an unusual but logical choice for Heller, because in a sense he had three fathers–Jesse, Saul, and God–and lost them all. One of the novel's climactic moments occurs in the sixth chapter, where David's music brings Saul out of a catatonic melancholia. He regards Saul lovingly as a paternal savior–but not for long: "I felt redeemed–now he would be more indebted to me than ever before. I gazed at him in happiness. The next thing I knew, the crazy son of a bitch was lunging to his feet for his javelin and casting it at my head with all his might!" Up to this point in his career Heller depicted fathers as figures of betrayal. Now they become positively murderous. David yearns for a father, only to be rejected. In one of the best reviews of this novel, Mordechai Richler argued that Heller "doesn't so much tell a story as peel it like an onion–returning to the same event again and again." Saul is indeed a figure that David keeps coming back to in an effort to understand his puzzling outbursts of mania. David's attempt to reclaim this father, who is at the same time the king he has deposed, constitutes an attempt to cling to a belief in rational causality; the two tragic events in David's narrative are Saul's enactment of murderous hostility and God's killing of David and Bathsheba's child.

The potential issue of polygamy is replaced by the overwhelming importance to David of his relationship with Bathsheba. Heller considered working the whole novel into an erotic narrative but concentrated the eroticism within specific sections and scenes. For instance, the image of Bathsheba bathing on the roof recurs constantly throughout David's narrative, but Bathsheba exists as more than just spectacle. In dialogues she repeatedly questions David's explanations of his own motives and actions. Even the deity plays a crucial role in this process.

Heller draws on the biblical books of Samuel and Kings in order to dramatize David's restiveness against his divine calling. When a dialogue is recalled between Moses and God (the burning bush episode), the voice of God operates primarily to question Moses' assumptions. Similarly, in the dialogues between David and God, the latter never answers questions directly but makes either enigmatic or skeptical responses. The deity therefore emerges in this novel as inscrutable. Heller has explained that Jehovah "owes no explanation to man for any behavior." He simply *is*. Because his words and actions are so difficult to understand, pious acceptance would scarcely be appropriate to this narrative. David demonstrates what William James would call a "will to believe," but constantly recoils from unpleasant possibilities such as the existence of hell. Dialogue carries a certain reassurance within itself since utterance confirms the existence of the other. After the killing of Bathsheba's baby, that tragedy is compounded by the lack of communication with God: "I could not make sense of the quiet in the universe," David reflects, yearning for a response. By the end of his narrative David has come to reenact the position of Saul after he had lost God's favor. Right to the last, David struggles in his thoughts against the loneliness and isolation of old age.

It has been suggested that Heller's work was continuing the tradition of the Midrash, the Jewish scriptural commentary that constantly revises the original narratives. His inspiration, however, was to an important degree linguistic. It was the perceived values embedded in the cadenced phrasing of the King James Bible that he targets through anachronisms and contemporary speech idioms. The covenanted promise of a homeland, for instance, becomes a series of liabilities enumerated by a patriarch-turned-kvetch: "Some Promised Land [. . .] To people in California, God gives a magnificent coastline, a movie industry, and Beverly Hills. To us He gives sand [. . .] To people who didn't know how to wind a wristwatch He gives underground oceans of oil. To us He gives hernia, piles and anti-Semitism." Heller deploys humor, which diminishes its subjects, especially the status of biblical figures such as Solomon, reduced from a sage to an obsequious sycophant, who tries to copy down David's words for posterity. In particular Heller wanted to question the image of David as a hero-king, which he felt the details of the biblical story contradicted. Accordingly he plays the King James idiom against modern speech styles, revising the action subtly and, above all, undermining the decorum of the earlier text.

Whatever else he does, David is a consummate stylist who presents himself as an underappreciated author. He promises the reader insider knowledge ("you want to hear the real story?") and goes through an extended performance where his earlier self is distanced and ridiculed. David as narrator quotes at various times from William Shakespeare, Percy Bysshe Shelley, and John Milton, for example, thereby identifying his voice as the cumulative modern view, not only of his own biblical story but of other writers' versions of it. The quotations and allusions represent his criticism of those stories; for example, Milton's *Samson Agonistes* (1671) is attacked for its florid rhetoric, whereas Robert Browning's poem, "Saul" (published in its partial state in *Dramatic Romances & Lyrics,* 1845, and complete, in *Men and Women,* 1855), receives more detailed attention, perhaps because it is closer in tone to Heller's own work. The very nature of a biblical narrative presumes a familiarity with its events on the reader's part. Heller's David delivers a strikingly self-conscious narrative that expresses an awareness of literary reworkings.

In December 1981, while in the middle of writing *God Knows,* Heller was suddenly struck down by a serious disease that attacks the nervous system, Guillain-Barré Syndrome, which for a time paralyzed him completely. He later published an account of his ordeal, cowritten by his friend Speed Vogel, in *No Laughing Matter* (1986). Heller describes the worst stage of his illness as a figurative descent into hell where he felt the "mortal dread" of succumbing to an urge to sleep that would be his last. Once he had recovered, a second difficulty emerged: Heller had repeatedly stated his dislike for the factual precision needed in nonfiction. During his illness he was given a copy of Norman Cousins's *Anatomy of an Illness* (1979) that describes a process of self-therapy administered during a disease of the connective tissues. *No Laughing Matter* bears little resemblance to this work since Heller was content to be a relatively passive patient. What was much more important to him was his capacity to speak, which restored his contact with the outside world. Vogel's chapters were written first, and then Heller produced his own. The result is a good-humored dialogue between friends who sometimes give contrasting versions of the same event, and a narrative that also reveals the differences between what Heller experienced and what those around him saw. Death is either referred to in a matter-of-fact way or defused by comedy, as when Vogel writes a pastiche sentimental account of Heller dying in his arms. There are three subplots to *No Laughing Matter:*

the comedy of Mel Brooks's interference with the hospital authorities, the drawn-out legal wrangling of Heller's divorce, and the growing love between himself and his nurse, Valerie Humphries, whom he married a year after the book was published.

With the passing of his illness Heller experienced a new surge of productivity, completing *God Knows,* writing his chapters of *No Laughing Matter,* and publishing articles on his illness. In addition he started his next novel, *Picture This* (1988), which has proved more difficult to assess than any of his other works. The book has a double subject—Rembrandt and seventeenth-century Dutch culture, and the history of Athens from the Peloponnesian War (431–404 B.C.) to the death of Socrates (399 B.C.). Structurally the two periods are linked by an artifact—Rembrandt's painting *Aristotle Contemplating a Bust of Homer* (1653). From Gary Schwartz's 1985 biography, *Rembrandt: His Life, His Paintings,* Heller took the model of tracing out the painter's relation to patrons. He drew also on Simon Schama's massive book *The Embarrassment of Riches: An Interpretation of Dutch Culture in the Golden Age* (1987), which relates painting and other cultural activities to the newly independent Netherlands' desire for self-legitimation. (The Netherlands' independence from Spanish rule was enacted by the Treaty of Westphalia in 1648.)

Heller has stated he intended his new work to sound "more like a lecture than a written work," and when he supplies a brief biography of Rembrandt, he is careful to show how the artist's life becomes subsumed by the developing fortunes of his country. For Heller the dominant factor in Rembrandt's life is money; even his marriage is presented as the prelude to a series of financial negotiations. One sign of the commercial rise of the Netherlands is that paintings become commodified into valuable objects. Drawing partly on John Lothrop Motley's *Rise of the Dutch Republic: A History* (1856), which is quoted directly, Heller questions the idealized image of a "golden age" in Dutch history by reminding the reader of the negative side to this prosperity and by bringing out the contradictions within the culture—the poverty of the textile workers in Leiden, the subjugation of the East Indies, and so forth. The Dutch, for instance, forbade domestic slavery but willingly shipped slaves to their South American plantations.

Rembrandt is used as a figure to link the socioeconomic context of his culture to issues of representation. Chapter 21 in particular raises questions about Rembrandt's portrait by setting up a dialogue between the painter and his subject Aristotle. When the latter states, "I'm enquiring about this painting of me," Rembrandt replies, "It's not of you. It's a painting of Aristotle," thereby drawing a distinction between Aristotle the

Dust jacket for Heller's novelistic meditation on death

man and Aristotle the cultural icon. Heller juxtaposes such exchanges with the information that the paintings of one of Rembrandt's pupils are selling better than his own. Similarly, in representational terms Aristotle has become "Aristotle," a cultural figure reified by portraits and writings, just as David had taken shape from his descriptions in *God Knows*. With the recession of the original subject a representation can take on a quality of its own. Heller was familiar with the discussion of mimesis in Aristotle's *Poetics* as he implies in *Picture This:* "the painting of which he and Homer were part was much more than an imitation. It had a character uniquely its own, with no prior being, not even in Plato's realm of ideas." For one thing, the painting depicts a human figure contemplating a representation of another artist. It is thus a representation of a representation. Heller's imagination is vocal by nature, giving voice to rival attitudes and points of view. *Picture This* can be taken as a comic refutation of the position advanced in Plato's *Phaedrus* where the reader is told that paintings "maintain a solemn silence." Heller gives Aristotle a voice in order to dramatize the interaction

between artifacts and to question presumptions of a simple correspondence between originals and their artistic representations.

Heller links the Netherlands to ancient Greece as two cultures thriving on imperial conquest. In the Greek sections of *Picture This* Heller displays clear sympathy for Aristophanes' irreverent parodies and targets figures like the demagogue Cleon as if he were a Cold War hawk fighting against "subversion." In the block of chapters dealing with the Peloponnesian War, Alcibiades is portrayed as another manipulator of rhetoric, this time a self-seeking moralizer. But the Greek chapters are overwhelmingly dominated by a stark contrast between Aristotle and Plato: "Plato had his head in the clouds and his thoughts in the heavens . . . Aristotle had his feet on the ground and his eyes everywhere." By using contemporary terms like "gulag" out of context, Heller encourages the reader to compare historical periods, especially ancient Greece, the seventeenth-century Netherlands, and the periods of Nazism and the Cold War. Chapter 11 ("The Rise of the Dutch Republic") makes this process most explicit, using side-by-side examples of Cold War rhetoric, allusions to Hitler's speeches, and again a description of Cleon. Rembrandt's painting then functions rather like the protagonist of a picaresque narrative traversing history and revealing fluctuations in the art market.

One of the problems reviewers had with *Picture This* was how to classify it. The book moves across genres in engaging with its subject, resembling a history at one point, a novel at another. Most startlingly, Heller uses substantial quotations from classical works by Plato, Diogenes Laertius, and Thucydides. This practice is more common in twentieth-century epics than in prose, but Heller never merely transcribes the original. Selection, paraphrase, and verbal revision are all used to appropriate these works for Heller's purposes. For instance, Plato's *Symposium* is condensed to heighten the contrast between Socrates and Alcibiades. As in *God Knows,* Heller wants the reader to attend to issues more implicit in the original narratives. Again and again he returns to the importance of rhetorical manipulation in totalitarian politics (demonstrating considerable skepticism toward democracy) and to the vulnerability of law to exploitation (the trial of Socrates is a set piece).

Closing Time (1994) was publicized as the long-awaited sequel to *Catch-22;* though it continues and revises many motifs from the earlier novel, the new work replaces a uniform absurdism with a mixed mode, combining satire with surrealism. Heller focuses on different dimensions of time, especially in relation to the ultimate ending of death. To highlight the latter theme, the cover of the first edition portrayed black figures silhouetted in the dance of death. The novel is saturated with references to time and repeatedly privileges the act of remembering, starting from the opening chapter, where Sammy Singer, a wartime friend of Yossarian's, looks back through old photographs and mementos. For the main characters of *Closing Time,* most things have already happened. Sammy remembers his grandfather being mocked for his World War I regalia, but the novel positions itself, partly through Sammy's memories, at an historical moment where the generation that has lived through World War II–Heller's own, in other words–is on the verge of extinction. The more recent war will also recede into an anonymous past; "soon . . . there will be no more of us left," Sammy reflects. Time is valued as a rare commodity about to run out.

Remembering, in *Closing Time,* is either collaborating, as when old wartime friends meet up again, or reminiscing to the reader as if to a familiar companion. In this way the reader is drawn into the circle of Yossarian's friends, who themselves describe collective experiences from their youth, such as collecting bottles or playing games at Coney Island. Two of these characters play important roles in defining one of the novel's main themes–that of illness. Lew Rabinowitz is the son of a salvage dealer, a giant of a man who, according to his wife, hungered for everything American. Lew witnesses and experiences illness, succumbing finally to cancer; whereas his friend Sammy Singer loses his wife to the same disease. Because Lew has narrated his own memories before his death, his wife's recall of his physical vitality becomes a particularly moving section of the novel, as does Sammy's extended monologue in book 10 on his own dead wife. Since Lew dies within the present of the novel, the reader experiences his death as a loss far more immediate than if Lew had been merely a subject of reference. From *Catch-22* onward, Heller's fiction had focused on individual deaths. In *Closing Time* the emphasis falls more on the common fate of all the characters.

By creating a continuity between the events of *Catch-22* and the present of the new novel, Heller writes into *Closing Time* the reader's implied knowledge of the earlier work, and also of both novels' authorship. So a minor character called "Joey Heller" figures as a one-time friend to some of the leading figures who are held together by common memories. Heller is careful to mix fact and fiction to suggest that memory expands from the individual consciousness into a cultural pool where authors and their characters jostle each other on a common level of reality. This idea is made quite explicit in one of the novel's many divergences from realism where Yossarian descends into the underground region of the dead and meets William Saroyan and Ernest Hemingway, authors who influenced Heller's early works. When a friend of Sammy's looks back on the war, his contacts include Kurt Vonnegut. Perhaps as a gesture of friendship to Vonnegut, Heller includes Lew's account of living through the Dresden firebombing, thereby reenacting the narrative of Billy Pilgrim in *Slaughterhouse-5*. The description heightens Lew's consciousness of the individual's insignificance within historical events: "They were dead in the street, burned black into stubs and turned brown by the ash still dropping from the layers of smoke going up everywhere." The reduction of humans to inert matter recalls less gorily the deaths of Snowden and Kid Sampson in *Catch-22,* this time making the remains into an emblem of mortality that anticipates the apocalyptic finale of the novel. Heller's incorporation of *Slaughterhouse-5* was strategic because Vonnegut was also addressing the necessity of keeping alive memories of a key event in World War II. Written during the anti-Vietnam protests, *Slaughterhouse-5* describes the difficulty of writing a war novel without simply repeating earlier treatments in fiction and motion pictures. Heller repeats Vonnegut's use of the Dresden bombing as an event overshadowed by Hiroshima.

There are two key locations in *Closing Time:* Coney Island (the place of the past) and New York. Heller commemorates the Coney Island Luna Park through its historical presiding genius, George C. Tilyou, who is described as an orchestrator of "collaborative pretense," building a "Steeplechase which wasn't a steeplechase, an artist of the fairground who created devices for the comic discomfiture of his customers." Tilyou stands at the opposite extreme to all the manipulators in Heller's novel, whether they are politicians, lawyers, or businessmen, because his means were so concrete and immediately visible like his rollercoaster and hall of mirrors. *Closing Time* takes as one of its premises the continuing existence of figures after their death, and Tilyou is no exception. Although his Luna Park burned down long ago, Tilyou's consciousness persists in the novel, albeit underground, where he has constructed a model of his previous structure in miniature. Tilyou then focuses Heller's nostalgia for a lost world. Even while he was alive, he represented the imminent demise of a "gilded age."

Heller layers vertical space in this novel to suggest that the past is not irretrievable. Tilyou's yellow house still exists in the "tunnel" of his afterlife, whereas on the surface (in the present) it has become a vacant site. Extrapolating on the concept of death being "in the earth," underground represents the location of past places and people, transformed through memory. In this way the novel counteracts time as a process of erasure literally wiping out landmarks. Spatial layering is also used to depict the extreme contrasts of wealth and poverty in New York. Yossarian, now a prosperous executive, lives in a high-rise block of luxury apartments well above the growing squalor of the streets, which concentrate most graphically in the Port Authority bus terminal. Heller uses Yossarian as a witness to social decay, taking the terminal symbolically as the culture's end point. Descriptions of this location draw on the Rome section of *Catch-22,* ironically presenting the underside of America's supposed national prosperity in peacetime.

Like Dante's Inferno, this location is layered through levels accessed through emergency stairwells, the upper ones becoming constantly clogged by the traces of human activity: "the maintenance men had been through with their hoses and face masks to clean away the messes of excrement, trash, and garbage left the night before, the charred matchsticks and empty vials from dope, the soda cans, needles, wine bottles, and used condoms and old Band-Aids. The astringent smell of caustic disinfectant hung ineradicably in the air like the carbolic harbinger of a remorseless decay." Yossarian is guided through such scenes by a terminal official who takes him through the concealed door in the

back of a closet down deeper and deeper below street level. His vertiginous descent leaves social observation behind, taking him into what appears to be an enormous nuclear shelter. The darkness at these depths and the visual obscurity of the place disorient Yossarian and the reader into admitting fantastic possibilities, such as the existence of an underground monster. The latter is "explained," equally fantastically, as a recording of a "ferocious and petrifying bedlam of piercing barks and deafening roars" triggered automatically to terrify intruders. These levels can be understood as representing dimensions of time from street level (squalid present), through the nuclear shelter (Cold War), down to unspecified depths, where figures from the historical past circulate as simulacrums on a reconstituted rollercoaster. As he descends, Yossarian notes the absence of sound and shadows and catches fleeting glimpses of objects; just as in the Rome section of *Catch-22,* he registers snapshot images of random violence; and these objects displace him from commonsense presumptions of a stable reality: "They had come out of nowhere and gone away someplace, and he had the unearthly sense that he had only to think of an object to bring it into an unreal reality before him."

Part of Yossarian's descent involves the discovery of what is apparently a secret, deep-level nuclear shelter, and this discovery bears on a political continuity between *Catch-22* and *Closing Time.* In the latter novel the reader is told: "the cold war was over and there was still no peace on earth." *Catch-22* recurs again in the Freedom of Information Act, which prescribes that government agencies are compelled to release information except for the information they do not want to be released; so when Yossarian receives his FOIA file, he finds all the pages blackened out. Far from guaranteeing freedom, the agency simply confirms institutional secrecy. The world of *Closing Time* is just as paranoid as that of *Catch-22,* the difference being that it is now Yossarian's lawyer, Gaffney, who seems to have contacts everywhere. "You know enough to be God," Yossarian exclaims to him, and it is through Gaffney the reader learns how routine surveillance has become in this society. Gaffney not only points out the ubiquity of bugs; he also embodies the culture of surveillance by constantly changing disguises, and presiding over a labyrinthine network of front companies. Gaffney claims to know everything, but his knowledge is based on a premise that officialdom is infallible: "the records never lie," he insists to Yossarian.

Although the Cold War has ended, surveillance has evidently increased, and the arms business proves to be alive and well. Chaplain Tappman is brought back into the novel once again to play out the role of victim. Ironically, because he tried to contact Yossarian

University of South Carolina President John Palms, Heller, and USC Dean of Libraries George Terry at the F. Scott Fitzgerald Centenary banquet in Columbia, South Carolina, 1996 (photograph by Michael Rogers)

under the Freedom of Information Act, he is "spirited away" by secret service once it is discovered that he is passing heavy water and emitting tritium gas in his flatulence. Since both substances are priceless in their applications to nuclear weapons, the hapless chaplain becomes reified into a military-industrial commodity under constant scrutiny. Like a radioactive isotope, he is transported around the country in a sealed lead-lined train, a paradoxical "man of God who might be developing within himself the thermonuclear capability for the destruction of life on the planet." The chaplain becomes the centerpiece of the "Wisconsin Project," a fantasy repetition of the Manhattan Project, presided over by the long-dead former security head, General Groves.

The second arms project of the novel centers on Milo Minderbinder, who plays a central role in procuring funds for a top-secret plane resembling the Stealth bomber, a "weapon for the close of the century." This plane constitutes the ultimate absent referent in the novel. It represents a "projection" that takes on specifics from the ridiculous language of the planning group. It is a plan that paradoxically will do it its job "yesterday," unlocatable in time. When Milo hisses "Shhh" at the others, this sound—as befits a silent plane—becomes the name of the project. When a character raises the question of "angles" on the plane, he is told that all parts will

be rounded. The plane therefore has only a verbal existence and, true to the continuing mind-set of the planners, it does not ultimately matter whether it works or even exists, because "its chief value is to deter." Milo's main rival for this project is Dr. Harold Strangelove, a master strategist who encourages the administration to continue to function in opposition to an unnamed enemy. Milo illustrates the overlap between politics, the military, and business, symbolized in the Washington MASSPOB building (Military Affairs Special Secret Projects Office Building), where a successful shopping center is sandwiched between higher and lower levels, floors to which only the authorized have access. Like William Gaddis in his 1975 novel *JR*, Heller demonstrates for the reader an awareness of the capacity for money to be "manufactured out of nothing," and, even more strikingly, the novel confirms the persistence of vested interests where Cold War enemies have to be invented to justify expenditure on arms projects. The rivalry between Milo and Strangelove evaporates when they "blend" together in a bizarre form of corporate merger.

Both projects are ultimately directed toward death, which is the central theme of *Closing Time*. It is no coincidence that Yossarian's favorite author is Thomas Mann, who perceived so clearly where the "ungovernable machinery" of civilization was heading. Two of

Mann's works are referred to: *Doctor Faustus* (1948), which makes an historical analysis of the irrational in recent history, culminating in Nazism (Yossarian's own perception is more succinct: "Nothing made sense."); and *Death in Venice* (1925) because Yossarian identifies with Gustav Ashenbach, the anachronistic protagonist ("he and his era were coming to a close") whose death goes unnoticed as an anticlimax.

Heller's climactic set piece in the novel orchestrates a wedding between two of the richest American families (the "Wedding of the Close of the Century") as a preapocalyptic spectacle of lavish consumption. The bus terminal is taken over and converted into simulations of Versailles and of itself, with actors playing hustlers. This *Satyricon* resembles F. Scott Fitzgerald's *Gatsby* dinners in the sheer quantity of consumables: the wedding cake, for instance, is a "wondrous monument of whipped cream, spun sugar, innumerable icings," so high that it needs acrobats to cut it. The term "monument" is pointedly used here, because nothing could be less permanent. The reception is shown to be a spectacle instantly converted into news media reports where the participants come to see and be seen, but without any consciousness of time. Once again, Yossarian acts as commentator. He recognizes the analogy between Richard Wagner's *Götterdämmerung* (Twilight of the Gods, 1874), the last work in Wagner's tetralogy *Der Ring des Nibelungen* (1853–1874), and the fate of the revelers, for whom it is "almost closing time." A cacophony from fictional composer Adrian Leverkühn's *Apocalypse* (in Mann's *Doctor Faustus*) makes a sardonic comment on the whole spectacle ("crashing choirs of ruthless laughter"), which concludes with ominous signs of impending apocalypse in the video monitors, where the sun goes black and the ships in the harbor appear inverted.

The finale to the novel is initiated by the one figure conspicuous by his absence from the wedding feast—the U.S. president. Throughout the novel he is presented as a diminished ("call me Prick") and infantilized figure who has reduced the size of the Oval Office to make space for a video games room. Here he plays *Victory in Vietnam, The Gulf War,* and a nuclear war game called *Triage.* Seemingly incapable of distinguishing game from reality, he launches the nation's nuclear weapons and only then realizes that he has lost control over events. Hence the appropriate monologue by Harold Strangelove from a deep-level shelter that everything has been thought of except (unlike his prototype in the 1963 film *Dr. Strangelove*) taking women down with him. The finale consists of a rapid montage of scenes assembling different perspectives on nuclear doom. The contrails of missiles are witnessed from a transatlantic jet "going east into nightfall" when the sun is seen "as gray as lead." Ascents alternate with descents, Yossarian taking an elevator again into the depths below New York, where he sees a train carrying the forms of dead politicians. Even the lawyer Gaffney participates in these variations on closure by planning a novel that would reverse the biblical story of the Creation, running backward from the sixth day. The final note is given to Sammy Singer, who waits for the ending of Gustav Mahler's Fifth Symphony (used as the theme music for the 1971 movie version of *Death in Venice*) and imagines with horror the decomposition of his own body after death. In this finale Heller weaves together different themes on death like musical motifs, ending with a grim final image of the imminent death of civilization before the nuclear winter sets in: "The yellow moon turned orange and soon was as red as a setting sun."

In *Closing Time* Heller partly mounts an extended reexamination of his own youth. *Now and Then: From Coney Island to Here* (1998) completes this process by documenting further the importance Coney Island had for him as spectacle and as an early education against expecting value for money. This memoir fills out the information on Heller's early reading that previously had only been available in scattered interviews. His favorite authors included the humorists Robert Benchley and P. G. Wodehouse, and the realists who offered models for his own first stories, Irwin Shaw and William Saroyan. The memoir also sheds new light on Heller's own satirical interests when he records his enthusiasm for H. L. Mencken's attacks on "hokum." Looking back on his life, Heller quietly identifies a recurring tendency to "stifle painful emotion"; *Now and Then* reverses this denial by his recalling of all those events where he came close to death: swimming out to the Coney Island bell for example, or almost having his fingers sheared in a blacksmith's shop. Heller's memoir completes a process of self-examination that had begun decades ago with personality tests (alerting him to the countless reminders of mortality in *Catch-22*) and periods of psychotherapy. Above all, *Now and Then* reinstates the figure of the missing father who has recurred throughout Heller's writing and who is now recognized: "I know him by his absence." This understated autobiography makes an excellent companion to Heller's fiction, in its commentary on the central themes of his novels and its account of origins.

Joseph Heller died of a heart attack on 12 December 1999 at the age of seventy-six. Throughout his almost forty years as a novelist, Heller used humor and satire to give expression to the horrors of war and to a distrust of bureaucracy and government that reached its peak during the Vietnam War. His fiction radically altered a whole generation of readers' perception of America.

Friend and fellow novelist Kurt Vonnegut spoke for that generation in describing Joseph Heller's death as a "calamity for American letters." At the time of his death, Heller left a completed novel titled "Portrait of the Artist as an Old Man."

Interviews:

Adam J. Sorkin, ed., *Conversations with Joseph Heller* (Jackson: University Press of Mississippi, 1993);

Charlie Reilly, "An Interview with Joseph Heller," *Contemporary Literature,* 39 (Winter 1998): 507–533.

Bibliographies:

Joseph Weixlmann, "A Bibliography of Joseph Heller's *Catch-22*," *Bulletin of Bibliography,* 31 (1974): 32–37;

Robert M. Scotto, *Three Contemporary Novelists: An Annotated Bibliography of Works by and about John Hawkes, Joseph Heller, and Thomas Pynchon* (New York: Garland, 1977);

Jonathan Eller, "Catching Up: An Updated Bibliography of Joseph Heller's *Catch-22,* 1973–1988," *Bulletin of Bibliography,* 47 (1990): 9–21.

References:

David M. Craig, *Tilting At Mortality: Narrative Strategies in Joseph Heller's Fiction* (Detroit: Wayne State University Press, 1997);

Brenda M. Keegan, *Joseph Heller: A Reference Guide* (Boston: G. K. Hall, 1978);

Frederick Kiley and Walter McDonald, eds., *A Catch-22 Casebook* (New York: Crowell, 1973);

Robert Merrill, *Joseph Heller* (Boston: Twayne, 1987);

James Nagel, ed., *Critical Essays on Catch-22* (Encino, Cal.: Dickenson, 1974);

Nagel, ed., *Critical Essays on Joseph Heller* (Boston: G. K. Hall, 1984);

Sanford Pinsker, *Understanding Joseph Heller* (Columbia: University of South Carolina Press, 1991);

Stephen W. Potts, *Catch-22: Antiheroic Antinovel* (Boston: Twayne, 1989);

Potts, *From Here to Absurdity: The Moral Battlefields of Joseph Heller,* second edition (San Bernardino, Cal.: Borgo Press, 1995);

Judith Ruderman, *Joseph Heller* (New York: Continuum, 1991);

David Seed, *The Fiction of Joseph Heller: Against the Grain* (New York: St. Martin's Press, 1989).

Papers:

The largest collection of Joseph Heller's correspondence and manuscripts is in the Joseph Heller Archive, Department of Rare Books and Special Collections, Thomas Cooper Library, University of South Carolina, Columbia. The Joseph Heller Collection in the Archival and Manuscript Collections of the Brandeis University Library, Waltham, Massachusetts, holds manuscripts of early stories (published and unpublished), correspondence, and the manuscript of *Catch-22.*

Jamaica Kincaid

(25 May 1949 –)

Diane Simmons
Borough of Manhattan Community College

See also the Kincaid entry in *DLB 157: Twentieth-Century Caribbean and Black African Writers, Third Series.*

BOOKS: *At the Bottom of the River* (New York: Farrar, Straus & Giroux, 1983; London: Pan, 1984);

Annie John (New York: Farrar, Straus & Giroux, 1985; London: Picador, 1985);

Annie, Gwen, Lilly, Pam and Tulip, text by Kincaid, lithographs by Eric Fischl (New York: Library Fellows of the Whitney Museum of Modern Art, 1986);

A Small Place (New York: Farrar, Straus & Giroux, 1988; London: Virago, 1988);

Lucy (New York: Farrar, Straus & Giroux, 1990; London: Cape, 1991);

The Autobiography of My Mother (New York: Farrar, Straus & Giroux, 1996; London: Vintage, 1996);

My Brother (New York: Farrar, Straus & Giroux, 1997; London: Vintage, 1998);

Poetics of Place, text by Kincaid, photographs by Lynn Gessaman (New York: Umbrage Editions, 1998);

My Garden (Book) (New York: Farrar, Straus & Giroux, 1999).

RECORDING: *Jamaica Kincaid Reads Annie John (The Red Girl Section), At the Bottom of the River (Girl and My Mother Sections) and Lucy (Excerpts),* Columbia, Mo., American Audio Prose Library, AAPL 11021, 1991.

OTHER: Mariana Cook, *Generations of Women: In Their Own Words,* introduction by Kincaid (San Francisco: Chronicle Books, 1998);

My Favorite Plant: Writers and Gardeners on the Plants They Love, edited, with an introduction, by Kincaid (New York: Farrar, Straus & Giroux, 1998; London: Vintage, 1999).

SELECTED PERIODICAL PUBLICATIONS–
UNCOLLECTED: "West Indian Weekend," by Kincaid and George W. S. Trow, *New Yorker,* 50 (30 September 1974): 30–31;

Jamaica Kincaid (photograph © by Marianna Cook; from the dust jacket for The Autobiography of My Mother, *1996)*

"Jamaica Kincaid's New York," *Rolling Stone,* no. 249 (6 October 1977): 70–73;

"Antigua Crossings: A Deep and Blue Passage on the Caribbean Sea," *Rolling Stone* (29 June 1978): 48–50;

"Ovando," *Conjunctions,* 14 (1989): 75–83;

"On Seeing England for the First Time," *Harper's,* 283 (August 1991): 13–17;

"Flowers of Evil," New Yorker, 68 (5 October 1992): 154–159;

"A Fire by Ice," *New Yorker,* 69 (22 February 1993): 64–67;

"Song of Roland," *New Yorker,* 69 (12 April 1993): 94–98;

"Alien Soil," *New Yorker,* 69 (21 June 1993): 47–51;

"This Other Eden," *New Yorker,* 69 (23–30 August 1993): 69–73;

"Putting Myself Together," *New Yorker,* 71 (20–27 February 1995): 93–94, 98, 100–101;

"In Roseau," *New Yorker,* 71 (17 April 1995): 92–99;

"Homemaking," *New Yorker,* 71 (16 October 1995): 54–64;

"The Flowers of Empire," *Harper's,* 292 (April 1996): 28–31;

"Looking at Giverney: A Walk Through Monet's Elusive Landscape," *Architectural Digest,* 55 (November 1998): 138, 142, 148;

"Those Words That Echo . . . Echo . . . Echo Through Life," *New York Times,* 7 June 1999, p. E1.

"The space between the idea of something and its reality is always wide and deep and dark," Jamaica Kincaid writes in the essay "On Seeing England for the First Time" (1991). And it is this space, which "starts out empty . . . but rapidly becomes filled up with obsession or desire or hatred or love–sometimes all of these things," that the West Indian American author has insisted on inhabiting throughout her literary career. Whether she is writing about the loss of a mother's love, the cruelty and narcissism of the colonial environment, her brother's death from AIDS, or the plants in her garden, Kincaid holds in solution a sense of endless loss and betrayal that is complicated by a love for the betrayer. This love, once inculcated in the trusting young heart, can never truly die, despite what one may later learn. In inhabiting this space, Kincaid has made herself a rare, one-woman monument, not only to the legacy of European conquest and domination of the world's places and peoples but also to the immense paradox of that legacy. While her work has always been critically acclaimed–her nonfiction book, *My Brother* (1997), was nominated for the National Book Award– Kincaid has at the same time, through her insistence on the paradox of her experience, managed to get under the skin of people on all points of the political spectrum. Reviewing the 1988 essay *A Small Place,* the *New Statesman and Society* (7 October 1988) excoriated Kincaid's "inexplicable" descent into a "sniveling attack on the sins of the nasty–and long-departed colonial power" that had dominated her West Indian home of Antigua. Her *New Yorker* colleagues were upset to see portrayals that paralleled their own lives in Kincaid's *Lucy* (1990), a novel that explores the experiences of a young West Indian au pair in the home of upper-middle-class Manhattanites. The characters are composites, Kincaid

responded in a 1990 *New York Times Magazine* interview, but she added, "I would never say I wouldn't write about an experience I've had." Audrey Edwards of *Essence* magazine asked in 1991 whether her marriage to a white man, Allen Shawn, son of *New Yorker* editor William Shawn, was a "contradiction." "I'm a person," Kincaid answered. "Not a political entity." And in a 1997 *Mother Jones* interview, Marilyn Snell asked Kincaid to explain her "insistence on provocation and unpleasantries." "I don't know how to say this without sounding pompous," Kincaid replied. "Why this insistence on the truth?"

While none of Kincaid's fiction can be formally described as autobiographical, it is clear from her remarks that all of her work, both fiction and nonfiction, is based on the personal odyssey of a girl born 25 May 1949 on the tiny island of Antigua as Elaine Potter Richardson, daughter of Annie Richardson and a father she did not know. She was raised by her mother and her stepfather, a carpenter. When she was nine, the first of her three brothers was born, and Richardson felt expelled from the "paradise" of her mother's love, as she recounts in her first novel, *Annie John* (1985). At about the same time, she became aware of the islanders' subservience to the British, a status she questioned but that others seemed to accept. Though exceptionally bright, she began to be considered a problem in school; as punishment she was forced to memorize long passages of John Milton's *Paradise Lost* (1667), a work she later credited with first suggesting the subversive idea that one may rebel against even overwhelming power.

The children were drilled in English history and literature until, as Kincaid writes, "On Seeing England for the First Time": "England was to be our source of myth and the source from which we got our sense of reality, our sense of what was meaningful, our sense of what was meaningless–and much about our own lives and much about the very idea of us headed that list." Although Kincaid later saw that the colonial education constituted an "erasure" of her own identity, which was replaced by a love of all things British, her childhood love of English literature was intense, and she became a voracious reader. This fascination with books irritated her mother, Kincaid recounts in *My Brother,* and when she neglected baby-sitting duties to read, her mother doused all of her books with kerosene and set them on fire. Though her teachers thought that she had a chance at winning a prized secondary-school scholarship, Richardson's mother felt that she could not be spared at home. When family finances worsened, the girl was sent to the United States to work as a nanny and send money home. Her first employers in Scarsdale, New York, were "very nice and protective," Kincaid wrote in a 1977 article in *Rolling Stone,* and were amused by their

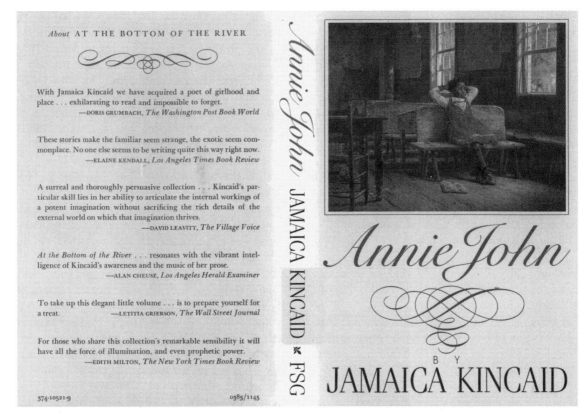

About AT THE BOTTOM OF THE RIVER

With Jamaica Kincaid we have acquired a poet of girlhood and place . . . exhilarating to read and impossible to forget.
—DORIS GRUMBACH, *The Washington Post Book World*

These stories make the familiar seem strange, the exotic seem commonplace. No one else seems to be writing quite this way right now.
—ELAINE KENDALL, *Los Angeles Times Book Review*

A surreal and thoroughly persuasive collection . . . Kincaid's particular skill lies in her ability to articulate the internal workings of a potent imagination without sacrificing the rich details of the external world on which that imagination thrives.
—DAVID LEAVITT, *The Village Voice*

At the Bottom of the River . . . resonates with the vibrant intelligence of Kincaid's awareness and the music of her prose.
—ALAN CHEUSE, *Los Angeles Herald Examiner*

To take up this elegant little volume . . . is to prepare yourself for a treat.
—LETITIA GRIERSON, *The Wall Street Journal*

For those who share this collection's remarkable sensibility it will have all the force of illumination, and even prophetic power.
—EDITH MILTON, *The New York Times Book Review*

374-10521-9   0385/1145

Dust jacket for Kincaid's first novel (1985), which draws on her childhood in the West Indies

young baby-sitter's fascination with New York City. Soon Richardson left Scarsdale for another nanny job in New York City, this time, like the protagonist of *Lucy,* looking after the children of a well-to-do family. The young nanny became interested in photography and took courses at the New School for Social Research. She attended Franconia College in New Hampshire for a time but returned to New York to find her first job in publishing at a magazine called *Art Direction,* only to be fired, as she recalled in a 1988 interview with Selwyn R. Cudjoe, for an article she wrote on black American advertising. She applied for jobs at *Mademoiselle* and *Glamour* but was hindered by her inability to type. Then a story idea submitted to the magazine *Ingenue*–a proposal to ask Gloria Steinem what she was like when she was seventeen–was accepted. The article was a success and turned into a series.

Around this time, in 1973, Elaine Potter Richardson became Jamaica Kincaid, a move she has described as a way of shucking family disapproval of her writing and gaining a sort of anonymity. The choice of name was not particularly political, she has said, just something she thought up, sitting around with friends. Twenty years later in a *New Yorker* gardening piece,

however, Kincaid put the act of renaming into a deeper context, seeing that the "naming of things" is "crucial to possession. . . . It is not surprising that when people have felt themselves prey to [conquest], among the first acts of liberation is to change their names." The name change was not Kincaid's only act of liberation. She cut her hair short, dyed it blond, and wore extreme clothing, apparently removing herself as far as possible from the proper, faux-English schoolgirl in her gray linen uniform.

Kincaid's first journalistic successes produced others, and a chance acquaintance with the *New Yorker* writer George W. S. Trow resulted in lunch with William Shawn, *New Yorker* editor, and an assignment to write her first *Talk of the Town* piece for the magazine: an account of the annual West Indian parade in Brooklyn. The piece was the first of eighty *Talk of the Town* pieces spanning a decade. Even in her first article, "West Indian Weekend" (30 September 1974), Kincaid's autobiographical bent can be seen, as she confesses that at carnivals at home her mother would not let her "jump up." Others pieces profile her stepfather and his love of Americans, offer humorous tips on how to decorate a tiny apartment to make it seem bigger, and comment on a Jamaican beauty contest in Manhattan.

Another turning point came in 1978 when Kincaid, under the influence of the Elizabeth Bishop poem "In the Waiting Room," wrote the short story "Girl" in a single afternoon. The one-sentence story was published in *The New Yorker*, filling one magazine page. Later widely anthologized, "Girl" became Kincaid's first published fiction and the first story in her collection *At the Bottom of the River* (1983). The voice here is quite different from that of Kincaid's journalism. The long, detailed lists that frequently mark her earlier work are still here, along with the minute observations, but the slightly self-conscious tone of a smart, defiant, but careful schoolgirl has vanished, as has any conventional sense of story and direction. The voice now speaks to and for itself, as if in a dream or a deep reverie; the connections are those of the subconscious. That afternoon, she remembers, she knew she had found her voice as a writer. Not surprisingly, the voice she found is that of a mother whose nurturing instructions camouflage the seeds of betrayal. As she related in the Cudjoe interview, the freedom of New York and the empowerment of success as a journalist allowed Kincaid not only to see that her mother was the "fertile soil" of her creative life but also to dare finally to dig into that soil.

Kincaid's breakthrough was not only psychological. It was also the result of an examination of her basic assumptions about writing. So well taught was she in the classics of English literature that she assumed that all literature was created in the past, never imagining that people were still writing. As a result, Kincaid told Cudjoe, she never thought of writing herself. Also, the premodernist storytelling mode she learned from the British works did not seem useful in exploring her own world, one still strongly influenced by beliefs in obeah magic. Here there was no reliable realism, and things and people could never be trusted to be what they seemed to be. Further, Kincaid had come to believe that a directional narrative was almost never an attempt to tell a true story but was almost always a way of creating self-serving lies. But two things changed Kincaid's thinking about writing. One was a French movie, *La Jeteé* (1962), made up of black-and-white still photographs, and the other was the work of the experimental French writer Alain Robbe-Grillet. Both works showed Kincaid that there was a way to write without recourse to a storytelling mode she had come to see as archaic and dishonest. In her earliest work, as in the nonnarrative scenes of Robbe-Grillet, both writer and reader are freed of the need to make conventionally coherent arrangements of experience and reality and are invited instead to follow a chain of subliminal connections to find psychological, if not rational, sense.

Kincaid had not, however, jettisoned all aspects of her colonial education. Milton's *Paradise Lost,* for example, gave her the first notion of what later became her own central theme, the relationship of the powerful to the powerless. As she relates in Moira Ferguson's *Jamaica Kincaid: Where the Land Meets the Body* (1994), reading *Paradise Lost* and identifying with Lucifer "left me with this feeling of [the possibility of] articulating your own pain, as Lucifer did. It seemed if you couldn't say what was wrong with you, then you couldn't act." Although Kincaid sees writing as an act of liberation, she refuses to claim membership in any literary "army." While she acknowledges that feminism has probably contributed to her success, she does not want to be categorized as a woman writer. Nor does she want to be categorized as a black writer. While she refuses to see herself as a "political entity," she also believes that people have to keep their "history" in mind. Of her own history—descending from both African slaves and Carib Indians—she says in *Jamaica Kincaid,* "there was an attempt, successful, by English colonization to make a certain kind of person out of me, and it was a success. . . . I do not spend my present time trying to undo it. I do not now, for instance, spend my life now attempting to have some true African heritage. My history is that I came from African people who were enslaved and dominated by European, British people and that is it. And there is no attempt to erase it."

By 1983, seventeen years after leaving Antigua to work as a servant, Jamaica Kincaid was a literary star. Her first book, *At the Bottom of the River,* a collection of *New Yorker* stories, including the breakthrough story "Girl," won the Morton Dauwen Zabel Award of the American Academy and Institute of Arts and Letters, was nominated for the PEN/Faulkner Award, and was widely reviewed by critics who were often adulatory and always respectful, even when puzzled by the surreal nature of the book. In the ten dreamlike stories speakers are unidentified, identities merge, and fantasy and reality are inseparable. Taken together, the pieces trace a journey of mourning over the loss of a prelapsarian world, a childhood paradise of perfect love and harmony in which time stands still and in which betrayal—including the great betrayal of death—is unknown.

The pieces move through the stages of mourning—from denial, through anger and depression, to a vision of peaceful acceptance. The first four stories, "Girl," "In the Night," "At Last," and "Wingless," deny the permanence of the loss but seek a way of going back, of being once again the child, the infant, or even the fetus in the womb, swimming "in a shaft of light, upside down." The next group, "Holidays," "The Letter from Home," and "What I Have Been Doing Lately," are told from the perspective of one who has left the childhood world but is still in limbo, recording a collection of sensations that do not quite add up to a separate mature identity. In "What I Have Been Doing Lately," for example, a dream journey seems to entrap the narrator in an endless cycle of departure, yearning, and awareness of the impossibility of return. In the final group of stories, "Blackness," "My Mother," and "At the Bottom of the River," the narrator squarely faces the crisis of loss, feeling herself to have been erased, numbed, and silenced. This feeling, similar to an emotional crisis Kincaid recorded later in *Annie John,* is experienced as a "blackness" that silently falls all around, soft and dense as soot. In "My Mother" the narrator begins her actual journey of departure, leaving a mother, then finding what appears to be another mother, one with whom there is a sense of openness, of fertility, of a future, of rooms that "are large and empty, opening on to each other, waiting for people and things to fill them up." In "At the Bottom of the River" the narrator replaces the lost perfection of childhood life and innocence with a mature joy in her understanding of the impartiality and implacability of creation, a force "unmindful of any of the individual needs of existence, and without knowledge of future or past." Creation is still innocent, timeless, and perfectly itself, whatever one's personal loss. Though one vision of light and beauty has been lost, another has been found. With this vision Kincaid's narrator may move on into maturity and into her own life; she may "emerge" from the "pit," "step into a room and . . . see that the lamp is lit," and she may feel her own name "filling up [my] mouth."

At the Bottom of the River was followed in 1985 by the more accessible *Annie John,* also originally published as a series of short stories in *The New Yorker*. The book was one of three finalists for the 1985 international Ritz Paris Hemingway Award, and this time the reviews were almost universally laudatory. In this novel Kincaid covers similar emotional ground as in *At the Bottom of the River,* but in a less surrealistic, more autobiographical form. The book charmed some reviewers with its picturesque scenes of uniformed colonial schoolgirls and graceful West Indian women in big, brightly colored skirts and with its stories of schoolgirl crushes and coming-of-age angst. Behind the book's deceptively simple surface, however, looms an overpowering specter of betrayal and death. While the traditional coming-of-age story traces the often painful journey from youth to maturity, in Annie's world, as defined both by the all-powerful mother and the colonial education system, there seems to be no viable maturity. For in her mother's kingdom—and by reflection in colonial Antigua—the coming-of-age black girl is expected to have only one preoccupation: to imitate as much as possible the white English girl, whom she can never become and to whom she will always be deemed inferior.

It is perhaps not surprising that Kincaid's coming-of-age novel, taking place in a world where a black girl's maturation inaugurates a lifelong struggle to avoid the death of the spirit, begins with an obsession with death, and particularly the death of little girls. What may seem surprising is that Annie does not see death coming to her at the hands of the colonial power; rather, she associates death with her mother, who is often accidentally present when someone dies, who bathes the dead, and who seems to carry death on her hands. The mother has not exactly suffered spiritual death herself, but when it comes to coping with her daughter's burgeoning maturity, she seems to have internalized Rudyard Kipling's "half devil and half child" characterization of colonized people. It follows that if Annie is no longer part child, she must be all devil. The mother who has previously been able to see her daughter as having the innocent perfection of any child now sees the same girl as a liar, a thief, and a "slut" who most be expelled from the "paradise" of mother's love into the living death of a loveless purgatory. Annie struggles to deny, and then rebels against, the loss of childhood paradise. Finally, however, she can no longer hold up against the tide of grief that has been building as she comes to see that the world around her has grown murderous, intent on killing all that is authentic within her. As Annie slides into collapse, grief begins to collect like a "mist," blotting out the world.

The girl is only revived by a visit from her grandmother, Ma Chess, who still commands ancient obeah magic and is oblivious to and untainted by the demands of the colonial presence. Ma Chess sees immediately that the child must be remothered until she finds a sense of self again. "Sometimes at night," Annie recounts, "when I would feel that I was all locked up in the warm falling soot and could not find my way out, Ma Chess would come into my bed with me and stay until I was myself—whatever that had come to be by then—again." Indeed, Annie seems to be taken back into the womb as she lies beside her grandmother, "curled up like a little comma." Annie is revived, but only to accept that she is at odds with everything around her and has no choice but to leave her home forever. Her departure—on a ship to England, where she is to study nursing—is not in triumph, however. In the last image in the book Annie listens to the ship's sounds "as if a vessel filled with liquid had been placed on its side and was now slowly emptying out." There is desolation in this image, which can be read as an image of death, as blood flowing from the body. But it is also an image of impending renewal, for, if the vessel is not too fragile to sustain its own emptiness, the old content is making way for the new.

In 1979 Kinkaid married the composer Allen Shawn, the son of William Shawn, and by 1985 the couple had a baby daughter, Annie, followed three years later by a son, Harold. Rather than seeing a family as a hindrance to writing, Kincaid seems to see it as an almost necessary condition, describing herself in 1993 to interviewer Donna Perry as a person who reduces "everything to a domestic situation. . . . It's not anything deliberate or a statement or anything, that's just how I understand things." The family lives in Bennington, Vermont, where Allen Shawn is on the faculty of Bennington College.

If Kincaid has written herself into domestic contentment, community prominence and literary success, she has also come to discover her own mind. Another thing she discovered, as she told Perry, was a great deal of anger. She was bothered, she said, when people called her work "charming." This anger was expressed directly for the first time in the long essay *A Small Place*. Kincaid withdraws the surreal dreamscape of *At the Bottom of the River* and the gentle, sad tones of *Annie John*. In this work, the writer addresses the reader, whom she assumes to be a relatively privileged *New Yorker* subscriber: "You are a tourist, a North American or European—to be frank, white." An unrelenting attack takes up the first quarter of the eighty-one-page essay. Kincaid shows the white tourist as repeating the pattern of racial and cultural domination begun by slaveholding European colonists. White tourists, Kincaid allows, may feel a few twinges of guilt when they visit a country like Antigua, a "slightly funny feeling" about "exploitation, oppression [and] domination" or the continued relationship of the so-called first world to the so-called third world. This feeling, if allowed to persist, could "ruin" a holiday, and to avoid such unpleasantness the tourist is determined to see the black Antiguans as picturesque objects rather than as thinking, feeling human beings. Kincaid is just as determined to reveal the Antiguans as subjects and to show exactly the sort of object the "incredibly unattractive, fat, pastry-like-fleshed" white tourists may appear to be in their eyes. The tourists may be "nice" and "attractive" people at home, Kincaid allows. Only when they enter into the narcissistic role of tourist do they become ugly; only when they seek to reduce others to objects, to empty others of content, do they themselves become empty. The tourists, she concedes, like the Europeans who colonized the West Indies, would probably be good people if they had stayed home.

The white reader who can get through the first two sections—many cannot, it seems, judging from the reviews that frequently refer only to the first portion of the essay—are rewarded in the second part by an unusual and painfully frank portrait of the postcolonial Caribbean and the way in which the new native rulers continue the pattern of greed and oppression. Kincaid details the shambles that has been made of the island since the end of colonial rule and the awful fear she feels that things may actually be worse than before. The second part of the essay may help explain the ferocity of the first. These are painful matters, Kincaid's method seems to indicate, not to be discussed with people who insist on always acting superior, who are unwilling to be told that white people and white flesh can on occasion be grossly unattractive. It is only with white readers who are willing to shed any sense of innate superiority—as is required to get through the first half of the essay—and who are willing to consider their own continued participation in the domination of others that Kincaid is willing to share her anguish over what she sees when she looks back to her own home and people. The essay does not, as one reviewer claimed, back the white reader into a corner but seeks to do the opposite: to allow him or her out of the corner of racial anxiety and paralysis by showing that what separates people is not, finally, racial difference. No one's essential nature is good or bad, Kincaid writes. Rather, all are dehumanized who allow themselves to be defined in terms of power relationships. Kincaid strives to explain to white readers the incredibly complex effect on white and black of centuries of domination, showing them their own continued participation in a way that may not have been apparent to them before. She also seems to be describing, perhaps to herself as well, the psychological effects and aftermath of slavery and colonialism on the black residents of Antigua. Finally, she writes, only by throwing off the role one has assumed in an environment ordered by power relationships can all people, white or black, be fully human: "Of course, the whole thing is, once you cease to be a master, once you throw off your master's yoke, you are no longer human rubbish, you are just a human being, and all the things that adds up to. So, too, with the slaves. Once they are no longer slaves, once they are free they are no longer noble and exalted; they are just human beings."

William Shawn liked the piece, but it was rejected as too angry by Robert Gottlieb, the editor who replaced Shawn. It was published in book form by Farrar, Straus and Giroux in 1988, and certainly no one found it "charming." Nor did reviewers miss the anger. Salman Rushdie described it as "a jeremiad of great clarity and a force that one might call torrential were the language not so finely controlled" (*Wall Street Journal,* 16 October 1990). Many reviewers, such as Michiko Kakutani of *The New York Times* (16 July 1988), did not find the anger at "Europeans and North Americans who routinely patronized and humiliated the Antiguans" misplaced, but Alison Friesinger deemed the book "distorted" by Kincaid's anger (*The New York Times Book Review*, 10 July 1988). And the reviewer for the British journal *New Statesman and Society* (7 October 1988) appears to have been infuriated by the book. Adewala Maja-Pearce wrote, "Unfortunately the author quickly loses control of her material and inexplicably descends into a sniveling attack on the sins of the nasty–and long-departed–colonial power." The disapproval *A Small Place* met in some quarters, however, did not seem to dismay Kincaid, and she told Perry: "As I go on writing, I feel less and less interested in the approval of the First World, and I never had the approval of the world I came from, so now I don't know where I am. I've exiled myself yet again."

Despite the disagreement over *A Small Place, The New Yorker* continued to publish Kincaid's fiction, and in 1990 five of these stories were collected and published as the novel *Lucy*. While *Lucy*, whose title character is named for Milton's great rebel Lucifer, contains little of the overt political anger of "A Small Place," it is still a work obsessed by the question of how domination hinders the formation of authentic identity. The stories take up where *Annie John* left off, showing the further progress of a West Indian girl who leaves her mesmerizing mother and her Caribbean home, going out to make her way in a new world and becoming the nanny to a beautiful and wealthy white family that seems to present a portrait of perfection until the X-ray vision of the young girl reveals a turmoil that will soon break the family apart.

Lucy's mother predicts that the girl's throat will be cut on a subway if she stays in a place like New York, and Lucy is well aware of the danger present in both of her options–staying in the West Indies, a place where she cannot really be at home, or journeying to a place where she will be a vulnerable outsider. But she refuses to accept that these are the only choices: "In this great big world, why should my life be reduced to these two possibilities?"

Lucy thus rejects the available identities offered by her mother, Antiguan society, and the British Empire. But she also rejects the identity offered by her loving employer Mariah, the American man who finds her exotic, and her employers' African American maid, who thinks Lucy's manner of speaking and acting is disgustingly prim and proper. All of these people seem to offer Lucy a role based on their perception of her place in a framework of essentialized oppositions, whether racial, cultural, sexual, or geographical. Lucy's first task of self-definition is to reject proffered roles, the sense of self is first formed in the negative. Lucy's clearest statement of her new identity in her first year in America is expressed as what she is not: "I had been a girl of whom certain things were expected, none of them too

Dust jacket for Kincaid's 1990 novel, about a West Indian girl who becomes an au pair for a wealthy Manhattan family

bad: a career as a nurse, for example; a sense of duty to my parents, obedience to the law and worship of convention. But in one year of being away from home, that girl had gone out of existence." Lucy cannot say what exactly will replace that girl. She only knows that she is following a powerful instinct to find a self that feels authentic: "I understood that I was inventing myself more in the way of a painter than in the way of a scientist. I could not count on precision or calculation; I could only count on intuition. I did not have anything exactly in mind, but when the picture was complete I would know. I did not have position, I did not have money at my disposal. I had memory, I had anger, I had despair." Like Lucifer in Milton's *Paradise Lost*, all she has left is an "unconquerable will" and "courage never to submit or yield."

Set apart from her old world but not yet a part of the new, Lucy can see the manipulative power of both empire and the "white West" quite clearly. At home she memorized William Wordsworth's famous poem about the daffodil, a flower beloved by the British but never seen by West Indian children. On being shown her first daffodil in New York, Lucy reacts with fury, understanding it to be a brilliantly disguised weapon of imperial domination, subtly and disarmingly advancing the notion that everything English is better than anything found in the West Indies.

While Annie John only slowly comes to understand the hypocrisy of her world—apparent benevolence that is actually based on the assumption of and desire for, power rather than on true concern and generosity—Lucy has a newcomer's quick eye for contradictions. She studies her happy, affectionate employer, Mariah, for example, always aware of the gap that exists between Mariah's desire to be loving and sympathetic and her understanding of what life is like for people less privileged than herself. Indeed, Kincaid's creation of this character tells the reader something important about her investigation of the white world. The threat to Lucy does not come in the form of racists, either crude or subtle, for these do not appear in the work. Even class discrimination, practiced by those friends of Mariah's who see Lucy as merely "the girl who takes care of the children," is placed in the background as a kind of minor irritation. The threat to Lucy and to the self she is trying to create will not come from those who scorn or hate her but from those who possess many admirable and even lovable qualities and who reach out in friendship. In the world of Kincaid's protagonists, the great danger is not in overt hostility and brutality but in being presented with something that one will love too much and, through that love, being lost to oneself. Like a bed of beautiful daffodils, which "looked simple, as if made to erase a complicated and unnecessary idea," Mariah's golden existence seems to invalidate the complication and difficulty of Lucy's life. Conversely, if Lucy's experience is to be valid, then Mariah's simple assumptions must be invalidated. So, as Lucy is overcome with a desire to kill the daffodils to which Mariah has lovingly introduced her, she also demonstrates a determination to demolish Mariah's innocence, to insist that life is much more complex and morally ambiguous than Mariah has yet grasped. Thus, she complicates Mariah's appreciation of the daffodils by showing how they were used to make West Indian children, forced to memorize Wordsworth's poem, love a world to which they could never belong. And she deflates Mariah's simple joy at the sight of freshly plowed fields out the train window as they travel toward Mariah's childhood home on the Great Lakes by reminding her of the historical link between physical labor and domination based on race, remarking with "a cruel tone" in her voice, "Well, thank God I didn't have to do that."

While Kincaid casts the white Mariah as a representative of the narcissistic power against which Lucy must fight if she is to forge a separate, authentic identity, Mariah, in another sense, seems to mirror Lucy herself, the happy child summarily expelled from paradise. In this case Mariah's husband proves unfaithful, and the perfect family is broken up. Thus, while Lucy at first feels the need to ruffle the perfection of Mariah's life, she comes to see that it is not really necessary, that even the "golden" and privileged Mariah cannot stay in paradise forever. As Lucy sees Mariah's life begin to unravel, she becomes less paralyzed by the grief of her own loss. Lucy is able to see loss as part of the human condition, not as a special punishment reserved for those who somehow, like Lucifer, have fallen. If Mariah and Lucy begin the book as gleaming God and grieving Lucifer, they end it as a version of Adam and Eve making their way out of the garden of Eden, sadder but wiser.

The triumph in *Annie John* is the girl's departure from Antigua, even if it is a triumph that is experienced as an "emptying out" and feels more like losing than like winning. The triumph in *Lucy* is the achievement of solitude. Lucy has not only escaped those at home who would keep her in a scenario of colonial or racial domination but has also managed to avoid replacing those left behind with people who would use her in a similar way, however subtle or unconscious their desire to do so might be. It is a triumph for Lucy to find herself alone at last; yet, as with Annie's departure from her island home, Lucy's achievement of solitude in her own apartment in the immensity of New York City is accompanied by an immense sense of loss, the love for the home she has renounced still so great "that I could die from it."

But even if grief may at times blur the picture, Lucy is not, like the girl at the end of *Annie John,* entirely afloat in loss. Her new solitary life may be frightening, but Lucy quickly grounds it in steadying domestic detail. She cannot replicate the beautiful, powerful mother of her infancy, but she can replicate the details of cooking, cleaning, and arranging that were the locus of life and love when mother and daughter were united. Here, in spite of the grief that soaks her solitude, Lucy is, for the first time, mistress of her own home, her own small world. After this world has been set to rights one hears an echo, albeit a strangely peaceful one, of the mother's voice that opens Kincaid's first story, "Girl": "I did all sorts of little things; I washed my underwear, scrubbed the stove, washed the bathroom floor, trimmed my nails, arranged my dresser, made sure I had enough sanitary napkins. When I got into bed, I lay there with the light on for a long time doing nothing."

With her next work of fiction, *The Autobiography of My Mother*, published in 1996, Kincaid continues to explore her sense that the instinct to dominate others, as enacted by the colonial powers in the West Indies, is born in a narcissistic emptiness that sends people out in the world on a mission of conquest and control. It is this fundamental narcissism on the part of the English who find themselves in the West Indies that Kincaid seeks to probe in *The Autobiography of My Mother*. To accomplish this probing, Kincaid creates Xuela, a young West Indian woman who has been born into a climate that is entirely narcissistic but who, by virtue of her mother's early death, has, unlike everybody else in the book, never developed any illusions about the world in which she lives. Unlike Annie John, who still perceives her early childhood to have been "paradise," Xuela experiences from birth a brutal world in which there is no genuine nurture, no selfless love. Also, Xuela understands that the narcissistic demands placed on the weak by everyone in her society are a result of slavery and colonial domination. "That the first words I said," Xuela remarks, "were in the language of a people I would never like or love is not now a mystery to me; everything in my life, good or bad, to which I am inextricably bound is a source of pain."

For Xuela, there is no hope for magical rebirth, no "restoration of lost paradise," as there is for Annie John. When, in *Annie John,* the beloved mother suddenly turns on the girl, apparently disgusted by everything about her, Annie is saved by a substitute mother figure, the magical Ma Chess, a self-knowing, self-loving woman of the earth, possessed of ancient obeah magic, who symbolically rebirths the girl, thus allowing her to go on. In *The Autobiography of My Mother,* however, the substitute mother figure has become the brutal, self-hating Ma Eunice, who is given the care of the motherless child. Ma Eunice treats Xuela as she does her own children, with the thoughtless cruelty that, Kincaid writes, "in a place like this . . . is the only real inheritance." Kindness and nurture, Kincaid claims, cannot exist in the colonial environment. Deprived of the self-esteem that allows selflessness, all contend with one another within the desperate economy of narcissism; all struggle to get from others the respectful regard of which they have been deprived. Thus, Xuela says, "to distrust each other was just one of the many feelings we had for each other, all of them the opposite of love, all of them standing in the place of love. It was as if we were in competition with each other for a secret prize, and we were afraid that someone else would get it; any expression of love then would not be sincere, for love might give someone else the advantage." Appropriately, Ma Eunice loves only one thing: a china plate painted with a scene of the

Dust jacket for Kincaid's 1996 novel, in which a West Indian girl seduces and destroys a member of the white ruling class

English countryside, labeled "Heaven." Also appropriately, one of Xuela's first acts is to smash the beloved object.

Understanding how the needs of those around her result in the desire to dominate others, Xuela is in a position to use the needs of the English doctor, Philip, as a weapon against him as she seduces and then destroys him. And Philip is surprisingly ripe to be taken in this way. Historically he is the victor, but he is also the dispossessed, as an inheritance of conquest has placed him "at the end of the world." With nothing to do but to play the assigned role of victor in a scenario of domination, he has become sterile, emptied out. He, like those who play the role of vanquished in the same scenario, is cut off from any authentic self. He is, Xuela says, "empty of real life and energy, used up, too tired even to give himself pleasure." Since his identity has come to be based solely on his position in an artificial hierarchy, Xuela understands that in defeating her he has defeated himself. Xuela, understanding the emptiness at the heart of the need for power, understands how to destroy him. "In my defeat," she says, "lies the beginning of my great revenge."

Xuela takes Philip "into the mountains, into the land where my mother and the people she was of were born." There she causes the Englishman to become utterly disoriented, reducing him to such a degraded version of his former self that he will never find the will to escape her trap. In so doing she reverses the terms of engagement between those of African and those of English descent. As black West Indians have been taught to adore a magical Englishness they can never attain, Xuela denies the white Philip the love she has made him crave, denying him her magical self, on which, like a child, he now depends: Xuela says, "He grew to live for the sound of my footsteps, so often I would walk without making a sound; he loved the sound of my voice, so for days I would not utter a word."

Philip, who cannot quite grasp that he is no longer in charge, struggles ineffectually to organize and control his world. He cultivates odd plants, captures and observes animals, organizes and reorganizes his books. But, like Xuela, he has nowhere to go, no possibility of escape or rebirth. British colonial power has stolen first home, then freedom, then self-esteem from the descendants of African slaves; now Xuela takes these same things from Philip, denying him every avenue back to himself. His attempts to recall history do not bring him peace, for now "he lives in a world in which he could not speak the language," and Xuela, who must translate for him, "blocks off his entrance into all the worlds he had come to know." When he begins to reminisce about the England of his childhood, Xuela cuts him short, ordering him onto his knees to please her sexually, always demonstrating that he exists only to serve her and that even a nostalgic re-creation of identity will be crushed. Philip dies a "lonely man, far away from the place where he was born," far from anyone who might have loved him. He has been reduced, in short, to the situation in which Xuela has found herself from the moment of her birth.

At the end of Xuela's own life her body is "withering like fruit drying on the vine" but not "rotting like a fruit that has been picked and lies uneaten on a dirty plate." In this conclusion there is some sad triumph. She has not really lived, has never managed to love or be loved. Though she has aged, she has not matured. Her only accomplishment is that, at least, she has not allowed herself to be used. Still, as she looks at the life she and Philip have led and, by extension, all relationships based on power, she must ask, "Did so much sadness ever enclose two people?"

The Autobiography of My Mother is perhaps the most painful of Kincaid's books to read. Cathleen Schine, while praising the beauty of the author's prose, declared that Kincaid had written a "truly ugly meditation on life" (*The New York Times Book Review,* 4 February 1996). To Schine, Xuela, "an abstraction of an entire people's suffering and degradation," was "almost unbearable–without ever feeling real." In a review in *The New York Times* (16 January 1996) Kakutani did not find Xuela a "terribly sympathetic heroine" but noted, "if we are repelled by Xuela's bitterness, we are also made to understand it in the context of her own history and her perception of the history of her island."

In 1997 Kincaid published *My Brother,* the nonfiction account of the death of her half brother, Devon Drew, of AIDS. The third child of Kincaid's mother and stepfather, Drew was three when Kincaid left Antigua for the United States. Kincaid had warned her brother to protect himself from the AIDS virus and was assured by him that "Me no get dat chupidness, man." She tells of returning to Antigua when she learns of her brother's illness and finding him in a decrepit hospital room: "The walls of the room were dirty, the slats of the louvered windows were dirty, the blades of the ceiling fan were dirty, and when it was turned on, sometimes pieces of dust would become dislodged. This was not a good thing for someone who had trouble breathing. He had trouble breathing." The hospital and the attitude toward AIDS generally–there is no real effort to treat the disease, no funds for the expensive drugs, and no support from her brother's friends, who do not visit him in the hospital–seems to represent her home in microcosm as a place that is broken and where there is no attempt at repair. Leaving the hospital, she comes to a "major crossing where there was a stoplight, but it was broken and had been broken for a long time; it could not be fixed because the parts for it are no longer made anywhere in the world; in Antigua itself nothing is made." Despite her proven ability to make things–art, a family, the means to import the AZT that enables her brother's short-term recovery–the author is suddenly pulled into this world where nothing can be made to work; she feels herself "falling into a deep hole . . . swallowed up in a large vapor of sadness." She yearns for the "hard-earned order of my life, my life of children and husband, and they love me and love me again, and I love them."

Kincaid's brother, too, is broken–not just by the disease but by the life he has lived, a life in which he, and other men like him, are "only urges to be satisfied." When Drew makes what appears to be a miraculous recovery as a result of the AZT that Kincaid has been able to import from America, he returns to a life of drugs and random sex, both heterosexual and homosexual, as little concerned for the well-being of others as for his own. He makes no attempt to earn a living or undertake any adult responsibilities but continues to

Kincaid in her garden at her home in Bennington, Vermont (photograph by Annie Liebovitz; from the dust jacket for My Garden [Book], *1999)*

live with his mother despite their mutual antagonism. Although Kincaid has drawn a portrait of a man whose life is fundamentally rotten, she also shows that it was not inevitable that it be this way. While Drew's life was a dead end, and he had flirted with criminality, he had also been an excellent student, one who read and took an interest in the history of the West Indies, even though these things were not encouraged by his environment. His sister remembers, too, how he "crossed a swelling river" to save a dog, his "sense of humor," his smile. "He was not meant to be silent. He was a brilliant boy, a brilliant man. Locked up inside him was someone who would have spoken to the world in an important way. I believe this. Locked up inside him was someone who would have found satisfaction speaking to the world in an important way."

As she is drawn back into the life she seemed so firmly to have left behind, Kincaid revisits a theme from which she has never gained much distance: that of her betrayal at the hands of a once-beloved mother. In seeing the failure of her mother's love for children other than herself, she is able to see the mother in a more realistic light, moving beyond the portrayals of near-magical maternal power in earlier works to the harsh details of parental cruelty: the mother's habit of verbally humiliating her children, which she continues to exercise on Devon, even as he is dying; a moment in the mother's backyard as she indulges in her habit of saying "bad things to each of us about the others behind our backs" and at the same time uproots the lemon tree that the dying brother had planted and that would have been one of the few monuments to his life. Kincaid quotes another brother, the one who broke the mother's neck by throwing her to the ground when she refused to stop throwing stones at him, who said: "Mom's evil you know." She remembers the mother who, irritated with her reading, doused her books with kerosene and set them on fire. And she recounts, for the first time in decades of autobiographical writing, that her only possible avenue to an education was blocked by her mother: "Some time before I was sixteen years of age, I might have taken a series of exams that, had I passed them, would have led me to be educated at a university, but just before all of that my mother removed me from school. There was no real reason for me to be removed from school, she just did it, removed me from school. My father was sick, she said, she needed me at home to help with the small children, she said. But no one would have died had I remained in school, no one would have eaten less had I remained in school. . . ."

At the same time, Kincaid acknowledges that throughout Drew's illness the mother has spent her days preparing food and taking it to the hospital–often traveling on foot through the heat–feeding and bathing her son, dressing him and changing his sheets. Here is the same mother who, as seen in *Annie John,* created a paradise for her tiny daughter, only to turn her back on the growing girl. Finally, Kincaid knows this about her mother:

> Her love for her children when they are children is spectacular, unequaled I am sure in the history of a mother's love. It is when her children are trying to be grown-up people–adults–that her mechanism for loving them falls apart; it is when they are living in a cold apartment in New York, hungry and penniless because they have decided to be a writer, writing to her, seeking sympathy, a word of encouragement, love, that her mechanism for loving falls apart. Her reply to one of her children who found herself in such a predicament was, "It serves you right, you are always trying to do things you know you can't do." Those were her words exactly. All the same, her love, if we are dying, or if we are in jail, is so wonderful, a great fortune, and we are lucky to have it. My brother was dying; he needed her just then.

In her involvement with her brother's death and the life that preceded it, Kincaid revisits her own childhood from a different perspective than that of the young woman who wrote *Annie John* a dozen years before. *Annie John,* and to a large extent *Lucy* as well, are suffused with the grief of Kincaid's own loss and her sense of betrayal both by her mother and by a mythical England she was taught to adore. In both novels the young protagonists take steps toward creating an identity despite these betrayals, but both books close with images of emptiness and the loss of once-great love. The sound Annie John hears as she boards a ship to take her to a new life is that of a vessel "slowly emptying out." Lucy achieves the independence of her own apartment in New York, but the book closes in a blur of tears and the "shame" of desiring to "love somebody so much I could die from it." There is shame because Lucy is not entirely sure that she will escape the degradation of allowing her life to be determined by those who have their own interests, rather than hers, at heart, who would create in her an object on which they may project their own desires, fears, hatreds, and needs.

But as Kincaid writes *My Brother,* she knows that she has not succumbed to this form of degradation. She knows it as she looks at her brother's life with all its inherent promise and imagines the failure her own life

could have been: "It frightened me to think that I might have continued to live in a certain way, though, I am convinced, not for very long. I would have died at about his age, thirty-three years, or I would have gone insane." Part of Kincaid is "angry" at her brother for dying in such a way, for succumbing to a life that has made such suffering inevitable. While few people have written more directly about the way in which whites have sought to dominate blacks, and the way in which this domination goes beyond physical, political, or economic oppression to the deepest psychic "erasure," Kincaid is not willing to lay her brother's situation entirely at the feet of racism–as an AIDS counselor, a "British woman of African descent," suggests. Kincaid, who has insisted on being a person, not a "political entity," recoils at the suggestion and records a "bitter" thought:

> How unlucky people are who cannot blame the wrong, disastrous turns life can sometimes take on racism; because the hardness of living, the strange turns in it, the luck of it, the good chance missed of it, the therebut-for-the-grace-of-God part of it is so impossible to accept and it must be, in some way, very nice to have the all too real evil of racism to blame. But it was not racism that made my brother lie dying of an incurable disease in a hospital in the country in which he was born; it was the sheer accident of life, it was his own fault, his not caring about himself and his not being able to carefully weigh and adjust to and accept the to-and-fro of life, the feasting and the famine of life or the times in between, the fact that he lived in a place in which a government, made up of people with his own complexion, his own race, was corrupt and did not care whether he or other people like him lived or died.

Kincaid has written of her home in other contexts, particularly in *The Autobiography of My Mother,* as a place where a history of slavery and colonialism colors every aspect of life, where relationships are "redolent . . . in every way of the relationship between captor and captive, master and slave, with its motif of the big and the small, and the powerful and the powerless, the strong and the weak." At the same time, however, Kincaid refuses to accept that these ills make up the whole of one's existence, that they exempt one from the broader range of human success and failure. As if to underscore this refusal, Kincaid closes the book in mourning not for her brother but for William Shawn, her father-in-law and a *New Yorker* editor, who died in 1992. For many years, she says in *My Brother,* she wrote for Shawn: "Whenever I thought of something to write, I immediately thought of him reading it, and the thought of this man, William Shawn, reading something I had written only made me want to write it more. . . ." If Shawn, to some extent, made writing possible, then he also allowed Kincaid to undo, methodically and over time, some of the ills of her childhood environment. For, she writes in *My Brother*, "It would not be so strange if I spent the rest of my life trying to bring those books (that were destroyed in her mother's bonfire) back to my life by writing them again and again until they were perfect, unscathed by fire of any kind."

Interviews:

Selwyn R. Cudjoe, "Jamaica Kincaid and the Modernist Project: An Interview," *Callaloo,* 12 (Spring 1988): 396–411;

Leslie Garis, "Through West Indian Eyes," *New York Times Magazine,* 7 October 1990, pp. 43–44, 70, 78, 80, 91;

Audrey Edwards, "Jamaica Kincaid Writes of Passage," *Essence,* 22 (May 1991): 87–90;

Allan Vorda, "An Interview with Jamaica Kincaid," *Mississippi Review,* 20 (1991): 7–26;

Donna Perry, "Jamaica Kincaid," in her *Backtalk: Women Writers Speak Out: Interviews by Donna Perry* (New Brunswick, N.J.: Rutgers University Press, 1993), pp. 127–141;

Moira Ferguson, "A Lot of Memory: An Interview with Jamaica Kincaid," *Kenyon Review,* 16 (Winter 1994): 163–188;

Pamela Buchman Muirhead, "An Interview with Jamaica Kincaid," *Clockwatch Review: A Journal of the Arts,* 9, nos. 1–2 (1994–1995): 39–48;

Ivan Kreilkamp, "Jamaica Kincaid: Daring to Discomfort," *Publishers Weekly,* 243 (1 January 1996): 54–55;

Marilyn Snell, "Jamaica Kincaid Hates Happy Endings," *Mother Jones,* 22 (September–October 1997): 28–31;

Jeannine De Lombard, "My Brother's Keeper: An Interview with Jamaica Kincaid," *Lambda Book Report,* 6 (May 1998): 14;

Dwight Garner, "Jamaica Kincaid," *Salon,* on-line magazine <www.salon1999.com/05/features/kincaid.html>.

References:

Frank Birbalsingh, *Jamaica Kincaid: From Antigua to America* (New York: St. Martin's Press, 1996);

Harold Bloom, ed., *Jamaica Kincaid* (Philadelphia: Chelsea House, 1998);

Keith Byerman, "Anger in a Small Place: Jamaica Kincaid's Cultural Critique of Antigua," *College Literature,* 22 (February 1995): 91–102;

Louis F. Caton, "Romantic Struggles and the Bildungsroman: Mother-Daughter Bonding in Jamaica Kincaid's *Annie John,*" *MELUS: The Journal for the Study of Multi-Ethnic Literature of the United States,* 21 (Fall 1996): 125–142;

Nancy Chick, "The Broken Clock: Time, Identity, and Autobiography in Jamaica Kincaid's *Lucy,*" *CLA Journal,* 40 (September 1996): 90–103;

Giovanna Covi, "Jamaica Kincaid and the Resistance to Canons," in *Out of the Kumbla: Caribbean Women and Literature,* edited by Carole Boyce Davies and Elaine Savory Fido (Trenton, N.J.: Africa World Press, 1990), pp. 345–354;

Alison Donnell, "Dreaming of Daffodils: Cultural Resistance in the Narratives of Theory," *Kunapipi,* 14, no. 2 (1992): 45–52;

Donnell, "She Ties Her Tongue: The Problems of Cultural Paralysis in Postcolonial Criticism," *Ariel: A Review of International English Literature,* 26 (January 1995): 101–116;

Donnell, "When Daughters Defy: Jamaica Kincaid's Fiction," *Women: A Cultural Review,* 4 (Spring 1993): 18–26;

Wendy Dutton, "Merge and Separate: Jamaica Kincaid's Fiction," *World Literature Today,* 63 (Summer 1989): 406–410;

Barbara Edlmair, *Rewriting History: Alternative Versions of the Caribbean Past in Michelle Cliff, Rosario Ferré, Jamaica Kincaid and Daniel Maximin,* Austrian Studies in English, volume 84 (Vienna: Braumüller, 1999);

Mary Louis Emery, "Refiguring the Post Colonial Imagination: Tropes of Visuality in Writing by Rhys, Kincaid, and Cliff," *Tulsa Studies in Women's Literature,* 16 (Fall 1997): 259–280;

Moira Ferguson, *Jamaica Kincaid: Where the Land Meets the Body* (Charlottesville: University Press of Virginia, 1994);

Ferguson, "*Lucy* and the Mark of the Colonizer," *Modern Fiction Studies,* 39 (Summer 1993): 237–259;

Ferguson, "A Small Place: Glossing Annie John's Rebellion," in her *Colonialism and Gender Relations from Mary Wollstonecraft to Jamaica Kincaid: East Caribbean Connections* (New York: Columbia University Press, 1993), pp. 116–138;

Patricia Harkins, "Family Magic: Invisibility in Jamaica Kincaid's Lucy," *Journal of the Fantastic in the Arts,* 4 (1991): 53–68;

R. B. Hughes, "Empire and Domestic Space in the Fiction of Jamaica Kincaid," *Australian Geographical Studies,* 37 (March 1999): 11;

Louis James, "Reflections and the Bottom of the River: The Transformation of Caribbean Experience in the Fiction of Jamaica Kincaid," *Wasafiri,* 9 (Winter 1988–1989): 15–17;

Bénédicte Ledent, "Voyages into Otherness: Cambridge and *Lucy*," *Kunapipi*, 14, no. 2 (1992): 53–63;

Kristen Mahlis, "Gender and Exile: Jamaica Kincaid's *Lucy*," *Modern Fiction Studies*, 44 (Spring 1998): 164–183;

Bryant Mangum, "Jamaica Kincaid," in *Fifty Caribbean Writers: A Bio-Bibliographical Critical Sourcebook*, edited by Daryl Cumber Dance (Westport, Conn.: Greenwood Press, 1986), pp. 255–263;

Deborah Mistron, *Understanding Jamaica Kincaid's Annie John* (Westport, Conn.: Greenwood Press, 1999);

H. Adlai Murdoch, "The Novels of Jamaica Kincaid: Figures of Exile, Narratives of Dreams," *Clockwatch Review: A Journal of the Arts*, 9, nos. 1–2 (1994–1995): 141–154;

Murdoch, "Severing the (M)Other Connection: The Representations of Cultural Identity in Jamaica Kincaid's *Annie John*," *Callaloo*, 13 (Spring 1990): 325–340;

Roni Natov, "Mothers and Daughters: Jamaica Kincaid's Pre-Oedipal Narrative," *Children's Literature*, 18 (1990): 1–16;

Edyta Oczkowicz, "Jamaica Kincaid's *Lucy*: Cultural 'Translation' As a Case of Creative Exploration of the Past," *MELUS: The Journal for the Study of Multi-Ethnic Literature of the United States*, 21 (Fall 1996): 143–157;

Lizabeth Paravisini-Gebert, *Jamaica Kincaid: A Critical Companion* (Westport, Conn.: Greenwood Press, 1999);

Donna Perry, "Initiation in Jamaica Kincaid's *Annie John*," in *Caribbean Women Writers: Essays from the First International Conference*, edited by Selwyn Cudjoe (Wellesley, Mass.: Callaloux, 1990), pp. 245–253;

Muriel Lynn Rubin, "Adolescence and Autobiographical Fiction: Teaching *Annie John* by Jamaica Kincaid," *Wasafiri*, 8 (Spring 1988): 11–14;

Diane Simmons, "Coming of Age in the Snare of History: Jamaica Kincaid's *The Autobiography of My Mother*," in *The Girl: Constructions of the Girl in Contemporary Fiction by Women*, edited by Ruth O. Saxton (New York: St. Martin's Press, 1999), pp. 107–118;

Simmons, "In Dialogue with the Canon: John Milton, Charlotte Bronte, and Jamaica Kincaid," *MELUS: The Journal for the Study of Multi-Ethnic Literature of the United States*, 23 (Spring/Summer 1998): 65–85;

Simmons, *Jamaica Kincaid* (New York: Twayne, 1994);

Simmons, "Jamaica Kincaid: Conjure Woman," *Journal of Caribbean Studies*, 11 (Fall 1996): 225–241;

Simmons, "Loving Too Much: Jamaica Kincaid and the Dilemma of Constructing a Postcolonial Identity," in *Postcolonialism & Autobiography: Michelle Cliff, David Dabydeen, Opal Palmer Adisa*, edited by Alfred Hornung and Ernstpeter Ruhe (Amsterdam & Atlanta: Rodopi, 1998), pp. 233–245;

Simmons, "The Mother Mirror in Jamaica Kincaid's *Annie John* and Gertrude Stein's *The Good Anna*," in *The Anna Book: Searching for Anna in Literary History*, edited by Mickey Pearlman (Westport, Conn.: Greenwood Press, 1992), pp. 99–104;

Simmons, "Rhythm and Repetition: Jamaica Kincaid's Incantatory Lists," *World Literature Today* (Summer 1994): 466–472;

Craig Tapping, "Children and History in the Caribbean Novel: George Lamming's *In the Castle of My Skin* and Jamaica Kincaid's *Annie John*," *Kunapipi*, 11, no. 2 (1989): 51–59;

Helen Tiffin, "Cold Hearts and (Foreign) Tongues: Recitation and the Reclamation of the Female Body in the Works of Erna Brodber and Jamaica Kincaid," *Callaloo*, 16 (Fall 1993): 909–921;

Tiffin, "Decolonization and Audience: Erna Brodber's *Myal* and Jamaica Kincaid's *A Small Place*," *Span*, 30 (April 1990): 27–38;

Helen Pyne Timothy, "Adolescent Rebellion and Gender Relations in *At the Bottom of the River* and *Annie John*," in *Caribbean Women Writers: Essays from the First International Conference*, edited by Selwyn Cudjoe (Wellesley, Mass.: Callaloux, 1990), pp. 233–242;

Eleanor Ty, "Struggling with the Powerful (M)Other: Identity and Sexuality in Kogawa's *Obasan* and Kincaid's *Lucy*," *International Fiction Review*, 20, no. 2 (1993): 120–126.

Frederick Manfred

(6 January 1912 – 7 September 1994)

Nancy L. Bunge
Michigan State University

See also the Manfred entries in *DLB 6: American Novelists Since World War II, Second Series,* and *DLB 212: Twentieth-Century American Western Writers, Second Series.*

BOOKS: *The Golden Bowl,* as Feike Feikema (St. Paul, Minn.: Webb, 1944);

Boy Almighty, as Feikema (St. Paul, Minn.: Itaska Press, 1945; London: Dobson, 1950);

This Is the Year, as Feikema (Garden City, N.Y.: Doubleday, 1947);

The Chokecherry Tree, as Feikema (Garden City, N.Y.: Doubleday, 1948; London: Dobson, 1949; revised edition, Denver: Swallow Press, 1961);

The Primitive, as Feikema (Garden City, N.Y.: Doubleday, 1949);

The Brother, as Feikema (Garden City, N.Y.: Doubleday, 1950);

The Giant, as Feikema (Garden City, N.Y.: Doubleday, 1951);

Lord Grizzly (New York: McGraw-Hill, 1954; London: Transworld, 1957);

Morning Red: A Romance (Denver: Swallow Press, 1956);

Riders of Judgment (New York: Random House, 1957);

Conquering Horse (New York: McDowell, Obolensky, 1959);

Arrow of Love (Denver: Swallow Press, 1961);

Wanderlust (Denver: Swallow Press, 1962)—comprises revised editions of *The Primitive, The Brother,* and *The Giant;*

Scarlet Plume (New York: Trident, 1964);

The Man Who Looked Like the Prince of Wales (New York: Trident, 1965); republished as *The Secret Place* (New York: Pocket Books, 1967);

King of Spades (New York: Trident, 1966);

Winter Count Poems, 1934–1965 (Minneapolis: James D. Thueson, 1966);

Apples of Paradise and Other Stories (New York: Trident, 1968);

Eden Prairie (New York: Trident, 1968);

The Manly-Hearted Woman (New York: Crown, 1976);

Milk of Wolves (Boston: Avenue Victor Hugo, 1976);

Frederick Manfred, March 1978 (photograph by James Studio; from the dust jacket for The Wind Blows Free, *1979)*

Green Earth (New York: Crown, 1977);

Hubert Horatio Humphrey: A Memoir (St. Paul, Minn.: Minnesota Historical Society, 1978);

The Wind Blows Free: A Reminiscence (Sioux Falls, S.Dak.: Center for Western Studies, Augustana College, 1979);

This Is the Year (Boston: Gregg Press, 1979);

Sons of Adam (New York: Crown, 1980);

Dinkytown (Minneapolis: Dinkytown Antiquarian Bookstore / West Branch & Loc, Iowa: Toothpaste Press, 1984);

Winter Count II: the Poems of Frederick Manfred (Minneapolis: James D. Thueson, 1987);

Prime Fathers (Salt Lake City: Howe, 1988);

Flowers of Desire: A Novel (Salt Lake City: Dancing Badger Press, 1989);

No Fun On Sunday (Norman: University of Oklahoma Press, 1990);

Of Lizards and Angels: A Saga of Siouxland (Norman: University of Oklahoma Press, 1992);

Duke's Mixture (Sioux Falls, S.Dak.: Center for Western Studies, Augustana College, 1994).

Collections: *Buckskin Man Tales,* 5 volumes (Boston: Gregg Press, 1980)–comprises *Lord Grizzly, Riders of Judgment, Conquering Horse, Scarlet Plume,* and *King of Spades;*

The Frederick Manfred Reader, edited by John Calvin Rezmerski (Duluth: Holy Cow! Press, 1996).

OTHER: "The Mystique of Siouxland," in *A Common Land, a Diverse People: Ethnic Identity on the Prairie Plains,* edited by Harry F. Thompson, Arthur R. Huseboe, and Sandra Olsen Looney (Sioux Falls, S.D.: Nordland Heritage Foundation, 1987), pp. 71–88.

SELECTED PERIODICAL PUBLICATIONS–UNCOLLECTED:

FICTION

"Child Delinquent," *Northwest Life,* 16 (March 1944): 26–27;

"Horse Touch," *Northwest Life,* 18 (May 1945): 18–20;

"Judith: A Fragment," *Plainsong,* 2 (Winter 1950): 4–13;

"Omen of Spring," *Minnesota Quarterly* (Winter 1950): 4–13;

"The Voice of the Turtle," *South Dakota Review,* 11 (Autumn 1973): 89–105;

"Where the Grass Grows Greenest," *Farmer,* 72 (6 June 1953): 14–15, 32–33; (20 June 1953): 10, 25.

NONFICTION

"Sinclair Lewis: A Portrait," *American Scholar,* 23 (Spring 1954): 162–184;

"Backgrounds for Western Writing," *Denver Westerner's Monthly Roundup,* 17 (August 1961): 4–11;

"The Western Novel–A Symposium: Frederick Manfred," *South Dakota Review,* 2 (Autumn 1964): 7–9;

"Sinclair Lewis' Funeral, and In Memoriam Address," *South Dakota Review,* 7 (Winter 1969–1970): 54–78;

"Of Holders and Probers," *South Dakota Review,* 28 (Spring 1990): 19–23;

"The Siouxlander," *Papers of the Dakota History Conference* (1990): 669–677.

Critics such as Robert C. Wright have called Frederick Manfred the "midwest's William Faulkner." Like Faulkner, who created the mythical Yoknapatawpha County, Manfred produced a mythic and fictional version of Siouxland, where Minnesota meets South Dakota, Nebraska, and Iowa–the area where the Big Sioux and Missouri Rivers mingle and Native Americans encountered a variety of European immigrants and their descendants. Manfred built two houses for himself against rocky hillsides in Luverne, Minnesota, at the site of the Sioux quarry for ceremonial pipes. His choice of site reveals his emotional attachment to the land. The first house was built in 1960 at the southernmost outcropping facing south toward Doon, Iowa, where he was born. This house was built into the solid rock facing, and only Manfred's high, windowed study, which he called his "tipi," could be seen from the road below. He built his second house in 1975, just across the valley from the first, after the government purchased the land on which his earlier home sat to create Blue Mounds State Park. From these houses he surveyed the landscape that inspired his work.

Although living in the region he wrote about helped to guarantee the accuracy of his fiction, Manfred supplemented his native knowledge by doing scholarly research into history and language and by replicating, as much as possible, the experiences of his characters. He always tried to tell his stories simply. As he explained it, "Homer wouldn't have been repeated orally for two, three, four hundred years if there had been a lot of philosophy or moral instruction in it. It was a great story. . . . A good story is basic to human enjoyment, so I go for the story line." Despite the grounding of Manfred's novels in fact and plot, the broad themes that always fascinated him and permeated his talk inevitably enlarged his work. As Wallace Stegner remarked in his foreword to John R. Milton's *Conversations with Frederick Manfred* (1974), "The movement of Fred Manfred from reality and history to myth is as inevitable as the expansion of gas to fill an empty space."

Manfred often explained that he loved to learn, and evidence of his lifelong emotional and intellectual education pervades his novels. He was elated when his writing took him into new territory:

I rub my hands in glee whenever I hit a wall in my manuscript and I don't know where to go next. There's a damn good reason why: it's something I don't want to look at. If I can push through and get into that area, I'll find something not only about myself, but something that may be of real value to someone else. And, inadvertently, everything you need, the theme, the plot, will jump right out at you as you go along.

Throughout his career Manfred's curiosity, persistence, and vitality kept his mind and fiction expanding and deepening.

Frederick Manfred was born Frederick Feike Feikema in Doon, Iowa, on 6 January 1912, to Aaltje (Alice) Van Engen and Feike (Frank) Feikes Feikema VI, of Saxon and Frisian descent. Manfred wrote under the Frisian name Feike Feikema until he legally changed it to Frederick Manfred in 1952, after his seventh novel. He remained proud of his Frisian heritage all his life, claiming that it made him more English than the English and gave him a special tie to Geoffrey Chaucer. For high school and college, he attended institutions run by the Christian Reformed Church: Western Academy in Hull, Iowa, and Calvin College in Grand Rapids, Michigan (where to his embarrassment, he failed freshman English). While in college he published sketches and poems in *The Chimes,* the college paper, and *Prism,* the college magazine. After graduating from Calvin College in 1934, he continued his informal education by hitchhiking west, journeying to Yellowstone National Park, Passaic, New Jersey, Sioux Falls, and places between. During these travels he also did many odd jobs, working in a U.S. Rubber factory as a warehouse employee and then as a columnist for several small newspapers. Because of his 6'9" height, he was for a short time a professional basketball player for a small local team and was proud of once scoring fifty-seven points in a single game. In 1937 he became a sports reporter for the *Minneapolis Journal.* While spending two years in a sanatorium recovering from tuberculosis (1940–1942), he met Maryanna Shorba, whom he married on 31 October 1942 and with whom he had three children: Freya, Marya, and Frederick. They were divorced in October 1978.

After leaving the hospital in 1942, Manfred took a job on the editorial staff of *Modern Medicine,* leaving in 1943 to begin writing full time. The following year he won a Minnesota Regional Writing Fellowship. In 1945 he was awarded $1,000 by the American Academy of Arts and Letters and moved to Bloomington, Minnesota. His work soon attracted the friendship and encouragement of established writers such as Robert Penn Warren and Sinclair Lewis. Although sales and critical assessments of his novels fluctuated as the decades passed, Manfred held to his course, writing about Siouxland until his death on 7 September 1994.

In the autobiographical novel *Green Earth* (1977) Manfred offers a vivid description of how his fiction-writing career began. In the late 1930s, after working late at the *Minneapolis Journal,* he dragged himself to a friend's party, hoping to meet a new girlfriend. Instead, he found himself the center of attention as he talked about his hitchhiking days. His first attempts at fiction tended to mimic the style of any novelist whose work he had just read, but on his way home from the party he realized that he had told his story in his own

voice and decided to write it down just as he had spoken it. He stayed up writing all night and far into the next day. When he reread his story Monday night after work, he realized that he had discovered his voice and that it was the voice of a writer. His first novel, *The Golden Bowl* (1944), about a hobo he had encountered while hitchhiking west, grew directly from the anecdote he told at the party. The critics agreed that Frederick Manfred, or Feike Feikema as he then called himself, was a noteworthy novelist.

Manfred's next book, *Boy Almighty* (1945), offered a fictionalized account of his two years in a tuberculosis sanatorium. He wrote this book because his forgetfulness about this period made him fear he was closing off his emotions: "A callus or a veil or something was growing across my brain and shutting that whole experience out, and I didn't know whether I wanted that or not." The main character, Erik Frey, is based on Manfred's roommate at the sanatorium, Howard Anderson. Manfred had assumed that Anderson's fighting spirit would keep him alive, but it did not. When Anderson died, Manfred said to himself, "Look buddy, you should have died but you didn't," and he emerged from that experience "a raging bull." The book received lukewarm reviews; while the critics recognized the author's potential, their response to *Boy Almighty* was ambivalent.

In his next novel, *This Is the Year* (1947), Manfred explored his Frisian background, producing a brief family history beginning with Alde Romke, who immigrates to Siouxland from Frisia. Writing this book allowed Manfred to imagine the perspectives of his ancestors, and he produced moving portraits of the homesick Alde and his son, Piers, who takes over the family farm only to lose it because he and his father have misused the land. Manfred said that the novel is ultimately about the importance of respecting the land rather than attempting to exploit it. Yet, he also saw heroism in Piers's determination to start over after all his goods have been auctioned.

The book did well with reviewers and was named the Associated Press Book Reviewers' best novel of the year. Sinclair Lewis and Van Wyck Brooks praised it, and Harrison Smith was among the reviewers who admired its "vitality of an epic narrative" (*Saturday Review,* 29 March 1997). The novel was also a best-seller in 1947, spending four weeks on *The New York Times* list and two weeks on *The New York Herald Tribune* list.

Manfred next created a character even more remote from himself than Alde and Piers. In *The Chokecherry Tree* (1948) the main character, Elof Lofbloom, has trouble finding a sense of direction. He aspires to be an accountant but in the meantime earns

Dust jacket for Manfred's 1976 novel, based on the story of an Arapaho named Flat War Club in
David Lavender's Bent's Fort *(1954)*

money any way he can. He tries sales, but his distaste for manipulating potential customers makes him largely ineffective. He wants to do something important but cannot find his way. Critics also admired this novel. Writing on 8 April 1948 for *The New York Times,* Nash Burger called it "moving and persuasive."

Manfred's World's Wanderer trilogy—*The Primitive* (1949), *The Brother* (1950), and *The Giant* (1951)—brought him the first of a long series of negative reviews from eastern critics, and Manfred's refusal to change his course in response to their objections led to conflict with his publisher, Doubleday. They parted ways in 1953. The issue of heroism continues to play a central role in the Wanderer novels. The main character, Thurs, much like Manfred himself, raises embarrassing questions about Christianity at his religious college two months before graduation, pursues music late in life even though doing so will cut him off from the financial support of his benefactor, and supports his mentor, Professor Maynard, when the board of trustees decides to fire him. Maynard, however, accepts the board's decision with quiet dignity, refusing to allow their action to upset him or change his course. Manfred commented that this character came totally from his imagination and that "I think that Mr. Maynard is somebody that I

think maybe I'll grow to be." In continuing to write what he considered his best work, whether the critics' reaction to his fiction was positive or negative, Manfred may, in fact, be compared to the professor. The Wanderer trilogy offers interesting insights into Manfred's values and state of mind, but reviewers characterized the three novels in terms such as "shapeless," "juvenile," and "grotesque."

Discontented with the thinness of the characters in the trilogy, Manfred decided to write next about a character based in history. When he happened on the story of Hugh Glass in a book of South Dakota history, Manfred felt certain that he had found an appropriate hero and spent ten years doing research for *Lord Grizzly* (1954), the first of his five *Buckskin Man Tales*—*Lord Grizzly, Riders of Judgment* (1957), *Conquering Horse* (1959), *Scarlet Plume* (1964), and *King of Spades* (1966). If they are arranged in the chronological order of the periods in which they are set, the order would be *Conquering Horse* (1800), *Lord Grizzly* (1823–1824), *Scarlet Plume* (1862), *King of Spades* (1876), and *Riders of Judgment* (1892). Manfred's biggest commercial and critical success to this point, *Lord Grizzly* tells the colorful story of Hugh Glass, whose companions abandoned him after he received massive injuries in a fight with a grizzly bear. The novel focuses on his arduous fight for survival despite his injuries, which included a broken leg he had to reset himself. The true drama of the story is psychological, for when he tracks the men who left him, Glass finds he has forgiven them. While writing this novel Manfred not only researched historical documents but also put himself in Glass's physical circumstances as best he could, following Glass's probable path through South Dakota, binding up his leg in the kind of device Glass used, and crawling as Glass must have done. Manfred also stated that to create the character of Glass convincingly, he had to stretch his capacity for love, hate, and, especially, forgiveness, learning from the example of his brother, who had been falsely accused of a crime and forgave his accuser. Manfred was especially proud of *Lord Grizzly:* "I've never written better. It's as if I actually lived back in 1823–24 and actually was Old Hugh Glass." The novel appeared on *The New York Times* best-seller list and garnered extensive critical approval. Victor Hass (26 September 1954) praised Manfred's "robustness," "ranginess," and "engaging lustiness of style and expression."

Set in cattle country in 1892, *Riders of Judgment,* the volume of the *Buckskin Man Tales* that Manfred wrote next, is considered the weakest novel of the series by many critics. Far more successful was Manfred's next effort, *Conquering Horse,* which focuses on a brave called No Name because he has never had a vision. He eventually has two visions requiring him to perform daunting tasks to prove his courage and earn honor. Writing for *The New York Times Book Review* (16 February 1975), Madison Jones praised the novel, especially the "living breathing image of that part of Mother Earth that he [Manfred] has rendered for us with so much love and eloquence."

In *Scarlet Plume,* another successful contribution to the *Buckskin Man Tales* series, Manfred challenged the critics' expectations by choosing a female protagonist. The novel begins during the Sioux uprising of 1862 when Judith Raveling wanders into an Indian attack while visiting her sister in Minnesota, is kidnapped by the Yangton tribe, and eventually escapes. On her long trek back to St. Paul, Judith learns to accept what Manfred calls the "Old Lizard," the animal wisdom within her: "Our civilization, and all the other levels of nations we have gone through, and all the things we've learned to do by reason and because of common sense, has gradually wiped out our most powerful ally. And that is our primate nature. What I call the Old Lizard. Or the Old Leviathan."

Although she is a strong character, Judith is clearly no feminist heroine. Yet, the book expresses feminine values in its focus on her love for Scarlet Plume, a brave who has followed her on her journey to protect her. In this novel Manfred's so-called Buckskin Men soften; the emphasis shifts from hand-to-hand combat with grizzly bears or murderous attacks by humans to caring attitudes toward others.

In *Scarlet Plume* Manfred again demonstrates the value of Native American culture, stressing the strong tie between human beings and animals and the futility of disowning this link. The novel was popular with readers, but as Manfred went on to explore daring, sometimes even disturbing, psychological themes in subsequent novels, the critical response to his work became less positive and sales declined.

The last of the *Buckskin Man Tales, King of Spades* is a Black Hills version of the story of Oedipus. In Manfred's novel the son, Roddy King, kills his father, takes the name Earl Ransom, and has a sexual relationship with a woman whom he does not recognize as his mother. The book opens with a passage about the lizard that explains the logic of Roddy's behavior:

> The first great miracle to appear on earth was the emergence of love in the mother lizard. And the first great bewilderment to appear on earth was the emergence of taboo: having learned of love from his mother, a son was not to return this love to his mother.
> Caught in flesh and caught by flesh.

The reader is not surprised when the book ends tragically.

Although the *Buckskin Man Tales* as a whole enjoyed critical praise as well as wide sales, reviewers had mixed reactions to *King of Spades.* Victor P. Haas wrote in *The Chicago Tribune* (20 November 1966): "It has been a long time since I have read a novel as distasteful, absurdly violent, and luridly melodramatic." Yet, Jack Conroy, writing for *The Chicago Daily News* (29 October 1966), disagreed: "Manfred's narrative power . . . was never displayed to greater advantage." In their edition of Manfred's letters, Nancy Owen Nelson and Arthur R. Huseboe attributed the ambivalent critical response to the "violence, melodrama, and explicit sex" in the novel. As always, Manfred ignored the critics.

Eden Prairie (1968) continues Manfred's exploration of relationships and incest, this time focusing on two brothers who are closer to each other than they are to the women in their lives. When one brother and his wife have a child, the other brother kills himself. For this novel Manfred drew on the lives of two of his uncles, who were so close to each other that they could not relate intimately to their wives. In a comment included in *The Frederick Manfred Reader* (1996), Manfred explained: "the brothers were deeply in love with each other. Maybe not incestuous, but the two were so attached, that they couldn't break out of it to get into a woman. . . . That's the duty of the artist. When you run across something like that, you've got to explore it." Although this statement might be a valid artistic stance, by frankly addressing such controversial themes, Manfred risked losing his audience.

In his next novel, *The Manly-Hearted Woman* (1976), Manfred returned to the theme of Native American culture. He began thinking about the story after someone gave him twenty pages of David Lavender's *Bent's Fort* (1954), which includes the story of Flat War Club, an Arapaho who had dreams his tribe considered feminine. The story failed to interest Manfred until he thought of pairing Flat War Club with a woman whose achievements were those normally associated with men. *The Manly-Hearted Woman* focuses on sex and gender roles and illustrates that the deepest and most heroic characters combine the strengths of both sexes.

Later in his career Manfred turned more to summary and synthesis. *Milk of Wolves* (1976) could be read as a parable of Manfred's success in making writing his central activity. The main character, Juhl Melander, knows from a young age that he loves working with stone and eventually realizes that creativity involves loyalty to one's deepest artistic yearnings: "Down with the barriers of skin and learned response." Juhl eventually retreats to an island, where he practices his art and becomes even more sensitive and obedient to his body's demands. Through his love for Fleur, an Indian woman, he finds "something that awoke in him a profound respect for the sacred," and his work improves. Though tragedy—Fleur's death and the loss of his island—soon overwhelms him, he is able to begin again. The book argues directly and passionately for committing oneself to one's art and sexuality as fully as possible. In *The Frederick Manfred Reader* Manfred is quoted as saying that the two urges are strongly yoked: "God wouldn't have made sex so pleasant if it were just for procreation. Sex drive and creativity seem to go together into a great flowering of energy."

In *Green Earth* Manfred produced another rendition of what he calls a "rume," a novel built around autobiography. In this novel Manfred drew on his early years, and he has said that of all his creations, Free, or Alfred Alfredson, the central character in *Green Earth*, comes the closest to himself. *Green Earth* describes growing up in Siouxland between 1909 and 1929, focusing on the impact of Alfredson's mother and father and trying to describe the values of both. In the preface to the book, Manfred describes the "two societies" that coexisted in the Midwest at the time: "When you get over there to the ministers' and women's side, then you object somewhat to my vivid language and my lively language. Then, over on the males' side, you object once in a while when I write about some of them, like

in *Eden Prairie,* where they pray so much." Indeed, in *Green Earth* Manfred put aside his usually critical stance toward religion to allow Alfred's mother some lovely moments in prayer.

While examining the impact of the father's and the mother's perspectives, the novel also examines the psychological basis for Manfred's life as a writer. Like Manfred, Free first announces his aspirations to authorship in a conversation with an aunt. When his aunt proclaims poetry writing the most difficult task in life, young Free responds: "Then that's what I'll be someday. A poet. Because I want to be like my pa. Be the best there is." Like Manfred, young Free admires Mark Twain's down-to-earth language and enjoys getting lost in a story, but he aspires to produce fiction that plunges deeper into reality than Twain's: "The whole problem was to get down to the really real. That was the trouble with most writers. They never quite managed to get into where the real was really real."

Manfred's repeated attempts to tell his parents' stories testify to his conviction that "good fiction" and a true account of his own life both demanded a solid rendering of his father and mother. Many readers consider *Green Earth* his masterpiece. The critic for *Publishers Weekly* (19 September 1977) wrote that "Manfred does stretch some of his scenes excessively, but his insistent accumulation of detail somehow gives the novel a compelling kind of life." Russel Roth in the *Minneapolis Tribune* (27 November 1977) described the book as "a strong and compelling story that gains rather than loses power and momentum from its ever-accumulating mass of interwoven detail. It is meticulously historical, larger-than-life in its characterizations, and full of a Rabelais-cum-Breughel good humor in its depiction of a humanity still rooted in and drawing its primary force—whether willingly or not—from the soil."

In 1988 Manfred published *Prime Fathers,* a collection of essays about men who had served as his role models. One of these men is Manfred's father, who—although he was illiterate until in his eighties, he taught himself to read—encouraged and admired his son's literary achievements. Manfred's account of his father reveals him to have been extremely bright with a sharp eye for landscapes, a careful ear for music, and a tender heart. He cared deeply about the people around him, visiting his son every month at the tuberculosis sanatorium to hold his hand, but he was also a resourceful survivor who could realize as he fell fifty feet from a rotting windmill that he needed to land like a cricket.

Another father figure for Manfred was Sinclair Lewis, who not only praised Manfred's work but also took a personal interest in his career, helping him to sign with Doubleday and urging him above all to work hard. When Lewis died, Manfred delivered the grave-

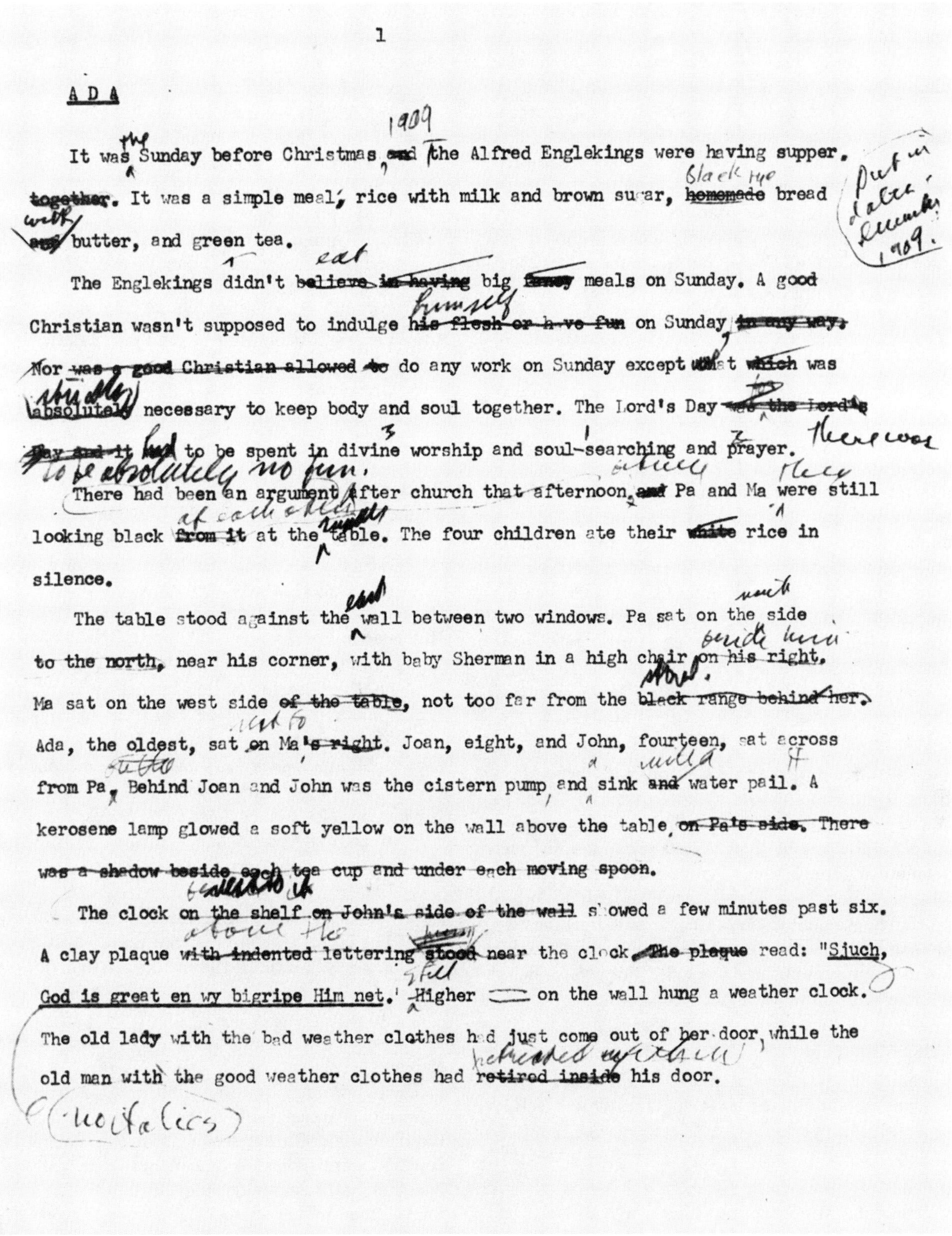

1

A D A

1909

It was Sunday before Christmas, ~~and~~ the Alfred Englekings were having supper.
~~together.~~ It was a simple meal, rice with milk and brown sugar, ~~homemade~~ bread
with butter, and green tea.

The Englekings didn't ~~believe in having~~ big ~~fancy~~ meals on Sunday. A good
Christian wasn't supposed to indulge ~~his flesh or have fun~~ on Sunday ~~in any way.~~
~~Nor was a good Christian allowed to~~ do any work on Sunday except ~~what~~ which was
~~absolutely~~ necessary to keep body and soul together. The Lord's Day ~~was the Lord's~~
~~Day and it had~~ to be spent in divine worship and soul-searching and prayer.

There had been an argument after church that afternoon, ~~and~~ Pa and Ma were still
looking black ~~from it~~ at the ~~table.~~ The four children ate their ~~white~~ rice in
silence.

The table stood against the wall between two windows. Pa sat on the side
to the north, near his corner, with baby Sherman in a high chair on his right.
Ma sat on the west side ~~of the table,~~ not too far from the ~~black range behind her.~~
Ada, the oldest, sat on ~~Ma's right.~~ Joan, eight, and John, fourteen, sat across
from Pa. Behind Joan and John was the cistern pump and sink ~~and~~ water pail. A
kerosene lamp glowed a soft yellow on the wall above the table. ~~on Pa's side.~~ There
~~was a shadow beside each~~ tea cup and under each moving spoon.

The clock on ~~the shelf on John's side of the wall~~ showed a few minutes past six.
A clay plaque with ~~indented~~ lettering ~~stood~~ near the clock. ~~The plaque~~ read: "Sjuch,
God is great en wy bigripe Him net.' ~~Higher~~ on the wall hung a weather clock.
The old lady with the bad weather clothes had just come out of her door, while the
old man with the good weather clothes had ~~retired inside~~ his door.

(*no italics*)

Page from the revised typescript for Green Earth *(1977) (Frederick Manfred Papers; Manuscripts Division, University of Minnesota Libraries)*

side eulogy, praising Lewis's ethical commitment: "Red heard The Call too. Not to preach, or to admonish in particular, or to hurl unctuous maxims and hellfire anathemas at us. But The Call to lift a light, a lamp, so that the rest of us could clear away the lies, the deceit, the sloth, the sins of omission and of commission that beset us as humans." At the end of the eulogy, Manfred reminded his listeners that it fell to them to keep Lewis's integrity alive. Manfred never forgot this responsibility. As John Calvin Rezmerski comments in *The Frederick Manfred Reader*, "Substitute the names Manfred for Lewis, Fred for Red, and the piece is still 95 percent accurate in describing its subject." Like Lewis, in *Prime Fathers* Manfred offers insight into examples of decency and persistence that shaped his life and career.

Because Manfred explained that "my dream was to write a history of Siouxland and environs from the year 1800 to the day I die," it seems appropriate that his last published novel, *Of Lizards and Angels: A Saga of Siouxland* (1992), provides a history of a fictional Siouxland family, beginning in 1880 and ending one hundred years later. The novel also explores the union of instinctual and spiritual truth that Manfred strove always to render in his fiction. His last book, like his first and all those in between, is filled with vivid characters, earthy realism, and great stories. In *Western American Literature* (May 1993) Dexter Martin praised Manfred's honesty: "Manfred offers the suppressed truth about the early settlers of his Siouxland. The novel should become a maverick classic."

Manfred's work evolved during the course of his career, but his books share a persistent determination to describe the heroism of ordinary lives while focusing on the place he knew best. He always strove to satisfy his definition of "true fiction": "where the reader, no matter what the intelligence is, gets lost in the story." When asked if he would not sometimes like to "forget the long view and do something else," Manfred replied: "No. It's fun to be always like this. I like to be wide awake. Being wide awake, you've got all the doors open."

Letters:

The Selected Letters of Frederick Manfred, 1932–1954, edited by Arthur R. Huseboe and Nancy Owen Nelson (Lincoln: University of Nebraska Press, 1988).

Interviews:

"West of the Mississippi: An Interview with Frederick Manfred," *Critique,* 2 (Winter 1959): 35–36;

John R. Milton, *Conversations with Frederick Manfred* (Salt Lake City: University of Utah Press, 1974);

Mark Vinz, "Milton, Manfred, and McGrath: A Conversation on Literature and Place," *Dacotah Territory,* 8/9 (Fall–Winter 1974–1975): 19–26;

Nancy Bunge, "Frederick Manfred," in her *Finding the Words: Conversations with Writers Who Teach* (Athens, Ohio: Swallow Press/Ohio University Press, 1985), pp. 68–82;

Robert W. Smith, "Frederick Manfred: Outsize Man and Writer," *North Dakota Quarterly,* 55 (Spring 1987): 139–150;

Leslie Whipp, *An Interview with Frederick Manfred* (East Lansing, Mich.: Midwestern Press, 1992);

Nancy Bunge, "'Something Magical and Important is Going On': Interviews with Frederick And Freya Manfred," *North Dakota Quarterly,* 61 (Spring 1993): 19–36.

Bibliography:

Rodney J. Mulder and John H. Timmerman, *Frederick Manfred: A Bibliography and Publishing History* (Sioux Falls, S.Dak.: Center for Western Studies, Augustana College, 1981).

References:

Joseph Flora, *Frederick Manfred,* Western Writers Series, no. 13 (Boise, Idaho: Boise State University, 1974);

Freya Manfred, *A Daughter Remembers* (Minneapolis: Minnesota Historical Society, 1999);

John R. Milton, *Sinclair Lewis and Frederick Manfred* (Vermillion: University of South Dakota, 1969);

Nancy Owen Nelson, ed., *The Lizard Speaks: Essays on the Writings of Frederick Manfred* (Sioux Falls, S.Dak.: Center for Western Studies, Augustana College, 1998);

Leslie Whipp, "Frederick Manfred's *The Golden Bowl*— The Novel and Novelist Emerging," *South Dakota Review,* 27 (Autumn 1989): 100–128;

Robert C. Wright, *Frederick Manfred* (Boston: Twayne, 1979).

Papers:

Frederick Manfred's correspondence, journals, and manuscripts are available in the Manfred Collection in the University of Minnesota Archives, St. Paul. Photocopies of correspondence and manuscripts, as well as Manfred's personal library, may be found in the Center for Western Studies at Augustana College, Sioux Falls, South Dakota.

Paule Marshall

(9 April 1929 –)

Joyce Pettis
North Carolina State University

See also the Marshall entries in *DLB 33: Afro-American Fiction Writers After 1955* and *DLB 157: Twentieth-Century Caribbean and Black African Writers, Third Series.*

BOOKS: *Brown Girl, Brownstones* (New York: Random House, 1959; London: W. H. Allen, 1960);

Soul Clap Hands and Sing (New York: Atheneum, 1961; W. H. Allen, 1962);

The Chosen Place, The Timeless People (New York: Harcourt, Brace & World, 1969; London: Longman, 1970);

Praisesong for the Widow (New York: Putnam, 1983; London: Virago, 1983);

Reena and Other Stories (Old Westbury, N.Y.: Feminist Press, 1983); republished as *Merle: A Novella and Other Stories* (London: Virago, 1985);

Daughters (New York: Atheneum / Toronto: Maxwell Macmillan Canada / New York: Maxwell Macmillan International, 1991; London: Serpent's Tail, 1992);

Language Is the Only Homeland: Bajan Poets Abroad, Sir Winston Scott Memorial Lecture, no. 19 (Bridgetown: Central Bank of Barbados, 1995);

The Fisher King: A Novel (New York: Scribner, forthcoming 2000).

Editions: *Brown Girl, Brownstones,* afterword by Mary Helen Washington (Old Westbury, N.Y.: Feminist Press, 1981);

Soul Clap Hands and Sing, introduction by Darwin T. Turner (Washington, D.C.: Howard University Press, 1988).

RECORDING: *Paule Marshall Reads from Browngirl* [sic], *Brownstones, The Chosen Place, the Timeless People, and Praisesong for the Widow,* Columbia, Mo., American Audio Prose Library, AAPL 4131, 1984.

OTHER: "Some Get Wasted," in *Harlem U. S. A.,* edited by John Henrik Clarke (Berlin: Seven Seas, 1974), pp. 364–375;

Paule Marshall (photograph © Jerry Bauer)

"Characterizations of Black Women in the American Novel," in *In the Memory and Spirit of Frances, Zora, and Lorraine: Essays and Interviews on Black Women and Writing,* edited by Juliette Bowles (Washington, D.C.: Institute for the Arts and the Humanities, Howard University, 1979), pp. 76–79;

"Black Literature in the '90s: The Past as Prologue to 'The New Wave,'" in *Defining Ourselves: Black Writers in the 90s,* edited by Elizabeth Nunez and Brenda M. Greene (New York: Peter Lang, 1999), pp. 25–33.

SELECTED PERIODICAL PUBLICATIONS–
UNCOLLECTED: "Shaping the World of My Art," *New Letters,* 40 (October 1973): 97–112;
"Chez Tournon: A Homage," *New York Times Magazine,* 18 October 1992, II: 28–34.

Paule Marshall's fiction makes a distinctive addition to African American and American literature. She uses her literary imagination to invoke experiences of the African Diaspora. Since her first novel, *Brown Girl, Brownstones* (1959), Marshall's work has consistently explored conflicts, themes, and events particular to people of African descent. The ideas in her fiction are explored against a geographically diverse canvas that includes the Caribbean with its history of European colonization and the segregationist history of the United States. Thus, history and community, shapers of the past and the present, are vital subtexts in the lives of Marshall's characters. Just as important, Marshall explores the notion of cultural continuity through identification with African heritage and culture as a means of healing the psychic fragmentation that has resulted from colonization and segregation. Her fiction is noted for its artistry—for finely crafted structures, fluid narrative, for language that conveys the nuances of the spoken word, and for characters that are especially complex and rich. Because Marshall's settings include both the United States and the Caribbean, she has the distinction of being claimed by both places as one of their own.

Her first three novels—*Brown Girl, Brownstones* (1959), *The Chosen Place, The Timeless People* (1969), and *Praisesong for the Widow* (1983)—were conceived of as a trilogy. Their unity, while achieved through a striking mix of themes, issues, and motifs, is largely dependent on the author's intention of finding acceptable answers to personal and public issues. *Daughters* (1991) can be called the author's post-trilogy fiction. Although it continues several of the issues familiar in the trilogy, its protagonist struggles toward a different kind of discovery and independence. *Soul Clap Hands and Sing* (1961), Marshall's second book, consists of four novellas named for geographical locations. It focuses on aging male protagonists who in the autumn of their lives confront striking personal inadequacies. In turning to young, fertile women for spiritual salvation, they anticipate one of the hallmarks of Marshall's canon. While the male characters of these novellas, as well as those in

the novels, are memorable and generally convincingly drawn, it is her women characters who especially command attention for their abilities to define themselves. Marshall's women are provocative, complex, interesting, conscious of community, and agents of their own interior transformation; they are, in varying mixtures, brash, bold, silent, determined, young, and elderly.

Paule Marshall's interest in characters of the so-called third world is logically linked to her biography. Born in Brooklyn, N.Y., on 9 April 1929, her father and mother, Samuel and Ada Clement Burke, were Barbadian immigrants in characteristic search for the American dream. They had arrived in Brooklyn after World War I, her father entering the United States illegally by way of Cuba. Like many young West Indian men, he had been lured there by promises of success as a worker on a government scheme. Mr. Burke joined Father Divine's religious organization, the "kingdom," in Harlem, and pretty much disappeared from the life of his family. In an interview with Daryl Dance in *Southern Review* (1992), Marshall comments on the effect her father's rejection had on her over the years. The love and loss of their relationship is mirrored in her first novel and in *Daughters*. Growing up in a transplanted West Indian community and also surrounded by relocated black southerners, Marshall was on promising ground for learning the values of each group, including their suspicion and distrust of each other. These conflicts, among others, are integrated into her first novel.

Several experiences of Marshall's formative years in Brooklyn are transformed in her fiction. For example, when Marshall was nine years old, she made her first trip to Barbados, her parents' homeland. Financial resources for the trip came from money left to the family after the death of Ada Burke's brother, a worker on the Panama Canal. Like many other West Indian men working in the insect-infested swamps and jungles of Panama, he failed to survive the diseases native to the region. Ada Burke's decision to use the inheritance for transporting her children "home" for a visit was fraught with difficulty. Samuel Burke wanted to invest the money in a brownstone. To complicate matters, Ada Burke lost the money in an unwise investment with a fellow Barbadian travel agent. Nevertheless, they finally made the trip. The influence of the island on Marshall's budding imagination was immeasurable.

One discernible influence became her strategic use of the Caribbean landscape. Although the setting is significant in all of her fiction, Marshall's use of landscape transcends physical qualities to embrace what Barbara Christian has termed an "interdependency of character and culture." Originally published in *New World Magazine* (1976) and later collected in *Reena and Other Stories* (1983), "To Da-Duh, in Memoriam," Mar-

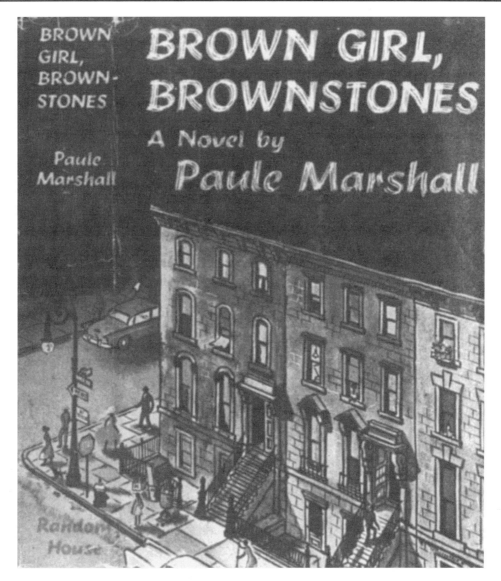

Dust jacket for Marshall's first novel, about West Indian immigrants living in Brooklyn

shall's most autobiographical story, is characteristic of this use and is linked in several ways with her first visit to Barbados. Her maternal grandmother, Da-Duh, was something of a myth in her own family. She had had fourteen children (including two sets of twins), farmed her own land after her husband's untimely death, and sent her children to America with the hope of improving their lives. In one of a series of interviews in 1991–1992 with Joyce Pettis for *MELUS,* Marshall spoke of her grandmother as an "overpowering figure of the matriarch in the most positive sense of the powerful." The story describes the first meeting in Barbados between a New York child and her Barbadian grandmother. Through this simple encounter, Marshall explores themes of knowledge versus inno-

cence, the natural versus the mechanical, and the destructive might of the West over noncompetitive geographical entities. Like the young city girl in the story who had only seen an urban landscape, Marshall was awed by the natural beauty of the Caribbean. The author states in the interview, "I remember too the sense of a place that was completely, it seemed to me, covered in sugar cane. I didn't know anything about sugar cane, but there were all of these tall canes all over this place. . . . That I remember. There was always the sense that the West Indies was in some way important to my understanding my self. . . . Then, too, there was the practical, technical aspect to it. I found that because the islands were small, they permitted me to deal with a manageable landscape. I could use that to say what I wanted to about the larger landscapes, the metropoles. . . ."

When Marshall's artistic sense began its process of reviving and transforming, it drew from her family, her community, and from her early island visit. Her impressive memory of her maternal grandmother, affectionately called "Da-Duh," became the model for the ancestor that appears in Marshall's subsequent novels. Marshall recalls Da-Duh walking to meet them through the disembarkation shed in Barbados. She was "a very small, dry, wiry, quick stepping, very black old woman, the grandmother" who, transcribed into Marshall's fiction, becomes Mrs. Thompson in *Brown Girl, Brownstones;* Medford in *The Chosen Place, The Timeless People;* Aunt Cuney and Lebert Joseph in *Praisesong for the Widow;* and Celestine in *Daughters.* This ancestor figure becomes an enabler, a conduit of cultural continuity, and a bridge for familial history, as well. The responsibility in instructing a new generation in the old ways of survival is taken seriously.

Marshall's island visit lasted a year, during which she was enrolled in the British school system there. She found it intolerable because of its strictness and its practice of punishing the children by caning. She could not bear to be whipped nor to witness the pain of her classmates, so she did not continue enrollment. She returned to Brooklyn with a Barbadian accent and the classic silver wrist bangles, both of which, in response to the teasing of her classmates, she tried to lose.

During her adolescent school years, Marshall developed her insatiable appetite for reading. She frequented the Macon Street Branch of the Brooklyn Public Library. Not encouraged to read black writers, she thus remained unaware that Zora Neale Hurston and Nella Larsen had published fiction, that the Harlem Renaissance had taken place, or that Richard Wright at that point in time was widely popular. The only work by a black writer that she encountered was the poetry of Langston Hughes. Her dominant literary exposure was to American and European establishment writers.

The memorable community of West Indian women and their melodic language in *Brown Girl, Brownstones,* however, comes from Marshall's youthful observance of her mother and other island women who gathered in the kitchen of their Brooklyn brownstone. Marshall has immortalized these intimate scenes both in *Brown Girl, Brownstones* and in the essay "The Making of a Writer: From the Poets in the Kitchen," originally published in *The New York Times Book Review* (9 January 1983). Thus, she credits the highly visual and metaphoric language of these women with the power of restoration and healing after a week of labor in New York factories or domestic kitchens.

In 1950 she married Kenneth E. Marshall, with whom she had one son, Evan, (the couple divorced in 1963) and received her B.A. degree from Brooklyn College in 1953. She began attending Hunter College in 1955 while working for a magazine called *Our World,* a journal in competition with and very much like *Ebony.* Marshall did not care for the work but nevertheless credits the experience with teaching her discipline. This quality became a much-needed asset when she began her novels. In fact, she began writing *Brown Girl, Brownstones* at night, at the time she was writing for *Our World.* She left the magazine in 1956 and completed her first novel in Barbados.

When Marshall began writing and publishing fiction in the 1950s, the decade did not seem a promising one for African American women writers. Black women had not published collectively in significant numbers since the Harlem Renaissance of the 1920s; poets such as Georgia Douglass, Alice Nelson Dunbar, Helene Johnson, and Gwendolyn Bennett were undervalued in comparison to their male counterparts. Novelists Jessie Fauset and Nella Larsen had offered their visions of middle-class women; and Zora Neale Hurston had offered her short stories in the 1920s and her novels in the 1930s. Whatever nurturing had been forthcoming from women writers or readers disappeared amidst the economic struggles of the Depression years. Marshall, however, was aware of Ann Petry's work of the 1940s and 1950s and of the Gwendolyn Brooks novella *Maud Martha* (1953); she credits Brooks's example with influential insight on navigating the black woman's psychological interior.

Marshall began writing during a period still dominated by male writers, including Richard Wright, Ralph Ellison, and James Baldwin. Notably, *Brown Girl, Brownstones* was published on the eve of the 1960s, the decade of civil rights that spawned attendant interest in out-of-print and forgotten black literature, including women's writing. Marshall's first novel, however, is not overtly protest literature. Rather, it marks the beginning of her journey through fiction to examine several issues. Chief among them are biculturalism, issues of race, gender, and class, and spiritual reconciliation. Her interests transcend physical borders in recognition of an African heritage for black Americans and Caribbeans. Her fiction questions and exposes the political and economic power of the West in relationship to emerging third-world countries. While these are significant issues whose impact can be destructive to the individual, Marshall's focus centers primarily on character and heterogeneous cultural experiences. These interests are manifested in her first novel through the main cast of characters, Caribbean immigrants seeking the American dream as well as economic and social assimilation in New York City. *Brown Girl, Brownstones* reveals the coming of age of Selina Boyce, born in the United States, but equally a daughter of the Caribbean through heritage and more practically, through her daily experiences. In *The Chosen Place, The Timeless People,* published in 1969, the only work whose setting is completely in the Caribbean, Marshall explores the contrast between the West and an economically impoverished island. In protagonist Merle Kinbona, the conflicted cultural strands of Africa, Europe, and the Caribbean rage until she can attain some degree of spiritual reconciliation. The West is represented by a Jewish researcher, his wife, and his associate, who, with the financial backing of a philanthropic association, live among the islanders while formulating strategies for ameliorating some of their persistent economic problems.

The protagonist in *Praisesong for the Widow,* published in 1983, is an elderly widow from White Plains, New York, whose Caribbean vacation cruise results in an unanticipated spiritual journey. *Praisesong for the Widow,* winner of the Before Columbus Award, is Marshall's most critically reviewed and most frequently taught novel, culminating inquiries that have been left unanswered in the first two works of the trilogy. *Soul Clap Hands and Sing,* a collection of four novellas, falls outside this trilogy, but nevertheless explores many of its relevant issues.

In *Brown Girl, Brownstones* Marshall draws from many of the experiences she knows. She localizes the Brooklyn, New York, West Indian community, incorporates her mother's women friends as poets of the kitchen, and provides an ancestor as the youthful protagonist's mentor. Nevertheless, *Brown Girl, Brownstones* transforms and transcends the biographical to become an elaborate study of intricate conflicts, themes, symbols, and complex characters.

The novel recounts the coming-of-age experience of Selina Boyce in the household of her parents, Deighton and Silla, and the older sister, Ina, a quiet, self-effacing counterpart to her sister's liveliness. Selina is age ten when the narrative begins and age twenty-one at its conclusion. The transplanted West Indian immigrants and their pursuit of the American dream become significant contexts for the maturation process of the protagonist. *Brown Girl, Brownstones* thus initiates Marshall's ongoing exploration of the relationship between work and capitalist profit through the oppressions of race, class, and gender. Laboring for the goal of achieving the American dream and all its promises—homes, business, college education, and professions for their children—animates the Boyces and their close-knit community. But Deighton envisions the dream and its outcome differently from his wife, and therein lies the conflict that ultimately derails their marriage and intensifies the

already complex coming-of-age process for their daughter Selina. Deighton's dream is to acquire capital sufficient to return to Barbados and to build a house there on his inherited land. Silla's goal is to own the Brooklyn brownstone where they live in New York and to educate their daughters for a lucrative profession in the United States. Their different goals illustrate the differing degree to which they both are willing to assimilate to the dominant culture.

Through Deighton's character, Marshall exposes and explores the psychic damage that occurs when a character is a romantic dreamer unsuited by disposition to the frenzied race for material acquisition. The New York Barbadian community, united in its absorption in the American dream, symbolically rejects Deighton as does the capitalist system. The difference between Deighton's and Silla's responses to the capitalist system is dramatically illustrated through its primary symbol of technology—the machine. Physically, Deighton's arm is mangled in an accident in a mattress factory. Psychologically, the mangled arm is indicative of a psychic mangling that began before he left Barbados. After physical recuperation, Deighton attends to his psychic needs by joining a cultlike religious organization. Deserting his family in his commitment to "father's kingdom," as it is called, signals his alienation from a capitalist society. In retaliation, his wife reveals his illegal status, which results in his deportation. Rather than return to Barbados in disgrace, he apparently throws himself overboard before the boat reaches the island.

In contrast, at the munitions factory where she works, Silla's movements are unified with the machinery, as if her fingers and arms were its extensions. This image symbolizes her rapport with a system bigger and more powerful than the individual. She becomes its symbolic hand, rejecting those—even her husband—who seemingly threaten her progress. She also rejects her boarder, fellow Barbadian Suggie Skeete who, like Deighton, resists assimilation, and Silla apparently scares the old boarder, Miss Mary, to death to speed her ejection from the brownstone. Nevertheless, the powerful, threatening Silla Boyce, whom Selina refers to as "the mother," also has a convincingly tender and thoughtful side that renders her one of Marshall's most complex characters. Although glimpses of this quality surface in her relationship with her husband, it is most apparent in a scene with the distraught Selina when she learns of her father's deportation. Presented with the precision of a still-life tableau, Selina rises out of her bed, repeatedly calling her mother "Hitler." When Silla approaches "the dangerous orbit around the bed," Selina grabs her mother's dress and brings her fist down on her mother's shoulder, methodically striking it, and saying the hated name. Silla endures and permits

Marshall in the late 1950s (photograph by Edmund Edwards; from the dust jacket for Brown Girl, Brownstones, *1959)*

Miss Thompson, an aged hairdresser from the South. Miss Thompson, the ancestor in this work, gives Selina her first curls, a significant event in the life of a young black girl, and teaches her about tolerance. Selina's journey to young adulthood includes her painful introduction to the reality of race, her sexual initiation with a failed Barbadian artist, and her rebellious betrayal of the Barbadian Homeowners Association, of which her mother is a member. She feigns allegiance to the group in order to win its scholarship money to escape Brooklyn and her mother. She confesses her plan, however, and reconciles with her mother, though the taint of her disgrace lingers. Selina's emergence into maturity is illustrated by her confession and her plans to leave Brooklyn for travel to Barbados. In the last scene of the novel, she throws one of her bracelets on the site of a demolished brownstone but keeps the other. This behavior recognizes her Brooklyn experience but also acknowledges that she is neither home nor whole. Poised for travel to Barbados, Selina is also positioned to seek a spiritual peace that has eluded her in the first segment of her life. The way the novel ends is Marshall's nod to the second and third novels of her trilogy, both of which feature the cultural journeys of women protagonists.

Although well received by reviewers and acknowledged as a critical success, *Brown Girl, Brownstones* was not a commercial success and, like most black fiction of the time, went out of print in the United States until the early 1980s. The novel has benefited from the interest in women's writing that emerged in the aftermath of the civil rights struggle and the women's rights campaign. Florence Howe of the Feminist Press expressed interest in republishing the book in response to several inquiries about it. Marshall gave permission, and *Brown Girl, Brownstones* enjoyed a spectacular comeback after the Feminist Press edition was published in 1981.

While Marshall completed *Brown Girl, Brownstones* in Barbados, she encountered the nucleus of the second novel of her trilogy, *The Chosen Place, The Timeless People*. Knowing the extensive research and time that her incomplete idea required, she wrote a second book in the interval. Its title, *Soul Clap Hands and Sing,* is taken from the poem "Sailing to Byzantium" by William Butler Yeats: "An aged man is but a paltry thing, / A tattered coat upon a stick, unless / Soul clap its hands and sing. . . ." These lines unambiguously convey the thematic focus of the book. It is a work about self-confrontation and action that is too little, too late, when aged men face their vacuous lives. In their panic, the old men turn to the vitality of young women for salvation. The dominant male presence in the stories is, in part, a response to queries raised from the first book— whether

this behavior until Selina is physically and mentally exhausted. Silla lifts her daughter, carries her into the parlor, and sits there holding her. "Then, almost reverently, she touched the tears that had dried white on her dark skin, traced with her finger the fragile outline of her face and rested her hand soothingly on her brow. . . . Yet, despite the tenderness and wonder and admiration of her touch, there was a frightening possessiveness. Each caress declared that she was touching something which was finally hers alone."

The brownstone has both literal and symbolic meaning as Silla's passionate quest for the promise of the American dream. Its importance also extends as the primary site for unfolding the protagonist's maturation. Selina carefully negotiates its physical and psychological spaces, trying, for example, to avoid encounters with her parents' conflicts. Several spaces in the brownstone hold particular lessons for her, aside from the mother's sterile white kitchen space and her father's pink suffused sunroom. In Suggie's room, Selina learns about woman's sexuality, while in Miss Mary's room, she becomes acquainted with the dangers of oppressive immersion in one's past history and with the way a distorted memory can obfuscate present time. As Selina's growth moves her outside the confines of the brownstone to the larger physical community, she encounters

Marshall could depict male characters as well as female characters. Each of the four novellas that make up the work has a geographic place name as its title. This naming strategy conveys Marshall's interest in the experiences of African Diaspora peoples.

In "Barbados" the seventy-year-old protagonist, Mr. Watford, unlike Deighton Boyce, achieves his dream of returning "home" to the island after fifty years in Boston and buying property and a home. He discovers himself sadly out-of-step with the place and its youthful energy, however. Watford is unaffected by the island's lush beauty as he settles into an unrelieved work routine. The presence of a girl hired for housekeeping chores eventually affects him, but only after he has spurned her uncomplicated offer of friendship. Watford's life has been solitary, except for occasional female company. His effort to join the human community comes too late.

Like Watford, Max Berman, a Jewish man in "Brooklyn," reaches old age without having experienced love, although he has had two wives. Teaching a summer French class, he is drawn through recognition of a kindred loneliness to a young black southern student. His intent, to exploit her loneliness, fails when she easily sees through his plan and rejects him. "Barbados" and "Brooklyn," the most reprinted selections from the book, both depict young earth-identified women through descriptive imagery. For example, "The girl" to whom Watford appeals has "feet like strong dark roots amid the jagged stones, her face tilted toward the sun. . . . But it was the bold and sensual strength of her legs which completely unstrung Mr. Watford." Both these women have the ripeness of life about and within them, but understanding the selfish, self-preserving instincts of Watford and Berman, respectively, the women refuse the exploitation that the men offer them.

As in the first two stories, issues of aging and spiritual sterility are evident in "British Guiana," and "Brazil." However, the latter two stories expand to embrace the complex Caribbean issues of identity and class. In "British Guiana" Gerald Motley, as his surname suggests, represents an amalgam of European, African, and East Indian racial heritages. His conflict thus involves his identity and class. Motley represents Marshall's fledgling exploration of interdependency among character, culture, and place. Motley's psychological predicament is linked not to a lack of human caring so much as to uncertainty about his identity. Both his race and his class issues originate in a legacy of slavery and colonization and subsequently rigid social and economic barriers. Motley embraces his creole identity that places him in better economic and social positions, but he relinquishes that component of his heritage that is African derived. His problem is thus his refusal or inability to accept all the strands of his heritage without privileging any one of them. The young woman in this story is not the object of an intended exploitation, but an object of blame for Motley's inability to confront his "self."

In "Brazil" similar issues of race and class reoccur but with a twist. Heitor Guimares, whose stage name is O Grande Caliban, is an entertainer whose identity merges completely with that of the comic character he plays. The crisis of identity occurs because with retirement imminent, Caliban will have no public audiences to affirm his identity. To locate that identity, he begins a literal and psychic journey back to the old section of Rio where he had worked before becoming a celebrity. Yet, expecting a source outside oneself to confirm identity assures failure since identity recognition must emerge from within. Like Milkman Dead Jr. did later in Toni Morrison's *Song of Solomon* (1977), Caliban returns to the old community wearing the trappings of success but fails in his quest for identity. Caliban, unlike the men of the other stories, has both a young wife and a mistress (his stage partner), but neither of them can assist him in his quest. Moreover, the socio-sexual stage roles between Caliban, the dark but small Brazilian, and Miranda, the tall, statuesque lover, complicate rather than simplify his quest.

Meaning, purpose, and spiritual redress in their empty lives thus elude these four men. They are nothing more than stick figures, and that is all they can be without a means of binding up their fragmented selves. Significantly, women in these four stories are symbols of vitality, nourishment, and fertility. They anticipate Marshall's fashioning of women protagonists as those most capable of interior transformation.

In addition to the novellas, Marshall has written other short fiction, including "Reena," a story originally published in *Harper's Magazine* in 1962, which has received considerable attention. Reprinted in *Reena and Other Stories* in 1983, it was commissioned by the magazine for a special issue titled "The American Female," and Marshall's piece represented their inclusion of the black female writer. Languishing after its debut, the story has become popular since its placement in Toni Cade Bambara's anthology, *The Black Woman* (1970). Marshall admits to writing about women like herself in this story, lower-middle or middle-class urban working women of a West Indian American background who had attended New York City colleges in the 1940s and 1950s. The situation is a relative's funeral, and Reena and her friend meet and talk at the wake after the burial service.

The nucleus of the second novel in Marshall's trilogy, *The Chosen Place, The Timeless People,* was emerging even as she wrote the novellas of *Soul Clap Hands and Sing.* The work that was to become the most monumental effort of her corpus began from the author's observation of a group of social scientists in Barbados for summer fieldwork. She thought that with further elaboration, her observations might constitute the outline for a novel. As the outline materialized, Marshall understood the massive research requirements in order that the historical context might be accurate. *The Chosen Place, The Timeless People* is her only novel exclusively set in the Caribbean.

The novel depicts the static peasant population of an imaginary but representative, postcolonial island called Bourne. The entire island is featured in the work, but its central action occurs in the community of Bournehills. Both the island, its towns, and its people are captives of their historical past. In addition, a complex network of myth and ritual animates the story and is integral to its history, community, and people. The emphasis on history is immediately apparent through the epigraph, borrowed from the Tiv of West Africa: "Once a great wrong has been done, it never dies. People speak the words of peace, but their hearts do not forgive. Generations perform ceremonies of reconciliation but there is no end." An early description in the novel establishes the link between Bournehills people and their African forebears: the island faces "east, the open sea, and across the sea, hidden beyond the horizon, the colossus of Africa." This diasporic connection is maintained throughout the novel.

Peasant existence on the island is at once vigorous and rich but also staid and poverty infected. The population levels above the peasants include the colored at the middle range and the wealthy, business people, mostly white, at the top. The protagonist, Merle Kinbona, is a mix of all three groups: her parentage (white colonial father and servant mother), her European education, and property-owning status situate her among the middle class. Colonialism occupies the same social and hierarchical structures as slavery, and Merle's parentage mirrors the personal and commercial relationships between white patriarchy and the African Caribbean population.

Bourne Island is a symbolic as well as a literal representation in the novel. Physically, it symbolizes other ravished localities, and its inhabitants mirror the fate of other peoples whose existence includes forced servitude and colonialism. This relationship between place and people so central to the vision of the novel is revealed in various ways, but primarily through the economic structure that privileges the upper classes and disenfranchises the poor. The peasant population, the cane-field workers, remain bound to the earth in a seemingly never-improving relationship. A determining quality about the Bournehills peasants is their resistance to technological advances that others have tried to intro-

duce to them. They remain rooted to their history, particularly in the person of Cuffee Ned, a slave revolutionary.

Through Cuffee Ned, Marshall weds history, myth, ritual, and festival. This history, recorded in the formal texts of the people, plays a vigorous role in the daily lives of the Bournehills poor. During their annual carnival pageant, they celebrate the feat of Cuffee Ned, who led a slave insurrection and provided the leadership for repelling the British. At the local rum tavern, the men's friendly argument about Cuffee Ned's exploits assumes mythic proportion and ritual patterning. Even the physical landscape keeps his exploits visible. The hill where Cuffee Ned burned his slave owner's manor looks as if the event happened recently. They call the site Pyre Hill. The reverence given Cuffee transcends folk-hero status and becomes instead a revitalizing symbol of the community's potential for self-empowerment.

This effort is visible in the annual carnival pageant where the Bournehills residents re-create Cuffee Ned's finest hour. Their masque, a physical rendering of Pyre Hill and an enactment of the revolt and the resistance, takes on mythic and ritualistic overtones. As myth it marks the past commencement of a new way of existence that the population renews and sustains through oral tradition and festive reenactment. As ritual, it is repetitive, organized, dramatized, and group sustaining. Cuffee is the cultural hero, and his deeds are seen as bringing about an ideal community. "Reaping our crops together, sharing whatsomever we had with each other. We was a people then, man; and it was beautiful to see," one character boasts. Their masque as ritual revitalizes and heals for an additional year. They take strength for the future from the resistance of one of their own. The peasant population and the history of Bourne Island are thus integral to the vision of *The Chosen Place, The Timeless People*.

Within this context of history and myth, of class and caste, and of a colonial mentality, Marshall examines the issues of philanthropy and western intervention through the research team headed by the Jewish Saul Amron, who brings his wife, Harriet, and his assistant, Allen Fuso. Saul's method differs from previous research teams in his effort to interact with and to understand the culture and motivation of the people whose economic lives he hopes to improve. Coming from an historical background of suffering, Saul can empathize with the dispossessed people of Bourne island and make credible his behavior with them. Through him Marshall examines the figure of the cultural intruder who enters a community with noble intentions of assistance. His goals are not achieved, but he makes friends and moves beyond a superficial understanding of what is required. Saul's sincerity is evident in many ways, including his camaraderie with the village men in the rum shop and his participation in communal rituals such as Whitsun, the pig killing, and Carnival. His political identification with them is perhaps best illustrated by his involvement in their struggle to transport their sugarcane crops to another market after the local processing factory shuts down.

As a receptive character, Saul is capable of being altered by his encounter with Bourne Island. So is Allen Fuso, who confronts his homosexuality on the island. Harriet Amron, however, proves incapable of introspection and personal change. As Saul's character has been shaped by identification with historical suffering, Harriet's has been shaped by a history of hegemony. Through her, Marshall explores the relationship between Western economic power and monetarily disenfranchised localities. She also reveals a little-known fact of women's investment in the slave trade, the industry that financially enriched Harriet's female forebears. Her connections to wealth and privilege and her refusal to engage their meaning effectively isolate her character from any growth. Her seeming engagement with the women of Bourne Island remains superficial. She is thus antithetical to her husband, and her positions prove disruptive to her marriage and to her husband's work.

The complex ideologies of this novel are tightly balanced by a large cast of island characters, including the sugarcane workers. Marshall conveys through them the drudgery and hardship of harvesting sugarcane and the ravages of their historic past. She succeeds, too, in conveying an internal vitality that somehow fuels their resistance to modernization brought from outside while they await salvation from within their community. They refuse, for example, to use tools brought as part of a "government scheme" to ease their economic deprivation. Pipes for irrigation systems lie rusting in the small cane fields; a factory intended for pottery production decays because people refuse to work there; an experimental banana grove intended eventually to replace small cane plots fails for lack of participation. Intuitively, perhaps, the men and women understand that the economic assistance from the West to third-world countries, in whatever guise, will ultimately extend the exploitation and destruction already in place. Thus, within the structures of British colonialism that persist in spite of formal independence, the workers continue as they are.

In her work, Marshall often employs the automobile as a symbol of the industrial might of the West and its ability to shape or to destroy a people's self-perception. Merle Kinbona, for example, drives a Bentley, an obvious symbol of the prestige and authority formerly

Dust jacket for Marshall's 1969 novel, set on a fictional island in the West Indies

given to the colonial governor. Like colonialism, however, by the time Merle is driving the car, it is a battered shell of its former self, although it is still operating. Gerald Motley, in the novella "Brazil," having acknowledged his hollowness and yet unable to reconcile his identity, dies when his Jaguar crashes. In the case of Vereson Walkes (Vere), a German-originated automobile is used to illustrate the destructive capability of the West in the shaping of Caribbean identity, even outside the island. In significant ways, Vere is another version of Deighton Boyce, the Barbadian immigrant in *Brown Girl, Brownstones*. Vere leaves Bourne Island on a government plan for Caribbean men. He finds himself in Florida cutting cane in the same kind of menial labor he could have experienced at home. Failing to discover his definition of manhood, he returns to the island still in search of self-definition, and seeks it through his plan to win the Whitmonday race. He purchases a wreck of an old car, an Opel with a German motor and American body, to rebuild. "It's got to be fire red, so when people see me coming they'll know for certain it's me." As a symbol of prestige, power, and speed, the automobile is a likely object with which a young man in search of definition might align himself. But for Vere, reconstructing the car is equal to self-reconstruction, as he revisions himself though the tools of the West. "It's the car make him feel he's a man," the people say, as they agree that it "meant him no good." Having readied and tested the car, he enters the race, envisioning victory. On the last lap, however, the Opel behaves as if it "possessed a mind, an intelligence, that for some reason had remained unalterably opposed to Vere, so that while doing his bidding and permitting him to think he was making it over into his own image to express him, it had also at the same time been conspiring against him and waiting coolly for this moment to show its hand. . . . [Perhaps the collapse flowed] out of a profoundly self destructive impulse within the machine itself." The Opel crashes, and Vere is killed.

The remaining structures of the colonial past, its economic and psychological fracturing, the interdependency between the people and the land, and most important, the necessity of self-definition, are all stunningly brought together in the dynamic protagonist named Merle Kinbona. Her mixed parentage reflects the power structure on Bourne Island. Her failure of self-definition is symbolically reflected through dress iconography in which her African, European, and Caribbean strands seem at war with each other. Having gone to London to study history, Merle returns with little but the failure of an exploitative lesbian relationship and a troubled marriage. Her husband, an African student, leaves her and takes their daughter to East Africa on learning of her deception about her London lover. Merle's unresolved issues are treacherous to her mental and physical health; nevertheless, she is feisty, politically minded, and desperately in love with the island and her people. She is a forceful vitality, a contrast in a mainly lethargic setting, a streak of red energy in an otherwise gray-blue landscape.

Although the cane cutters of Bourne Island are connected to the ravages and plight of the land, Merle is the symbolic embodiment of this interdependency. Barbara Christian has characterized this phenomenon as "the delineation of personal characters . . . to show how individuals are distinctive features of the seemingly impersonal face of history. Time and timelessness and character and culture exist in a continual movement." The island's history is recalled through Merle in her many significant personal losses. As an adult having returned (or retreated) to the island, she feels its losses and, even more keenly, recognizes her inability to affect any change. Attempting to teach youngsters history, perhaps aiming for long-term change, she is fired for teaching about Cuffee Ned. Although she has a forceful

personality, Merle's activism is largely confined to vitriolic discourse. She rails about conditions, and when the sugarcane processing plant is shut down after the cane of the colonial landowners is harvested before the workers' individual plots, she verbally attacks the plant manager. Her talk is ineffectual in island politics but can help salvage her "self," and it is the self that must first be healed.

Merle comes to recognize that the beginnings of self-healing lie within herself, through her ability to talk and her identity with the land. In the wake of the ritual of Carnival and overcoming her fear of another rejection, Merle plans to travel to Uganda to find her husband and child. The novel thus ends without answering the question of Merle's success or failure on her venture. It ends as *Brown Girl, Brownstones* does, with the protagonist poised for flight to a significant place in her continuing search for psychic salvation.

In *Praisesong for the Widow,* the journey is completed. Avatara (Avey) Johnson, the widowed protagonist, crosses over to the other side in a reverse journey from spiritual death to spiritual life. Evoking the literal triangular middle passage across the Atlantic Ocean, through happenstance, myth, and the intercession of the ancestors, Avey crosses from the island of Grenada to the smaller island of Carriacou, where she is symbolically and literally reconciled to her heritage and to wholeness. The African Diaspora is represented on Carriacou through its dispersed people and through West African cultural traditions, including the Big Drum and ancestral worship. Avey Johnson thus completes the journeys left incomplete for Selina Boyce and Merle Kinbona.

Praisesong for the Widow is told largely through flashback and memory. The economic success that animated Silla Boyce, and to a lesser degree, Deighton, in *Brown Girl, Brownstones* becomes a reality in *Praisesong for the Widow.* Avey and her husband, Jerome (Jay), marry, live in New York, and begin work. Jay's plan for economic betterment, work during the day and accounting school at night, is threatened by failure when their three children are quickly born. Financial pressures strain the couple's marriage. Nevertheless, Jay is single-minded in his grueling schedule, and after more than twelve years the couple begins to see some success. The question that plagues Avey during her flashbacks to this period of their marriage, and also that the novel asks, is how they might have achieved financial comfort without losing a significant part of themselves to materialism? Marshall dramatizes their loss through double exposures, as when Avey does not recognize herself in a mirror and when Jay shaves off his mustache and looks unlike himself to his wife. The consequence of loss, however, is shown to be a culturally unmoored self more than a physically changed body.

During the summer when Avey was a child, her mother sent her "down South" to visit great aunt Cuney. Aunt Cuney (and later Lebert Joseph) is the ancestor of this novel, responsible for teaching Avey a crucial lesson that she forgets as an adult in the modern world. Similar to the Africans who flew back to the homeland, Aunt Cuney narrates the story of the Ibos, who, on being brought out of the slave ship at Ibo Landing in South Carolina, looked around, saw the future in America, turned their backs on it, and walked across the water back home. As in traditions of African storytelling, this story is being passed on. Aunt Cuney's gran had told it to her, and Aunt Cuney now tells it to Avey. The gran had added a coda: "Her body she always usta say might be in Tatem but her mind, her mind was long gone with the Ibos." This crucial lesson for survival—if escape is impossible, protect the division between the physical place of the body and the psychological space of the mind—is lost to Avey. But as West African tradition believes, Aunt Cuney reasserts herself in the widow Avey's dreams in order to redirect her path. When a living intercessor is necessary, Lebert Joseph on the island of Grenada takes on the role. Significantly, he is a Legba figure, one who has one leg in this world and one in the next. Thus, he limps and fluctuates between looking incredibly old and acting surprisingly youthful. Moreover, he has the gift of knowing what is unsaid. He convinces Avey to delay her departure to New York a day or so longer to go to Carriacou to attend a Big Drum ceremony.

Carriacou is a legitimate choice for Avey's spiritual reconnection because of its particular history. Marshall visited the island in the 1960s and discovered its retention of a full-fledged ancestor cult and the Big Drum or Nation Dance. This ceremony—a recognition of African nation groups and an occasion of reverence for the elderly, living and dead, through drumming, singing, and dancing—still thrives on Carriacou, a small island accessible by boat from Grenada. When Avey participates in the ceremony, its familiarity comes from having stood in South Carolina with Aunt Cuney and having watched the ring shout, a religious dance practiced in the rural churches. This diasporic link is thematically crucial. This ceremony, as Christian has recognized, ritualistically joins several black societies: "the Ring Dances of Tatem, the Bojangles of New York, the voodoo drums of Haiti, and the rhythms of the various African peoples brought to the new world." Other research has also illustrated the presence of the ring shout during slavery, illustrating its unifying qualities among different African peoples. The dance functions to restore Avey to her cultural roots and to her commu-

nity. Symbolically, the dance takes place on a bare hill, because the earth in African tradition is life-giving and a place of stability for humans. Avey is restored to herself and speaks her true name, Avatara, which suggests the descent of a deity to the earth in an incarnate form. Her journey has become one of self-discovery.

Following the paradigm of the mythic hero, Avatara plans to return home and then to Tatum, South Carolina, where Aunt Cuney had lived. She will keep the tradition alive, inviting her grandchildren for the summer, and telling them the story of the Ibos. In New York, as well, "Her territory would be the street corners and front lawns in their small section of North White Plains . . . the office buildings of Manhattan . . . the entranceways of the skyscrapers." She will be a woman involved in saving youth, in saving her community. Thus, the ending of *Praisesong for the Widow* fulfills the promise of the trilogy.

In its departure from the trilogy, *Daughters* embraces other issues. As if to emphasize its difference, in *Daughters* Marshall alters the style of the narrative from the conventional modes seen in her earlier novels. In *Daughters,* as she explains in her interview with Daryl Dance in *Southern Review,* character monologues are extensively used to reveal the personalities of others. The silence that results for some of the characters is deliberately representative of silence about personal issues.

Daughters is set in New York and in the Caribbean on a fictional island called Triunion. The symmetry of the narrative is carefully balanced. Estelle, a black American reared in Connecticut, marries Primus Mackenzie, a Triunion politician, and moves there where their daughter, Ursa, is born and reared to high-school age. Ursa completes her education in the United States and lives and works in New York. Juxtaposing characters in the city and on the island allows Marshall to investigate issues in common between the two localities. Thus, the remnants of colonialism on a so-called third-world island are shown to be remarkably similar to political decisions and controls in a black city community. The need for revolutionaries in present times continues as it did during slavery. The personal remains the political.

Although Ursa is clearly the protagonist, she shares the stage with a constellation of other "daughters" whose significance to the unfolding narrative is conveyed through a design where their names identify the chapters or monologues of the book. In this multivocal text, the daughters of Triunion—Malvern, Astral Forde, and Celestine—comprise three different gendered experiences and illustrate three examples of self-definition. Estelle, who might have been characterized as a cultural interloper, is rather a psychically whole woman

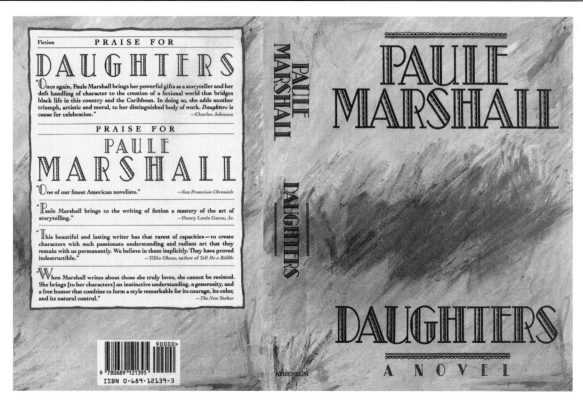

Dust jacket for Marshall's 1991 novel, about an African American woman who marries a West Indian politician

who identifies with the impoverished women of Triunion and with its revolutionary history, particularly women's role in that history. Finally, Viney, Ursa's New York friend, is the modern woman, a successful single mother balancing a good job against raising a well-rounded son. All of these women, with the exceptions of Malvern and Viney, form a constellation around Primus Mackenzie or the PM, a Triunion politician, whose idealism deteriorates over the years until it becomes a betrayal of his constituency. Primus, a well-drawn, charismatic man, exemplifies patriarchy and the ineffectual politician constrained and ultimately defeated by remaining colonial structures. Like Marshall's other male characters, his personal flaws contribute to his defeat. Primus's charisma holds Estelle, Celestine, and Astral Forde in orbit about him. Primus and Estelle's first years of marriage, like those of Avatara and Jerome in *Praisesong for the Widow,* are loving and romantic. The love remains, but its character alters when Estelle discovers his long-term infidelity with Astral Forde, called in island terminology, his "keep miss." Though older than Primus, Celestine, who became a young housemaid in the home of Primus's mother and continued as housekeeper in his home, has loved him over the years.

The force of his magnetism, in fact, is at the core of the conflict between Ursa and her father, for he rep-

resents the stifling hegemonic impulse of colonialism in his dual roles as politician and biological father. Ursa's physical separation from the island is insufficient for her total liberation. A more significant and personally intrinsic act is necessary. The resolution, which necessitates Ursa's return to Triunion, unites daughter and mother, joins the personal and the political, and suggests hope for the island's future through a new generation. Ursa's determination to be her own woman on her own terms, the characterization of Viney as a politically conscious, self-defined contemporary mother and worker, and the depiction of other women characters creates feminist interest in this text. Marshall's ability to draw women of complexity and intrigue while still making them accessible is nothing new to her work.

Paule Marshall's work has won several prestigious awards, including a Guggenheim Fellowship in 1960; the Rosenthal Award from the National Institute of Arts and Letters, 1962, for *Soul Clap Hands and Sing;* Ford Foundation grants in 1964–1965; or a National Endowment for the Arts grant, 1967–1968; the New York State Governor's Arts Award for Literature in 1987; and the John Dos Passos Award for Literature in 1989. Winning the MacArthur Fellowship in 1992 is perhaps her grandest honor to date. In addition to writing, Marshall has held many university teaching positions, including Regents Professor at the University of California at Berkeley in 1984 and professor of English and creative writing at Virginia Commonwealth University beginning in 1987.

Interviews:

Joyce Pettis, "A *MELUS* Interview: Paule Marshall," *MELUS,* 17, no. 4 (1991–1992): 117–129;

Daryl Dance, "Interview with Paule Marshall," *Southern Review,* 28 (1992): 1–20;

Molara Ogundipez-Leslie, "'Re-Creating Ourselves All Over the World': A Conversation with Paule Marshall," in *Moving Beyond Boundaries, II: Black Women's Diasporas,* edited by Carole Boyce Davies (New York: New York University Press, 1994), pp. 19–26;

Angela Elam, "To Be in the World: An Interview with Paule Marshall," *New Letters,* 62 (1996): 96–105.

Bibliography:

Harihar Kulkarni, "Paule Marshall: A Bibliography," *Callaloo: A Journal of African American and African Arts and Letters,* 16 (Winter 1993): 245–267.

References:

Barbara Christian, *Black Women Novelists: The Development of a Tradition* (Westport, Conn.: Greenwood Press, 1980), pp. 80–136;

Eugenia Collier, "The Closing of the Circle: Movement from Division to Wholeness in Paule Marshall's Fiction," in *Black Women Writers (1950–1980): A Critical Evaluation,* edited by Mari Evans (New York: Anchor, 1984), pp. 295–315;

Eugenia C. DeLomotte, *Places of Silence, Journeys of Freedom: The Fiction of Paule Marshall* (Philadelphia: University of Pennsylvania Press, 1998);

Dorothy Hamer Denniston, *The Fiction of Paule Marshall: Reconstructions of History, Culture, and Gender* (Knoxville: University of Tennessee Press, 1995);

Shanna D. Greene, "Paule Marshall (1929–   )," in *Contemporary African American Novelists: A Bio-Bibliographical Critical Sourcebook* (Westport, Conn.: Greenwood Press, 1990), pp. 295–303;

Joyce Pettis, *Toward Wholeness in Paule Marshall's Fiction* (Charlottesville: University of Virginia Press, 1995).

Marge Piercy

(31 March 1936 –   )

Sue B. Walker
University of South Alabama

See also the Piercy entry in *DLB 120: American Poets Since World War II, Third Series.*

BOOKS: *Breaking Camp* (Middletown, Conn.: Wesleyan University Press, 1968);

Hard Loving (Middletown, Conn.: Wesleyan University Press, 1969);

Going Down Fast (New York: Trident, 1969);

Dance the Eagle to Sleep (Garden City, N.Y.: Doubleday, 1970; London: W. H. Allen, 1971);

4-Telling, by Piercy, Emmet Jarrett, Dick Lourie, and Robert Hershon (Trumansburg, N.Y.: New/Books, 1971);

Small Changes (Garden City, N.Y.: Doubleday, 1973; Harmondsworth, U.K.: Penguin, 1987);

To Be of Use (Garden City, N.Y.: Doubleday, 1973);

Living in the Open (New York: Knopf, 1976);

Woman on the Edge of Time (New York: Knopf, 1976; London: Women's Press, 1979);

The High Cost of Living (New York: Harper & Row, 1978; London: Women's Press, 1979);

The Twelve-Spoked Wheel Flashing (New York: Knopf, 1978);

Vida (New York: Summit, 1979 [i.e., 1980]; London: Women's Press, 1980);

The Last White Class: A Play About Neighborhood Terror, by Piercy and Ira Wood (Trumansburg, N.Y.: Crossing Press, 1980);

The Moon Is Always Female (New York: Knopf, 1980);

Circles on the Water: Selected Poems (New York: Knopf, 1982);

Braided Lives (New York: Summit, 1982; London: Allen Lane, 1982);

Parti-Colored Blocks for a Quilt (Ann Arbor: University of Michigan Press, 1982);

Stone, Paper, Knife (New York: Knopf, 1983; London: Pandora, 1983);

Fly Away Home (New York: Summit, 1984; London: Chatto & Windus, 1984);

My Mother's Body (New York: Knopf, 1985; London: Pandora, 1985);

Marge Piercy (photograph by Robert M. Shapiro; from the dust jacket for Vida, *1980)*

Gone to Soldiers (New York: Summit, 1987; London: Joseph, 1987);

Available Light (New York: Knopf, 1988; London: Pandora, 1988);

Summer People (New York: Summit, 1989; London: Joseph, 1989);

The Earth Shines Secretly: A Book of Days, by Piercy and Nell Blaine (Cambridge, Mass.: Zoland, 1990);

He, She, & It (New York: Knopf, 1991); republished as *Body of Glass* (London: Joseph, 1992);

Mars and Her Children (New York: Knopf, 1992);

The Longings of Women (New York: Fawcett Columbine, 1994; London: Joseph, 1994);

Eight Chambers of the Heart (London: Penguin, 1995);

City of Darkness, City of Light (New York: Fawcett Columbine, 1996; London: Joseph, 1997);

What Are Big Girls Made Of ? (New York: Knopf, 1997);

The Art of Blessing the Day (London: Five Leaves, 1998; New York: Knopf, 1999);

Storm Tide, by Piercy and Wood (New York: Fawcett Columbine, 1998);

Written in Bone: The Early Poems of Marge Piercy (London: Five Leaves, 1998); republished as *Early Grrrl: The Early Poems of Marge Piercy* (Wellfleet, Mass.: Leapfrog Press, 1999);

Three Women (New York: Morrow, 1999; London: Piatkus, 2000).

RECORDINGS: *Marge Piercy: Poems,* New York, Radio Free People, 1969;

"Laying Down the Tower," in *Black Box 1,* New York, Radio Free People, 1972;

Reclaiming Ourselves, by Piercy, the Painted Women's Ritual Theater, and Jeriann Hilderley, New York, Radio Free People, 1974;

The Ordeal of the Woman Writer [panel discussion with Toni Morrison and Erica Jong], New York, Norton, 1974;

Reading and Thoughts, Deland, Florida, Everett/Edwards, 1976;

At the Core, Washington, D.C., Watershed Tapes, 1976.

OTHER: "The Grand Coolie Damn," in *Sisterhood is Powerful: An Anthology of Writings from the Women's Liberation Movement,* edited by Robin Morgan (New York: Random House, 1970), pp. 421–438;

"Women's Liberation: Nobody's Baby Now," in *Defiance: A Radical Review,* edited by Dotson Rader (New York: Paperback Library, 1970), pp. 134–162;

"Mirror Images," in *Women's Culture: The Women's Renaissance of the Seventies,* edited by Gayle Kimball (Metuchen, N.J. & London: Scarecrow Press, 1980), pp. 187–194;

"Starting Support Groups for Writers," in *Words in Our Pockets: The Feminist Writers Guild Handbook,* edited by Celeste West (San Francisco: Bootlegger, 1981), pp. 1–11;

Early Ripening: American Women's Poetry Now, edited, with an introduction, by Piercy (New York: Pandora, 1987; London & Boston: Pandora, 1987);

Ellen Messer and Kathryn E. May, *Back Rooms: Voices from the Illegal Abortion Era,* foreword by Piercy (New York: St. Martin's Press, 1988);

"Active in Time and History," in *Paths of Resistance: The Art and Craft of the Political Novel,* edited by William Zinsser (New York: Houghton Mifflin, 1989), pp. 89–123;

"Simone de Beauvoir," in *Daughters of de Beauvoir,* edited by Penny Forster and Imogen Sutton (London: Women's Press, 1989), pp. 112–123;

"The Dark Thread in the Weave," in *Testimony: Contemporary Writers Make the Holocaust Personal,* edited by David Rosenberg (New York: Random House, 1989), pp. 171–191;

"Fame, Fortune and Other Tawdry Illusions," in *Written in Water, Written in Stone,* edited by Martin Lammon (Ann Arbor: University of Michigan Press, 1996), pp. 171–180.

SELECTED PERIODICAL PUBLICATIONS–
UNCOLLECTED:

"Going over Jordan," *Transatlantic Review,* 22 (Fall 1966): 148–157;

"The Foreign Policy Association: 50 Years of Successful Imperialism," *CAW,* no. 1 (February 1968): 6–10;

"Love Me Tonight, God," *Paris Review,* 43 (Summer 1968): 185–200;

"Do You Love Me?" *Second Wave,* 1, no. 4 (1972): 26–27, 40;

"Somebody Who Understands You," *Moving Out,* 2, no. 2 (1972): 56–59;

"Books for the Daughters," *Margins,* no. 7 (August/September 1973): 1–2;

"Little Sister, Cat and Mouse," *Second Wave,* 3, no. 1 (1973): 9–12, 41;

"From Where I Work: A Column," *American Poetry Review,* 5, no. 1 and no. 5 (1976); 6, no. 3 (1977);

"I Will Not Describe What I Did," *Mother Jones,* 7 (February/March 1982): 44–56.

Marge Piercy's reputation as an important fiction writer began with the appearance of her first published novel, *Going Down Fast,* in 1969. Especially with *Gone to Soldiers* (1987) and *City of Darkness, City of Light* (1996), her genius for transforming history is realized. In all her novels Piercy examines women's roles, especially those traditionally relegated to men.

In an interview published in *Ways of Knowing: Essays on Marge Piercy* (1991), Piercy defines her fictional concerns by stating that she is "conscious of being very strongly in a women's tradition: an oral Jewish women's tradition transmitted to me by my

Piercy   Anna VI-2

green. The sky was pale ~~and~~ ~~cloudy,~~ but the sun smote the
street glaringly. In a block she unbuttoned her coat again.
The big yellow envelope felt conspicuous. ~~She dreaded running~~
~~into someone who'd ask, Hey Anna, what's in that?~~ ~~Hastily~~ Duck-
ing into the Oriental Institute, she hurried across the lobby,
past the guard and into the first big exhibition room. Leon,
Leon where are you, damn your eyes. ~~Nowhere.~~ Slowly she walked
the central aisle between cases of Egyptian artifacts. ~~Nowhere.~~
Oh, that completely unreliable bastard. Why couldn't he get up
when he had to?

Toward the great Assyrian winged bull ~~she walked,~~ letting
the envelope ~~just~~ trail the floor between two fingers, toward the
sideways walking wallhigh winged bull with the face and beard of
a man. ~~Right up to the velvet rope.~~ Strong and full of dignity
it spread, surmounting photographs of its excavation. The ~~man's~~
legs were muscular pillars, with sexual cannon; the man's fore-
head was broad and deep. The beard extended itself square and
curly like a cultivated field. ~~She realized she was smiling.~~
Beast ~~A strange emblem~~ proclaimed by the sign a cherub: Menal
did ~~cherub,~~ how your name decline to pink-assed tutti? As she
stepped back to admire the brawny legs, the stout chest, ~~the~~ owl
heavy, fullfeathered wings, she knew it reminded her of Rowley.
Still she smiled, feeling ripples; I should never have let you
into my life. Do you really think it right to have thrown me
over for a chit like Caroline, no matter how pretty? I would

— going down
fast —

Page from the typescript, with Piercy's revisions, for her 1969 novel, Going Down Fast
(The Marge Piercy Papers, Special Collections Library, University of Michigan)

mother and grandmother, first of all; second, a woman's tradition in writing; third, a contemporary community of women writers from whom I learn and with whom I share the discoveries each of us makes." Although women's issues always underlie Piercy's examination of history and culture and race and ethnicity, her fiction moves beyond particular causes to the question "who can bear hope back into the world," as she asks in *Stone, Paper, Knife* (1983).

Born on 31 March 1936, Marge Piercy grew up in inner-city Detroit within a patriarchal working-class family. Her father, Robert Douglas Piercy, who was born into a Presbyterian family but observed no religion, came from Welsh-English stock, grew up in a soft-coal mining town in Pennsylvania. He worked for Westinghouse all his adult life but was laid off for a year and a half during the Depression. Piercy's mother, Bert Bernice Bunnin Piercy, grew up in poverty and never finished the tenth grade. She taught her daughter to observe closely, value curiosity, and love books, fostering in her the characteristics that Piercy claims made her a poet and writer of fiction.

Piercy was particularly fond of her maternal grandmother, Hannah Bunnin Adler, who remarried some years after her first husband was murdered. Hannah Adler was born in Lithuania, the daughter of a rabbi; it was she who gave her granddaughter the Jewish name Marah and who, along with Marge's mother, brought her up in the Jewish faith, a heritage Percy affirms throughout her work. Piercy has one sibling–Grant Courtade, her mother's son by a previous marriage, who is fourteen years her senior. In a series of poems about him in *What Are Big Girls Made Of?* (1997) she says that although she and her brother "grew out of the same mother, they never spoke real words since she turned twelve." Despite this distance between them, however, Courtade had an important role in shaping his sister's psyche. From him she acquired what she has called "a license / for the right of the body to joy." This license allows Piercy to depict the faces of poverty, violence, and the ugliness of oppression, but still to hold out hope that religions and races can live together harmoniously. As clearly as any writer of her time, Marge Piercy conveys what it is to be a Jewish woman writer with strong links to her family and beliefs.

After attending public schools in Detroit, Piercy enrolled at the University of Michigan, winning Hopwood Awards for poetry and fiction in 1956 and for poetry in 1957. She earned her B.A. in 1957, having been elected to Phi Beta Kappa and Phi Kappa Phi. After earning an M.A. from Northwestern University in 1958, Piercy married Michel Schiff, a Jewish particle physicist, and went with him to live in France. Piercy ascribes the breakup of this marriage to Schiff's inability to pay serious attention to her writing conventional views on the roles of women. Divorced at twenty-three Piercy supported herself with various part-time jobs: secretary, switchboard operator, department-store clerk, artists' model, and instructor at the Gary extension of Indiana University (1960–1962). During this time she wrote several unpublished novels and also became active in the Civil Rights movement.

In 1962 Piercy married Robert Shapiro, a computer scientist. The open marriage that they established meant that other men and women often shared the house with them. Over the next few years the couple lived in Cambridge, Massachusetts, San Francisco, and Boston. In spring 1965 Piercy and her husband moved to New York City, where she did research on the CIA, helped found North American Congress on Latin America (NACLA), and continued to be active in Students for a Democratic Society (SDS). As she continued writing and attempting to get her work published, Piercy and her husband became increasingly active in the anti–Vietnam War movement. Her time was consumed by these political and literary activities during 1969, the year in which her first published novel appeared.

Growing out of her political involvement during the 1960s, *Going Down Fast* demonstrates how power corrupts even when it seems to represent progress. Such progressive developments as urban renewal and the building of a university extension may result in mere demolition, which Piercy likens to legalized rape. In this novel, Anna Levinowitz, a Jewish teacher at the university extension in Gary, Indiana, watches helplessly as her former home is destroyed:

> The crane stood beside her building with neck bowed and suppliant, head resting on the ground. Her old rooms lay open. The outer wall and circlet of windows were gone to dust. The pale blue walls of her bedroom, the white wall of her kitchen were nude to the passerby. She felt a dart of shame.

In *Going Down Fast* and the novels that followed, Piercy's radical beliefs about the oppression of women found literary expression. In "A Fish Needs a Bicycle," an essay published in *Parti-Colored Blocks for a Quilt* (1982), she says that she finds it "absolutely essential as a poet and novelist to . . . draw from Marxism . . . a sense of class." Along with anarchism and feminism, these "three equally old radical collections of theory and practice . . . have shaped my political activities, my political thinking and all my writing." In *Going Down Fast* Anna confronts the questions: "what have I done with my life? where am I going?" Because sexual relationships confer possession and function, it is not surprising that while she is cooking in the kitchen, her lover pinches her from behind. Not only is Anna serving veal in sour cream, she is serving a man as a sexual object. Piercy finds that men often see their relations to women as taming and dominating. Anna's friend, Leon, tells her a story that illustrates this point:

> A man got himself a pretty bright-colored bird because he liked the way it sang. He took it home and put it in a cage, but it wouldn't sing when it couldn't fly. Every day the bird got smaller and smaller; it wouldn't eat and drink and finally got so small it flew out like a mosquito through the wire mesh. That goes to show you, the man said, I should've invested in a better cage.

In the years following the publishing of *Going Down Fast* the political movement Piercy was part of gradually fragmented, and she became involved in the women's movement—writing articles, organizing consciousness-raising groups, and attending feminist functions. In 1971 Piercy and her husband, Robert Shapiro, moved to Cape Cod, where she still lives. Once there, Piercy's creativity and sense of peace blossomed. She discovered that she loved gardening, became active with local women's groups, and made frequent trips to Boston. Piercy's marriage began to fail. She and Shapiro were divorced in 1980.

During these years, Piercy's fiction grew progressively stronger, and her intense interest in history and politics is again evident in *Dance the Eagle to Sleep* (1970). Classified as dystopian science fiction, the novel recalls the author's experiences as a member of SDS and anticipates her later interest in futuristic worlds. In this novel she depicts marginalized groups such as the Dakota Indians dancing a world into being, a "world in which things had been happy and good, and right. As in much of Piercy's fiction, the story is told from multiple points of view: in this case those of Corey, a half-Indian leader; Billy, a high-school whiz kid; Sean/Shawn, a musical rock star; and Jill/Joanna, a runaway teenager. *Dance the Eagle to Sleep* also deals with the effects of violence on and by political groups.

In *Small Changes* (1973) Piercy takes these ideas further, registering the meager alterations in the lives of women in spite of the so-called radical movements of the 1960s. Piercy says that this novel was designed to raise the consciousness of women about various entrapments—especially those of marriage. The question of what it means to be a "real" woman is addressed through the liberation of the protagonist, Beth Phail. The novel demonstrates how being a woman is traditionally grounded in male-centered biases that deny the validity of people often labeled as poor, white, black, lesbian, disabled, and transsexual. Piercy shows that such categorization often results in inaccurate and judgmental definitions. Through telling their stories, women are able to emancipate themselves from enclosure in patriarchal definitions.

In an autobiographical essay in volume one of *Contemporary Authors Autobiography Series,* Piercy says that her next novel, *Woman on the Edge of Time* (1976), arose from "a tension between the harshness of much of my earlier life and the gratitude I felt toward the land where I was living. . . . It was also the first of my works to pay some sort of homage backward to my mother, for there is a lot of her in the character of Consuelo Ramos." As she explains in *Parti-Colored Blocks for a Quilt,* Piercy's women are bound by sex roles that divide "humanity into winners and losers, makers and made, doers and done. . . ." Who, she asks, "wants to be passive, moist, cold, receptive, unmoving, inert; sort of a superbasement of humanity?" Although the fictional Mattapoisett falls short of being Eden, it does hold out the possibility of a better world.

Envisioning gardens of Eden where there are none is one way Piercy affirms hope in a compromised world. She unearths beauty in squalor and believes that lessons can be learned from horror. Describing the Detroit of her childhood in *Parti-Colored Blocks for a Quilt,* she says it "sprawls . . . willfully ugly mile after flat smoggy mile," yet her tiny backyard was filled with produce and flowers: "tomatoes, beans, herbs, lettuce, onions, Swiss chard. . . . Pansies, iris, mock orange, wisteria, hollyhocks along the alley fence, black-eyed Susans, goldenglow whose stems were red with spider mites, bronze chrysanthemums, a lilac bush by the compost pile." Only her mother, she felt, was more beautiful than the flowers blooming in that yard; beauty and fear, oppression and hope grow in the same garden patch. If the past is made present, it can be a corrective and of use.

In her essay for the *Contemporary Authors Autobiography Series,* Piercy says that in *The High Cost of Living* (1978) she used her observations "of students and of young people generally, of the changing pressures of class, of the confusion between morality and politics so common in our culture." The novel deals with academia and exposes the consequences of choices, especially those made by women—both heterosexual and homosexual, mothers and virgins." These women make "work choices, living choices, sexual choices" that refigure their lives and represent the high cost of living in the present time. In an interview with Richard Jackson in *Parti-Colored Blocks for a Quilt,* Piercy says that she is always concerned with

what it means as a woman to be able to choose. These are difficult issues today in general, and especially for women on a political and social level. Feminism provides a point of view through which to understand problems, but I wouldn't say everything should be reduced to that. Racism is very real; the class struggle is very real. Feminism involves a strong sense of history, a strong sense of ourselves in nature, in natural cycles, and a sense of responsibility to each other whenever we need aid.

This imperative is succinctly stated in "The Sabbath of Mutual Respect," a poem Piercy collected in *The Moon Is Always Female* (1980): "praise any woman / who chooses, and make safe her choice." *The High Cost of Living* looks at the cost of succeeding in male disciplines.

Vida (1979), Piercy's fifth novel, juxtaposes two sisters, one of whom, the author says in *Parti-Colored Blocks for a Quilt,* "is a woman whose politics is based on a sense of her own oppression, her own situation, and who becomes a feminist, and the other sister is a woman whose politics is based primarily on the oppression of other people, and who is involved in the more traditional causes." Through her characterization of Vida, Piercy explores what it is to be a nonfeminist—though Vida is not indifferent to feminist actions and politics. Piercy explains in *Parti-Colored Blocks for a Quilt* that for Vida the experience of being a political fugitive

is the experience of being an invisible woman, instead of a token woman. She was much less open to feminism when she was a token woman, a charismatic woman sharing the stage with men. As a fugitive, invisible and necessarily anonymous, she has none of that—her experiences are much closer to the experiences of ordinary women, and she becomes much more open to the ideas of feminism, though she could never be called a feminist.

Reviewing the novel in the *National Review* (30 May 1980), Norma B. Hawes praised *Vida* for examining the antiwar movement of the 1960s from a "viewpoint that deals with people and their relationships rather than ideas and ideals" and without the anger that often characterizes feminist literature. Again, Piercy's ability to portray the lives of individual women caught up in significant historical moments is the major strength of her work.

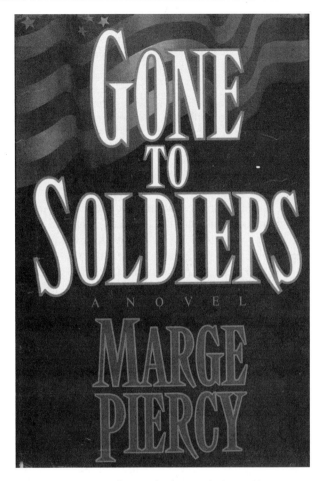

Dust jacket for Piercy's 1987 novel, about twin sisters separated during World War II

On 2 June 1982 Piercy married Ira Wood, whom she had known for six years. Early in their relationship they wrote a play, *The Last White Class* (1979), and poems. Later they wrote a novel, *Storm Tide* (1998). Piercy credits Wood with giving her an emotional and artistic security that nourishes her activism and her writing.

Although it is the most autobiographical of her novels, Piercy says that *Braided Lives* (1982) is not just "autobiography—it is far more novel than memoir. . . . I would call it a heightened fantasy on certain autobiographical themes." Like her character Jill, Piercy left home to escape the stultifying relationship with her mother, which she describes so poignantly in her poem "My mother's body." Here a daughter recognizes that her mother is her twin, sister, and lost love, and she says: "I carry you in me like an embryo / as once you carried me." The mother's body, alive in her daughter's, dares to be reborn and is a part of her child's personhood. The theme of motherhood and its concomitant metaphors of child-birth may testify to the traditionally creative and maternal. As Sara Ruddick pointed out in a 1994 essay,

> A child is mothered by whoever protects, nurtures, and trains her. Although it is a material, social, and cultural fact that most mothers are now women, there is no difficulty in imagining men taking up mothering as easily as women–or conversely, women as easily declining to mother.

Piercy often argues that to be a woman is not so much a sex as an attitude. In *Braided Lives* Jill makes this point when she says: "I don't know a girl who does not say, I don't want to live like my mother." But in reference to the way lives are entwined, she asks: "Is it our mothers, ourselves, or our men who mold us?" Piercy shows that untangling the strands that make up the braid of our lives can be a daunting task.

Although Ellen Sweet, reviewer for *Ms* (March 1984), claims that *Fly Away Home* (1984) has the hackneyed theme of self-realization through divorce, the novel again affirms the need and the right of women to make personal choices. Daria Walker, the central figure in the novel, whose 140-year-old house is "her treasure, her artwork, her outer skin," attempts to separate the self from imperatives of ownership and possession. She realizes that a woman is not her house, and she does not have to "think thin" and diet because of the dictates of fashion or men. She can be a cook if she wishes, and the smell of barbequed pork emanating from the kitchen may, in her imagination, be "her husband spitted over a slow fire." In keeping with this metaphor of cooking, which signifies woman's traditional role and her rage at being part of such a stew, Piercy playfully says that in some recipes "before cooking is commenced, the disparate ingredients must sit together for a time: it is called the marrying of the herbs, the spices. At a certain point the flavor is different than the sum of its parts. That is happening . . . we are making a new whole." Daria finds that as she establishes her identity as a woman in her own right, she can move toward more creative and satisfying relationships. At the end of the novel she is a better woman for being on her own. At the party that follows their divorce, Daria and Ross Walker are pronounced "woman and man, strangers to each other bodily, emotionally and in all of their values until the time of their death."

Piercy's next novel, *Gone to Soldiers,* takes a bold step forward. The book is a war story that examines women's position in what has traditionally been mas-culine terrain. Piercy uses war to present a religious, gay, feminist-psychological slant on ethnicity. She disrupts the rootedness of family and place, the stability of jobs in the traditional, established, patriarchal work force, and shows that equality in relationships may be only a dream. Twins who call one another by their Hebrew names, Rivka and Naomi, rather than Renée and Nadine, their legal French names, are separated because of World War II. Their alienation from one another, their family, and their home and homeland is the theme that unifies the novel as ten characters reenact the historical lessons of a ravaged past that is still alive in the present–a postmodern conjunction that Susan Rubin Suleiman defines as

> that moment of extreme (perhaps tragic, perhaps playful) self-consciousness when the present–our present–takes to reflecting on its relation to the past and to the future primarily as a problem of repetition. How does one create a future that will acknowledge and incorporate the past–a past that includes, in our very own century, some of the darkest moments in human history–without repeating it? How does one look at the past with understanding, yet critically, . . . which has to do with discrimination and choice in the present?

As Piercy states in *Gone to Soldiers,* her novel "is conceived in the imagination," but she "wanted nothing to happen in it that had not happened somewhere in the time and place I was working with." She says that she has "relied heavily on my own memory and on the memories of my family and of families" she had known well. It is through this re-creation of memory that she is able to make Jewishness–particularly that of female Jewishness–central to the history of mankind. Jacqueline speaks out, naming the atrocities she suffers and telling how it is to be victimized by those who are "crazy with power." She describes being lashed and beaten and tells about being "stripped, tattooed, shaved of . . . head and body hair." In relating what it is like to have no name, "no clothing, nothing individual," and "to live in terror as if it were the air we take into our lungs," she shows that it is only by articulating one's ethical beliefs that acting ethically may become possible. *Gone to Soldiers* and *City of Darkness, City of Light* may well be Piercy's finest achievements.

Piercy's tenth novel, *Summer People* (1989), unveils the nature of relationships within a *ménage à trois:* Dinah, an avant-garde composer, Willy, a sculptor and fashion designer, and Susan, Dinah's lover and best friend. The psychological boundaries of three-somes illustrate the complexity of such relationships whether they exist among women and men, women and women, or men and men. The novel is important partly as a study of sexuality that emphasizes hidden issues within nontraditional alliances—issues such as intimacy, fear of abandonment, jealousy, commitment, power, and control.

In *He, She, & It* (1991) language—specifically the power of naming—is central, as it often is in Piercy's work, and she does not fail to speak of failed relationships, violence, oppression, and man's inability to conserve and use well the habitable earth. As a character in this novel says,

> when we give a name to something in our lives, we may empower that something, as when we call an itch love, or when we call our envy righteousness; or we may empower ourselves because now we can think about and talk about what is hurting us, we may come together with others who have felt this same pain, and thus we can begin to do something about it.

In *He, She, & It* Piercy claims that "we construct the world out of words," connecting "with powers beyond our own fractional consciousness to the rest of the living beings we all make up together." She notes that the Hebrew word *davar* means both "word" and "thing."

In 1993 *He, She, & It* won the Arthur C. Clarke Award for Best Science Fiction Novel published in the United Kingdom during the previous year. Patricia Doherty calls it "Another of Piercy's creative utopian stories" and notes that it "alternates between the story's setting in a Jewish settlement in the middle of the twenty-first century offset by the retelling of the legend of the golem of seventeenth-century Prague." This shift in time and emphasis allows Piercy to address a postmodern concern—that of the interface between human and machine—especially during the Industrial Revolution, when people became exploitable labor. The multi-envisioned world of Norika easily breaks traditional boundaries—such as human and nonhuman, physical and nonphysical—and places reader and character alike in a new age where technology and the availability of body parts make who and what human beings are problematic. Piercy conflates biology, technology, ecology, capitalism, militarism, class, gender, new sexualities, and ethnicities. Humans who are tool users and makers create selves, stories, and new worlds. A golem and a cyborg are both material-semiotic generative cells of production. Both human and divine natures are the manifestation of space, place, and text—all of which interface and mediate information exchange. At the end of the novel Piercy reminds the reader of human responsibility and shows that it is imperative to ques-

tion—as Shira does—the desire to "feel empowered to make a living being who belongs to me as a child never does and never should." The human race does not own the earth or any living thing, and the terrible power to possess, to create, and to destroy must be examined again and again. As Malkah says in fashioning the cyborg Yod:

> Creation is always perilous, for it gives true life to what has been inchoate and voice to what has been dumb. It makes known what has been unknown, that perhaps we were more comfortable not knowing. The new is necessarily dangerous. You, too, must come to accept that of your nature, Yod, for you are truly new under the sun.

In *The Longings of Women* (1994) Piercy joins the lives of three women. As Kerstin Westerlund Shands explains, "The three protagonists are brought together through plot and characterization as well as through imagery of marginal or open spaces juxtaposed with tropes of invisibility, dissimulation, and camouflage integral to the novel's exploration of women's encapsulation in patriarchal codes and their methods of actualizing some measure of autonomy and authenticity." Piercy's intent, as expressed throughout her work and especially in this novel, is to examine the longings of women whether they command a place in academe, are homeless, or are trapped within the boundaries placed around the working-class poor. For all women, issues of identity are paramount. Despite a need for her husband to be "as physically smitten with her as she was with him," Professor Leila Landsman, a forty-five-year-old writer who knows more about literary than actual love, recognizes that one of the reasons for the length of her marriage was "that I and my husband led separate lives and spent part of every year apart." But is such a relationship love? Perhaps women want power when they say they want love. Another character, Becky Souza Burgess, loves the way Sam "was always trying to do what she told him"—especially when she gives him directives about making love. Becky wants to escape the shabby house where her mother struggled to raise seven children, and she wants security and position. She also wants to be in love, but she confuses love with lust. An actress in a theater group, she plays roles—and fails to achieve the position of power she desires. Unable to manage even the condo for which she spends most of her salary, she is a victim of her own longings, which lead her to kill. Leila Landsman calls love a disease—a "long and tedious delusion. . . . a one-person brainwashed cult." Why then, Piercy questions, are women so enraptured by love? The third woman,

Piercy with her husband, the novelist Ira Wood (photograph © by Debi Milligan; from the dust jacket for Piercy's Storm Tide, *1998)*

homeless Mary Burke, offers another perspective, emphasizing the accommodations of women. Trying to pass as a respectable middle-class woman rather than a bag lady, she goes through department stores trying samples of makeup and spraying herself with perfume. A woman wearing lipstick, makeup, and powder is deemed respectable. If Mary could look right and smell right, she believes, she would not be thought homeless and a vagrant. Mary, like Becky, assumes a mask. Even her daughter, who runs the "Goddess Shop" for oversized women who would not be thought of as goddesses, does not understand her mother's plight. Mary Burke's name alludes to Edmund Burke, the eighteenth-century British philosopher who wrote that death is the loss of self. Buying into the myth "that if you were pretty and smart, you would get what you wanted," Mary says that when her husband wanted her out of his way, he treated her "like a piece of cheese that had turned bad." In the end Leila finds a way to give Mary an opportunity to return to the middle class. Through such characters, the novel carefully examines how much personal space a woman needs to be happy and successful.

Piercy's next novel was an important literary achievement. *City of Darkness, City of Light* views the French Revolution from a feminist perspective. Piercy employs six viewpoint characters: Maximillien Robespierre, George Danton, Condorcet,

Madame Roland, Pauline Leon, and Claire Lacombe. Historians of the period have praised Piercy's portrayal of Robespierre, who Piercy views with a mixture of admiration and horror at what he became. The novel also focuses on the roots of modern feminism in the French Revolution, examining how revolutionaries abandon their original ideals as they become corrupted by power. Two of the main characters are feminists: Particularly compelling are Piercy's fictionalized versions of three Revolutionary women. Pauline Leon, an unmarried chocolate maker, and Claire Lacombe, an actress who founded the Society of Revolutionary Republican Women in 1793. The members of this most radical women's group of the French Revolution wore red liberty caps, tricolor ribbons, and trousers, carried pistols and daggers, and were, Piercy writes,

> far more visible than the men who always outnumbered them. They were scarier than they should have been. Most men saw them as bloodthirsty Amazons about to do something unspeakable. That they had seized the male prerogatives of weapons and bold demands seemed to scare the men the most, as if some enormous charade on which their power depended might topple. That was their most potent weapon: the perception of them as unnatural, out of control and therefore wild and dangerous. . . . but it was male fear that gave them their edge.

Setting her novel in France between 1789 and 1794, Piercy explores structures of dominance and subordination as they relate to class and caste, race and religion, and social and economic reform. Indeed she constructs the force of women witnessing the world. She contrasts the views of Jean-Jacques Rousseau, a philosopher and antifeminist who argued that women were domestic creatures designed to please husbands and bear children, and of the profeminist Marie-Jean-Antoine-Nicolas de Caritat, Marquis de Condorcet, who contended in "On the Admission of Women to the Rights of Citizenship" (1790) that women possessed rights equal with men. He was, Piercy says,

> almost alone in his new ideas, but he observed in the salons that educated women were as intelligent and able in argument, in pointed discourse, as any of the men, and often as witty. He could see no basis in his own experience for the universal belief that women were mental or emotional children. Some no doubt were, since they were given little useful training and no real education; but then, a great many men were idiots or mental incompetents. Freedom was a universal right of all humans or an intellectual contradiction. If only some were born free, then freedom could not exist except as a greedy privilege.

For Piercy ethnic concerns are never separate from those associated with race, class, and gender, and she is particularly interested in the plight of Mendès Herrera, who, as an outcast Jew, had "no rights, no legal status," and was "hardly viewed as human." She emphasizes again the power of language, saying that it "is the great tool by which we manipulate each other socially and are manipulated. Poverty of life goes with poverty of mind. What we can't speak about, we can't think about." Human beings "do each other in," as Georges Danton says at the end of the novel. "It's a disease. The poison is power." Louis Capet lost his head, but the Revolution marched on. Life and times changed, but not necessarily for the better. If the world is to become a safe place for all classes and religions, then, Piercy asserts, power must not be abused but administered with accountability and care.

Three Women (1999) tells the story of a mother, grandmother, and daughter who find themselves, after a period of independence, trying to coexist in one house. At the age of forty-nine, Suzanne Blume, a successful trial lawyer and law professor, finds herself the caregiver for her mother, Beverly, who has suffered a stroke and is no longer able to live alone in her own apartment. Suzanne's unemployed daughter, Elene, in her late twenties, returns home and conducts a clandestine affair with her mother's friend's husband.

Examining issues associated with aging, disability, and health care, Piercy shows that it is not easy for three generations to live harmoniously together when each is deprived of a place of her own. Yet, woman is traditionally the healer, and it is she who is able to transcend personal tragedy.

During her distinguished literary career, Piercy has taught or been a writer in residence at schools such as the University of Kansas (1971), Thomas Jefferson College and Grand Valley State College (1975–1976, 1978, and 1980), Holy Cross University (1976), State University of New York at Buffalo (1977), University of California at San Jose (1984), Ohio State University (1985), University of Cincinnati (1986), and University of Michigan (1992). She has also taught at many writers' conferences. In addition to the honors mentioned previously, she has received the Borestone Mountain Poetry Award (1968 and 1974), the Literature Award from the Massachusetts Governor's Commission on the Status of Women (1974), a National Endowment for the Arts Award (1978), the Rhode Island School of Design Faculty Association Medal (1985), the Carolyn Kizer Poetry Prize (1986 and 1990), the Sheaffer Eaton-PEN New England Award for Literary Excellence (1989), the Golden Rose Poetry Prize (1990), the New England Poetry Club (NEPC) Award (1990, 1991, and 1992), the May Sarton Award (1991), the Brit ha-Dorot Award of Shalom Center (1992), the Barbara Bradley Award (1992), and the Orion Scott Award in Humanities (1993).

From the beginning Piercy's novels have expressed a fundamental belief in the possibilities of freedom for all people, regardless of age, sex, race, religion, or sexual preference. She recognizes history as a continuing lesson in how people may exist together as true individuals while creating a stable society based on understanding and respect. Her fiction and poetry have social and literary value. It is clear that Piercy will continue writing fiction, and if her most recent novels are any indication, her best novels may lie ahead of her.

Interviews:

"An Interview With Marge Piercy," *Kalliope*, 4 (Winter 1982): 37–45;

"Interview with Ira Wood and Marge Piercy," *Pulp*, 8, no. 1 (1982);

Richard Jackson, "Shaping Our Choices," in his *Acts of Mind: Conversations with Contemporary Poets* (University: University of Alabama Press, 1983);

Interview with Kay Bonetti [recording], Columbia, Mo.: American Audio Prose Library, AAPL 168-1, 1986;

Kathy Shorr, "Marge Piercy," *Provinceton Arts Magazine*, 90 (1990);

Mickey Pearlman and Katherine Usher Henderson, *Inter/View: Talks With America's Writing Women* (Lexington: University Press of Kentucky, 1990), p. 65;

Lisa Davis, "Marge Piercy on Cooperative Living," *Communities: Journal of Cooperative Living*, 82 (Spring 1994): 57–58.

Bibliography:

Patricia Doherty, *Marge Piercy: An Annotated Bibliography* (Westport, Conn.: Greenwood Press, 1997).

References:

Francs Bartkowski, "The Kinship Web: Joanna Russ's *The Female Man* and Marge Piercy's *Woman on the Edge of Time*," in her *Feminist Utopias* (Lincoln: University of Nebraska Press, 1989);

Diane P. Freedman, "The Ecology of Alchemy, or, Recycling, Reclamation, Transformation in Marge Piercy, Tess Gallagher, Alice Walker, Susan Griffin," in her *An Alchemy of Genres: Cross-Genre Writing by American Feminist Poet-Critics*

(Charlottesville: University of Virginia Press, 1992);

Elaine Tuttle Hansen, "The Double Narrative Structure of *Small Changes*," in *Contemporary American Women Writers: Narrative Strategies,* edited by Catherine Rainwater and William J. Scheick (Lexington: University of Kentucky Press, 1985);

Lisa Maria Hoegland, *Feminism and Its Fictions* (Philadelphia: University of Pennsylvania, 1998);

Anne Hudson Jones, "Feminist Science Fiction and Medical Ethics," in *The Intersectional of Science Fiction and Philosophy,* edited by Robert E. Myers (Westport, Conn.: Greenwood Press, 1983);

Margaret Keulen, *Radical Imagination: Feminist Conceptions of the Future in Ursula Le Guin, Marge Piercy, and Sally Miller* (New York: Peter Lang, 1991);

S. Lilian Kremer, *Feminism and Its Fictions* (Lincoln: University of Nebraska Press, 1999);

Susan Kress, "In and Out of Time," in *Future Females: A Critical Anthology,* edited by Marlene Barr (Bowling Green: Bowling Green State University Popular Press, 1981);

Magali Cornier Michael, *Feminism and the Postmodern Impulse: Post-World War II Fiction* (Albany: State University of New York Press, 1996);

Elaine Orr, "Mothering as Good Fiction: Instances from Marge Piercy's *Woman on the Edge of Time,*" *Journal of Narrative Technique,* 23 (Spring 1993): 61–79;

Sara Ruddick, "Thinking Mothers/Conceiving Self," in *Representations of Motherhood,* edited by Donna Bassin, Margaret Honey, and Meryle Mahrer Kaplan (New Haven: Yale University Press, 1994), pp. 29–45;

Joanna Russ, "Recent Feminist Utopias," in *Future Females,* edited by Marlene Barr (Bowling Green: Bowling Green State University Popular Press, 1981);

Kerstin Westerlund Shands, *The Repair Of The World* (Westport, Conn.: Greenwood Press, 1994);

Robert Shelton, "The Social Text as Body: Images of Health and Disease in Three Recent Feminist Utopias," *Literature and Medicine,* 12 (Fall 1993): 161–177;

Christine W. Sizemore, "Masculine and Feminine Cities: Marge Piercy's *Going Down Fast* and *Fly Away Home,*" *Frontiers: A Journal of Women Studies,* 13, no. 1 (1992): 90–110;

Pia Thielmann, *Marge Piercy's Women: Visions Captured and Subdued* (Frankfurt, Germany: R. G. Fischer, 1986);

Sue Walker and Eugenie Hamner, eds., *Ways of Knowing: Essays on Marge Piercy* (Mobile, Ala.: Negative Capability Press, 1991).

Papers:

The Harlan Hatcher Graduate Library at the University of Michigan has a collection of Marge Piercy's manuscripts and memorabilia.

Ayn Rand

(2 February 1905 – 6 March 1982)

Laurence Miller
Western Washington University

BOOKS: *We the Living* (New York: Macmillan, 1936; London: Cassell, 1936; revised edition, New York: Random House, 1959);

Night of January 16th: A Comedy-Drama in Three Acts, edited by Nathaniel Edward Reeid (New York: Longmans, Green, 1936; revised edition, New York: World, 1968);

Anthem (London: Cassell, 1938; Los Angeles: Pamphleteers, 1946);

The Fountainhead (Indianapolis: Bobbs-Merrill, 1943; London: Cassell, 1947);

Atlas Shrugged (New York: Random House, 1957);

For the New Intellectual: The Philosophy of Ayn Rand (New York: Random House, 1961);

The Virtue of Selfishness, a New Concept of Egoism, with articles by Nathaniel Branden (New York: New American Library, 1964);

Capitalism, the Unknown Ideal, with articles by Branden, Alan Greenspan, and Robert Hessen (New York: New American Library, 1966);

Introduction to Objectivist Epistemology (New York: Objectivist, 1967);

The Romantic Manifesto: A Philosophy of Literature (New York: World, 1969; revised, 1975);

The New Left: The Anti-Industrial Revolution (New York: New American Library, 1971); republished with additional material as *Return of the Primitive: The Anti-Industrial Revolution,* edited by Peter Schwartz (New York: Meridian, 1999);

Philosophy, Who Needs It (Indianapolis: Bobbs-Merrill, 1982);

The Early Ayn Rand: A Selection from Her Unpublished Fiction, edited by Leonard Peikoff (New York: New American Library, 1984);

The Voice of Reason: Essays in Objectivist Thought, edited by Peikoff (New York: New American Library, 1989);

The Ayn Rand Column: A Collection of Her Weekly Newspaper Articles, written for the Los Angeles Times; *with Additional, Little-Known Essays,* edited by Schwartz (Oceanside, Cal.: Second Renaissance Books, 1991); revised as *The Ayn Rand Column: Written for the* Los

Ayn Rand in a photograph inscribed to her brother-in-law, Nick O'Connor (Butterfield Butterfield & Dunning auction catalogue, sale 6865Z, 18 November 1998)

Angeles Times (New Milford, Conn.: Second Renaissance Books, 1998);

Ayn Rand's Marginalia: Her Critical Comments on the Writings of Over 20 Authors, edited by Robert Mayhew (New Milford, Conn.: Second Renaissance Books, 1995);

Journals of Ayn Rand, edited by David Harriman (New York: Dutton, 1997);

The Ayn Rand Reader, edited by Peikoff and Gary Hull (New York: Plume, 1999).

PLAY PRODUCTIONS: *Penthouse Legend,* produced as *Woman on Trial,* Hollywood, Hollywood Playhouse, October 1934; produced as *Night of January 16th*, New York, Ambassador Theater, 16 September 1935;

The Unconquered, New York, Biltmore Theatre, 14 February 1940.

PRODUCED SCRIPTS: *Love Letters,* motion picture, Paramount, 1945;

You Came Along, motion picture, Paramount, 1945;

The Fountainhead, motion picture, Warner Bros., 1949.

OTHER: *The Objectivist Newsletter,* volumes 1–4, edited by Rand and Nathaniel Branden, 1962–1965; republished in one volume (New York: Objectivist, 1967);

The Ayn Rand Letter, volumes 1–4, edited by Rand, 1971–1976; republished in one volume (Palo Alto, Cal.: Palo Alto Book Service, 1979);

The Objectivist, volumes 5–10, edited by Rand and Branden, 1966–1971; republished in one volume (Palo Alto, Cal.: Palo Alto Book Service, 1982).

Ayn Rand's novels *The Fountainhead* (1943) and *Atlas Shrugged* (1957) manifest a development of her own philosophy of Objectivism, which challenged conventional values by emphasizing laissez-faire capitalism, individualism, and opposition to altruism. After her novels, Rand promoted Objectivism in several works of nonfiction and three periodicals during the 1960s and 1970s. Though it developed into a movement, Objectivism was eventually undermined by personal conflicts between Rand and her followers. Still, in the time since her death in 1982, her books continue to sell and inspire admiration and even devotion or conversion to her philosophy or "sense of life," as she called it.

Ayn Rand was born Alice (Alysia) Rosenbaum on 2 February 1905, in St. Petersburg, Russia. Her father, Franz Rosenbaum, was a faculty member in the chemistry department at the local university. Rand's mother, Anna Rosenbaum, cared for the house and entertained frequently. Rand, who felt that her father was indifferent to her and was contemptuous of her mother's preoccupation with socializing, was a precocious and highly intelligent child who eschewed friendships in favor of intellectual endeavors and the world of ideas. She attended the University of Petrograd from 1918 to 1924 and graduated with honors in history.

Rand read widely and avidly in her early years, and several key events between childhood and college influenced her writing. A child who knew by the age of eight that she wanted to be a writer, she was most influenced by the writings of Maurice Champagne, Victor Hugo, and Friedrich Nietzsche. Rand read Champagne's adventure story "The Mystical Valley" in a French magazine in 1914; for her, its protagonist, Cyrus, a totally self-confident man of action, intelligence, and courage, became an ideal of manhood. In fact, Cyrus became the basis for all the fictional heroes and heroines she later created.

She gained a sense of what a novel should be from Hugo—the creation of heroic, larger-than-life characters and complex, ingenious plots unfolding on a grand and unexpected scale that still managed to incorporate themes, ideas, and action. Although Rand disagreed with much of what Nietzsche believed, she viewed him as a spiritual ally who had a similar view of man that emphasized the heroic, defended individualism, and despised altruism. Like Rand, Nietzsche held the opinion that an individual man's purpose should be directed toward his own personal happiness.

Rand's development was further influenced by dramatic events in Russia. Believing that people should be free to determine their own actions and goals, she vigorously opposed government authority. For her, Communism meant living for the State. Rand and her family suffered severe deprivations at the hands of the Communists, and Rand remained a lifelong staunch anti-Communist. She was also a lifelong atheist, believing that the concept of God was rationally indefensible and degrading to man because it focused on mysticism rather than reason.

Rand's intellectual and philosophical foundation was thus firmly in place when relatives who had previously immigrated to New York City provided for her to immigrate to America in 1926. Along the way she changed her first name to Ayn, after a Finnish writer, and her last name to Rand, after her Remington-Rand typewriter. She spent her early years in America in the movie industry, working in the prop and costume departments and also as an extra in movies. She married another extra, Charles Francis "Frank" O'Connor, in 1929 and became an American citizen in 1931. Most important, from the viewpoint of her later career, she spent these initial years cultivating and honing her writing skills, learning English, and writing several unpublished short stories and screenplays.

Rand's career as a novelist began with her first published book, *We the Living* (1936). The novel took three years to complete, largely because her work in the movie industry placed heavy demands on her time. Moreover, while learning to write in a new language, she continued to be a perfectionist, demanding clarity and precision in her writing. Nevertheless, the book was rejected by several publishers. A play Rand wrote in 1933 called *Penthouse Legend* premiered in 1934 at the Hollywood Theater as *Woman on Trial.* The play was produced on Broadway in 1935 as *Night of January 16th,* and published under the same name in 1936 by Longmans, Green. The play, more an entertainment than a reflection of her beliefs and philosophy, did not, however, truly represent her emergence as a significant writer. It did at least help her to become known in East Coast cultural circles.

More importantly, Macmillan published *We the Living* in April 1936. The Russian setting of the novel reflects Rand's earlier experiences under Communism. Its plot focuses on a young female protagonist, Kira Argounova, who becomes the mistress of a Communist, Andrei Taganov, in order to save the life of the man she loves, Leo Kovalensky. The interplay of these three characters against a background of villainous and statist Communism allowed Rand to introduce her essential philosophy. The story ends as Andrei finds out about Kira and Leo, realizes the evils of Communism, and kills himself. Leo, broken in spirit and without hope in a Communist society, leaves Kira, who then attempts to escape from Russia but is shot at the border.

Rand was pleased with the structure and plot of the book. Valorizing the sanctity of human life rather than the supremacy of the state, the novel emphasizes that the state, though able to destroy a person, cannot destroy the individual spirit. Rand, however, became dissatisfied with parts of the book, believing them to be overwritten. She thought that her writing was too romantic and lush, and Kira too openly emotional. Rand realized that in order to obtain the strongest emotional response from her readers, she needed to be more subtle and less explicit in her writing. In her later novels, emotions were minimized or subordinated to intellect, and reason was implicitly and indirectly expressed through actions. For Rand, reason was man's only means of perceiving reality and his only guide to action; feelings, she asserted, revealed nothing about facts and did not facilitate cognition.

Though Rand was commended for her narrative and dramatic skills, *We the Living* was reviewed negatively. In a time when Communism was viewed by many influential intellectuals as a noble ideal, the anti-Communist tone and argument of the book were especially criticized. Initial sales of the novel were slow but picked up dramatically within a year because of favorable publicity. Unfortunately, by that time, Macmillan had already destroyed the type and the novel was out of print.

In 1935 Rand began work on *The Fountainhead*. While *The Fountainhead* was considerably more complicated in theme, plot, and character than *We the Living*, Rand was in command throughout stylistically and intellectually, and she clearly and persuasively presented complex ideas. The book is quite remarkable in its literary style and plot, the complexity and interest of its several memorable characters, the interweaving of

Poster for the 1949 movie adaptation of Rand's 1943 novel, for which she wrote the screenplay

her philosophy within the framework of fiction, and its epic scope and grandeur.

Through overt philosophizing, *The Fountainhead* expresses Rand's concept of the ideal man. Her characters reflect her philosophical principles, which in turn direct her characters' behavior. Rand referred to her style "of writing in essentials and in terms of universal values" as "Romantic Realism." Writing *The Fountainhead* did not proceed uninterrupted in large part because financial exigencies forced Rand to divert her attention to other, more short-term projects. Two plays, "Ideal" (1934) and "Think Twice" (1939), went

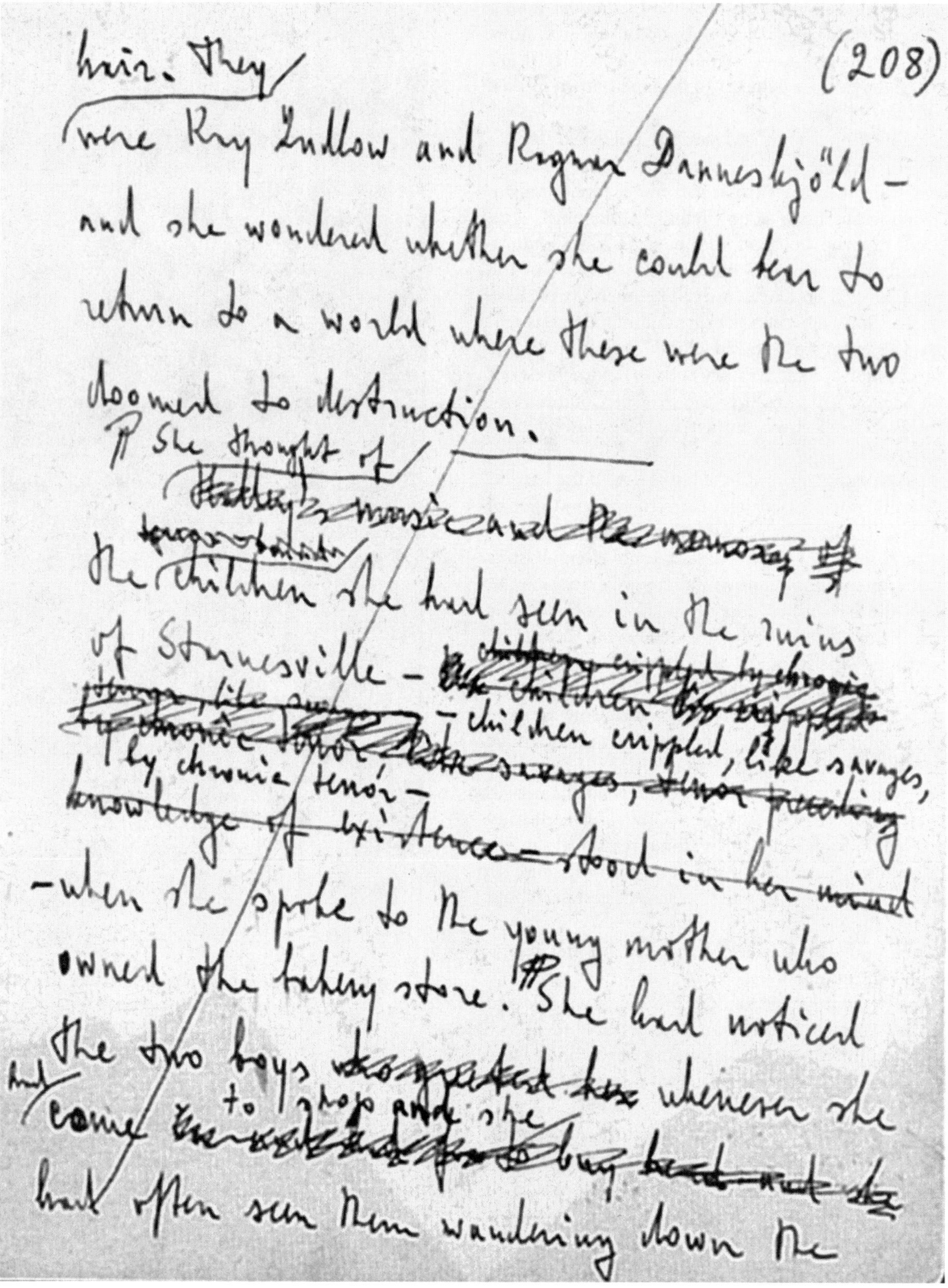

(208)

min. They

were Kay Ludlow and Ragnar Danneskjöld —
and she wondered whether she could bear to
return to a world where these were the two
doomed to destruction.

She thought of
~~~~ music and ~~~~
the children she had seen in the ruins
of Starnesville — ~~the children crippled by chronic~~
~~~~ — children crippled, like savages,
~~by chronic~~ ~~tenor~~ —
knowledge of existence — stood in her mind
— when she spoke to the young mother who
owned the bakery store. She had noticed
the two boys ~~~~ whenever she
come ~~~~ to shop ~~~~ she
had often seen them wandering down the

unproduced. A play version of *We the Living,* titled *The Unconquered,* was produced in 1940 but closed after only five performances.

The Fountainhead is an idiosyncratic vision of egoism, good and evil, individualism, and the human spirit, dramatized in fiction. In this novel, life is depicted not as it is, but as it could be and should be. Thematically, the book concerns the struggle of individualism versus collectivism, with Rand's fundamental premise being that one's existence and well-being depend on actions that promote survival. The book emphasizes that reason, guided by an appropriate code of values and morality, makes possible truly meaningful action. Moreover, such reason is possible only for the heroic individualist, who is entirely independent, self-sufficient, and productive. His convictions, values, and goals are the product of a clear intelligence and a rational mind and come entirely from within himself. He exerts man's fundamental right to enlightened self-interest, the virtue of selfishness. One must, the novel argues, live for the self without placing others above the self. The collectivist, in contrast, is controlled and shaped by other men, a soulless second-hander lacking inner direction. He is an altruist, placing the welfare of others above his own, thus subverting productivity and creativity. The novel insists that, in the end, good will triumph because only good can build and create. Evil is impotent and self-defeating because it can only destroy.

The Fountainhead chronicles the struggles of architect Howard Roark, who exemplifies Rand's ideal man. Rand chose architecture for the subject because she viewed the skyscraper as the perfect symbol of man's greatest achievements. Roark's struggle and ultimate triumph over an evil society is made engaging and memorable by his conflicts with a colorful cast of imperfect people. The heroine, Dominique Francon ("Myself in a bad mood," Rand observed), is an emotionally withdrawn and self-destructive idealist. Gail Wynand, the newspaper publisher, has the potential to become heroic like Roark, but destroys himself by seeking power and yielding to the collective masses. Peter Keating, also an architect, is the opposite of Roark. He is the ultimate "second-hander," a man devoid of original thought and independent action. Finally, Ellsworth Toohey, the architectural critic who insidiously and deliberately attacks and tries to destroy all that Howard Roark personifies, represents the quintessentially evil man.

Prior to *The Fountainhead,* Rand had published another enduring work of fiction, the novella *Anthem* (1938). Told as a sequence of flashbacks, it is a fascinating blend of science fiction and fantasy with an uncharacteristically lyrical style. In fact, Barbara Branden, in her biography, *The Passion of Ayn Rand* (1986), compared

Rand after completing the 1,168-page manuscript for Atlas Shrugged *(photograph by Barbara Branden)*

Anthem to a prose poem. *Anthem* is entirely consistent with Rand's philosophy. In a totally collectivized world the words "I" and "He/She" have been replaced by "We" and "They." All past achievements in art, industry, and science have disappeared from life and from memory. The hero, determined to acquire knowledge, rediscovers the electric light. Subsequently, he and his woman friend are forced to flee into an uncharted wilderness, where they rediscover the meaning of the words "I" and "We" and formulate plans to establish a new society. Rand initially failed to find an American publisher for *Anthem;* Branden suggested that, as with *We The Living,* it was too political and antisocialist. Rand did, however, succeed in getting the novel published in England; it was not published in America until 1946.

Initial attempts to publish *The Fountainhead* paralleled the same bleak experience of *We The Living.* Twelve publishers rejected it as being commercially unsuitable because it was too politically and philosophically controversial, too intellectual, too improbable a story, too long, poorly written, and dull, and because it employed an unsympathetic hero. Finally, an editor at Bobbs-Merrill, Archie Ogden, was favorably impressed and recommended that the book be published. In one of those legendary stories in book publishing, the front office rejected Ogden's recommendation. In true Randian heroic fashion Ogden replied, "If this is not the book for you, then I am not the editor for you." The reply was, "Far be it from me to dampen such enthusiasm. Sign the contract. But the book better be good." Thus in May 1943 *The Fountainhead* was published.

The debut of the book was anything but auspicious. Advertising and early reviews misrepresented the book as being about architecture and slum dwellers. Many major publications did not review it, and many of the reviews that did appear were negative. The most notable exception was *The New York Times Book Review* (16 May 1943), in which Lorine Pruette praised the power, brilliance, beauty, and thought-provoking quality of Rand's writing and correctly recognized that the central concern in *The Fountainhead* was individualism.

When initial sales of *The Fountainhead* were slow, Rand worried that the book would suffer the same obscurity as *We The Living;* but as the book began to find its audience, a second printing appeared, and sales accelerated dramatically. The paperback edition was published in 1952, and a decade later more than one million copies were in print. The novel struck an undeniable chord in many readers. Rand received enormous amounts of mail telling how the book had changed individual lives and motivated people to work for a new vision. Nathaniel Branden, later Rand's protégé and intellectual heir, was fourteen when he read the book, and later recalled "the sense of a door opening, intellectually, spiritually, psychologically—a passageway into another dimension, like a summons from the future."

Rand wrote the screenplay for the 1949 movie version of *The Fountainhead,* which starred Gary Cooper and Patricia Neal. The reception of *The Fountainhead* gave Rand financial independence and allowed her, for the first time, to devote herself to full-time writing. Her new celebrity status provided her considerable exposure; for instance, in 1947 she appeared before the House Un-American Activities Committee to express her concern about the influence of Communism in American movies. (Rand had written a pamphlet that year, *Screen Guide for Americans,* for an anti-Communist organization, in which she discussed these concerns.) She insisted, however, that she would testify only on ideological issues. Rand called the hearings a disgusting spectacle and in later years expressed ambivalent feelings about her appearance.

In October 1957 Rand published *Atlas Shrugged,* which took more than a decade to write. It is 1,168 pages long, features a sixty-page speech, and represents the maturation of Rand's evolving philosophy. The focus shifts from architecture to the railroad, the central industry that touched all other industries and was the

circulatory system that kept America alive. *Atlas Shrugged* is a mystery and an action tale written on a grand scale, combining, Rand said, "metaphysics, morality, economics, politics and sex." This time, Atlas represented Rand's ideal man—a man of the mind supporting the world on his shoulders and making civilization possible. When Atlas is manipulated and subjugated by an increasingly collectivist society, he rebels, and society collapses.

The incarnation of Atlas and the apotheosis of human potential, John Galt instigates and leads the revolt featured in the novel. Practicing unbreachable rationality—the commitment to fully use his mind and to respect facts, reality, and logic—Galt epitomizes intelligence, serenity, and joy in living, productivity, self-esteem, courage, and a profound contempt of evil. Galt is complemented by a cast of memorable characters. Dagny Taggart is Rand's conception of the ideal woman, a female version of Howard Roark ("Myself, with any possible flaws eliminated"). In Barbara Branden's *The Passion of Ayn Rand* Rand states that Hank Beardon is "the American businessman at his best, self-made, inventive, resourceful, unself-pitying—and much too innocent for his own good." Francisco d'Anconia, who is on the same level as Galt, his best friend and comrade-in-arms, willfully destroys his own multibillion-dollar industry in support of Galt's principles. James Taggart is Dagny's brother and her philosophical antithesis. Rand described Lillian Rearden, Hank's wife, as "the archetype of the humanitarian liberal pseudointellectual who despises and hates the industrialist."

Atlas Shrugged, while further developing themes introduced in *The Fountainhead,* presents important new aspects of Rand's still-evolving philosophy of Objectivism. In the later novel, she differentiates between errors of knowledge and breaches of morality. Even though Dagny Taggart and Hank Rearden commit errors of knowledge by not immediately joining the strike, they are still depicted as honorable and good people. Implicit in the novel is the idea that evil results only from breaches of morality; and a related concept, "sanction of the victim," concerns honorable and able people allowing evil to occur. Rand argues that, by being altruistic and conceding moral superiority to their oppressors, such people permit their virtues to be used unjustly against them. Against such sanction of the victim, John Galt organizes the strike of the mind. Finally, *Atlas Shrugged* rejects the dichotomy of body and mind (soul), which Rand believed led to the denigration of activities as diverse as sex and industrial production as mindless and purely material activity. Rather, the novel insists that mind and body are one, and all of these activities flow naturally from a free mind.

Rand believed that capitalism is the only moral economic system because it is based on the inviolability of human rights, and *Atlas Shrugged* is a paean to unfettered laissez-faire capitalism. The novel argues that capitalism symbolizes the importance of work and gives man the right to his own mind and to his happiness. Industrial achievement and innovation are synonymous with intelligence, courage, and integrity, while altruism, the belief that man's first duty is to sacrifice his individual right to exist in the interest of the common good, is incompatible with capitalism.

In a capitalist economy run by ideal people of the highest moral integrity, the well-being of all citizens is maximized. To achieve such a state, in the words of John Galt,

> Man must hold these things as the supreme and ruling values of his life: Reason–Purpose–Self-esteem. Reason, as his only tool of knowledge–Purpose, as his choice of the happiness which that tool must proceed to achieve–Self-esteem, as his inviolate certainty that his mind is competent to think and his person is worthy of happiness, which means worthy of living.

Atlas Shrugged was Rand's last work of fiction. In the novel, she had presented her philosophy to her satisfaction and felt there was nothing more to say. The reviews echoed those of her earlier works and in fact were even worse. Although there were several good reviews, most of the big-city, major-market reviewers savaged the book, charging it with being drab, cumbersome, lumbering, and terribly written. Further, the novel was accused of being pro-Nazi, immoral, antireligious, undemocratic, hateful, and destructive. When initial sales of *Atlas Shrugged* were less than expected, Random House feared the book would fail. Once again, however, after the book reached its audience, sales increased dramatically, and the novel eventually became a runaway success in both hardback and paperback.

Readers who consider *Atlas Shrugged* a masterpiece point to Rand's first-rate narrative skill and mastery of plot construction; her proficiency at suspense; the fast pace of action; and the melodramatic, spectacular scene. In addition, Rand's followers praise her attention to detail and her mastery and control in organizing complex themes and ideas; the elaborate structure of the text; and its compelling power and drama. *Atlas Shrugged* has come to be viewed as a provocative, stimulating, and revolutionary book of ideas.

Nevertheless, *Atlas Shrugged* reads like an overstated, pedantic, and dry primer of Objectivism. The interactions between characters are, at times, didactic and lacking in feeling, emotion, and spontaneity. In par-

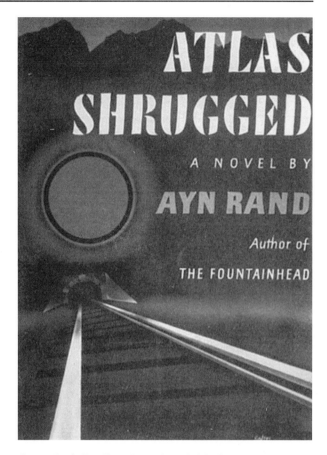

Dust jacket for Rand's 1957 novel, in which leading entrepreneurs and industrialists stage a worldwide "strike" in response to government "looting" of their enterprises

ticular, John Galt comes across as a mysterious, symbolic abstraction rather than a flesh-and-blood human being. It should be pointed out that Rand intended Galt to be godlike, and as she stated, "One does not approach a god too closely–one does not get too intimate with him–one maintains a respectful distance from his inner life." The characters (as Rand herself could be) often seem overly harsh, contemptuous, judgmental, and unforgiving of individuals to whom they are philosophically opposed.

The favorite Rand characters of many readers are Hank Rearden and Kira Argounova, precisely because they come across as being the most emotional and human of her creations. Rand has been criticized for disparaging and minimizing emotions. Nathaniel Branden observed, for instance, that the characters in *Atlas Shrugged* are unable to listen to their feelings, reflect on them, and gain insights that could modify thinking. Rand repeatedly admitted she knew nothing about psychology, and had she known more about it, she might have given emotions a more central and trusted place in her philosophy.

Some readers have detected sadomasochistic undertones and sexual violence in her work and see such concerns as reflecting Rand's lifelong hero worship and belief in the physical and sexual dominance of men. Indeed, Rand stated that "Dagny is a man worshiper, as any heroine of mine would have to be. Man is the ultimate." The most famous instance of sexual violence in her fiction is the so-called rape scene in *The Fountainhead*. After considerable verbal foreplay, Howard Roark has what some critics have interpreted as forced sex with Dominique Francon. The feminist Susan Brownmiller, in her 1975 work *Against Our Will: Men, Women and Rape,* decried this scene as the central shame of modern fiction and accused Rand of being a traitor to her own gender. Rand countered that no rape occurred and that any such act would be disgusting and unthinkable to any of her heroes. Of what happened to Dominique, said Rand, "If that was rape—it was rape by engraved invitation."

Still others, while praising Rand's comprehensive, systematic, closely reasoned, and rigorously logical philosophy, dispute the validity of some of the fundamental premises of that philosophy. Hiram Haydn, Rand's editor in chief at Random House, considered her philosophy to be "one kind of arid intellectual triumph, a tour de force that commanded admiration," but believed that its social and political consequences were troubling.

In 1959 a revised edition of *We the Living* was published. The most controversial of the revisions, because Rand did not mention it in her introduction, was her excision of a passage, reminiscent of Nietzsche, in which Kira justifies the use of force in the name of right and debates the propriety of bloodshed under certain circumstances. Eventually, Rand rejected the use of force as a means to an end and argued that it was justified only in response to force initiated by someone else.

After publication of *Atlas Shrugged,* Rand wrote only nonfiction essays about Objectivism, a philosophy that stimulated considerable interest. She received many requests to provide more information concerning it. With Rand's full support, Nathaniel Branden (born Nathan Blumenthal) founded the Nathaniel Branden Lectures (later called the Nathaniel Branden Institute or NBI) in 1958. These lectures on specific aspects of Objectivism were given by members of Rand's inner circle of friends and associates (the "Collective" or "The Class of '43"). Rand answered questions following the lectures. A four-page monthly newsletter, *The Objectivist Newsletter,* edited by Rand and Branden, was started in 1962 and by 1966 had grown into a small monthly magazine, *The Objectivist*. In addition, Rand wrote pamphlets and articles that analyzed various issues and subjects from an objectivist viewpoint. By the 1960s, the increasing success of the NBI and Rand's popularity had attracted many followers, and Objectivism was now a genuine movement.

Rand published eight more books after her last novel. *Night of January 16th* was republished in 1968 with an introduction by Rand, while the other seven books, ranging over a variety of subjects from an objectivist perspective, were largely collections of her previously published essays with new introductions by her, though some of the books included new material. The titles of these collections of nonfiction are *For the New Intellectual: The Philosophy of Ayn Rand* (1961), *The Virtue of Selfishness, a New Concept of Egoism* (1964), *Capitalism, the Unknown Ideal* (1966), *Introduction to Objectivist Epistemology* (1967), *The Romantic Manifesto: A Philosophy of Literature* (1969), *The New Left: The Anti-Industrial Revolution* (1971), and *Philosophy, Who Needs It* (1982).

Despite Rand's success and fame, her life after the publication of *Atlas Shrugged* was unhappy and difficult. Her husband's health deteriorated because of a progressive dementia, and he died in 1979. Rand also suffered serious health problems that drained her energy and made it difficult for her to write. She severed ties with many of her best friends because of her intolerance for their presumed deviation from objectivist principles or because they failed to meet unreasonable demands she made of them. Rand's primary goal was to foster the acceptance of Objectivism and to change America, but her personal relationship with Nathaniel Branden destroyed this goal.

According to Branden, Rand saw in him the character traits she celebrated in her writing. The affair ("It's a rational universe: this *had* to happen," Rand said) was conducted with the full knowledge but less than wholehearted approval of their respective spouses. It began in June 1954 and was intended to be only platonic. Not wanting to look foolish by being involved with a much younger man, Rand originally envisioned the relationship as lasting only a year or two. Nevertheless, four months after it began, the relationship became sexual, and it continued until 1958.

In 1958, after *Atlas Shrugged* was published, Rand suffered severe depression caused by a combination of factors: a letdown from the exhilaration and drive of writing the book; the vitriolic criticism directed against her; the misrepresentation of her ideas; and the lack of support from anyone of intellectual substance whom she admired. She became increasingly isolated, withdrawn and bitter at what she felt to be the mediocrity of the world. Unable to write, she put her relationship with Branden on hold.

With the passage of time, the mushrooming popularity of Objectivism, and the success of the NBI, Rand's spirits slowly revived. In 1964, now nearly

Barbara and Nathaniel Branden with Rand and her husband, Frank O'Connor, in 1963

sixty, she tried to rekindle the relationship with the thirty-five-year-old Branden, unaware that in the interim Branden had become intimately involved with a married NBI student. Not until four years later did Branden tell Rand about this relationship.

A stunned, humiliated, and angry Rand sought retribution and removed Branden from any role in the NBI and *The Objectivist*. His name on the dedication page of *Atlas Shrugged* and Rand's concluding acknowledgment of him were omitted in later editions. Ultimately, Rand severed all direct communication with Branden and tried unsuccessfully to prevent a book he had written (*The Psychology of Self-Esteem*, 1969) from being published. In the May 1968 issue of *The Objectivist* (published in October), she wrote a six-page article informing her readers of the break and giving reasons for it, although she never revealed their affair or accepted any responsibility for what had happened. Instead, the article was a litany of accusations concerning Branden's personal and professional conduct, some of them half-truthful and others outright lies. The article created divided loyalties and disillusionment, basically ending Objectivism as an organized movement. Rand severed her ties with the NBI in September 1968, effectively killing it. *The Objectivist* was replaced in 1971 with *The Ayn Rand Letter,* irregularly published until 1976 for a dwindling audience. Rand spent her remaining years caring for her increasingly ill husband, writing

relatively little, making some public appearances, working on a television miniseries of *Atlas Shrugged* that was never produced, and becoming increasingly bitter and disenchanted with the direction in which the world was moving. Her health slowly deteriorated from the postoperative effects of surgery, first for lung cancer and later for gallstones, and she died on 6 March 1982.

Critics have accused Rand of being a hypocrite and of proving the inconsistency of her philosophy, with particular attention directed at her lack of insight into and control of her own motivations and emotions. (Rand had claimed that "I've never had an emotion I couldn't identify or an emotion that clashed with reason.") Her supporters argue, however, that she transcended her personal limitations and imperfections to effectively convey a vision of humankind at its best and most heroic. What is important is her continuing popularity. Her books annually sell three hundred thousand to five hundred thousand copies; and in 1991, the Library of Congress reported that *Atlas Shrugged* was surpassed only by the Bible as the book considered to be the most influential in the lives of its readers. Study groups and conferences concerning her work continue to be widely held. An article in *The Economist* (25 December 1993 – 7 January 1994) ranked Rand favorably with other important figures in influence, originality, intellectual coherence, and devotion of followers.

Despite the indifference and even hostility of academic opinion, Ayn Rand developed a philosophy that offers an accessible and compellingly cogent view of life and man that nevertheless raises legitimate points of disagreement. Nathaniel Branden, for example, objected to an "intellectualized" or premeditated self-regard that neglected the more natural and latent quality of emotions, kindness, and compassion. Instead, Rand's form of idealism stressed independence, honesty, productivity, and self-responsibility. Readers found in both Rand's literary characters and in her expository writing a moral philosophy that helped them grow and direct their lives toward the rational (hence moral) ends of productivity and happiness.

Rand emerges then as a distinctive combination of novelist and philosopher who successfully expressed serious philosophical and existential themes through the conventions of popular fiction. However flawed or tragic a figure, her complex, determined, and single-minded persona ensured her a place as one of the most controversial, colorful, and influential writers of the twentieth century.

Letters:

Letters of Ayn Rand, edited by Michael S. Berliner (New York: Dutton, 1995).

Interview:

Alvin Toffler, "A Playboy Interview: Ayn Rand," *Playboy,* 11 (March 1964): 35–64.

Bibliography:

Vincent L. Perrin, *Ayn Rand–First Descriptive Bibliography* (Rockville, Md.: Quill & Brush, 1990).

Biographies:

Barbara Branden, *The Passion of Ayn Rand: A Biography* (Garden City, N.Y.: Doubleday, 1986);

Nathaniel Branden, *Judgment Day: My Years with Ayn Rand* (Boston: Houghton Mifflin, 1989).

References:

James Thomas Baker, *Ayn Rand* (Boston: Twayne, 1987);

Harry Binswanger, ed., *The Ayn Rand Lexicon: Objectivism from A to Z* (New York: New American Library, 1986);

Nathaniel Branden, *My Years with Ayn Rand* (San Francisco: Jossey–Bass, 1999);

Branden and Barbara Branden, *Who Is Ayn Rand?* (New York: Random House, 1962);

Douglas J. Den Uyl and Douglas B. Rasmussen, eds., *The Philosophic Thought of Ayn Rand* (Urbana: University of Illinois Press, 1984);

Peter F. Erickson, *The Stance of Atlas: An Examination of the Philosophy of Ayn Rand* (Portland, Ore.: Herakles Press, 1997);

Mimi Reisel Gladstein, *The Ayn Rand Companion* (Westport, Conn.: Greenwood Press, 1984; revised and enlarged, 1999);

Gladstein and Chris Matthew Sciabarra, eds., *Feminist Interpretations of Ayn Rand* (University Park: Pennsylvania State University Press, 1999);

Tibor R. Machan, *Ayn Rand* (New York: Peter Lang, 1999);

Ronald E. Merrill, *The Ideas of Ayn Rand* (La Salle, Ill.: Open Court, 1991);

William F. O'Neill, *With Charity toward None: An Analysis of Ayn Rand's Philosophy* (New York: Philosophical Library, 1971);

Michael Paxton, *Ayn Rand: A Sense of Life: The Companion Book to the Feature Documentary, Ayn Rand: A Sense of Life* (Layton, Utah: Gibbs Smith, 1998);

Leonard Peikoff, *Objectivism: The Philosophy of Ayn Rand* (New York: Dutton, 1991);

Claudia Roth Pierpont, "Twilight of the Goddess," *New Yorker,* 71 (24 July 1995): 70–81;

Sciabarra, *Ayn Rand: The Russian Radical* (University Park: Pennsylvania State University Press, 1995);

Jeff Walker, *The Ayn Rand Cult* (Chicago: Open Court, 1999).

Papers:

A collection of Ayn Rand's papers, including drafts, galleys, and proofs of her novels, is housed at the Library of Congress; archives that include her journals are housed at the Ayn Rand Institute, Marina del Rey, California.

Ishmael Reed

(22 February 1938 –   )

Julian Cowley
University of Luton

See also the Reed entries in *DLB 2: American Novelists Since World War II; DLB 5: American Poets Since World War II, First Series; DLB 33: Afro-American Fiction Writers After 1955; DS 8: The Black Aesthetic Movement;* and *DLB 169: American Poets Since World War II, Fifth Series.*

BOOKS: *The Free-Lance Pallbearers* (Garden City, N.Y.: Doubleday, 1967; London: MacGibbon & Kee, 1968);

Yellow Back Radio Broke-Down (Garden City, N.Y.: Doubleday, 1969; London: Allison & Busby, 1971);

catechism of d neoamerican hoodoo church (London: Breman, 1970; Detroit: Broadside Press, 1971);

Mumbo Jumbo (Garden City, N.Y.: Doubleday, 1972);

Conjure: Selected Poems, 1963–1970 (Amherst: University of Massachusetts Press, 1972);

Chattanooga: Poems (New York: Random House, 1973);

The Last Days of Louisiana Red (New York: Random House, 1974);

Flight to Canada (New York: Random House, 1976);

A Secretary to the Spirits (New York: NOK, 1978);

Shrovetide in Old New Orleans: Essays (Garden City, N.Y.: Doubleday, 1978);

The Terrible Twos (New York: St. Martin's Press/Marek, 1982; London: Allison & Busby, 1990);

God Made Alaska for the Indians: Selected Essays, Critical Studies on Black Life and Culture, volume 24 (New York: Garland, 1982);

Reckless Eyeballing (New York: St. Martin's Press, 1986; London: Allison & Busby, 1989);

Cab Calloway Stands in for the Moon (Flint, Mich.: Bamberger, 1986);

New and Collected Poems (New York: Atheneum, 1988);

Writin' Is Fightin': Thirty-Seven Years of Boxing on Paper (New York: Atheneum, 1988);

The Terrible Threes (New York: Atheneum, 1989; London: Allison & Busby, 1993);

Airing Dirty Laundry (Reading, Mass.: Addison-Wesley, 1993);

Japanese By Spring (New York: Atheneum, 1993; London: Allison & Busby, 1994).

Ishmael Reed (photograph © by Jerry Bauer; from the dust jacket for Japanese by Spring, *1993)*

PLAY PRODUCTIONS: *Hell Hath No Fury . . .,* New York, The Playwrights and Directors Project of the Actors Studio, June 1980;

Savage Wilds, Berkeley, Cal., Julia Morgan Theater, January 1988;

Hubba City, Black Repertory Theatre, 1988;

The Preacher and the Rapper, New York, Nuyorican Poets Cafe, 1994.

PRODUCED SCRIPT: *Personal Problems,* video, script by Reed and Al Young, 1980.

RECORDING: "Sky Diving," read by Reed, *Big Ego,* New York, Giorno Poetry Systems Records, GPS 012–013, 1978.

OTHER: *The Rise, Fall, And . . .? of Adam Clayton Powell,* edited by Reed as Emmett Coleman (New York: Bee-Line, 1967);

19 Necromancers from Now, edited by Reed (Garden City, N.Y.: Doubleday, 1970);

Yardbird Reader, 5 volumes, edited by Reed (Berkeley, Cal.: Yardbird Publishing Cooperative, 1972–1976);

Yardbird Lives!, edited by Reed and Al Young (New York: Grove, 1978);

Calafia: The California Poetry, edited by Reed (Berkeley: Y'bird Books, 1979);

"The American Literary Scene as a White Settler's Fortress," in *The Art of Literary Publishing: Editors on Their Craft,* edited by Bill Henderson (Wainscott, N.Y.: Pushcart Press, 1980), pp. 100–105;

Quilt, edited by Reed and Young (Berkeley, Cal.: Reed & Young, 1981);

The Before Columbus Foundation Fiction Anthology: Selections from the American Book Awards 1980–1990, edited by Reed, Kathryn Trueblood, and Shawn Wong (New York & London: Norton, 1992);

Richard Nagler, *Oakland Rhapsody: The Secret Soul of an American Downtown,* introduction by Reed (Berkeley, Cal.: North Atlantic Books, 1995);

Reginald Martin, ed., *Dark Eros,* foreword by Reed (New York: St. Martin's Press, 1997).

SELECTED PERIODICAL PUBLICATION–
UNCOLLECTED: *Savage Wilds, Callaloo,* 17, no. 4 (1994): 1158–1204.

Ishmael Reed is one of America's leading proponents of multiculturalism. His commitment to the transformation of America into a truly multicultural society has informed his writing and has also been evident in his energetic activity as editor, publisher, and cultural entrepreneur. As a satirist he has been compared to not only William S. Burroughs but also Jonathan Swift. Characteristically, Reed counters such comparisons with the assertion that there is an African or Afro-American tradition within which his writing can more accurately be placed, and of which his critics are woefully ignorant. Similarly, he views the tendency to place

his work conveniently in the company of white post-modernists as evidence of the narrowness of critics' terms of reference. In a 1988 interview with Shamoon Zamir that was collected in *Conversations with Ishmael Reed* (1995), Reed returned to a point he had made regularly before: "I think that avant-garde movements tend to take themselves too seriously and believe that they are originating forms which are, in fact, ancient."

In a 1971 interview published in *The New Fiction: Interviews with Innovative American Writers* (1974) John O'Brien described Reed as a writer who had been "planting bombs in our imaginations, disrupting our sense of what a novel should be as well as our belief about what America is." This striking image of Reed as terrorist of the imagination, subverting expectations of both literary form and cultural orthodoxies, remains appropriate nearly a quarter of a century later, although his approach to literary form has grown less disruptive. He is in a real sense a political writer, but he distanced himself from the highly visible radical groups that dominated the media coverage of American politics during the 1960s, and that to a degree have continued to do so. As his fiction shows, he is alert to ways in which oppositional militants replicate the habits of their oppressors. Yet, he has shown remarkable resistance to cynicism; there is an enduringly affirmative element that forms the primary value of his work. Reed has affirmed that he writes religious books, and he has formulated his own aesthetic of Neo-HooDoo.

Ishmael Scott Reed was born in Chattanooga, Tennessee, on 22 February 1938 to Henry LeNoir, a fundraiser for the Young Men's Christian Association (YMCA), and Thelma V. Coleman, a salesperson in a department store. His mother subsequently married Bennie Stephen Reed, who worked in an automobile factory, and her son took his stepfather's surname. In the interview with Zamir, Reed not only asserted that he has Cherokee Indian ancestry on his father's side but also laid claim to Irish ancestry. When he was four, the family moved to Buffalo, New York. He began writing stories while in the second grade. An interest in music became evident during his school career; he played trombone and was second violin in a string quartet. William M. Banks, in his *Black Intellectuals: Race and Responsibility in American Life* (1996), quotes Reed's reminiscence of his schooldays: "Writing and reading were things I enjoyed doing. I was a kind of loner. Nobody would choose me for their basketball teams. Sports was a big thing and I was good at sports up to a point, but I wasn't interested in sports anymore. I got along with kids, but I didn't belong to their clubs, I didn't see myself as being anybody exceptional. I just liked to be alone. Although I'm still friends with many of them, I never socialized. A lot of stuff they were talking about was foreign to what I was going through. I did straight things like go to the YMCA." In 1955 he won a trip to Paris to attend an international convention of the YMCA. Reed attended Buffalo Technical High School between 1952 and 1954 and graduated from East High School in 1956. He worked as a clerk for the public library system to support himself through night school at Millard Fillmore College. "Something Pure," a short story depicting the Second Coming of Jesus as an advertising agent, impressed his English instructor, who facilitated Reed's entry to the University of Buffalo's Bachelor of Arts program. He majored in American Studies. In retrospect, Reed views this period as one of indoctrination in Western cultural attitudes, although exposure to writers such as William Blake and William Butler Yeats, who espoused heterodox, syncretic, and highly personal systems of belief, was to prove useful to him. Severe financial difficulties forced him to withdraw without a degree after two and a half years.

In 1958, while a student, he founded a YMCA community drama workshop and performed in Jean Anouilh's *Antigone*. In September 1960 he married Priscilla Rose Thompson. The couple moved to Buffalo, and their daughter, Timothy Bret Reed, was born. Reed was employed in 1961 as staff correspondent for the *Empire Star Weekly*. As the father of a young child, living in Talbert Mall Projects, he was particularly sensitive to the harsh conditions endured by his neighbors. Starting to write creatively, he was, at the same time, producing committed journalism that helped form what he calls in *Writin' Is Fightin': Thirty-Seven Years of Boxing on Paper* (1988), his "pungent writing style." Also in 1961, with Joe Walker, editor of the *Star,* he cohosted "Buffalo Community Roundtable," a politically radical and formally innovative show on radio station WVFO. The program was canceled following an interview with Malcolm X, conducted by Reed. His interest in acting continued, and he was given a part in Edward Albee's *The Death of Bessie Smith* at Buffalo's Jewish Center's Theater in the Round.

In 1962, the Reeds moved to New York City. He wrote his first play, "Ethan Booker," about conflict between Muslims and conservatives on a Southern campus, but the manuscript was lost. Reed separated from his wife in 1963. In that year he joined the *Umbra* Workshop and "began to become acquainted with the techniques of Afro-American literary style." His poem, "Time and the Eagle," was published in *Umbra* magazine. His work also appeared in the *Liberator*. He remained in New York until 1967, taking a variety of jobs. He worked in hospitals, packed boxes in a factory, acted as a clerk in an unemployment office, and did market research. During this period he shared an apart-

Dust jacket for Reed's first book, a satiric novel about a naive black man's nightmarish journey into "the heart of whiteness"

ment with Askia Muhammed Toure, née Ronald Snellings, and Charles and William Patterson.

In 1964, the final issue of *New Masses* included his poem "The Arse Belching Muse." At Tenth Street Gallery he met Carla Blank, a dancer whom he later married. In 1965 they appeared together in "Black," a multimedia show at the Bridge Theater, on St. Mark's Place. He founded and acted as editor in chief for *Advance,* a weekly community newspaper published in Newark, New Jersey. The *Umbra* group, which included Tom Dent, David Henderson, and Calvin Hernton, congregated at a bar run by Stanley Tolkin. There Reed met and gave support to the painter Walter Bowart, establishing *The East Village Other,* which Reed named. He was instrumental in setting up the influential St. Mark's Project and in 1966 ran its first fiction workshop.

Among his acquaintances at that time were musicians Cecil Taylor, Albert Ayler, and Sun Ra. He has continued to feel an affinity between his own work and that of the late Sun Ra, whose work similarly married innovation with a strong awareness of musical tradition and was infused with mythic elements. Generally, Reed feels that musicians have responded to the rhythm in his writing, just as visual artists have been more alert and more sympathetic than literary critics to his use of collage techniques. So, while a reviewer in *The Nation* compared him to Mark Twain and another in *The New York Times* referred to him as the North American equivalent to Gabriel García Márquez, the great drummer Max Roach has identified Reed as "the Charlie Parker of American fiction."

In the mid 1960s in New York, he became friends with Langston Hughes and Walter Lowenfels. Lowenfels included Reed's work in *Poets of Today: A New American Anthology* (1964) and in *Where Is Vietnam? American Poets Respond; an Anthology of Contemporary Poems* (1967). In Reed's discussion with Zamir in 1988, Reed acknowledged the powerful personal influence of Hughes: "He's a model for me, and I try to help young writers as he did and I live in a black ghetto just as he lived in a Harlem neighbourhood." Hughes included a poem by Reed in the anthology, *The Poetry of the Negro,* and introduced him to Anne Freedgood, who accepted Reed's first novel, *The Free-Lance Pallbearers,* in 1966 for Doubleday.

The Free-Lance Pallbearers was published to some critical acclaim the following year, after Reed's move to Berkeley, where he took up a teaching post at the University of California. The book contains Reed's most sinister landscape, a grim image of modern America filtered through the literary Gothic and deriving features from expressionist art and cinema. Reed, in a 1971 interview with O'Brien published in his *Interviews with Black Writers,* compared its world to that of Robert Wiene's "German Voodoo film," *The Cabinet of Dr. Caligari* (1920). Moreover, just as the *bokor,* or magician, in Wiene's movie sends out a zombie to destroy his enemies, Reed directed his satirical novel at a corrupt world. Initially, it had a much more limited focus, satirizing the local political situation in Newark, New Jersey. It evolved, however, into a nightmarish vision of the death of individual freedom, couched in bleakly comic terms.

The novel is set in HARRY SAM, a place, but also the personification of a degenerated society. HARRY SAM is the state that consumes its own offspring, and Reed offers no easy alternative to the cannibalistic structures that make this novel so grim. He allows no party to escape his corrosive wit. As he observed in 1988 in *Writin' Is Fightin','* "I don't have a predictable, computerized approach to political and social issues in a society in which you're either for it or agin' it. Life is much more complex."

The novel is crucially concerned with the efforts of its black protagonist to conform to the cultural norms established by the ruling elite of white men. Bukka Doopeyduk is a naive figure, carried along from one compromising situation to another, always discovering his identity in terms offered by others. Reed not only satirizes the training of the compliant Nazarene

apprentice Bukka's Christian orthodoxies, but he also attacks the militant Elijah Raven, whose separatist position is alien to Reed's vision of polycultural America. At the end of the novel, Bukka discovers the grossly unpalatable physical reality underlying the rhetoric of HARRY SAM. In a concerted act of demystification he confronts the structure of control that has contained him. Nonetheless, once HARRY SAM is toppled, Bukka aspires to the same kind of power, replicating the oppressive ways of the tyrant: "I WAS GOING TO RUN THE ENTIRE KIT AND KABOODLE. ME DICTATOR OF BUKKA DOOPEYDUK."

Finally, he is subjected to a parodic crucifixion, broadcast on network television. A giant ball of manure hangs suspended above the state, symbolic of the Western intellectual tradition that hangs as destructively as an atomic bomb above a subservient population. Part of Reed's strategy in countering the monolithic nature of that tradition has been incorporation of materials and forms from popular culture. As he told O'Brien in 1971: "I've watched television all my life, and I think my way of editing, the speed I bring to my books, the way the plot moves, is based upon some of the television shows and cartoons I've seen, the way they edit." The perverse logic of cartoons and the fragmented structure of television viewing, both inherit the tradition of vaudeville, which Reed reveres as an expansive vernacular art form. Since his first novel he has shared in that inheritance, discovering creative modes of engaging with American realities that do not conform to the repressive expectation that black writing should be either confessional or social-realist. Conformity to such an expectation is, for Reed, tantamount to perpetuation of slavery by other means.

In *The Free-Lance Pallbearers* hoodoo is subjected to a degree of ridicule, but in 1967 Reed started serious investigation of this syncretic religion, and its voodoo sources. Its importance for Reed since then cannot be overstated. It provided a vital metaphor for the affirmative vision that took him beyond the ostensible impasse of that first novel, and it has given his varied cultural activities meaningful shape. In a 1977 interview with Jon Ewing, collected in *Shrovetide in Old New Orleans* (1978), he declared: "Voodoo is the perfect metaphor for the multiculture. Voodoo comes out of the fact that all these different tribes and cultures were brought from Africa to Haiti. All of their mythologies, knowledges, and herbal medecines, their folklores, jelled. It's an amalgamation like this country. Voodoo also teaches that past is present. When I say I use a Voodoo aesthetic I'm not just kidding around."

Reed's mission is to promote pluralistic values, and he opposes ferociously the threat to multicultural richness posed by exclusive systems. In his early work Christianity was his principal target, enabling him to bypass antagonisms grounded in crude racial differentiations of black and white and to engage with a structure of belief that he saw as fueling the motor of intolerance. Reed has spoken of his own books as religious texts, but his Neo-HooDoo has no dogma, and its forms of worship are manifold.

His researches have uncovered an alternative, African American literary tradition. He remarks in *Shrovetide in Old New Orleans* that "when one reads early HooDoo tales one is struck by the free use of what professors call 'the vernacular,' the lack of division between the natural and the supernatural, animism, the discontinuous sense of time, the listing of rites, and the talking of that talk (talking in codes . . .)." In his introductory remarks to *19 Necromancers from Now* (1970), he states his belief in "the American experience as rooted in slang, dialect, vernacular, argot, and all of the other put down terms the faculty uses for those who have the gall to deviate from the true and proper way of English." Viewed in this perspective, his work is not innovative in any way that suggests mere novelty, but is continuous with a submerged tradition of American writing, literatures that have been suppressed or that have remained long hidden.

It should not be assumed that Reed's espousal of non-European cultural forms requires uncritical rejection of European art. In addition to expressionism, he has acknowledged the impact on him of Dada and Surrealist art. These manifestations of early-twentieth-century European culture take their place alongside native American, African, and Oriental practices within the array of cultural resources available to him.

In 1969 Reed organized the second American Festival of Negro Art (he had participated in the first in 1965). That same year he taught at the University of Washington, Seattle, and his second novel was published. *Yellow Back Radio Broke-Down* is a variant on the Western, a genre that thrives on binary opposition, the law versus the outlaw, the man in white versus the man in black. His novel sets out to undermine the currency of such polarities. Reed has explained, in "The Writer as Seer: Ishmael Reed on Ishmael Reed," his 1974 self-interview (collected in *Shrovetide in Old New Orleans*), that the title suggests a technical guide and follows the lead of a poem by Lorenzo Thomas called "Modern Plumbing Illustrated" (1966). The "Yellow Back" was a Western novel, recounting tales of cowboy heroism between standard yellow covers. The action was customarily sensational, and Reed works his singular variations on that convention. Radio scripts inspired the second part of the title. Reed wanted to write a book in which dialogue was to the fore, with readers projecting the setting and scenery just as listeners to broadcast dramas were accustomed to doing. The opening paragraph leaves no doubt as to his intention to write an "oral" book, tapping into traditions other than the recognizably literary: "Folks.

This here is the story of the Loop Garoo Kid. A cowboy so bad he made a working posse of spells phone in sick. A bullwhacker so unfeeling he left the print of winged mice on the hides of crawling women. A desperado so onery he made the Pope cry and the most powerful of cattlemen shed his head to the Executioner's swine."

After the unremitting gloom of *The Free-Lance Pallbearers,* this second novel is unmistakably upbeat, a West Coast book, whereas its predecessor sprang from the housing projects of the East. HooDoo assumes an entirely constructive role and is ever present, on the surface and in the undercurrents of the fiction. Loop Garoo, the HooDoo cowboy, is its incarnation. He arrives in Yellow Back Radio with a circus and discovers that the frontier town is run by children who have driven out their tyrannical parents. Drag Gibson, a wealthy rancher, organizes a violent reprisal. Only Loop and two of the children survive. They take to the hills and set about working HooDoo against Gibson.

They preserve a utopian vision of the Seven Cities of Cibola, bearing the stamp of Buckminster Fuller and other prophets of postindustrial culture. It is accessible only to young people, uncorrupted by materialism. Foremost amongst the agents of corruption that Reed identifies are "Stupid historians who are hired by the cattlemen to promote reason, law and order—toad men who adore facts—say that such an anarchotechnological paradise where robots feed information into inanimate steer and mechanical fowl where machines do everything from dig irrigation ditches to mine the food of the sea help old ladies across the street and nurture infants is as real as a green horse's nightmare."

In O'Brien's 1971 interview, Reed declared that *Yellow Back Radio Broke-Down* wages "artistic guerrilla warfare against the Historical Establishment." He added: "I think the people we want to aim our questioning toward are those who supply the nation with its mind, tutor its mind, develop and cultivate its mind, and these are the people involved in culture. They are responsible for the national mind and they've done very bad things with their propaganda and racism." It is scarcely surprising then that the self-proclaimed saboteur of historical orthodoxy has increasingly directed his critical attention as a writer to the role of television, and more recent electronic technologies, in the formation of collective horizons.

The second section of the novel contains a concise aesthetic manifesto that has become one of Reed's most frequently cited declarations of intent. It occurs in the course of an attack on Bo Shmo, leader of the neosocial-realist gang of critics. Reed is squaring up to the East Coast Leftist intelligentsia that he has accused of exploiting black people's experience to its own political ends. Shmo criticizes Loop for being a "crazy dada nigger," prone to fantasy and indifferent to details. In opposition

Folks . This here is the story of the Loop Garoo Kid . A cowboy so bad he made a

working posse of spells phone in sick . A bullwhacker so unfeeling he left the print

of winged mice on hides of crawling woth . A desperado so onery he made the Pope cr-

y and the most powerful of Cattlemen shed his head to the hangman's swine . *Executioner's*

A terrible cuss of a thousadn shivs he was who wasted whole herds , made the fruit *thousand*

black and womy dryed up the water holes and caused people's eyes to grow from tiny

black dots into slap jacks where ever his feet fell .

Now , he wasn't always bad trump over hearts diamonds and clubs . Once a wild

joker he cut the fool before bemused Egyptians , dressed like Mortimer Sner and spil- *Egyptians*

led french fries on his lap at Las Vegas' top of the strip .

Booted out of his fatner's house after a quarrel whores snapped at his heels and *father's*

trick dogs did the fandango on his belly .

Men called him brother only to cop his coin and tell malicious stories about his

cleft one foot .

I mean-see night tripper he moved from town to town quoting Thomas Jefferson and

allowing bandits to build a flophouse about his genius .

A funny blue hippo who painted himself with water flowers only to be drummed

out of each tribe dressed down publicly his medals ripped off .

Finally he joined a small circus & happily performed with his fellow 86-D . A *cut*

Juggres a dancing Bear a fast talking barker and Zozo Labrique charter member of

the American Hoo-Doo church .

Their fame spread through out the frontier and bouquest of flowers greeted them in *bouquets*

every town until they moved into that city which seemed a section of Hell chipped

off and shipped upstairs .

Yellow Back Radio , where even the sun was afraid to show it's bottom .

Page from the revised typescript for Yellow Back Radio Broke-Down *(University of Delaware Library)*

to the "suffering books" endorsed by these critics, with their ideological commitment to verisimilitude, Loop asks: "What if I write circuses? No one says a novel has to be one thing. It can be anything it wants to be, a vaudeville show, the six o'clock news, the mumblings of wild men saddled by demons."

His literary circus is characterized by surprising disjunctions, dramatic structural shifts, which for Reed evoke the practice of revered artists of the vaudeville stage. In his fourth novel, *The Last Days of Louisiana Red* (1974), he returned to vaudeville forms with the dialogues of Kingfish Stevens and Andy Brown, replicating the exchanges of straight man and clown. In *Shrovetide in Old New Orleans* he pays tribute to "the artistic accomplishments of the American Medicine Shows, Newspapers, Vaudeville, Minstrelsy," and he counters the high seriousness of most literary criticism with the "fool stories that have taught generations of people how to be wise" and that have been perpetuated in the work of comedians such as Bert Williams, W. C. Fields, Lenny Bruce, and Richard Pryor.

In 1970 Reed obtained a formal divorce from his first wife and married Carla Blank. Also in 1970, Reed's *catechism of d neoamerican hoodoo church,* a book of poems, and *19 Necromancers from Now,* an anthology of innovative work by black writers, edited by Reed, was published. He dedicated the anthology to Chester Himes. In 1972 it was awarded a Certificate of Merit from the California Association of English Teachers. In 1971, consolidating and extending the project undertaken in that collection, he established, with Steve Cannon and Al Young, the Yardbird Publishing Company. He acted as its editorial director until 1975. This cooperative organization, named in honor of Charlie Parker, was committed to the promotion of multicultural creativity. In his introduction to *Yardbird Reader 1,* in 1972, Reed recounted how "One day, early in 1971, a few of us living in Northern California were comparing notes concerning the treatment of Afro-American artists by callous publishers, editors and others. It was decided that we are treated as commodities; mute dictaphones recording someone's often ludicrous political and social notions—slaves standing on an auction block as our proportions and talents are discussed." Reed's conviction is that slavery has in fact been internalized and continues to the present day in the form of conditioning of attitudes and expectations. As writer, publisher, and cultural entrepreneur, he has sought to raise awareness of that conditioning and to open up routes of escape.

In the 1978 retrospective anthology *Yardbird Lives!* he testified that the experience of editing the journal was one of "learning firsthand the extraordinary and ingenious job Western aggression had done in keeping slaves in slavery, and how some of the slaves actually encour-

aged this arrangement!" Nonetheless, *Yardbird Reader* was characterized by generosity and expansiveness. In the fifth issue, published in 1976, he proclaimed: "*Yardbird reflects cultural exchange!* A fact of everyday ordinary existence in the complex civilization in which we live. We feel that there are enough Black Worlds, Yellow Worlds, Red Worlds, Brown Worlds, and White Worlds for people who crave that." *Yardbird Reader* received two Pushcart Prizes for small press writing, and a complementary enterprise, Reed, Cannon & Johnson Communications, was set up in 1972.

Reed was nominated for the National Book Award for the two books he published in 1972: *Conjure: Selected Poems, 1963–1970* and *Mumbo Jumbo. Conjure* includes the important "Neo-HooDoo Manifesto," which first appeared in the *Los Angeles Free Press* in September 1970. In 1973, the year *Chattanooga: Poems* was published, *Conjure* was nominated for a Pulitzer Prize in poetry and for the Richard and Hilda Rosenthal Foundation Award. The novel *Mumbo Jumbo* parodies the detective story, deploying familiar conventions of the literary and cinematic genres to Reed's satirical ends. The detective here is Papa LaBas of Mumbo Jumbo Kathedral. His name alludes to Legba, the central figure of the Voodoo spirit altar, who acts as medium between the material and spiritual realms.

The novel met with a notably more enthusiastic critical reception than its predecessors, with an appreciative front-page review in *The New York Times.* His variations not only deploy and disrupt familiar literary patterns, they also work with clichés of cinematic practice. So the novel ends: "(Locomobile rear moving toward neoned Manhattan skyline. Skyscrapers gleam like magic trees. Freeze frame.)" The story is set in Manhattan, and its action follows the spread of the anti-plague, Jes Grew. In *Mumbo Jumbo* it is a "psychic epidemic" that is "electric as life and is characterized by ebullience and ecstasy. Terrible plagues were due to the wrath of God; but Jes Grew is the delight of the gods." Against its spread are marshaled the forces of the Wallflower Order, the backbone of the Atonist faith, whose deadening aesthetic "is thin flat turgid dull grey bland like a yawn." Papa LaBas, who holds within him the ancient mysteries of Jes Grew, is pitted against their leader, Hinckle Von Vampton, crusader against paganism. Both search for the Book of Thoth, sacred text of Jes Grew. Thoth, who presided over writing, was held in ancient Egypt to have been the first choreographer; he wrote down the Dance of Osiris in order to contain its energies for constructive use, to prevent its dispersal in wasteful action. Reed offers this conjunction of writing and dancing as an antidote to the European perception of writing as sedentary and solitary practice. He has defined his own task, and that facing like-minded writers, as a search for literary form to match the spirit pervading the

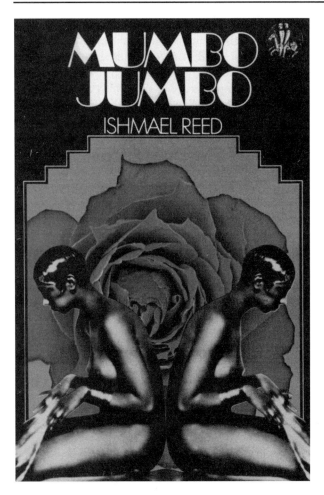

Dust jacket, with mirror-image photographs of dancer Josephine Baker, for Reed's 1972 novel, set in Harlem during the 1920s

music of his contemporaries: James Brown, Otis Redding, Albert Ayler, Sun Ra, and John Coltrane.

Fats Waller is also important to Reed, and he has asserted that Waller was "in" *Mumbo Jumbo*. His music was particularly appropriate because Reed felt that scrutiny of the rhythms of American civilization in the 1920s could elucidate the rhythms of contemporary life. *Mumbo Jumbo* invokes the Harding era as a way of comprehending the age of Richard Nixon, with the Harlem Renaissance played against the creativity of contemporary writers. Photographs and other pictorial illustrations are included to reinforce the parallels and—as Reed would have it—to allow revelations to occur.

One of the villains in the book is former police commissioner Biff Musclewhite, who, as curator of the Center of Art Detention, presides with armed guard over a large collection of "fetishes," the sacred art treasures of other cultures. Restoration of these icons to "aesthetically victimized civilizations" is the goal of a multicultural gang of art thieves, led by Berbelang, once a colleague of LaBas and a man feared by Musclewhite because he "is

aware of his past and has demystified ours." But the sacred book is destroyed by Abdul Hamid, a black Muslim, whose puritanical attitudes the author clearly finds equally unpalatable. Still, LaBas sounds the positive note that was heard throughout *Yellow Back Radio Broke-Down:* "I'll bet that before this century is out men will turn once more to mystery, to wonderment; they will explore the vast reaches of space within instead of measuring more 'progress' more of this more of that." *Mumbo Jumbo* remains the novel in which Reed has most dramatically embodied his Neo-HooDoo aesthetic, in which his skill in composing a whole from fragments of startlingly diverse material is at its most evident.

As work in progress toward *Mumbo Jumbo,* Reed wrote *Cab Calloway Stands in for the Moon,* which became his own contribution to *19 Necromancers from Now* and was separately published in 1986. Calloway is another influential figure for Reed, who assigned the singer's character "Minnie the Moocher" a key role in his next novel, *The Last Days of Louisiana Red.* In a review of that book, included in his *Fabulation and Metafiction* (1979), Robert Scholes declared that Reed "seems gifted with a kind of fundamental high-spiritedness and good humour that keep his satire close to comedy and prevent his black art from sinking into the futilities of literary rage." Nonetheless, *The Last Days of Louisiana Red* is an angry book, and, perhaps because verbal pyrotechnics and formal ingenuity are more muted than in its predecessors, it appears still more venomous.

In 1973 Reed started to publish under the imprint I Reed Books. As its manager he has assumed responsibility for publishing black male writers, whose work he believes has been systematically neglected by the major houses in favor of writing by black women. As he told Zamir in 1988: "I'm trying to remedy this by buying novels by black men from publishers. I can keep them in print. I recently bought works by Cecil Brown and William Demby. I've kept the novels of Calvin Hernton and Al Young in print for many years. I know that I'm being published, but that's not enough, because when black male writers lose, I lose." Publishing these books is a political act: "We use our plays, novels and other writings as a way of talking back." In recent years the imprint has embraced more writing by women.

Reed has been emphatic in his support for hardworking black people who have been severely disadvantaged as a consequence of romanticized media focus on atypical figures who, Reed argues, deserve condemnation rather than respect. *The Last Days of Louisiana Red* developed this concern within a fiction and heightened his unpopularity with black nationalist and Left-wing groups. The novel also expresses Reed's sense that some black American women have been complicit with white men in perpetuating the oppression of black men. Unsurprisingly, this idea had an incendiary effect on feminist readers and reviewers. Charges of misogyny were leveled against him; not for the last time. Reed has always welcomed, even courted, controversy. For him, controversy is a sign that literature is working, rather than gathering dust on a shelf.

The book received a mixed reception, but it had its champions; it won the National Institute of Arts and Letters Award for the best noncommercial novel of 1974. It was a good year for Reed in terms of recognition, as he also won the John Simon Guggenheim Memorial Foundation Award for fiction and received a National Endowment fellowship for creative writing. Papa LaBas recurs in this novel to investigate a case of industrial espionage involving murder. A subplot carries the story of Antigone, as reinterpereted by a figure modeled on the Chorus of ancient Greek drama. The Chorus, the voice of traditional wisdom, disinherited due to current perversity, followed Reed's own path to Berkeley from the East Coast, where the commercial demands of the box office dominate. And like his author the Chorus is "seeking his natural diction between reading writing and watching television."

In the retelling, Antigone is transformed from a free spirit resisting tyranny to Minnie, Queen of the Moochers, "The Sphinx who ate men raw." Her followers are Reed's principal targets: "They are the moochers who cooperate with their 'oppression,' for they have the mentality of the prey who thinks his destruction at the fangs of the killer is the natural order of things and colludes with his own death." Ed Yellings, on the other hand, runs Solid Gumbo Works, a HooDoo business. His mission is to end Louisiana Red, Reed's term for psychological stress and consequent violence in contemporary American life, grounded in competitiveness of a kind that creates rifts in the fabric of society. Indeed, "if Louisiana Red is anything, it's Crabs in the Barrel. Each crab trying to keep the other one from reaching the top." Yellings creates a Gumbo to cure cancer, but when he sets out to combat heroin addiction, he is murdered by industrial assassins. *The Steve Cannon Show,* an audiocassette magazine issued by Reed, Cannon & Johnson Communications, featured a dramatized episode from *The Last Days of Louisiana Red,* performed by Al Young, Ray Johnson, and Victor Cruz.

In 1975 Reed taught at the State University of New York at Buffalo. In the next year *Flight to Canada* was published, and Reed was at the height of his powers, this time raising parallels between contemporary America and the time of the Civil War. The parallels are anchored in his understanding that "words built the world and words can destroy the world," suggesting that the account that has long prevailed has determined the course of history as it has subsequently unfolded. Reed's

task is to revise the story in order to open up opportunities for a multicultural future, replete with creative possibilities for all Americans. Interrogating the reader's reception of conventional accounts of the 1860s, he asks: "Why isn't Edgar Allan Poe recognized as the principal biographer of that strange war? Fiction, you say? Where does fact begin and fiction leave off? Why does the perfectly rational, in its own time, often sound like mumbojumbo? Where did it leave off for Poe, prophet of a civilization buried alive, where, according to witnesses, people were often whipped for no reason. No reason?" Repression is revealed as the dynamic undercurrent of the history of slavery. It casts up monsters in the form of sadism, masochism, and necrophilia.

Alert as ever to myths that impose cultural coherence, in *Flight to Canada* Reed presents the Old South as "an Anglican Grand Design," with Arthurian legend providing a model for holy war conducted against the deities of Native American and African peoples. Raven Quickskill, fugitive slave and antislavery lecturer, has assumed the mantle of the artist-priest, and plantation owner Arthur Swille anxiously remarks: "We gave him Literacy, the most powerful thing in the pre-technological pre-postrational age—and what does he do with it? Uses it like that old Voodoo—that old stuff the slaves mumble about. Fetishism and grisly rites, only he doesn't need anything but a pen he had shaped out of cock feathers and chicken claws."

Reed's belief that slavery has been internalized is expounded throughout his fiction with memorable incisiveness. The American monoculture has replaced the plantation overseer, and multiculturalism is the much needed escape route—the flight to Canada. In 1970, introducing *19 Necromancers from Now,* Reed noted the fashion for "Neo-Slave Narrative" and criticized the ease with which writers adopting this form managed to "confuse their experience with that of thirty million other people." He also remarked on "a frenzy for this kind of writing in publishing circles," elevating its authors to celebrity status "on the lecture circuit." His fifth novel parodies slave narrative, subverting that genre's traditional reliance on an amalgam of confessional and vivid social realism, which he considers enslaving modes. "Flight to Canada" is the title of a poem by Quickskill, annunciating his cultural liberation: "His writing was his HooDoo. Others had their way of HooDoo, but his was his writing. It fascinated him, it possessed him; his typewriter was his drum he danced to." A subsequent stage version of *Flight to Canada* was scripted by William Cook. In the staging the story was framed within a performance by a company of minstrels.

In 1976, with Victor H. Cruz and Bob Callahan, among others, Reed established the Before Columbus Foundation, which has served primarily as a small press

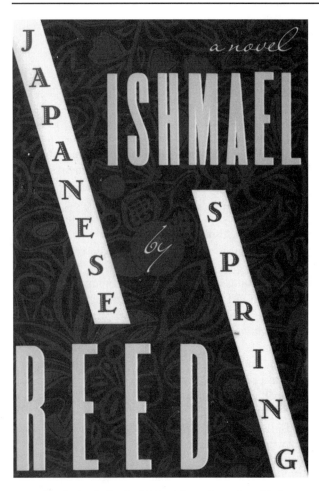

Dust jacket for Reed's 1993 novel, a satire on the political maneuvering that takes place at American universities

outlet. He won New York City's Poetry in Public Places Award for "From the Files of Agent Franklin" and collaborated with his wife and Suzushi Hanayagi on a mystery play for America's bicentennial, *The Lost State of Franklin*. His daughter Tennessee Maria was born in 1977. That same year he failed to secure tenure in the English Department at Berkeley. He traveled to Paris to attend a conference on "The New American Novel" and was asked to become advisory board chairman for the Coordinating Council of Literary Magazines, a post he held until 1979. In 1978 Reed published *A Secretary to the Spirits,* a volume of poetry, and *Shrovetide in Old New Orleans,* essays on various topics. Additionally, he was awarded the Lewis H. Michaux Literary Prize by the Studio Museum in Harlem and the American Civil Liberties Award, organized the first American Book Awards, and acted as editor in chief of *Y'Bird* magazine from 1978 until 1980.

In 1979 Reed taught at Yale University and held the Edward Butler Chair at Buffalo. He used the latter opportunity to help students organize a magazine called

Buffalo. Similarly, he has encouraged student writing at Berkeley, assisting in organization of *The National Student Anthology.* He received a Pushcart Prize for his essay "American Poetry: Is There A Center?" That same year he moved into a working-class area in North Oakland, which he describes in *Writin' Is Fightin'* as "the kind of neighborhood I grew up in before leaving for New York in 1962." *Calafia,* an anthology of Californian poetry for which he had acted as project director, was also published in 1979. In his preface Reed celebrated the cultural vitality of the state: "*Calafia* is an anthology of poetry, but I'm sure that an anthology of Dance, Painting and Music would also show that, out of the high tides and pounding winds of its history, California has produced America's truly world state, and if, as they say, California is the United States' window on the future, then the prospects for a diverse, national poetry, instead of the various sects of the moment, are good."

In 1980 Reed was a judge for the National Poetry Competition and for the King's County Literary Award, chair of the Berkeley Arts Commission, and lecturer at Dartmouth College. He and Al Young initiated publication of a successor to *Yardbird Reader,* the journal *Quilt,* which continued until 1985. Reed has become increasingly involved in television work, recognizing the medium as a powerful controlling influence. *Personal Problems,* a television soap opera, premiered at the Georges Pompidou Museum, Paris, in November 1980. Reed was its executive producer and collaborated with Al Young on script treatments. The program won the Japan Foundation Award, toured, and was shown on cable television. Reed explained to an interviewer for the *Oakland Tribune:* "We chose the soap opera format because the soap opera is an American invention, and for that reason not much has been done to develop it by 'serious artists.'"

If the creative diversity of California fueled Reed's optimism, the elevation of California's governor Ronald Reagan to president of the United States had quite the opposite effect. *The Terrible Twos,* prompted by Reed's profound distaste for that administration, was published in 1982. The novel is set in 1990 when Dean Clift, a former male model, occupies the White House, and the commercialization of Christmas is complete. The title signals Reed's contention that many Americans are intellectually and emotionally immature: "Their plates will be full but they'll have their eyes on everybody else's plates, or they'll have a cookie in their hand and yet ask for another cookie, or the whole bag of cookies." Reed tries to convey that this world, where the idealism of the 1960s, "days of thunder and days of drums. Brave hearts exploding like tropical flowers," has grown entirely alien. Reed is well aware of the violent reality that accompanied that idealism, and he foresees the return of violence in reaction to a bleak, deadening cultural conservatism.

"A Past Christmas," the first section of the novel, portrays white male backlash against erosion of its power by a range of liberal and progressive causes. The reaction includes revived affiliation with Nazi groups and an alliance between the Soviet Union and the United States to defend Northern interests against the southern hemisphere. Reed shares the inclination to weave conspiracy theories so evident in much of contemporary fiction. *The Terrible Twos* throws up Operation Two Birds, a plan to drop a nuclear bomb on New York, blame Nigeria, and then devastate that country. The plan has been conceived in order to eradicate surplus population. Less dramatically, but with unmistakable anger, Reed portrays this country as one in which the poor starve on the streets, while the extremely wealthy can indulge every whim.

The figure of Santa Claus links the perceived immaturity of Americans with inveterate consumerism. Exclusive rights to the figure are granted to Oswald Zumwalt and his North Pole Development Corporation. Reed has always been aware that control of the symbols is the key to power in any society. As is usually the case in his fiction, a covert opposition is active. Its work is to reclaim St. Nicholas, and his assistant Black Peter, for compassion, generosity, and affirmation of life.

President Clift is converted by the intervention of St. Nicholas and determines to divert resources from weaponry into realization of a terrestrial paradise. He is declared insane and confined to an asylum. State Troopers use tear gas to suppress opposition to the status quo. Reed may advocate release of imagination as an antidote to cultural malaise, but he never ignores or underestimates the material difficulties involved in liberating creative and constructive energies. The role of the artist is to sustain those energies and give them direction. At the end of *The Terrible Twos,* St. Nicholas flies across the city, empowered by language and Reed's vision. Below, a manhunt is underway, on the trail of the saint and his accomplice. Nonetheless, HooDoo magic is at work.

In 1982 Reed was associate fellow of Calhoun College, at Yale, and guest lecturer for the University of Arkansas at Fayetteville and for the Sitka Community Association, in Alaska. He also published a collection of essays that year titled *God Made Alaska for the Indians.* Jerome Klinkowitz, who recognizes a common method in Reed's approach to writing novels and essays, refers to the book in his *Literary Subversions: New American Fiction and the Practice of Criticism* (1985) as the "decade's most insightful literary critique of American morals and manners." He adds that the eight essays "range across contemporary America to indicate how one-sided and exclusionary its standards of cultural authority still are. And not just

for black Americans." In the process, they encapsulate Reed's "adversary vision."

During 1983 Reed worked on a television production of *Mother Hubbard* and taught at Columbia University. American Clavé produced a compact disc titled *Conjure Music for the Texts of Ishmael Reed,* produced by Kip Hanrahan. The band Conjure, which had been brought together for the occasion, included such luminaries as Taj Mahal, Allen Toussaint, David Murray, and Carla Bley. Reed's novel *Reckless Eyeballing* (1986) is dedicated to the musicians who made the recording.

In December 1981, in the foreword to Elizabeth A. and Thomas A. Settle's annotated bibliography of his work, Reed wrote: "I am still conscious of the fact that I am a black male writer, who is treated as shabbily as any other black male (until they find out who I am), and that I am a member of a class which has been cast to the bottom of the American caste system, and from those depths I write a vision which is still strange, often frightening, 'peculiar' and 'odd' to some, 'ill-considered' and unwelcome to many." That unsettling vision, fueled by his disgust at the ways in which "the media has created the image of black men as rapists, muggers, and brutes," makes *Reckless Eyeballing* uneasy reading. Interviewed by Mel Watkins in 1985, Reed suggested that the novel "is basically about the parallelism between Jewish and Afro-American experiences." He repeated the point in 1988, when he told Zamir that it not only is "a trickster novel," alluding to Native American mythology, but also contains elements derived from a tradition of Judaism, which his researches persuaded him could be considered "Hebrew Obeah."

Reed had been doing research in comparative religions, but he had also been investigating the historical reality of the Nazi movement. With characteristic boldness he drew analogy, during his discussion with Watkins, between the treatment of Jewish men during the rise of Nazism and the fate of black males, stereotyped as potential rapists within certain kinds of feminist discourse. The novel is an outspoken response to such rhetoric. Its protagonist, Ian Ball, is a black writer who is working on a play about Ham Hill, lynched for "eyeballing" a white woman. Hill is clearly based on the notorious case of Emmett Till, murdered in 1955. Ball struggles against Becky French, a producer who rejects his work in favor of a play about Eva Braun, and playwright Tremonisha Smarts, who is overtly compared to "those women who collaborated with the Nazis." *Reckless Eyeballing* is Reed's most provocative work to date. It touched raw nerves and was met with considerable hostility from many reviewers.

In 1987 Reed taught at Harvard University and was made an associate fellow of the Harvard Signet Society. He also became the thirteenth writer in residence for the *San Francisco Examiner*. In the same year he founded There City Cinema, in Oakland. This multicultural foundation has staged annual motion-picture festivals. In January 1988 Reed's play *Savage Wilds* was performed at the Julia Morgan Theater in Berkeley, and it was produced by Reed. *Savage Wilds* was published in the journal *Callaloo* in 1994. The Black Repertory Theater then commissioned another full-length play, *Hubba City,* which premiered later that year.

In 1988 Reed was regents lecturer at the University of California, Santa Barbara, and published *Writin' Is Fightin'.* The volume is subtitled *Thirty-Seven Years of Boxing on Paper* but actually comprises essays and occasional pieces from the mid 1980s. A second *Conjure* compact disc, *Cab Calloway Stands in for the Moon,* was recorded in 1988. It features Bobby Womack, Eddie Harris, and Don Pullen as well as Tennessee Reed, who contributes to the New Magic Chorus. In accompanying notes, Don Palmer writes: "Like an itinerant bluesman, Reed spins fables that raise demons of the forlorn and frustrated only to banish them with a trickster's cackle."

The Terrible Threes was published in 1989. It is a continuation of *The Terrible Twos,* features the same cast of characters, and recaptures much of the action of its predecessor. Reed is especially concerned to establish the essentially pagan figure of Black Peter as the key to restoring the festival of Christmas as a life-enhancing, celebratory occasion rather than an annual consumerist indulgence. The book is disappointing in that it reiterates so much. But such a judgment is incidental to Reed's approach to writing. If the reader can acknowledge that Reed sends out his books to counter oppressive forces at work in the contemporary world, then it is a purposeful fiction that addresses an ethos of hopelessness and impotent despair, "the Terribles which have plagued the nation since Dallas, November 22, 1963."

During 1989 Reed taught at both the University of California, Santa Barbara, and the University of Washington, Seattle. *Savage Wilds* played at the Zephyr Theater in San Francisco and in 1990 at the Nuyorican Poets Cafe in New York. *Konch,* the journal that succeeded *Quilt,* was launched in 1989 and continued publication until 1995. In 1992 Reed received a commission from the San Francisco Opera Company to write a libretto for music by Bobby McFerrin. *Gethsemane Park* was completed in 1994. Reed attended a conference in 1992 in Paris, "African Americans in Europe," and acted as co-editor for two anthologies issued by the Before Columbus Foundation.

Japanese By Spring, Reed's 1993 novel, is a concerted attack on the pretensions, prejudices, and shortcomings of the academic community. Academic parasites had been featured in earlier novels, such as U2 Polglot in *The Free-Lance Pallbearers* and Maxwell Kasavubu in *The Last Days of Louisiana Red.* In *Japanese By Spring* "Chappie" Puttbutt is the focus for a full-blown satire on the politics of American universities. Clearly for Reed the real cultural work is to be done away from the campus, institutional politics, and academic self-interest. In his 1988 interview with Zamir, Reed noted the increasing conservatism of Afro-American departments and suggested that this suited the "academic bureaucrats and commissars who'd be out of a job if a whole new era of multicultural writing was ushered in." This observation is amplified into a broadside in the novel. Puttbutt is an opportunist who presented himself as a radical in the 1960s but has assumed the conciliatory guise of the neoconservative as he maneuvers his way through life at Jack London College. His reactionary posturing fails to win him tenure, and Reed attacks with evident relish the factions engaged in this academic community's struggles for power.

Puttbutt's latest bravura act of opportunism is to learn Japanese, sensing a swing of economic and cultural power to the East. When the college is taken over by Japanese sponsors, he is rocketed to a position of great influence. As the narrative unfolds, however, the new regime is shown to be just as flawed as the old. The transition from one intolerant and repressive group to another may recall the ending of Reed's first novel, where the Chinese takeover of HARRY SAM leaves the status quo intact.

Reed enters this novel as a character in the manner fashionable some years ago with writers such as Ronald Sukenick and Steve Katz. The effect here is to close palpably the gap between Reed's fiction and nonfiction work. The *Terribles* series found Reed on the ropes but still swinging punches, his appearance here evidence of a writer revived and determined to seize control of the bout. Reed incorporates essayistic points (notably with reference to the beating of Rodney King) without sacrificing any of the exuberance of the novel, and in the epilogue he offers an upbeat reading of the condition of America. The affirmation comes from engagement with Yoruba culture, which offers the multiculturalists in the novel the model that Japan failed to deliver. Yoruba is a touchstone for Reed's Neo-HooDoo, enabling him even to accommodate Christian ceremony within his expansive sense of creative cultural possibilities.

In *Japanese By Spring,* The Terribles, that condition that has afflicted the nation since the death of John F. Kennedy, a traumatic assassination of hope and loss of innocence, still persists. *Japanese By Spring* acknowledges that all is far from well: "If, of all the indexes of a nation's health, the condition of the children was the most important, then the United States was deeply troubled. Black male children were killing each other. White children and Native American children were killing themselves. Millions of children were mired in poverty and had no health care." Despite this diagnosis, the concluding pages of the novel celebrate the burgeoning multiculturalism of California, which is symptomatic of a national trend.

In 1993 Reed received the Sakai Kinu Award from Osaka Community Foundation. *Airing Dirty Laundry,* published that year, corroborates the sense that Reed's pungent essays should be viewed in conjunction with the fiction, as an integral part of the same project. In 1994 the author received an award for literary excellence from the Morgan State University Alumni, and he was chosen by Gwendoline Brooks to receive the George Kent Award. His play *The Preacher and the Rapper* was performed at the Nuyorican Poets Cafe. In 1995 he was awarded an honorary doctorate in letters from the State University of New York at Buffalo. Reed continues to teach at the University of California, Berkeley.

Ishmael Reed has long held that technology holds keys to cultural liberation, and his inclination has been to identify creative applications of technology as "black." In his 1988 conversation with Zamir, he expressed continued optimism: "With software publishing and new high tech video technology we will go to town." For all the ferocity of which he is capable, Reed's work has been driven by a remarkable resource of affirmative energy. While other contemporary writers may herald the apocalypse or bemoan entropic drift, Reed works to make things happen. Critics may try to locate him within literary traditions, but Reed is a hands-on writer. His fiction, his poetry, his essays, and his multifarious other activities are seamlessly linked in the service of liberating the many voices that make up the American experience, moving toward genuine establishment of the multiculture.

Interviews:

Robert Gover, "An Interview with Ishmael Reed," *Black American Literature Forum,* 12 (1978): 12–19;

"Ishmael Reed," in *The Imagination on Trial: British and American Writers Discuss Their Working Methods,* edited by Alan Burns and Charles Sugnet (London: Allison & Busby, 1981), pp. 133–148;

Reginald Martin, "An Interview with Ishmael Reed," *Review of Contemporary Fiction,* 4, (1984): 176–187;

Kevin Bezner, "An Interview with Ishmael Reed," *Mississippi Review,* 20, (1991): 110–119;

Cameron Northouse, *Ishmael Reed: An Interview,* Glen Cove Interviews, no. 1 (Dallas: Contemporary Research, 1993);

Bruce Dick and Amritjit Singh, eds., *Conversations with Ishmael Reed* (Jackson: University Press of Mississippi, 1995).

Bibliography:

Elizabeth A. Settle and Thomas A. Settle, *Ishmael Reed: A Primary and Secondary Bibliography* (Boston: G. K. Hall, 1982).

References:

William M. Banks, *Black Intellectuals: Race and Responsibility in American Life* (New York: Norton, 1996);

Jay Boyer, *Ishmael Reed,* Boise State University Western Writers Series, no. 110 (Boise, Idaho: Boise State University, 1993);

Keith E. Byerman, "Voodoo Aesthetics: History and Parody in the Novels of Ishmael Reed," in his *Fingering the Jagged Grain: Tradition and Form in Recent Black Fiction* (Athens & London: University of Georgia Press, 1985), pp. 217–237;

Julian Cowley, "What If I Write Circuses?: The Space of Ishmael Reed's Fiction," *Callaloo,* 17, no. 4 (1994): 1236–1244;

Bruce Allen Dick and Pavel Zemliansky, eds., *The Critical Response to Ishmael Reed* (Westport, Conn.: Greenwood Press, 1999);

Jerome Klinkowitz, "Ishmael Reed," in his *The Life of Fiction* (Urbana: University of Illinois Press, 1977), pp. 117–127;

Klinkowitz, "Ishmael Reed's Multicultural Aesthetic," in his *Literary Subversions: New American Fiction and the Practice of Criticism* (Carbondale: Southern Illinois University Press, 1985), pp. 18–33;

Reginald Martin, *Ishmael Reed and the New Black Aesthetic Critics* (Basingstoke, U.K.: Macmillan, 1986; New York: St. Martin's Press, 1988);

Patrick McGee, *Ishmael Reed and the Ends of Race* (New York: St. Martin's Press, 1997);

Jeffrey Melnick, "What You Lookin' At? Ishmael Reed's *Reckless Eyeballing,*" in *The Black Columbiad: Defining Moments in African American Literature and Culture,* edited by Werner Sollors and Maria Diedrich (Cambridge, Mass.: Harvard University Press, 1994), pp. 298–311;

Robert Scholes, *Fabulation and Metafiction* (Urbana: University of Illinois Press, 1979);

Richard Walsh, "'A Man's Story Is His Gris-Gris': Cultural Slavery, Literary Emancipation and Ishmael Reed's *Flight to Canada,*" in his *Novel Arguments: Reading Innovative American Fiction,* Cambridge Studies in American Literature and Culture, no. 91 (Cambridge & New York: Cambridge University Press, 1995), pp. 65–83.

Hubert Selby Jr.

(23 July 1928 -)

James R. Giles
Northern Illinois University

See also the Selby entry in *DLB 2: American Novelists Since World War II.*

BOOKS: *Last Exit to Brooklyn* (New York: Grove, 1964; London: Calder & Boyars, 1966);
The Room (New York: Grove, 1971; London: Calder & Boyars, 1972);
The Demon (New York: Playboy Press, 1976; London: Marion Boyars, 1977);
Requiem for a Dream (New York: Playboy Press, 1978; London: Marion Boyars, 1979);
Song of the Silent Snow and Other Stories (London: Marion Boyars, 1986; New York: Grove, 1987);
The Willow Tree: A Novel (New York & London: Marion Boyars, 1998).

SELECTED PERIODICAL PUBLICATIONS– UNCOLLECTED: "Lou/s Labour/s Lost," *Black Mountain Review,* 3 (Autumn 1957): 169–186;
"Fat Phil's Day," *Evergreen Review,* 11 (August 1967): 52–53;
"Solving the Ice-Cream Cone Problem," *Evergreen Review,* 12 (August 1968): 57–58;
"Happy Birthday," *Evergreen Review,* 13 (August 1969): 35–37;
Review of *Lament* by David Carson, *Village Voice,* 1 November 1973, p. 28;
"Beauty and the Beatnicks," *Hollywood Review,* 1 (Spring 1991): 146–150;
"Lost and Found," *Hollywood Review,* 1 (Spring 1991): 151–154.

Hubert Selby Jr.

The advent of Hubert Selby Jr. on the international literary scene in 1964 was dramatic and controversial. After charges of obscenity were filed against *Last Exit to Brooklyn* (1964) in Great Britain, Selby's sensational and innovative first novel became the subject of an intense debate in the House of Commons. The novel was subsequently banned in Italy. In fact, some of the material that appears in the novel inspired controversy in the United States even before the book was published by Grove Press. In 1960, after "Tralala"– which became part 4 of the novel—was published in *The Provincetown Review,* the editor of that little magazine was arrested for selling pornography to a minor. As Selby later told interviewer S. E. Gontarski, "it turned out the minor wasn't a minor; he was nineteen years old." Although a lower court found the editor guilty, the case was eventually thrown out. Word of Selby's manuscript then reached Grove Press editor Barney Rosset, who acquired it for publication. Almost instantly the novel achieved the status of an underground classic and received some favorable and important attention from mainstream publications as well. Grove, in fact, cited the enthusiastic *Newsweek* review in its promotion of the novel.

Given his background, it is somewhat surprising that the cause of all this controversy became a writer at all. Born at Victory Memorial Hospital in Brooklyn, New York, on 23 July 1928, Hubert Selby Jr. was the son of Hubert Selby Sr., an engineer, and Adalin Layne Selby. Like many other middle-class American families, the Selbys suffered economically during the Great Depression. After graduating from Public School 102, Selby attended Peter Stuyvesant High School for only one year before dropping out at age fifteen to join the U.S. Merchant Marines. While in Europe in 1946 he contracted tuberculosis and later almost died of an extreme reaction to streptomycin while undergoing surgery. Selby spent most of the next three and a half years convalescing in New York City hospitals. Selby has been married three times—to Inez Taylor in 1953, Judith Lumino in 1964, and Suzanne Shaw in 1969— and is the father of two daughters and two sons. He lives alone in Los Angeles. Though he is a private person by nature, he was a technical adviser for, and made a cameo acting appearance in, Uli Edel's 1989 movie version of *Last Exit to Brooklyn*.

In a 1981 interview with John O'Brien, Selby discussed the pain that his decision to quit school early caused his parents:

> I broke my parents' hearts when I left home. They wanted me to go to school and have an easy life and not have to suffer. And when I was young I had a very good mind, even though I never liked school.

Selby has also described his pain and alienation, particularly during the period after his surgery. As he told Bill Langenheim in a 1988 interview, "I was kind of surviving, you know. . . . I'd stay in the hospital for a year and then leave and stay drunk awhile." Nevertheless, during this time he became part of an impressive group of young writers and artists, which included LeRoi Jones (Amiri Baraka), Joel Oppenheimer, Robert Creeley, Edward Dahlberg, and Gilbert Sorrentino (a novelist with whom he developed an especially close and lasting friendship). Selby also read extensively, participated in the formation of at least two literary magazines, and began to write and publish fiction. The main product of this literary activity was *Last Exit to Brooklyn*.

The novel comprises five sections, each of which can also stand alone as an independent story. The volume then ends with a coda. A horrific vision of life among the working class and the Lumpenproletariat during the early 1950s, the novel is held together by the composite characterization of the young members of a Brooklyn street gang. Originally published in *New Directions* (1961), the brief first section, "Another Day Another Dollar," sets the tone of what follows, recounting in brutal detail the gang's sadistic physical assault on a Southern soldier who is trying to return to his Brooklyn army base after a squabble with a neighborhood prostitute. More sketch than story, this episode establishes the gang as roaming predators and introduces the claustrophobic atmosphere of Selby's Brooklyn.

The title of the first section emphasizes the pervasive boredom and pointlessness of Brooklyn life, thus implying one explanation for the sudden outbreaks of savage violence that occur throughout the novel. Vinnie, Harry, Tony, Hal, and the other young gang members respond to the frustration of their purposeless, powerless lives by lashing out occasionally and randomly at vulnerable individuals. Above all, *Last Exit to Brooklyn* constitutes a definitive expression of the rage and despair that characterize the lives of modern American city dwellers. Selby may well be described as a poet of urban powerlessness.

The gang also makes an appearance in the next section, "The Queen Is Dead," which was first published in the *Evergreen Review* (December 1964). Narrating the destruction of a drag queen named Georgette, Selby makes his sympathy clear in the opening paragraph of "The Queen Is Dead," explaining:

> Georgette was a hip queer. She (he) didnt try to disguise or conceal it with marriage and mans talk, satisfying her homosexuality with the keeping of a secret scrapbook of pictures of favorite male actors or athletes or by supervising the activities of young boys or visiting turkish baths or mens locker rooms, leering sidely while seeking protection behind a carefully guarded guise of virility. . . .

Instead, Georgette flaunts her gay identity in dress, behavior, and language. She falls in love with Vinnie, one of the most brutal and selfish of the gang members, a mistake that leads inexorably to the drag queen's humiliation and psychological destruction.

In a 1992 interview with Allan Vorda, Selby explained that his fictional drag queen had a real-life model in Brooklyn:

> There was a real kid named George. Georgie must have felt like an outcast who was totally alienated. . . . I've always felt like an outcast who was alienated all my life. So Georgie and I had that point of identification although this was totally unconscious. I had a tremendous sympathy for George.

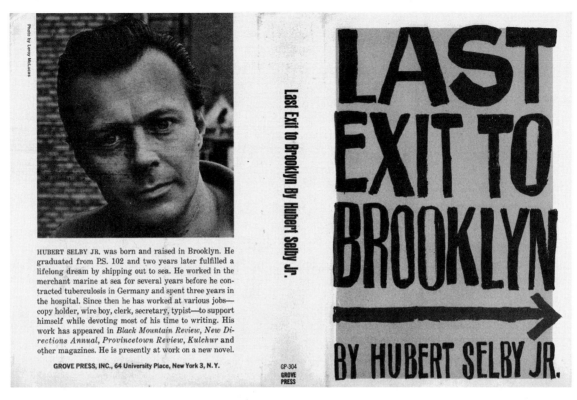

HUBERT SELBY JR. was born and raised in Brooklyn. He graduated from P.S. 102 and two years later fulfilled a lifelong dream by shipping out to sea. He worked in the merchant marine at sea for several years before he contracted tuberculosis in Germany and spent three years in the hospital. Since then he has worked at various jobs—copy holder, wire boy, clerk, secretary, typist—to support himself while devoting most of his time to writing. His work has appeared in *Black Mountain Review*, *New Directions Annual*, *Provincetown Review*, *Kulchur* and other magazines. He is presently at work on a new novel.

GROVE PRESS, INC., 64 University Place, New York 3, N. Y.

GP-304
GROVE
PRESS

Dust jacket for Selby's controversial first novel, a pessimistic view of street life in Brooklyn

A few years after Selby got to know him, George died of a drug overdose at about age twenty. According to Selby, "I guess I felt Georgie needed more than a death in the street. He needed a memorial. . . . Thus, in a very real way, Georgie is responsible for the book *Last Exit to Brooklyn*." Selby also confirmed that his obvious sympathy for his character had the unexpected result of making readers assume he was a homosexual, though he is not. In 1964 this misperception added to Selby's reputation as an underground writer.

"Tralala," the story that resulted in the Provincetown lawsuit, is the most powerful section of *Last Exit to Brooklyn*. The chronicle of the psychological and physical destruction of a prostitute who works in cooperation with the street gang to rob male victims, this section is a study of urban violence and exploitation. Having accepted her community's definition of her body as a commodity, Tralala derives her sense of self-worth through repeatedly selling her body. Each "trick" momentarily confirms her value. The underlying assumptions of Tralala's world are shattered when she meets and starts sleeping with an army officer, who then falls in love with her. Just before being shipped overseas, the officer leaves her a love letter rather than the money she has expected. Confronted with an equation of sex with love instead of monetary reward, she is completely disoriented and willfully initiates a process of self-destruction, which culminates in a horrific and extensively described gang rape. Tralala is a new and revolutionary kind of character in American literature—a woman so thoroughly objectified that she seems not to possess a spiritual dimension. In contrast, the depictions of such alienated female protagonists of American fiction as Stephen Crane's Maggie and Ernest Hemingway's Lady Brett Ashley seem almost sentimental.

The longest part of the novel is its climactic fifth section, "Strike," the harrowing account of another self-induced destruction, this time of a male character. Harry Black is "the worst lathe operator of the more than 1,000 men" employed in a Brooklyn factory and a married man who—though he verbally abuses "queers"—has started to feel strong attractions for neighborhood drag queens. Harry's moment of prominence comes when a strike is declared at his factory, and he is asked to manage the strike headquarters, an assignment no one else wants. To Harry, though, the appointment seems a belated confirmation of his importance. He abuses his position, spending union funds to entertain the street gang, and begins to haunt gay bars, starting an affair with a drag queen named Regina.

When the strike is settled, ending Harry's brief prominence, Regina becomes terrified by the rage that so obviously is close to exploding in Harry and drops him. Harry then makes a sexual advance to a young boy, who tells the gang about it. As punishment, the gang administers a grotesquely savage beating to Harry, at one point hanging him, in a position of crucifixion, on a fence. As if to complete his damnation, Harry, though barely conscious, utters what he believes to be the ultimate blasphemy by accusing God of a homosexual act. In a 1974 article Richard A. Wertime argued that the street gang functions throughout the novel and most memorably in Harry's story, as emblematic figures representing a primitive kind of "retributive justice." Indeed, the entire novel has the feel of primitive art. Its narration is almost totally unmediated, consisting of the more-or-less direct responses of its raging and powerless characters.

"Landsend," the coda to *Last Exit to Brooklyn,* is a grimly satiric account of life in a Brooklyn housing project. In a 1969 article, Charles D. Peavy described Selby as a moral satirist in the tradition of Jonathan Swift, and most of the inhabitants of the Landsend project do seem closer to being "Yahoos" than human beings. One voice in this coda, the "Women's Chorus," expresses enjoyment in watching an abandoned infant who has crawled onto the window ledge of a fourth-floor apartment and encouraging the baby to "fly." Selby's point seems to be that Americans have come to the end of the American promise of renewal, that the American Dream is not only dead but completely forgotten. As a result, sheer animal survival remains. An unmistakable implication of this dark pessimistic novel is that Americans have truly reached "landsend," and—even more ominous—the nation has plunged into the depths of human rage and alienation. It is interesting that several of the characters in the Landsend project have the same names as members of the street gang. Vinnie, Harry, and the others end up trapped in the tedious existence of housing-project life. Gerd Hurm has analyzed the subtext on the deterioration of government-subsidized public housing in Selby's novel.

While in 1964 *Last Exit to Brooklyn* seemed to express the ultimate vision of urban despair, Selby offered a still darker picture in his second novel, *The Room* (1971). *The Room* grew out of a short story called "The Sound," written in 1967. In quite different ways, *The Room* is as innovative a text as *Last Exit to Brooklyn.* Virtually plotless, it consists almost entirely of the ravings of a nameless man, who—before the novel opens—has been arrested and imprisoned on a charge that is never specified. In its dramatic situation and deliberate formlessness, *The Room* echoes Jean Genet's *Our Lady of the Flowers* (1944), a novel that Selby has said influenced him. As with Harry Black, the powerlessness of an unnamed protagonist in *The Room* contributes to the dementia of his rage.

In his interview with Langenheim, Selby remarked, "*The Room* was the most disturbing book I have ever read. I mean, it is really a *disturbing* book. . . . I didn't read it for twelve years after I wrote it." Selby told Vorda that he himself had spent "some time in jail," charged with driving under the influence of drugs, "an extension of all the addictive medication I had when I was in the hospital" in the late 1940s.

As in *Last Exit to Brooklyn,* the narrative voice of *The Room* is unmediated and usually raging. Still, *The Room* features a variety of styles, each of which reveals a different aspect of the unnamed prisoner's consciousness—all united by tropes from mainstream and underground American culture. For instance, in the prisoner's long early fantasy of clearing his name through the legal process, the ideas, language, and imagery come from American popular movies and pulp fiction of the 1940s and 1950s. Later his mind shifts to a revenge fantasy in which he dehumanizes and punishes the two police officers who arrested him by treating them as dogs. In this section the style and logic are that of pornography, an approach that easily allows the consciousness of the protagonist to slide into an imagined assault of a woman, Mrs. Haagstromm, by the two officers. Here, Selby is committing a kind of calculated assault—his aesthetic of rage and hate is a deliberate violation of his American contemporaries' boundaries for polite and respectable fiction. The horrific detail and raging obsession of this narrative strategy have the desired effect of shocking the reader out of complacency into complete, if unwilling, attention. Moreover, the imagined rape of Mrs. Haagstromm provides a point from which the narrator's tortured consciousness can recall his experiences with women, which have been consistently repressive and unfulfilling. His mother gradually assumes a defining and oppressive presence in the narrative, a trope that leads Eric Mottram to argue that the novel "is a modern classic of oedipal fantasies against law, authority and the impersonality of victimizing justice, with the mother functioning as a pillow for tears and comfort for the lying self-righteousness of an infantile son."

The proof of Selby's art in *The Room* is his ability to move the reader to compassion for the protagonist even after the most elaborate and horrifying of his sadistic fantasies. Repeatedly, his obsessive imagination fails him, and he is brought back to his own desperate and alienated situation. In a 1969 article in *Critique,* Peavy pointed out that Selby's characters "are all victims of *hubris* who fail because of a narcissistic pride or self-love which is also self-destructive." Self-love in Selby's fiction becomes self-destruction

Dust jacket for Selby's 1978 novel, which portrays the destructive effects of drug addiction

because it is inextricably linked to guilt and self-hatred. In the case of the protagonist of *The Room,* his guilt is especially overwhelming because its cause is kept vague and secret. For this reason several critics have discussed Selby as an existentialist writer—the only real cause of the guilt that consumes his characters is their humanness.

The novel ends with the prisoner emptied of fantasy and alone in his narrow cell. Unbearable as its horrific detail often is, *The Room* is an exceptionally successful piece of writing, representing in many ways the peak of Selby's art. One cannot find a more powerful depiction of the rage of the powerless lower-class urban male in American fiction.

Selby's next novel, *The Demon* (1976), represents a departure for him. In style and form it is his most conventional work, and it focuses on a protagonist from the upper class. Harry White, obviously a double of Harry Black in "Strike," is a business executive who moves to the top of the corporate ladder before his uncontrollable obsessions destroy him. Initially

his behavior, while cynical and exploitative, is only moderately dangerous. He compulsively seduces married women, always imagining discovery by their jealous husbands. When this behavior begins to damage his career, he marries a beautiful young woman named Linda for whom he initially feels only lust. He hopes that marriage to her will allow him to control his obsessive womanizing. Harry and Linda start a family, and he rises to the top of the corporation for which he works, but his attempt to control his obsessive urges through marriage does not succeed. The epigraph to the novel acts as a gloss on the title: "A man obsessed is a man possessed by a demon." Harry is unable to control his obsessive behavior for any extended period of time. Soon seducing anonymous women during his lunch breaks ceases to be enough for him. He begins a secret life, working late and taking occasional breaks to steal expensive equipment from his office. Eventually this level of criminality does not pose enough risk for him, and he begins to steal from other offices in his own and nearby buildings, managing to avoid detection because no one would ever suspect a person in his position. There is no apparent reason for his senseless criminality, and he quickly and randomly discards the items that he steals.

Yet, theft is not the ultimate transgression, and Harry finally succumbs to the irresistible temptation to commit a murder. In one of the most horrifying scenes in all Selby's fiction, Harry pushes a stranger into the path of an approaching subway train. Selby spared no detail in his description of the man's gory death. Even this horrible crime, however, does not suffice for Harry because it was committed secretively and did not include a genuine risk of detection. Thus, Harry murders twice more in increasingly public ways.

His last victim is a religious media celebrity, Cardinal Leterman, who has just recovered from a near-fatal heart attack. With the help of newspapers and television, Leterman has managed to transform his having been pronounced dead and then revived into a reenactment of the resurrection of Christ. By killing him, Harry can symbolically fulfill the ultimate existential challenge of killing God. Selby emphasizes this thematic overtone by having the murder of the cardinal take place during a communion service "televised all over the world" and packing the scene with symbolism echoing biblical accounts of the Crucifixion and Resurrection. This thematic emphasis becomes trite, though Selby does succeed in conveying, in an indirect manner, Harry's sexual arousal during the murder. Sickened rather than exhilarated by having committed such a daring and unforgivable sin, Harry commits suicide at the end of the novel.

The critical response to *The Demon* was largely negative. Dean Flower's review in *The New York Times Book Review* was typical, calling the novel Selby's "most ludicrous to date." Flower criticized "the obsessive grossness of Selby's style. No wit, irony, qualification, contingency, credibility, subtlety, social or moral complexity appears to detract the monologuist from his dreary exercise." While finally unsuccessful and indeed implausible in places, *The Demon* is an important addition to the Selby canon. It clarifies that social class, while a contributory factor, is not the central cause of his characters' powerlessness. Rather, the inhabitants of Selby's world are doomed by a spiritually empty society and their own all-consuming pride and guilt. Writing for *Newsweek* (1 November 1976), Paul D. Zimmerman perceptively commented that the shift in setting and characterization, while essential, contributed to the artistic failure of the novel because of Selby's apparent lack of knowledge about the upper class. This unfamiliarity leads at times to a triteness of language and description that one finds nowhere else in Selby's fiction.

Just as obsession is the thematic emphasis in *The Demon,* addiction is the main theme of Selby's next novel, *Requiem for a Dream* (1978). Throughout his career Selby has been intrigued by obsessive, addictive personalities. *Requiem for a Dream* is also more conventional in form and language than *Last Exit to Brooklyn* or *The Room,* and, like *The Demon,* it was largely dismissed by critics. The innovative novelist Paul Metcalf denounced *Requiem for a Dream* as a betrayal of Selby's art. Yet, it is a good novel, a harrowing account of the destruction of four central characters by their uncontrollable addictions. Three of the four characters in *Requiem for a Dream* are closely bonded in their personal lives. Harry Goldfarb lives with his girlfriend, Marion, a dropout from the upper reaches of society, and they are both close to the African American Tyrone C. Love. The fourth protagonist, Harry's mother, Sara Goldfarb, is a widow who lives alone in an apartment building surrounded by other senior citizens. Harry, Marion, and Tyrone are all addicted to heroin, while pretending to be able to give up the drug at any time.

Requiem for a Dream is in part a drug novel in the tradition of Nelson Algren's *The Man With the Golden Arm* (1949). Like Algren, Selby is not primarily concerned with writing an exposé of the American drug culture (though both writers document the dominant practices and behaviors of that culture) but with exploring the nuances of the addictive mentality. Nevertheless, *Requiem for a Dream* includes some harrowing images of a New York City turned into a frozen jungle by the drug trade. Most memorable is a detailed depiction of city streets during a "panic," or controlled heroin shortage:

All the neighborhood streets were filled with dope fiends, even in the snow and sleet, looking for something, anything. Every hallway was cluttered with sick faces with runny noses and bodies shivering with the cold and junk sickness, the cold cracking the marrow of their bones as they broke out in sweats from time to time.... When someone did cop he then had to make it safely to his pad, or some place, where he could get off without someone breaking down the door and stealing his dope and maybe getting killed, or killing, if he didnt want to part with something more precious, at that particular moment, than his life....

It is important to the message of Selby's novel that this nightmarish scene, while controlled by organized crime, is directed by the police. The drug trade, *Requiem for a Dream* clearly implies, is a vital, if officially disapproved, part of the dominant capitalistic structure in the United States.

Harry and Tyrone progress from using heroin to dealing it and soon become obsessed with a fantasy of getting "a pound of pure" heroin, selling it, and becoming financially secure for life. They tell themselves that economic security will inevitably lead to happiness, but their quest destroys them, as well as Marion. The three characters' love for and loyalty to each other and to their individual selves are consumed and perverted. One of the most chilling aspects of Selby's narration is his account of the various ways in which Harry, Tyrone, and Marion betray each other in order to feed their addictions. Harry asks Marion to prostitute herself to feed their all-consuming habit, and she agrees, initially selling herself to her psychiatrist and then to a cynical drug dealer who delights in debasing her.

Sara Goldfarb is destroyed by another form of addiction. She constantly watches television and is especially fond of quiz programs and commercials, knowing most of the latter by heart. Desperately lonely and purposeless since her husband's death, Sara dreams of discovering in American consumerism some meaning for her life and an end to her isolation. After receiving a telephone call from a man claiming to represent the McDick Corporation and informing her that she has been chosen as a future contestant on a television quiz program that the corporation sponsors, she thinks she has found both meaning and community. Desperate to become thin for her appearance, she starts taking, and quickly becomes addicted to, diet pills. Of course, she never again hears from the McDick Corporation, which has "dicked" or used her.

Having nearly starved herself with the diet pills, Sara descends into mental illness, which is intensified by the hospital to which she is committed. Selby depicts the mental institution as another McDick Corporation, an uncaring, impersonal organization concerned only

Dust jacket for Selby's 1998 novel, which, he says, investigates the possibility of "redemption through forgiveness"

with the power of those who run it. It is also, like the drug trade, a segment of the capitalist power structure in which those who fall under its control are reduced to victims. At the end of the novel Sara has been reduced by shock therapy and other senseless cruelties to a nearly vegetative state.

Harry and Tyrone also suffer horrible fates. While the ending does descend somewhat into cliché, *Requiem for a Dream* is an underrated novel. There are few more powerful depictions of the psychic destruction resulting from mass consumerism in American literature. All four of Selby's protagonists are guilty of the sin of pride and seek relief from their spiritual emptiness and guilt in modes of consumerism. Such quests, the novel strongly implies, are inevitably doomed. Before their rapid descents into destruction, the characters in *Requiem for a Dream* are middle class—making clear the underlying thesis of Selby's fiction: all of American society, not just its upper and lower economic classes, is suffering from spiritual emptiness and the despair of

powerlessness. Kenneth Tindall has pointed out the connection of style and theme in *Requiem for a Dream*, noting that Selby's characters "are prisoners of their idiom. So restricted by their language . . . does their possibility for conceiving ways out appear that the problem is almost one of philology."

Selby's first short-story collection, *Song of the Silent Snow and Other Stories* (1986), is his finest achievement since *The Room*. Most of the stories focus on familiar Selby motifs and settings, but the cumulative effect of the collection nevertheless represents something new in Selby's work. In his interview with Selby, Langenheim mentioned detecting a kind of affirmation and hope in several of the stories that is absent from the novels, and Selby did not contradict him. In *Song of the Silent Snow* Selby does give some of his protagonists more reason for hope than he ever had before. They represent all socio-economic levels of American society, with most initially suffering from the same isolating pride and spiritual emptiness that permeates the novels. Yet, here there is a clearer focus on the problems plaguing his protagonists than one commonly finds in Selby's fiction, with most of them suffering from various psychological disorders ranging from relatively common forms of depression to debilitating schizophrenia. Exploration of the forms and effects of mental illness is a central motif in the volume. Some of the characters find unexpected relief from, if not precisely cures for, their pain.

The stories vary in tone and mood, with one bearing comparison to a romantic musical composition. Selby has more than once emphasized the importance of music to his work, saying that Ludwig van Beethoven is his only conscious influence. A short, intensely lyrical sketch that offers a variation of transcendentalism, "Of Whales and Dreams," is an unexpected and especially rewarding addition to the Selby canon, recalling the poetry of Walt Whitman and the prose of Herman Melville and Thomas Wolfe. Nature also provides a life-affirming epiphany for the protagonist of the title story, one of the many Selby characters named Harry. To a degree that is unusual in Selby's work, the story communicates a sustaining sense of family. As in "Of Whales and Dreams," nature, which barely exists in Selby's novels, is treated as being inherently redemptive. Another story, "The Musician," recalls the Henry James stories "The Real Thing" (1892) and "The Death of the Lion" (1894) in its idea that the creative urge can be sustained by any genuinely appreciative audience, no matter how small. Little affirmation, however, comes to the central characters in "The Coat," the longest story in the collection, or "The Sound," which Selby has identified as the origin of "the concept" for *The Room*. "The Sound" recalls the fiction of Edgar Allan Poe, a writer echoed in other Selby works as well. Two other stories, "Hi Champ" and "Liebesnacht," depict the destructive effects on men of the cult of machismo, while "Fortune Cookie" examines the insecurities inherent in capitalist competition. "I'm Being Good" is a brilliant epistolary study of a woman who has been psychologically destroyed by a misogynistic society. While its feminist sensitivity is initially a surprising thing to find in a Selby story, it reflects his overriding compassion for victims. All in all, *Song of the Silent Snow* is a rewarding volume that confirms the innovative brilliance of Selby's fiction.

The Willow Tree (1998), Selby's first novel in twenty years, continues the turn toward affirmation seen in several of the stories in *Song of the Silent Snow*. Selby has called the novel an investigation of the theme of "redemption through forgiveness." Set in New York City, it describes the evolution of a loving bond between Bobby, an African American teenager from the South Bronx, and a man who calls himself Moishe, an aged survivor of a Nazi concentration camp who lives alone in an apartment that he has deliberately made almost invisible from the street. Near the beginning of the novel a Hispanic street gang attacks Bobby and his Chicana girlfriend Maria, throwing acid in Maria's face. Unable to bear the horrible pain and dawning knowledge of her disfigurement, she commits suicide while still in the hospital. Following the code of the streets, Bobby plans revenge on the gang members who destroyed Maria–"thas the way it is . . . I got to get up side their heads"–and begins to stalk the young Hispanics. He commits two especially brutal acts of vengeance (cutting off a Puerto Rican boy's ear) and, in the climactic moment of the novel, nearly murders the leader of the Hispanic gang before abruptly rejecting the hatred that has consumed him since Maria's death.

Moishe, who has virtually adopted the young boy, is the catalyst for Bobby's repudiation of violence and hatred. The old man's real name is Werner Schultz. In Germany he was falsely identified as a Jew and sentenced to a death camp, where at first he blamed and hated the Jews in the camp. He learned, however, that such hatred would destroy him and survived the camp by accepting a spiritual brotherhood with them. He is gradually able to teach this ideal to Bobby, for whom the hardest part of living it–as it was for Moishe–is to accept the necessity of forgiving and embracing one's enemies at least spiritually.

As in his earlier fiction, Selby depicts urban America as a war zone. In *The Willow Tree* he specifically creates a parallel between the brutal gang warfare of New York and the wartime destruction of Europe. At one point in the novel, however, Moishe thinks that while the urban landscape in which he lives seems somewhat like "Europe right after the war," that scene of postwar desolation "was another time, another life . . . hopefully."

The link between Bobby and Moishe accentuates the post-Holocaust vision that runs throughout Selby's work. While not as original as *Last Exit to Brooklyn* or *The Room, The Willow Tree* is still a convincing novel. It succeeds most of all because of Selby's skill in making the bond between Bobby and Moishe believable and in communicating his vision of redemptive forgiveness. The most powerful moments of the novel are those dramatizing the terror that accompanies the rejection of a hatred that has been the sustaining basis of identity.

In Europe as well as in the United States, Selby has been increasingly recognized as one of the most innovative post–World War II American novelists. He has undeniably been an influential figure for younger American writers, such as Richard Price.

Interviews:

John O'Brien, "Interview with Hubert Selby, Jr.," *Review of Contemporary Fiction,* 1 (1981): 315–335;

Bill Langenheim, "Interview with Hubert Selby, Jr.," *Enclitic,* 10 (1988): 14–28;

S. E. Gontarski, "Last Exit to Brooklyn: An Interview with Hubert Selby," *Review of Contemporary Fiction,* 10 (1990): 111–115;

Michael Lally, "Last Exit to L.A.: Interview with Hubert Selby, Jr.," *Hollywood Review,* 1 (Spring 1991): 155–187;

Allan Vorda, "Examining the Disease: An Interview with Hubert Selby, Jr.," *Literary Review,* 35 (Winter 1992): 288–302.

References:

Kenneth John Atchity, "Hubert Selby's *Requiem for a Dream:* A Primer," *Review of Contemporary Fiction,* 1 (1981): 399–405;

Roland Binet, "The Mirror of Man," *Review of Contemporary Fiction,* 1 (1981): 380–388;

Robert Buckeye, "Some Preliminary Notes Towards a Study of Selby," *Review of Contemporary Fiction,* 1 (1981): 374–375;

Jack Byrne, "Selby's Yahoos: The Brooklyn Breed, A Dialogue of the Mind with Itself," *Review of Contemporary Fiction,* 1 (1981): 349–353;

Richard Gehr, "Last Exit to Brooklyn," *American Film,* 15 (May 1990): 34–39, 48;

James R. Giles, "The Game of Mum as Theme and Narrative Technique in Hubert Selby's *Last Exit to Brooklyn,*" in his *The Naturalistic Inner-City Novel in America: Encounters with the Fat Man* (Columbia: University of South Carolina Press, 1995), pp. 119–138;

Giles, *Understanding Hubert Selby, Jr.* (Columbia: University of South Carolina Press, 1997);

Josephine Hendin, "Angries: S-M as a Literary Style," in her *Vulnerable People: A View of American Fiction Since 1945* (New York: Oxford University Press, 1978), pp. 53–71;

June Howard, "Documents, Dramas, and Discontinuities: The Narrative Strategies of American Naturalism," in her *Form and History in American Literary Naturalism* (Chapel Hill: University of North Carolina Press, 1985), pp. 142–182;

Gerd Hurm, "Hubert Selby: *Last Exit to Brooklyn*," in his *Fragmented Urban Images: The American City in Modern Fiction from Stephen Crane to Thomas Pynchon* (Frankfurt am Main & New York: Peter Lang, 1991), pp. 273–299;

Frank Kermode, "'Obscenity' and the 'Public Interest,'" *New American Review,* 3 (April 1968): 224–229;

James B. Lane, "Violence and Sex in the Post-War Urban Novel: With a Consideration of Harold Robbins's *A Stone for Danny Fisher* and Hubert Selby, Jr.'s *Last Exit to Brooklyn*," *Journal of Popular Culture,* 8 (1974): 295–308;

Harry Lewis, "Some Things I Want to Say About Hubert Selby's Work," *Review of Contemporary Fiction,* 1 (1981): 413–415;

Paul Metcalf, "Herman and Hubert: The Odd Couple," *Review of Contemporary Fiction,* 1 (1981): 364–369;

Eric Mottram, "Free Like the Rest of Us: Violation and Despair in Hubert Selby's Novels," *Review of Contemporary Fiction,* 1 (1981): 353–363;

Joyce Carol Oates, "The Nightmare of Naturalism: Harriette Arnow's *The Dollmaker*," in her *New Heaven, New Earth: The Visionary Experience in Literature* (New York: Vanguard, 1974), pp. 99–110;

John O'Brien, "The Materials of Art in Hubert Selby," *Review of Contemporary Fiction,* 1 (1981): 376–379;

Joel Oppenheimer, "Memories," *Review of Contemporary Fiction,* 1 (1981): 397–398;

Charles D. Peavy, "Hubert Selby and the Tradition of Moral Satire," *Satire Newsletter,* 6 (Spring 1969): 35–39;

Peavy, "The Sin of Pride and Selby's *Last Exit to Brooklyn*," *Critique,* 11 (1969): 35–42;

Gilbert Sorrentino, "Addenda 1981: After *Last Exit to Brooklyn*," *Review of Contemporary Fiction,* 1 (1981): 346–348;

Sorrentino, "The Art of Hubert Selby," *Kulchur,* 13 (Spring 1964): 27–43;

Michael Stephen, "Hubert Selby, Jr.: The Poet of Prose Masters," *Review of Contemporary Fiction,* 1 (1981): 389–397;

Tony Tanner, "On the Parapet," in his *City of Words: American Fiction, 1950–1970* (New York: Harper & Row, 1971), pp. 344–371;

Kenneth Tindall, "The Fishing at Coney Island: Hubert Selby, Jr. and the Cult of Authenticity," *Review of Contemporary Fiction,* 1 (1981): 370–373;

Richard A. Wertime, "On the Question of Style in Hubert Selby, Jr.'s Fiction," *Review of Contemporary Fiction,* 1 (1981): 406–413;

Wertime, "Psychic Vengeance in *Last Exit to Brooklyn*," *Literature and Psychology,* 24 (4 November 1974): 153–166.

Jane Smiley
(26 September 1949 –   )

Neil Nakadate
Iowa State University

BOOKS: *Barn Blind: A Novel* (New York: Harper & Row, 1980; London: Flamingo, 1994);

At Paradise Gate: A Novel (New York: Simon & Schuster, 1981; London: Flamingo, 1995);

Duplicate Keys (New York: Knopf, 1984; London: Cape, 1984);

The Age of Grief: A Novella and Stories (New York: Knopf, 1987; London: Collins, 1988);

Catskill Crafts: Artisans of the Catskill Mountains (New York: Crown, 1988);

The Greenlanders (New York: Knopf, 1988; London: Collins, 1988);

Ordinary Love; & Good Will: Two Novellas (New York: Knopf, 1989); republished as *Ordinary Love: Two Novellas* (London: Collins, 1990);

The Life of the Body: A Story, illustrated by Susan Nees, Espresso Editions (Minneapolis: Coffee House Press, 1990);

A Thousand Acres (New York: Knopf, 1991; London: Collins, 1991);

Moo (New York: Knopf, 1995; London: Flamingo, 1995);

The All-True Travels and Adventures of Lidie Newton: A Novel (New York: Knopf, 1998; London: Flamingo, 1998);

Horse Heaven (New York: Knopf, 2000).

OTHER: "Turnpike," in *Voices Louder Than Words: A Second Collection,* edited by William Shore (New York: Vintage, 1991), pp. 97–113;

"Can Mothers Think?" in *The True Subject: Writers on Life and Craft,* edited by Kurt Brown (St. Paul, Minn.: Graywolf Press, 1993), pp. 3–15;

Untitled commentary on "Lily," in *American Voices: Best Short Fiction by Contemporary Authors,* edited by Sally Arteseros (New York: Hyperion Press, 1993), pp. 213–214;

"Can Writers Have Friends?" in *Between Friends: Writing Women Celebrate Friendship,* edited by Mickey Pearlman (New York: Houghton Mifflin, 1994), pp. 44–55;

Jane Smiley (photograph by Robert Blakeman; from the dust jacket for The All-True Travels and Adventures of Lidie Newton, *1998)*

Kathy Kiernan and Michael M. Moore, eds., *First Fiction: An Anthology of the First Published Stories by Famous Writers,* introduction by Smiley (Boston, New York, Toronto & London: Little, Brown, 1994);

Introduction to "The Interview" by Ruth Prawer Jhabvala, in *You've Got to Read This: Contemporary American Writers Introduce Stories That Held Them in Awe,* edited by Ron Hansen and Jim Shepard (New York: HarperCollins, 1994), p. 272;

"The Bathroom," in *Home: American Writers Remember Rooms of Their Own,* edited by Sharon Sloan Fiffer

283

and Steve Fiffer (New York: Pantheon, 1995), pp. 106–115;

"Full Cry," in *Women on Hunting,* edited by Pam Houston (Hopewell, N. J.: Ecco Press, 1995), pp. 186–198;

The Best American Short Stories 1995, edited by Smiley and Katrina Kennison, with an introduction by Smiley (Boston & New York: Houghton Mifflin, 1995);

Untitled essay, in *The Logophile's Orgy: Favorite Words of Famous People,* edited by Lewis Burke Frumkes (New York: Delacorte, 1995), pp. 180–181;

"Afterword: Gen-Narration," in *Family: American Writers Remember Their Own,* edited by Sharon Sloan Fiffer and Steve Fiffer (New York: Pantheon, 1996), pp. 241–247;

"The Life of the Body," in *Prize Stories 1996: The O. Henry Awards,* edited by William Abrahams (New York: Doubleday, 1996), pp. 251–269;

"Two Plates, Fifteen Screws," in *The Healing Circle: Authors Writing of Recovery,* edited by Patricia Foster and Mary Swander (New York: Plume, 1998), pp. 99–106;

Thomas Hardy, *The Return of the Native,* introduction by Smiley (New York: Signet, 1999);

"What Stories Teach Their Writers: The Purpose and Practice of Revision," in *Creating Fiction: Instruction and Insights from Teachers of the Associated Writing Programs,* edited by Julie Checkoway (Cincinnati: Story Press, 1999), pp. 244–255;

"You Can Never Have Too Many," in *The Barbie Chronicles: A Living Doll Turns Forty,* edited by Yona Zeldis McDonough (New York: Touchstone, 1999), pp. 189–192.

SELECTED PERIODICAL PUBLICATIONS–UNCOLLECTED:

FICTION

"And Baby Makes Three," *Redbook,* 149 (May 1977): 231–234;

"I In My Kerchief and Mama In Her Cap," *Redbook,* 150 (January 1978): 157–161;

"New Poems," *Fiction,* 5 (Spring 1978): 136–153;

"Good Intentions," *Playgirl,* 6 (May 1979): 36–39;

"Sex," *Mademoiselle,* 86 (July 1980): 154, 156–159;

"The Blinding Light of the Mind," *Atlantic,* 252 (December 1983): 48, 50–52, 55–58;

"Firing Jennifer," *TWA Ambassador* (October 1984);

"A Spy Story," *Poet and Critic,* 16 (Winter 1985): 32–52;

"The Age of Grief," *Quarterly,* 1 (Spring 1987): 104–189;

"What the Women Said," *Wigwag* (August 1990): 48–52;

"The Nickel Plan," *McCall's,* 118 (October 1990): 112–114, 144–146, 150–151;

"Fahrvergnügen," *Playboy,* 38 (December 1991): 102–104, 112, 196–199;

"Gregor: My Life as a Bug," *Harper's,* 285 (August 1992): 36–37;

"A Quarrelsome Peace," *New York Times Magazine,* 20 December 1992, pp. 26–28, 46.

NONFICTION

"As Time Goes By," *Savvy,* 9 (January 1988): 95–96;

"Getting Away from Daddy," review of *The Right Thing to Do* by Josephine Gattuso Hendin, *New York Times Book Review,* 13 March 1988, p. 29;

"Searching for Secrets on This Side of the 'Moon,'" review of *Moon Palace* by Paul Auster, *USA Today,* 17 March 1989, p. D4;

"Someone's in the Kitchen With Freud," review of *Family Pictures* by Sue Miller, *New York Times Book Review,* 22 April 1990, pp. 1, 45;

"In One Small Town, the Weight of the World," review of *Animal Dreams* by Barbara Kingsolver, *New York Times Book Review,* 2 September 1990, p. 2;

"The Wild West Show," review of *Buffalo Girls* by Larry McMurtry, *Chicago Tribune Books,* 21 October 1990, pp. 6–7;

"Matters of Appearance," review of *Two Girls, Fat and Thin* by Mary Gaitskill, *Chicago Tribune Books,* 17 February 1991, p. 3;

"In the Shadow of a Big Bad Boy," review of *Treetops: A Family Memoir* by Susan Cheever, *New York Times Book Review,* 10 March 1991, p. 6;

"You'd Never Suspect Kathleen," review of *The Rise of Life on Earth* by Joyce Carol Oates, *New York Times Book Review,* 5 May 1991, p. 9;

"Caribbean Voices," review of *Daughters* by Paule Marshall, *Chicago Tribune Books,* 6 October 1991, p. 3;

"Mirror Images," *Life,* new series 15 (March 1992): 87;

"Horse Love," *Victoria,* 6 (May 1992): 38–40;

"Vogue Arts: Books," review of *Playing in the Dark* and *Jazz* by Toni Morrison, *Vogue,* 182 (May 1992): 158, 160;

"All-American Garden," *House and Garden,* 164 (June 1992): 122–129, 156;

"Imposing Values," *New York Times Magazine,* 20 September 1992, pp. 28–29;

"The Undresser," *Allure,* 2 (October 1992): 96–98;

"New Wine from the Grapes of Wrath," review of *Fruit Fields in My Blood: Okie Migrants of the West* by Toby F. Sonneman and Rick Steigmeyer, and *Rising in the West: The True Story of an "Okie" Family From the Great Depression Through the Reagan Years* by Dan Morgan, *Los Angeles Times Book Review,* 11 October 1992, pp. 2, 7;

"Fiction in Review," review of *WLT* by Garrison Keillor, *Paradise News* by David Lodge, *Hello Darling, Are You Working?* by Rupert Everett, *Foolscap* by Michael Malone, *The Easy Way Out* by Stephen McCauley, and *She Needed Me* by Walter Kirn, *Yale Review,* 81 (January 1993): 148–162;

"Wisconsin: Three Visions Attained," *New York Times Magazine,* 7 March 1993, II: 28–29, 42, 44, 46, 48;

"Snap, Crackle, Pop In Battle Creek," review of *The Road to Wellville* by T. Coraghessan Boyle, *New York Times Book Review,* 25 April 1993, pp. 1, 28;

"From the New World,"review of *The Infinite Plan* by Isabel Allende, *Boston Sunday Globe,* 16 May 1993, B39, B42;

"The Worth of a Bookstore," *Victoria,* 7 (August 1993): 71;

"Reflections on a Lettuce Wedge," *Hungry Mind Review,* no. 27 (Fall 1993): 13;

"Something Extra," *New York Times Magazine,* 10 October 1993, p. 8;

"In Distant Lands of Ice and Sun," review of *Smilla's Sense of Snow* by Peter Hoeg, *Washington Post Book World,* 24 October 1993, pp. 1, 11;

"Something Is Wrong With This Life," review of *They Whisper* by Robert Olen Butler, *New York Times Book Review,* 13 February 1994, p. 12;

"So Shall We Reap," *Sierra,* 79 (March/April 1994): 74–80, 82, 140–141;

"Borges, JCO, You, and Me," *Antaeus,* no. 73/74 (Spring 1994): 56–57;

"The Call of the Hunt," *Outside,* 19 (November 1994): 114–122;

"Tornadoes," *Outside,* 20 (March 1995): 72;

"Jane Austen's Heroines," *Victoria,* 9 (May 1995): 28–29;

"Idle Hands," *Hungry Mind Review,* no. 33 (Spring 1995): 13;

"Puissance," *Flyway: A Literary Review,* 1 (Spring 1995): 23–32;

"North Carolina's Equestrian Heaven," *New York Times Magazine,* 17 September 1995, II: 55–57, 60, 64;

"Yes, Please, and One of Those . . . ," *Mirabella,* 7 (September/October 1995): 66, 68;

"The Big Soak," *Vogue,* 185 (October 1995): 256, 258, 260;

"Confess, Early and Often," *New York Times Magazine,* 8 October 1995, pp. 62–63;

"My Gelding Myself," *Outside,* 20 (November 1995): 112–118, 159;

"And Moo to You Too," *Civilization,* 2 (November/December 1995): 75;

"Say It Ain't So, Huck: Second Thoughts on Mark Twain's 'Masterpiece,'" *Harper's,* 292 (January 1996): 61–67;

"There Is Nothing Like a Dane," *Town & Country,* 150 (February 1996): 62–63;

"The Affair: Why It's Not Worth It," *Mirabella,* 7 (March/April 1996): 78–79;

"Okay, Go Ahead," *Hungry Mind Review,* no. 37 (Spring 1996): 13;

"Losing the Farm," review of *Fields Without Dreams* by Victor Davis Hanson, *New Yorker,* 72 (3 June 1996): 88–92;

"Greenland," *Islands,* 16 (1 July 1996): 118;

"Back to School," review of *Great Books* by David Denby, *Chicago Tribune Books,* 8 September 1996, pp. 1, 11;

"Shakespeare In Action," *New York Times,* 2 December 1996, A13;

"Making Enemies: Your Bad Review," *Hungry Mind Review,* no. 40 (Winter 1996–1997): 21;

"Dream House," *Architectural Digest,* 54 (November 1997): 46, 48, 52;

"Mothers Should," *New York Times Magazine,* 5 April 1998, pp. 37–39;

"Taking It All Back," *Washington Post Book World,* 21 June 1998, pp. 1, 8;

"Catting Around," review of *Tomcat in Love* by Tim O'Brien, *New York Times Book Review,* 20 September 1998, pp. 11–12;

"Sex, As It Ought to Be," *Washington Post,* 25 October 1998, C1–C2;

"A Reluctant Muse Embraces His Task, and Everything Changes," *New York Times,* 26 April 1999, B1;

"A Week's Worth of Sorrys," *Civilization,* 6 (April/May 1999): 64, 66;

"Suddenly, More Than I Ever Wanted," *Washington Post,* 28 November 1999, B3;

"The Good Lie," *New York Times Magazine,* 7 May 2000, pp. 58–59;

"Oaxaca: Baroque Jewel in a Pre-Hispanic Setting," *New York Times Magazine,* 14 May 2000, II: 24–25, 40, 42, 44–45.

The range and variety of Jane Smiley's work as a writer of fiction have resulted in a great deal of critical attention, a wide and committed readership, and several different perceptions of her achievement. Smiley's novels, particularly those following *The Greenlanders* (1988), are typically the products of serious research and imaginative rethinking of fundamental cultural issues. At the same time Smiley draws on per-

"*Even readers who have never set foot in a stirrup will be awed by this tense and elegant family novel.*"
— Jane Howard

JANE SMILEY was born in Los Angeles, grew up in St. Louis, and studied at Vassar, at the Writer's Workshop of the University of Iowa, and at the University's graduate school, where she received her Ph.D. in 1978. It was in a February in Iceland, where she was researching her dissertation, that she began *Barn Blind*, "wishing to imagine summer." She lives in Iowa City with her husband, a historian, and their small daughter.

0-06-014016-X

JANE SMILEY

BARN BLIND

BARN BLIND
A Novel by
JANE SMILEY

Harper & Row

Dust jacket for Smiley's first novel, about a family of horse breeders in Illinois

sonal experience of various kinds—equestrian sports, marriage and parenting, environmental issues, autonomous and shared living situations, domestic conversation, and family stories—for the material and ideas that shape her work. Clearly possessing a sensibility attuned to late-twentieth-century life, Smiley was initially inspired by the careers of Jane Austen and George Eliot and the fiction of modernists such as Virginia Woolf. She has long been fascinated by medieval European culture.

Smiley's books include an epic of a doomed Nordic settlement in fourteenth-century Greenland and several family-focused novels, including *A Thousand Acres* (1991), a tragic portrait of an Iowa farm family, which won the 1992 Pulitzer Prize in literature. She is also the author of *Moo* (1995), a comic novel about academic life. In complementary fashion, she has written a large number of essays, articles, occasional pieces, and book reviews. In both her fiction and nonfiction the salient issues and common focuses include environmental vigilance, the role and disposition of power in domestic life, the implications

of food production and preparation, and reading, writing, and culture.

Jane Graves Smiley was born on 26 September 1949 in Los Angeles County Hospital to James LaVerne Smiley and Frances Graves Smiley, both Midwesterners. Her parents met in Paris during World War II, while Frances Graves was an army journalist and James Smiley an army officer. When the war ended, they resumed independent lives; she began a career in journalism in Memphis, and he a career in aeronautical engineering in Los Angeles. Their relationship was eventually re-established by letter, and they were married in December 1948. When Smiley was four, her parents divorced, her father having started to undergo treatment for mental problems (possibly because of trauma suffered during his wartime service). Jane Smiley and her mother moved to St. Louis, Missouri, where Frances Smiley wrote and edited for the *Globe Democrat* and the *Post-Dispatch*. Jane Smiley grew up with her maternal grandparents and had frequent contact with the families of her mother's siblings, Jane, Ruth, and David, enjoying the secure environment of this large, close extended family, all of whom were storytellers. Smiley has said that the first "novel" she ever knew was her family. Several of the family stories Smiley heard as a child were eventually recast as episodes in her fiction, particularly in *At Paradise Gate* (1981).

When Smiley was eleven, her mother married William J. Nuelle, and the family moved to Webster Groves, Missouri, where Jane grew up with two step-siblings and two half siblings and attended public and private schools. In the course of two years during early adolescence Smiley grew from five to six feet in height—well on her way to her adult height of six feet, two inches. While this physical characteristic complicated her adolescent relationships, it later contributed to her sense of self-possession in public and professional life.

Smiley's adolescent interests were literature, history, and horses, with riding horses her true passion. Smiley's reading at this time included several works that have remained strong in her memory and influenced her writing: O. E. Rölvaag's *Giants in the Earth* (1924–1925), for its stark realism; John H. Storer's *The Web of Life, a First Book of Ecology* (1953), for its treatment of ecological and environmental issues; Charles Dickens's *David Copperfield* (1849–1850), for its development of the novel as a form; and several plays by William Shakespeare, including *King Lear*. In particular Storer's introduction to the concepts of species variety and the interconnectedness of all life on earth should not be underestimated as an early source of themes that are crucial to some of Smiley's fiction, including *The Greenlanders* and *A Thousand Acres,* and at the heart of several thematically linked articles and reviews, such as "Reflections on a Lettuce Wedge" (1993), "So Shall We Reap" (1994), and "Losing the Farm" (1996).

Smiley enrolled at Vassar College in the fall of 1967 and graduated in 1971. While studying at Vassar, she read a great deal of English literature and was introduced by Professor Harriet Hawkins to the notion of reinterpreting Shakespeare. Smiley also met her first husband, John B. Whiston, then a student at Yale University. Married on 4 September 1970, they lived in a leftist commune in New Haven, Connecticut. Working in electronics factories there, Smiley developed a sense of social consciousness. After graduation, Smiley and Whiston moved to Iowa City, where Whiston began graduate work in medieval history at the University of Iowa, and Smiley subsequently entered the graduate program in English literature, earning an M.A. in 1975. In a rented farmhouse outside of Iowa City, Smiley and Whiston lived a version of back-to-the-land existence. Smiley read a

great deal, including Barry Commoner's *The Closing Circle: Nature, Man, and Technology* (1971). Her experiences during this period contributed significantly to her fiction writing, perhaps most strikingly to the novella *Good Will* (1989) and *A Thousand Acres*.

Although she had been turned down for admission to the Iowa Writers' Workshop, Smiley's friends encouraged her to continue writing and reapply. She studied the fiction of students already enrolled in the program, worked on her technique, and was accepted in 1974. She received her M.F.A. in 1976. Smiley's graduate studies included not only fiction writing, literature, and theory but also courses in Gothic, Sanskrit, Old Irish, Old and Middle English, and Old Norse. Smiley spent the 1976–1977 academic year in Iceland, under a Fulbright-Hays study grant. She returned to Iowa City having read a great deal of European fiction, written several short stories, and developed outlines for two novels. Smiley also returned with the conviction that she should write a creative dissertation to complete the requirements for her Ph.D., which she earned in 1978. Having divorced Whiston in 1975, Smiley married historian William Silag on 1 May 1978.

Barn Blind (1980) and *At Paradise Gate* (1981), the novels conceived during Smiley's time in Iceland, might properly be considered ambitious efforts by a rapidly maturing writer. There is some awkward writing in these novels; both emphasize structure at the expense of plot. *Barn Blind* concerns a rural Illinois family whose consuming preoccupation is horse breeding and competitive riding and whose ethos is effectively imposed by the mother. Kate Karlson is domineering, manipulative, and obsessive, while her husband, Axel, is an oddly passive and ineffectual husband and father, a limited male presence in the book. The novel is interesting primarily as a study of the virtually unchecked exercise of maternal power and the responses of the four Karlson children to it. While the ending of the Karlsons' story is perhaps too easy to anticipate, *Barn Blind* is notable as an exercise in creating in multiple points of view and as Smiley's first attempt to examine the troubled and often-hidden dynamics of domestic life in general and marriage in particular.

At Paradise Gate examines the long but troubled marriage of Anna and Ike Robison and the failed relationships of their three adult daughters, Helen, Claire, and Susanna. Smiley extends her study into a third generation by juxtaposing to Anna's story that of Helen's daughter, Christine. As in her first novel, Smiley pursued the drama of family life—occasionally, as in *Barn Blind,* shading into melodrama—but *At Paradise Gate* takes a more promising approach to generational

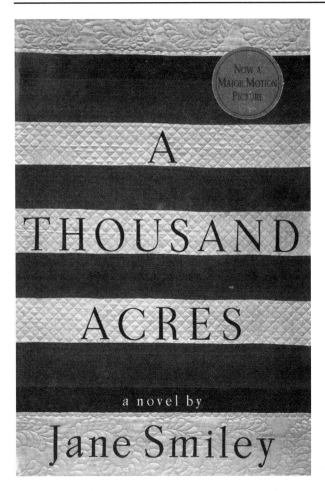 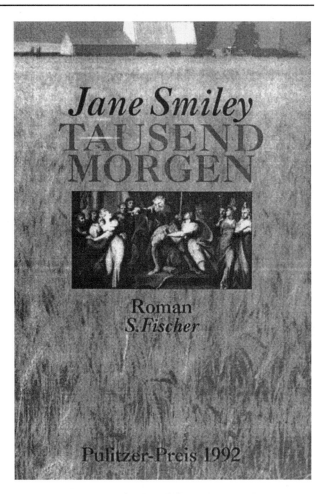

Dust jackets for the American and German editions of Smiley's 1991 novel, a modern version of William Shakespeare's King Lear

conflict. The novel is also interesting for the shift of Smiley's interest from matriarchal oppression to the long-term impact of patriarchal tyranny–in part manifested as physical abuse–an issue revisited in *A Thousand Acres* and *Good Will.* Yet, the ending of *At Paradise Gate* seems hurried and oddly unsatisfactory. Smiley's first two novels may also strike some readers as apprentice-like. In theme and tone they reveal Smiley's admiration for the twentieth-century modernist fiction of writers such as Virginia Woolf. Both *Barn Blind* and *At Paradise Gate* were briefly noted and reviewed as accomplished work by a developing young writer.

In 1981 Smiley accepted a position in the English department at Iowa State University, moving to Ames with Silag and their daughter, Phoebe. Their second daughter, Lucy, was born in Ames. At Iowa State, Smiley taught courses on literature and fiction writing. The murder mystery *Duplicate Keys* (1984), which she completed during her second pregnancy, was a conscious attempt on Smiley's part to learn how

to construct a plot by analyzing and working within the conventions of an established genre in which motivation and action are dominant considerations. In writing her third novel Smiley followed her inclination to seek intellectual and creative challenges. That is, she pursues fiction writing in terms of projects that present new problems of content, conceptualization, and style. Thematically, *Duplicate Keys* can be linked to a between-semesters visit Smiley made to New York City during her Fulbright year. She stayed for three weeks with an hospitable Iowa City friend who had given out so many keys to her apartment that she could not account for all of them. In Smiley's novel, librarian Alice Ellis's promising relationship with an appealing and devoted suitor is compromised by the bewilderment that follows the murders of two old friends from Minnesota, members of a struggling rock band. Unwilling to accept the disintegration of the close-knit group of Minnesota friends with whom she first came to the city or to alter her expectations of her increasingly unreliable friends, Alice comes in contact with a police detective named Honey and her long-time friend Susan Gabriel, toward whose erotic energy and personal strength Alice is drawn as her familiar world falls away. *Duplicate Keys* reveals the ongoing influence of social and cultural energies of the late 1960s and early 1970s.

In the spring of 1984, with *Duplicate Keys* soon to be published, Smiley began a period of extensive research and writing that finally ended in July 1985. After preliminary work in Ames, she took a long research trip to England, Denmark, and Greenland, and eventually completed a 1,100-page manuscript for the novel *The Greenlanders* (1988), her epic story of a doomed fourteenth-century colony. Smiley had become so completely involved in rendering the violent, oppressive ethos of the colony in restrained, narration-resistant language that she immediately sought compensatory activity in writing a radically different kind of work. First published in *The Quarterly* (Spring 1987), *The Age of Grief* was composed during July 1985. During her research trip for *The Greenlanders,* Smiley had begun to recognize that her marriage was failing. Driven by emotions set loose by the failure of her marriage and its impact on all concerned, Smiley employed an emotional and introspective language in *The Age of Grief* that was precluded by the artistic premises of her Greenland saga. Smiley and Silag divorced in February 1986. On 25 July 1987 Smiley married Stephen Mortensen, whom she had met in Iowa City in 1973. They have one son, Axel James. A few months after her marriage, Smiley's novella of chastened domesticity was published with some earlier and more-recent short stories. *The Age of Grief: A Novella and Stories* (1987) was nominated for the 1987 National Book Critics Circle Award.

The Age of Grief is a tour de force of sustained introspective narration. The novella is essentially the story of David Hurst's largely unvoiced (but occasionally acted out) response to his discovery that his wife and dental partner are having an affair and his recognition that to survive—and enable his family to survive—this deeply wounding (but perhaps not fatal) age of grief may demand more in the way of endurance than action and may involve more pathos than heroics. The story succeeds in part because it acknowledges the humbling, frustratingly melodramatic aspects of the Hursts' situation and in part because it renders convincingly the tenacious hope and quotidian obligations that shape David's behavior. Dana Hurst is convincingly presented as a woman who has long recognized that she has what it takes to compete successfully in a male-dominated society and who is willing to prove it. *The Age of Grief* is another of Smiley's examinations of the disposition of rights and pre-rogatives within a family, not only between spouses, but also among parents and children. Taken together, they contributed to limiting notions of Smiley as a writer of "domestic fiction," but this perception had earned her a large following of readers.

The publication in 1988 of *The Greenlanders*—558 pages of frequently brutal events described by a grim narration reminiscent in mode and spirit of the Icelandic sagas—surprised these and other readers. Smiley's epic, which she considers the true "masterpiece" of her body of work, is a synthesis of her many years of studying medieval languages and literature, as well as a tribute to the Nordic heritage of her mother's family. *The Greenlanders* is the first in a series of novels through which Smiley has systematically explored the possibilities of the epic, tragic, comic, and romantic modes of Western literature. *The Greenlanders* marks Smiley's conscious (as well as striking) departure from her formal training in fiction writing and from her imaginative affiliation with twentieth-century modernists. Like her extended acquaintance with solitude, desolation, and the dark-gray North Atlantic while in Iceland, writing this novel was a transforming experience for Smiley. The history and eventual disappearance of the Greenland settlement are a matter of record (and a few of her characters are based on real people). Smiley's challenge was to bring to life the culture of a medieval Nordic "frontier" and then to recount its slide toward extinction. Beyond that, she had also to investigate, ponder, and render through character and event the possible reasons for the demise of an outpost that actually flourished for several generations. She accomplished this feat by focusing on the lives of Asgeir Gunnarson and his immediate descendants, mainly Gunnar Asgeirsson and Margret Asgeirsdottir, whose passions and imaginations are treated as alien in the straitened twilight of the Greenlanders' tenure, but whose gifts are among their available resources for survival. The result is a harsh lesson in history and archaeology. The novel is also a cautionary tale regarding the conduct and "progress" of Western civilization in relationship to a resource-rich but inevitably unforgiving natural world. Smiley suggests that cultural prejudices and obliviousness to environmental realities combined with other factors to doom the Greenlanders. *The Greenlanders* was translated into Danish, Finnish, French, German, Icelandic, and Swedish, and extensively reviewed in western Europe.

Also in 1988, Smiley published a book of nonfiction, *Catskill Crafts: Artisans of the Catskill Mountains,* a project that speaks to her long-standing interest in indigenous cultures and subsistence living. Smiley's remarkable composition of four books and an impres-

71

Chapter Six: I Enter Kansas Territory

I did not speak to Mr. Newton of my moment of fear, for surely that was what it was--the effects of a moment so short that it lasted only so long as it took for the patrons at the table to see the dishes of food and then reach for them--and yet it leaked into and colored every subsequent moment. Even now, as I recall our ride to Lawrence, the rolling golden prairie with its lines of distant trees and its distant dome of blue seem infused with shadows. The road, for the most part, was hard enough and Mr. Graves knew where all the mirey spots were and avoided them. Nor was there solitude to oppress us--we met men, women, and children, wagons and walkers and riders, and everyone shouted out in the friendly way that westerners have on the road (it is only when they have made claims and staked the boundaries of THEIR OWN territories that they become suspicious and *trigger-happy). The landscape was just as we expected it to be, and contained the expected open sort of beauty. Even so, the very sunshine looked dark to me and the heat of the day, which was waxing moment by moment, seemed cold. I could not imagine any cabin, any town, any society that would relieve my spirits.

Mr. Newton, on the other hand, admired the country and was pleased as he could be to have arrived, and he spoke to Mr. Graves with thorough animation and lack of reserve. Eavesdropping, I added to my knowledge of my husband.

"I knowed you was a preacher," said Mr. Graves.

"I was for a few months, only," said Mr. Newton. "After leaving Harvard College. But the work didn't suit me. When members of my flock sought my counsel, it struck me dumb."

"That an't bad," said Mr. Graves. "Most folks like to talk themselves into whatever it is that they want to do, anyway. I did some work in the preaching line myself, but it didn't pay. Folks expect the word of God to be free for the asking."

Page from the typescript for The All-True Travels and Adventures of Lidie Newton *(Collection of Jane Smiley)*

sive number of shorter works between 1985 and 1988 marks this period of her career as one of experimentation, variety, and confirmation.

The novella *Good Will*–published with *Ordinary Love* in 1989–provides a chastened vision of twentieth-century man as steward of the land and head of the family, a kind of negative companion piece to *Catskill Crafts*. The designation "man" is appropriate here because Bob Miller, the point-of-view character, is clearly the author of an Edenic autocracy in rural Pennsylvania, the smug master of all he surveys. *Good Will* is a particularly striking critique of patriarchy in Western culture. With Liz Miller struggling for self-definition in the face of her husband's iron will–which is reinforced by his intelligence and practical skills–the fundamental conflict of the story is provided by their young son, Tommy, ultimately an abused victim of his father's ideology, enthusiasms, and ego. In *Good Will* the rebellious son represents human nature struggling for recognition in the face of the father playing God. The narration is traditionally linear, and its lessons are not surprising. By contrast, *Ordinary Love* was nontraditional from its conception and proved difficult for Smiley to write. Rachel Kinsella's revelation to her children of the affair that destroyed her marriage and their family–the most intimate and dramatic part of the story–occurs fairly early, and the painful description by both parent and children of their succeeding days and years lays claim to the greater part of the story. Like Bob Miller, Rachel has made a life and altered the terms of her family's existence, but in her telling "ownership" has more to do with wonder and responsibility than control. As a juxtaposed pair, *Ordinary Love* and *Good Will* play tradition against innovation, allowing Smiley to address the premises of patriarchy and the problematics of alternative choices. *Ordinary Love* is also a companion piece to *The Age of Grief,* both having been undertaken by Smiley in an attempt to accommodate the emotions generated by her second divorce.

The environmental awareness triggered by Smiley's reading *The Web of Life, The Closing Circle,* and similar writings was reinforced by her living in Iowa, where the apparent contamination of the land and the water supply in the course of food production was overlooked as a matter of politics, economics, and cultural habit. Since her time as a student at the University of Iowa, Smiley had observed how established farming practices were threatening the environment. This awareness is at the heart of *A Thousand Acres,* her Pulitzer Prize–winning novel of heartland tragedy and the agricultural crisis of the 1980s. In addition, Smiley's story of the abuse suffered on Larry Cook's Iowa farm is a carefully undertaken recasting of

Shakespeare's *King Lear,* a play whose standard interpretation Smiley had come to mistrust. While writing *A Thousand Acres,* she was teaching Shakespeare's play in her world-literature course. The novel focuses on the narrator, Virginia "Ginny" Cook, and her sisters, Rose, and Caroline (Smiley's versions of Shakespeare's Goneril, Regan, and Cordelia), examining the women's relationships with each other, their husbands and lovers, and their father. Smiley's Lear, Larry Cook, is hardly the injured parent of Shakespeare's play, whose pathos derives more from his daughters' betrayal and disrepect than from the errors and thwarted intentions of old age. Larry is irascible, egotistical, autocratic, and capriciously malevolent, so when events conspire against him, he does not receive the sympathy accorded the father of Cordelia. Instead, the reader feels concern for Rose and Ginny, and the cathartic theatricality of Shakespeare is for the most part replaced by revelation and articulate contemplation–the sisters' shared assessment of the hidden costs of their kingdom of a thousand acres and Ginny's synthesis of their observations.

Some reviewers questioned the viability of so much smart but "talky" meditation, or Smiley's displacement of the Lear figure from center stage. Others considered her reworking of *King Lear* forced or criticized her combination of environmental, feminist, economic, and incest themes, arguing that it made the book overloaded. A different set of reviewers found much to admire in the novel (including Smiley's feminist reinterpretation of the daughters' behavior) and considered the book deserving of praise. The decision of the 1992 Pulitzer Prize committee corroborated the evaluation of this group and ensured the ongoing success of the novel. Perhaps the appropriately ironic postscript to *A Thousand Acres* as a commentary on an unexamined ethic of ownership and commodification is its having been made into a motion picture–on which Smiley eschewed opportunities for input. In 1994 Smiley was named a fellow of the American Academy of Arts and Letters.

While *A Thousand Acres* was less widely reviewed than might have been expected, given the success of her earlier work, *Moo,* Smiley's comic and warmly satirical 1995 send-up of academic life, was a reviewing and interviewing event. The book was widely noted and discussed, eliciting a mixture of puzzlement, negative criticism, and praise. Like *The Greenlanders,* Smiley's comic novel was criticized for not meeting the expectations of readers who thought of Smiley as the author of *The Age of Grief.* Many considered *Moo* atypical of Smiley as a brilliant delineator of domestic space, calling *Moo* insufficiently biting in its satire and not consistently funny. Yet, *Moo* is the product of Smi-

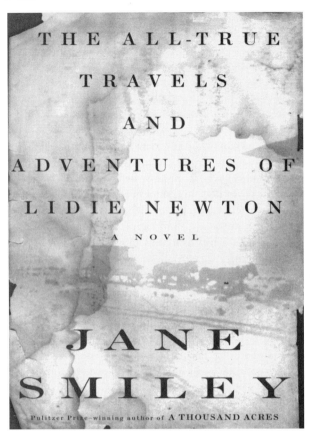

Dust jacket for Smiley's 1998 novel, about an abolitionist's wife

ley's long and productive association with the academy in general and (at Iowa State) with land-grant higher education in particular. Her novel reflects a compassionate, almost protective affinity for the university as a commensal community—especially the Moo U. under fire from Governor Orville T. Early, treated as a means of grant-getting and ego-grooming by Professor Lionel ("Homo Economicus") Gift, and administered by the likes of the "albino" Nordic twins Nils and Ivar Harstad. In Smiley's rendering of cow-college culture, Moo U. is by turns provincial, ego-ridden, and beset by professional jealousies and ambitions, but it is also surprisingly diverse, remarkably concupiscent, occasionally endearing, and more often than not a successful enterprise despite its shortcomings. It is, after all, the home of (among a score of others) administrative secretary Loraine Walker, the powerful but unseen guiding hand of the university; Horticulture Chairman X, a stubborn holdover activist from the 1960s; an engaging cluster of undergraduates whose ambitions and preoccupations might surprise their parents considerably but the student-counseling service not at all; and an exceptionally

large, pink Landrace hog named Earl Butz, whose life-work is unfettered consumption.

With epic, tragic, and comic novels already written, Smiley needed a romance to complete her long-term plan to produce fiction in four major traditional modes. Her ambitious work plan (reminiscent of the one that produced *The Greenlanders*) called for Smiley to research yet another subject and master the social circumstances, political realities, and discourse conventions of another time and place, in this case Kansas Territory in the 1850s. The result was a kind of "anti-romance," *The All-True Travels and Adventures of Lidie Newton* (1998). Smiley brings human nature, social and political forces, and the often intemperate climate of the Kansas prairie to bear on mid-nineteenth-century sentimental notions regarding domestic life and romantic or overimagined assumptions regarding migration to the expanding West. As her allusive title suggests, such a realist critique of the sentimental and romantic implicitly extends the argument of "Say It Ain't So, Huck," a 1996 *Harper's* article in which Smiley takes issue with the largely unchallenged canonical status of Samuel Langhorne Clemens's *Adventures of Huckleberry Finn* (1884) as realistic commentary on slavery and freedom in America. In her article Smiley argues that Harriet Beecher Stowe's *Uncle Tom's Cabin* (1852) is a more candid and responsible treatment of this theme. In *Lidie Newton* she illuminates slavery as an issue by tying it to issues central to female identity and domestic life, both of which are also central to Stowe's novel.

Lydia Harkness Newton, Smiley's twenty-one-year-old heroine, is both a representative woman and an extraordinary individual. In the first of the two "books" into which the novel is broken, Lidie recounts her orphaned girlhood, her uneasy "adoption" into the family (and the domestic ethos) of her sister, her brief courtship and sudden marriage to Massachusetts abolitionist Thomas Newton, and her migration to "K.T." (Kansas Territory), which in 1855 was less a haven for idealists than a violently contested borderland caught up in the question of whether Kansas should become a free state or a slave state. She reports her transformation from a wife who is nominally privileged through marriage—but inevitably patronized by her culture—into a tragically unencumbered woman for whom gender is less a presumed condition than a matter of self-conscious behavior and a calculated strategy for survival. In book 2 of *The All-True Travels and Adventures of Lidie Newton,* the social, philosophical, and economic debates that transform Kansas from a land promoter's dream into a battlefield over slavery inevitably skew Lidie's attempts to achieve a new identity; she must negotiate territory dominated by violence and the exercise of masculine prerogatives. Her "all-true adventures" while fleeing Missouri with the runaway slave Lorna constitute a novelistic counterpoint to *Huckleberry Finn* (particularly the closing section of Clemens's novel, in which Tom Sawyer and Huck Finn play at helping Jim escape from the Phelps farm) and a late-twentieth-century realist's less-than-sanguine sense of the likely fate of social relationships determined by gender in a country destabilized by slavery.

Smiley wrote *The All-True Travels and Adventures of Lidie Newton* in Carmel Valley, California, following a cross-country move in 1996 that enabled her to engage on a full-time basis her writing and her passion for equestrian pursuits. The novel appeared shortly after her resignation from the faculty at Iowa State and in the wake of the dissolution of her marriage to Mortensen. Two years later, returning to the panoply-of-characters format of *Moo* and employing her knowledge of thoroughbred horses and horse people, Smiley published *Horse Heaven* (2000), a geographically diverse, variously populated novel about the sprawling world of the racehorse.

This ninth major work of fiction has a picaresque quality. The reader is asked to follow the constant movement of horses, money, and a Dickensian range of characters from New York to Maryland, Florida, and California, with Texas, France, and other points around the globe also included. Hardly intimidated by the bewildering mix of power, money, heredity, and hope at the racetrack, Smiley finds there a Vanity Fair of breeders, ranchers, owners, trainers, groomers, jockeys, veterinarians, con artists, and bettors. Given that human ambitions are always informed by passions, quirks, appetites, superstitions, hunches, and ego, Smiley offers no apology for a California channeler who can read horses' minds or for equine characters with individual personalities and practical intelligence rendered as points of view. In fact, Mr. T., Justa Bob, and the rest of the field have an inevitably clear sense of who they are and what they are about. The world of *Horse Heaven* is an interesting one in which genetic inheritance and animal integrity often prove more trustworthy than human thought and motive.

Smiley's adventurous intelligence and creative energy, along with the often surprising turns of her life, make any speculation concerning the nature of the fiction yet to come highly problematic. To paraphrase more than one Smiley character, her readers should just pay attention and see what happens.

Interviews:

Marcelle Thiébaux, "*PW* Interviews: Jane Smiley," *Publishers Weekly*, 233 (1 April 1988): 65–66;

Suzanne Berne, "Belles Lettres Interview," *Belles Lettres*, 7 (Summer 1992): 36–38;

Mickey Pearlman, "Jane Smiley," in her *Listen to Their Voices: Twenty Interviews with Women Who Write* (New York & London: Norton, 1993), pp. 99–111;

Alexander Neubauer, "Jane Smiley," in *Conversations on Writing Fiction: Interviews with Thirteen Distinguished Teachers of Fiction Writing in America*, edited by Neubauer (New York: HarperCollins, 1994), pp. 209–227;

Richard Grant, "Jane Smiley: Homebody Makes Good," *Telegraph Magazine*, 20 May 1995, pp. 36–39;

Darragh Johnson, "Paradise Found," *Sacramento Bee*, 29 April 1998, E1–E5;

Ron Fletcher, "Bringing a Timeless Humanity to Writing," *Christian Science Monitor*, 30 April 1998, B2;

Marie Arana-Ward, "A Bard of the Midwest," *Washington Post Book World*, 21 June 1998, p. 8;

Kay Bonetti, "An Interview with Jane Smiley," *Missouri Review*, 21, no. 3 (1998): 89–108;

Teresa K. Weaver, "A Willing Vessel: Smiley Gives Words Free Rein," *Atlanta Journal-Constitution*, 28 February 1999, L1, L9;

Conan Putnam, "Distance Runner," *Chicago Tribune Magazine*, 25 July 1999, pp. 18–19;

Dan Cryer, "Thoroughbred Writer," *Newsday*, 25 April 2000, B6–B7.

References:

Jane S. Bakerman, "'The Gleaming Obsidian Shard': Jane Smiley's *A Thousand Acres*," *Midamerica XIX* (1992): 127–137;

Bakerman, "Renovating the House of Fiction: Structural Diversity in Jane Smiley's *Duplicate Keys*," *Midamerica XV* (1988): 111–120;

Bakerman, "Water on Stone: Long-term Friendships in Jane Smiley's *Duplicate Keys* and Charlaine Harris's *A Secret Rage*," *Clues: A Journal of Detection*, 10 (Fall/Winter 1989): 49–63;

Kate Chedgzoy, "Wise Children and Foolish Fathers," in her *Shakespeare's Queer Children: Sexual Politics and Contemporary Culture* (Manchester & New York: Manchester University Press, 1995), pp. 49–58;

Peter Conrad, "Expatriating Lear," in his *To Be Continued: Four Stories and Their Survival* (Oxford: Clarendon Press, 1995), pp. 131–151;

Sara Farris, "American Pastoral in the Twentieth-Century: *O Pioneers!, A Thousand Acres,* and *Merry Men,*" *Isle,* 5 (Winter 1998): 27–48;

Dana Heller, "Father Trouble: Jane Smiley's *The Age of Grief,*" in her *Family Plots: The De-Oedipalization of Popular Culture* (Philadelphia: University of Pennsylvania Press, 1995), pp. 94–112;

Justin Kaplan, "Selling *Huck Finn* Down the River," *New York Times Book Review,* 10 March 1996, p. 27;

Steven G. Kellman, "Food Fights in Iowa: The Vegetarian Stranger in Recent Midwest Fiction," *Virginia Quarterly Review,* 71 (Summer 1995): 435–447;

Tim Keppel, "Goneril's Version: *A Thousand Acres* and *King Lear,*" *South Dakota Review,* 33 (Summer 1995): 105–117;

Jack Temple Kirby, "Rural Culture in the American Middle West: Jefferson to Jane Smiley," *Agricultural History,* 70 (Fall 1996): 581–597;

Amy Levin, "Familiar Terrain: Domestic Ideology and Farm Policy in Three Women's Novels About the 1980's," *NWSA Journal,* 11 (Spring 1999): 21–43;

Carl D. Malmgren, "The Lie of the Land: Heartland Novels by Smiley and Kinsella," *Modern Fiction Studies,* 45 (Summer 1999): 432–456;

Kelly A. Marsh, "The Neo-Sensation Novel: A Contemporary Genre in the Victorian Tradition," *Philological Quarterly,* 74 (Winter 1995): 99–123;

Neil Nakadate, *Understanding Jane Smiley* (Columbia: University of South Carolina Press, 1999);

Katie Roiphe, "Making the Incest Scene," *Harper's,* 291 (November 1995): 65–71;

Margaret Rozga, "Sisters in a Quest—*Sister Carrie* and *A Thousand Acres:* The Search for Identity in Gendered Territory," *Midwestern Miscellany,* 22 (1994): 18–29;

James A. Schiff, "Contemporary Retellings: *A Thousand Acres* as the Latest *Lear,*" *Critique,* 39 (Summer 1998): 367–381;

John Seelye and others, "Letters: Twain Sold Down the River?" *Harper's,* 292 (April 1996): 6–7, 83–85;

Deborah Slicer, "Toward an Ecofeminist Standpoint Theory: Bodies as Grounds," in *Ecofeminist Literary Criticism: Theory, Interpretation, Pedagogy,* edited by Greta Gaard and Patrick D. Murphy (Urbana: University of Illinois Press, 1998), pp. 48–73.

John Updike

(18 March 1932 –   )

Donald J. Greiner
University of South Carolina

See also the Updike entries in *DLB 2: American Novelists Since World War II, First Series; DLB 5: American Poets Since World War II; DLB 143: American Novelists Since World War II, Third Series; DBL 218: American Short-Story Writers Since World War II; DLB Yearbook: 1980; DLB Yearbook: 1982;* and *DS 3: Saul Bellow, Jack Kerouac, Norman Mailer, Vladimir Nabokov, John Updike, Kurt Vonnegut.*

BOOKS: *The Carpentered Hen and Other Tame Creatures* (New York: Harper, 1958); republished as *Hoping for a Hoopoe* (London: Gollancz, 1959);

The Poorhouse Fair (New York: Knopf, 1959; London: Gollancz, 1959);

The Same Door (New York: Knopf, 1959; London: Deutsch, 1962);

Rabbit, Run (New York: Knopf, 1960; London: Deutsch, 1961);

The Magic Flute (New York: Knopf, 1962; London: Deutsch & Ward, 1964);

Pigeon Feathers (New York: Knopf, 1962; London: Deutsch, 1962);

The Centaur (New York: Knopf, 1963; London: Deutsch, 1963);

Telephone Poles and Other Poems (New York: Knopf, 1963; London: Deutsch, 1964);

Olinger Stories (New York: Vintage, 1964);

The Ring (New York: Knopf, 1964);

Assorted Prose (New York: Knopf, 1965; London: Deutsch, 1965);

A Child's Calendar, illustrated by Nancy Ekholm Gurkert (New York: Knopf, 1965); republished, with illustrations by Trina Schart Hyman (New York: Holiday House, 1999);

Of the Farm (New York: Knopf, 1965; London: Deutsch, 1966);

Verse (Greenwich, Conn.: Fawcett, 1965);

The Music School (New York: Knopf, 1966; London: Deutsch, 1967);

Couples (New York: Knopf, 1968; London: Deutsch, 1968);

John Updike (photograph by Martha Updike; from the dust jacket for Bech at Bay, *1998)*

Midpoint and Other Poems (New York: Knopf, 1969; London: Deutsch, 1969);

Bottom's Dream (New York: Knopf, 1969);

Bech: A Book (New York: Knopf, 1970; London: Deutsch, 1970);

Rabbit Redux (New York: Knopf, 1971; London: Deutsch, 1972);

Seventy Poems (London: Penguin, 1972);

Museums and Women (New York: Knopf, 1972; London: Deutsch, 1973);

Buchanan Dying (New York: Knopf, 1974; London: Deutsch, 1974);

A Month of Sundays (New York: Knopf, 1975; London: Deutsch, 1975);

Picked-Up Pieces (New York: Knopf, 1975; London: Deutsch, 1976);

Marry Me: A Romance (New York: Knopf, 1976; London: Deutsch, 1977);

Tossing and Turning (New York: Knopf, 1977; London: Deutsch, 1977);

The Coup (New York: Knopf, 1978; London: Deutsch, 1979);

Too Far to Go (New York: Fawcett Crest, 1979); republished as *Your Lover Just Called* (Harmondsworth, U.K.: Penguin, 1980);

Problems and Other Stories (New York: Knopf, 1979; London: Deutsch, 1980);

Rabbit Is Rich (New York: Knopf, 1981; London: Deutsch, 1982);

Bech Is Back (New York: Knopf, 1982; London: Deutsch, 1983);

Hugging the Shore (New York: Knopf, 1983; London: Deutsch, 1984);

The Witches of Eastwick (New York: Knopf, 1984; London: Deutsch, 1984);

Facing Nature (New York: Knopf, 1985; London: Deutsch, 1986);

Roger's Version (New York: Knopf, 1986; London: Deutsch, 1986);

Trust Me (New York: Knopf, 1987; London: Deutsch, 1987);

S. (New York: Knopf, 1988; London: Deutsch, 1988);

Self-Consciousness: Memoirs (New York: Knopf, 1989; London: Deutsch, 1989);

Just Looking (New York: Knopf, 1989; London: Deutsch, 1989);

Rabbit at Rest (New York: Knopf, 1990; London: Deutsch, 1990);

Odd Jobs (New York: Knopf, 1991; London: Deutsch, 1992);

Memories of the Ford Administration (New York: Knopf, 1992; London: Hamilton, 1992);

Collected Poems: 1953–1993 (New York: Knopf, 1993; London: Hamilton, 1993);

Brazil (Franklin Center, Pa.: Franklin Library / New York: Knopf, 1994; London: Hamilton, 1994);

The Afterlife and Other Stories (New York: Knopf, 1994; London: Hamilton, 1995);

A Helpful Alphabet of Friendly Objects (New York: Knopf, 1995);

Rabbit Angstrom: A Tetralogy (New York: Knopf/Everyman, 1995;

Golf Dreams: Writings on Golf (New York: Knopf, 1996; London: Hamilton, 1997);

In the Beauty of the Lilies (Franklin Center, Pa.: Franklin Library / New York: Knopf, 1996; London: Hamilton, 1996);

Toward the End of Time (New York: Knopf, 1997; London: Hamilton, 1998);

Bech at Bay: A Quasi-novel (New York: Knopf, 1998);

More Matter (New York: Knopf, 1999);

Gertrude and Claudius (New York: Knopf, 2000).

A reader would be hard pressed to name a contemporary author other than John Updike whose work is more in tune with the way most Americans live. Unconcerned with apocalypse in his fiction, undeterred by the universal absurdity that threatens to negate the bravest and the best, Updike writes about ordinary people leading ordinary lives. Man, wife, home, children, job—these mundane concerns have rested at the heart of his art since he published his first book, a volume of poetry titled *The Carpentered Hen and Other Tame Creatures,* in 1958, and they have continued to help him dissect, lovingly and clearly, the daily routine of Middle America in small town and suburb.

War is generally not an issue for Updike, and neither are the problems of space weapons, worldwide hunger, or the fouling of the planet. The concerns in Updike's writing do not make front-page news, but they do matter because Updike knows that "something fierce goes on in homes." He may not write about murder and mayhem and madness, but, in an exquisitely lyrical style that even his detractors admire, he probes the crises that sear the human spirit: how does a man cling to a mistress when he fears leaving his wife; how does he explain his guilt to his children when he knows that love is all that matters; how does he get his life going again when the applause heaped on him in high school has shattered into silence; how does he fill the void when religious faith seems faltering and false; and how does he grow along with his children who, overnight, seem to know more but care less?

Moralist, stylist, chronicler of the American middle class, Updike investigates the inner lives of families and the common details that define them. He knows that the insignificant particulars of a life are both signs of God's handiwork and hints of humanity's needs: finely crafted furniture, a carefully mown field, a perfect tee shot, a groping prayer, and, unfortunately, the halting march toward death.

Updike can tell of these lives because he has been there. Born on 18 March 1932 in Shillington, Pennsylvania, John Hoyer Updike grew up an only child in a relatively poor family. His father, Wesley R. Updike, taught mathematics in the local high school, but at age thirteen Updike; his father; his mother, Linda G. Hoyer Updike; and her parents, John F. and Katherine Z.

Hoyer, moved from the town to a farm from which he and his father had to commute daily. His memoir "The Dogwood Tree: A Boyhood" (*Assorted Prose,* 1965) captures the centrality of his Shillington years, and he has since implied that the loneliness uncovered by the move to the farm fired his imagination.

He now jokingly confesses that his adolescent imaginings were partly devoted to the problem of "how to get out of here," and his exquisitely paced short stories such as "A Sense of Shelter" and "Flight" (*Pigeon Feathers,* 1962) examine the contradictory urges that define most high-school students: longing to break free from home yet fearing the flight itself. Updike "flew" imaginatively through the cartoons and fiction in *The New Yorker* and physically when he won a scholarship to Harvard University. His lifelong commitment to prose style, to the sheer sound of words artfully selected and rhythmically grouped to suggest resonance and tone, was developed at Harvard. While an undergraduate English major, he drew cartoons and wrote for the *Harvard Lampoon,* which he later edited; after he was graduated summa cum laude in 1954, he studied for one year on a Knox Fellowship at the Ruskin School of Drawing and Fine Arts in Oxford, England.

Updike has revealed that his true ambition was to be a cartoonist, if not for Walt Disney then at least for *The New Yorker:* "What I have become is a sorry shadow of those high hopes." Still, the beginnings of his career as a writer are associated with *The New Yorker,* for that magazine published his first professional story, "Friends from Philadelphia," on 30 October 1954. Following his return from Oxford in 1955, he joined the staff of *The New Yorker,* and for the next two years he contributed to the "Talk of the Town" columns. Although he ended his formal ties with the magazine's editorial staff in 1957 and moved to Ipswich, Massachusetts, to concentrate on writing, he continued his relationship with the periodical, which has been publishing his poems, stories, essays, and reviews regularly for more than four decades. The move from New York to Ipswich brought the anticipated results, for by 1959 Updike had had three books published: *The Carpentered Hen* (1958), *The Poorhouse Fair* (1959), and *The Same Door* (1959).

Critical recognition soon followed. In 1959 he was awarded the Guggenheim Fellowship and then the Rosenthal Foundation Award of the National Institute of Arts and Letters for *The Poorhouse Fair* in 1960; his novel *The Centaur* (1963) won the National Book Award for fiction in 1964; several of his short stories have been honored with O. Henry Awards; and he was elected to the National Institute of Arts and Letters in 1964 and to the American Academy of Arts and Letters in 1977. *Rabbit Is Rich* (1981) won the Pulitzer Prize, the National

Book Critics Circle Award, and an American Book Award, and his collection of essays *Hugging the Shore* (1983), won the National Book Critics Circle Award for criticism. *Rabbit at Rest* (1990) won the Pulitzer Prize and the National Book Critics Circle Award.

Although his popular reputation rests primarily on his novels, Updike is a master of four genres: novel, short story, poetry, and essay. In each case his care for the rhythms of language shapes his dismay at the secularization of life, but this is not to suggest that he writes in the 1990s the way he began in the 1950s. Committed in his novels, for example, to the realistic depiction of mundane affairs, he has nevertheless written about the comic intransigence of language in *A Month of Sundays* (1975), about the way that language controls both culture and global politics in *The Coup* (1978), and about the fine line between fantasy and reality in *The Witches of Eastwick* (1984), a humorous novel that is closer to the magic realism of contemporary Latin American authors than to Updike's earlier work.

Similar variations mark the development of his short fiction. The most accomplished American short-story writer since John O'Hara, Updike has moved from the nostalgia of *The Same Door* and some of the tales in *Pigeon Feathers* to the lyrical meditations of such stories as "Wife-wooing" (*Pigeon Feathers*) and "The Music School" (*The Music School,* 1966), toward the irony of *Museums and Women* (1972), *Problems and Other Stories* (1979), and *Trust Me* (1987). His decades-long love affair with this peculiarly American genre has helped change the shape of the short story, for the narrative element associated with the tales in *The Same Door* is often subordinated to a lyrical, meditative use of language in later pieces. His general topic is diminishment, and the reader of Updike's short-story collections will note how the loss of the high-school years in *The Same Door* and *Pigeon Feathers* gives way to the loss of family through betrayal and divorce in *The Music School* and *Museums and Women,* which look toward, in *Problems and Other Stories* and *Trust Me,* the declining potency brought on by the specter of loss of life. Updike stirs the emotions while he challenges the intellect.

Varied interests also direct Updike's poetry. Blessed with a sense of humor and thus able to laugh at the flaws of life and the foibles of language, he has always been intrigued by the intricate verbal demands of light verse. Indeed, most of the poems in *The Carpentered Hen and Other Tame Creatures* and the first half of *Telephone Poles and Other Poems* (1963) sparkle with linguistic wit. But while Updike has maintained his joyous appreciation of the playfulness of words in his later volumes of verse, he has altered his emphasis. The decline of religious sureties is a prominent consideration in *Telephone Poles and Other Poems* and *Midpoint and Other Poems*

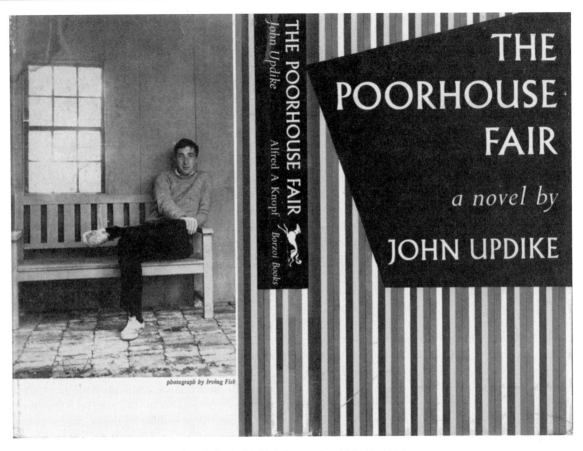

Dust jacket for Updike's first novel, published in 1959

(1969), and the diminishment of life itself results in the somber tone of many of the poems in *Tossing and Turning* (1977). The odes to natural processes in *Facing Nature* (1985) are challenging displays of intellect and humor, but they also indicate, however indirectly, the inadequacy of humanity before the inexorable increments of nonhuman otherness.

Updike formally discusses many of these concerns in the fourth genre at which he excels—the essay. *Assorted Prose, Picked-Up Pieces* (1975), *Hugging the Shore, Just Looking* (1989), *Odd Jobs* (1991), and *More Matter* (1999) illustrate not only a curious mind but also an astonishing range of interests. Small-town America, Central Park, baseball, mimesis, Nathaniel Hawthorne, the general state of the art of fiction, theology, and painting are just a few of the topics that engage his delighted enthusiasm for the things of his world. Yet, as with all his work, significant changes have marked his essays since *Assorted Prose*. Largely a collection of parodies, occasional pieces that Updike wrote for the "Talk of the Town" section of *The New Yorker*, memoirs, and reviews, *Assorted Prose* is primarily notable for four distinguished essays: "The Dogwood Tree: A Boyhood";

"Hub Fans Bid Kid Adieu," a justly famous account of Ted Williams's last baseball game for the Boston Red Sox; "Faith in Search of Understanding," an analysis of Karl Barth's rigorously conservative theology; and "More Love in the Western World," an essay on the history of romantic love in literature.

Picked-Up Pieces, on the other hand, is necessary reading for the student of Updike primarily because it includes his speeches on the genre of fiction and his essay-reviews of the work of many non-American authors in which he develops his understanding of mimesis. European writers continue to hold Updike's focus in *Hugging the Shore,* but in this collection he discusses for the first time some of his American predecessors: Walt Whitman, Herman Melville, and Hawthorne. His interest in American literature also often prompts him to invoke the achievement of Henry James when evaluating the books of other writers.

In *Just Looking* Updike shifts his focus from writers to painters. Despite the self-effacing tone of his title, he offers nearly two dozen essays on artists as various as Richard Estes, Jan Vermeer, and Andrew Wyeth. Of special interest, when one considers Updike's long association with *The New Yorker,* are the essays on *The New Yorker* cartoonist Ralph Barton and on writers who were also artists of sorts, including Edgar Allan Poe, Oscar Wilde, and Updike himself. *Odd Jobs* has a similarly self-deprecatory title, but Updike's seriousness is apparent in the sheer bulk of the collection—nearly nine hundred pages of essays and reviews. Commentaries on William Dean Howells, Franz Kafka, Isak Dinesen, and Graham Greene are especially illuminating, as are the multiple reviews of Updike's contemporaries John Cheever and Philip Roth. Typically, however, Updike features analyses of non-American writers, especially those from Africa and Europe.

The concerns that Updike elaborates in his essays shape the themes that he develops in his novels: the malaise of the spirit, the glory of common details, the shrinking of the family center, the enticing lure of adultery, and the ever-beckoning shadow of decay. His first novel, *The Poorhouse Fair,* is a case in point. Unlike most beginning authors who write about youthful initiation from the perspective of personal experience tentatively explored, Updike considers the plight of old folks in a charity home who have no place to turn except toward death. Published in 1959, *The Poorhouse Fair* is set in the imagined future of the 1970s as Updike predicts a welfare society where all needs but spiritual health are met. Writing in the lyrical style that would become the hallmark of his achievement, he exposes the potential sterility of a nation that supplies everything except the right to be eccentric, individual, and alone.

Detailing the one day in the county poorhouse when the inmates are permitted to hold a fair for the citizens of the town, the novel centers on the conflict between Conner, the efficient administrator, and Hook, the aging ward. The problem is not that Conner fails to care but that he fails to see. He can offer blankets for the beds and food for the table, but he cannot understand that marking the rocking chairs with nameplates denies the individuality of choice. The former schoolteacher Hook senses that "not busyness but belief" is the issue, that belief means not only that God dwells in both telephone poles and trees but that faith inspires the craftsmanship that shapes everything from handcarved furniture to the nation itself. What happens to the soul of a country, asks Updike, when machine-sewn blankets count for more than hand-stitched quilts? On the day of the fair, the poorhouse inmates show off their carved peachstones and trinkets, and Updike celebrates their feeble yet stubborn rebellion against manufactured welfare and impersonal regard.

Announcing his presence in American fiction with an admirable first novel of verbal skill and significant concerns, Updike also previewed a theme that would become increasingly important in his canon:

the necessity for belief—for faith—above all else. An informal student of modern theology, he has shaped his own religious thought from the strict tenets of Karl Barth and his predecessor Søren Kierkegaard. Drawn especially to Barth's insistence that God is "Wholly Other," that humanity cannot reach God and that only God can touch humanity, Updike stresses Barth's call for belief. Hook has this belief and thus a faith that permits him to maintain calm in the face of care. Harry "Rabbit" Angstrom has belief, too, but he lacks Hook's capacity for thought.

Rabbit, Run (1960), the first volume of the Rabbit chronicle that includes *Rabbit Redux* (1971), *Rabbit Is Rich,* and *Rabbit at Rest,* continues to be Updike's most shocking novel, but many of its themes are variations of those initiated in *The Poorhouse Fair.* Although Rabbit (Harry Angstrom) is only twenty-six while Hook is ninety, both men sense the dead ends of their lives. Both also accept Barth's notion of religious commitment. Whereas Hook possesses the serenity that comes with age and the ability to articulate his faith, Rabbit reveals the uncertainty of youth and the inability to express his fear.

Called by Stanley Edgar Hyman "the most gifted novelist of his generation," Updike began to fill the void left by the decline of William Faulkner and Ernest Hemingway. But, while initiated readers responded to Updike's lush style and sympathetic probing of the pain of American life, the general public was shocked by Rabbit's sexual exploits and by his wife's accidental drowning of their baby. *Rabbit, Run* continues to disturb readers because of Updike's skill at generating sympathy for a troubling young man who inadvertently causes pain. Updike takes a common American experience—the graduation from high school of a star athlete who has no life to lead once the applause diminishes and the headlines fade—and turns it into a subtle exposé of the frailty of the American dream.

Rabbit's dilemma has occupied Updike for his entire career (see, for example, "Ex-Basketball Player" in *The Carpentered Hen and Other Tame Creatures* and "Ace in the Hole" in *The Same Door*), and it is now clear that he has written a saga of middle-class America in the second half of the twentieth century. Not liking what he has but never defining what he wants, Rabbit is a decent, unintelligent man who finds that the momentum that sustained him during his basketball years has slowed to a crawl in a dingy apartment where the dinner is always late and the wife has stopped being pretty. Written entirely in the present tense—an unusual technique in American fiction—and thus stressing the immediacy of Rabbit's crisis, the novel details the sterility of a society that offers television sets and cars but ignores spiritual loss and belief.

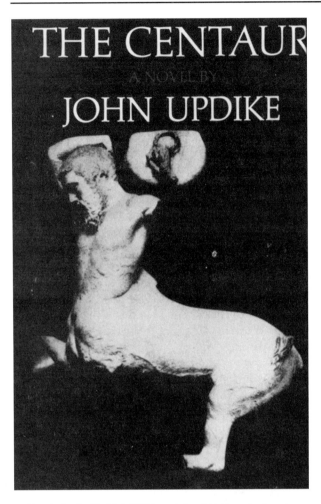

Dust jacket for Updike's 1963 novel, in which the main character, George Caldwell, is based on the author's father

Bewildered by her husband's restless agony, by his inarticulate need to run, Janice personifies all that clogs Rabbit's life. Updike's astonishing facility with language is used not only to suggest Rabbit's need for order and style but also to describe the junk that surrounds him via Janice: dirty ashtrays, droning television sets, disorganized closets. All she wants is for him to be like other husbands, to give in to the nine-to-five routine of selling Magi-peelers in the local dimestore, but Rabbit senses that loss of life's momentum means loss of life itself. So he runs.

And as he runs he becomes Updike's religious quester, momentarily stalled between the right way (Janice) and the good way (freedom), but determined to save himself despite the consequences. The Reverend Jack Eccles tries to help him, but Updike shows that Eccles lacks Rabbit's Barthian sense of belief, that in his passion for good works Eccles is a cousin of Conner in *The Poorhouse Fair*. When the frustrated Eccles badgers Rabbit to explain what he wants, all the inartic-

ulate quester can do is hit a perfect tee shot on the golf course, point to the fluidity and grace of the soaring ball, and shout, "That's it!" The last word of the novel– "Runs"–suggests Rabbit's inability to find that grace.

A decade later, in 1971, Updike reintroduced Rabbit at age thirty-six. In *Rabbit Redux* ("Rabbit led back"), however, the junk of ashtrays and closets that Harry has run from earlier is replaced by national events that threaten to overwhelm him: Vietnam, the Civil Rights movement, and the drug culture. Framing these disasters–as Rabbit considers them to be–is the excitement of the first moon shot; but try as he might to turn the space flight into a metaphor for his own need to soar gracefully and far, he understands that the moon adventure is sterile, merely a triumph of impersonal technology making contact with a dead rock. In *Rabbit Redux* Harry's dash for open territory has taught him that America no longer promises places to run to, so he returns to his dingy house in the plastic suburb.

What he finds is a metaphor for the upheaval of the 1960s: Janice has left him for a lover, although she would come home if Harry would ask; his son, Nelson, is suddenly a teenager who needs and deserves guidance; a hippie girl and a black Vietnam vet, both drug-crazed, invade his house; and Rabbit finds himself succumbing to physical sloppiness and spiritual despair. The fire that destroys the Angstrom house at the end of the novel is Updike's ironic apocalypse, his signal that nothing earth-shattering is going to happen to Rabbit, that Rabbit will have to rebuild his little life by himself. Rabbit attempts to rebound when, in the final scene–all but forgetting his earlier need for grace–he leads Janice to a motel. The last words of the novel–"Sleeps. O.K.?"–are a long way from "Runs."

Rabbit Redux is the least intriguing of the Rabbit tales, for Harry is a more interesting character when he quests instead of halts. But the third Rabbit novel, *Rabbit Is Rich,* is one of Updike's best, and it was published within a year of the resurrection of another of Updike's favorite characters, Henry Bech, in *Bech Is Back* (1982). Read together as installments in Updike's sagas, the two volumes illustrate the expanse of his range: Rabbit sells Toyotas; Bech writes books.

Each Rabbit novel records the tone of a decade. *Rabbit Is Rich* is about the 1970s, and the rainbow that Harry chases in the 1950s and 1960s has shrunk as the American dream goes sour with the bad taste of middle age and aimless youth. Farmland turns into shopping malls; overflowing garbage cans stand beside unsuccessful plywood restaurants; and people reel from a combination of less energy and higher prices. Now forty-six years old, Rabbit does not blame anyone for *Skylab* falling or Exxon's greed, but death leers on the horizon, and he is afraid of running out of gas. When

Rabbit looks over his shoulder at the glory of early fame too easily won on the basketball court and thinks of himself as "king of the lot" and "the star and spear point" of the flourishing Toyota dealership his family owns, the reader knows that he has not changed much from the man whose value system was defined in terms of athletic prowess.

Yet, he has changed some: golf has replaced basketball, and he rumbles rather than runs with a forty-two-inch waist and a tendency to avoid mirrors when he used to love reflections of himself. Still, Rabbit is rich in the ironic sense of being able to afford cashews instead of peanuts. Life is sweet. For the first time in twenty-five years he is happy to be alive, even happy with his marriage to Janice. Deserted by Harry in the first Rabbit novel and deserting him in the second, Janice fits snugly into a middle-age routine, plays tennis at the country club, and, says Rabbit, "never looked sharper." She still drinks too much, and she rarely serves meals on time, but she finally enjoys sex and even manages now and then to stand up to her husband.

Despite Janice, golf, and money, Rabbit needs to run, not as fast and not as far, but somewhere. He muses on "the entire squeezed and cutdown shape of his life," and he realizes that middle age is upon him, a time when dreams decline to awareness of limits and stomachs take on a noticeable sag. The strained jollity of the country-club set, "the kind of crowd that will do a marriage in if you let it," makes him uneasy, but his flight in this novel is not as urgent as it is in *Rabbit, Run* and thus not as poignant. He knows that he is a "soft and a broad target."

Aiming at the target is his son, Nelson, twenty-two-years old, a surly college dropout, and, in Rabbit's eyes, "humpbacked and mean, a rat going out to be drowned." Hitchhiking home to a hurry-up marriage to a pregnant secretary, Nelson wants a job at Rabbit's Toyota dealership. Updike sketches the father/son tension with superb detail so that the reader understands Rabbit's lament: "How can you respect the world when you see it's being run by a bunch of kids turned old?" But that old bunch was once Rabbit's bunch, and Nelson will be right behind them. He is tired of being young, but he does not know how to grow up. Nelson lacks fluidity and grace. Sympathy for his fear of being trapped is not easy to give because, unlike his father, he has no intuitive sense of joy, no yearning. His wife is correct: he is a spoiled bully. Nelson runs but without Rabbit's faith; the son runs from while the father runs toward.

Later Rabbit "glimpses the truth that to be rich is to be robbed, to be rich is to be poor." In part he means spiritually poor, though he would not say it that way, so

he and Janice break from his mother-in-law and buy their own home. Maybe his rainbow is in the suburbs. He still longs for a world without ruts, but God has become a "raisin lost under the car seat." In the earlier novels Rabbit runs toward transcendence, toward what he calls "it," but now he has only a vacation in the Caribbean to rejuvenate him. There, engaged in wife-swapping where he once pursued life's rhythm, he even misses his dream girl when he is paired with his second choice. Sex is part of Rabbit's scampering, his questing, as Updike established years ago.

Rabbit returns home to find that his son has drifted back to college, and his granddaughter has been born. The birth calms him for a moment, soothes his undefined sense of unsettledness, but he knows that it is also a giant step toward extinction: mortality looms beyond the middle years.

Late in *Rabbit at Rest,* the final novel of the celebrated tetralogy about Harry Angstrom, Rabbit looks at his overweight, middle-aged body and sees "an innocuous passive spirit that doesn't want to do any harm, get trapped anywhere, or ever die." All three desires are denied him. At long last, Updike's Rabbit stops running.

Like James Fenimore Cooper's Leatherstocking, Hawthorne's Hester, and Mark Twain's Huck, Harry is one of the immortal literary characters who first absorb and then define a national culture. Now fifty-six and stuck in the United States of the 1980s with its cocaine addiction and condos—in what Rabbit calls "Reagan's reign"—Harry still worries about sex and death, religion and belief, but he is not as certain as he used to be, not as confident. Personal limitation mirrors national malaise. His America is depleted, and his dreams are deferred. He now lives part of the year in a Florida condo, but, when he looks at the imported Toyotas that have brought him the easy life of golf and profits, he thinks not of success but of the eerie presence of lurking death: "Most of American life is driving somewhere and then driving back wondering why the hell you went." Similar witticisms throughout the novel create a comic frame for Rabbit's gloom.

No longer the hopeful Rabbit of his basketball-playing days in the 1950s, he is similarly distanced from the grace he once pursued with inarticulate fear. Like many Americans of his indulgent generation, Harry suffers from heart trouble, the physical sign of his spiritual dread. Never articulate, he continues to define abstractions with the metaphors of sports. Golf, he reasons, now has a greater relevance to his life than basketball: the golf ball starts wide before falling into a small hole in the ground. Perhaps the only immortality he will find is the "little genetic quirk" that he passes on to his granddaughter: "You fill in a slot for a time and then move out." Death means making room for someone else.

Yet, for all his fear, Harry continues his quest to break free of limitations. He is Updike's American dreamer, a mundane Jay Gatsby whose daily dissatisfaction cloaks a lifelong spiritual yearning. In *Rabbit at Rest* Updike describes the hairstyles, the inane pop songs, the dismal TV programs such as *Roseanne,* the physical-fitness nuts, and the racial prejudices to illustrate the uneasiness of the United States in 1988–1989 and to generate sympathy for a character who is similar to many readers who will buy the novel but also one they normally will not much like.

Despite material accumulation during the Reagan years, life in America is usually a matter of "mostly missed signals." Rabbit fails to acknowledge both his son's drug addiction and his own failing heart. His youthful running has been slowed to gliding over immaculate fairways in golf carts, aware, sadly, that the most depressing agony about aging is "the lessening of excitement about anything."

Clearly, Updike reread the earlier Rabbit novels in preparation for the finale. Harry's many memories include events dramatized in the first three books, and quotations of his thoughts from past years indicate the long continuity of his quest, the never-ending fever of his fear. In this way Updike suggests that a person's life establishes unalterable patterns, as when Rabbit nearly loses his granddaughter in a boating mishap and thus relives the horror of his wife's accidental drowning of their daughter decades ago when he still believed in the promise of possibility. Harry's wife thinks that he is at peace now. Updike and the reader know better.

Watching a TV monitor to see inside his own heart during angioplasty, Rabbit witnesses a preview of his own death. Yet, with an irony that readers of the entire tetralogy will appreciate, Updike shows how Harry's wife accepts middle age as a springboard to move enthusiastically into the world even as her husband retreats inside his own shrinking space.

Despite the transgression of adultery, then, the reader cheers when, in the last movement of the novel, Rabbit runs one final time–away from complications, away from stasis, away from a catastrophe that he himself has helped cause. He no longer runs toward his ill-defined goal of "it," but at least he moves forward, "jostling for his space in the world as if he still deserves it." He even returns to the basketball court despite his weight, his age, and his heart. In short, he tries, but his fear presages the final stillness. The last word of this splendid novel is "Enough." Death is, as it always was, the still center of Rabbit's frantic life of motion.

It is sad to think of death setting its snare for Rabbit Angstrom because, after four decades and four long novels, he has joined the pantheon of American literary heroes. Yet, a glimpse of final defeat is the price to be paid for membership in that exclusive club. Like Natty Bumppo, Ahab, Huck Finn, Gatsby, Ike McCaslin, and Holden Caulfield, Harry learns that, no matter how far he runs in space, he cannot outrace time.

Henry Bech has all but stopped running. In *Bech Is Back* Henry returns to the literary scene with a new wife and a new novel, but his old bewilderment is still intact. His former mistress knows that his book is lousy, but the ad-fed public adores it anyway. Henry suspects that her judgment is correct; yet, after suffering through a silence lasting more than a decade, he wonders how he can reject the royalties and the fanfare, since he has poured enough sex and violence into his latest novel to guarantee a best-seller all but created by media hype. Silence, he reasons, offers only limited rewards.

Bech is Updike's favorite writer, a character who promises to have the longevity of Rabbit in the Updike canon and who allows Updike the opportunity to work out the frustrations that inevitably trap the successful artist in America. When last seen in *Bech: A Book* (1970), Bech had published enough fiction to shape a reputation with the intelligentsia; had fallen into the hell of writer's block that, ironically, increased his reputation; and had emerged as a kind of artifact that Uncle Sam paraded around the globe to fulfill various cultural exchanges. Bech is Updike's joke on himself. More to the point, he is also Updike's joke on the discouraging hoopla with which Americans surround their authors in order to worship not the writing but the writer.

The laughs begin on the first page of *Bech: A Book.* There Updike reveals a letter to himself from Bech in which Bech says, with his ego showing, "Well, if you must commit the artistic indecency of writing about a writer, better I suppose about me than about you." The laughs continued through the 1970s when Updike kept up the charade of Henry Bech as real author by publishing bogus interviews between Bech and himself in *The New York Times.*

Yet, there is a serious tone to the laughter. The jokes about Bech may illustrate the appalling way America treats its authors, but Updike is just as concerned with the fate that dooms many American writers to lesser and lesser achievement. While the royalty checks jump to six figures and the talk-show appearances multiply, the quality of the writing diminishes. In 1974 Updike said in a speech, "Why Write?": "*To remain interested*–of American novelists, only Henry James continued in old age to advance his art."

How right he is–but only up to a point. Those who care about American fiction may now place Updike's name beside James's. The point is not that he rivals James but that, unlike Hawthorne and Melville,

2/9/70

~~RABBIT REDUX~~   POP/MOM/MOON

Men emerge *pale* from the little printing plant at four sharp, ghosts for an instant, blinking, ~~even in clean shirts looking into~~ until the outdoor light overcomes the ~~atmosphere~~ *air* of constant ~~blue~~ indoor light clinging to them. ~~They are pale from work.~~ In winter ~~the street~~ *Pine Street* at this hour is dark, darkness pressed down from the mountain that hangs above this stagnant city of Brewer, but now in summer the ~~mixed housefronts and hopeful porches wince~~ granite *curbs* starred with mica and the ~~housefronts of~~ *mixed row houses differentiated by speckled* bastard sidings and the hopeful ~~small porches~~ with their ~~milk-bottle boxes and their~~ *boxes for milk bottles* jigsaw brackets and ~~gray~~ *gray milk* ~~old people's chairs~~ and the gingko trees and the ~~hot~~ *baking* curbside cars wince beneath a brilliance like a frozen explosion. The city, attempting to revive its dying downtown, has torn away blocks of buildings to create parking lots, so that a desolate ~~rubbled-weedy~~ *weedy and rubbled,* openness, spills through the ~~once-packed~~ *once-packed* streets, exposing church façades ~~that~~ had never ~~been~~ seen *from* a distance and generating new perspectives of rear entryways and half-alleys and intensifying the cruel breadth of the light. The sky is cloudless yet colorless, hovering blanched humidity, in the way of these Pennsylvania summers, good for nothing but to make green things grow. Men don't even tan; *filmed by sweat they turn* yellow,

~~A man and his son.~~ *A man and his son,* Earl Angstrom and Harry, are among the printers released from work. ~~The father~~ *The father* Earl is near retirement, aged, a thin man with no excess left to him, his face washed empty by a river of grievances and caved in above the protruding slippage of bad false teeth. ~~Harry his~~ *The* son is five inches taller and fatter; ~~life still can take from him.~~ His prime is soft, somehow pale and sour.

Revised typescript page for the second novel (1971) of Updike's trilogy about Harry "Rabbit" Angstrom (Houghton Library, Harvard University)

unlike Twain and Hemingway, unlike, arguably, even Faulkner, Updike has continued to advance his art.

Henry Bech is not so lucky. In *Bech Is Back* irony irritates his life. Even enduring reputation smarts: "Though Henry Bech, the author, in his middle years had all but ceased to write, his books continued, as if ironically, to live, to cast shuddering shadows toward the center of his life, where that thing called his reputation cowered." This sentence begins the book, and one thinks immediately of Bech's fellow author J. D. Salinger. Salinger's silence seems noble. Rejecting the show-biz of big-time publishing, he may be writing his books only for himself. Bech's silence is more demeaning. Languishing in the success of his first novel, he is paralyzed by an old-fashioned writer's block. Silent before his public for almost fifteen years, Bech has become, to his dismay, a kind of myth.

Silence does not mean invisibility, however. If Americans cannot recognize true artists, they are proficient at worshiping stars. Rather than let Henry suffer privately from his inability to write, they send him around the world again to give the speech "The Cultural Situation of the American Writer" and inadvertently to act the patsy to third-world audiences who use literature for political ends.

Henry's travels are the slowest part of *Bech Is Back,* but the entire book is a delight. Rebounding, for example, from the disillusion of meeting an avid collector who hoards Bech's novels for their potential value on the rare-book market, Henry agrees for a price to sign his name to 28,500 of his books. Transported to a balmy island for the chore and ministered to by his mistress, Bech confronts a stunning silence: he cannot even write his own name.

When he finally does dodge the spotlight for a moment and inches his way toward true literary recognition, he is selected for, of all things, the Melville Medal, "awarded every five years to that American author who has maintained the most meaningful silence." This kind of humor sparkles throughout *Bech Is Back.* Success, it seems, is unavoidable. Marrying his mistress's sister and moving to her family home in Ossining, New York, he gives in to his wife's nudges to free his blocked inspiration with pep talks, changes the working title of his novel in progress from *Think Big* to *Easy Money,* and accepts the degradation of advertising's stranglehold on literature when Madison Avenue turns the book into a best-seller. "Bech is back," scream the hucksters, but, Henry and Updike muse, at what cost? Lionized as the latest rage, surrounded by New York's prettiest at a gaudy white-on-white party, he closes with a word that typifies the entire experience: "unclean."

For all Bech's troubles, however, one hopes that he will rebound again in ten years or so. For Updike has more to say about the paradox that afflicts writers: their craving for applause and their need for privacy. The conflict between easy money and noble silence is deadly to American artists. Rather than pontificate about this cultural trap in ponderous essays, Updike uses sharp wit and evocative prose to create a memorable character who lives the dilemma.

Standing between the silent but articulate Bech and the questing but inarticulate Rabbit are Updike's family novels (*The Centaur* and *Of the Farm,* 1965); his marriage novels (*Couples,* 1968; *A Month of Sundays; Marry Me: A Romance,* 1976; and *The Witches of Eastwick*); and his unexpected novel about language and Africa (*The Coup*). Updike has occasionally named the award-winning *The Centaur* his favorite. One can see why. Beautifully written and imaginatively conceived, *The Centaur* is an homage to his father, Wesley Updike, who sacrificed his own dreams to keep his family together during the disruptive trauma of the Great Depression.

Interestingly, Updike originally thought of *The Centaur* as a contrasting companion to *Rabbit, Run.* Both novels suggest that the threat of death can be defined as a loss of grace before an onslaught of the mundane yet overwhelming details that any head of a family faces in his daily routine; but, whereas Harry scampers from drudgery in pursuit of "it," George Caldwell plods painfully through the snow to escort his teenaged son Peter back home. Harry is a rabbit while Caldwell is a horse, and the story of his sacrifice is a modern tale of heroism.

Told from Peter's perspective when he is a middle-aged, second-rate painter in New York, *The Centaur* develops in a complicated manner along two parallel lines of narration. The first is the realistic level as Peter recalls his high-school days in Olinger, Pennsylvania, and the agony that his mocked and martyred father suffers while teaching science to uncaring clods. The second is the mythic level as Peter adapts the Greek tale of Chiron, the centaur injured in war but beloved by Zeus, to highlight Caldwell's heroism. Dreading the shrinking of his future by the dispiriting grind of the high school and the destruction of his body by disease, Caldwell bravely yet comically bumbles his way through the day, unselfishly giving himself, unaware that the unruly students love him. Mocked, jeered, and metaphorically shot through the ankle with the "arrow" of laughter, Caldwell rarely challenges his duty and never dodges his fate.

The primary question in the novel, then, is not whether Caldwell will succumb to routine duties but whether Peter will step toward a creative life. Updike's style works its magical best in *The Centaur* as Peter's reminiscence transforms ancient Olympus into modern Olinger via lyrical descriptions of love, uncertainty, and fear. The epigraph from Karl Barth once again recalls Updike's insistence on the tenet of belief, and at the end of the novel George Caldwell trudges back through the snow toward his high school in order to guarantee the stability his son needs while growing up. Peter's narration is both an expression of gratitude and his greatest "painting," and the reader suspects that Peter is ready now to break out of his skepticism, ready now to live.

Of the Farm is the companion novel to *The Centaur*. Although the characters' names are changed, the situations are similar: both novels explore how a middle-aged son comes to terms with an aging parent who has personal myths of the family's past. The focus in *Of the Farm,* however, is on the mother, and Mrs. Robinson (whose husband is named George) is one of Updike's most intricately conceived characters. Strong, willful, jealous, brave, and afraid, Mrs. Robinson is an old woman who fears that death will beckon before her grown son, Joey, can fulfill the myth that she has dreamed for him and that he resists. She has set her life on his becoming a poet and a protector of her farm, but Joey has fled her distorting myth for a career in advertising and the concrete of New York. This short but highly charged novel is a psychological thriller that takes place during one weekend when Joey brings his second wife, Peggy, and his stepson to the farm for Mrs. Robinson's blessing.

He does not get it. In many ways *Of the Farm* is about the failure of forgiveness: Joey blames his mother for ruining his first marriage and threatening his second; Mrs. Robinson blames Peggy for enticing her son beyond poetry and the farm with the lure of uninhibited sexuality; and Peggy blames Mrs. Robinson for destroying Joey's father by forcing him to move to the lonely farm.

Framing these crosscurrents of guilt and fear is the counterpoint between the weakness of the son's resolve and the strength of the mother's myth. Joey admits that he is weak, that he has turned to Peggy's earthy sexuality as a substitute for the farm: "My wife is a field." Yet, he also understands the force of his mother's ability to reshape her past to accommodate her present. Trapped within her warping myth of the farm as a "people sanctuary," he falls victim once again and betrays Peggy to Mrs. Robinson's disparaging dismissal. Listening to a sermon in which the minister quotes Barth on the notion that women are "an appeal to the kindness of Man," Joey must realize that he has fallen short. Unlike Peter Caldwell in *The Centaur,* he cannot use the proven glory of his command

of words (the novel itself) to illuminate the potential glory of his own life.

Updike's marriage novels continue his probing of the relationship between the physical and the spiritual, but in these particular books he wonders whether sexuality can fill the void left by the decline of faith in the "post-pill paradise." In the short story "The Music School" (*The Music School*), for example, the narrator muses, "We are all pilgrims, faltering toward divorce." Separation seems the ironic goal of Updike's married couples. But the reader should understand that, although adultery is a consequence, unbridled sensuality is not the issue. Like Rabbit and Bech, the men in these novels fear for the loss of their souls, and, when they fail to find assurance in religion, they look to the carnal for the promise that they will never die.

The fate of Piet Hanema in *Couples* is an example. A builder who, like Hook, appreciates the strength of Calvinism and the permanence of fine carpentry, Piet becomes afraid when he suspects the inability of contemporary religious practices to hold back the darkness of his doubt. Thus when he abandons wife Angela (angel) for mistress Foxy (animal), he knows that his search for love triggers his fall to the world. Like the falls suffered by Hawthorne's characters (for example, in *The Marble Faun,* 1860), however, his plunge from grace may mean the fulfillment of his humanity. Piet's predicament is the most complex of the various adulteries in *Couples,* and the novel itself is Updike's most detailed evocation of the microcosm of the middle-class suburb. The reader must thus be careful to keep the lyrical descriptions of sex from obscuring the seriousness of Updike's concern for the ineffectuality of religion.

Updike's uncertainty about the value of Piet's effort is reflected in *Marry Me: A Romance,* a novel that exchanges the realism of *Couples* for the fable of Hawthorne, for what the earlier author called "romance." Clearly not meant to be realistic, *Marry Me* proposes three illusory endings to Jerry Conant's adulterous affair with Sally, but in each case Jerry is still searching for assurance—be it spiritual or physical—that his life matters. Exclaiming that "I am married to my death," he cannot understand his wife Ruth's calm in the face of mortality. Neither can he understand how Ruth's own adulterous affair causes her blossoming as a woman. Although relatively slight as a novel, *Marry Me* includes, in Ruth, Updike's finest portrait of a woman. She, too, remains trapped by the Puritan insistence on the separation of the body and the soul, and her quest for love and selfhood parallels Jerry's quest for faith.

If *Marry Me* is the slightest of the marriage novels and *Couples* the most famous, *A Month of Sundays* is the most important. It is also the most difficult, the most comic, and the most ignored. Once again openly bow-

Updike in his office above the Dolphin Restaurant in Ipswich, Massachusetts, in 1972

ing to Hawthorne, Updike places his minister, Tom Marshfield (the echo of Dimmesdale is clear), in an omega-shaped motel in the desert to which he has been banished for seducing his organist, and in which he is to write a journal about his spiritual recovery. Marshfield has as much trouble with the intransigence of his language as with the flimsiness of his vows, and much of the comedy in this rich novel derives from the inadvertent puns and Freudian slips that he finds himself writing. Language, suggests Updike, is just as troubling to master as faith, and *A Month of Sundays* is on one level a novel about an author writing a novel in which the novelist is the main character.

The comedy also has its serious side, for Marshfield is another of Updike's Barthian believers. Armed with his faith and aware of the weakness of his flesh, the wayward minister is convinced (as is Updike) that body and soul must be reunited if belief is to survive in a secular world. He pursues this conviction through a progression of often specious theological speculations and a longing for physical contact with women. His final affair with the mysteriously silent Ms.

Prynne (a modern Hester) signals his success, and the novel ends with a serious prayer shaped by a comic embrace of the flesh.

A decade after *A Month of Sundays,* Updike published two novels that, when added to that work, comprise his trilogy on Hawthorne's *The Scarlet Letter* (1850). In *Roger's Version* (1986) and *S.* (1988) he reimagines Roger Chillingworth and Hester Prynne from a late-twentieth-century perspective. *Roger's Version* is especially challenging because of its focus on the antagonism between computer technology and theology.

Those readers who regard Updike as only the deft describer of suburban sexuality and prayerful flight should recall his careerlong fascination with science. From the astonishing first chapter of *The Centaur,* through the poem "Midpoint" (1969), to the collection *Facing Nature,* Updike has argued that, while science may be a metaphor for the mystery of creation, it is not a substitute for faith. In *Roger's Version* he offers a dazzling display of arcane knowledge that takes shape around the proposition that "wherever theology touches science, it gets burned." To, one suspects, the secret joy of most humanists, the person who gets burned in this novel is a computer freak.

Epigraphs from Karl Barth and Kierkegaard suggest not only that Updike is calling on past thinkers whose intellectual complexities have echoed throughout his work but also that he is setting a confrontation between faith and reason. To his usual interplay of sex, sin, and salvation, he adds the murky theories of science. One thinks immediately of Hawthorne's Aylmer ("The Birthmark," 1843) and Rappaccini ("Rappaccini's Daughter," 1844).

The Reverend Roger (that is, Chillingworth) Lambert, professor in a divinity school, prefers the sanctuary to the laboratory. As he says, "It is very important for my mental wellbeing that I keep my thoughts directed away from areas of contemplation that might entangle me." But entangled he becomes with the introduction of Dale (that is, Dimmesdale) Kohler, a research assistant in the computer lab. Roger tells his tale with a droll self-irony that enhances his wit and extols his modesty. No self-righteous fundamentalist, he is skeptical and irreverent, but he does believe. His faith in "the Lord's unsleeping witness and strict accountancy" has little patience with the crass zeroes and ones of a mainframe computer.

Yet Dale, himself one of the faithful, thinks that he can use computers to prove God's existence, and he needs Roger's help in securing a grant to support his research. Wondering whether the proof of reason will diminish the mystery of faith, Roger suspects that to reveal God's face is to eliminate God's majesty. (Updike's original title for the novel was "Majesty.") Thus Updike explores the ancient dilemma of humanity's need to know and its fear of knowledge, and he asks an equally ancient question: is religious faith stronger when long-held beliefs are protected from scrutiny or when they are subjected to challenge? Why, asks Roger, should he revere a God who allows himself to be "intellectually trapped"? Lambert knows his Barth: such a God would not be God. But he also argues that universities should fund something more "substantial than black or feminist studies," and thus he ostensibly backs Dale's project while indirectly teaching Dale a hard lesson: that the formulas of science are no match for the unreason of faith.

But this is an Updike novel; domestic crises also matter: Roger's wife Esther (that is, Hester) is bored. Like many of Updike's women, Esther is a nonbeliever. Domestic disaster masks religious uncertainty because God, Updike insists, blesses the flesh as well as the spirit. Updike dovetails these various strands confidently, convincingly, and comically. When, for example, Roger calls on Tertullian's ancient opinion that carnal attraction does not threaten religious belief and that flesh does not oppose soul, he illustrates Updike's interest in America's disturbing need to separate body and spirit.

Comic, troubling, and erudite, *Roger's Version* is Updike's most intellectually challenging novel. In addition to Barth and Kierkegaard, Updike refers to, among others, Friedrich Nietzsche, Gian Bernini, Lucretius, Martin Luther, Marcion, Thomas Aquinas, Paul Dirac, Albert Einstein, Paul Tillich, Ludwig Wittgenstein, Ferdinand de Saussure, Dietrich Bonhoeffer, and Charles Darwin as well as the physics of the Big Bang Theory, Boolean algebra, and Christian heresies. Hawthorne would have been pleased.

Hawthorne's Hester finds her contemporary voice in S. Updike has explained that *S.* is an effort to placate feminist detractors of his canon by celebrating "a woman on the move." Yet, as Sarah Worth, the forty-two-year-old discontented heroine, flees the rich life of her patriarchal, philandering husband, she moves from gaudy materialism to Asian spiritualism in such a rush that she unconsciously personifies feminism gone delightfully wacky. Sarah descends from the Prynnes and bears a daughter named Pearl, but she wants no part of Hester's stateliness and reserve in public. Where Hester is unusually quiet, S. (Sarah) is usually talking— or writing, one should say: *S.* is an epistolary novel built on Sarah's lively letters to her husband, daughter, mother, hairdresser, and dentist.

S. begins her rebellion by moving out of her present and into her future, resentful of her husband of twenty-two years and of all the "dark unheeding illegible male authority." American women, she complains, are raised to enjoy "the smell of a man in the house." Updike's grin is delightfully wide as he details Sarah's swing from an American love of things to a religious pursuit of spirit. For Updike refers again to arcane theology, and thus he understands that chasing the spirit means enjoying the erotic: "Ego is the enemy," S. preaches; "love is the goal." Love, she decides, may be found by joining an arhat's religious commune in Arizona, and she fills her letters with the exotic words of Eastern worship while she dresses in "love colors" and helps build an eyesore called the Hall of Millionfold Joys.

The reader soon realizes that Updike's voluptuous S. is much more sexually active than Hawthorne's voluptuous Hester. Much of the fun of this witty novel comes from following Sarah's account of her pilgrimage to what she hopes is the perfect theological blending of active body and prayerful spirit. Her arhat asks, for example, whether she has "any venereal disease and how much money was I bringing to the Treasury of Enlightenment." Updike's bemused tone undercuts the illusion of blissful freedom for

Dust jacket for Updike's 1976 novel, which includes one of his most fully realized depictions of a female character

female or male, and, unlike *S.*, the reader understands that the arhat lusts after both women and cash. Some of the wittiest moments are shaped in letters that *S.* types for the bogus spiritual leader and that expose his oily methods of soliciting funds. Alluding to the religious scandals of Jim Bakker and Jimmy Swaggert, *S.* is as timely as it is funny. Religion sells, and in America a sucker is born every minute. *S.* is one of those suckers. She even defends the arhat's nationwide chain of "regional meditation and massage centers." The reader waits, of course, for the moment when the arhat lures her to his lair.

Although a Christian believer, Updike is no puritan. He is amused by Sarah's diatribe against "the Atrophied Puritan theology" that has, she insists, conspired for centuries against the liberation of women. Trying to free her willing body from the outdated Christian notion of Eve as defiler, she explains feminine power convincingly. Yet, her naive belief in total freedom and in a huckster who builds a residence "Park" for the faithful suggests that her independence is an illusion.

As if she were aware of Updike's final joke in *The Witches of Eastwick* when the divorced women remarry, *S.* is horrified to learn that her daughter plans to drop out of college and marry a man. Men and women, it seems, need each other. Worse, she discovers that the arhat from India is really Art from Massachusetts. Her lesson takes hold: "Follow the fashion and trust biology to override culture." One assumes she means that gender politics is finally sterile. "We all have a number of skins," writes *S.*, "especially women . . . because society makes us wriggle more." At the end Sarah has wriggled herself into a tentative freedom with money and goodies to spare. *S.* is Updike's funniest novel, a meditation on the unexpected combination of American femininity and spiritual grace.

The comedy is even more audacious in *The Witches of Eastwick*, a novel that lacks the weight of *A Month of Sundays* and *Roger's Version* but that extends Updike's novelistic experiments beyond his earlier commitment to realism. The magic realism of such Latin American masters as Carlos Fuentes, Gabriel García Márquez, and Isabel Allende is in the background. Tennis balls turn into furry things, and suburban witches cast a spell of adultery, but the novel is finally a celebration of duty and art. The time is the late 1960s; the place is Rhode Island; and the witches are three thirty-ish mothers who have divorced their husbands in the name of womanhood and freedom. Updike's sense of history sets the frame. Famous at its founding as a refuge for liberal believers looking to escape the rigors of Massachusetts Puritanism, Rhode Island was once described by Cotton Mather as the "fag end of creation." Anne Hutchinson, banished to Rhode Island in 1637, hoped to found a covenant of grace there, but today's witches of Eastwick have established instead a coven of transgression.

Jane, Sukie, and Alexandra shrink from the word *man* as an "assertive" noun that can negate the peaceful aura of a calm morning. *Man* carries such dreary connotations for the three divorced women that they deny witchhood to a friend merely because she still has a husband. "Magic," writes Updike, "occurs all around us as nature seeks and finds the inevitable forms," and for much of the novel the inevitable form for the three liberated witches is freedom from "the armor of patriarchal protector" in the hope of indulging the fecundity women think they will find when single.

Alexandra, for example, becomes a witch when, in her middle thirties, she realizes she has a right to exist, not as "an afterthought and companion–a bent rib," and thus less than a man, but as "the mainstay of the continuing Creation, as the daughter of a daughter." Her initial tricks are often the result of "maternal wrath," and she argues that "a conspiracy of women upholds the world."

If all this sounds good to today's housewife, consider Updike's irony: becoming a witch frees Alexandra only from the obligations of wearing high-heeled shoes and controlling her weight. Blooming selfhood has its foolish extremes, too. As the narrator wryly says, "This was an era of many proclaimed rights." Updike's bemused tone directs the first half of the novel: "Being divorced in a small town is a little like playing Monopoly; eventually you land on all the properties."

In the post-Christian era, promiscuity is no more than a game. The only burnings these witches suffer are a hot bath with a ridiculous devil and the tongues of indignant opinion. Although these women are a long way from Mather's scorched victims, they initially earn Updike's concern as well as his laughter. When frustrated housewives receive Tofrinal from doctors and suspect advice from ministers, domestic rebellion is just around the next corner, coming home with the children.

The complications begin when Darryl Van Horne, an unmarried, monied musician and dabbler in science, moves to Eastwick. In the waning 1960s, a time the narrator calls "this hazy late age of declining doctrine," the wealthy lord of the underworld easily makes his way. He may be ineffective and vulgar, but he fascinates the locals. Van Horne is, after all, their dark prince, the odd defiler who does not bother with God.

Updike finally sympathizes not with the sexy witches and their mysterious mentor but with the anonymous citizens who plod "through their civic and Christian duties." While Van Horne sardonically collects the "permanized garbage" of the culture as mocking works of sculpture, the dutiful suburbanites have to live with the junk. The devil in the novel is not godless science but ministers who exchange belief for the latest college course, dropouts who do not wash and cannot think, and wives who save the world but ruin their homes.

The Witches of Eastwick laughs at these absurdities until a murder and suicide change the tone. Satire and sadness mix. Updike has written a novel of ebb and flow, spring and fall, life and death; a novel in which evil seems so potent that nothing can combat it except art. In an age of little faith, Johann Sebastian Bach counts for more than war protesters, Paul Cézanne for more than politics. Love, too, matters. The witches regain humanity when they find new husbands.

Updike's commitment to art and duty reaches a comic climax in *The Coup*. Africa has long been for Updike "an invitation to the imagination": "I've always been attracted to hidden corners." Drawing on that strange land as "the emptiest part of the world I could think of," he made *The Coup* a novel with noticeable

though not dramatic differences from his other fiction. The most obvious difference is that the land of Kush is a long way from the lawns of suburbia. In addition, *The Coup* has a comic tone sustained largely by the sardonic observations of the narrator, Colonel Hakim Felix Ellelloû. Ellelloû describes Kush, for example, as a constitutional monarchy "with the constitution suspended and the monarch deposed." Among Kush's natural resources, which seem largely to be comprised of drought and desert, is what Ellelloû calls "the ample treasury of diseases." Finally, the narrator's conscious manipulation of narrative voice is distinctive in the Updike canon. Colonel Ellelloû, the recently ousted president of Kush, tells of his presidency primarily in the third person even while he is much aware of the first person who experienced the events. A narrator watching his own presence in the tale, he interrupts his story, for example, to comment on how his manuscript is blurred in places by a wet ring from a glass of Fanta.

Part of the comedy, then, results from Ellelloû's distancing himself from himself with the device of third-person narration and yet relying on first person when convenient: "There are two selves: the one who acts, and the 'I' who experiences. This latter is passive even in a whirlwind of the former's making, passive and guiltless and astonished. The historical performer bearing the name Ellelloû was no less mysterious to me than to the American press." The point is that Ellelloû writes his story as much to find out who he is, to distinguish public mask from private man, as to explain the coup that has forced him to take up his pen. He understands now that the "he" carried the "I" here and there, and that the "I" never knew why but submitted. As a result, the "I" suffers the effects of the "he's" actions. A man of disguises and anonymous travels throughout Kush, he is a leader whose "domicilic policy is apparently to be in no place at any specific time." Even his languages are "clumsy masks" that "his thoughts must put on."

Ellelloû is a mystical leader without pragmatic talent because he believes primarily in "the idea of Kush." Yet one of his problems is that his obsession with his country is but the other side of his distrust of the world, an obsession that nurtures his determination to burn food offered by bungling America while his people go hungry. A true son of the Third World, he understands how gifts bring humans who in turn bring oppression, but his hatred of America is comically undercut by the clichés of revolution in his speeches. In light of the childish rhetoric of the Iranian revolution, Updike's portrait of the Islamic nationalist is especially interesting. America, for example, is "that fountainhead of obscenity and glut," but in Kush "the land itself is for-

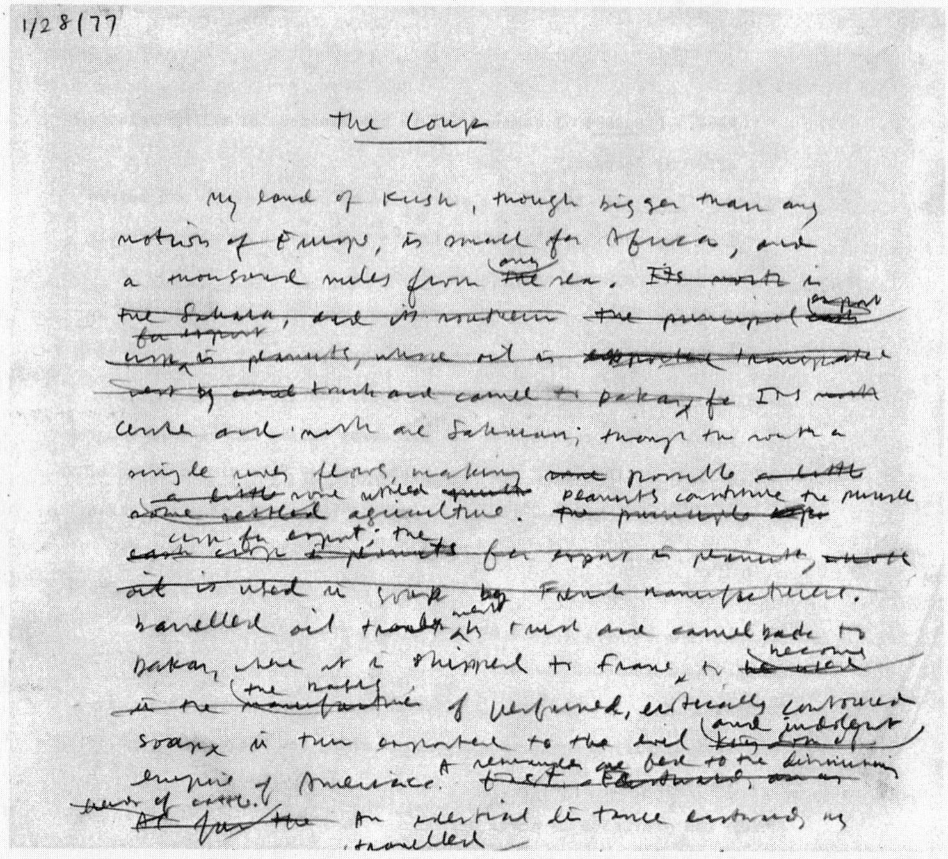
1/28/77

The Coup

My land of Kush, though bigger than any nation of Europe, is small for Africa, and a thousand miles from any sea.

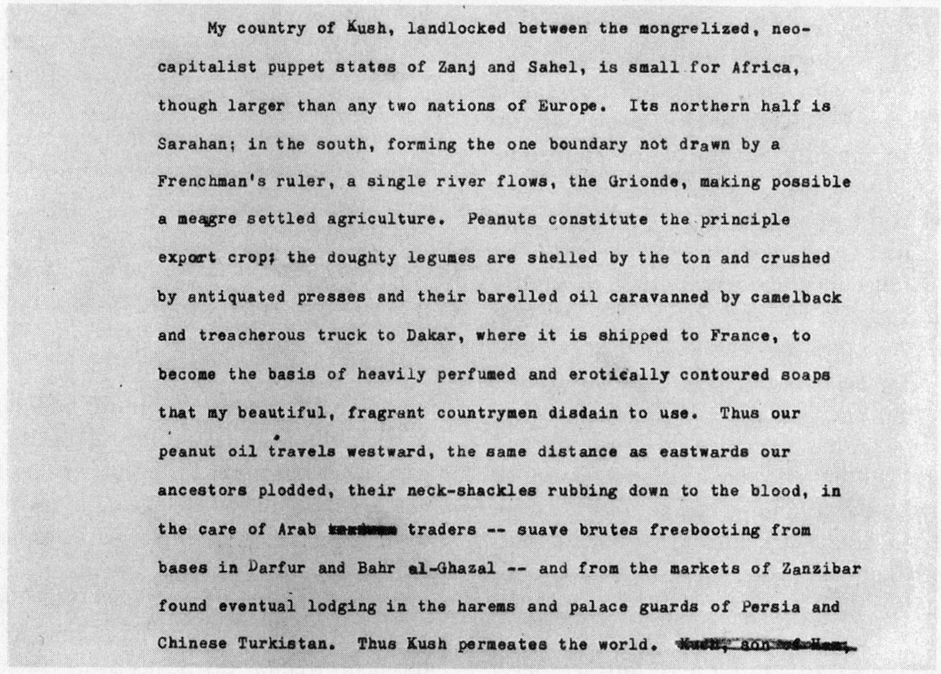
My country of Kush, landlocked between the mongrelized, neo-capitalist puppet states of Zanj and Sahel, is small for Africa, though larger than any two nations of Europe. Its northern half is Sarahan; in the south, forming the one boundary not drawn by a Frenchman's ruler, a single river flows, the Grionde, making possible a meagre settled agriculture. Peanuts constitute the principle export crop; the doughty legumes are shelled by the ton and crushed by antiquated presses and their barelled oil caravanned by camelback and treacherous truck to Dakar, where it is shipped to France, to become the basis of heavily perfumed and erotically contoured soaps that my beautiful, fragrant countrymen disdain to use. Thus our peanut oil travels westward, the same distance as eastwards our ancestors plodded, their neck-shackles rubbing down to the blood, in the care of Arab ~~[illegible]~~ traders -- suave brutes freebooting from bases in Darfur and Bahr al-Ghazal -- and from the markets of Zanzibar found eventual lodging in the harems and palace guards of Persia and Chinese Turkistan. Thus Kush permeates the world. ~~Kush, son of Ham,~~

Pages from two early drafts for Updike's 1978 novel (Houghton Library, Harvard University)

getful, an evaporating pan out of which all things human rise into blue invisibility."

The first meeting between Ellelloû and a goodwill bureaucrat from America is simultaneously ludicrous and pointed. Updike's two-pronged satire of the misguided American gift of a mountain of Trix cereal and potato chips to drought-stricken Kushites and of the indignant Ellelloû, who burns both the junk food and the bureaucrat, is a comic set piece that underscores how America's mindless need to be loved and the Third World's rigid ideology clash while people starve. One is reminded of Updike's earlier story "I Am Dying, Egypt, Dying" (*Museums and Women*) with its portrait of the benign, rich American who cannot return the affection he seeks.

The comedy of this ideological sparring match depends on the speech of the antagonists. Full of pop slang and bureaucratese, the American urges, "These cats are *starving*. The whole world knows it, you can see 'em starve on the six o'clock news every night. The American people want to help. We know this country's socialist and xenophobic." Ellelloû's response is little better: "Offer your own blacks freedom before you pile boxes of carcinogenic trash on the holy soil of Kush!" Updike's control of speech tones and language is so superb in *The Coup* that in one sense language itself is the hero of the novel.

Style is the triumph of *The Coup*, the primary means by which Updike makes fun not only of America's need to help despite its vexation by Vietnam and President Richard Nixon but also indirectly of President Jimmy Carter's fortune in peanuts. Typical of the comic tone is the following comment by one of Ellelloû's advisers when he learns that the national fad of dieting in America has caused a drop in consumption of peanut butter and a corresponding increase in the exporting of peanuts: "Nothing more clearly advertises the American decline and coming collapse than this imperative need, contrary to all imperialist principles, to export raw materials." The laughter cuts both ways, for American peanuts on the open market threaten Kush's own crop of peanuts, which it must sell to purchase Czech dynamos. Updike understands that the intricacies of shifting political alliances often depend upon the supply of hardly strategic items such as peanut oil, so he creates Ellelloû, an African revolutionary educated in America, a leader who despises that country as a meddling superparanoid, to personify these contradictions that may be ridiculous but are nevertheless lethal.

Longing to find a mystical cause for Kush's deprivation, Ellelloû travels the country only to collide with his Americanized side in a metropolis of McDonald's and Coke. On his final journey through Kush, he stumbles into a surprise: a bustling, illegal city named for him. Drugstores sell deodorant ("God sees the soul; men smell the flesh"), women wear miniskirts and halters, and the people go Western. Ready capital and comfort undermine Spartan tradition and myth. In this plastic town, with its commitment to upward mobility and declining quality, Ellelloû discovers that he is considered the curse on Kush. The coup achieved, he takes refuge as a short-order cook and parking attendant, searching the newspapers for news of himself, before accepting exile in France to write *The Coup*. The last lines reemphasize his dual narrative perspective: "He is writing his memoirs. No, I should put it more precisely: Colonel Ellelloû is rumored to be working on his memoirs."

Black Muslims, prejudiced whites, "double-speak" bureaucrats, liberal college students, revolutionary Africans, dull Russians—all are targets for Updike's comic darts. His love for caricatures and parodies, for James Thurber and Max Beerbohm, once manifested in his boyhood desire to draw cartoons for *The New Yorker*, works itself out in *The Coup*.

A similar comedy of politics and language informs *Memories of the Ford Administration* (1992). In 1974, at the beginning of the Gerald Ford presidency, Updike published *Buchanan Dying*, the most curious but least read of his many books. A closet drama in three acts with an eighty-page afterword, *Buchanan Dying* chronicles the presidency of James Buchanan, Updike's fellow Pennsylvanian. Updike claims the play remains "my favorite among my books." The statement appears to be accurate, for Buchanan reappears in *Memories of the Ford Administration* as the obsession of the narrator, Alfred Clayton.

A history professor at Wayward Junior College, Clayton receives a request from an historians' association for his memories of the Ford era. He obliges, but accounts of both his domestic chaos and his scholarly research on Buchanan's doomed administration become entangled in his explanations of the sexually liberated 1970s associated with Ford. The result is a comic novel of such erudition as to confirm once again Updike's preeminence among contemporary American novelists.

Clayton's rationalization to the historians who solicit his analysis of Ford is that he hopes not to rehabilitate but to reanimate Buchanan. One of Updike's jokes, however, is that the narrator becomes more sedentary as Buchanan becomes more lively. Stories tend to consume storytellers. Thus part of the fun of *Memories of the Ford Administration* is its occasional self-reflexivity, its use of footnotes and asides to the reader to document not only the difficulty of writing but also the proximity of history and fiction.

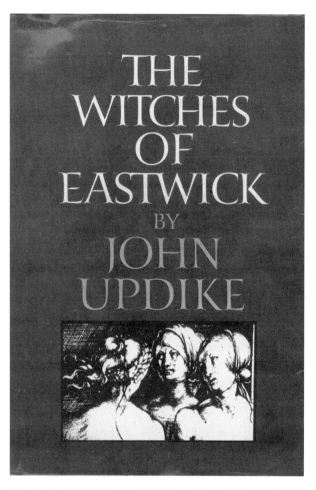

Dust jacket for Updike's comedic 1984 novel, in which three suburban Rhode Island women become sorceresses in the 1960s

blessing—the discredited academic fad known as deconstruction, and his struggle to complete both his book and his memoirs shows not only that history is narrative but also that reconstruction of the past is infinitely more important than deconstruction of texts.

Updike's subject, as always, is the mystery of America. Like Buchanan before the disaster of the Civil War, and like Ford after the near disaster of Watergate, he ponders the national quandary: "Our American problem is, we have land and climate enough for a number of nations, and seek to be only one." Updike succeeds admirably in the daunting task of counterpointing the formal vocabulary of Buchanan's nineteenth-century American oratory and the informal speech rhythms of Clayton's contemporary slang, and he does not hesitate to mock his own ornate style to illustrate humanity's tendency to embroider the historical record: "the careless desperate cascade of Mankind's enormous annals." The accounts of Buchanan's meetings with Andrew Jackson and Hawthorne are Updike's gems of historical reconstruction. Yet, the value of *Memories of the Ford Administration* is finally its concern with language, humanity's primary means of communication. Late in the novel the narrator muses, "When . . . what we strive to achieve has been undone by history, the words we write remain, and will plead for us." Updike's artist figures—Marshfield, Roger, Sarah Worth, Ellelloû, and Clayton among them—know this truth.

In *Brazil* (1994) Updike revisits the magic realism that he employed with irreverent glee in *The Witches of Eastwick*. He explains in the afterword that he used sources by authors as varied as Claude Lévi-Strauss, Theodore Roosevelt, Clarice Lispector, and Elizabeth Bishop, but it is fair to say that *Brazil* is less historical romance than a tale of consuming romantic love that embraces fantasy. Taking the doomed love of Tristan and Iseult for his cultural frame, Updike creates black and poor Tristao and white and wealthy Isabel as lovers determined to overcome the limitations of race and class. They fail insofar as Tristao's murder severs their physical relationship, but they triumph insofar as their love fires them to contest the prohibitions that contemporary society places on such a union.

Readers of *Brazil* would do well to refer to the chapter in *Self-Consciousness: Memoirs* (1989) titled "A Letter to My Grandsons." Writing a family history for his two grandsons of African descent via their father, Updike begins, "We are all of mixed blood." This truth informs the entirety of *Brazil,* which begins "Black is a shade of brown. So is white, if you look." Using the freedoms of magic realism, Updike sends the lovers through not only the realistic details of contemporary Brazil but also the exotic layers of Brazilian

The breakup of the family unit during what Clayton calls the "paradise of the flesh" in the Ford administration parallels the shattering of the Union under Buchanan. Skillfully detailing his familiar subject matter of husband, wife, mistress, and child, Updike suggests—albeit humorously—that Clayton's refusal to choose between wife and mistress reflects Buchanan's failure to embrace either South or North. "There is a civilized heroism to indecision," explains Clayton.

No wonder, then, that Clayton cannot finish his study of Buchanan. Satirizing scholarship even as he shows off his own research with an astonishing re-creation of America on the eve of the Civil War, Updike smiles at lesser mortals who cannot turn research into narrative, history into action. Intermingling direct quotations from Buchanan's papers, Clayton's unfinished book on Buchanan, and Clayton's memories of the Ford years, Updike implies that all history is fiction. Clayton writes from the perspective of 1992, and he has as much trouble remembering Ford as refashioning Buchanan. He mocks—with, one understands, Updike's

history. Tristao and Isabel's love even takes them beyond the colonial past of Brazil to the magical, numinous world of its first inhabitants. The more they love, the more they are transformed until, in the most astonishing feat of fantasy in the novel, they exchange race: Isabel becomes black, Tristao white. A love letter to his black grandsons, *Brazil* is also Updike's dream of a multicultural America.

In the Beauty of the Lilies (1996) features the probing of cultural and family history illustrated by *Brazil* and "A Letter to My Grandsons." It also recalls such earlier Updike short stories as "Son" (*Problems and Other Stories*) and "The Family Meadow" (*The Music School*) in which he ponders the heavy weight of familial antecedents. The title, of course, is taken from "The Battle Hymn of the Republic" (1862), and Updike has described this famous line as "in its surreal sadness summing up a world of Protestant estrangement." Although *In the Beauty of the Lilies* chronicles the persistent and, it would seem, irreversible decline of religious faith in American culture, it also details the fall of America itself.

Magisterial in its profundity, *In the Beauty of the Lilies* is Updike's homage to his country at the end of the millennium. Indeed, the novel concludes with an apocalypse that recalls the tragedy of a religious cult in Waco, Texas, but it begins in 1910. Investigating what has become known as "the American century," Updike focuses on one family to trace America's slide from grace. The Reverend Clarence Wilmot, a Presbyterian minister in a middle-class town, abruptly suffers a loss of faith, "a visceral surrender, a set of dark sparkling bubbles escaping upward." Readers should consult Updike's essay in *Self-Consciousness* titled "On Being a Self Forever," for his personal insistence on a lifelong pursuit of faith offers an informative frame for Wilmot's shock of recognition. Reverend Wilmot is based on Updike's grandfather Harley Updike, who also abandoned the ministry, but *In the Beauty of the Lilies* soars beyond family history to examine an entire culture.

In much of Updike's fiction, theology and love provide the interface that structures the tale, but the interface of *In the Beauty of the Lilies* is composed of theology and of movies and television. When God retires, the images manufactured by the visual media rush in to fill the void. Intimations of this cultural disaster were present at the dawn of the century, as Updike shows when he begins the novel with an account of D. W. Griffith directing the film *The Call to Arms* with Mary Pickford, but in that era of relative faith few people heeded the portent. Tracing four generations of the Wilmot family from the moment that Reverend Wilmot's fall intersects with Hollywood's rise, Updike meticulously and lyrically chronicles the specific details of

American life in the twentieth century. The novel is so well informed and so well written that it earns George Steiner's tribute in *The New Yorker* (11 March 1996): "John Updike's genius, his place beside Hawthorne and Nabokov have never been more assured, or chilling."

Toward the End of Time (1997) is the companion piece to *In the Beauty of the Lilies*. Whereas the latter reprises the American century from the perspective of the end of the millennium, the former imagines America in the year 2020. It is not a pretty picture. Set after a war of annihilation between China and the United States, *Toward the End of Time* describes the life of an upper-middle-class American suburbanite after the world has irrevocably changed. Despite its somber premise, however, the novel mixes fantasy and humor as Updike takes his aging narrator, Ben Turnbull, through the ravages of the future.

The title refers to Updike's long interest in cosmology, quantum physics, and theories of the existence of parallel time; thus Updike moves Ben "backward" to debate theology with St. Paul and "forward" to the comical moment when civil security in a postapocalyptic world is guaranteed by FedEx. As Ben says, "I split—so it feels—into a number of disinterested parties." The novel is similarly "split" into a series of elegant meditations on love, theology, science, and the arcane mysteries of natural processes (which recall *Facing Nature*). Some readers might complain that Ben's musings overpower the other characters. Yet, *Toward the End of Time* is not meant to be a realistic tale. It is, rather, Updike's most erudite novel since *Roger's Version,* an astonishingly learned treatise on the mystery of mortality.

Despite the triumphs of his African novel, his reconstruction of James Buchanan, and his millennial meditations, Updike remains fascinated primarily by the intricate workings of the American family. His short stories illustrate that interest. Beginning with *The Same Door,* he has traced the changing curve of the stability of family life. Read as a whole, his short-story volumes offer a social commentary on American domesticity since mid century, and, while the prose is always lyrical and the observations always sharp, a tone of sadness—wistfulness—prevails. For Updike shows in his tales that the instability of the family reflects the shakiness of the nation, and the nostalgia associated with *The Same Door* and *Pigeon Feathers* finally gives way to the incisiveness of irony and the shadow of mortality in *Problems and Other Stories* and *Trust Me.*

An important example of family instability in *Problems and Other Stories* is the end of "Separating," where the father, Richard Maple, tells his oldest son about the impending divorce. When the son asks "Why," the query cuts Richard to the quick. Facing a

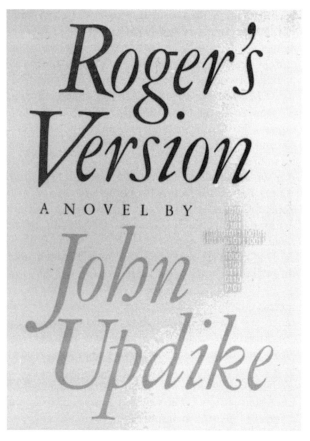

*Dust jacket for Updike's 1986 novel, in which he updates
Nathaniel Hawthorne's* The Scarlet Letter
(1850) for the computer age

darkness that is suddenly grim, he realizes that he has no answer: "*Why.* It was a whistle of wind in a crack, a knife thrust, a window thrown open on emptiness. The white face was gone, the darkness was featureless. Richard had forgotten why." Depicting that one lapse of memory, Updike dissects the breakdown of traditional values that seemed inviolable in the 1950s and became baffling in the 1970s. (The Maple stories are collected in *Too Far to Go,* 1979.) Paul Theroux in *The New York Times Book Review,* on 8 April 1979, writes, "Updike is one of the few people around who has given subtle expression to what others have dismissed and cheapened by assuming it is a nightmare." The point is well taken. No American author is currently writing about the mystery of family with such patience and grace as Updike.

Problems and Other Stories is largely a gathering of stories about such trauma. Teenaged sons criticize the rest of the family; daughters go away to live with red-bearded harpsichord makers; unhappy fathers forget why; and guilt creeps through suburbia. The stories were written from 1971 to 1978, a period of unsettling family conditions for Updike himself. Although the tales are not autobiography, the specter of domestic

loss, of love moving forward from all sides toward a contact barely reached, hovers around most of them. It is not that love is denied but that it is difficult to sustain. Updike supplies a definition in "Love Song, for a Moog Synthesizer": "Love must attach to what we cannot help–the involuntary, the telltale, the fatal. Otherwise, the reasonableness and the mercy that would make our lives decent and orderly would overpower love, crush it, root it out." These stories detail the problems suffered when the threats to love do not stay hidden behind the bedroom wall. As Updike writes in the author's note, "Seven years since my last short-story collection? There must have been problems . . . the collection as a whole, with the curve of sad time it subtends, is dedicated lovingly" to his children.

The plunge to domestic problems takes place immediately, for in "Commercial," the first story, Updike contrasts the manufactured familial snugness of a television commercial for natural gas with the calm, unspoken, and finally hesitant familial tension of a suburban home. "Commercial" is vintage Updike in many ways. Nothing "happens": a husband, having watched the ad for natural gas late at night, shuffles and urinates, tosses and turns, tries to doze. Yet, the reader knows that all is not well: the husband's fretfulness, the wife's sleepiness, the cold room. The little details are exact: the cat's need to go out, the noise of the hamster's wheel. The prose is exquisite: "The sharp bright wires of noise etched on darkness dull down into gray threads, an indistinct blanket." And the saving grace of comedy occurs here and there: "GRANDMOTHER-LINESS massages her from all sides, like the brushes of a car wash." Tone is finally all. In eight pages Updike conveys the bewilderment of sadness, the bleakness of loss. The implied question is, why cannot the long years of the man's domestic life equal the thirty seconds of the commercial's ideal family? The particulars behind this question are not important, but the final word of the story is "Nothing."

Other stories touch on the unspectacular but felt burden of religious belief in a secular community: the comic allegory "Minutes of the Last Meeting" and the thoughtful "Believers." "How to Love America and Leave It at the Same Time," a lyrical meditation reminiscent of the stories in *The Music School,* contrasts with Nabokov's satire of America's ubiquitous motels and fast-food restaurants in *Lolita* (1955): "America is a vast conspiracy to make you happy." The most unusual stories are "Augustine's Concubine," a meditation in defense of the saint's mistress that recalls the less successful "Four Sides of One Story" (*The Music School*), and "The Man Who Loved Extinct Mammals," a comic tale of the relationships between love and extinction that echoes "The Baluchitherium"

(*Museums and Women*) and has in it the following metaphor, an example of Updike's sparkling language: "And the child's voice, so sensible and simple up to this point, generated a catch, tears, premonitions of eternal loss; the gaudy parade of eternal loss was about to turn the corner, cymbals clanging, trombones triumphant, and enter her mind."

Except for the two stories about the Maple family, the finest tale in *Problems and Other Stories* is "The Gun Shop." With touches of *The Centaur*, "Home" (*Pigeon Feathers*), and "Leaving Church Early" (*Tossing and Turning*), "The Gun Shop" is a story of fathers and sons filled with the gestures of domestic particulars that Updike at his best details with delicacy and care. In this portrait of generations, in which the unnecessary tension caused by a grandson's disappointment with a malfunctioning .22 rifle is eased into harmony, Updike shows the ambiguities of love that bind grandfather, son, grandson, and surrogate father into a moment of communication free of the embarrassment that close proximity always nurtures.

"The Gun Shop" is not a lyrical meditation as are "Leaves" and "The Music School"; that is, dialogue, characterization, and pacing carry the burden instead of meditative prose. Yet, nuance takes the place of overt drama as Updike writes of the complications encountered when a country-bred but city-dwelling father brings his city-bred son back to the farmhouse of his parents. To the father the farm is a field of memories and echoes, but to the son it is a promise of experience: he is always permitted to shoot the old Remington .22 following Thanksgiving dinner. Updike focuses on the contrasts between the ways fathers handle sons. Aware that his tendency to respond to his son's distress with gentle irony is a reaction against his own father's embarrassing habit of good-humored acceptance, the father watches as the grandfather turns the boy's disappointment into the expectation of adventure. The grandfather knows just the man to fix the rifle.

Dutch, the gunsmith, is the hero of the tale, a man to be admired and loved, for although gruff, grimy, and direct, he is an artist with machine tools, a country-bred man who can both repair the firing pin and communicate with a stranger's boy familiar with the language of skiing and golf but not of gun shops. The father is out of place in the shop. Rejecting the grandfather's life of blundering forays and unexpected breakdowns, he has made his life in Boston a model of propriety and caution. He says all the wrong things in the gun shop, makes all the wrong gestures. The grandfather makes most of the right ones. With the insight of a man who is open to the world, the grandfather knows that the grandson is like Dutch and that even the father should have had Dutch for a parent. The rare combination of

love and skill emanates from the gunsmith. The story ends with the father remembering his childhood and the son firing the rifle. Pride and relief are heard in the father's final laugh. The irreconcilable tensions between generations of a family will never completely dissolve, but for the moment communication offers its balm.

None of these touches is forced, for "The Gun Shop" is a story not of commentary but of reverberation. Nor does the father have an epiphany that promises to narrow the distance between his son and himself. His retort to his wife's comment that he is too hard on the boy shows that the lesson in the gun shop is observed but not absorbed: "My father was nice to me, and what did it get him?" Indeed the final paragraph suggests that the son is on the verge of his own rebellion. For the moment at least, the family holds on, as it does in another story, "Son," where the boy is the family's "visitor" and "prisoner." Fathers always fail their children, who are always beautiful.

It is not outrageous to say that *Problems and Other Stories* will eventually be judged as one of the major collections of American short stories published in the twentieth century. John Romano (*The New York Times Book Review*, 28 October 1979) supports this opinion: "*Problems and Other Stories* won't be surpassed by any collection of short fiction in the next year, and perhaps not in the next 10. Its satisfactions are profound, and the proper emotion is one of gratitude that such a splendid artistic intelligence has been brought to bear on some of the important afflictions of our times." Updike remains America's foremost family chronicler because he understands that little incidents, grace notes as it were, make up the true drama of a home. The woman in "Nevada" who cries out "that it was nobody's *fault,* that there was nothing he could *do,* just let her *alone*" is a more convincing snapshot of a troubled wife than a dozen descriptions of women who survive on tranquilizers and thoughts of suicide. In this sense *Problems and Other Stories* is a volume of middle age. Wives' accusations are "moralistic" reflexes, and husbands' responses are full of "predictable mockery." As Updike writes in "The Egg Race," "The stratum of middle age has its insignia, its clues, its distinguishing emotional artifacts." Unlike *The Same Door* and *Pigeon Feathers,* which focus on the nostalgia felt for a time left far behind with the dogwood tree and youth, this collection is closer to *Museums and Women,* which details the love that lingers after the marriage goes bad. Not every story is about family, and not every story is about loss, but the fact remains that *Problems and Other Stories* reemphasizes Updike's move in his fiction from pastoral Olinger, Pennsylvania, to surburban Tarbox, Massachusetts. He had taken this step a long time ago, of course. The differ-

Updike circa 1989 (photograph by Hana Hamplova; from the dust jacket for Self-Consciousness: Memoirs*)*

youth. Trusting his father's promise to catch him in the swimming pool if he will only jump from the safety of the side, he remembers that the father instead let him hit the water and slip chokingly to the bottom in a botched lesson of sink or swim. The parallel to "The Gun Shop" and the contrast with *The Centaur* are intriguing. Yet most of the variations on trust in *Trust Me* are less dramatic. Quiet, subtle, and lurking, the undermining of confidence more often takes its time, inching its way through a life or a marriage toward its final goal of disintegration and pain.

Adultery and divorce are not always the issues, as Updike shows in the stately "Made in Heaven." Once again ironic, the title refers to the long, apparently successful marriage of Brad and Jeanette Henderson. Interestingly for an Updike story, Brad is first attracted to Jeanette not by her promise of carnal mystery but by her confidence in what she calls "the salvation of my soul." Her surety negates his gloom, his sense that Karl Marx and H. L. Mencken were correct when they announced the death of religion. As Brad becomes more active in the church during the many years of their marriage, Jeanette, however, becomes less so, even to the point of rejecting an offer of Communion as she confronts her final illness. Only then does he learn that his trust in her religious certainty violated her belief that spiritual matters are a private undertaking, an exploration that cannot tolerate crowding: "Since you took it from me. . . . It didn't seem necessary, for the *two* of us to keep it up." Recrimination is not the issue. Loss is, and, as Updike shows in *Trust Me,* little losses sear.

Updike extends his exploration of the enormity of loss in *The Afterlife and Other Stories* (1994). Although the title immediately suggests the after-domain of the religiously faithful, the stories dissect the emotional and physical diminishment of a declining life. However ridiculed, faith in an afterlife shores up the modest human need for faith in the assurance that the very next moment of one's earthly existence will be a continuation of all that has come before. Such is not the case, of course, and thus Updike muses in this exquisitely written collection on how the miracle of memory can periodically thwart the looming of mortality.

"Nobody belongs to us," Updike writes in "Grandparenting," "except in memory." These are the final words of the book, and they suggest the inevitable link between the dance toward death and the imperative of recall. "A Sandstone Farmhouse" eloquently illustrates the linkage. A meditation on the death of Updike's mother, "A Sandstone Farmhouse" won the O. Henry Award as the year's most distinguished short story when it was first published in 1990. The intertextual connection with *Of the Farm* is clear as Updike names the protagonist Joey and then details the furnish-

ence is that, whereas in *Museums and Women* he occasionally glances back over his shoulder at the tranquil, "voluptuous" 1950s, a time "when everyone was pregnant," in *Problems and Other Stories* his stories document the plunge into middle age when wives and husbands finally separate, when children unexpectedly grow up, when the soul grows calluses, and when guilt, oddly, both lacerates and soothes.

A similar diminishment informs *Trust Me.* With a title that is largely ironic, the collection chronicles the crumbling of domestic order in what would seem at first glance to be an impregnable citadel of trust and ease: the civilized suburbs and rural retreats of the upper middle class. "The Ideal Village" concludes, "Man was not meant to abide in paradise," and this acknowledgment of dwindling expectations illustrates the enormous difference between the tales in *Trust Me* and the early, much-admired "Pigeon Feathers," which ends with David Kern's certainty that God would let him live forever.

The title story sets the tone for the collection as a middle-aged man recalls the shock of recognition in his

ings of the house that he once suspected had trapped him: "On the same principle, an invisible giant, removing only one day at a time, will eventually dispose of an entire life." Updike knows that in discarding a dead parent's belongings, a son displaces his own past. However inhibiting and enclosing, a parent's home provides shelter. Thus the "afterlife" in this much-honored tale is, ironically, the adult child's life following the death of the parents. All through childhood, muses Updike, offspring struggle to escape the home, to plunge into the center of things. Only by recalling the parents in memory do the children finally learn otherwise. "A Sandstone Farmhouse" ends with a sentence that summarizes this poignant collection: "He had always wanted to be where the action was, and what action there was, it turned out, had been back there."

Similar variations direct Updike's poetry, except that the comic element is more pronounced in the verse than in the tales. Updike takes his poems seriously, as much more than diversions between completing one novel and planning the next, but the public wrongly defines his poetry merely as light verse in the spirit of Ogden Nash. This misconception is unfortunate, for his collections of poems show a change in tone and mood from the humor of *The Carpentered Hen,* through the lyrics of *Telephone Poles* and the autobiographical poems of *Midpoint,* to the meditations on death in *Tossing and Turning* and the celebration of nature in *Facing Nature.* This is not to say that he abandons humor after *The Carpentered Hen,* but only to suggest that the poems of comic rhyme and verbal pyrotechnics are but one side of Updike the poet. The place to begin a reading of his verse is not with *The Carpentered Hen* but with his essay "Rhyming Max," a review of Beerbohm's parodies first published in *The New Yorker* (7 March 1964) and collected in *Assorted Prose.*

Understanding Beerbohm's verse parodies to be a kind of verbal cartooning, Updike points to the art of rhyme as an agency of comedy. Replete with regularity and rigidity, rhyme reflects the mechanical action that Henri Bergson termed a primary cause of laughter. Updike writes, "By rhyming, language calls attention to its own mechanical nature and relieves the represented reality of seriousness." Assonance and alliteration perform a similar function and join rhyme as means by which humanity asserts control over things. Light verse for Updike "tends the thin flame of formal magic and tempers the inhuman darkness of reality with the comedy of human artifice . . . it lessens the gravity of its subject." *The Carpentered Hen* illustrates his argument. Beneath his celebration of the delightful artificiality of words is a respect for language itself.

Many of these early poems take to task the inane writing of journalists, advertisers, and editors. Combin-

ing verbal acrobatics such as puns and traditional stanza forms organized with amusing twists, he often parodies the venerable art of the occasional poem when he appends to many of the verses prose statements usually lifted verbatim from an ad or editorial. Thus "Duet, with Muffled Brake Drums" pokes fun at an advertisement in *The New Yorker* claiming that the meeting of Rolls and Royce made engineering history, while "An Ode: Fired into Being by Life's 48-Star Editorial, 'Wanted: An American Novel'" comically exposes the muddled thinking of those who argue that the Great American Novel may be written to order to reflect the surface prosperity of the 1950s. Quoting parts of the editorial and designating sections of his poem as strophe, antistrophe, and epode (parts of the Pindaric ode), he writes a parody of inspiration.

Not all the poems are this amusing. As if foreshadowing the more somber poetry of his later collections, Updike also includes serious pieces of social observation such as "Ex-Basketball Player" and "Tao in the Yankee Stadium Bleachers." These poems illustrate his lifelong interest in sports, but, more important, they comment upon the ephemeral nature of physical prowess, reputation, and life itself. Readers of the story "Ace in the Hole" (*The Same Door*) and the novel *Rabbit, Run* will recognize the situation in "Ex-Basketball Player" as Updike describes the plight of the aging athlete whose current circumstances no longer equal the glory of past headlines. "Tao in the Yankee Stadium Bleachers" is a better poem, which muses on the proposition that "Distance brings proportion." Referring to passages of Eastern philosophy such as "the dead rule longer than any king," Updike couches his thoughts on mutability in a metaphor of athletics. The inner journey is "unjudgeably long," and every man eventually flies out while small boys in the grandstands wait to take their places.

These two poems look forward to the short stories in which Updike effectively comments upon the sense of diminishment and loss that age inexorably brings. Yet, the dominant tone of *The Carpentered Hen* is not melancholy but joy. The book appropriately ends with the twelve-page poem "A Cheerful Alphabet," which is an updated *McGuffey's Reader* designed to teach his son the wonder of a versatile vocabulary. *A* stands no longer for the apple of sin and Eden but for the still lifes of Cézanne. Designating *T* for trivet, for example, and *X* for xyster, Updike shows that alphabets can be cheerful and that language is alive.

Updike's witty efforts to guard language from the stultifying effects of jargon and cliché, a primary feature of *The Carpentered Hen,* are continued in the first half of *Telephone Poles.* The occasional poem is again parodied, as in "Recital," which quotes a headline in *The New York Times,* "Roger Bobo Gives Recital

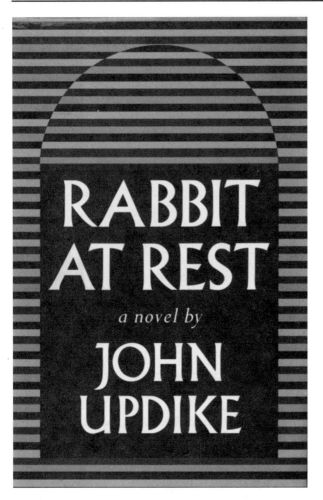

Dust jacket for Updike's 1990 novel, the final
installment of the Rabbit tetralogy

Updike writes, "The Nature of our construction is in every way / A better fit than the Nature it displaces." He does not mean that trees, for example, are less valuable than telephone poles, but that poles testify to humanity's ingenuity in meeting its needs in the natural world, which must endure the yearly cycle of death and rebirth. Telephone poles may not offer much shade, but unlike elms they are both stable and utilitarian. Since their "fearsome crowns" at the top may literally "stun us to stone," the poles also serve as updated versions of ancient myths, in this case the myth of gorgons' heads.

Perhaps the most memorable poem in *Telephone Poles* is "Seven Stanzas at Easter." Noting how contemporary humanity is caught between the demands of reason and faith, Updike insists that the miracle of the Resurrection must withstand the challenge by the mind if the Christian Church is to survive: "Make no mistake: if He rose at all / it was as His body." The dilemma is nicely suggested in the key word *if* and in the speaker's description of the miracle in the rational discourse of scientific language. If Christ rose, he did so not metaphorically but literally. Symbols may not replace fact as the cornerstone of faith. The poet's uncertain tone reflects the predicament of intelligent modern people who would believe even while they doubt.

Updike's most ambitious collection of poems is *Midpoint*. Published when the poet was thirty-seven years old, the title poem is a forty-one-page analysis of his life to age thirty-five, midpoint in the biblical span of three score and ten years. "Midpoint" is an impressive combination of autobiography, homage to past poets (Dante, Edmund Spenser, Alexander Pope, Walt Whitman, and Ezra Pound), scientific knowledge, experimental typography, and comic tone. Defining the intellectual bearings of his first thirty-five years in order to prepare for the second half of his life, Updike explains that "Midpoint" is both "a joke on the antique genre of the long poem" and "an earnest meditation of the mysteries of the ego." "Midpoint" is not entirely successful because the parts are more impressive than the whole, but it must be read carefully by those interested in Updike's career.

The general movement of the poem illustrates the poet's growth from youthful solipsism to an acceptance of his connection with all humanity. *Point* is the key word both thematically and in terms of the poem's arrangement, for Updike not only shows that he needs an acceptable point of view to understand his relationship with the highpoints of history, but he also fills the second canto with a maze of dots that take shape as photographs from his family album when held at arm's length.

on Tuba," and which goes on to play with the outrageous rhymes associated with light verse. For all the pleasures of the light verse, however, *Telephone Poles* is a significant collection primarily because of the serious lyrics in the second half. These poems treat many of the themes that readers of Updike's fiction have come to expect: the attractions of memory, the threat of mutability, and the pleasure of the mundane. As Updike writes in the foreword to *Olinger Stories* (1964), he needs the "quiet but tireless goodness that things at rest, like a brick wall or a small stone, seem to affirm." These poems look more to Shillington than to Ipswich, as if he were trying to secure a still point before facing the changes of middle age. A testimony to his close observation of common things, the volume illustrates his statement that "a trolley car has as much right to be there, in terms of aesthetics, as a tree."

The title poem is the center of the collection. Praising the relative permanence of human-made objects and their place in the modern imagination,

From his midlife perspective he understands that as a child he saw himself as the most prominent point in a radius of dots all secondary to him. Each person may view experience from a single point of view at a given moment in his or her life, but the solipsism of the child must be toned down if the child is to accept a place in the world. The pointillistic photographs illustrate Updike's most immediate connection–the family–and the opening line parodies Whitman's celebration of self: "Of nothing but me, me / –all wrong, all wrong–." Whitman may be a significant dot in the myriad points of Updike's past, but nineteenth-century beliefs are not necessarily reliable for a twentieth-century person. The importance of appropriate points is again established in the third canto, about the composition of solids, which Updike now understands to be made up of compressed particles and dots. Finally he accepts the truth that identity depends upon love and the willingness to see life as a progression toward a metaphorical point that clears the vision of the eye/I.

Three other sections join the title poem to make up *Midpoint:* "Poems," "Love Poems," and "Light Verse." Of the three, "Love Poems" is the most impressive because the mixed emotions of desire and guilt that are a hallmark of Updike's best short stories are poignantly expressed. These poems reflect what the shift from remembering his past to concentrating on his present has meant to his imagination.

Updike's recognition in *Midpoint* that he is on the downside of what he calls the "Hill of Life" forms the emotional center of *Tossing and Turning,* his most accomplished volume of poetry. He does not abandon the subject of his past, as the fine "Leaving Church Early" shows, but he focuses more than ever on the challenges of success and suburbia. The persistence of memory, a primary factor in his earlier poems and tales, gives way to the encroachment of age. The title of the collection suggests his restlessness, and a line from "Sleepless in Scarsdale" describes his dilemma: "Prosperity has stolen stupor from me."

Two of the three long poems in *Tossing and Turning* recall Updike's boyhood in Shillington and youth at Harvard: "Leaving Church Early" and "Apologies to Harvard," the Harvard Phi Beta Kappa poem for 1973. The aloneness that later becomes insomnia is detailed in the former as Updike describes the absence of communication in his family "kept home by poverty, / with nowhere else to go." The need to forgive is a condition of their misery. The latter poem may be read along with "The Christian Roommates," a story from *The Music School,* as one of Updike's few accounts of university days.

Yet, the richest poems in *Tossing and Turning* are the shorter lyrics in which Updike acknowledges his step

across midpoint in the direction of what he calls "Nandi." Surrounded in suburbia by the trappings of material success and a happy family, he nevertheless finds himself restless and afraid. The stupor that prosperity steals has a double meaning. He cannot find the stupor he needs to sleep because his life is now "too clean," and his success has lulled him into a stupor that clouds his artistic vision, his spiritual sustenance. Too much success "pollutes the tunnel of silence."

It also makes him afraid. More than the other collections, *Tossing and Turning* shows the poet's uncertainty about death and annihilation. In "You Who Swim" and "Bath after Sailing," two of his finest poems, Updike uses water to illustrate the unbeatable immensity of nonhuman otherness. The former is a sixteen-line description of his lover, who is such an expert at the dead man's float that she seems at home on both land and water. She splashes and plays and excels at love, but death lurks just out of sight. The final line–"We swim our dead men's lives"–suggests that all people return to the water that made them. The fear is just as great in "Bath after Sailing." Safely back from another confrontation with the deep, the poet is aware of the ironic change from overwhelming ocean to soothing tub. The "timeless weight" of the sea may threaten, and the gentle swell of the bath may cleanse, but the tub so resembles a coffin that his fingertips shriveled by the water remind him of death. The last trip to the final destination is described in "Heading for Nandi" as the lonely poet takes a night flight across the endless ocean.

Not all the poems in *Tossing and Turning* are as bleak, for Updike also includes a section of light verse that recalls the verbal antics and dedication to a lively language that characterize *The Carpentered Hen.* Burlesques such as "The Cars of Caracas" and "Insomnia the Gem of the Ocean" are fun to read. But the public's misconception of Updike the poet as a mere versifier of witty rhymes and sparkling puns could be corrected by close readings of his more serious poems, especially those in the second half of *Telephone Poles* and most of *Tossing and Turning.*

The light verse placed at the end of *Facing Nature* similarly recalls the linguistic fun of *The Carpentered Hen,* but in his fifth collection of poetry Updike searches primarily for a balance between dread and desire. The sonnets in this volume meditate on mutability and death, but these inexorable laws of nature are then celebrated in "Seven Odes to Seven Natural Processes," in which Updike suggests that nature's "rot," "evaporation," and "fragmentation" are inextricable from nature's "growth," "crystallization," and "healing." Death and life are one. In these challenging odes Updike reveals intellectual curiosity and verbal precision to hint that the order of art reflects the wholeness of nature.

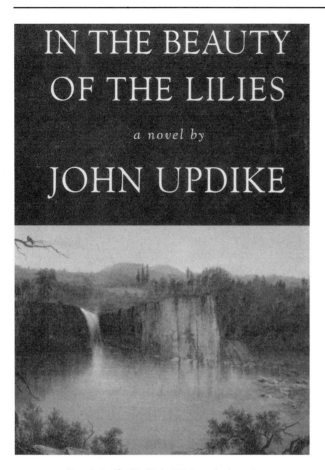

Dust jacket for Updike's 1996 novel, about the decline of religious faith in the United States

Gathering his poetry in 1993 for *Collected Poems: 1953–1993,* Updike formalizes a long-apparent distinction when he divides the collection into two sections: poetry and light verse. Though the collection covers a span of forty years, it is not "the complete poems of John Updike." Although he includes seventy poems that had not been previously published in book form, he also omits eleven poems from his earlier collections as well as seven originally published in *The New Yorker* but never gathered in a volume. In a short preface he describes his poetry as "the thready backside of my life's fading tapestry," and thus he suggests that the poems take second place to the fiction. The suggestion is accurate, yet the point remains that the poetry offers a different angle of vision on his career-long concerns: domesticity, natural processes, the significance of little things, faith, and death.

Supporting Updike's achievement in poetry, short stories, and novels is a body of essays large and varied enough to fill a half-dozen volumes. Including everything from parodies and autobiography, to celebrations of baseball and golf, to erudite ruminations on the practice of fiction, Updike's collections of nonfiction testify to a lively mind joyously receptive to worldly vagaries and common details. What finally amazes the reader is the range of his curiosity, a range illustrated by the heart of each volume: the essay reviews.

Beginning with *Assorted Prose* and *Picked-Up Pieces* and expanding in *Hugging the Shore,* Updike has assembled a substantial body of commentary on authors that not only directly investigates the literature of his day but also indirectly analyzes his own writing. The award-winning *Hugging the Shore* shows him at his most challenging, as one of the few men of letters who can write intelligently about Wilson and Nabokov, Henry Green and Iris Murdoch, Saul Bellow and Kurt Vonnegut, Louis-Ferdinand Céline and Robert Pinget, Italo Calvino and Günter Grass, Karl Barth and Paul Tillich, Roland Barthes and Claude Levi-Strauss. Few other contemporary writers can clarify so much or can help the reader see relations among so many branches of knowledge. Few except Updike have managed such enthusiasm for the life of the mind and continued to comment sanely and generously on artists who do not write or think the way he does.

As *Hugging the Shore* illustrates, Updike is primarily an appreciator. Not driven to possess his subject with an academic thoroughness, he nevertheless responds with such knowledge and wit that he cannot be dismissed as a dilettante. In *Hugging the Shore* he writes about theology, New England churches, and—incredibly—more than 130 authors with so much tact that the reader feels comfortable in the presence of his sparkling mind.

He does not rant and rave; he does not scold and scorn; and he does not stumble into the trap that ensnares many critics and makes them unable to treat other authors' books as anything except disappointing versions of what they themselves might have written. The hallmark of *Hugging the Shore* is sympathy for the writer's dilemma, concern for the writer's chore. About Nabokov, Updike writes, "He asked, then, of his own art and the art of others a something extra–a flourish of mimetic magic or deceptive doubleness–that was supernatural and surreal in the root sense of these degraded words." About Muriel Spark and Murdoch: "The two of them together reappropriate for their generation Shakespeare's legacy of dark comedy, of deceptions and enchantments, of shuddering contrivance, of deep personal forces held trembling in a skein of sociable truces." Such sympathy abounds.

Yet, for all the joy of reading this book, the initiated reader might squirm just a bit. Updike's insistence on realism echoes throughout. It is not that he regards realism as a literary convention like Romanticism or modernism but that he somehow drags in his acknowledged Christian perspective and affirms the marriage of realism and morality. Of Calvino's fiction, for example, he writes, "There is little that sticks in the mind as involuntarily real, as having been other than intellectually achieved." Updike clearly prefers the touch of grace gained by hard contact with the real. His uneasiness with writers who stress the play of language over the reflection of the world is disquieting.

Especially rewarding are three longish lectures on three American giants–Hawthorne, Whitman, and Melville–which, he explains, were undertaken to "educate the speaker as much as the audience." That one comment perhaps best catches the spirit of *Hugging the Shore.* Updike learns as he reads and does not pontificate as he writes.

One is finally grateful for such gems as "A sensation of blasphemous overlapping, of some vast substance chemically betraying itself, is central to the Gothic tradition of which Hawthorne's tales are lovely late blooms." The question of religious belief not only unites the lectures on Hawthorne, Whitman, and Melville but also defines Updike's attitude toward his own life and art. A believer himself, he is drawn as if by paradox to the shudder of Melville's uncertainty: "Moby Dick represents the utter blank horror of the universe if Godless, a horror so awesome as to excite worship."

If, as Updike suggests in *The Witches of Eastwick,* art counters emptiness, then his essays on painters collected in *Just Looking* are more than an amateur's mere musings, as the self-effacing tone of the title might imply. Reading this wide-ranging volume, one remembers Updike's boyhood appreciation of Disney, his own drawings for the *Harvard Lampoon,* and his year of study at the Ruskin School of Drawing and Fine Arts in Oxford following graduation from Harvard. His initiation into the complexities of cartoon art recalls his skill with light verse and is amply illustrated in the twenty-page essay on Ralph Barton, perhaps the most famous of *The New Yorker* cartoonists: "A cartoon traditionally aims to give all its information at a glance; it is a kind of calligraphy, which reduces marginal details to the most quickly readable scribble. But in Barton the background presses toward the foreground with an insistence found in Oriental art, and again in Cubism."

Although Updike discusses the seriousness of melancholy as the frame of Barton's drawings, he devotes most of *Just Looking* to remarks on what many readers would call "true" artists. Of Pierre-Auguste Renoir he writes, "Renoir does not quite rank with the heroic masters of early modern painting–specifically, with his friends Monet and Cézanne. Compared with either, he didn't look hard enough"; of John Singer Sargent: "Sargent had an underindulged instinct for the marginal"; of Edgar Degas: "This scrupulous real-

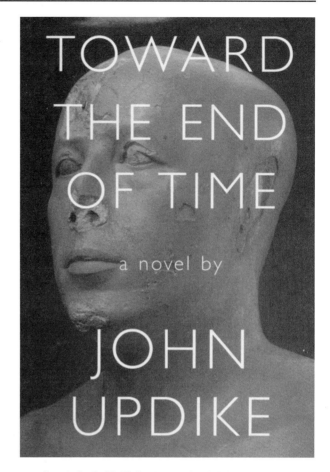

Dust jacket for Updike's 1997 novel, which depicts suburban American life in a postapocalyptic world

ist found the perfect modern excuse for the female nude . . . bathing"; of Jan Vermeer (one of Updike's favorites): "He could paint anything." An appreciation of precision, of the objects of the world observed fondly and rendered accurately, marks these essays, and thus Updike's interest in painting reflects his commitment to writing. Both are means of investigating what he calls "details."

A similar discriminating curiosity sparkles throughout his most comprehensive collection of essays, *Odd Jobs.* Comically blaming the sheer bulk of the book on his acquiring a word processor, Updike describes himself as "aging into a shaky sort of celebrity" as he writes more and more "prefaces and puffs." Yet, the bantering tone belies the seriousness illustrated, as in *Hugging the Shore,* by his sympathetic but astute opinions about writers from South America, Europe, Asia, and Africa. He muses, for example, on John Barth's use of Latin American authors to distinguish between modernism and postmodernism, on Zhang Xianliang's novel about love in the "drastically desexed culture" of China, on the fusing of oral narrative and written fiction in recent novels from Nigeria, and on such American giants as Ralph Waldo Emerson and William Dean Howells.

Part of *Odd Jobs* is composed of what Updike terms "Fairly Personal" and "Literarily Personal," and, in the absence of biographies, journals, and collections of letters, the reader who longs to know more about the writer might consult these sections. Such a reader would be better off with *Self-Consciousness: Memoirs,* a sly, partly revealing portrait of the author written, Updike explains, as a repudiation "of someone wanting to write my biography–to take my life, my lode of ore and heap of memories, from me! The idea seemed so repulsive that I was stimulated to put down, always with some natural hesitation and distaste, these elements of an autobiography."

In a series of six chapters Updike tells only what he wants to tell–eloquently and, more important, shrewdly–for in these pieces he nudges the reader away from biography and back toward what should be the reader's primary interest: the novels, tales, poems, and essays. Thus, the exquisitely paced "A Soft Spring Night in Shillington," a memoir of Updike's return to his hometown in middle age, should be read in context with the short stories in *The Same Door* and *Pigeon Feathers.* "On Not Being a Dove," a revelation of his complex and perhaps unexpected position during the Vietnam War, should be read with *Rabbit Redux* and "Marching through Boston" (*Museums and Women*). The long "A Letter to My Grandsons" is especially notable when one understands that Updike's daughter is married to a West African, and thus the "letter" gives added resonance to *The Coup* and to Updike's many essays about African writers. Readers who have followed the subtleties of Updike's struggle with religion and who know his essay "Faith in Search of Understanding" (*Assorted Prose*) and his various analyses of Karl Barth and Kierkegaard will profit from "On Being a Self Forever." Yet, perhaps the most revelatory chapters in *Self-Consciousness* are "At War with My Skin" and "Getting the Words Out," in which Updike describes his decades-long battle with psoriasis and stammering. The story "From the Journal of a Leper" in *Problems and Other Stories* is relevant here, but more significant is that Updike refuses to use his afflictions as a catalyst for complaint. Rather, he shows how physical problems shape his response to the world and thereby his writing: "I groped for the exact terms I knew were there but could not find. . . . My stuttering feels like an acknowledgment, in conversation, of the framework of unacknowledged complexity that surrounds the simplest exchange of words." One need hardly reiterate that Updike "got the words out."

Particularly eloquent is *Golf Dreams: Writings on Golf* (1996), a happy combination of fiction and essays about the sport that Updike considers to be the most physically frustrating yet spiritually challenging of all human diversions. Most of the pieces have not been previously collected, but all are written with the ease and grace evident in his finest sparkling prose. *Golf Dreams* is no mere hodgepodge, no hasty gathering from the clipping file. Divided into three sections–"Learning the Game," "Playing the Game," and "Loving the Game"–the volume impresses upon the reader the inevitable connection between physical exertion and moral imperative. Such titles as "Is There Life after Golf?" and "Is Life Too Short for Golf?" are for Updike more than witty asides. They are queries about the looming burden of mortality. Golf is a sport that nearly always results in a defeat for the participant, and thus Updike ponders the "momentary amplification of myself within a realm larger than life."

A poet of the physical, the golf pro murmurs to a frustrated adult discouraged enough to quit taking lessons, "Golf is life . . . and life is lessons" ("The Pro"). The trek down the fairway becomes a journey through a lifetime, a metaphor of starting in a wide space before falling into a small hole. The quest is inevitably unsettling as, when Updike writes in "Intercession," "the angle of a metal surface striking a rubber sphere counted far more with God than the keenest human hope." Readers interested in the religious element that pervades the Updike canon will want to consult *Golf Dreams,* a collection of thoughtful meditations on the inexplicable continuum of a human life.

There are those who argue that Updike does not demand enough in his essays, that he refuses to ask hard questions. To insist, however, on more than the enormous amount that he already offers is to require academic specialization from one of America's finest creative writers. The happy union of lyrical prose and intellectual probing that is the highlight of his fiction shows itself everywhere in his nonfiction. John Updike may hug the shore in his criticism, but he remains one of the most perceptive men of letters in the United States since Edmund Wilson and Henry James.

Interview:

James Plath, ed., *Conversations with John Updike* (Jackson: University Press of Mississippi, 1994).

Bibliographies:

Michael Olivas, *An Annotated Bibliography of John Updike Criticism, 1967–1973* (New York: Garland, 1975);

Elizabeth A. Gearhart, *John Updike: A Comprehensive Bibliography with Selected Annotations* (Norwood, Pa.: Norwood Editions, 1978);

Cameron Northouse, ed., *John Updike: A Bibliography of Research and Criticism, 1970–1986* (Dallas: Contemporary Research Associates, 1988);

Jack DeBellis, *John Updike: A Bibliography, 1967–1993* (Westport, Conn.: Greenwood Press, 1994).

References:

Harold Bloom, ed., *John Updike: Modern Critical Views* (New York: Chelsea House, 1987);

Lawrence R. Broer, *Rabbit Tales: Poetry and Politics in John Updike's Rabbit Novels* (Tuscaloosa: University of Alabama Press, 1998);

Rachael C. Burchard, *John Updike: Yea Sayings* (Carbondale: Southern Illinois University Press, 1971);

Robert C. Detweiler, *John Updike,* revised edition (New York: Twayne, 1984);

Elizabeth A. Falsey, *The Art of Adding and the Art of Taking Away: Selections from John Updike's Manuscripts: An Exhibition at the Houghton Library* (Cambridge, Mass.: Harvard College Library, 1987);

Donald J. Greiner, *Adultery in the American Novel: Updike, James, and Hawthorne* (Columbia: University of South Carolina Press, 1985);

Greiner, *John Updike's Novels* (Athens: Ohio University Press, 1984);

Greiner, *The Other John Updike: Poems/Short Stories/Prose/Play* (Athens: Ohio University Press, 1981);

Alice and Kenneth Hamilton, *The Elements of John Updike* (Grand Rapids, Mich.: Eerdmans, 1970);

George Hunt, *John Updike and the Three Great Secret Things: Sex, Religion, and Art* (Grand Rapids, Mich.: Eerdmans, 1980);

Robert M. Luscher, *John Updike: A Study of the Short Fiction* (New York: Twayne, 1993);

William R. Macnaughton, ed., *Critical Essays on John Updike* (Boston: G. K. Hall, 1982);

Joyce B. Markle, *Fighters and Lovers: Theme in the Novels of John Updike* (New York: New York University Press, 1973);

Modern Fiction Studies, special Updike issue, edited by William Stafford and Margaret Church, 20 (Spring 1974);

Modern Fiction Studies, special Updike issue, edited by William J. Stuckey, 37 (Spring 1991);

Judie Newman, *John Updike* (New York: St. Martin's Press, 1988);

Dilvo I. Ristoff, *Updike's America: The Presence of Contemporary American History in John Updike's Rabbit Trilogy* (New York: Peter Lang, 1988);

Charles Thomas Samuels, *John Updike* (Minneapolis: University of Minnesota Press, 1969);

James A. Schiff, *Updike's Version: Rewriting The Scarlet Letter* (Columbia: University of Missouri Press, 1992);

George J. Searles, *The Fiction of Philip Roth and John Updike* (Carbondale: Southern Illinois University Press, 1985);

Larry E. Taylor, *Pastoral and Anti-Pastoral Patterns in John Updike's Fiction* (Carbondale: Southern Illinois University Press, 1971);

David Thorburn and Howard Eiland, eds., *John Updike: A Collection of Critical Essays* (Englewood Cliffs, N.J.: Prentice-Hall, 1979);

Stanley Trachtenberg, ed., *New Essays on Rabbit, Run* (Cambridge: Cambridge University Press, 1993);

Suzanne Henning Uphaus, *John Updike* (New York: Ungar, 1980);

Edward P. Vargo, *Rainstorms and Fire: Ritual in the Novels of John Updike* (Port Washington, N.Y.: Kennikat Press, 1973);

James Yerkes, ed., *John Updike and Religion: The Sense of the Sacred and the Motions of Grace* (Grand Rapids, Mich.: Eerdmans, 1999).

Papers:

John Updike's manuscripts and letters are at the Houghton Library, Harvard University.

Gerald Vizenor

(22 October 1934 –   )

Alan R. Velie
University of Oklahoma

See also the Vizenor entry in *DLB 175: Native American Writers of the United States.*

BOOKS: *Poems Born in the Wind* (Minneapolis, 1960);

The Old Park Sleepers: A Poem (Minneapolis: Obercraft, 1961);

Two Wings the Butterfly: Haiku Poems in English (St. Cloud, Minn.: Privately printed, 1962);

South of the Painted Stones: Poems (Minneapolis: Callimachus, 1963);

Raising the Moon Vines: Original Haiku in English (Minneapolis: Callimachus, 1964);

Seventeen Chirps: Haiku in English (Minneapolis: Nodin Press, 1964);

Slight Abrasions: A Dialogue in Haiku, by Vizenor and Jerome Downes (Minneapolis: Nodin Press, 1966);

Empty Swings (Minneapolis: Nodin Press, 1967);

Thomas James White Hawk (Minneapolis: Four Winds, 1968);

The Everlasting Sky: New Voices from the People Named the Chippewa (New York: Crowell-Collier, 1972);

Tribal Scenes and Ceremonies (Minneapolis: Nodin Press, 1976);

Wordarrows: Indians and Whites in the New Fur Trade (Minneapolis: University of Minnesota Press, 1978);

Darkness in Saint Louis Bearheart (St. Paul, Minn.: Truck Press, 1978); revised as *Bearheart: The Heirship Chronicles* (Minneapolis: University of Minnesota Press, 1990);

Earthdivers: Tribal Narratives on Mixed Descent (Minneapolis: University of Minnesota Press, 1983);

The People Named the Chippewa: Narrative Histories (Minneapolis: University of Minnesota Press, 1983);

Matsushima: Pine Islands: Haiku (Minneapolis: Nodin Press, 1984);

Griever, An American Monkey King in China: A Novel (Normal: Illinois State University / New York: Fiction Collective, 1987);

The Trickster of Liberty: Tribal Heirs to a Wild Baronage (Minneapolis: University of Minnesota Press, 1988);

Gerald Vizenor

Crossbloods: Bone Courts, Bingo, and Other Reports (Minneapolis: University of Minnesota Press, 1990);

Interior Landscapes: Autobiographical Myths and Metaphors (Minneapolis: University of Minnesota Press, 1990);

Landfill Meditation: Crossblood Stories (Hanover, N.H.: Wesleyan University Press/University Press of New England, 1991);

The Heirs of Columbus (Middletown, Conn.: Wesleyan University Press / Hanover, N.H.: University Press of New England, 1991);

Dead Voices: Natural Agonies in the New World (Norman: University of Oklahoma Press, 1992);

Manifest Manners: Postindian Warriors of Survivance (Hanover, N.H.: Wesleyan University Press, 1994); republished as *Manifest Manners: Narratives on Postindian Survivance* (Lincoln: University of Nebraska Press, 1999);

Shadow Distance: A Gerald Vizenor Reader, introduction by A. Robert Lee (Hanover, N.H.: Wesleyan University Press, 1994);

Hotline Healers: An Almost Browne Novel (Hanover, N.H.: Wesleyan University Press/University Press of New England, 1997);

Fugitive Poses: Native American Indian Scenes of Absence and Presence (Lincoln: University of Nebraska Press, 1998);

Postindian Conversations, by Vizenor and Lee (Lincoln: University of Nebraska Press, 1999);

Cranes Arise: Haiku (Minneapolis: Nodin Press, 1999);

Chancers, A Novel (Norman: University of Oklahoma Press, 2000).

PRODUCED SCRIPT: *Harold of Orange,* motion picture, Native American Public Broadcasting Consortium Video, 1984.

OTHER: *Summer in the Spring: Lyric Poems of the Ojibwe,* edited by Vizenor (Minneapolis: Nodin Press, 1965); revised as *Anishinabe Nagamon* (Minneapolis: Nodin Press, 1970); republished with *Anishinabe Adisokan,* edited by Vizenor (Minneapolis: Nodin Press, 1970), as *Summer in the Spring: Ojibwe Lyric Poems and Tribal Stories* (Minneapolis, Minn.: Nodin Press, 1981); enlarged as *Summer in the Spring: Anishinaabe Lyric Poems and Stories* (Norman: University of Oklahoma Press, 1993);

Escorts to White Earth, 1868–1968: 100 Year Reservation, edited by Vizenor (Minneapolis: Four Winds, 1968);

Touchwood: A Collection of Ojibway Prose, edited by Vizenor (St. Paul, Minn.: New Rivers Press, 1987);

Narrative Chance, Postmodern Discourse on Native American Literatures, edited by Vizenor (Albuquerque: University of New Mexico Press, 1989);

"Luminous Thighs," in *The Lightning Within: An Anthology of Contemporary American Indian Fiction,* edited, with an introduction, by Alan R. Velie (Lincoln: University of Nebraska Press, 1991), pp. 67–90;

Native American Literature: A Brief Introduction and Anthology, edited by Vizenor (New York: HarperCollins, 1995).

Gerald Vizenor is often called the most prolific and controversial writer of the American Indian literary renaissance that began in 1968. He has written nine books of poetry, a collection of short stories, seven novels, and eight books of nonfiction, mostly political and autobiographical essays. Among his awards are the 1983 Film in the Cities screenplay prize from the Sundance Institute for *Harold of Orange* (1984), which also won "Best Film" in the category of American Indian Films at the San Francisco Film Festival in 1984; the New York Fiction Collective Award (1986) and the American Book Award (1988) for *Griever, An American Monkey King in China* (1987); and the Josephine Miles Award for Excellence in Literature from PEN-Oakland for *Interior Landscapes: Autobiographical Myths and Metaphors* (1990).

Gerald Vizenor's paternal ancestors were of mixed blood, Anishinaabe (the traditional tribe name that many Chippewa still prefer) and French Canadian. His Anishinaabe forebears were members of the Crane Clan, the tribal elite who during the eighteenth century settled on the land that is now the White Earth Reservation in Minnesota . Vizenor comes by his facility with words naturally; the members of the Crane Clan were the orators of the tribe. Vizenor traces his ancestors back to Keeshkemun, an eighteenth-century chief who was awarded the George Washington Peace Medal. Keeshkemun's grandson Clement Beaulieu (whose name Vizenor has frequently adopted as a nom de plume) was a fur trader and a commissioned colonel in the Pioneer Guards of northern Minnesota. Clement's son Charles was a company commander in the Union Army during the Civil War, and Clement's nephew Theodore Beaulieu started the White Earth Reservation newspaper, *The Progress,* in 1886.

As Vizenor relates in *Interior Landscapes* (1990), the Vizenors were Metis, mixed-blood French Canadians and Indians. The name *Vizenor* is an Indian agent's "despotic transcription" of Vezina. Vizenor's father, Clement William, was born on White Earth Reservation but moved to Minneapolis, Minnesota, where he worked as a housepainter. In the spring of 1934 Clement Vizenor married LaVerne "Lovey" Peterson, a white woman. Their son, Gerald, was born on 22 October 1934, at General Hospital in Minneapolis.

When Vizenor was eighteen months old, his father was murdered. A story in the *Minneapolis Journal* (30 June 1936) reported that the police sought a "giant Negro" as a suspect, but they made little attempt to solve the crime. In *Interior Landscapes* Vizenor discounts race as a motive for the killing and raises the possibility that his father, who was fond of gambling, was a victim of organized crime. Some twenty-five years later when Vizenor questioned the policeman in charge of investigating the case, the officer said, "We never spent much time on winos and derelicts in those days. . . . Who knows, one Indian vagrant kills another."

Clement and Gerald Vizenor in Minneapolis, 1936 (Collection of Gerald Vizenor)

LaVerne Vizenor periodically put her son in foster families or left him with his grandmother on the reservation. His closest attachment during childhood was to a stepfather, Elmer Petesch, with whom Gerald lived after his mother decamped to California. Although Petesch was cruel to Gerald at first, they soon formed a bond and lived happily for some months until Petesch met a violent death, falling into an elevator shaft on Christmas Eve, while Gerald waited for him at home to celebrate the holiday.

Vizenor dealt with the constant changes in his home situation by using trickster ways to keep himself amused. He developed a rich interior life based on a relationship with a woodland elf named Erdupps Mac-Churbbs, a tiny trickster who visited him frequently.

At fifteen Vizenor lied about his age to join the Minnesota National Guard, becoming a "proud soldier between the wars . . . a mixed-blood featherweight, more trickster than warrior, more earnest than comic;

the headband in my helmet liner rested on my ears." Two years later he left high school without graduating to join the U.S. Army. His social worker tried to convince him to finish, but Vizenor told her, "this school is death, graduation is death, and compared to that, the military is my liberation."

Since adolescence Vizenor has considered himself a living avatar of Nanabozho, the Chippewa Trickster. Nanabozho, like other tricksters down through the ages, such as Coyote, Odysseus, Renard the Fox, and Br'er Rabbit, is an amoral figure who plays tricks, is the victim of tricks, and generally gives in to every impulse. He has an immense appetite for adventure, mischief, sex, and experience. Vizenor continued his mischievous ways in the army, harassing his superiors, playing tricks, and cavorting with prostitutes. One angry officer consigned Private Vizenor to combat in Korea, but the war ended just as his ship arrived. Vizenor was sent to Japan, where he spent time with geishas and learned to write haiku. His greatest tricks in Japan involved leading a group of soldiers to visit prostitutes while they were ostensibly going for dental checkups and capturing and humiliating enemy commanders during war games. Despite pulling stunts worthy of Nanabozho, Vizenor flourished as a soldier. The army eventually sent him to a theater workshop, and he ended his tour as entertainment director at a large base near Sendai, Japan.

When Vizenor left the army in 1955, he enrolled at New York University, where he studied writing with Eda Lou Walton, who had been an office mate of Thomas Wolfe when he taught there. The verbal exuberance of Wolfe's fiction had exerted a strong influence on the style of Vizenor's early attempts at writing, and Vizenor was excited about working with someone who had known the novelist. Walton, who had published collections of Blackfoot and Navajo verse, also introduced Vizenor to Native American poetry. After two semesters at New York University and a series of arguments with the administration over his high-school diploma, which he had earned by passing a high-school equivalency test in the army, Vizenor transferred to the University of Minnesota, where he majored in child development and Asian area studies. At Minnesota he discovered "the source of my second liberation," Professor Edward Copeland, with whom he studied Japanese culture, literature, art, and language.

In 1959, while still in college, Vizenor married Judith Horns, an elementary-school teacher. Their son, Robert, was born in 1960. The family moved into a narrow attic apartment near the university, where Vizenor began to write poetry, particularly haiku. After he graduated in 1960, he took a job with the Minnesota Department of Corrections as a social worker and corrections agent. He continued to write verse and took graduate courses at the university in 1962–1965.

Although Vizenor's reputation is based primarily on his novels and nonfiction, his earliest books were collections of poetry. He published five books of verse—*Poems Born in the Wind* (1960), *The Old Park Sleepers: A Poem* (1961), *Two Wings the Butterfly: Haiku Poems in English* (1962), which was printed by the inmates at the Minnesota State Reformatory, *South of the Painted Stones: Poems* (1963), and *Raising the Moon Vines: Original Haiku in English* (1964)—before founding Nodin Press and publishing three collections of haiku: *Seventeen Chirps: Haiku in English* (1964), *Slight Abrasions: A Dialogue in Haiku*, with Jerome Downes (1966), and *Empty Swings* (1967).

In his introduction to *Shadow Distance: A Gerald Vizenor Reader* (1994), A. Robert Lee explains that haiku serves as "an especially intimate signature for Vizenor." Vizenor's fascination with haiku stems not only from his love of Japanese literature but also from its resemblance to Indian song, particularly as it appears in printed form. He compares the visual dreamscape of the haiku to the sense of natural human connections to the earth found in tribal music, dream songs.

The Anishinaabe were traditionally the most musical of the Indian tribes. Musicologist Frances Densmore wrote in *Chippewa Music* (1910) that when an Anishinaabe visited another reservation, "one of the first questions asked on his return was, 'What new songs did you learn?'" Inspired by Densmore, Vizenor edited a collection of her English translations of Anishinaabe songs: *Summer in the Spring: Lyric Poems of the Ojibwe* (1965), which was revised in 1970 as *Anishinabe Nagamon* (Songs of the People). In 1970 Vizenor also edited *Anishinabe Adisokan* (Tales of the People), a collection of stories originally published in *The Progress*. In 1981 both collections were published together as *Summer in the Spring: Ojibwe Lyric Poems and Tribal Stories,* and an enlarged edition was published in 1993 as *Summer in the Spring: Anishinaabe Lyric Poems and Stories.*

From 1964 to 1968 Vizenor worked as a community organizer for the Indians in Minneapolis, and from 1966 to 1968 he also served as director of the American Indian Employment and Guidance Center. He organized demonstrations to call attention to "racism and failure in the Bureau of Indian Affairs" and began writing magazine articles critical of governmental organizations created to help urban Indians. Later when urban radicals in Minneapolis formed the American Indian Movement, Vizenor became disillusioned with them, criticizing them for corruption, flamboyant poses, and inflammatory rhetoric.

In 1968 Vizenor took a job as a staff writer with the *Minneapolis Tribune*. Many of the articles and editorials he wrote during that time have been collected in *Tribal Scenes and Ceremonies* (1976) and *Crossbloods: Bone Courts, Bingo, and Other Reports* (1990). The tribal people Vizenor met as a reporter, most of them Anishinaabe, became the subjects of the essays and sketches he published in 1978 as *Wordarrows: Indians and Whites in the New Fur Trade*. The line between fiction and nonfiction in Vizenor's work is never entirely clear, and the subjects of his articles and essays often turn up later as characters in his novels.

In 1969 Vizenor was divorced from Judith Vizenor, and the following year he took a job as an English instructor at Lake Forest College in Illinois. He has since taught at Bemidji State in Minnesota, where he was director of Indian Studies (1971–1973); the University of California, Berkeley (1976–1980); the University of Minnesota, where he was James J. Hill Professor (1978–1987, with a joint appointment at Berkeley); at the University of California, Santa Cruz (1987–1990), where he was provost of Kresge College as well as professor of literature and American Studies; the University of Oklahoma (1991–1992), where he held the David Burr Chair of Letters; and again at Berkeley, teaching in the American Studies program.

In 1978 Vizenor published his first novel, *Darkness in Saint Louis Bearheart*. The narrator, Saint Louis Bearheart, is a trickster who, while serving as a minor functionary in the Bureau of Indian Affairs (BIA), has been devoting most of his time to writing a novel, his contribution to "the new tribal word wars." The frame of *Darkness in Saint Louis Bearheart* is a scene in which Bearheart seduces a young Indian radical who has broken into the BIA. Bearheart ridicules her for dressing in chicken feathers but has sex with her anyway and gives her his novel, *Cedarfair Circus,* a futuristic fantasy of what happens when America runs out of gasoline.

The hero of Bearheart's novel is Proude Cedarfair, an Anishinaabe from the Red Cedar Reservation in Minnesota. Cedarfair represents the trickster in his role of savior or culture hero; he is resourceful and benevolent, a leader. There is a darker side to tribal tricksters, however; they can be amoral pariahs who violate sacred tribal taboos. For instance, Nanabozho, the Anishinaabe trickster who serves as the archetype for Vizenor's characters, is a hero when he kills the dreaded *windigoo,* but a pariah when he kills his own grandmother. The dark side of the trickster in *Darkness in Saint Louis Bearheart* is played by Benito Saint Plumero, an irresponsible, violent, oversexed scoundrel. Benito, who looks as if "he must have been put together from broken clowns," has an enormous penis known as "president jackson." (Andrew Jackson is the president least loved by Indians. In the 1830s he forcibly removed them from their ancestral homelands in

Vizenor in Japan, 1954, during his service in the U.S. Army
(Collection of Gerald Vizenor)

the East, making them walk in winter to new lands in Oklahoma.) Splitting the trickster into two figures, as Vizenor does in *Darkness in Saint Louis Bearheart,* is not uncommon in mythology. Prometheus, who was a benefactor to man by stealing fire from the gods, and his brother Epimetheus, who owned the box that Pandora opened to bring evil into the world, are a classical example of a trickster pair.

The novel includes examples of what Vizenor calls "mythic verism," a combination if realism and fantasy. As Vizenor explained in "Trickster Discourse," a paper he presented at the School of American Research, Santa Fe, in June 1986: "Verisimilitude is the appearance of realities; mythic verism is discourse, a critical concordance of narrative voices, and a narrative realism that is more than mimesis or a measure of what is believed to be natural in the world." Mythic verism is related to but fundamentally different from the magical realism practiced by American Indian writers such as Louise Erdrich, N. Scott Momaday, or Leslie Silko. Magical realism is an example of what literary theorist Tzvetan Todorov defines as "the fantastic," a type of writing in which the reader cannot tell whether supernatural events actually happen or are imagined. For instance, in Erdrich's Chippewa tetralogy the Indians believe that Fleur Pillager comes back from the dead

three times, that she periodically turns into a bear, and that she kills Boy Lazarre with her magic. The reader cannot tell whether she really does these things or the Indians merely imagine them. The ambiguity is a result of the writer's simultaneous use of two different codes of reality, the traditional Indian code and the scientific code of mainstream America.

In Vizenor's work bizarre events are seldom ambiguous. Some are wildly improbable. Sir Cecil's practice of gambling with people for their lives, for example, is clearly a fantasy of the science-fiction variety—events that have not happened but could if present conditions, such as the depletion of the American gas supply, were extrapolated. A supernatural event that is not ambiguous, that clearly happens within the context of the novel, is Proude's passage from this world (the third), into the fourth, another dimension. What is important to Vizenor is not measuring events in a work of fiction against reality, but measuring them "against what is natural in the world of the work." In the introduction to *Wordarrows,* Vizenor quotes literary critic Monroe Berger's observation about the "reader's desire for a combination of the recognizable and the unusual." The novel ends with Proude entering the fourth world, leaving his wife behind looking mournfully at his footprints in the snow. Vizenor revised the novel in 1990 and changed the title from *Darkness in Saint Louis Bearheart* to *Bearheart: The Heirship Chronicles.*

In May 1981 Vizenor married Laura Hall, an ethnic-studies scholar from London, who received her Ph.D. at Berkeley in 1995 and now teaches there. In 1983 he published two books, *Earthdivers: Tribal Narratives on Mixed Descent,* a collection of essays and short stories, and *The People Named the Chippewa: Narrative Histories,* a series of historical essays about his tribe.

In *Earthdivers* the pieces are variations on the theme of being "mixedblood," a term Vizenor says possesses "no social or scientific validation because blood mixture is not a measurement of consciousness, culture, or human experiences. . . ." He proudly claims his heritage as a descendant of the Metis, or mixedbloods, of Canada. The title of the collection comes from the Anishinaabe creation myth, in which Muskrat, with the help of Nanabozho, creates the earth by diving to the bottom of the boundless waters and bringing up several grains of sand. Vizenor explains that the "Metis, or mixedblood, earthdivers in these stories dive into unknown urban places now, into the racial darkness in the cities, to create a new consciousness of coexistence."

The best of the stories in *Earthdivers* is "The Chair of Tears," an absurdly comic depiction of the search for a chair of a department of American Indian Studies. The pieces in the book vary from such wild fantasies to primarily factual works, such as "Sand Creek Survi-

vors," about a young Indian boy who hangs himself in jail. It may seem odd to find fiction and nonfiction in the same collection, but in Vizenor's work these forms are not distinct genres. They exist on an imaginative continuum. Vizenor's creative powers are obvious in shaping the material of "Sand Creek Survivors," and although he sticks close to the facts, the reporter he calls Clement Beaulieu is Vizenor himself.

Many of the events in "The Chair of Tears" are extrapolations and exaggerations of things that happened in the Department of Native American Studies at Berkeley. Over the years Vizenor has drawn heavily from his academic life in his work. Pink Stallion, the satyromaniacal professor of "Satirical Stallion," is a caricature of Vizenor's former chairman Terry Wilson, who appears frequently in Vizenor's works. At times Vizenor borrows Wilson's name and little else. Twelve-wives Wilson in *Bearheart* and Battle Wilson in *Griever* have little to do with Terry Wilson. On other occasions, as with Terrocious PanAnna in *The Trickster of Liberty: Tribal Heirs to a Wild Baronage* (1988) and Pink Stallion in *Earthdivers,* Vizenor caricatures Wilson by exaggerating events from his colorful life.

The People Named the Chippewa: Narrative Histories seems a straightforward title for a book of essays about Vizenor's tribe, but it is not. The word *named* is a verb, the subject of which is people (that is, "white colonists"). As Vizenor points out, "In the language of the tribal past, the families of the woodland spoke of themselves as the Anishinaabe until the colonists named them Ojibwe and Chippewa." Whites encouraged, even forced, tribes to abandon their languages and to forget their history. To redress this insult to his people Vizenor writes his own history of his tribe, drawing heavily on Anishinaabe accounts.

One of Vizenor's major points in *The People Named the Chippewa* is that culture is more than a matter of blood. People invent their cultures; they define themselves existentially by telling stories about themselves. The stories Vizenor tells in these narratives range from historical accounts of nineteenth-century fur trappers to contemporary tales of urban reformers, radicals, and alcoholics.

Vizenor won the 1983 Film in the Cities screenplay award for *Harold of Orange,* a comic movie about a trickster who bilks a foundation into funding imaginary projects. Harold Sinseer, the trickster, asks the foundation to fund a coffee plantation on the reservation so that Indians can open coffeehouses. Then, he predicts, Indians will give up alcohol for coffee and engage in the radical discussions endemic to coffeehouses. The movie ends with a hilarious softball game between foundation whites and reservation Indians. *Harold of Orange* was released as a motion picture in 1984 with Oneida comic

Charlie Hill in the role of Harold Sinseer. The screenplay was published as *Shadow Distance* (1994).

In 1985 Vizenor introduced his most interesting trickster hero, Griever de Hocus, who serves as his fictional alter ego. Griever is from White Earth, Vizenor's ancestors' reservation in northern Minnesota. He first appeared in "Luminous Thighs," a short story first published in the academic journal *Genre* (Summer 1985) and later collected in *The Lightning Within: An Anthology of Contemporary American Indian Fiction* (1991). In that story Griever and China Browne, an old friend from the reservation, are tourists at Cambridge University.

In Vizenor's 1987 novel, *Griever, An American Monkey King in China,* Griever teaches English at Tianjin University, as Vizenor himself did in 1983. As critic Louis Owens says, the novel is "somewhat paradoxically autobiographical while at the same time determinedly nonrepresentational." Vizenor once again takes people who actually exist and events that really happened and exaggerates them to the point of fantasy.

Griever, like all tricksters, is a rebel against authority, and he devotes his efforts in China to liberating whomever and whatever he can. Most of his efforts, however, are in vain. He begins with a nightingale, but when he lets it out of its cage, it flies back in. He next buys chickens in a market to free them from death at the hands of a butcher. The chickens refuse to fly off. He frees prisoners on their way to execution by hijacking their truck, but some of the prisoners will not leave the truck, and the rest are shot as they flee.

In depicting Griever, Vizenor combines the Anishinaabe trickster Nanabozho with Monkey, the trickster hero of Chinese folktale and opera. The folk epic *Journey to the West* tells how Monkey plays tricks on the Jade Emperor, the Queen of Heaven, and even Buddha himself. After punishing Monkey for his audacity, Buddha sends him on a quest to India to bring back sacred teachings. Monkey is accompanied on his quest by Pigsy and Sandy, spirits who have been transformed into monsters as punishment for their sins.

In *Griever,* when the Chinese insist that Griever have a photograph taken for his identification card, he paints his face to resemble Monkey as he is depicted in Chinese comic opera. As Griever does battle with the Chinese cadres, he is helped by modern avatars of Pigsy and Sandy. Yet, Griever, like most tricksters, loses as often as he wins. The woman he loves is murdered for carrying his baby, and Griever barely escapes, heading for Macao in a tiny airplane powered by a snowmobile engine sent to him from White Earth Reservation. The book does not reveal if he makes it, but in 1994 Vizenor went to Macao to examine the setting for another, as yet unpublished, Griever novel.

Robert Redford, Vizenor, and Charlie Hill at the Sundance Film Festival in 1983, the year Vizenor won the Sundance Institute Film in the Cities Screenplay Award for his motion picture Harold of Orange *(Collection of Gerald Vizenor)*

Griever is a minor character in *The Trickster of Liberty,* which Vizenor calls a novel but is more a collection of sketches and stories. The book is set on White Earth Reservation, Griever's home, and the reader learns of Griever's origin:

> Griever was born without a name, the child of a caravan called the Universal Hocus Crown. His mother told him that she met his father at three places on the reservation . . . and then "the caravan and your father, gone in less than a week." She never even learned his real name.

The name Griever comes from his father's manual *How to Be Sad and Downcast and Still Live in Better Health than People Who Pretend to Be So Happy,* which includes an exposition of "Griever time meditation," a method of curing "colds, headaches, heartaches, tired feet, and humdrum blood."

Most of *The Trickster of Liberty* is taken up with the adventures of the Browne family, the nobility of White Earth Reservation. Most notable among this clan are Griever's friend China Browne, a magazine writer who goes to China to find Griever; Tune Browne, who founds the New School of Socioacupuncture "under his hat on Sproul Plaza at the University of California"; and Tulip Browne, a private investigator who solves a case involving witchcraft and a stolen computer in the

Native American Mixedblood Studies Department at Berkeley (based on a real incident in Vizenor's department). Another character is Eternal Flame Browne, a former nun who establishes a "scapehouse" for wounded reservation women. The reappearance of the scapehouse, first introduced in *Bearheart,* is an indication of Vizenor's reluctance to say goodbye to characters and places at the end of a work. Finally, there is a Slyboots Browne, the inventor who in *Griever* sends Griever the microlight airplane he uses in his escape attempt from China. Slyboots sets out with "three airborne warriors" for China, where he sells his microlights while searching for Griever.

In *The Trickster of Liberty* Vizenor again uses fantasy as a vehicle for his trenchant social and political commentary. The best episode of the book, which could easily stand alone as a short story, is "The Last Lecture on the Edge." A former priest called Father Mother Browne establishes a "tavern and sermon center" called the Last Lecture next to a precipice called The Edge of the White Earth. People who want to change their lives stand up in the tavern, give a lecture, make a last phone call, and drop over the edge.

Among the lecturers are Marie Gee, a mixedblood educator, one of the "first generation of Indian experts." She admits to selling out the children she taught "for the power and money bestowed on us by liberal whites." The second lecturer is Coke de Fountain, "an urban pantribal radical and dealer in cocaine," based on one of the AIM leaders Vizenor had come to despise. The final lecturer, Homer Yellow Snow, is a white writer who has made a career of pretending to be Indian. He promises that "Within the hour . . . the Indian author you thought you knew will step over the edge and become a Greek, an Italian, perhaps a Turk, but no more will I be your Indian." Yellow Snow is a slightly disguised version of Jamake Highwater, a writer of Greek descent who posed as an Indian to write a series of books about American Indian philosophy.

In 1990 Vizenor published *Crossbloods: Bone Courts, Bingo, and Other Reports,* a collection of essays, and *Interior Landscapes: Autobiographical Myths and Metaphors,* an autobiography. The word *crossbloods* is a Vizenor neologism, another term for mixedbloods, but one that Vizenor invests with new connotations: "Crossbloods are a postmodern tribal bloodline, an encounter with racialism, colonial duplicities, sentimental monogenism, and generic cultures."

Crossbloods includes Vizenor's views on contemporary political issues in Indian country. One important issue is the question of ownership of the remains of tribal members. Whereas the remains of whites, blacks, and most other ethnics are held sacred, the bones and possessions buried with Indians have frequently been dug up and exhibited in museums. In Iowa in the 1970s, for example, a bulldozer operator dug up an unmarked cemetery, uncovering the bodies of twenty-seven people. Twenty-six were immediately reburied; the other, identified as an Indian girl, was taken by the state archeologist, who insisted he had a right to the body under Iowa law. Because of the efforts of Vizenor and others, such Indian remains are being returned to their tribes for reburial.

Another controversy is bingo, a source of enormous revenue to tribes. Some Indians and whites have attacked Indian gaming on moral grounds or because it attracts organized crime, but Vizenor, while acknowledging the problems and dangers of bingo, points out that "Bingo has earned millions of dollars for the tribal community near Red Wing, Minnesota; roads have been paved, each child in the community has a trust fund, health and dental care are provided, and members of the tribal community receive a cash dividend once a month. Where other economic development ventures have failed, high stakes bingo has resolved the unemployment problems in the first few months of operation."

In general Vizenor takes the middle ground on Indian issues. In *Crossbloods* he ridicules Ronald Reagan for saying, "Maybe we made a mistake in trying to maintain Indian cultures. Maybe we should not have humored them in wanting to stay in that kind of primitive lifestyle." Yet, Vizenor also pillories the politically correct "romantics and culture cultists" of the Left, who have "homogenized tribal philosophies and transvalued tribal visions into counterculture slogans and environmental politics."

Interior Landscapes covers Vizenor's life from 1934 to 1989, focusing mainly on his youth, with a full account of his childhood, adolescence, military career, and university education and saying little about his life since the early 1970s. He leaves out his adventures in academe, his second marriage, his lecture tours, and his other travels, which have taken him all over the globe.

In *Interior Landscapes* Vizenor explicitly states his ideas on autobiography: "Gerald Vizenor implies that autobiographies are imaginative histories," he says, discussing himself in the third person, "a remembrance past the barriers, and wild pastimes over the pronouns." He attempts to imagine and invent himself by "loosening the seams in the coarse shrouds of imposed identities." The subtitle of the volume, *Autobiographical Myths and Metaphors,* refers to Vizenor's struggle to transcend quotidian reality. His wild metaphors, often mixed, exemplify what grammarians call "catachresis," using words in strained and unaccustomed ways. Catachresis, then, is Vizenor's trademark, his attempt to expand the bounds of language, and therefore reality. Vizenor quotes the critic George Steiner's observation that "language is the main instrument of man's refusal to accept the world as it is." Vizenor is most catachrestic when discussing writing and its relationship to identity: "My survival is mythic, an imaginative transition, an intellectual predation, deconstructed as masks and metaphors at the water holes in autobiographies."

The chronology of *Interior Landscapes* is haphazard, omitting long periods and moving back and forth in time because, Vizenor says, "Some stories choose their best time to be told, and other stories take their chances." As a result, he has painted a highly impressionistic self-portrait, and an illuminating one.

In 1991, just before the five-hundredth anniversary of Christopher Columbus's discovery of America, Vizenor published *The Heirs of Columbus,* a postmodern historical novel. Whereas most Indians who spoke out about Columbus during the quincentennial decried the desecration of their Eden by white colonialists, Vizenor depicts Columbus favorably—and as Indian descended from Mayas by way of Sephardic Jews. *The Heirs of Columbus* includes historical events but abandons verisimilitude for absurdist fantasy. Columbus fathers a child

Dust jacket for Vizenor's 1987 novel, for which he won an American Book Award

by an Indian from Samana Cay. His descendants, Anishinaabe from the White Earth Reservation, become wealthy from bingo and other enterprises and eventually set up a utopian republic at Point Assinka in Washington, where they heal maladjusted and deformed people through gene therapy, using the powerful genes of Christopher Columbus.

The plot may seem preposterous in an historical novel, especially if the reader expects something like Sir Walter Scott's *Ivanhoe* (1820), but the events in *The Heirs of Columbus* are not much more farfetched than Ivanhoe's adventures with Robin Hood or Scott's Crusader novel *The Talisman* (1825). The difference is that Scott packaged fantasy to look like historical reality, and Vizenor depicts real historical relations between whites and Indians by using fantasy.

Vizenor domesticates Columbus, thus rendering him harmless for Indians. As Vizenor says in the epilogue to *The Heirs of Columbus:* "Columbus arises in tribal stories that heal with humor the world that he wounded; he is loathed, but he is not a separation in

tribal consciousness. The Admiral of the Ocean Sea is a trickster overturned in his own stories five centuries later." *The Heirs of Columbus* is Vizenor's most accessible and entertaining novel, despite its bewildering array of characters, a new one in every chapter or what A. Robert Lee calls "a Jacobean plenty of a cast."

Vizenor's 1992 book, *Dead Voices: Natural Agonies in the New World,* is a novel comprising a series of stories. The narrator is identified only as Laundry, a university professor who lectures on tribal philosophies and meets a mixedblood woman named Bagese, who "reeked of urine, and the marbled sweat on her stout neck had a wicked stench." Vizenor, as usual, fights to find beauty in the ugliest of beings. Bagese introduces the narrator to the game of *wanaki,* played with special cards marked with animals. As Bagese turns up the cards in succession, the animals tell their stories. In these stories–Vizenor's most wildly imaginative yet–bears live in mirrors; fleas wage war on an exterminator; a squirrel forgives the hunter who shoots it; Nanabozho makes anthropologists out of feces; and a crossblood woman can empower birch trees to create paper products by speaking an unknown tribal language to them.

Vizenor employs odd points of view to convey his political and cultural ideas. For instance, the fleas are not only concerned about the exterminator; they are also worried about how they can survive the poisons in the blood of humans. When the fleas discuss declaring war on the exterminator, the fleas that live on doves are for peace, while those that fed on the sparrows favor war. The fleas enlist the support of the birds and drive off the exterminator, who is pecked and flea bitten almost to death.

The sources for many of the stories are traditional Anishinaabe tales, but Vizenor also draws on his imagination and experiences, recycling some of his old stories. The story of Ducks the squirrel is an example of Vizenor's adaptation of life into art. After a hunter wounds the squirrel, he fires four more shots into its head trying to put it out of its misery. By the last shot the hunter is in tears, begging the squirrel for forgiveness. In *Interior Landscapes* Vizenor tells virtually the same story about himself. After he killed the squirrel, he gave up hunting because it caused a "separation from the natural world." This separation, a natural consequence of urban life, is a major theme of *Dead Voices.*

The title, *Dead Voices,* refers to the speech of the "wordies," white Americans whose voices have always been dead and who have killed the tribal voices as well: "The tribes are dead, our voices are traced, published and buried, our voices are dead in the eye of the missionaries." Vizenor contrasts the living oral tradition of tribal stories with the lifeless transcriptions of them made by anthropologists and missionaries and says, "We must go on, we must go on and be heard over the dead voices." Vizenor is of course aware of the irony that here and elsewhere he has written down the oral stories, but he does not justify it. He has the narrator explain how Bagese would disapprove of what he has done and how she might return to pummel him for his act.

In *Manifest Manners: Postindian Warriors of Survivance* (1994), a collection of essays, Vizenor, who has long been interested in critical theory, applies poststructuralist ideas to questions of Indian identity and culture. When the whites overwhelmed traditional tribal cultures, they imposed identities on the Indians, pressuring them to accept the "manifest manners of domination." In the place of the Indians of the eighteenth and nineteenth centuries there are now "postindians" who must invent themselves out of the detritus of their cultures. As Vizenor puts it: "The postindian warriors hover at last over the ruins of tribal representations and surmount the scriptures of manifest manners with new stories. . . . The postindian arises from the earlier inventions of the tribes only to contravene the absence of the real with theatrical performances; the theatre of tribal consciousness is the recreation of the real, not the absence of the real in the simulations of dominance."

Having laid the theoretical basis of his ideas in the initial essay, "Postindian Warriors," Vizenor goes on to examine aspects of tribal life, for example, gambling, which he favors for the revenue it provides, and AIM: "The American Indian Movement, two decades after the occupation of Wounded Knee, is more kitsch and tired simulation than menace or moral tribal visions."

A controversy surrounded the appearance of *Shadow Distance: A Gerald Vizenor Reader* in 1994. The cover illustration is a color reproduction of a work by German artist Dirk Gortler. This "expressionistic montage," as Vizenor describes it, includes a portrait of Vizenor and an "androgynous nude trickster figure" facing a large bear standing on its hind legs. When it was displayed in a case at the Ethnic Studies Department at Berkeley, the department chair, Elaine Kim, ordered the book cover removed because it offended the women of the department. Vizenor was offended by the removal and eventually left Ethnic Studies for American Studies.

Hotline Healers: An Almost Browne Novel (1997) continues the saga of the Browne clan of White Earth. Almost, a distant relative of Griever and a trickster in his own right, is another Vizenor alter ego: a lecturer in the humanities who bounces from one American university to the next much in the manner of his creator. Almost, the son of a native nun, Eternal Flame Browne, and a native priest, Father Mother Browne, lives to tease: "We live forever in stories, not manners, so, tease the chance of conception, tease your mother."

Dust jacket for Vizenor's 1997 book, his second novel about the Browne family of White Earth Reservation

As Almost travels from university to university, Vizenor parodies several of his former colleagues. His description of an absurd faculty meeting of the English department at Oklahoma University, for example, settles a few scores and gives some comfort to his old allies.

Fugitive Poses: Native American Indian Scenes of Absence and Presence (1998) is a collection of essays about "academic surveillance, simulations, resistance, natural reason, survivance, and *transmotion* of native sovereignty." Vizenor starts his observations by recounting his experiences in Tianjin University, which he fictionalized in *Griever,* and reminding the reader of the similarities between the Chinese trickster Monkey and Nanabozho, the Chippewa trickster. Stories about Monkey were subject to "communistic censure" in China, while Nanabozho stories were expurgated by missionaries in the United States. Vizenor goes on to compare the kinds of censorship one encounters in China and the United States. At Tianjin University authorities did not allow books in his courses; they Xeroxed sections for each class. When they read and were appalled by the homosexual sex scenes in Jerzy Kosinski's *Being There* (1970), they claimed the Xerox machine was broken.

In California students at two colleges strongly objected to the graphic depictions of sexual violence in *Bearheart* and were outraged with Vizenor and the instructors who had assigned it. "Students were the new censors," Vizenor complained. Vizenor points out that stories have a liberating power, so small-minded tyrants instinctively try to block their dissemination. Censorship is harsher in China, he argues, but it is not unknown in the United States.

The title essay in *Fugitive Poses* addresses simulations and survivance. "Survivance," a Vizenor neologism, implies "more than survival, more than endurance or mere response; the stories of survivance are an active presence." For Indians survivance means persisting authentically in the face of attempts by mainstream society (and some Indians) to portray Indians in various simulations. "The *indian* is an imprinted picture, the pose of a continental fugitive. The simulation of the other is the absence of the native; the *indian* is the imprimatur of a theistic civilization." Vizenor cites French theorists Michel Foucault, Roland Barthes, and Jean Baudrillard on the topic of simulation to show how and why the image of the Indian in America today is an invention based on fiction and lies.

Vizenor is fond of pointing out similarities among figures whom no one else would see as having anything in common. In the introduction to *Fugitive Poses* he compares Che Guevara and Thomas Jefferson on the subject of race, and in the title essay he shows the basic similarity in outlook between Theodor de Bry, the sixteenth-century engraver who made gruesome engravings of Indians as savages, and Russell Means, the American Indian Movement firebrand who led the Red Power movement in the 1970s. Means posed for Andy Warhol's *American Indian* series, played Chingachgook in the 1992 remake of the motion picture *The Last of the Mohicans,* and was an adviser to Disney for the 1995 movie *Pocahontas.* Vizenor finds Means's portrayal of Indians no more authentic than he does de Bry's depictions of savages; however, he holds Means more accountable, because he expects more from someone who presents himself as a spokesman for Indians.

Vizenor continues to write essays, poetry, and fiction. One of the most versatile, innovative, and productive American writers, he is widely regarded as a leading American Indian writer and as a major presence in American letters.

Interviews:

Joseph Bruchac, "Follow the Trickroutes: An Interview with Gerald Vizenor," in his *Survival This Was: Interviews with American Indian Poets* (Tucson: University of Arizona Press, 1987);

Laura Coltelli, "Gerald Vizenor," in her *Winged Words: American Indian Writers Speak* (Lincoln: University of Nebraska Press, 1990), pp. 155–184;

Helmbrecht Breinig and Klaus Losch, "Gerald Vizenor," in *American Contradictions: Interviews with Nine American Writers,* edited by Breinig and Wolfgang Binder (Hanover, N.H.: Wesleyan University Press/University Press of New England, 1995);

Dallas Miller, "Mythic Rage and Laughter: An Interview with Gerald Vizenor," *Studies in American Indian Literatures,* 7 (Spring 1995): 77–95;

Larry McCaffery and Tom Marshall, "On Thin Ice, You Might As Well Dance: An Interview with Gerald Vizenor," in *Some Other Fluency: Interviews with Innovative American Authors,* edited by McCaffery (Philadelphia: University of Pennsylvania Press, 1996), pp. 287–309;

Hartwig Isernhagen, "Gerald Vizenor," in his *Momaday, Vizenor, Armstrong: Conversations on American Indian Writing* (Norman: University of Oklahoma Press, 1999).

References:

Kimberly M. Blaeser, *Gerald Vizenor: Writing in the Oral Tradition* (Norman: University of Oklahoma Press, 1996);

Richard F. Fleck, ed., *Critical Perspectives on Native American Fiction* (Washington, D. C.: Three Continents Press, 1993), pp. 145–181;

A. Robert Lee, ed., *Loosening the Seams: Interpretations of Gerald Vizenor* (Bowling Green, Ohio: Bowling Green State University Popular Press, 2000);

Louis Owens, "Ecstatic Strategies: Gerald Vizenor's Trickster Narratives," in his *Other Destinies: Understanding the American Indian Novel* (Norman: University of Oklahoma Press, 1992), pp. 225–254;

James Ruppert, "Mythic Vision: *Bearheart: The Heirship Chronicles*," in his *Mediation in Contemporary Native American Fiction* (Norman: University of Oklahoma Press, 1995), pp. 92–108;

Studies in American Indian Literatures, special Vizenor issue, edited by Owens, 9 (Spring 1997);

Alan R. Velie, "Beyond the Novel Chippewa-Style: Gerald Vizenor's Post-Modern Fiction," in his *Four American Indian Literary Masters: N. Scott Momaday, James Welch, Leslie Marmon Silko, and Gerald Vizenor* (Norman: University of Oklahoma Press, 1982), pp. 123–148.

Papers:

Some of Gerald Vizenor's papers are in the Manuscript Collection at the Minnesota Historical Society in St. Paul and in the Kerlan Collection at the University of Minnesota Library, Minneapolis.

Edmund White

(13 January 1940 –   )

Nicholas F. Radel
Furman University

BOOKS: *When Zeppelins Flew,* by White and Peter Wood (New York: Time-Life Books, 1969);

The First Men, by White and Dale Browne (New York: Time-Life Books, 1973);

Forgetting Elena (New York: Random House, 1973); republished as *Forgetting Elena; and, Nocturnes for the King of Naples* (London: Picador, 1984);

The Joy of Gay Sex: An Intimate Guide for Gay Men to the Pleasures of a Gay Lifestyle, by White and Charles Silverstein (New York: Crown, 1977);

Nocturnes for the King of Naples (New York: St. Martin's Press, 1978; London: Deutsch, 1979 [i.e. 1980]);

States of Desire: Travels in Gay America (New York: Dutton, 1980; London: Deutsch, 1980);

A Boy's Own Story (New York: Dutton, 1982; London: Pan, 1983);

Caracole (New York: Dutton, 1985; London: Pan, 1986);

The Darker Proof: Stories from a Crisis, by White and Adam Mars-Jones (London: Faber & Faber, 1987; New York: New American Library, 1988);

The Beautiful Room is Empty (New York: Knopf, 1988; London: Pan, 1988);

Genet: A Biography (New York: Knopf, 1993; London: Chatto & Windus, 1993);

The Burning Library: Essays, edited by David Bergman (New York: Knopf, 1994); republished as *The Burning Library: Writings on Art, Politics, and Sexuality, 1969–1993* (London: Chatto & Windus, 1994);

Sketches from Memory: People and Places in the Heart of Our Paris, by White and Hubert Sorin (London: Chatto & Windus, 1994); republished as *Our Paris: Sketches from Memory* (New York: Knopf, 1995);

Skinned Alive: Stories (New York: Knopf, 1995; London: Chatto & Windus, 1995);

The Farewell Symphony (London: Chatto & Windus, 1997; New York: Knopf, 1997);

Marcel Proust (New York: Viking, 1999); republished as *Proust* (London: Weidenfeld & Nicolson, 1999);

The Married Man (London: Chatto & Windus, 2000); republished as *The Married Man: A Love Story* (New York: Knopf, 2000).

Edmund White (photograph by Anne de Brunhoff)

Editions: *States of Desire: Travels in Gay America,* afterword by White (New York: Plume, 1991);

A Boy's Own Story, introduction by White (London: Picador, 1994).

PLAY PRODUCTIONS: *The Blueboy in Black,* New York City, Masque Theater, April 1963;

Trios, Leicester, Haymarket Studio, November 1990; London, Riverside Studios, July 1993; Cork, Ireland, The Granary, September 1995.

RECORDING: *Edmund White Reads Nocturnes for the King of Naples (Chapter Eight) and A Boy's Own Story*

(Excerpt). Edmund White Reads The Beautiful Room is Empty (Chapter Two), Columbia, Mo., American Audio Prose Library, 1989.

OTHER: "Goldfish and Olives," in *New Campus Writing No. 4,* edited by Nolan Miller and Judson Jerome (New York: Grove, 1962), pp. 110–131;

"The Beautiful Room is Empty," in *The Other Persuasion: An Anthology of Short Fiction about Gay Men and Women,* edited by Seymour Kleinberg (New York: Viking, 1977), pp. 279–299;

"The Passionate Friends," in *On the Line: New Gay Fiction,* edited by Ian Young (Trumansburg, N.Y.: Crossing Press, 1981), pp. 21–34;

Jean Genet, *Fragments . . . et autres textes,* preface by White (Paris: Gallimard, 1990);

Genet, *Prisoner of Love,* translated by Barbara Bray, introduction by White (London: Picador, 1990);

The Faber Book of Gay Short Fiction, edited, with an introduction, by White (London & Boston: Faber & Faber, 1991);

Coleman Dowell, *A Star-Bright Lie,* foreword by White (Normal, Ill.: Dalkey Archive Press, 1993);

Genet, *The Selected Writings of Jean Genet,* edited by White (Hopewell, N.J.: Ecco Press, 1993);

Denton Welch, *A Lunch Appointment,* foreword by White (North Pomfret, Vt.: Elysium Press, 1993);

Robert Mapplethorpe, *Altars,* text by White (New York: Random House, 1995; London: Cape, 1995);

Oscar Wilde, *The Picture of Dorian Gray,* introduction by White, Oxford World's Classics (Oxford & New York: Oxford University Press, 1999).

SELECTED PERIODICAL PUBLICATIONS– UNCOLLECTED:

FICTION

"The Hermaphrodite," *Review of Contemporary Fiction,* 16 (Fall 1996): 27–30.

NONFICTION

"The Library Without Walls," "Extracts from the Panel Discussions," *Shenandoah,* 33, no. 3 (1982): 10–18, 27, 31, 35–38, 41, 40, 42, 44–45;

"Residence on Earth: Living with AIDS in the '80s," *Life,* 12 (Fall 1989): 135;

"Edmund White Speaks With Edmund White," *Review of Contemporary Fiction,* 16 (Fall 1996): 13–20;

"Journals of the Plague Years," *Nation,* 264 (12 May 1997): 13–18;

"The Joy of Gay Lit," *Out* (September 1997): 110–197.

Edmund White is unarguably the preeminent author of the white gay male subculture. His career coincides almost exactly with the rise of the modern gay movement in the 1960s, and his work documents articulately and vividly the transition from a time when homosexuality was regarded as a sin or a disease, to our own era when gay writing and cultural production has moved front and center. White's works signal and celebrate this transformation. Like many important American novelists working within ethnic traditions, White reveals how a minority perspective can create a more universal interest. That he is one of the first and most prolific writers to do so from a self-conscious and perhaps politicized gay perspective marks him as singularly important.

More than any other contemporary gay male writer, White has achieved a large crossover following among heterosexual readers and critics. His autobiographical novel, *A Boy's Own Story* (1982), became a bestseller in the United States and England, and helped transform the gay narratological tradition of the "coming out" story into a newly respectable literary narrative. His works are reviewed not only in gay and lesbian publications but in such mainstream publications as *The New York Times, The Chicago Tribune, The Nation,* and *The New Republic.*

White's many honors include an American Academy and Institute for Arts and Letters award for fiction and a Guggenheim Fellowship, both in 1983. He won the National Book Critics Circle Award for *Genet: A Biography* in 1993, and the French government awarded him the Chevalier de l'ordre des arts et lettres the same year. White was made a member of the American Academy of Arts and Letters in 1997.

Edmund Valentine White III was born in Cincinnati, Ohio, on 13 January 1940, to Delilah Teddlie White, a child psychologist, and Edmund Valentine White II, a chemical engineer. His parents divorced when he was seven, and White, his mother, and his sister, the future psychotherapist Margaret Fleming, moved to Evanston, Illinois. Fleming told Leonard Schulman, who wrote a profile of White for *Time* magazine (1990), that the divorce had a profound effect on the future writer. White felt deeply rejected by his father, and that rejection is perhaps reflected in the many cold and distant father figures that appear in his fiction. After his parents' divorce White was sent to Cranbrook Academy, a boarding school near Detroit, Michigan, where he began the difficult process of coming to terms with his homosexuality. That period in his life provided the basis for one of his most significant books, *A Boy's Own Story,* because it was at that time that White learned firsthand about the self-hatred imposed on young gay men by a society that abominates homosexuality. After Cranbrook, White attended the University of Michigan, studying Chinese and graduating with a B.A. in 1962. He then moved to New York City, where he was accepted into a writer's training program for Time-Life Books. He worked there from 1962 until 1970.

At Time-Life White wrote *When Zeppelins Flew* (1969) with Peter Wood, and *The First Men* (1973) with Dale Browne. Although he has said that his job at Time-Life sapped the energy he might have devoted to creative work, White evidently wrote prolifically during this period, completing several novels and plays that remain unpublished. One play, *The Blueboy in Black,* was produced off-Broadway in 1963, but ran for only thirty-two performances. By 1970 White was ready to move on, and with the money he earned through the profit-sharing plan at Time-Life, he moved to Rome for a year; there, he told Kay Bonetti in a 1989 interview (published in 1990), he did no work at all. When he returned to New York, he worked as an editor at *Horizon,* did freelance editing and writing, and served as senior editor for *The Saturday Review.* Most important, he wrote his first published novel, *Forgetting Elena* (1973). White continued to write prolifically but was not able to make a living from his writing. Therefore, until the early 1980s he also worked as a journalist and as a ghostwriter of college textbooks. From 1977 to 1979 White was assistant professor of English at Johns Hopkins University, and from 1980 until 1982 he was adjunct professor of creative writing at Columbia University.

In 1983 White was able to move to Paris on money he received from the Guggenheim Foundation. Reviving a role played by American novelists from Henry James to Ernest Hemingway and James Baldwin, White continued to live and work in France until the early 1990s, when he was briefly employed as a full professor at Brown University in Providence, R.I. After leaving Brown, White returned to Paris until 1997, when he accepted a tenured position in creative writing at Princeton University.

White's work falls naturally into several major categories. The first includes his novels *Forgetting Elena* (1973), *Nocturnes for the King of Naples* (1978), and *Caracole* (1985). Only *Nocturnes for the King of Naples* deals with explicitly gay subject matter, but all the novels have similar styles, and each is set within an overly sophisticated society that provides the occasion for its exploration of character. The stories are conspicuously nonmimetic, deeply experimental, and highly wrought. White develops to its fullest the Baroque style that distinguishes much of his work and that has led him to be compared to major writers of the European tradition such as Marcel Proust and Vladimir Nabokov.

A second category of novels is made up of the semi-autobiographical, realistic works for which White is most famous, *A Boy's Own Story* (1982), *The Beautiful Room is Empty* (1988), and *The Farewell Symphony* (1997). These works explore what it is like to have been a gay

Dust jacket for White's 1982 novel, about a homosexual growing up in America in the 1950s

man in the United States from the 1950s to the present. In particular, the novels reveal the ways in which a gay white man from the American Midwest struggles against social and self-imposed restraints on his homosexuality. Although White has resisted viewing these novels as being about a representative type, many readers have perceived them almost as allegories of emerging gay self-awareness, both individual and communal. As a result, they have been both praised for their universality and denigrated for their narrow interpretation of gay experience in white, male, middle-class terms. No one, however, denies the power of these novels as psychological portraits nor their appeal as stylistic artifacts. In this second category of realistic works also belong many of White's short stories, which were written over a period of years. Most of them have been collected in two volumes: *The Darker Proof: Stories from a Crisis* (1987), which includes stories by Adam Mars-Jones, and *Skinned Alive* (1995). *The Married Man* (2000) also belongs in this category of semi-autobiographical writings, although this novel differs from the earlier ones in being set primarily in France.

White has also produced a significant body of nonfiction that has made him one of the foremost commentators on contemporary gay life and culture in the United States and that provides a richly mineable resource for understanding his fiction. The provocative and groundbreaking work, *The Joy of Gay Sex: An Intimate Guide for Gay Men to the Pleasures of a Gay Lifestyle* (1977), was co-authored with Dr. Charles Silverstein. Although White has been criticized for this work (especially in the hindsight of the AIDS crisis), the book nevertheless represented a high point of visibility and gay sexual self-definition in the 1970s. White continued to promote gay culture and visibility with the publication of *States of Desire: Travels in Gay America* (1980), a travelogue about gay life in different regions of the United States. This book represented the first example of what would become a subgenre of gay travel narratives written throughout the 1980s and 1990s. Even though it reflects the sexual mores and values of its time and the dominant assumptions of a relatively prosperous gay male community, some critics still judge *States of Desire: Travels in Gay America* to be the best work of its kind, primarily because it brings to its subject matter the master novelist's shrewd powers of observation. White's third major work of nonfiction, a magisterial biography of the great French author, Jean Genet, was published in 1993. Over the years White has also produced a significant number of essays on literary and cultural topics that have been collected in *The Burning Library: Essays* (1994). Largely occasional pieces, the essays nevertheless provide a good source for understanding many of the issues that defined gay communities in the United States in the 1980s. In 1999 White published a short biography and critical appreciation of Proust that addresses Proust's homosexuality and reveals the ways the author's experience of his sexuality helped shape *A Remembrance of Things Past* (1913–1927).

White has produced a few interesting miscellaneous works, as well. These works include an essay illustrated by his late lover Hubert Sorin, *Sketches from Memory: People and Places in the Heart of Our Paris* (1994), that appeared in Britain shortly after Sorin's death, as well as two collections: *The Faber Book of Gay Short Fiction* (1991) and *The Selected Writings of Jean Genet* (1993). Although White often caricatures himself as a lazy writer ("If I write a page a day, I'm lucky," he said in a 1988 *Paris Review* interview with Jordan Elgrably), he in fact writes prolifically and with passion about gay men's lives and experiences in the last half of the twentieth century. His place and position are, perhaps, best revealed by Michael Denneny, the editor at St. Martin's Press who published White's first explicitly gay novel,

Nocturnes for the King of Naples, after it had been turned down by twelve other publishers. According to Denneny, White is a literary hero of sorts. "Of all the gay writers who made it in the '70s," Denneny was quoted as saying in a 1990 *Time* magazine profile, "Edmund was the only one who had entree into the pre-existing literary circles, the sophisticated world of Susan Sontag and Richard Howard, but he turned his back on it. He wanted it known that he was a gay writer. That was a very brave decision on his part. For me, that made him a gay leader."

If White's openness and courage have made him one of gay America's most important writers and thinkers, it took a long time for his explicitly gay fiction to see its way into print. In the 1988 interview with Elgrably he said that during the 1960s he had "written five novels and six or seven plays." At least one of these novels involved gay characters and themes, for in the 1989 interview with Bonetti, White said that during that period he wrote an autobiographical gay book. He recalled in the interview with Bonetti that this early gay novel "was very long, very self-analytical, very uncritical. It went to twenty-five publishers and was rejected by everybody." He attributes the rejection, in part, to the fact that the novel was "about a middle-class homosexual," and in those days "publishers were prepared to publish books like those by John Rechy or Jean Genet or William Burroughs about freaky people, drug-takers, pimps, prostitutes, marginal gay people. . . . But it was more threatening to write about a person who was really quite like the presumably middle-class reader, except that he happened to be gay." Although these early works do not exist in print, White used passages from them in later novels, and he borrowed the title of one for *The Beautiful Room is Empty.* They became, he said in the interview with Elgrably, "a source for a lot of information, particularly about the fifties and sixties." The existence of these works suggests that White was planning to write the kind of autobiographical novel about white, middle-class gay male experience that is exemplified by *A Boy's Own Story, The Beautiful Room is Empty,* and *The Farewell Symphony,* long before the Stonewall uprising (riots that occurred at a gay bar in New York City in 1969 that precipitated the modern gay revolution). As White told Elgrably, however immodestly, "I was writing gay books well before gay liberation and before there was a recognized gay reading public."

That White's early works were rejected, however, was probably salutary, for it was the rejection of these early autobiographical writings that led him to produce his first published novel. He decided, he told Bonetti, to write a novel purely for himself, something that reflected his own taste in a way that nothing he had previously written did. The result was *Forgetting Elena,* a novel that is not, properly speaking, a gay novel, but one clearly envisioned within the refracting lenses of gay experience in the late 1960s. In a self-interview in *The Review of Contemporary Fiction* (Fall 1996), White describes its peculiar genesis on New York's Fire Island in 1969: "I had been reading Sei Shonagon's *The Pillow Book* as well as Lewis's *The Splendid Century* about Versailles. Reading about court life inflected my experience of gay life on Fire Island. I didn't make a decision to exclude homosexuality . . . but I wanted to tap the energies of homosexuality without drawing an explicit portrait of its folkways." The result is a novel that interviewers Larry McCaffery and Sinda Gregory call "hallucinogenic," because of its intricacies of style, structure, and narrative.

Forgetting Elena is primarily a satire of a society in which aesthetics have come to stand in the place of morality or ethics. It is set on an island kingdom reminiscent of the summertime society of Fire Island, a kingdom dominated by a feudal order seemingly more appropriate to the Middle Ages than the present. Part of the plot of the novel concerns the competition between two feudal groups for control of the island populace and its young prince, who narrates the novel, which is largely soliloquy. The prince's inability to remember who he is, or what his role in society should be, creates difficulties for the reader, who must piece together the context of the novel from the assorted and sometimes biased scraps of information the narrator provides. The prince seems to have been set adrift in a society in which he knows none of the rules and little about the people. It is a society in flux, one in which an "Old Code" of social and civil order has recently been replaced by a "New Code." The ethical leader of the new order is Herbert, in whose house the narrator is living at the opening of the novel. During the course of the narrative, the readers learns that Herbert has been made regent, responsible for the education of the prince and for overseeing one of the few social rituals left from the old society: the ceremonial return of the prince to the island to assume his position of leadership. One of Herbert's tasks seems to be directing the prince away from the "Old Code" faction, the Valentine family, and from Elena, a mysterious woman with whom the narrator seems to have had an affair, which he resumes over the course of the novel. Since the prince himself is a Valentine, the implication of the novel is that the internecine power struggles of the island represent the posturing of an extremely closed and provincial society.

Summary does little justice to the narrative or verbal texture of this novel, but it does help to isolate the satiric tensions at issue. *Forgetting Elena* is a novel about a society obsessed with the rules of social style even in the absence of any meaningful exposition of those rules

and about that society's hypocritical gestures toward egalitarianism and tolerance. The constant production of rules that cannot be clearly codified under the New Code produces a type of dulling conformity that one transgresses only at great cost. One could say that *Forgetting Elena* seems to expose the pretensions toward sexual and social equality that accompanied the moral experimentation in the United States in the 1970s, providing as it does so trenchant a critique of that brave and hedonistic new world. On this level, the novel is about the giving over of an old order that has, as the novelist Harry Mathews points out, tragic implications. For that giving over is symbolized in the death of Elena, a charming young woman whose portrait is vividly and sympathetically drawn by White. The novel thus serves as a cautionary tale about a world in which moral codes have been replaced by aesthetic ones. What makes *Forgetting Elena* even more interesting is that it does not simply posit its island society as a dystopic falling away from a more authentic utopia. In spite of its satiric critique of the New Code, there is no strong reason to believe that the Old Order was any better than the new. Although Elena writes a memoir in which she represents herself as the source of authenticity and sincerity who is tragically rejected by the narrator, the novel as a whole dramatizes a series of power strategies within a constantly changing order. As Elena puts it in her memoir: "Surely Herbert had known that by changing the Old Code to the New he had introduced the dangerous notion of change itself." The novel is a comedy of manners with no more clear moral center than the ruminations of its unreliable narrator and its rejected eponymous heroine.

Critics were almost unanimous in both their praise for and their confusion over *Forgetting Elena*. On one level, the novel was correctly identified as belonging to an existential tradition in its concern with the narrator's search for identity and authenticity. Some (including White, in the interview with McCaffery and Gregory) saw the prince's failure to know himself, his forgetting, as a strategic virtue that allows him to evade culpability, in particular responsibility for his multiple disloyalties to the various ruling factions and for his role in the suicide of Elena. So, while the narrator gains the trust and sympathy of the reader, he is gradually revealed to be unreliable and sometimes even duplicitous. It is a narrative strategy typical of White's early works, one he later used to great effect in *A Boy's Own Story*.

Alan Friedman in *The New York Times Book Review* (25 March 1973) was the only reviewer to raise the question of the narrator's sexual identity. To the extent that *Forgetting Elena* seems to represent a character who has been heterosexually involved but who has come to

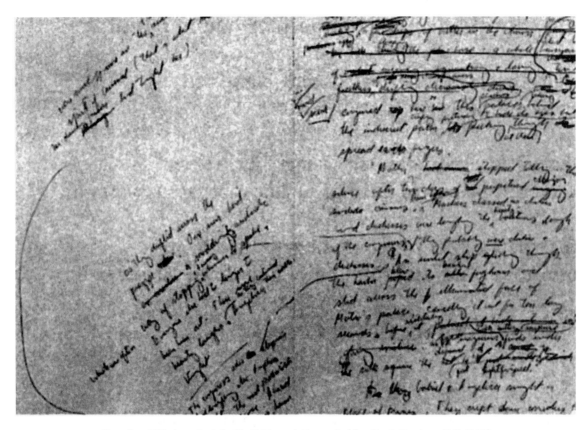

Page from White's notebook for his 1985 novel, Caracole *(from* Paris Review, *Fall 1988)*

live almost exclusively in a world of men much like the gay male milieu on Fire Island, the novel might be said to represent allegorically a kind of gay "coming out" story. If so, the prince's "arrival" on the island, his ceremonial assumption of an exalted place in society, his coming out, is, indeed, a type of productive forgetting. In such a reading, the prince himself might be seen as the newly emergent gay man, that blank slate on which a new social order can and will be written. *Forgetting Elena* becomes a Bildungsroman in reverse, a novel in which the narrator does not discover himself, but frees himself from the restraints of being who he was, or who he currently is.

Forgetting Elena need not, however, be read simply as gay allegory. During a panel discussion at a literary symposium at George Mason University in April 1982 (extracts from which were published in the journal *Shenandoah* that same year), White said that this strangely unrealistic book actually had its origins in autobiography: "I felt I was in some ways a Midwesterner who had come to New York and was completely puzzled by this very fancy Mandarin way of acting—which I think I've now at last acquired. But it took a lot of work. I think that in a way *Forgetting Elena* was a bit

about being initiated into this spooky and slightly artificial society, the whole novel is a kind of parable about that." For all its pretending to be about a prince searching for himself on a mysterious island, *Forgetting Elena* may, indeed, be more about White seeking his own voice, finding the proper cadence of irony, satire, and celebration of what was new in the life he was living as a gay man in New York in 1969. It is an interesting assessment, and one that at least discerns the outlines of a relationship between this early experiment and White's later, explicitly autobiographical fiction.

Despite the critical success of *Forgetting Elena*, White had difficulty getting his second but first explicitly gay novel published. In the late 1970s several important gay novels appeared in the United States—including Larry Kramer's *Faggots* (1978), Andrew Holleran's *Dancer from the Dance* (1978), and James Baldwin's *Just Above My Head* (1979). White had published *The Joy of Gay Sex* and was writing *States of Desire*. It was clearly a period when interest in gay writing was emerging in full force. Nevertheless, *Nocturnes for the King of Naples* was rejected by twelve publishers before Denneny of St. Martin's Press picked it up. When it was finally published in 1978, this small, arty novel took a place alongside the novels by Kramer, Holleran, and Baldwin in the vanguard of what became a new gay and lesbian literary movement in the United States in the 1980s.

Nocturnes for the King of Naples is a series of eight prose poems read by another anonymous narrator. It is a collection of melancholy meditations, poetic nocturnes that ultimately piece together a memoir of the narrator's life and his relationship with a lover he abandoned, a man who is, in a stunning narrative strategy, addressed throughout only as "you." As the reader comes to discover, the abandoned lover has subsequently died, and there is no chance that the narrator can ever rectify his error. He is doomed to be perpetually ineffective, always meditating on the thing that cannot be changed, and becoming, in his own words, a "ghost." To the extent that it does have a plot, *Nocturnes for the King of Naples* tells the story of what in the narrator's past life anticipated his relationship to the lost lover and what subsequently happened. White has said the novel derived from his own fantasies about the young actor Keith McDermott, who rejected White's affections. The sophisticated and famous older man of the novel, White adds, is based both on himself and the poet Frank O'Hara. There is a sense, then, in which the "you" the narrator addresses, the abandoned lover, refers to the author himself, and the novel can be seen as an entirely solipsistic fantasy of desire and revenge. The origins of the novel in autobiography, however, do not obscure its powerful evocations of obsessive love and desire, loss and absence, remembrance and regret.

The novel describes, with a good deal of psychological acuity, the relationship between an older man and a younger lover, who has yet to experience a stable relationship in his life. It details both the benefits of such a relationship and the tensions that finally drive the younger man to look for love elsewhere. Nevertheless, White takes this May-December arrangement seriously, recognizing its legitimacy, as David Bergman states in *Gaiety Transfigured: Gay Self-Representation in American Literature* (1991), in a homosexual world in which erotic desire may be entangled with love for the father. That same theme is hinted at in *Forgetting Elena* as the narrator struggles with his erotic and paternal entanglements with Herbert, and it is one that will be even more powerfully developed through the narrator's identification with his father in *A Boy's Own Story*. Here, however, White explores the multiple ironies of the relationship, showing that the narrator holds a good deal of power over the older lover, but that the lover threatens to subsume his younger partner entirely. The narrator himself, it seems, only comes to appreciate the ways in which this subsuming of his person might represent completion and not obliteration with the hindsight of his own aging. Exploring these ironies, *Nocturnes for the*

King of Naples becomes a character study bordering on tragedy.

Several critics have noted that *Nocturnes for the King of Naples* looks toward Europe in its allegiances, especially to that other great paean to homoerotic desire and regret, Proust's *Remembrance of Things Past*. *Nocturnes for the King of Naples* is, on one level, about the desire for one particular man, lost to the narrator forever, the abandoned lover, the *you* of the novel. On another level it is about the melancholy ubiquity and evanescence of desire. Having rejected what he calls the "perfect love," the narrator is bound to relive the search for him over and over. It is his condition at the beginning and at the end of the novel, where we hear him talking about the passengers onboard the boat on which he is traveling: "As I looked at the other passengers, I could easily pick out those expressionless, intriguing beauties I address as *you,* those same faces, dark or fair, brooding or elated, whom I'd always believed I could love. . . ." Desire is figured as an obsessive yearning for perfection that will never be attained, the perfect lover who does not exist, and it is a search for completion doomed to failure. If the narrator of *Nocturnes for the King of Naples* sees himself as a ghost, it is because the *I* of his speaking voice can find definition only in its relationship to the *you*—to the many *you*'s—it addresses in place of the lover who was rejected. J. D. McClatchy wrote that the novel is "the Pysche's reminiscence of Eros, and its characters are the narrator's meditations on the echoes of an original erotic transcendence in his subsequent affairs and menages, which comprise the world of experience fallen from a mysterious grace."

The sustained use of the rare second-person narrative in *Nocturnes for the King of Naples* produces stunning stylistic effects, what McClatchy termed "a heady, luxuriant prose, which White plies with a poet's prodigal finesse and a moralist's canny precision." It also, however, makes the work tremendously evocative in its themes, for the "you" addressed throughout demands metaphorical readings that lead in many different directions at once. For McClatchy, it invokes the narrator's and artist's poetic muse. For Nicholas F. Radel, in his essay on White's works in *Queer Words, Queer Images: Communication and the Construction of Homosexuality* (1994), it invokes the reader, who becomes both the topic of the novel and the signifying intelligence behind it, the person able to witness the confession of the narrator and confer or withhold absolution. For White himself, as he stated in the interview with McCaffery and Gregory in 1987, the second-person narrative implies a devotional level to the work, as if divinity itself were being addressed. The existence of these various levels of meaning suggests that *Nocturnes for the King of Naples* should be read as one would read a good poem. It repays careful, detailed analysis of its language, imagery, syntax, and structure. White has said that the novel was written quickly and with little revision, but its range of literary allusion, its thematic crosscurrents, and its precise use of language would indicate otherwise. Like *Forgetting Elena, Nocturnes* is a carefully worked experimental novel and is as different from White's first novel as that one is from any novel that appeared before it. White is not a novelist to repeat himself.

Appearing immediately after White published *The Joy of Gay Sex, Nocturnes for the King of Naples* was, to a certain extent, subjected to a type of critical scrutiny that *Forgetting Elena* was not, one proceeding from the recognition, or in some cases apparent shock, that the author was gay. A certain flippancy of tone, a seeming tendency not to take homosexuality seriously as a subject for fiction, for example, marred Jeffrey Burke's March 1979 review of six books in *Harper's*, "by, about, or for homosexuals," one of which was *Nocturnes for the King of Naples*. Although Burke found White's novel admirable, especially his "gifted, witty" prose and his attention "to every word, phrase, and sentence," it was the exception to an otherwise bad lot. The review in *The New York Times Book Review* (10 December 1978) by John Yohalem was more problematic. Yohalem praised White's "exquisite" prose but went on to compare it to an Italian pastry, "gooey and fantastic." It is, he said, "narcissistic" prose. He concludes that the novel is "self-indulgent," albeit, he concedes, its excess must have seemed necessary to someone who was also the author of *The Joy of Gay Sex*. It is as if in revealing himself to be gay, White somehow could be excused for his obvious indulgences. In hindsight, Yohalem's earlier image of White's prose as a puff pastry and his Freudian language of narcissism seem equally homophobic and patronizing. If both Yohalem and Burke recognized the clear superiority of White's novel and style, their ambivalent responses to gay subject matter nevertheless suggest that even in the late 1970s the unapologetic examination of gay male desire exposed a nerve in the social body. Their reviews provide evidence, if any were needed, that the present fascination with gay issues and gay literature is recent in origin and that writers of superior gay fiction such as White were, in part at least, responsible for helping to bring about a change in attitudes toward homosexuality; his next novel, however, would do the most in that regard.

A Boy's Own Story was hugely successful, and it received ecstatic reviews from French and American critics. Although the gay British novelist Alan Hollinghurst only cautiously praised it in *TLS: The Times Literary Supplement* (19 August 1983), it sold more than one hundred thousand copies in Britain alone. White's earlier novels were great critical successes, but *A Boy's Own Story* was his first true commercial one and the book that earned him an international readership. To understand what the novel truly achieves, the reader must look at the context in which White wrote it and in which it appeared. In 1980, two years after he published *Nocturnes for the King of Naples,* and three years after *The Joy of Gay Sex,* White published *States of Desire.* White was fast becoming the articulate spokesman for a gay minority culture in the United States. For all its many limitations in defining too narrowly what might legitimately be called gay America—which have been widely acknowledged by critics and the author himself—*States of Desire* rendered a compelling portrait and incipient critique of American gay culture at the end of the 1970s. It was, White said in the 1988 *Paris Review* interview, "an attempt to see the varieties of gay experience and also to suggest the enormous range of gay life to straight and gay people. . . ." More important, *States of Desire* seemed to be part of a larger political strategy emerging in gay writing: the deliberate attempt to write about gay life and gay people as if doing so were nothing special.

In "Edmund White and the Violet Quill Club" (1996), the gay novelist Felice Picano relates the origins of a small group of writers who banded together in New York City in the early 1980s under the name the Violet Quill Club. The Violet Quill consisted of seven writers in the forefront of creating gay fiction and literature in the late 1970s and 1980s: White, Christopher Cox, Andrew Holleran, George Whitmore, Robert Ferro, Michael Grumley, and Picano. These men have written books that, according to Picano, are still "in print, still read . . . as a group they've come to represent an early high watermark in gay writing." He went on to say that White "seemed the most intensely aware of us of the problems we faced within what we were writing. And there were problems in presenting this Brave Gay New World. Should we take old forms and remodel them to fit the material? Or should we break new formal ground? How much sex should we include in our books? As much as possible to push in straight faces? . . . Should we be utterly blasé, he wondered. . . ."

White, by this time, had grown acutely conscious of what it meant to produce gay writing in the United States. He seemed to know that he and other members of the Violet Quill were creating the groundwork for a new minority literature within the American melting pot. How they did so would have significant political implications for gay men and lesbians. One result of his musings on the problems was *A Boy's Own Story,* and judging from the critical reception it received, the novel succeeded brilliantly in writing about a particular gay life, as if it were an everyday matter.

A Boy's Own Story records the coming to sexual maturity of a young man. The novel succeeds in part because of the strength of its portrait of the young man's struggle to grow into a respectable adulthood. Most critics seemed to agree with Christopher Lehmann-Haupt, in *The New York Times* (17 December 1982), who said that "this is not exclusively a homosexual boy's story. It is any boy's story, to the marvelous degree that it evokes the inchoate longing of late childhood and adolescence, the sense that somehow, someday, somewhere, life will provide a focus for these longings, and the agonizing length of time that life seems to take in getting around to this particular piece of business. For all I know, it may be any girl's own story as well." The story is tougher and less sentimental than its early critics suggest, however. Although in her review of the book for the *New York Times Book Review* (10 October 1982), Catherine Stimpson saw the novel as a cross between J. D. Salinger and Oscar Wilde, in his 1996 article on *A Boy's Own Story,* author Robert Glück observes that the novel "at heart has more in common with *The Prince* than with *The Catcher in the Rye.*"

A Boy's Own Story seems to be an example of a gay coming-out story, but it is not a typical one. These stories generally detail, often in a sentimental way, the painful, personal experiences of young gay men as they first discover their sexual difference and as they act on and accept this difference. White's novel is hardly sentimental, for if his narrator, who remains nameless throughout, is the victim of the social prejudice around him, he is also a shrewd and intelligent manipulator. The novel begins with an idyllic picture of two teenage boys exploiting their own adolescent lusts at a lake house in the summer. But it ends the next school year with the narrator's calculated sexual betrayal of one of his teachers. *A Boy's Own Story* carefully juxtaposes two images of adolescent homosexuality, its idyllic romantic face and the contortions of its social one. In between, the reader learns of the boy's struggle to master the power differentials of adult sexuality in the United States in the 1950s. Ironically, the boy in this story does not so much accept his sexual difference from the heterosexual adults around him as he comes to ape their bad behavior, their willingness to exploit sex for their own ends. The novel transforms the coming-out story into a shrewd analysis of the workings of the nuclear family, and, even more, into an exploration of the forms and workings of power in sex. Equally important, it breaks the convention by which gay novelists were supposed to present only positive images of gay people. One of the important effects of White's novel was that it helped create the imperative for gay fiction to explore its characters and social issues complexly. White was not alone in helping the gay novel to mature in this way,

Dust jacket for White's 1988 novel, the second in his semi-autobiographical trilogy

but the fact that his novel was so widely read made his influence decisive.

Whereas the usual narrative of emerging gay self-awareness proceeds toward the revelation of a unified personality, the self-accepting gay man, in *A Boy's Own Story* White toys with an Eastern, Buddhist sense of self. The narrator decribes his belief in a self that is "merely a baggage depot where random parcels have been checked . . . soon enough to be collected by different owners, an emptying out that will leave the room blissfully vacant." The notion appeals, obviously enough, to a boy who wants to annihilate what he sees as his own aberrant impulses, and it seems to suit White's sense that the gay man must struggle to create a self within a homophobic environment. White's refusal to name his heroes appropriates the invisibility of the minority figure within the American mainstream that Ralph Ellison so memorably evoked in *Invisible Man* (1952). But the narrator's assertions opposing a unified self reflect White's own philosophy on the subject, so they seem the set the stage for the contradictory roles—the almost mutually exclusive positions—that define the narrator by the end of the story. While the novel as a form almost demands that its sentral characters achieve some type of coherence, White struggles against it. The same struggle led him to write about mysterious characters with no essential inner being in *Forgetting Elena* and *Nocturnes* and later led to his daring experiments with narrative form in *The Farewell Symphony*. In *A Boy's Own Story* this struggle raises intriguing questions about what it means to be gay and the ways in which the gay self can never be unified in a homophobic society.

A Boy's Own Story has come to be a victim of its own success. If it helped to make the coming-out story a popular genre of gay literature, a younger generation of gay and lesbian critics argue that the genre has been overused, has assumed too great an importance in gay life. They criticize it because it plays on heterosexuals' sympathy at the expense of gay strength. In other words, they see the coming-out story–and White's example of it–as portraying most young homosexuals as victims who are acceptable because they can be easily pitied by heterosexual readers. That criticism can only be partly true for White's novel, because its nameless hero is only partially the victim of social forces beyond his control. But other criticisms are more trenchant. For example, in his *The Queer Renaissance: Contemporary American Literature and the Reinvention of Lesbian and Gay Identities* (1997), Robert McRuer accuses White of fabricating white, gay, middle-class experience as if it were "the original gay tale," the story that defines most essentially what it is like to be gay in the United States. *A Boy's Own Story* has come to seem too representative, the superior example of the gay novel of sexual self-determination. Thus, it has come to stand synecdochically for everyone's experience of "coming out." But, McRuer points out that many people have different experiences than White's of what it means to be gay. The critique is valid, but it also must be said that it responds not to the failings of the novel but to its strengths.

What puts *A Boy's Own Story* in a category all its own is the author's mastery of style and intellection. Most early critics seemed to think that in this novel White had tamed what they often saw as the excesses of his Baroque style. The critic for *Harper's* (October 1982) said that the novel was "written with the flourish of a master stylist," and the novelist Thomas Disch said, in a review in the *Washington Post Book World* (17 October 1982), "I've seldom read a book so continuously and variously quotable." In *A Boy's Own Story*, White seemed to have married his technical virtuosity to realistic gay writing, writing that vividly described social reality in the 1950s and that drew a complex portrait of gay American adolescence. In so doing, he may not have placed his work beyond criticism, but he did

place it beyond the particular criticism that his subject matter was unimportant, trivial, or marginal. He finally succeeded in doing what he had set out to do in his unpublished autobiographical fiction from the 1960s: write about a young man who was like other, middle-class people, except that he was gay. It was a transformation that helped pave the way for the explosion in mainstream, middle-class gay and lesbian writing that took place in the United States and England in the 1980s and 1990s.

White's next novel, *Caracole* (1985), proceeded in an entirely different direction, away from the gay scene in the United States toward Europe, and away from the realistic mode of *A Boy's Own Story* back to the elaborate formulations of the novel as textual strategy found in *Forgetting Elena* and *Nocturnes for the King of Naples*. Like those works, *Caracole* reveals the direct influence of the European novel in its emphasis on psychology, its formal experimentation, and its existential ruminations on memory and identity, but *Caracole* betrays a firsthand knowledge of European culture. Throughout much of the 1970s and early 1980s, White spent his summers in Venice with his friend, the late scholar David Kalstone, and in 1983 moved to Paris. It is no surprise then that *Caracole* is set in a mythic city of palaces and canals, masqued balls, and tribal politics. Nor is it surprising that this city lacks a recognizable gay ghetto, a marginalized subculture, indeed, any gay characters. Even though its exoticism is filtered through an American sensibility–as novelist Neil Bartlett says in his 1996 essay on *Caracole,* the capital city portrayed is part Venice, part Paris, and part Manhattan, "that other offshore island of dreams"–the novel still represents a significant departure for White, whose work after *Forgetting Elena* had been almost exclusively and explicitly concerned with gay characters and themes. It was a departure that elicited confusion and even consternation as critics struggled to understand how a self-identified gay writer could write exclusively about heterosexuality (for like White's other books, this one is also about sex and desire) and how he could seem to betray his emerging gay audience. The concern itself, of course, is homophobic in its assumption that gay writers must always and exclusively write about gay issues. Nevertheless, it has seriously influenced readers of *Caracole,* who have either damned White for his betrayal or led them to emphasize what Bartlett sees as its "gay perspective"; that is, its analysis of heterosexual behavior from a consciously gay point of view.

One of White's persistent themes is that the social world, the world that is traditionally taken to represent bedrock reality–especially in the Anglo-American novel–is nothing more than a set of rules and codes of behavior that are arbitrary and fluid. The typical plot of

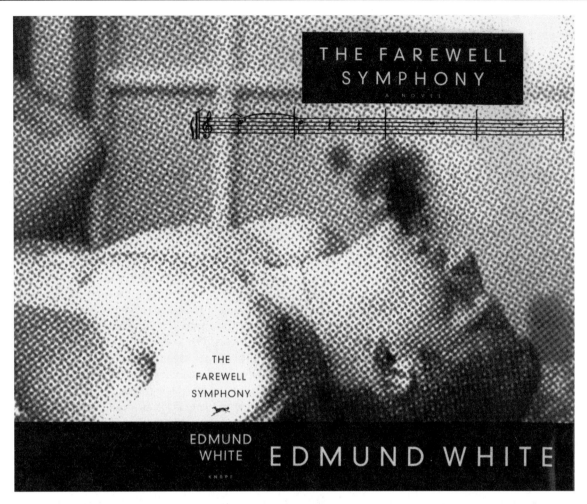

Dust jacket for White's 1997 novel, written in a style that he describes as a "new lyrical sexual realism"

a White novel concerns a young man trying to enter society. But to do so, he has to learn or invent a "self" appropriate to it. That is precisely the situation in *Caracole,* and the fact that the novel is about heterosexuals suggests that for White the problems of the self and its contingence on social circumstance are not limited to gay people. In *Caracole,* the search for self revolves around sexuality, desire, and intellect and the ways in which these do and do not provide a substantial basis of action in a world where genuine political power has been usurped. It is not hard to see beneath the surface of the fiction a reflection of New York City in the 1980s, where the tension between its artists and intellectuals and those commercial power brokers who dominate the American cultural landscape has always been strong.

For all its clarity of theme, *Caracole* is not always successful on a formal level. Like White's other "European" novels, the pleasures of *Caracole* reside chiefly in its language and in its not infrequent excursions into

commentary. The novel reflects on characters within a world evoked as fantasy. At its best, the strategy provides access to a voice familiar to readers of White's essays: the wise, observant voice of a narrator who has ideas about people and things and who articulates those ideas with enticing sonority. In a way, the novel can be seen as a testing ground for White's later fiction, for these also develop characters and stories as occasions for commentary. In the autobiographical works, this technique becomes a strategy for analyzing fully the quality of gay experience. In *Caracole,* however, the strategy sometimes allows the characters to become flat abstractions, propositions around which to debate principles. Much the same type of criticism has been made of its style. When it is good, the style displays the felicities of White at his best, although Bartlett concedes that the "reader can't quite be sure if . . . White's eclectic hunt for verbal precision is in the cause of accuracy or pleasure, of form or content." As the critic and novelist Julian Barnes noted in a 6 October 1985 review in the

Washington Post Book World, the style sometimes "tumbles into tranced Euphuism."

It is fair to say that *Caracole* stands with *Forgetting Elena* as a memorable and often brilliant evocation of a rarefied society in which sex, intellect, and aesthetics have become the basis on which people posit their personal identities and social politics. Its characteristically unsentimental exposure of the tenets of a world that White saw emerging in the 1970s and 1980s and its honesty about the ways in which sex and intellect both enhance and degrade individuals make *Caracole* a genuinely original achievement in American fiction. If the scope of the novel is small, the depth of its satiric portrait of intellectual life in the United States (and perhaps elsewhere) is nevertheless profound.

With the immense success of *A Boy's Own Story* and the literary debate over his "heterosexual" novel, *Caracole,* the middle of the 1980s signaled White's new position as America's most important and honored gay artist. His achievement, however, was about to be marked by the most tragic irony of gay life. At the same time that gay literature was making serious inroads into American consciousness, and writers such as White were exploring what it meant to be gay, a new and deadly disease called Acquired Immune Deficiency Syndrome (AIDS) was beginning to challenge that new-found power. White was living in New York at the outset of the epidemic, and he was, as he points out in the *Time* profile by Schulman, among those early leaders of the gay community who began to mobilize people in the struggle against the disease. Along with novelist and playwright Larry Kramer, he played a role in the founding of Gay Men's Health Crisis, an organization dedicated to AIDS education, advocacy, and community service. White tested positive for the HIV virus in 1985, and since then he has been an outspoken advocate for people with AIDS and a shrewd analyst of America's response to the disease. As might be expected, however, his greatest contribution has been literary. While struggling with his own diagnosis, White still managed to write, publishing three stories, "Palace Days," "An Oracle," and "Running on Empty," published in *The Darker Proof.* Together White and Mars-Jones helped forge and consolidate an emerging subgenre of AIDS literature in the United States and in England.

The stories in *The Darker Proof* are all written in a realistic mode, and although they focus on diverse characters in varied situations, they are thematically unified in at least one important respect: they all involve people who seem to be running away or toward something, as if AIDS itself could be evaded through geographical dislocation. These stories introduced a theme that would persist in the author's AIDS fiction up to and including his 1997 novel, *The Farewell Symphony:* the solitude of the survivor of AIDS; particularly poignant when considered in relation to White himself, who, as a longtime survivor of HIV infection, has outlived many of his closest friends and associates. The impact of this collection in the field of gay and AIDS literature has been great. In one story, "The Oracle," what, on the surface, seems to be a story of loss and grief has been variously interpreted as a positive fiction about gay achievement in the face of crisis. Robert D. Fulk, for instance, in a 1997 *College Literature* article, sees the story as an affirmation of gay culture within larger cultural and historical contexts, whereas, for Richard Dellamora, in an essay in *Writing AIDS: Gay Literature, Language, and Analysis* (1993), it becomes an exploration of the ways in which gay men's intimacies lead to new forms of strength and sociality.

The emphasis on what is strong in gay life and culture is defining in White's later work, and the theme emerges fully developed in his short stories. As is always the case in White's fiction, the stories in *The Darker Proof* self-consciously work out formal challenges to achieve their effects. White told interviewer Kay Bonetti that he and Mars-Jones used the short story as the forum for the AIDS-related fiction rather than the novel "because the novel has an inevitable trajectory to it. That is, you begin healthy and end sick and dead. We wanted to get into and out of the subject matter in a more angular and less predictable way." Thus, the stories are significant in that they avoid ending with the death of their protagonists. They end, instead, as Peter Christensen argues in his 1996 article, in epiphany, at their protagonists' moments of greatest awareness. The strategy allows White to present his characters without judging them and leaves it up to the reader to decide to what extent the character will be able to act on the insight he has had. What is resolutely missing from these stories is consideration of AIDS from a social or political standpoint. The characters seem isolated from those larger community activities that, especially in New York, supported gay men through the worst of the AIDS epidemic. The reason in part is that the stories were written early in the AIDS crisis, before these support systems were fully in place. Also, White seems to prefer to explore the individual in crisis. In these stories, White presents fully realized, complex, and flawed human beings. Their responses to their situations demonstrate something about their particular lives and integrity and the nature of the gay world that seems to set them apart from others. That has been one of White's greatest achievements from the beginning of his career, and it is brought to fruition in these stories.

The powerful sadness of White's early stories about AIDS and the disturbing reality of his own HIV status also provide a bitter backdrop to his next novel, the semi-autobiographical *The Beautiful Room is Empty.* This work continues the life of the still nameless hero of

A Boy's Own Story through the 1960s, and it ends with the Stonewall Riots in New York City. Even though the novel seems to be wholly divorced from the AIDS epidemic of the 1980s and 1990s, its themes and its ending are played out in ways that draw meaning from the monumental assault on the gay community that AIDS represented. In a general way, *The Beautiful Room is Empty* represents gay history in the later 1950s and 1960s as a period in which homosexuality is transformed from a medical diagnosis to the basis for a social community, an idea articulated by the narrator at the end of the novel, in response to the Stonewall Riots: "I caught myself foolishly imagining that gays might someday constitute a community rather than a diagnosis." Appearing at the height of the AIDS epidemic in the United States, *The Beautiful Room is Empty* can be seen as White's attempt to chronicle and affirm the utility and validity of gay communities at their moment of greatest threat. Surely, the persistent undercutting of the notion that homosexuality is an illness makes the book, on some level, a type of AIDS novel, even as it looks forward to that liberated period in gay history, the 1970s, when the slow-moving HIV virus insidiously began to infect members of gay communities.

What *The Beautiful Room is Empty* actually explores with "intelligence, candor, humor—and anger," as John Rechy put it in a review in the *Washington Post Book World* (3 April 1988), is that "most insidious aspect of oppression, that which causes the oppressed to judge himself, not the oppressor, to annihilate self-esteem, accept shame." *A Boy's Own Story* had ended, shockingly, with the narrator's betrayal of a teacher who had been intimate with him. It was an act at once repugnant and sensible, given the oppressive power dynamics of the society in which the boy lived. As the boy grows into the young man of *The Beautiful Room is Empty,* that same destructive impulse turns inward, and the narrator turns his own loathing of homosexuality and his priggish morality onto himself. Before the Stonewall Riots, he internalizes society's view of homosexuality. It is the narrator who comments that "Homosexuality did not constitute a society, just a malady, although unlike many other maladies it was a shameful one—a venereal disease." As White makes clear, the young man's reasoning that homosexuality is a disease blends imperceptibly into another dominant judgment—that it is a sin or crime. Radel states in his article "Self as Other: The Politics of Identity in the Works of Edmund White" that what lies at the heart of the novel is "the narrator's ironic inability to envision the homosexual as anything other than alien," even though he himself is homosexual. The book, then, works out in larger social terms the implications of the narrator's betrayal of his teacher at the end of *A Boy's Own Story.*

White at the time of The Farewell Symphony
(photograph © Jerry Bauer)

Beneath the surface of White's analysis of homophobia and the ways in which it works through internalization, *The Beautiful Room is Empty* launches a vigorous critique of American society. The author aligns himself on the side of what has been called the anti-assimilationist position in debates concerning the place and value of gay culture. White told Janet Saidi in an interview for the *San Diego Gay and Lesbian Times* (11 September 1997), "There are about six . . . powerful spokespeople who are always on the covers of magazines and are always urging us to get married, live in the suburbs, adopt children and live like straight people. And I mean, what's the point? If that's being gay, I might just as well become a monk."

Just as important, White characteristically links his critique of American life in *The Beautiful Room* to yet another theme that has been important throughout his work, the role of art and the artist. In *A Boy's Own Story,* the young hero was attracted to the arts, and his attraction was both a sign of his homosexuality and, he hoped, a way to absolve himself of what he saw as its sinfulness. In *The Beautiful Room,* this theme is developed fully at the beginning of the novel as White records the story of his narrator's friendship with a group of artists in the art school across the street from Eton, his fictional prep school. Art provides the narrator a bohemian world of ideas that is, ultimately, more suitable for a young gay man who sees himself as an outcast from bourgeois society. The novel seems to suggest, as Diane Johnson puts it in her 1996 article in *The Review of Contemporary Fiction,* that there is a secret world of art and a secret gay world and that the two overlap significantly. Both provide the narrator a treasured position of Otherness, a way to create a distinct identity different from what he regards as the stultifying provinciality of the Midwest and the unquestioned banalities of heterosexual, suburban life.

Given its unapologetic exploration of the differences between gay and mainstream lifestyles, *The Beautiful Room is Empty,* like some of White's earlier works, created problems for heterosexual critics especially, who were made "uncomfortable," as Christopher Lehmann-Haupt remarked in a review in *The New York Times* (17 March 1988), by the specific depiction of gay sex in the novel. According to reviewer Clark Blaise in *The New York Times Book Review* (20 March 1988), White shows the difference between gay and straight men through "the meticulous reconstruction of the very texture of [the narrator's] sexuality (much of it sordid, most of it unquotable in this review)." These critics were responding to an issue that even White's narrator would articulate as problematic when he begs his readers to indulge him in his portrayal of sex scenes that they might find offensive. There is a peculiar way, then, in which the novel rehearses gay sex as an uncomfortable reality for straight readers, and one of the effects is to show how the narrator makes himself complicit with the straight reader in his discomfort at reproducing it. If it works to White's advantage here, in a novel about how a gay man internalizes the objectifying and dismissive gaze of his heterosexual counterpart, it also raises the issue of how much—or how little—heterosexual readers might be expected to understand about the differences between gay and straight sex. It is an issue that, according to Picano, was constantly discussed by the members of the Violet Quill in the early 1980s and that for White has remained a central concern. In his introduction to *The Faber Book of Gay Short Fiction,* White implies that he has more sympathy with "frankly sexual writers" than with the "erotic conservatism" of some new younger gay writers. The latter, he feels, signals the emergence of a new kind of puritanism. If, however, *The Beautiful Room is Empty* raised the issue of how to portray gay sexuality, critics also saw that its appeal was not limited to gay audiences. This novel about overcoming abuse "should not be restricted to a limited audience," Rechy said in his *Washington Post Book World* review.

Critics were also quick to point out the maturing of White's style in *The Beautiful Room is Empty.* Here the writing was "tighter, less luscious than in *A Boy's Own Story,*" as T. O. Treadwell put it in *TLS* (22–28 January 1988).

Similarly, Rechy remarked that the style is "quietly elegant—the gauzy prose of earlier books is gone." If the story did not elicit the same sympathy as *A Boy's Own Story,* the style in which it was told evoked ever-increasing admiration.

White returned to the United States to teach at Brown University from 1990 to 1992, but returned to Paris after only a few semesters because his then partner, Hubert Sorin, who was French, had no health coverage in the United States (Sorin died in 1994). White devoted the next several years primarily to writing nonfiction. He edited *The Faber Book of Gay Short Fiction* in 1991 and *The Selected Writings of Jean Genet* in 1993, and he continued to provide essays to magazines and journals, some of which were collected in his book of essays titled *The Burning Library* (1994). On 15 December 1992, *Après le Deluge: Post War Paris,* a British documentary directed by David Thomas, was broadcast on Channel 4 Television; the program featured White discussing his connection with other expatriate American writers in Paris. The author was featured in *Life* and *Time* magazines, both of which focused on his HIV status. In 1993 he was made the subject of an insightful, short, comic television program directed by Bill Cory and called "A Day in the Life of Edmund White." The same year, on 28 February 1993, a British television documentary series, *The South Bank Show,* aired a program directed by Jack Bond, "The White World of Jean Genet," in which White discussed the great French writer's influence on his own life and work. Perhaps because writing a biography of a major literary figure proved to be more demanding than White anticipated, he produced no extended works of fiction in these years. What little fiction he did produce in the late 1980s and early 1990s was primarily in the form of short stories, and these were ultimately collected in *Skinned Alive* (1995).

All but two of the stories in *Skinned Alive* have to do with AIDS on some level and its effect on particular gay men—the various narrators and protagonists whose experience seems so often to overlap with White's own. Although a causal connection between White's experience of AIDS and his fiction cannot be established with any certainty, it is true that most of the fiction White has written after his HIV diagnosis is less formally structured than are his earlier works. At the same time, these works increasingly obscure the distinction between art or fiction and the artist's life. The stories in *Skinned Alive,* especially those that have to do with AIDS, seem to be reminiscences, collections of anecdotes and observations. What is remembered is often juxtaposed to memories of other times or places, and recalled in relation to what is happening in the present. They are stories in which loss is always contextualized through recollection and the fear of what is still to turn up missing; they are not simply about loss, but about how to live with the threat of loss. Like Proust's remembrance of the past, these stories are about learning to value the present. Each is a masterful achievement in subtle emotion and literary effect, astonishingly mature examples from a writer in complete control of his medium. Although every story belongs to the realistic vein of White's work, they all continue the experimentation with form and structure that mark White's European novels.

In his review of *Skinned Alive* for *The Nation* (4 September 1995), Alfred Corn wrote that "White has figured out that he writes best when his and his narrator's experience most closely coincide," a judgment confirmed by White when he describes his writing in *The Farewell Symphony* as hovering "just over the divide between invention and reportage." The narrator of White's novel argues that autobiographical fiction provides a way of revealing "a whole new world of experience." White says in his essay "Esthetics and Loss," it is the experience of gay men who were "oppressed in the 1950s, freed in the 1960s, exalted in the 1970s, and wiped out in the 1980s." The author asserts, however, that gay experience can be the source of "great occasions" and gay lives can serve as exemplary narratives. That is precisely the point of White's short stories about living with AIDS, and it is the point of connection between the stories and *The Farewell Symphony*. It is an experience that might otherwise have been lost except for writers like White, and one of his most enduring achievements may be that his works will bear witness to the cultural moment in which modern gay life arose and was metamorphosed by the AIDS epidemic.

In White's later fiction, the act of writing itself can, and does, legitimate. To forget that fact when reading White is to neglect its production within a hostile context in which gay voices and gay writers have worked deliberately to render their experiences important and worthy of equal representation. Additionally, to forget it is to misperceive the urgency with which White works to affirm the legitimacy of gay life in the face of AIDS, a disease which many have wrongly fastened on as corroborating the illegitimacy of gay lives and gay sex. The substance of *The Farewell Symphony* lies in its complex but nevertheless affirmative portrait of gay life.

The Farewell Symphony is the third novel in a trilogy that includes *A Boy's Own Story* and *The Beautiful Room is Empty*. But if *The Farewell Symphony* completes the story of the narrators of the two earlier novels, it does not, as they did, deal with the problem of coming to terms with one's homosexuality. The narrator of this novel no longer struggles with his homosexuality but embraces it and the lifestyle and cultures it spawned in post-Stonewall America. In the novel, the narrator says that he had predicted at one time that "gay men, who were now perceived as

the most promiscuous element in society, would someday go 'beyond' sexuality to find newer, richer forms of association." The novel itself is a confirmation of that prediction. This novel is not about what it means to be gay in a homophobic society; it is, instead, a novel about gay men, what they did, who they loved, and how they lived. That their lives are meaningful is taken for granted. That their lives provide the basis for new understandings of sex, love, and friendship is a proposition seriously explored in the novel. Nevertheless, the book is made poignant, and indeed almost tragic, by its recognition that even while the author is in the midst of recording them, this culture and its celebrants are slowly dying of a mysterious disease.

What distinguishes this novel in degree if not kind from White's earlier novels (and indeed from most other gay novels about the AIDS epidemic) is its unflinching examination of both the brilliant intellectual world of gay culture in New York in the 1970s and 1980s and its embracing of a darker and more mysterious world of unbridled sexuality and hedonism. As Nicholas Jenkins described *The Farewell Symphony* in a 2 May 1997 review in *TLS,* "White's novel is a world of masks and barriers, back rooms and sloppy apartments, in which intellectuals can enjoy the most demeaning physical roles without relinquishing their other, cerebral lives. . . ." For White, there seems to be no inconsistency.

In a January 1996 interview with Owen Keehnan, White said that one of the things he hopes to convey in *The Farewell Symphony* is that gay people did not simply fall into promiscuity in spite of themselves in the 1970s. We "actually cultivated and esteemed it." White does not back off from the assertion that the 1970s was a time of liberation and freedom from constraint that was productive in its rebellion against heterosexual norms. The novel, then, takes up an explicitly antipuritanical position about gay sex that White has articulated throughout both his fiction and nonfiction. If White recognizes the relationship between gay promiscuity and the threatened destruction of gay achievements, if he sees his world as poisoned by its own desire, what he never does in the novel is to denigrate that desire. *The Farewell Symphony* attempts to effect a balance between understanding the causal realities of AIDS and asserting the moral legitimacy of gay sex. The novel refuses to accede to the demands of traditional morality.

White's position is a bold and perhaps unpopular perspective, and it has made him the target of attack. In the 27 May 1997 issue of the gay and lesbian news magazine *The Advocate,* published after the appearance of *The Farewell Symphony* in England, Larry Kramer criticizes White's work for what he sees as its excesses in depicting the sex life of its protagonist in a time of sexual plague. If Kramer overstates the case by implying that *The Farewell*

Symphony portrays White's life as being little more than a perpetual orgy, it is certainly true, as Kramer charges, that *The Farewell Symphony* contains multiple and graphic descriptions of the sex life of gay Manhattanites in the 1970s and 1980s. White responded to Kramer's attack in "The Joy of Gay Lit" (*Out,* September 1997). He contrasts his own novel about AIDS to what he calls the anti-pornographic novel that repudiates gay sex in the face of AIDS, and with characteristic bravado he aligns himself with Rabelais, Sade, Genet, and Celine, "a quartet of immoral but immortal geniuses" whose vision took them "very far away from traditional morality." He champions what he calls a "new lyrical sexual realism" that is not pornographic "but rather a dissection of what actually goes on in the head of someone while he is having sex." From this perspective, *The Farewell Symphony* can be effectively read as an extended meditation on gay sex, gay desire, gay love, but not necessarily one that validates all the excesses of its narrator. In "The Joy of Gay Lit" White quotes Bartlett's review in *The London Independent* as comprehending the novel better than Kramer does. For Bartlett, "the narrator is . . . a mess. Sleeping his way through Manhattan, he fails to find an Esterhazy; he can't get his stuff published. He falls in love with the wrong guys; he never gets laid enough." If this position also overstates the case, it nevertheless articulates clearly the opposing terms in which the controversy over *The Farewell Symphony* must be played out.

In 1999 White published a short biography of Proust that confirms the French writer's importance in White's development. This work continues a critical interest that began at Cranbrook Academy, where, Barber reports, White wrote a long essay on Proust's obsession with memory. In a novel titled *The Married Man* (2000), White writes about an American writer in Paris who falls in love with a young, married Frenchman. Modeled on White's relationship with Hubert Sorin, *The Married Man* continues White's realistic exploration of his own life and desires. Thus, it seems clear that he will continue to illuminate the subject he has made so vital to American letters: contemporary sexuality and the nature of desire.

Like all good writing, White's is defined by the era in which it was produced. For White that has been the gay male subculture that emerged in the 1960s in the United States. His association with that minority community has left an indelible mark on all his writing. But White has also made the experience of that community reverberate in the larger world around it. His novels provide contemporary American literature with sympathetic and complex gay characters in forms that are undeniably the product of mainstream traditions. He has helped move questions about sex, sexuality, and desire—especially in their gay forms—into the main currents of Amer-

ican literary thought. But what gives his work an uncommon unity is its persistent revelation of the ways in which sex and sexuality intersect with and revise the rules of social behavior and public morality. His writing reveals sex as a powerful productive force within the construction of American society and, rather than denigrate that productivity, applauds it. Without being sentimental about sex or gay people, White locates the power of both to launch a sustained critique of outmoded values and an enduring celebration of what is new in American mores and culture.

Interviews:

Larry McCaffery and Sinda Gregory, eds., *Alive and Writing: Interviews with American Authors of the 1980s* (Urbana & Chicago: University of Illinois Press, 1987), pp. 257–274;

Jordan Elgrably, "The Art of Fiction CV: Edmund White," *Paris Review,* 108 (Autumn 1988): 46–80;

Kay Bonetti, "An Interview with Edmund White," *Missouri Review,* 13, no. 2 (1990): 89–110;

Adam Block, "An Interview with Edmund White," *Out-Look,* 10 (Fall 1990): 57–62;

Thomas Avena, "Interview with Edmund White (1992)," in *Life Sentences: Writers, Artists, and AIDS* (San Francisco: Mercury House, 1994), pp. 213–246;

Owen Keehnan, "A Writer's Own Story: A Chat With Award–Winning Author Edmund White," *Outlines: The Voice of the Gay and Lesbian Community* (Chicago), 9 January 1996, p. 26;

Janet Saidi, "Politics and Promiscuities: A Conversation with Author Edmund White," *San Diego Gay and Lesbian Times,* 11 September 1997, pp. 10–12.

Bibliographies:

Emmanuel S. Nelson, *Contemporary Gay American Novelists: A Bio-Bibliographical Critical Sourcebook* (Westport, Conn.: Greenwood Press, 1993), pp. 386–394;

David Bergman, "An Edmund White Checklist," *Review of Contemporary Fiction,* 16 (Fall 1996): 88–89.

Biographies:

Leonard Schulman, "Profile: Imagining Other Lives," *Time,* 136 (30 July 1990): 58–60;

Stephen Barber, *Edmund White: The Burning World* (London: Picador, 1998; New York: St. Martin's Press, 1999).

References:

Neil Bartlett, "Caracole," *Review of Contemporary Fiction,* 16 (Fall 1996): 61–68;

David Bergman, *Gaiety Transfigured: Gay Self-Representation in American Literature* (Madison: University of Wisconsin Press, 1991), pp. 9–10, 115–116, 128, 190, 192–196, 199–200, 202;

Bergman, "Introduction: Native Innocence, Alien Knowledge," *Review of Contemporary Fiction,* 16 (Fall 1996): 7–12;

Peter Christensen, "'A More Angular and Less Predictable Way': Epiphanies in Edmund White's *The Darker Proof,*" *Review of Contemporary Fiction,* 16 (Fall 1996): 73–83;

Richard Dellamora, "Apocalyptic Utterance in Edmund White's 'An Oracle,'" *Writing AIDS: Gay Literature, Language, and Analysis,* edited by Timothy F. Murphy and Suzanne Poirier (New York: Columbia University Press, 1993), pp. 98–116;

Keith Fleming, *The Boy with the Thorn in His Side* (New York: Morrow, 2000);

Robert D. Fulk, "Greece and Homosexual Identity in Edmund White's 'An Oracle,'" *College Literature,* 24, no. 1 (1997): 227–239;

Robert Glück, "A Boy's Own Story," *Review of Contemporary Fiction,* 16 (Fall 1996): 56–60;

Diane Johnson, "The Midwesterner as Artist," *Review of Contemporary Fiction,* 16 (Fall 1996): 69–72;

Larry Kramer, "Sex and Sensibility," *Advocate, no.* 734 (27 May 1997): 59–70;

Harry Mathews, "A Valentine for Elena," *Review of Contemporary Fiction,* 16 (Fall 1996): 31–42;

Robert McRuer, "Boys' Own Stories and New Spellings of My Name: Coming Out and Other Myths of Queer Positionality," in his *The Queer Renaissance: Contemporary American Literature and the Reinvention of Lesbian and Gay Identities* (New York & London: New York University Press, 1997), pp. 32–68;

Felice Picano, "Edmund White and the Violet Quill Club," *Review of Contemporary Fiction,* 16 (Fall 1996): 84–87;

Nicholas F. Radel, "Self as Other: The Politics of Identity in the Works of Edmund White," in *Queer Words, Queer Images: Communication and the Construction of Homosexuality,* edited by R. Jeffrey Ringer (New York: New York University Press, 1994), pp. 175–192;

Review of Contemporary Fiction, special Edmund White and Samuel R. Delany issue, edited by David Bergman and James Sallis, 16 (Fall 1996).

Books for Further Reading

This list is a selection of general studies relating to the contemporary novel. Fuller bibliographies can be found in Lewis Leary, *Articles on American Literature, 1950–1967* (Durham, N.C.: Duke University Press, 1970); the annual MLA International Bibliography; and *American Literary Scholarship: An Annual* (Durham, N.C.: Duke University Press, 1965–   ).

Aldridge, John W. *Classics and Contemporaries*. Columbia: University of Missouri Press, 1992.

Aldridge. *The Devil in the Fire: Retrospective Essays on American Literature and Culture, 1951–1971*. New York: Harper's Magazine Press, 1972.

Aldridge. *In Search of Heresy: American Literature in an Age of Conformity*. New York: McGraw-Hill, 1956.

Aldridge. *Talents and Technicians: Literary Chic and the New Assembly-Line Fiction*. New York: Scribners, 1992.

Aldridge. *Time to Murder and Create: The Contemporary Novel in Crisis*. New York: McKay, 1966.

Allen, Mary. *The Necessary Blankness: Women in Major American Fiction of the Sixties*. Urbana: University of Illinois Press, 1976.

Alter, Robert. *After the Tradition: Essays on Modern Jewish Writing*. New York: Dutton, 1969.

Auchincloss, Louis. *Pioneers and Caretakers: A Study of 9 American Women Novelists*. Minneapolis: University of Minnesota Press, 1965.

Bachelard, Gaston. *The Poetics of Space*, translated by Maria Jolas. New York: Orion, 1964.

Baker, Houston A. *Blues, Ideology, and Afro-American Literature: A Vernacular Theory*. Chicago: University of Chicago Press, 1984.

Baker, ed. *Three American Literatures: Essays in Chicano, Native American, and Asian-American Literature for Teachers of American Literature*. New York: Modern Language Association of America, 1982.

Balakian, Nona, and Charles Simmons, eds. *The Creative Present: Notes on Contemporary American Fiction*. Garden City, N.Y.: Doubleday, 1963.

Baumbach, Jonathan. *The Landscape of Nightmare: Studies in the Contemporary American Novel*. New York: New York University Press, 1965.

Bell, Bernard W. *The Afro-American Novel and Its Tradition*. Amherst: University of Massachusetts Press, 1987.

Bellamy, Joe David. *The New Fiction: Interviews with Innovative American Writers*. Urbana: University of Illinois Press, 1974.

Bercovitch, Sacvan, ed. *Reconstructing American Literary History*. Cambridge, Mass.: Harvard University Press, 1986.

Berman, Ronald. *America in the Sixties: An Intellectual History*. New York: Free Press, 1968.

Bigsby, C. W. E., ed. *The Black American Writer*. DeLand, Fla.: Everett/Edwards, 1969.

Blotner, Joseph. *The Modern American Political Novel, 1900–1960*. Austin: University of Texas Press, 1966.

Boelhower, William. *Through a Glass Darkly: Ethnic Semiosis in American Literature*. New York: Oxford University Press, 1987.

Bone, Robert A. *The Negro Novel in America,* revised edition. New Haven: Yale University Press, 1965.

Bradbury, John M. *Renaissance in the South: A Critical History of the Literature, 1920–1960*. Chapel Hill: University of North Carolina Press, 1963.

Bradbury, Malcolm. *The Modern American Novel,* revised edition. Oxford & New York: Oxford University Press, 1992.

Bredahl, A. Carl, Jr. *New Ground: Western American Narrative and the Literary Canon*. Chapel Hill: University of North Carolina Press, 1989.

Bremer, Sidney H. *Urban Intersections: Meetings of Life and Literature in United States Cities*. Urbana & Chicago: University of Illinois Press, 1992.

Bryant, Jerry H. *The Open Decision: The Contemporary American Novel and Its Intellectual Background*. New York: Free Press, 1970.

Byerman, Keith E. *Fingering the Jagged Grain: Tradition and Form in Recent Black Fiction*. Athens: University of Georgia Press, 1985.

Campbell, Jane. *Mythic Black Fiction: The Transformation of History*. Knoxville: University of Tennessee Press, 1986.

Carr, John, ed. *Kite-Flying and Other Irrational Acts: Conversations with Twelve Southern Writers*. Baton Rouge: Louisiana State University Press, 1972.

Chametzky, Jules. *Our Decentralized Literature: Cultural Mediations in Selected Jewish and Southern Writers*. Amherst: University of Massachusetts Press, 1986.

Christian, Barbara. *Black Women Novelists: The Development of a Tradition, 1892–1976*. Westport, Conn.: Greenwood Press, 1980.

Civello, Paul. *American Literary Naturalism and Its Twentieth-Century Transformations: Frank Norris, Ernest Hemingway, Don DeLillo*. Athens: University of Georgia Press, 1994.

Conversations with Writers, 2 volumes. Detroit: Bruccoli Clark/Gale Research, 1977, 1978.

Cook, Bruce. *The Beat Generation*. New York: Scribners, 1971.

Cook, M. G., ed. *Modern Black Novelists: A Collection of Critical Essays*. Englewood Cliffs, N.J.: Prentice-Hall, 1971.

Core, George, ed. *Southern Fiction Today: Renascence and Beyond*. Athens: University of Georgia Press, 1969.

Cowan, Louise. *The Fugitive Group: A Literary History*. Baton Rouge: Louisiana State University Press, 1959.

Cowley, Malcolm, *The Literary Situation*. New York: Viking, 1954.

Cunliffe, Marcus, ed. *American Literature Since 1900,* revised edition. London: Penguin, 1993.

Darby, William. *Necessary American Fictions: Popular Literature of the 1950s*. Bowling Green, Ohio: Bowling Green State University Popular Press, 1987.

Dekker, George. *The American Historical Romance*. Cambridge: Cambridge University Press, 1987.

Drake, Robert, ed. *The Writer and His Tradition*. Knoxville: University of Tennessee Press, 1969.

Eco, Umberto. *Travels in Hyperreality: Essays,* translated by William Weaver. San Diego: Harcourt Brace Jovanovich, 1983.

Eisinger, Chester E. *Fiction of the Forties*. Chicago: University of Chicago Press, 1963.

Elliott, Emory, ed. *The Columbia History of the American Novel*. New York: Columbia University Press, 1991.

Elliott, ed. *The Columbia Literary History of the United States*. New York: Columbia University Press, 1988.

Etulain, Richard W., and Michael T. Marsden, eds. *The Popular Western: Essays toward a Definition*. Bowling Green, Ohio: Bowling Green State University Popular Press, 1974.

Federman, Raymond, ed. *Surfiction: Fiction Now and Tomorrow*. Chicago: Swallow Press, 1975.

Feldman, Gene, and Max Gartenberg, eds. *The Beat Generation and the Angry Young Men*. New York: Citadel, 1958.

Folsom, James K. *The American Western Novel*. New Haven: College and University Press, 1966.

Fox, Robert Elliot. *Conscientious Sorcerers: The Black Postmodernist Fiction of LeRoi Jones /Amiri Baraka, Ishmael Reed, and Samuel R. Delany*. New York: Greenwood Press, 1987.

French, Warren, ed. *The Fifties: Fiction, Poetry, Drama*. DeLand, Fla.: Everett/Edwards, 1970.

Friedman, Melvin J., and John B. Vickery, eds. *The Shaken Realist: Essays in Modern Literature in Honor of Frederick J. Hoffman*. Baton Rouge: Louisiana State University Press, 1970.

Fuller, Edmund. *Man in Modern Fiction: Some Minority Opinions on Contemporary American Writing*. New York: Random House, 1958.

Gado, Frank, ed. *First Person: Conversations on Writers and Writing*. Schenectady, N.Y.: Union College Press, 1973.

Galloway, David D. *The Absurd Hero in American Fiction: Updike, Styron, Bellow, Salinger,* second revised edition. Austin: University of Texas Press, 1981.

Gass, William H. *Fiction and the Figures of Life*. New York: Knopf, 1970.

Gass. *On Being Blue: A Philosophical Inquiry*. Boston: Godine, 1976.

Gates, Henry Louis, Jr. *The Signifying Monkey: A Theory of Afro-American Literary Criticism*. New York: Oxford University Press, 1988.

Gayle, Addison, Jr. *The Way of the New World: The Black Novel in America*. Garden City, N.Y.: Anchor/Doubleday, 1975.

Gayle, ed. *Black Expression: Essays by and about Black Americans in the Creative Arts*. New York: Weybright & Talley, 1969.

Geismar, Maxwell. *American Moderns: From Rebellion to Conformity*. New York: Hill & Wang, 1958.

Gerstenberger, Donna, and George Hendrick. *The American Novel, 1789–1959: A Checklist of Twentieth Century Criticism*. Chicago: Swallow Press, 1970.

Giles, James R. *The Naturalistic Inner-City Novel in America: Encounters With the Fat Man.* Columbia: University of South Carolina Press, 1995.

Gilman, Richard. *The Confusion of Realms.* New York: Random House, 1969.

Glicksberg, Charles I. *The Sexual Revolution in Modern American Literature.* The Hague: Nijhoff, 1971.

Gold, Herbert, ed. *First Person Singular: Essays for the Sixties.* New York: Dial, 1963.

González Echevarría, Roberto. *The Voice of the Masters: Writing and Authority in Modern Latin American Literature.* Austin: University of Texas Press, 1985.

Gossett, Louise Y. *Violence in Recent Southern Fiction.* Durham, N.C.: Duke University Press, 1965.

Green, Martin. *Re-appraisals: Some Commonsense Readings in American Literature.* London: Hugh Evelyn, 1963.

Greiner, Donald J. *Women Enter the Wilderness: Male Bonding and the American Novel of the 1980s.* Columbia: University of South Carolina Press, 1991.

Greiner. *Women without Men: Female Bonding and the American Novel of the 1980s.* Columbia: University of South Carolina Press, 1993.

Griffin, Farah Jasmine. *"Who Set You Flowin'?": The African American Migration Narrative.* New York & Oxford: Oxford University Press, 1995.

Gruen, John. *The Party's Over Now: Reminiscences of the Fifties.* New York: Viking, 1972.

Guttmann, Allen. *The Jewish Writer in America: Assimilation and the Crisis of Identity.* New York: Oxford University Press, 1971.

Hamilton, Cynthia S. *Western and Hard-Boiled Detective Fiction in America: From High Noon to Midnight.* Iowa City: University of Iowa Press, 1987.

Handy, William J. *Modern Fiction: A Formalist Approach.* Carbondale: Southern Illinois University Press, 1971.

Harap, Louis. *In the Mainstream: The Jewish Presence in Twentieth-Century American Literature, 1950s–1980s.* New York: Greenwood Press, 1987.

Hardwick, Elizabeth. *A View of My Own: Essays in Literature and Society.* New York: Farrar, Straus & Cudahy, 1962.

Harper, Howard M., Jr. *Desperate Faith: A Study of Bellow, Salinger, Mailer, Baldwin, and Updike.* Chapel Hill: University of North Carolina Press, 1967.

Harris, Charles B. *Contemporary American Novelists of the Absurd.* New Haven: College & University Press, 1971.

Haslam, Gerald W., ed. *Western Writing.* Albuquerque: University of New Mexico Press, 1974.

Hassan, Ihab. *Contemporary American Literature, 1945–1972: An Introduction.* New York: Ungar, 1973.

Hassan. *The Postmodern Turn: Essays in Postmodernist Theory and Culture.* Columbus: Ohio State University Press, 1987.

Hassan. *Radical Innocence: Studies in the Contemporary American Novel.* Princeton: Princeton University Press, 1961.

Hassan. *The Right Promethean Fire: Imagination, Science, and Cultural Change.* Urbana: University of Illinois Press, 1979.

Hauck, Richard Boyd. *A Cheerful Nihilism: Confidence and "The Absurd" in American Humorous Fiction*. Bloomington: Indiana University Press, 1971.

Hicks, Granville, ed. *The Living Novel: A Symposium*. New York: Macmillan, 1957.

Hicks, Jack. *In the Singer's Temple: Prose Fictions of Barthelme, Gaines, Brautigan, Piercy, Kesey, and Kosinski*. Chapel Hill: University of North Carolina Press, 1981.

Hilfer, Tony. *American Fiction Since 1940*. London & New York: Longman, 1992.

Hill, Herbert, ed. *Anger and Beyond: The Negro Writer in the United States*. New York: Harper & Row, 1966.

Hobson, Fred. *Tell about the South: The Southern Rage to Explain*. Baton Rouge: Louisiana State University Press, 1983.

Hoffman, Daniel, ed. *Harvard Guide to Contemporary American Writing*. Cambridge, Mass.: Belknap Press of Harvard University Press, 1979.

Hoffman, Frederick J. *The Art of Southern Fiction: A Study of Some Modern Novelists*. Carbondale: Southern Illinois University Press, 1967.

Hurm, Gerd. *Fragmented Urban Images: The American City in Modern Fiction from Stephen Crane to Thomas Pynchon*. Frankfurt am Main & New York: Peter Lang, 1991.

Jackson, Blyden. *The History of Afro-American Literature,* volume 1. Baton Rouge: Louisiana State University Press, 1989– .

Johnson, Charles R. *Being and Race: Black Writing Since 1970*. Bloomington: Indiana University Press, 1988.

Jones, Peter G. *War and the Novelist: Appraising the American War Novel*. Columbia: University of Missouri Press, 1976.

Karl, Frederick Robert. *American Fictions, 1940–1980: A Comprehensive History and Critical Evaluation*. New York: Harper & Row, 1983.

Kazin, Alfred. *Bright Book of Life: American Novelists and Storytellers from Hemingway to Mailer*. Boston & Toronto: Atlantic/Little, Brown, 1973.

Kazin. *Contemporaries: Essays*. Boston: Little, Brown, 1962.

Kennard, Jean E. *Number and Nightmare: Forms of Fantasy in Contemporary Fiction*. Hamden, Conn.: Archon, 1975.

Kim, Elaine H. *Asian American Literature: An Introduction to the Writings and Their Social Contexts*. Philadelphia: Temple University Press, 1982.

Klein, Marcus. *After Alienation: American Novels in Mid-century*. Cleveland & New York: World, 1964.

Klein, ed. *The American Novel Since World War II*. Greenwich, Conn.: Fawcett, 1969.

Klinkowitz, Jerome. *The Life of Fiction*. Urbana: University of Illinois Press, 1977.

Klinkowitz. *Literary Disruptions: The Making of a Post-contemporary American Fiction*. Urbana: University of Illinois Press, 1975.

Klinkowitz. *The New American Novel of Manners: The Fiction of Richard Yates, Dan Wakefield, Thomas McGuane*. Athens: University of Georgia Press, 1986.

Klotman, Phyllis Rauch. *Another Man Gone: The Black Runner in Contemporary Afro-American Literature*. Port Washington, N.Y.: Kennikat Press, 1977.

Kort, Wesley A. *Shriven Selves: Religious Problems in Recent American Fiction*. Philadelphia: Fortress, 1972.

Kostelanetz, Richard. *The End of Intelligent Writing: Literary Politics in America*. New York: Sheed & Ward, 1974.

Kostelanetz. *Master Minds: Portraits of Contemporary American Artists and Intellectuals*. New York: Macmillan, 1969.

Kostelanetz, ed. *The New American Arts*. New York: Horizon, 1965.

Kostelanetz, ed. *On Contemporary Literature: An Anthology of Critical Essays on the Major Movements and Writers of Contemporary Literature*. New York: Avon, 1964.

Kostelanetz, ed. *The Young American Writers: Fiction, Poetry, Drama, and Criticism*. New York: Funk & Wagnal, 1967.

Kremer, S. Lillian. *Witness Through the Imagination: Jewish American Holocaust Literature*. Detroit: Wayne State University Press, 1989.

Krim, Seymour. *Shake It for the World, Smartass*. New York: Dial, 1970.

Lebowitz, Naomi. *Humanism and the Absurd in the Modern Novel*. Evanston, Ill.: Northwestern University Press, 1971.

Lehan, Richard. *The City in Literature: An Intellectual and Cultural History*. Berkeley: University of California Press, 1998.

Lehan. *A Dangerous Crossing: French Literary Existentialism and the Modern American Novel*. Carbondale: Southern Illinois University Press, 1973.

Ling, Amy. *Between Worlds: Women Writers of Chinese Ancestry*. New York: Pergamon Press, 1990.

Lipton, Lawrence. *The Holy Barbarians*. New York: Messner, 1959.

Litz, A. Walton, ed. *Modern American Fiction: Essays in Criticism*. New York: Oxford University Press, 1963.

Lord, William J., Jr. *How Authors Make a Living: An Analysis of Free Lance Writers' Incomes, 1953–1957*. New York: Scarecrow Press, 1962.

Ludwig, Jack. *Recent American Novelists*. Minneapolis: University of Minnesota Press, 1962.

Lupack, Barbara Tepa. *Insanity as Redemption in Contemporary American Fiction: Inmates Running the Asylum*. Gainesville: University Press of Florida, 1995.

Lutwack, Leonard. *Heroic Fiction: The Epic Tradition and American Novels of the Twentieth Century*. Carbondale: Southern Illinois University Press, 1971.

Madden, Charles F., ed. *Talks with Authors*. Carbondale: Southern Illinois University Press, 1968.

Madden, David, ed. *American Dreams, American Nightmares*. Carbondale: Southern Illinois University Press, 1970.

Madden, ed. *Rediscoveries: Informal Essays in Which Well-Known Novelists Rediscover Neglected Works of Fiction by One of Their Favorite Authors*. New York: Crown, 1971.

Malin, Irving. *New American Gothic*. Carbondale: Southern Illinois University Press, 1962.

Margolies, Edward. *Native Sons: A Critical Study of Twentieth-Century Negro American Authors.* Philadelphia & New York: Lippincott, 1968.

May, John R. *Toward a New Earth: Apocalypse in the American Novel.* Notre Dame, Ind.: University of Notre Dame Press, 1972.

McHale, Brian. *Postmodernist Fiction.* New York & London: Methuen, 1987.

McNamara, Kevin R. *Urban Verbs: Arts and Discourses of American Cities.* Stanford, Cal.: Stanford University Press, 1996.

Michaels, Walter Benn. *Our America: Nativism, Modernism, and Pluralism.* Durham, N.C.: Duke University Press, 1995.

Milton, John R. *The Novel of the American West.* Lincoln: University of Nebraska Press, 1980.

Moore, Harry T., ed. *Contemporary American Novelists.* Carbondale: Southern Illinois University Press, 1964.

Myers, Carol Fairbanks. *Women in Literature: Criticism of the Seventies.* Metuchen, N.J.: Scarecrow Press, 1976.

Newman, Charles. *The Post-modern Aura: The Act of Fiction in an Age of Inflation.* Evanston, Ill.: Northwestern University Press, 1985.

Newquist, Roy. *Counterpoint.* Chicago: Rand McNally, 1964.

Nin, Anaïs. *The Novel of the Future.* New York: Macmillan, 1968.

O'Brien, John, ed. *Interviews with Black Writers.* New York: Liveright, 1973.

Olderman, Raymond M. *Beyond the Waste Land: A Study of the American Novel in the Nineteen-Sixties.* New Haven: Yale University Press, 1972.

Olster, Stacey Michele. *Reminiscence and Re-creation in Contemporary American Fiction.* Cambridge: Cambridge University Press, 1989.

Panichas, George A., ed. *The Politics of Twentieth-Century Novelists.* New York: Hawthorn Books, 1971.

Parkinson, Thomas, ed. *A Casebook on The Beat.* New York: Crowell, 1961.

Pearce, Richard. *Stages of the Clown: Perspectives on Modern Fiction from Dostoyevsky to Beckett.* Carbondale: Southern Illinois University Press, 1970.

Peden, William. *The American Short Story: Front Line in the National Defense of Literature.* Boston: Houghton Mifflin, 1964. Revised and enlarged as *The American Short Story: Continuity and Change, 1940–1975.* Boston: Houghton Mifflin, 1975.

Pinsker, Sanford. *The Schlemiel as Metaphor: Studies in the Yiddish and American Jewish Novel.* Carbondale: Southern Illinois University Press, 1971.

Podhoretz, Norman. *Doings and Undoings: The Fifties and After in American Writing.* New York: Farrar, Straus, 1964.

Rocard, Marcienne. *The Children of the Sun: Mexican-Americans in the Literature of the United States,* translated by Edward G. Brown Jr. Tucson: University of Arizona Press, 1989.

Rodgers, Lawrence R. *Canaan Bound: The African-American Great Migration Novel.* Urbana & Chicago: University of Illinois Press, 1997.

Rosenblatt, Roger. *Black Fiction.* Cambridge, Mass.: Harvard University Press, 1974.

Rotella, Carlo. *October Cities: The Development of Urban Literature*. Berkeley: University of California Press, 1998.

Rubin, Louis D., Jr. *The Faraway Country: Writers in the Modern South*. Seattle: University of Washington Press, 1963.

Rubin, ed. *The American South: Portrait of a Culture*. Baton Rouge: Louisiana State University Press, 1979.

Rubin and Robert D. Jacobs, eds. *South: Modern Southern Literature in Its Cultural Setting*. Garden City, N.Y.: Doubleday, 1961.

Rubin and others, eds. *The History of Southern Literature*. Baton Rouge: Louisiana State University Press, 1985.

Ruland, Richard, and Malcolm Bradbury. *From Puritanism to Postmodernism: A History of American Literature*. New York: Viking, 1991.

Ruoff, A. La Vonne Brown, and Jerry W. Ward Jr., eds. *Redefining American Literary History*. New York: Modern Language Association of America, 1990.

Saldivar, Jose David. *Border Matters: Remapping American Cultural Studies*. Berkeley: University of California Press, 1997.

Scholes, Robert. *The Fabulators*. New York: Oxford University Press, 1967.

Scholes and Robert Kellogg. *The Nature of Narrative*. London & New York: Oxford University Press, 1966.

Schraufnagel, Noel. *From Apology to Protest: The Black American Novel*. DeLand, Fla.: Everett/Edwards, 1973.

Schulz, Max F. *Black Humor Fiction of the Sixties: A Pluralistic Definition of Man and His World*. Athens: Ohio University Press, 1973.

Schulz. *Radical Sophistication: Studies in Contemporary Jewish-American Novelists*. Athens: Ohio University Press, 1969.

Scott, Nathan A., Jr. *Three American Moralists: Mailer, Bellow, Trilling*. Notre Dame, Ind.: University of Notre Dame Press, 1973.

Sherzer, Joel, and Anthony Woodbury, eds. *Native American Discourse: Poetics and Rhetoric*. New York: Cambridge University Press, 1987.

Simonson, Harold P. *Beyond the Frontier: Writers, Western Regionalism and a Sense of Place*. Fort Worth: Texas Christian University Press, 1989.

Smith, Valerie. *Self-Discovery and Authority in Afro-American Narrative*. Cambridge, Mass.: Harvard University Press, 1987.

Sollors, Werner. *Beyond Ethnicity: Consent and Descent in American Culture*. New York: Oxford University Press, 1986.

Spiller, Robert, ed. *A Time of Harvest: American Literature, 1910–1960*. New York: Hill & Wang, 1962.

Stark, John. *The Literature of Exhaustion: Borges, Nabokov, and Barth*. Durham, N.C.: Duke University Press, 1974.

Stepto, Robert. *From Behind the Veil: A Study of Afro-American Narrative*. Urbana: University of Illinois Press, 1979.

Stuckey, William J. *The Pulitzer Prize Novels: A Critical Backward Look*. Norman: University of Oklahoma Press, 1966.

Sutherland, William O. S., ed. *Six Contemporary Novels: Six Introductory Essays in Modern Fiction*. Austin: University of Texas Department of English, 1962.

Tanner, Tony. *City of Words: American Fiction, 1950–1970*. New York: Harper & Row, 1971.

Tanner. *The Reign of Wonder: Naivety and Reality in American Literature.* Cambridge: Cambridge University Press, 1965.

Tate, Claudia. *Black Women Writers at Work.* New York: Continuum, 1983.

Taylor, J. Golden, and Thomas J. Lyon, eds. *A Literary History of the American West.* Fort Worth: Texas Christian University Press, 1987.

Tilton, John W. *Cosmic Satire in the Contemporary Novel.* Lewisburg, Pa.: Bucknell University Press, 1977.

Turner, Darwin T. *Afro-American Writers.* New York: Appleton-Century-Crofts, 1970.

Tuttleton, James W. *The Novel of Manners in America.* Chapel Hill: University of North Carolina Press, 1972.

Tytell, John. *Naked Angels: The Lives and Literature of the Beat Generation.* New York: McGraw-Hill, 1976.

Waldmeir, Joseph J., ed. *Recent American Fiction: Some Critical Views.* Boston: Houghton Mifflin, 1963.

Watkins, Floyd C. *The Death of Art: Black and White in the Recent Southern Novel.* Athens: University of Georgia Press, 1970.

Watson, Carole McAlphine. *Prologue: The Novels of Black American Women, 1891–1965.* New York: Greenwood Press, 1985.

Weber, Ronald, ed. *America in Change: Reflections on the 60's and 70's.* Notre Dame, Ind.: University of Notre Dame Press, 1972.

West, James L. W. *American Authors and the Literary Marketplace Since 1900.* Philadelphia: University of Pennsylvania Press, 1988.

Westbrook, Max, ed. *The Modern American Novel: Essays in Criticism.* New York: Random House, 1966.

Whitlow, Roger. *Black American Literature: A Critical History.* Chicago: Nelson Hall, 1973.

Wiget, Andrew. *Native American Literature.* Boston: Twayne, 1985.

Wiget, ed. *Critical Essays on Native American Literature.* Boston: G. K. Hall, 1985.

Wilde, Alan. *Middle Grounds: Studies in Contemporary American Fiction.* Philadelphia: University of Pennsylvania Press, 1987.

Williams, John A., and Charles F. Harris, eds. *Amistad I: Writings of Black History and Culture.* New York: Knopf, 1970.

Williams and Harris, eds. *Amistad II.* New York: Knopf, 1971.

Writers at Work: The Paris Review Interviews, series 1–9. New York: Viking, 1958–1992.

Contributors

Dennis Barone . . . . *Saint Joseph College*

Nancy L. Bunge . . . . *Michigan State University*

Mark Busby. . . . .*Southwest Texas State University*

Jane Campbell . . . .*Purdue University, Calumet*

Julian Cowley . . . . *University of Luton*

Tamas Dobozy . . . . *University of British Columbia*

Helen S. Garson . . . . *George Mason University*

James R. Giles . . . .*Northern Illinois University*

Ibis Gómez-Vega . . . .*Northern Illinois University*

Donald J. Greiner . . . . *University of South Carolina*

Carol MacCurdy. . . . .*California Polytechnic State University*

Patrick Meanor . . . . *State University of New York College at Oneonta*

Laurence Miller. . . . .*Western Washington University*

Neil Nakadate . . . .*Iowa State University*

William Nelles. . . . . *University of Massachusetts, Dartmouth*

Joyce Pettis . . . .*North Carolina State University*

Nicholas F. Radel. . . . .*Furman University*

Arthur Saltzman . . . .*Missouri Southern State College*

David Seed . . . .*Liverpool University*

Diane Simmons . . . . *Borough of Manhattan Community College*

Alan R. Velie. . . . . *University of Oklahoma*

Sue B. Walker . . . .*University of South Alabama*

Cumulative Index

Dictionary of Literary Biography, Volumes 1-227
Dictionary of Literary Biography Yearbook, 1980-1999
Dictionary of Literary Biography Documentary Series, Volumes 1-19

Cumulative Index

DLB before number: *Dictionary of Literary Biography,* Volumes 1-227
Y before number: *Dictionary of Literary Biography Yearbook,* 1980-1999
DS before number: *Dictionary of Literary Biography Documentary Series,* Volumes 1-19

B

D

I

S

T

ISBN 0-7876-3136-1

90000